# The Latino Studies Re

D0470556

A Gift of Global Knowledge from the
SACRAMENTO REGIONAL
CENTER FOR INTERNATIONAL TRADE DEVELOPMENT &
CALIFORNIA MEXICO TRADE ASSISTANCE CENTER
916/563-3200

**Center for International Trade Development**

A Los Rios Community
College/ED>Net
Initiative

CMTAC
California-Mexico
Trade Assistance Centers

In memory of Frankie Garcia
*(Cannibal and the Headhunters)*
who prepared us for the land of a thousand dances

# The Latino Studies Reader:
# Culture, Economy, and Society

Edited by

**Antonia Darder and Rodolfo D. Torres**

BLACKWELL
*Publishers*

First published 1998
Reprinted 1998

Blackwell Publishers Inc
350 Main Street
Malden, Massachusetts 02148, USA

Blackwell Publishers Ltd
108 Cowley Road
Oxford OX4 1JF, UK

*Library of Congress Cataloging in Publication Data*
The Latino studies reader: culture, economy, and society/edited by
Antonia Darder and Rodolfo D. Torres
p.   cm.
Includes bibliographical references and index.
ISBN 1–55786–986–3 — ISBN 1–55786–987–1
1. Hispanic Americans. I. Darder, Antonia. II. Torres, Rodolfo
D., 1949– .
E184.S75L3627   1998                          97–14134
305.868073—dc21                               CIP

*British Library Cataloguing in Publication Data*
A CIP catalogue record for this book is available from the British Library

Printed and bound in Great Britain
by T. J. International Limited, Padstow, Cornwall

This book is printed on acid-free paper

To my sister Mirna, my history keeper;
and to Tony, Olga, Gladys, and Lester
whom I never knew, yet carry in my heart
AD


To my brothers and sisters, Alfredo, Margaret,
Mary Lou, Joe, Michael, and Jim
RDT

# Contents

# Contributors

**Edna Acosta-Belén** is a professor of Latin American and Caribbean studies, and women's studies, State University of New York, Albany

**Gloria Anzaldúa,** poet and writer, and author of *Borderlands/La Frontera*

**Luis Aponte-Parés** is a professor in the Department of Community Planning, University of Massachusetts, Boston

**Lourdes Arguelles** is a professor in the Department of Education, Claremont Graduate School in California

**Antonia Darder** is a professor in the Department of Education, Claremont Graduate School in California

**María de los Angeles Torres** is a professor in the Department of Political Science, DePaul University in Chicago

**Raúl Fernández** is a professor of economics, School of Social Science, University of California, Irvine

**Gilbert González** is a professor of history, School of Social Science, University of California, Irvine

**Ramón Grosfoguel** is a professor in the Department of Sociology, State University of New York, Binghamton

**J. Jorge Klor de Alva** is a professor of anthropology and ethnic studies, University of California, Berkeley

**Rubén Martinez** is a journalist and poet

**Beatriz M. Pesquera,** is a professor in Chicana/o studies, University of California, Davis

**Roberto Rodriguez-Morazzani** is director of research, Centro de Estudios Puertorriquenos, Hunter College, City University of New York

**David Román** is a professor in the Department of English, University of Southern California

**Rosaura Sánchez** is a professor of literature, University of California, San Diego

**Carlos E. Santiago** is a professor of Latin American and Caribbean studies, and economics, State University of New York, Albany

**Denise A. Segura** is a professor in the Department of Sociology, University of California, Santa Barbara

**Earl Shorris** is a contributing editor to *Harper's Magazine*

**Ilán Stavans,** a novelist and critic, teaches literature at Amherst College in Massachusetts

**Rodolfo D. Torres** is a professor of comparative Latino studies and public policy, California State University, Long Beach, and visiting professor of education at the University of California, Irvine

**Victor Valle** is a professor in the Department of Ethnic Studies, California Polytechnic State University, San Luis Obispo

**Zaragosa Vargas** is a professor in the Department of History, University of California, Santa Barbara

**Cornel West** is a professor in the Harvard University School of Divinity and the Department of African-American Studies

# Acknowledgments

We want to thank our editor at Blackwell, Susan Rabinowitz, for her support and patience in the preparation of this book, and Sandra Raphael for her fine editorial assistance. *Mil gracias* to Daryl Smith, Lourdes Arguelles, Michele St Germaine, and Zaragosa Vargas for their valuable comments on an earlier version of the manuscript. We also wish to express our appreciation to the authors whose work is included in this volume for their contributions to the ongoing debates on Latino culture, economy, and society. Last but not least, Rudy would like to thank Patricia for all those early-morning walks on the beach; Antonia thanks Guido for his music and love.

For permission to reprint the papers collected in this volume, the editors are grateful to the following publishers:

EDNA ACOSTA-BELÉN and CARLOS E. SANTIAGO, "Merging Borders," from the *Latino Review of Books* (Spring 1995), pp. 2–12;

MARÍA DE LOS ANGELES TORRES, "Encuentros y Encontronazos," from *Diaspora*, 4/2 (1995), pp. 211–38;

J. JORGE KLOR DE ALVA, "Aztlán, Borinquen, and Hispanic Nationalism in the United States," from *Aztlán: Essays on the Chicano Homeland*, ed. R. Anaya and F. Lomeli (Albuquerque: University of New Mexico Press, 1989), pp. 135–71;

GILBERT G. GONZÁLEZ and RAÚL FERNANDEZ, "Chicano History," from the *Pacific Historical Review*, 63 (1994), pp. 469–97 (© 1994 by Pacific Coast Branch, American Historical Association);

ROSAURA SÁNCHEZ, "Mapping the Spanish Language along a Multiethnic and Multilingual Border," from *Aztlán: A Journal of Chicano Studies*, 21/1–2 (1992–6), pp. 49–95 (Regents of the University of California, UCLA Chicano Studies Research Center; not for further reproduction);

ANTONIA DARDER, "The Politics of Biculturalism," from *Culture and Difference*, ed. A. Darder (Westview, CN: Bergin and Garvey, 1995), pp. 1–20;

ROBERTO P. RODRIGUEZ-MORAZZANI, "Beyond the Rainbow," from *Centro*, 7/1–2 (1996), pp. 151–69;

GLORIA ANZALDÚA, "Chicana Artists," from *NACLA Report on the Americas*, 27/1 (July/August 1993), pp. 37–42 (© 1993 by the North American Congress on Latin America, 475 Riverside Drive, # 454, New York, NY 10115–0122);

RUBÉN MARTÍNEZ, "The Shock of the New," from the *Los Angeles Times Magazine* (January 30, 1994), pp. 10–16, 39 (© 1994 by Rubén Martínez);

JORGE KLOR DE ALVA, EARL SHORRIS, and CORNEL WEST, "Our Next Race Question," from *Haper's Magazine* (April 1996), pp. 00–00 (© 1996 by *Harper's Magazine*. All rights reserved);

DENISE A. SEGURA and BEATRIZ M. PESQUERA, "Chicana Feminisms," from *Women: A Feminist Perspective*, ed. J. Freeman (Mountain View, CA: Mayfield, 1995), pp. 617–31;

LOURDES ARGUELLES, "Crazy Wisdom: Memories of a Cuban Queer," from *Sisters, Sexperts, Queers: Beyond the Lesbian Nation*, ed. Arlene Stein (New York: Plume, 1993), pp. 196–204;

DAVID ROMÁN, "Teatro Viva! Latino Performance and the Politics of AIDS in Los Angeles," from *¿Entiendes? Queer Readings, Hispanic Writings*, ed. Emilie L Bergmann and Paul Julian Smith (Durham, NC: Duke University Press, 1996), pp. 346–69;

ILAN STAVANS, "The Latin Phallus," from *Transition*, 58 (5/1, Spring 1995), pp. 48–68 (© 1995, W. E. B. Dubois Institute, Harvard University. Reprinted by permission of Duke University Press);

ZARAGOSA VARGAS, "Rank and File: Historical Perspectives on Latino/a Workers in the US," from the *Humboldt Journal of Social Relations* (1996), pp. 11–23;

VICTOR VALLE and RODOLFO D. TORRES, "Latinos in a 'Post-industrial' Disorder," from the *Socialist Review*, 23/4 (1994), pp. 1–28;

LUIS APONTE-PARÉS, "What's Yellow and White and Has Land All Around It? Appropriating Place in Puerto Rican *Barrios*," from *Centro*, 7/1 (1995), pp. 9–20;

RAMÓN GROSFOGUEL, "Caribbean Colonial Immigrants in the Metropoles," from *CENTRO*, 7/1 (1995), pp. 82–95.

# Introduction

# Latinos and Society: Culture, Politics, and Class

## *Antonia Darder and Rodolfo D. Torres*

> Culture is historically derived, fluid, composed of both positive and negative aspects, and is malleable to conscious action. In domination and resistance, culture is of salient importance. It is inseparably interrelated to the life of a people and their struggle. Culture is the context in which struggle takes place; however conflict or resistance is primarily economic and political and constitutes class resistance. The relationship between culture and class is a historical phenomenon, observable over time.
>
> *Juan Gomez-Quiñonez*[1]

In this important, but neglected essay, published in 1977, Juan Gomez-Quiñonez, a leading Chicano historian, proclaimed the inseparability of culture and class in an effort to understand and address the political economy of Mexican communities in the United States. Twenty years later, despite the changing political economy and its "observable" deleterious effects on the Latino population, we find ourselves still struggling to contextualize the analysis of Latinos in this country within an economic sphere that forthrightly engages material conditions, class structure, and cultural change as central to the discourse.

Without question, the closing years of the twentieth century represent the culmination of major changes in the socioeconomic landscape of US society. Nowhere is this more evident than in the "Latinization" of the United States. Latinos currently number 24 million and, according to recent Census Bureau data, Latinos will become the largest ethnic minority group by the year 2009. Despite this increase in population and the political, educational, and economic advances of Latinos during the last 20 years, 30.3 percent (or 8.4 million) of Latinos continue to live in poverty. Latino workers continue to occupy the lowest rungs of the US economy, finding themselves increasingly displaced and reconcentrated in conditions of structural underemployment and unemployment.

These economic conditions faced by Latino communities in the United States are linked to the transnational realities shared by populations of Latinos in Latin America and the Caribbean, despite specific regional histories which give rise to particular sociocultural configurations – configurations that are fundamentally shaped within the context of the ever-changing global economy.

## LATINOS AND THE GLOBALIZATION OF THE ECONOMY

The current socioeconomic conditions of Latinos can be directly traced to the relentless emergence of the global economy and recent economic policies of expansion, such as the North American Free Trade Agreement (NAFTA), which have weakened the labor participation of Latinos through the transfer of historically well-paying manufacturing jobs to Mexico and other "cheap labor" manufacturing centers around the world. Such consequences highlight the need for scholars to link the condition of US Latinos to the globalization of the economy.[2] This is to say that the study of the social, cultural, economic, and political changes that have historically taken place in the conditions of Latinos must be understood with respect to the particular role that Latinos, as a racialized group, have played in the economic system of this country. In his work on the global economy and Latino populations in the US, William Robinson (1993) argues that:

> Much sociological writing on Latino groups has focused on demographic phenomena, language, culture, and other descriptive or ascriptive traits. Other studies have stressed emerging ethnic consciousness, pan-Latino political action, and other subjective factors as causal explanations in minority group formation. These factors are all significant. However, in my view there are broad, historic "structural linkages" among the distinct groups that constitute the material basis and provide the underlying causal explanation for Latino minority group formation. In other words, cultural and political determinations are relevant, but subsidiary, in that they only become "operationalized" through structural determinants rooted in the U.S. political economy and in an historic process of capital accumulation into which Latinos share a distinct mode of incorporation. (pp. 29–30)

In light of this perspective, the history of US Latinos can only be fully understood and articulated within the context of the US political economy and the new international division of labor. Without question, the United States is the wealthiest country in the world today; yet it is the nation-state with the greatest economic inequality between the rich and the poor and with the most disproportionate wealth distribution of all the "developed" nations of the world. To overlook these facts in the analysis of Latino populations is to ignore the most compelling social phenomenon in US society – the growing gap between rich and poor.[3]

Further, we must address the impact of US economic globalization on cultural production, particularly that of popular culture, in this country and worldwide. Stuart Hall's (1991) writings on culture, globalization, and the world system clearly address the relationship between global mass culture

(which he identifies as American) and the economy.

> Global mass culture is dominated by the modern means of cultural production, dominated by the image which crosses and recrosses linguistic frontiers much more rapidly and more easily, and which speaks across languages in a much more immediate way. It is dominated by all the ways in which visual and graphic arts have entered directly into the reconstitution of popular life, of entertainment and of leisure. It is dominated by television and by film, and by image, imagery, and styles of mass advertising. Its epitome is in all those forms of mass communication of which one might think of satellite television as the prime example. Not because it is the only example but because you could not understand satellite television without understanding its groundings in a particular advanced national economy and culture and yet its whole purpose is precisely that it cannot be limited any longer by national boundaries. (p. 27)

Hall's analysis of the globalized economy and its impact on transnational cultural formations has a theoretical and political significance for understanding the concept of *mestizaje* as transcultural styles of Latino border crossing. Victor Valle and Rodolfo D. Torres (1995) argue that, although the notion of *mestizaje* has links to Mexican and Latin American history, its lived experience is radically transformed amid the realities of US political economy. They describe this phenomenon in the following manner.

> Mestizaje on this side of the border thus expresses a refusal to prefer one language, one national tradition, or culture at the expense of others. Culturally speaking, then, mestizaje is radically inclusive. At other times, it takes the form of a deliberate transgression of political borders. These transgressions, however, are not overtly ideological, but adaptive and strategic. Stated in economic terms, the globalization of capital, with its power to penetrate and

dominate regional markets and undermine native economies, obliges the Mexican peasant or Guatemalan worker to ignore state boundaries to survive. (p. 148)

The globalization of capital and its changes in class relations form the very backdrop of contemporary Latino politics and cultural formations, but is conspicuously absent in most contemporary "postmodern" accounts of Latino life in the US – accounts which ignore the increasing significance of class and the specificity of capitalism as a system of social and political relations of power.

## LATINOS AND THE "POSTMODERN" PROJECT

At this precipitous historical juncture, when an analysis of and challenge to capitalism is so urgently needed (perhaps more than in previous decades) many Chicano and Latino scholars have largely conceptualized the ideas of capitalism, labor, and class struggle out of existence. The increasingly fashionable trends of social and literary theories of "post-Marxism," with their rejection of Marxist theories of history, class, and the state, have failed to engage subtantively the dynamics of racialization within the context of the capitalist world economic system.

An acerbic critic of "culturalist" arguments, Ellen Meiksins Wood (1995) forcefully challenges the underlying assumptions that give rise to the postmodern project. Postmodernists claim that an epochal shift from modernity to postmodernity took place in the early 1970s. This "structural" shift is considered to move the economic priorities of capitalists from the mass production of standardized goods and the forms of labor associated with it to "flexible accumulation" with its new forms of production, diversification of commodities for niche markets, a flexible workforce, and mobile capital. This movement is primarily attributed to the development of new technologies, new forms of communication, the internet, and the "information superhighway."

Wood (1996) begins her analysis by challenging the tendency of the postmodernist to equate capitalism with "modernity" and to see capitalism as a "natural" outcome of technological development, a notion which, she argues, not only "disguises the specificity of capitalism" as a particular social form of domination and exploitation but is also false. Secondly, she forcefully criticizes postmodern "blanket" arguments against the Enlightenment project (particularly its universal human emancipatory ideal) as fundamentally destructive to the project of human rights and social justice. And most importantly, Wood argues that constant technological changes and changes in the marketing strategy do not constitute a major epochal shift in capitalist logic and capitalism's laws of motion. In addressing more specifically this point, she writes:

> The old fordism used the assembly line as a substitute for higher-cost skilled craftsmen and to tighten the control of labor-process by capital with the obvious objective of extracting more value from labor. Now, the new technologies are used to the same ends: to make products easy and cheap to assemble . . . to control the labor-process, to eliminate or combine various skills in both manufacturing and service sectors, to replace higher with lower wage workers, to downsize workers altogether – again to extract more value from labor. So what is new about this so-called new economy is not that the new technologies represent a unique kind of epochal shift. On the contrary, they simply allow the logic of the old mass production economy to be diversified and extended. (p. 35)

We acknowledge that changes in the economy have occurred, but there is a question as to how we can best analytically characterize these changes.[4] And if a historical shift actually took place, it would be more accurately identified in the mid-twentieth century when capitalism approached becoming a universal system that managed to penetrate every aspect of life, the state, the practices and ideologies of the culture of society. From this analysis, capitalism is alive and well, as a totalizing force that must be confronted and addressed frontally in order to restore the possibility of effective emancipatory movements worldwide. Postmodern arguments that refuse to engage with the universalizing phenomenon of capitalism and any notion of a universal human emancipatory project are problematic in guiding our efforts to transform a political economy of greed that creates and sustains the subordination and exploitation of racialized groups.

## LATINOS AND IDENTITY POLITICS

Over the last three decades, there has been a tendency among Latino studies scholars to primarily focus on the question of "Latino culture," following the scholarly tradition of many African American intellectuals who have historically focused on the problem of "race" as the central category of analysis for interpreting the social conditions of inequality and marginalization faced by African Americans. The resulting discourses, which have often focused on a politics of identity, have led to a serious blind spot or absence of depth in much of the theoretical writing about Latino life and culture in the US.

As we consider the conditions of Latinos today and the responses to these conditions by theories and practices shaped by identity politics, we must wholeheartedly agree with the criticisms articulated by Wood (1994) in her article entitled "Identity Crisis." Here we are reminded that capitalism is the most totalizing system of social relations the world has ever known. Yet, in most "postmodernist" or cultural-based accounts of Latinos, capitalism as a totalizing system does not exist. And even when it is mentioned, the emphasis is primarily on an undifferentiated plurality of identity politics and particular oppressions, while ignoring the overwhelming tendency of capitalism to homogenize rather than to diversify human experience.

No matter where one travels around the world, there is no question that racism as an ideology is integral to the process of capital accumulation. The failure of scholars to confront this dimension in their analysis of Latinos as a racialized group or to continue treating class as one of a multiplicity of (equally valid) perspectives, which may or may not "intersect" with the process of racialization, is a serious shortcoming. In addressing this issue, we must recognize that identity politics, which generally glosses over class differences and/or ignores class contradictions, have often been used by even radical intellectuals and activists within Latino communities in an effort to build a political base. By so doing, they have unwittingly perpetuated the dangerous notion that the political and economic are separate spheres of society which can function independently – a view that firmly anchors and sustains prevailing class relations of power in society and fails to deconstruct the cultural myths and internalized notions that serve to perpetuate the advancement of capitalist formations in the US and around the world.

Ramón Grosfoguel and Chloé S. Georas (1996) posit that "social identities are constructed and reproduced in complex and entangled political, economic, and symbolic hierarchy" (p. 193). Given this complex entanglement, what is needed is a more dynamic and fluid notion of how we think about Latino identities in this country. Such a perspective of identity would support our efforts to deconstruct static and frozen notions that perpetuate ahistorical, apolitical, and classless views of life. However, how we analytically accomplish this is no easy matter. Yet again, we are inspired by the words of Wood (1995)

> We should not confuse respect for the plurality of human experience and social struggles with a complete dissolution of historical causality, where there is nothing but diversity, difference and contingency, no unifying structures, no logic of process, no capitalism and therefore no negation of it, no universal project of human emancipation. (p. 263)

We must fundamentally reframe the very terrain that gives life to our understanding of what it means to live and work in a society with widening class differentiations and ever-increasing inequality. Through such an analytical process of reframing, we can expand the terms by which Latino identities are considered, examined, and defined, recognizing that reconfigurations of Latino identities are fundamentally shaped by the profound organizational and spatial transformations of the economy.

## THE LANGUAGE OF "RACE"[5]

The unproblematized "common sense" acceptance and use of "race" as a legitimate way to frame social relations finds its way into the literature on Latinos in this country. The use of this term among Latino scholars in the 1960s can be linked to academic acts of resistance to the term "ethnicity," and theories of assimilation which were generally applied to discuss immigrant populations of European descent. In radical efforts to distance Chicano (and Latino) history from this definition and link it to a theory of internal colonialism, cultural imperialism, and racism, Latinos were discussed as a colonized "racial" group in much the same manner that Marxist theorists[6] positioned African Americans. Consequently, the term's association with power, resistance, and self-determination has veiled the problematic of "race" as a social construct. Protected by the force of liberation movement rhetoric, "race" as an analytical term remained a "paper tiger"[7] – seemingly powerful in discourse matters but ineffectual as an analytical metaphor, incapable of moving us away from the notion of "race" as an innate determinant of behavior.

We recognize that we would be hard pressed to find a progressive scholar writing about Latinos who would subscribe to the use of "race" as a determinant of specific social phenomena associated with inherent (or genetic) characteristics of a group. Yet the use of "race" as an analytical category continues to maintain a stronghold in both academic and popular discourse. What does it mean to attribute analytical status to the idea of "race" and use it as an explanatory concept in theoretical discussion of Latinos? The use of "race" as an analytical category means to position it as a central organizing theoretical principle in deconstructing social relations of difference.

Unfortunately, the continued use of the notion of "race" in the literature and research on Latinos upholds a definition of "race" as a causal factor. In other words, significance and meaning are attributed to phenotypical features, rather than the relationship of difference to the historically reproduced complex processes of racialization. Further, the use of the term "race" often serves to conceal the particular set of social conditions experienced by racialized groups that are determined by an interplay of complex social processes, one of which is premised on the articulation of racism to effect legitimate exclusion (Miles and Torres, 1996).

Yet, despite the dangerous forms of distortion which arise from the use of "race" as a central analytical category of theory-making, scholars seem unable to break with the hegemonic tradition of its use in the social sciences. Efforts to problematize the reified nature of the term "race" and consider its elimination as a metaphor in our work are quickly met with major resistance even among progressive intellectuals of all communities – a resistance that is expressed through anxiety, trepidation, fear, and even anger. Often these responses are associated with a fear of delegitimating the historical movements for liberation that have been principally defined in terms of "race" (raza) struggles or progressive institutional interventions that have focused on "race" numbers to evaluate success. Although understandable, such responses nonetheless demonstrate the tenacious and adhesive quality of socially constructed ideas and how through their historical usage these ideas become common-sense notions that resist deconstruction. As a consequence, "race" is retained as "an analytical category not because it corresponds to any biological or epistemological absolutes, but because of the power that collective identities acquire by means of their roots in tradition" (Gilroy, 1991).

It is within the historical and contemporary contexts of such traditions that differences in skin color have been and are signified as a mark which suggests the existence of different "races." As a consequence, a primary response among many progressive scholars when we call for the elimination of "race" as an analytical category is to reel off accusations of a "color-blind" discourse. This is not what we are arguing. What we do argue is that the visibility of skin color is not inherent in its existence but is a product of signification. This is to say, human beings identify skin color to mark or symbolize other phenomena in a variety of social contexts in which other significations occur. When human practices include and exclude people in the light of the signification of skin color, collective identities are produced and social inequalities are structured (Miles and Torres, 1996).

In order to address these structural inequalities, an analytical shift is required, from "race" to a plural conceptualization of "racisms" and their historical articulations with other ideologies. This plural notion of "racisms" more accurately captures the historically specific nature of racism and the variety of meanings attributed to evaluations of difference and assessments of superiority and inferiority of people. In other words, progressive scholars, whether in the social sciences, humanities, or in the new legal genre of critical race theory, should not be trying to advance a critical theory of "race."[8] For to persist in attributing the idea of "race" with analytical status can only lead us further down a theoretical and political dead-end. Instead, the task at hand is to deconstruct "race" and detach it from the concept of racism. This is to say, what is essential for scholars is to understand that the construction of the idea of "race" is embodied in racist ideology that supports the practice of racism. It is racism as an ideology that produces the notion of "race," not the existence of "races" that produces racisms (Guillaumin, 1995).

Hence, what is needed is a clear understanding of the plurality of racisms and the

exclusionary social processes that function to perpetuate the racialization of Latinos. Robert Miles (1993) convincingly argues that these processes can be analyzed within the framework of Marxist theory without retaining the idea of "race" as an analytical concept.

> Using the concept of racialisation, racism, and exclusionary practice to identify specific means of effecting the reproduction of the capitalist mode of production, one is able to stress consistently and rigorously the role of human agency, albeit always constrained by particular historical and material circumstances, in these processes, as well as to recognise the specificity of particular forms of oppression. (p. 52)

Miles' work also supports the notion that efforts to construct a new language for examining the nature of differing racisms requires an understanding of how complex relationships of exploitation and resistance, grounded in differences of class, ethnicity, and gender, give rise to a multiplicity of ideological constructions of the racialized Other. This knowledge challenges the traditional notion of racism as solely a Black/White dichotomous phenomenon and directs us toward a more accurately constructed, and hence more politically and analytically useful way to identify a multiplicity of historically specific racisms.

There are critics, even within Latino studies, who cannot comprehend a world where the notion of "race" does not exist. Without question, mere efforts to undo and eliminate the idea of "race" as an analytical category in the social sciences is not sufficient to remove its use from the popular or academic imagination and discourse of everyday life. Moreover, in a country like the United States, filled with historical examples of exploitation, violence, and murderous acts rationalized by popular "race" opinions and scientific "race" ideas, it is next to impossible to convince people that "race" does not exist as a "natural" category. So in Guillaumin's words "Let us be clear about this. The idea of race is a technical means, a machine, for committing murder. And its effectiveness is not in doubt" (p. 107). But "races" do not exist. What does exist is the unrelenting idea of "race" that fuels racisms around the world.[9]

## RETHINKING ETHNICITY

In the sixties, the common academic practice of using "ethnicity" to refer to Latino populations declined and "race" became the term of analysis. This shift in terms represented a major political strategy by Chicano and other Latino intellectuals to embrace the "race" paradigm of the internal colony model, widely prevalent in the major writings of radical scholars addressing the conditions of African Americans. Thus, in addition to distancing Latinos from traditional assimilation theories of ethnicity used to explain the process of incorporation of other European ethnic groups, the idea of Latinos as the (brown) "race" provided a discursively powerful category of struggle and resistance upon which to build in-group identity and cross-group solidarity with African Americans. This mostly unchallenged appropriation of the term "race" (or *raza*) was widely reflected in the academic and popular discourses of Chicano and Puerto Rican intellectuals, literary writers, and activists. This was particularly the case, for example, with the identity politics of "Chicanismo" which "meant identifying with 'la raza' (the race or people), and collectively promoting the interests of 'carnales' (brothers) with whom they shared a common language, culture, and religion" (Gutierrez, 1995: 214).

In rethinking ethnicity and its potential as a category of analysis in Latino studies, the intellectual project of diaspora should not be ignored. A critical definition of "ethnicity" is also of vital concern to diasporan scholars, particularly those who are rethinking notions of Puerto Rican, Cuban, and Dominican identities here and in the homeland. There is no question that the assumptions of such a term as "ethnicity" are inextricably linked to the ideology and figurative language that gives rise to the media debates and the public policy discourse on Latinos and other racialized populations in the United States. But the assumption that seems most promising to a radical politics of diaspora is the notion that ethnicity is "a mobile and unstable entity which contains many possibilities, including that of becoming a diaspora" (Tölöyan, 1996: 27).

Further, Khachig Tölöyan (1996) argues that the lines which divide ethnic groups from diasporas are not clear-cut, changing in response to the complex transnational dynamics of political events and the global economy. But what seems most characteristic of diasporan populations is an emphasis on the collective identity of the dispersed community and its connection to the homeland.

> For example, the Cuban-American "community" contains a few assimilated members identifiable only by name and kinship affiliation, but otherwise wholly inactive in and for the community; a much larger number of ethnics, a group whose size is fervently debated, that forms an "exile" community, which is committed to the overthrow of Cuban communism and to a physical return to the island; and a diasporan fraction which is active in political and cultural representation, cares about maintaining contact with Cuba and Cuban communities in other countries, like Mexico and Spain, and re-turns, turns repeatedly towards Cuba, without actually intending a physical return. (pp. 17–18)

The ideologies of group identity and the specific terms used to identify particular populations cannot be overlooked as important political dimensions of Latino life. As with all historically racialized populations, Latino "identities are never complete, never finished . . . always as subjectivity itself is, in process" (Hall, 1996). Further, this process is driven by a variety of efforts to build community, engage tensions surrounding class and nationality differences, revitalize and expand cultural boundaries, and redefine the meaning of group identity within the context of an ever-worsening economy. This phenomenon is influenced by persistent efforts by Latinos to establish a "sense of place" from which to counter changing relations of material and cultural domination. In light of this, we can draw from the work of Hall (1990) who argues that a critical notion of ethnicity is required in order to "position" the discourse of racialized populations within particular histories related to the structure of class formations, regional origins, and cultural traditions. This is particularly the case with US Latino populations whose different national, class, gender, and sexual identities have been homogenized in terms of public policy under the all-encompassing categorical label of "Hispanic"[10] which, not surprisingly, is divided in terms of "white" and "non-white" subcategories.

As scholars attempt to move away from a language of "race" and the common practice of negating the multiplicity of Latino identities, critically rethinking the category of ethnicity comes to the forefront as an important intellectual and political project. Robert Blauner (1992), a major early proponent in the 1960s of the internal colony and the "race" paradigm, has begun to rethink the category of "race" and the common distinction between "race" and ethnicity, acknowledging that the "peculiarly modern division of the world into a discrete number of hierarchically ranked races is a historic product of Western colonialism" (p. 61). Moreover, he argues that:

> Much of the popular discourse about race in America today goes awry because ethnic realities get lost under the racial umbrella. The positive meanings and potential of ethnicity are overlooked, even overrun, by the more inflammatory meanings of race. (p. 61)

We must point out that rethinking the category of ethnicity does not imply that scholars should simply substitute the term "ethnicity" for "race." For in our intellectual pursuit of more precise and accurate language to reflect the conditions of Latino populations in this country, we must keep in mind Miles' (1982) warning that the theoretical use of "ethnicity" divorced from its historical and material context would be marred with a number of "analytical, logical, and empirical contradictions" constituting another analytical trap.

## THE LIMITS OF CULTURAL NATIONALISM

The politics of "cultural nationalism" has commonly been used to consolidate power within Latino communities, often ignoring or deliberately obfuscating serious class differences and severe contradictions present among different sectors of the Latino population. Conflicting views on the validity of this position among Latino intellectuals has been the topic of ongoing debate since the early 1970s. Carlos Muñoz (1989), in his seminal work on the Chicano movement, documented the criticisms of Chicanos who at a 1973 student conference urged the adoption of a Marxist ideology. These students framed their objections to cultural nationalism in the following manner.

> Cultural nationalism . . . points to a form of struggle that does not take into account the inter-connectedness of the world and proclaims as a solution the separatism that the capitalist has developed and perpetuated in order to exploit working people further . . . It promotes the concept of a nation without a material basis and solely on a spiritual basis and tends to identify the enemy on a racial basis, ignoring the origin of racism and that it is simply an oppressive tool of capitalism. (p. 91)

But for Puerto Ricans, as Clara Rodriguez (1995) points out, the politics of cultural nationalism was more akin to that of Native Americans. Puerto Ricans shared with Native Americans "a historical and still unresolved issue – political sovereignty in relation to the United States" (p. 224). Unlike the "imagined" homeland of Aztlán for Chicanos, Puerto Ricans contended with the 1898 invasion and conquest of Puerto Rico (Borinquen) and its continued status as a US colony. Drawing strength from the Cuban socialist revolution, there was a greater tendency among Puerto Rican intellectuals and activists to frame arguments about conditions that Puerto Ricans faced within the context of US imperialism and capitalist development. Under the legendary leadership of Frank Bonilla, faculty, staff, and students associated with the Centro de Estudios Puertorriquenos at Hunter College produced theoretically rich structural analysis of economic factors affecting Puerto Ricans in the United States and in the homeland. Many of these works focused on the political economy of migration within the context of a colonial relationship and the world capitalist system.

Yet, in much the same way, Chicano and Puerto Rican cultural nationalists discussed the construction of identity in terms of colonialism and the struggle for nationhood, while remaining noticeably silent about gender issues, heterosexism, and racialized relations among Puerto Ricans here in the US and on the island (Ramos, 1995). Addressing this issue of racism within the Puerto Rican community, Roberto Rodriguez-Morazzani (1996) explains:

> The question of "race" and racism proved difficult and problematic within the context of an anti-colonial struggle based on a nationalistist imaginary that denied or subordinated the significance of the African, and denied or subordinated the question of racism as it existed within Puerto Rican society. (p. 157)

Alma Garcia's (1989) writings on Chicana feminist discourse echo the disagreements of Latina feminists across the country with the ideological tenets of cultural nationalism.

> One source of ideological disagreement between Chicana feminism and cultural nationalist ideology was cultural survival. Many Chicana feminists believed that a focus on cultural survival did not acknowledge the need to alter male-female relations within Chicano communities . . . They chal-lenged the view that machismo was a source of masculine pride for Chicanos and therefore a defense mechanism against dominant society's racism. Chicana feminists called for changes in the ideologies responsible for distorting relations between women and men. One such change was to modify the cultural nationalist position that viewed machismo as a source of pride. (pp. 177–8)

A blatant absence of commitment to address sexism, heterosexism, and homophobia within the social and political milieu of cultural nationalism forcefully silenced and alienated Latino gays and Latina lesbians within movement organizations. In a political environment that already viewed feminist ideology as divisive and destructive to the Latino community, lesbians and gays experienced much hostility and political attack from "within." Without question, a cultural nationalist ideology that utilized its power, on the one hand, to perpetuate stereotypical images of Latina women as sacrificing and long-suffering mothers and wives, and on the other, to legitimate an unrelenting machismo, could hardly support a politics of inclusion and equality for homosexuals and lesbians who were considered a danger to the "raza."

In considering these serious limitations, most troubling is the recognition that the primacy of cultural nationalism in political discourse and its effectiveness as a tool of mass mobilization in the Latino community rests on the unfortunate fact that a national (or racialized) consciousness is generally much more developed than class consciousness. Furthermore, whatever its historical specificities, cultural nationalism as an ideology tends to not only grossly ignore or negate the legitimacy of class, gender, and sexual oppression, but also serves to block the development of critical consciousness in Latino communities.

## GENDER, SEXUALITY, AND POWER

The significant omissions in the intellectual and political discourse of Latinos in the US

can best be attributed to the powerful ideological hegemony of patriarchy that shaped
much of the collective ideal of cultural nationalism and its steady retreat from class analysis
over the last 20 years. The ideological formations of class rooted in the "naturalist
discourse" of machismo are considered by
many Latina feminists to represent the
building blocks of gender and sexual oppression. Antonia Castañeda (1993) argues that
"women are placed in opposition and in an
inferior position to men, on the assumption
that in the divine order of nature, the male sex
of the species is superior to the female" (p. 27).
Here, we can also turn to the writings of the
French sociologist, Colette Guillaumin (1995),
on racism, sexism, power, and the belief in
nature.

> Each of our actions, each of the actions
> which we engage in in a specific social
> relationship (speaking, laundering, cooking,
> giving birth, taking care of others) is attrib-
> uted to a nature which is supposed to be
> internal to us, even though that social
> relationship is a class relationship imposed
> on us by the modalities and the form of our
> life. (p. 229)

Despite the courageous efforts of many
Latina feminists to break down the sexist
barriers which prevented their full participation in the movement, their challenge to
patriarchal ideology was often perceived as a
threat to political unity. Unfortunately, attacks
against Latina feminists were not limited to
men. Chicana "loyalists," for example,
insisted that Chicana feminism was anti-
family, anti-cultural, anti-men, and therefore
anti-Chicano movement. Such attacks often
contributed to both the suppression of feminist activities and the erosion of critical
political analysis (Garcia, 1989). In shedding
light on this conflict and its impact, we once
again turn to the work of Guillaumin.

> But an ideology characteristic of certain
> social relations is more or less accepted by all
> the actors concerned: the very ones who are
> subjected to the domination share it up to a

certain point – usually uneasily, but sometimes with pride and insistence. Now the
very fact of accepting some part of the
ideology of the relationship of appropriation
(we are natural things), deprives us of a large
part of our means, and some of our potential,
for political thinking. And this is indeed the
aim of this ideology, since it is precisely the
expression of our concrete reduction to
powerlessness. (p. 232)

The conflicts and inequality reproduced by
exclusionary practices and the reluctance to
address the growing contradictions posed by
class, gender, and sexual differences among
Latinos served as primary catalysts for the
development of Latina feminist, lesbian, and
gay scholarship and organizations. Radical
Latinos who had been formerly silenced in
movement organizations boldly challenged
traditional social norms, deconstructed
languages of oppression, and publicly
renounced the power relations which perpetuated inequality and discrimination within
and outside of Latino communities.

It is worth noting here that, since the early
1900s, the involvement of Latinas in social
movements, labor unions, civic activities, and
church organizations was an important step
toward a growing political consciousness. The
political influence of Mexicana feminists in
Mexico was definitely felt by Chicana women
in this country. These influences can be linked
to the establishment of feminist organizations
such as the Liga Feminil Mexicanista in 1911
and direct involvement or support of a variety
of labor strikes in the Southwest (Cotera,
1977). In a similar vein, Puerto Rican organizations such as the Liga Feminea de Puerto
Rico in 1917 and the Liga Social Sufragista in
the 1920s were established. Puerto Rican
women working in the tobacco industry and
needlework joined together, demanding
improved conditions, an end to sexual harassment, and greater social opportunities.
Yamile Azize-Vargas (1990), in her writings
on the roots of Puerto Rican feminism, argues
that the oppression faced by Puerto Rican
women "in the needlework and tobacco
industries contributed to conditions for the

emergence of class and feminist conscious-ness" (p. 77). But alongside, she reminds us of the strident opposition of the Catholic Church to feminist demands, claiming "it could inter-rupt women's destiny, according to God and Nature, to be mothers and housewives" (*El Mundo*, September 4, 1920).

Such opposition points to the fact that as Latinas became more vocal about the power relations that reproduced conditions of sexism within Latino communities, labor, and social movement organizations, many of these women were ridiculed, slandered, and ostra-cized by their male counterparts. In a seminal essay, Maria Linda Apodaca (1986) eloquently addresses the dilemma of women within the Chicano movement.

> Chicanas were integral in the Chicano movement, but in time they began to ques-tion their lack of recognition as leaders within the movement. Their ideas regarding political strategy and action were also being ignored or considered insignificant. When demands of these women became too loud, or when Chicano men were forced to accept Chicana leadership, the Chicana was chided for her unwomanly behavior. The chastizing increased when Chicanas began to focus on women's issues, like abortion, forced steril-ization, and discrimination on the job. As conflict within the group increased, Chicanas began to re-evaluate their primary task and primary role. It became a question of deciding which came first: change as indi-viduals, change as women, or over-all social change? (p. 107)

In their efforts to counter the sexism they faced within Chicano and Latino organiza-tions, many Latinas turned their focus on the women's movement in this country. For most, this move was disappointing. Although now women's issues were at the forefront of the political rhetoric, issues of working-class and racialized women were nowhere to be seen. Latina women again faced a wall of silence. Some Latinas and Chicanas chose to continue their work for social change with in the political constraints of already existing organ-izations. Others began constructing and defining their own brands of feminism through the establishment of Latina com-munity, civic, and professional organizations. But as Apodaca is quick to point out, many of these efforts, founded on liberal feminist ideals, only nurtured the desires of aspiring middle-class Chicanas/Latinas and re-affirmed the political economy of mainstream interests.

Within the academy, scholars researched, theorized, and documented the lives of Latina women, seeking to construct feminist perspec-tives that would more accurately reflect the conditions faced by different populations of Latina women in the United States. Edna Acosta-Belén (1992) documents in her work the emergence of a literary cultural discourse among Latina writers that moved beyond national origins and more inclusively addressed issues of class position, sexual orientations, and racialized relations. But even with the best intentions, some of the most respected Latina scholars unwittingly continued to embrace essentialist arguments, depoliticized theories of culture, and/or "race"-centered arguments that often failed to engage with depth the notion of class structure and the differences in gendered class forma-tions among Latinas and other racialized women. Regretfully, few scholars responded to Rosaura Sánchez' (1990) call for more theoretical research grounded in a materialist analysis of Chicana (and Latina) life and culture in the United States.

The demons of naturalist discourse also reared their ugly heads in vehement attacks against Latino gays and lesbians, with accusa-tions that they were not only traitors to the movement, but to all Latinos. Addressing one dimension of this issue, Aida Hurtado (1996) speaks to the conflict between lesbianism and patriarchal notions of the "nature" of women.

> Lesbianism is subversive because it under-mines the unconquerable biological divide of patriarchal inheritance laws through biological ties. How can race (and to a certain extent class) privilege be maintained if there are no "pure" biological offspring?

Furthermore, the seat of patriarchal subordination is in the intimacy of the domestic sphere – how can lesbians be kept in check if the patriarch is only present in the public sphere? (p. 22)

In 1981, *This Bridge Called My Back,* edited by Cherrie Moraga and Gloria Anzaldúa hit the bookstores like a lightning bolt. It encompassed all of what Hurtado calls "the poetics of resistance" and loudly proclaimed that "radical women of color" would not be "kept in check." Latina, African American, Asian, and Native American women were not only collectively challenging the language, style, and discourse of the patriarchy, they were actively involved in counter-hegemonic activities that would open up political spaces where their particular issues and struggles would never again remain silent.

We are the queer groups, the people that don't belong anywhere, not in the dominant world nor completely within our own respective cultures. Combined we cover so many oppressions. But overwhelmingly oppression is the collective fact that we do not fit, and because we do not fit *we are a threat.* (p. 209)

Anzaldúa's words were a manifesto for the growing number of Latino radical intellectuals, artists, and activists who didn't "fit" into the narrow and confining definitions of political conservatives, cultural nationalists, or liberal feminists.

## IMMIGRATION AND THE LATINO METROPOLIS[1]

Despite an "official" national history shaped by the mass migration of European immigrants to the Americas, an increasingly "scapegoat" attitude toward new immigrants has been the prevailing force shaping the politics of (im)migration in this country. Much of the repression at the heart of immigration public policy today still stems from the growing problems left unresolved during the

period of industrial urbanization in this country. These unresolved problems later became exacerbated as the political economy of the United States strengthened its financial stronghold in the world and expanded its capitalist enterprises into the global arena. "Today, as military, political, and ideological power conspire to extend and consolidate the reach of the US global empire, the national economy continues its downward spiral and civil society descends further into breakdown and chaos" (Hamamoto and Torres, 1997: 3).

Although Mexican immigration to the Southwest, heavily influenced by Mexico's historical ties to the region and proximity to the border, represented an everyday occurrence, it was the 1924 Immigration Act restricting European migration to the United States that accelerated the massive migration of Caribbean migrants to New York. Several waves of Caribbean immigrants were to follow, along with refugee populations from Central America escaping from poverty and civil war in their countries. James Petras and Morris Morley (1995) argue that the new immigration from Latin America and other parts can be best understood as the direct outcome of the postwar advance of transnational capitalism while at the same time being symptomatic of US imperial decline.

Nowhere have the impact of anti-immigrant sentiments and the economic consequences of globalization been felt more than in the metropolitan areas of Los Angeles, Chicago, New York, Boston, and Miami. The increasing "Latinization" of these cities due to both legal and "illegal" immigration from Mexico, Central America, South America, and the Caribbean, coupled with higher birthrates among Latino immigrants, has come under attack by conservative anti-immigrant organizations. Despite numerous studies that show otherwise, poor and working-class Latino immigrants have been blamed for poor urban conditions, soaring welfare rates, and the deteriorating national economy. This rapidly increasing immigrant population has also had to face the growing tensions which stem from the reconfiguration of "race relations" beyond Black and White in the Latino Metropolis.[12]

In the early 1990s, the new nativism manifested itself in a number of Latino anti-immigrant political proposals in the state of California. Most recently, in 1994 Governor Pete Wilson and his constituents fought for the passage of Proposition 187. Latino educators, students, parents, community advocates, and their supporters launched a dramatic campaign across the state to defeat a proposition that, if passed, would not only prohibit school enrollment to undocumented students but eliminate the provision of all health services to immigrants who were not in the country "legally." In the end, Proposition 187 passed, but still remains in the courts, awaiting decision on its constitutionality.

Highly influenced by huge immigrant populations, Los Angeles and Miami represent excellent examples of the archetypal late twentieth-century "global city." Los Angeles has become a refuge to tens of thousands of Central Americans who began their flight to the US in the 1970s. The penetration of international capital and resultant economic dislocations, the war between El Salvador and Honduras, domestic political repression, and the availability of low-skill jobs in the US caused a huge leap in the number of Salvadoreans, Guatemalans, and Nicaraguans who joined both newly-arrived Mexicanos and well-established Mexican American communities in the state of California.[13]

While the historical pattern of Mexican settlement in Southwestern US cities such as Los Angeles continues, the nearly century-old colonial relationship between the United States and Puerto Rico becomes further strengthened as the world economy becomes ever more closely integrated, replenishing established ethnic enclaves in New York City, New Jersey, Chicago, and Boston.[14] The "circulating migration" of Puerto Ricans between the mainland and a home island economy dominated by US corporations benefiting from a combination of favorable tax policies, the availability of low-wage labor,

and lack of regulatory controls has resulted in the anomaly of fully 40 percent of the population living outside Puerto Rico. Although formally US citizens since 1917, albeit with limited political rights, the benefits accruing to Puerto Ricans as a result of such status have been minimal when compared to more recently arrived Latino groups such as Cuban Americans.

The post-revolutionary migration of Cubans to southern Florida during the 1960s illustrates the centrality of collective group identity and social class position as key determinants of immigrant success in the United States.[15] For among all Latino groups, Cuban Americans by all objective measures – average income, level of education, occupational status, political representation – stand alone as having achieved solidly a privileged class status within the larger society. The valorization of white European "Spanish" ethnic identity over that of Indian or African infusions and the well-educated urban professional composition (Habaneros in particular) of first-wave Cuban immigrants served them well in adapting to the new social setting. The rabid anti-communist fervor of the times further aided in the perception of Cubans as being "good" immigrants because of their explicit renunciation of state socialism led by Fidel Castro.

To better understand the Latino immigrant population of today, gender patterns must also be noted with analytical specificity.[16] Unlike earlier decades, newly arrived immigrants entering the country are more likely to be women, particularly among Caribbean-born US residents. The reason for this preponderance of female immigrants is the relative ease with which immigrant women can find work, often as domestics or in garment factories. A typical pattern is for a woman to migrate first, leaving her children and/or her husband behind, then to apply for their immigration as kin, after she has attained permanent resident status for herself (Sunshine, 1994). Hence, Catherine Sunshine (1994) provides the following description of the current prototype of the "new" Latino immigrant in New York.

... a woman from the Dominican Republic who migrates directly from her rural village. She leaves her children with her mother and goes to live with a cousin in a Manhattan tenement, earning $130 a week as a sewing machine operator. After she has been in the United States long enough to legalize her status, she sends for her children. The portion of her wages sent home are a major source of support for her extended family in the Dominican Republic. (p. 76)

The description above points to the notion that all Latino immigrant communities, to one extent or another, are connected to their native countries by transnational economic and social pressures. Whether we are speaking about the Cuban "exiles" in Miami who wield distinctive economic power there, or Puerto Ricans with fluid economic and migration patterns to and from the island, or seasonal Mexican laborers in California, or Dominican working women in New York, "the material forces that determine their migration, their present production relations, and their class positions are similarly determined by the larger social structure and the global economy" (Torres and Ngin, 1995: 60).

## THE READINGS: AN OVERVIEW

### Culture, history, and society: a conceptual map

Conventional historical accounts of the formative years of the United States tend to regard everything that preceded the establishment of the British thirteen colonies as unimportant . . . this confined view of U.S. territorial expansion and the formative years of the nation, tends to fragment or obscure the entire history of the past and its links to the present, leaving us with an impoverished understanding of how groups, such as Latinos, have been and continue to be an integral part of this country's multicultural patrimony and have at different times played a perceptible role in the shaping of

U.S. history and society.

*Acosta-Belén and Santiago (1995: 5)*

It is impossible to grasp the complexity of Latino culture and history, as well as the contemporary issues affecting Latinos in the United States, without reconstructing the boundaries of conventional perspectives. It is precisely this challenge that the writers in this section address through their efforts to develop new conceptual frameworks for rethinking the changing identities and cultural formations of Latinos in this country. These theoretical and analytical reformulations of traditional paradigms boldly engage a variety of highly provocative cultural, historical, and social themes.

In "Merging Borders: The Remapping of America," Edna Acosta-Belén and Carlos E. Santiago call for a rethinking of traditional notions of Latino culture in ways that discard reified conceptualizations that perpetuate static, ahistorical, apolitical, and classless views of life. US Latinos must be understood within a historical context of "a shared legacy of colonialism, racism, displacement, and dispersion," linking their conditions to the transnational realities of Latinos in Latin America and the Caribbean. Acosta-Belén and Santiago underscore the need to extend the cultural parameters of analysis beyond those already imposed by geographical frontiers or arbitrary boundaries. Further, they argue that contemporary discussions of US Latino identity must be reformulated within a conceptual framework where existing capitalist formations and economic inequality are central to any theory, practice, or public policy that claims to further cultural democracy.

The political theories and practices of "cultural nationalism" have united and divided radical scholars and activists committed to social and economic justice worldwide. In "Aztlán, Borinquen, and Hispanic Nationalism in the United States" Klor de Alva provides a strident critique of parochial notions of cultural nationalism and challenges the limitations of social movement ideologies founded exclusively on such a paradigm. He argues that although nationalism is shaped by socioeconomic imperatives, it tends to not only negate class but often serves to block the development of class consciousness. Central to Klor de Alva's analysis is the notion that "culture and identity are circumscribed by historical and material limitations, nevertheless people do not live out their lives as abstract categories." Through providing a comparative analysis of competing forms of nationalism in the political discourses of Chicano and Puerto Rican communities, Klor de Alva provides us with an opportunity to address current debates, given the renewed focus on cultural nationalism as a political and intellectual project in the US and around the world.

"Chicano History: Transcending Cultural Models" reinforces the dynamic and significant role of historical dimensions to understanding the changing conditions of Latino populations in this country. In this essay, Gilbert González and Raúl Fernández eloquently employ a Marxist framework that emphasizes a historical perspective founded on an integrated economic analysis. Moving away from culture-based models of history, they avoid perpetuating a traditionally narrow and stagnant cultural paradigm of Chicano life. Arguing against the distortions of traditional scholarship that keep culture and economic life in separate compartments, González and Fernández examine the systemic roots of conflict inherent in the prevalent economic organization of US society. González and Fernández accomplish this feat through providing a historical analysis that positions Chicanos and their participation in the US economy as central to their articulation of the social and cultural changes experienced by Spanish-speaking populations of the Southwest during the last two centuries.

In any text about Latinos, it is impossible to ignore the importance of language and its particular impact in shaping the cultural, social, and economic conditions of this population. Unlike traditional discussion of language issues in Latino communities, "Mapping the Spanish Language along a Multiethnic and Multilingual Border" takes a bold step in providing a linguistic analysis that is fundamentally linked to questions of the global political economy and the structure of class formations. Rosaura Sánchez argues against the popular notion of Latinos as a synthesis of "races" or a "mystical *raza cosmica.*" Instead, she posits that although a heterogeneous and politically fragmented population, Latinos are united by a history of conquest and colonialism, a history of proletarianization and disempowerment, and, to a large extent, by a common language – Spanish. And although language and culture may be considered irrelevant in political movements, Sánchez asserts that language, culture, and ethnicity are strategies for struggle because they are often tools used by hegemonic forces to oppress, exploit, and divide populations.

While paradigms founded on the notion of the diaspora have been quite abundant in the writings of African Americans, it is only recently that it has begun to emerge more consistently in the literature on Cubans and Puerto Ricans in the United States. Maria de los Angeles Torres in "Encuentros y Encontronazos: Homeland in the Politics and Identity of the Cuban Diaspora" calls for a "new vision of identity that requires a vision of power and organization across borders of nation-states" that "inevitably leads to an expansion of the boundaries of citizenship beyond any one single nation-state." This breakdown of physical boundaries, de los Angeles argues, creates a complex border place within struggle and affirmation in which there exists an ongoing process of cultural resistance and negotiation of internalized hegemonic notions that confront us daily. Most important, she stresses that the conditions faced by members of diaspora communities toss them into interactions with organizations which force them into constant negotiation of their identities and new ways of thinking about multiple identities.

### Cultural politics and border zones: recasting racialized relations

> Nepantla is the Nhuatl word for an in-between state, that uncertain terrain one crosses when moving from one place to another, when changing from one class, race or gender position to another, when traveling from the present identity into a new identity . . . The border is on a constant Napantla state. It is the locus of resistance, of rupture, of implosion and explosion, and of putting together the fragments and creating a new assemblage . . . Border artist cambian el punto de referencia. By disrupting the neat separations between cultures, they create a culture mix, una mestizada.
>
> *Gloria Anzaldúa (1993: 39–40)*

One of the most heavily contested theoretical terrains of our times is that of culture and identity. It is perhaps the arena in which traditional definitions of culture and identity have most failed in rendering a critical perspective of Latino populations in this country. Major limitations are found even in cultural studies and postmodernist articulations of ethnic and "racial" identities. "The Politics of Biculturalism: Culture and Difference in the Formation of Warriors for Gringostroika and the New Mestizas" represents a necessary move away from recurring essentialized notions of multiple identities. By considering the myriad of cultural, social, political, and economic forces at work in the formation of ethnic identities, Antonia Darder points to the complexity of issues that must be simultaneously addressed in order to arrive at an accurate conceptualization of difference within subordinate cultural communities. Drawing on recent works in cultural studies and political economy, Darder argues that an understanding of cultural identity formation must be fundamentally rooted in both political and economic theories of society.

The need to recast racialized relations in the social sciences is at the heart of Roberto P. Rodriguez-Morazzani's essay, "Beyond the Rainbow: Mapping the Discourse on Puerto Ricans and 'Race'." His work seeks to analyze the history of racial formation among Puerto Ricans, in an effort to better identify how social agents are defined or define themselves as racial subjects and the processes which result in the production of racialized and racializing practices within society. Rodriguez-Morazzani provides a useful review of the dominant discourses and counter-discourses on Puerto Ricans and "race" which he discusses through the use of the metaphor of "moments." Hence, his discussion moves the reader from looking at "race as sociopathology" (*The First Moment*) to a focus on "countering the dominant discourse" (*The Second Moment*) to an emphasis on "obfuscating racial formation and signification" (*The Third Moment*) with a discussion of its most prominent theory of the "rainbow people."

In her discussion of "Chicana Artists: Exploring Nepantla, El Lugar de las Fronteras" Gloria Anzaldúa ushers the reader into the place of *Nepantla*, an in-between zone of cultural production at "the border" where cultures are transformed and remade. "The border is a historical and metaphorical site, *un sitio ocupado*, an occupied borderland where individual artist and collaborating groups transform space and the two home territories . . . become one." As she attempts to unveil the complexity of border existence, Anzaldúa proclaims the strengths and difficulties associated with living multiple identities. For Chicana artists, for example, one of the many obstacles is simply being identified as a "border dweller" which places the artist in danger of illegitimacy in the eyes of the outside world. Given the existing social and economic conditions, Anzaldua argues that Chicanas must acknowledge the multiplicity of their identities as a strategy of resistance and survival.

In Rubén Martinez's "The Shock of the New" themes of resistance, survival, and the reconstruction of cultural identities are central to his poignant analysis of the "Mexican" Quebradita dance craze in the Southwest. In a most effective manner, the significance of popular culture as both a medium and site for cultural production and the formation of new hybrid cultural identities is powerfully illustrated. Martinez provides a revealing example of the transcultural dynamics of resistance inherent in the experience of border crossing, emphasizing that the forces of cultural assimilation are as much an "economic rite of passage as a cultural one."

Earl Shorris, a contributing editor of Harper's Magazine brought together two well-recognized scholars, Cornel West and Jorge Klor de Alva, to engage in a highly controversial and provocative debate. The stated intention was to move the discourse on power and ethnicity beyond black and white. The result of that debate, "Our Next Race Question: The Uneasiness between Blacks and Latinos," is included here to illustrate the range of views that can be found in the field of cultural studies. What is most apparent from this dialogue between West and Klor de Alva is their highly contrasting views on the analytical value of the term "race," despite their shared objection to essentialized concepts of "race" and the idea that differences are innate and outside of history. While Klor de Alva makes the case that West can only be considered Black "within a certain reductionist context," West asserts the value of continuing to identify himself as Black (a racialized label) "as a way of affirming ourselves as agents, as subjects in history." The debate becomes even more intensified when Klor de Alva argues that West is, in fact, an *Anglo* (an ethnic label) asserting that "Anglos may be of any race." A critical analysis of this debate supports the argument to eliminate the language of "race" from both academic and popular discourses and the need to make central the differing forms of racism(s) that impact on Latino and other racialized populations in this country – a feat that seems almost insurmountable given the historical discourses of power linked to the notion of "race" by both dominant and subordinate populations alike.

## Critical discourses on gender, sexuality, and power

Emerging from the experience of colonization, the *chignon/chingada* dynamic locks women into subordinate roles, inscribes inflexible definitions of masculinity and femininity, and on a larger scale, becomes the surveillance test of true nationalism. Whoever is penetrated, in other words, is immediately interpreted by dominant Latino culture as passive. Passivity, within this system, is understood to mean open to sexual betrayal and, and therefore, a threat to the nation.

*David Román (1995: 349)*

The expression of sexuality and its relationship to ethnicity, gender, and class relations cannot be overlooked in our efforts to understand the social, cultural, and political formations of men and women within Latino communities in the United States. Without question, we must engage critically the manner in which cultural productions emerging from gender and sexual relations are fundamentally rooted in relations of power. Further, it must be recognized that despite US Latino movements for liberation, the particular needs of Chicana and Latina women, Latina lesbians, and Latino gay men have often been either ignored or deemed divisive and destructive to the community by the powerful ideological hegemony of cultural nationalism that has shaped the history of these movements.

It is precisely the struggle against this powerful ideological hegemony of cultural nationalism, on the one hand, and the contradictions and exclusionary practices of the women's movement, on the other, that most informs the history and development of Chicana feminisms in the United States. In "Chicana Feminisms: Their Political Context and Contemporary Expression" Denise A. Segura and Beatriz M. Pesquera provide an excellent overview of the historical and contemporary views of Chicanas and their collective efforts to overcome their limited access as "second-class citizens." In their discussion they point to the destructive practice within the "male-dominated" Chicano movement of using labeling as "a tool of repression against Chicanas who advocated a feminist position." Segura and Pesquera also argue that class location has played a fundamental role in shaping the identity and political consciousness of Chicanas in this country. Of special interest is their description of Chicana organizations and their efforts to anchor feminist struggles within the social, economic, and political realities of the Chicano/Latino community at large.

Through the reflective power of youthful memories, Lourdes Arguelles, in "Crazy Wisdom: Memories of a Cuban Queer" ushers the reader through a series of "gender bending" recollections of two lesbian women in Cuba who disappeared from her life at the beginning of the Cuban revolution. It is, in many ways, an example of how Latina lesbians have often, quietly and inconspicuously, created spaces for themselves, even if only within the confines of their personal lives. Arguelles uses the knowledge gathered from her personal experiences with the two women to challenge the racialized "norms" of feminist psychology that have traditionally shaped concepts of individual freedom and fusion in intimate relationships.

David Román's essay, "Teatro Viva! Latino Performance and the Politics of AIDS in Los Angeles," examines questions of cultural production through the medium of Chicano theater and performance, linking his analysis to the realities faced by Latino gay and bisexual men with HIV or AIDS. Through carefully deconstructing the performance of *Culture Clash*, for example, Román exposes the unwitting perpetuation of oppressive discourses and images of sexuality that render gays and lesbians virtually invisible or a danger to Latino community life. Román clearly supports the notion that issues of people of color cannot be viewed without an analysis of race and class relations. Further, he critiques the limitations and contradictions of identity politics, particularly with respect to the manner in which cultural nationalism

conflates all Chicano experiences into a unified Chicano subject, failing to account for the differences in lifestyles, sexual orientation, and class location among Latino populations. In contrast, Román looks at the performances of Luis Alfaro to provide an example of the "multifocality" necessary to accurately depict the differences in class, gender, sexuality, and ethnicity among Latinos, and hence, to counter the hegemonic configurations that insist on the conflation of difference.

Ilán Stavan's treatise on "The Latin Phallus" boldly examines the persistent images and themes of machismo in Latino historical accounts and literary renditions of Latino sexuality. Stavans argues that patriarchal conquest, domination, and violent eroticism are overriding themes that continue to shape the sexual identity and attitudes of Latino men (and women) in this hemisphere, more than 500 years after the first Spanish *conquistadores* first set foot in the Americas. Reminiscent of Freudian analysis, Stavans describes the phallus "as an object of intense adoration, the symbol of absolute power and satisfaction . . . The Latin man and his penis are at the center of the Hispanic world." Yet despite such macho bravado, he identifies "a deep seated inferiority complex" at the root of this exaggerated obsession with the phallus. Through the writings of such major literary figures as Jorge Luis Borges, John Rechy, Julio Cortázar, Reinaldo Arenas, and Manuel Puig, Stavans further discusses the disturbing impact of an unrelenting machismo on Latino homosexuality.

### Labor and politics in a global economy: the Latino metropolis

The growth of America's Latino population in the last ten years, which includes the rapidly growing number of legal and undocumented Latino immigrants in the United States, is taking place within the context of economic globalization. Global economic integration has restructured the US . . . Latino workers are the workers most exposed to the ravages from the restruc-

turing of the American economy and therefore are persistently plagued by such ills as
high unemployment rates and a lack of job
security. Though Latinos represent a broad
range of working experiences, they undergo
a process of proletarianization exacerbated
by [racialization]. Along with African
Americans, Latinos occupy the lowest rungs
of a segmented labor market that has been
produced by the racism of employers,
unions, and US foreign policy in Mexico,
Central and Latin America and the Spanish-
speaking Caribbean.

*Zaragosa Vargas (1996)*

The failure to engage the logic of late capitalism and the changing modes of capital
accumulation worldwide is a serious limitation of "postmodern" discourses of identity
politics and Latino cultural studies. In a
counter-position to this problematic stance,
Zaragosa Vargas clearly addresses the global
changes in class formation and the social
structure of post-industrial capitalism and
how these changes have altered the face of
Latino immigration, labor force participation, and economic inequality in the US. In
"Rank and File: Historical Perspectives on
Latina/o Workers in the US" Vargas'
thoughtful, comparative discussion of these
issues provides a historical analysis of the
interplay of the restructuring of the
American economy and its destructive
impact on the power of unions and Latino
labor in this country. But despite the
economic difficulties faced by Latino communities, he argues against the folly of
utilizing "nationalism" to consolidate power
within Latino communities – a political strategy that has served to ignore or deliberately
obfuscate serious class differences and severe
contradictions present among different
sectors of the Latino population.

"Latinos in a 'Post-industrial' Disorder:
Politics in a Changing City" examines the
impact of "post-industrial" change in Latino
communities, with special emphasis upon the
contours of industrial development in Greater
East Los Angeles. Victor Valle and Rodolfo
D. Torres posit that the economic forces that

have transformed the Greater Eastside into
one of the nation's most dynamic industrial
landscapes requires a rethinking of Latino
politics, space, and culture. At the heart of
their rethinking of Latino political and
economic life is an overriding concern with
finding a conceptual language that can more
accurately depict the consequences of the
global economy's reorganization of industrial
production to poor and working communities. In addition, Valle and Torres argue that
an understanding of the dialectics of landscapes of consumption and production can
help significantly to reveal locations of actual
and potential political space. Finally, the
authors provide a framework for a "strategic
agenda" in a changing political economy. As
such, this work can be understood as a first
step toward creating a post-Fordist epistemology and politics that suggest new
opportunities for democratic economic
reform and social change in late twentieth-
century capitalism.

The concept of creating political space,
framed within a context of identity, resistance,
and survival, is also an overriding theme in
"What's Yellow and White and has Land All
Around It? Appropriating Place in Puerto
Rican Barrios." Through an analysis of the
phenomena of *casitas* in New York as
"architecture of resistance," Luis Aponte-
Parés eloquently challenges static and
absolute notions of Puerto Rican urban
culture. His work distinctly shows the significance of migration patterns to the
appropriation of urban space and the formation of *casitas* culture in Puerto Rican
communities. His discourse of Puerto Rican
*barrio* resistance in New York challenges us to
rethink the meaning of urban political space
and its relationship to cultural identity and
changing class relations.

"Caribbean Colonial Immigrants in the
Metropoles: A Research Agenda" contrasts
the experience of Caribbean immigrants
through a comparative study of the migration
process and societal modes of incorporation
for different Caribbean groups. Ramón
Grosfoguel accomplishes this through an
analysis of the impact of "race" and ethnic

relations upon economic public policies affecting different immigrant populations in the metropoles. Through his insightful analysis, he provides a critical framework for better understanding of the immigrant experience, based on a variety of significant factors. These factors include the origin of the immigrant population, institutional dimensions of the migration experience, the context of reception, and the cultural discursive impact associated with the process of incorporation in the receiving society. Most importantly, Grosfoguel's work strongly reinforces the use of a comparative research approach to studying the social and economic conditions of different ethnic populations.

## THE PURPOSE OF THE READER

In discussing our analytical framework in the first section of this introduction, we have attempted to draw attention to both competing and complementary theoretical narratives in the very diverse field of Latino cultural studies. Needless to say, the essays in this volume are not theoretically congruent or politically continuous with each other. The collection has incompatibilities, divergences, and edges of disagreement as to paradigms and theories used to understand Latino culture, politics, and society.

But one issue is very clear. Despite a rampage of critiques that argue against a return to theories of historical materialism and economic determinism, we call for a recovery and renewal of a critical historical materialism and class analysis of late capitalist formations as these relate to racialized relations in the US and abroad. We recognize that there is an apparent theoretical tension between our insistence on a structural analysis of class and class structure and the constructionist and discursive accounts of "race" and "identity." We argue, nonetheless, that much of the new analysis of the changing nature of American society and the much talked-about "Latinization" will be influenced by new approaches to class, inspired by a renewed Marxist political economy. In a recent inter-

view, Stuart Hall (1996) voiced concern about the silence of class and those theoretical writings that ignore the impoverishing consequences of capitalism. Upon being questioned on this issue, he responded:

> I do think that's work that urgently needs to be done. The moment you talk about globalization, you are obliged to talk about the internalization of capital, capital in its late modern form, the shifts that are going on in modern capitalism, post-fordism, etc. So those terms which were excluded from cultural studies . . . now need to be reintegrated . . . In fact, I am sure we will return to the fundamental category of "capital". The difficulties lie in reconceptualizing class. Marx it seems to me now, was much more accurate about "capitalism" than he was about class. It's the articulation between the economic and the political in Marxist class theory that has collapsed. (p. 401)

In addition, our intention was to include articles that represent major theoretical currents, rather than attempt to survey the discipline of Latino studies. The guiding perspectives that informed our choices are complex and multifaceted. But fundamentally they arise from an emphasis, to one extent or another, on the political economy and the globalization of capital, an understanding of capitalism as a worldwide phenomenon, the centrality of a renewed class analysis in theories of cultural life, a recognition of the traditional ideological expressions of power in prevailing views of women, gays, and lesbians, a view of Latinos as a diverse and changing population, the significance of immigration politics, and the overriding historical impact of these perspectives on the "Latinization" of large urban metropolitan areas in the United States.

But most importantly, the volume is informed by an urgency to break away from language and theoretical constructs that limit or obstruct our ability to address the changing conditions of late capitalism, as racialized structures, inequalities, and representations continue to be of immense importance. This includes calling for a new conceptual apparatus and critical lexicon to grapple with new racialized social relations and the ever changing class structure in late capitalism.

# Notes

1    J. Gomez-Quiñonez, *On Culture* (Los Angeles: UCLA Chicano Studies Center Publications, Popular Series No. 1, 1977).

2    We would like to emphasize here that the notion of globalization is not new. In fact, Marx and Engels recognized a shift in 1848, arguing that the State had begun to serve the interest of the global economy and in furthering this objective they predicted that modern industry would create a world market; the bourgeoisie would settle everywhere and establish connections everywhere; old-established national industries would be destroyed and replaced by new industries whose existence would become a matter of life or death for all nations; raw materials would be sought in the remotest regions; industry products would be consumed at home and worldwide; instead of self-sufficiency, universal interdependence would result; national one-sidedness and narrow-mindedness would become more impossible; and there would soon be a world literature and a world culture.

3    Economic inequality has been on the rise in the United States since the 1970s. Since 1992, when Bill Clinton charged that Republican tax cuts in the 1980s had broadened the gap between the rich and the "middle class," it has become more sharply focused as a political issue.

4    For an indispensable introduction to this debate, see *Post-Fordism: A Reader*, edited by Ash Amin (Blackwell, 1994).

5    Parts of this section have appeared in Miles and Torres, "Does Race Matter? Transatlantic Perspectives on Racism After 'Race Relations'" in *Resituating Identities: The Politics of Race, Ethnicity, and Culture*, ed. V. Amit-Talai and C. Knowles (Ontario: Broadview Press, 1996); and in Darder and Torres, "From Race to Racism: The Politics of 'Race' Language in 'Postmodern' Education,"

6    in *New Political Science*, 38/39 (Winter 1996). Critics of the internal colony model working within a Marxist political economy framework fell into a similar analytical trap in their failure to break away from the "race relations" paradigm. These writers representing different strands of "materialist" approaches retained "race" as an analytical concept, while working within the language of class, capital accumulation, and the reserve army labor. For more on this topic see Gilbert Gonzalez, "A Critique of the Internal Colonial Model," in *Latin American Perspectives* (Spring 1974), pp. 154–61. Also see, *Structures of Dependency*, ed. Frank Bonilla and Robert Girling (1973).

7    In addition to the works of Robert Miles (1989, 1993), the recent work by K. Anthony Appiah (1996) makes a similar argument on the problematic nature of the idea of "race."

8    For recent examples of scholarly works that focus on "critical theories of race," see *Critical Race Theory: The Cutting Edge*, ed. Richard Delgado (Philadelphia: Temple University Press, 1995); *Critical Race Theory: the Key Writings that Formed the Movement*, ed. Kimberle Crenshaw, Neil Gotanda, Gary Peller, and Kendal Thomas (New Press, 1995); and Critical Race Feminism: A Reader, ed. Adrien Katherine Wing, (New York University Press, 1997).

9    Additional works that have been important in shaping our analysis of racism, modernity, and identity include: *The Arena of Racism*, by Michel Wieviorja (London: Sage, 1995); *Racism*, by Robert Miles (London: Routledge, 1989); *Racialized Barriers: The Black Experience in the United States and England in the 1980s*, by Stephen Small (London: Routledge, 1994); *Racist Culture: Philosophy and the Politics of Meaning*, by David Theo Goldberg (Cambridge: Blackwell, 1993); *The Meaning of Race: Race, History and Culture in Western Society*, by Kenan Malik (New York University Press, 1996); *On Race and Philosophy*, by Lucius T. Outlaw (New York: Routledge, 1996); *Racial Formation in the United States: From 1860s to the 1990s*, by Michael Omi and Howard Winant, 2nd edn (New York: Routledge, 1994); *The Future of the Race* by Henry Louis Gates and Cornel West (New York: Knopf, 1996).

10    For an insightful discussion on the labeling of Latinos in the United States, see Suzanne Oboler, "The Politics of Labeling: Latino/a

Cultural Identities of Self and Others," in *Latin American Perspectives*, 19 4 (Fall 1992), pp. 18–36.

11    Excerpts from this section first appeared in the introduction of *New American Destinies: A Reader in Contemporary Asian and Latino Immigration*, ed. Darrell Y. Hamamoto and Rodolfo D. Torres (New York: Routledge, 1997).

12    See the path-breaking work of Andres Torres, *Between Melting Pot and Mosaic: African American and Puerto Ricans in the New York Political Economy* (Philadelphia: Temple University Press) 1995.

13    See "Central American Migration: A Framework for Analysis," by Nora Hamilton and Norma Stoltz Chinchilla, in *New American Destinies*, ed. D. Hamamoto and R. Torres.

14    For an excellent analysis of the past and present conditions of Latinos in New York, see *Latinos in New York: Communities in Transition*, ed. Gabriel Haslip-Viera & Sherrie L. Bauer, (University of Notre Dame Press, 1996).

15    For a book-length treatment of the history of Cubans in the United States, see Maria Cristina Garcia's *Havana USA: Cuban Exiles and Cuban Americans in South Florida, 1959–1994* (Berkeley: University of California Press, 1996).

16    For an excellent study of Mexican immigrants that treats gender with analytical primacy see *Gendered Transitions: Mexican Experiences of Immigration*, by Pierrette Hondagneu-Sotelo (University of California Press, 1994).

# Bibliography

Acosta-Belén, E. (1992). "Beyond Island Boundaries: Ethnicity, Gender, and Cultural Revitalization in Nuyorican Literature," *Callaloo*, 15/4, 979–98.

Amin, A. (1994). *Post-Fordism: A Reader*. Oxford: Blackwell.

Anzaldúa, G. (1981). "La Prieta," in *This Bridge Called My Back: Writings by Radical Women of Color*, ed. C. Moraga and G. Anzaldúa. Watertown, MA: Persephone Press.

Apodaca, M. L. (1986). "A Double Edged Sword," *Critica: A Journal of Critical Analysis*, 1 (Fall), 96–114.

Appiah, K. A. (1996). "Race, Culture, Identity: Misunderstood Connections," in *Color Conscious: The Political Morality of Race*, ed. K. A. Appiah and A. Gutman. Princeton, NJ: Princeton University Press.

Azize-Vargas, Y. (1990). "The Roots of Puerto Rican Feminism: The Struggle for Universal Suffrage," *Radical America*, 23/1, 71–9.

Blauner, R. (1992). "Talking Past Each Other: Black and White Languages of Race," *American Prospect*, 10 (Summer), 55–64.

Bonilla, F. and Girling, R. (1973). *Structures of Dependency*. Proceedings of Stanford University Colloquium.

Castañeda, A. (1993). "Sexual Violence in the Politics and the Policies of Conquest: Amerindian women and the Spanish Conquest of Alta California," in *Building with Our Hands*, ed. A. de la Torre and B. Pesquera Berkeley: University of California Press.

Cotera, M. (1977). *The Chicana Feminist*. Austin, TX: Information Systems Development.

Crenshaw, K., Gotanda, N., Peller, G., and Thomas, K. (eds) (1995). *Critical Race Theory: The Key Writings that formed the Movement*. Philadelphia: Temple University Press.

Darder, A. and Torres, R. (1996). "From Race to Racism: The Politics of 'Race' Language in 'Postmodern' Education," *New Political Science*, 38/39 (Winter), 89–96.

Delgado, R. (1995). *Critical Race Theory: The Cutting Edge*. Philadelphia: Temple University Press.

Garcia, A. (1989). "The Development of Chicana Feminist Discourse," *Gender & Society*, 3/2 (June), 217–38.

Garcia, M. C. (1996). *Havana USA: Cuban Exiles and Cuban Americans in South Florida, 1959–1994*. Berkeley: University of California Press.

Gates, H. L. and West, C. (eds) (1996). *The Future of the Race*. New York: Knopf.

Gilroy, P. (1991). *There Ain't No Black in the Union Jack*. Chicago: University of Chicago Press.

Goldberg, D. T. (1993). *Racist Culture*. Cambridge, MA: Blackwell.

Gomez-Quiñonez, J. (1977). *On Culture*. Los Angeles: UCLA Chicano Studies Center Publications, Popular Series No. 1.

Grosfoguel, R. and Georas, C. (1996). "The Racialization of Latino Caribbean Migrants in the New York Metropolitan Area," *Centro: Focus En Foco*. 8/1-2.

Guillaumin, C. (1995). *Racism, Sexism, Power and Ideology*. London: Routledge.

Gutierrez, R. (1995). "Historical and Social Science Research on Mexican Americans," in

*Handbook of Research on Multicultural Education,* ed. J. Banks and C. Banks. New York: Macmillan.

Hall, S. (1996). "Cultural Studies and the Politics of Internalization: An Interview with Stuart Hall by Kuan Hsing Chen," in *Stuart Hall: Critical Dialogues in Cultural Studies,* ed. D. Morley and K. H. Chen. London: Routledge.

—— (1991). "The Local and the Global: Globalization and Ethnicity," in *Culture, Globalization, and the World System,* ed. A. King. Binghamton, NY: State University of New York at Binghamton.

—— (1990). Ethnicity: Identity and Difference in Radical America. *Radical America,* 13/4, 9–20.

Hall, T. (1996). "The World-System Perspectives: A Small Sample from a Large Universe," *Sociological Inquiry,* 66 4 (November), 440–54.

Hamamoto, D. and Torres, R. (eds) (1996). *New American Destinies: A Reader in Contemporary Asian and Latino Immigration.* New York: Routledge.

Hamilton, N. and Stoltz Chinchilla, N. (1997). "Central American Migration: a Framework for Analysis," in *New American Destinies,* ed. D. Hamamoto and R. Torres. New York: Routledge.

Haslip-Viera and Bauer, S. (eds) (1996). *Latinos in New York: Communities in Transition.* Notre Dame: University of Notre Dame Press.

Hondagneu-Sotelo, P. (1994). *Gendered Transitions: Mexican Experiences of Immigration.* Berkeley: University of California Press.

Hurtado, A. (1996). *The Color of Privilege: Three Blasphemies of Race and Feminism.* Ann Arbor: University of Michigan Press.

Malik, K. (1996). *The Meaning of Race, History and Culture in Western Society.* New York: New York University Press.

Miles, R. (1993). *Racism After Race Relations.* London: Routledge.

—— (1989). *Racism.* London: Routledge.

—— (1982). *Racism and Migrant Labor.* New York: Routledge and Kegan Paul.

Miles, R. and Torres, R. (1996). "Does 'Race' Matter? Transatlantic Perceptives on Racism after 'Race Relations'" in *Resituating Identities: The Politics of Race, Ethnicity and Culture,* ed. V. Amit-Talai and C. Knowles. Ontario: Broadview Press.

Moraga, C. and Anzaldúa, G. (1981). *This Bridge Called My Back: Writings by Radical Women of Color.* Watertown, MA: Persephone Press.

Muñoz, C. (1989). *Youth, Identity, Power: The Chicano Movement.* London and New York: Verso.

Oboler, S. (1992). "The Politics of Labeling: Latino/a Cultural Identities of Self and Others," in *Latin American Perspectives,* 19/4 (Fall), 18–36.

Omi, M. and Winant, H. (1994). *Racial Formation in the United States: From 1960s to the 1990s,* 2nd edn. New York: Routledge.

Outlaw, L. (1996). *On Race and Philosophy.* New York: Routledge.

Petras, J. and Morley, M. (1995). *Empire of Republic? American Global Power and Domestic Decay.* New York: Routledge.

Ramos, J. (1995). "Latin American Lesbians Speak on Black Identity," in *Moving Beyond Boundaries.* Vol. 2. *Black Women's Diasporas.* New York: New York University Press.

Robinson, W. (1993). "The Global Economy and the Latino Populations in the United States: A World System Approach," *Critical Sociology,* 19/2, 29–59.

Rodriguez, C. (1995). "Puerto Ricans in Historical and Social Science Research," in *Handbook of Research on Multicultural Education,* ed. J. Banks and C. Banks. New York: Macmillan.

Rodriguez-Morazanni, R. (1996). "Beyond the Rainbow: Mapping the Discourse on Puerto Ricans and 'Race,'" *Centro: Focus En Foco,* 8/1–2, 151–69.

Sánchez, R. (1990). "The History of Chicanas: Proposal for a Materialist Perspective," in *Between Borders: Essays on Mexican/Chicana History,* ed. A. del Castillo. Encino: Floricanto Press.

Small, S. (1994). *Racialized Barriers: The Black Experience in the United States and England in the 1980s.* London: Routledge.

Sunshine, C. (1994). *The Caribbean: Survival, Struggle and Sovereignty.* Washington, DC: EPICA.

Tölöyan, K. (1996). "Rethinking Diaspora(s): Stateless Power in the Transnational Moment," *Diaspora,* 5/1, 3–37.

Torres, A. (1995). *Between Melting Pot and Mosaic: African American and Puerto Ricans in the New York Political Economy.* Philadelphia: Temple University Press.

Torres, R. and Ngin, C. (1995). "Racialized Boundaries, Class Relations, and Cultural Politics: The Asian American and Latino Experience," in *Culture and Difference: Critical Perspectives on the Bicultural Experience in the United States,* ed. A. Darder. Westport, CN: Bergin and Garvey.

Valle, V. and Torres, R. (1994). "Latinos in a 'Post-Industrial' Disorder: Politics in a Changing City," *Socialist Review,* 23 4, 1–28.

Valle, V. and Torres, R. (1995). "The Idea of Mestizaje and the 'Race' Problematic: Racialized Media Discourse in a Post-Fordist Landscape," in *Culture and Difference: Critical Perspectives on the Bicultural Experience in the United States*, ed. A. Darder. Westport, CN: Bergin and Garvey.

Wieviorja, M. (1995). *The Arena of Racism.* London: Sage.

Wing, A. K. (1997). *Critical Race Feminism: A Reader.* New York: New York University Press.

Wood, E. M. (1996). "Modernity, Postmodernity, or Capitalism," *Monthly Review*, 48/3, 21–39.

—— (1995). *Democracy Against Capitalism: Renewing Historical Materialism.* Cambridge: Cambridge University Press.

—— (1994). "Identity Crisis," *In These Times* (June), 28–9.

# Part I

*Culture, History, and Society:*
*A Conceptual Map*

# Merging Borders:
# The Remapping of America

## Edna Acosta-Belén and Carlos E. Santiago

In an era of increasing global interconnections, interdependence, and economic integration among nations and regions, paying due attention to the US Hispanic heritage, to the increasing presence of Latinos in the United States, and to the existing transnational linkages that (im)migrant groups maintain with their Latin American or Caribbean countries of origin, immediately suggests new challenges and changes in our conventional interpretations of the history and culture of the Americas, both North and South. For more than a century Latin American and Caribbean intellectuals have attempted to develop continental visions of the Americas that take into consideration the common experiences that bind together the colonized peoples and cultures of the hemisphere and recognize the basic oppression and estrangement of people of color in white-dominated societies, as well as the uneven distribution of wealth and power asymmetries within their own countries and between a developed North America and the undeveloped nations south of the border.

In this article we introduce some innovative and stimulating ways of looking at the cultural and racial diversity of the Americas – North and South – two intricate multicultural and multiracial spheres where we find diverse populations bound by a shared legacy of colonialism, racism, displacement, and dispersion; trying to outline ways in which it makes sense to transcend or redefine the conventional boundaries that have constrained our study and understanding of the peoples of Latin America and the Caribbean vis-à-vis their counterpart populations from these regions living in the United States. Some of the fundamental issues that merit further examination

are how the Americas are being bridged by existing transnational connections between the countries of Latin America and the Caribbean and their respective US diasporas; by the collective forms of cultural affirmation, resistance, and hybridization taking place among Latino groups within US society; and by overlapping issues of race, gender, nationality, ethnicity, and class. Our efforts at examining the interconnections among the cultures of the Americas across time and geographic divides aim to bring fresh insights into this cultural meeting ground as much as they attempt to modify the fragmented way in which we tend to look both at the US Latino experience and at the Latin American/Caribbean experience. In doing so, we underscore the need to extend the cultural parameters of analysis beyond those already imposed by spurious geographic national frontiers or constructed boundaries, rather than looking at two separate, unrelated, or closed cultural spheres of analysis. The approach we are suggesting here may encourage Latin Americanists, Caribbeanists, US Latino, and American studies specialists to move away from the monocultural, monolithic, and hegemonic conceptualizations of cultural identity, which, more often than not, have been predicated upon the active suppression or exclusion of the various forms of cultural diversity that we find in all of our societies.

Perhaps a good point of departure in this process of bridging the Americas is to "revisit" the concept of *Nuestra América (Our America)*, developed by the Cuban writer and patriot José Martí during the years he lived in New York City as a political émigré – that is, from 1881 to 1895, or a total of almost 14 years.

Martí came to New York when he was 28 and at 42 he went back to Cuba, where he was killed by Spanish troops shortly after his return to the island in 1895. Thus the New York period represents a significant part of his adult life. While in New York Martí organized the Cuban independence movement and published a good portion of his major writings. He was a frequent contributor to both Latin American and US newspapers and in 1892 founded *Patria*, the official newspaper of the Cuban Revolutionary Party. The reasons for choosing Martí as a significant point of departure in this cultural analysis of the Americas are twofold. First, it was during the time that he lived in New York that he produced the most important essays about his vision of the American continent and about the greatness and wretchedness of living in what he referred to as "las entrañas del monstruo" ("I have lived inside the monster and know its entrails," he once said). Secondly, he was an important figure during the formative years of the New York City *colonia hispana* – a period that is fundamental for the historical reconstruction of our US Latino communities, as we increase our knowledge about the links of solidarity between Puerto Ricans and Cubans in New York and other US cities during the late nineteenth-century independence struggles against Spanish colonial rule and of other joint efforts in the working-class struggles of the time. Similar connections, collaborations, and alliances also would flourish in the New York metropolis in subsequent decades among Spanish, other Latin American and Caribbean nationalities, and US groups around a wide range of cultural, political, and social issues, particularly during the years of the Harlem Renaissance, the Great Depression, the Spanish Civil War, World War II, the McCarthy Era, and in more recent decades, during the civil rights, ethnic revitalization, and women's movements.

From many of the essays that Martí produced while living in New York, we learn a great deal about the class and racial conflicts of the United States; about the clashes between capital and labor; about the detrimental conditions and discrimination faced by the US native and Black populations; and about the mighty threat of an emerging US imperialism looming over Cuba and other parts of Latin America. But most important from the perspective of this article is what we learn about Martí's continental vision – his efforts at capturing and defining the cultural elements that comprise Latin American identity, and his quest for a free and color-blind multicultural society not characterized by, as he would say, the "struggle of races" but by the "affirmation of rights."

Contrary to other intellectuals of his time, who viewed the future of Latin America in the emulation of imported "civilized" European or Anglo-American models, or who counterposed Western civilization to the purported "barbarism" of the indigenous, Black, mestizo, or peasant populations, Martí reaffirms the need to take into account those non-Western elements which are peculiar to the peoples of the Americas, in this way validating the multiplicity of cultures and classes autochthonous to the region and those resulting from a creolization process – that unprecedented mixing of races and cultural syncretism that took place in the Americas, and which perhaps has never reached a similar magnitude in any other part of the world. Martí emphatically called for "our mestizo America . . . to show itself as it is." And what is after all the true face of *Our America*, if not a place depopulated by conquest and colonization and repopulated by uprooted immigrants and slaves; the stage where the Spanish/European culture in exerting its domination converged and blended with the many indigenous and African cultures producing new and striking cultural configurations?

Perhaps one of Martí's most outstanding contributions to the Cuban independence struggle was his frontal attack on the racism that divided his native country and that could affect the common cause for Cuban independence. Two years before the 1892 founding in New York of the Cuban Revolutionary Party, he worked with Afro-Cuban émigrés in the City in the formation of *La Liga* (The League), which focused on the education and advancement of this working-class sector of the community. In this way he laid an important foundation for eradicating racism and promoting racial harmony and equality, and ameliorating social class divisions within the independence movement. When Martí declared that "Whoever foments and propagates antagonism and hate between the races, sins against Humanity" or when he delivered his oration "With all, and for the good of all," he was surpassing racial and class barriers in an attempt to unite the heterogeneous elements present within the Antillean independence movement. Although Martí is generally considered to be the major articulator of anti-imperialist thought in Latin America, he was as wary of US imperialism as he was of US racism and segregation. Through his innumerable essays about the two Americas – Anglo-Saxon and Hispanic – he articulates his continental political, social, and humanitarian vision about the future of the continent as much as his more specific concerns about the plight of the US native and Black populations.

The idea of equal dignity and harmony among the races was essential to Martí's concept of nation-building and the future of his own country. Yet, his affirmation of a multicultural and multiracial *Nuestra América* also takes on great contemporary significance as we strive to put an end to European and Anglo-American ethnocentricity by decolonizing and deconstructing the cultural mythologies and received knowledge about ourselves perpetuated within the dominant Western tradition. The essentialist cultural hegemony and parochialism of the Western nations has undermined the many subaltern cultural "others" of the so-called Third World, without properly acknowledging any shared system of cultural interactions, or by conceiving their realities and accomplishments in isolation from theirs.

While Martí developed the concept of *Nuestra América* in reference to a nineteenth-century Latin America that was struggling with the evils of tyranny and exploitative economic forces, even after most of the former

Spanish colonies had achieved independence, he realized that the destiny of the continent was inextricably linked to the Colossus to the North. From Martí's perspective, US government imperialist aims, its expressed desire to annex Cuba and other territories, and the expansionist ambitions of US wealthy investors, made Cuba, Puerto Rico, and other Latin American countries vulnerable to military and economic intervention or penetration. However, notwithstanding the man of vision that he was, Martí could not anticipate then the extent to which, almost a century later, some of those economic and political forces that he so much feared are pushing the peoples of Latin America and the Caribbean out of their countries and into the US metropolis in unprecedented numbers. Ironically, the incursion is reversing itself and more than ever before, the citizens of Martí's *Nuestra América* are caught in an intricate and complex web of international (im)migration and labor flows that are causing multiple population displacements from the peripheral to the advanced capitalist nations. Coupled with the political repression that continues to plague many Latin American and Caribbean countries, the journey to the prosperous *norte* remains one of the few viable surviving alternatives. *Nuestra América* has become a very palpable presence *in* the United States and this dramatic diasporic reality and the ongoing and projected changes in the demographic composition of the United States population, are forcing us both to come to terms with and expand the terms in which we see our Latino identity, or more accurately, to better understand the ways we juggle our multiple and fluid identities – those reconstituted or remolded from generation to generation from our cultural cross-connections with the native culture, with the US mainstream culture that marginalizes us, and with the cultures of other marginal groups.

Hispanics, as they are identified by government agencies, or Latinos, as they generally prefer to be called, all have been lumped together under a collective label that tends to eclipse the many different nationalities, cultural experiences, and histories shared by the individual groups. Under the Hispanic category used by the US Census are included the descendants of early Spanish settlers of the colonial period as well as the newcomers of our time; many were born in what is today US territory and others have come here as (im)migrants or as undocumented workers. Hence, the Latino presence of the United States is an unavoidable part of the past and present realities of this nation.

The fact that the diverse Latino nationalities may prefer not to identify themselves with the Hispanic or Latino panethnic label becomes less true every day. Ironically, the shorthand term is turning into a collective symbol of cultural affirmation and separate identity in a society that promoted the melting-pot assimilation ideology which viewed as desirable the suppression or rejection of cultural differences in the name of a unified or homogeneous American ethos. In reality, the myth of the melting pot overgeneralized the past assimilation patterns of white European immigrant groups and tended to obliterate or hide the long history of exclusion, racial discrimination, and social and civil rights struggles shared by people of color in US society. The Hispanic/Latino collective panethnic label is also proving to be useful in the political articulation of the pressing socioeconomic and educational needs and priorities of the various Latino communities. Therefore, even though each individual Latino group has a different sense of their own nationality and identity, to a large extent, Latinos are finding that their commonalities provide them with a more effective political voice.

An increasing Latino panethnic consciousness within US society is not, however, a contemporary phenomenon. On the contrary, it has had a long and vigorous tradition. It is not difficult to document in different historical periods many examples of the political alliances, cultural interactions, and exchanges that, although rooted in the US Latino communities, achieved a broad national or continental dimension. For contemporary US Latinos, learning about the pioneer communities and reconstructing a tradition within US society provide a sense of

continuity with the past and a vital source of collective identity and empowerment that helps to counteract the negative effects of their marginal status. This is particularly important for Latinos born or raised in the United States, who may have fewer ties or less contact with their families' countries of origin.

During the nineteenth century the United States, following its policies of territorial expansion, made its first incursions into Latin America by taking possession of about half of the territory that was part of the nation of Mexico, as a result of the Texas War of Independence and the Mexican-American War. The 1848 Treaty of Guadalupe Hidalgo transformed Northern Mexico into the US Southwest. The contemporary Chicano playwright and film-maker Luis Valdez succinctly summarized the disastrous outcome of this armed conflict when he stated that "We did not come to the United States at all. The United States came to us."

It was also in this century that the Colossus to the North appropriated the name America to signify the United States. In his book *The End of American History* (1985), historian David Noble argues that implicit in this change in the use of the name America is a profound commitment to isolating the US national culture and minimizing any major claims of cultural interdependence with other nations, when defining the country's national identity. The construction of the historical narrative of the US nation was guided not only by the political independence claimed in 1776, but also by the concept of a Chosen People coming into a Promised Land who developed

> a unique national culture that modified its colonial inheritance from its mother country, England . . . But American historians . . . have not used a concept that combines political independence with cultural interdependence to define our cultural identity. They have thought and written as if the United States was absolutely independent, standing apart in its uniqueness from the rest of the human experience. (p. 7)

Noble's interpretation is particularly illuminating if we consider that the United States always has been a necessary or unavoidable point of reference for the rest of the continent, while in contrast, the importance of Latin America and the Caribbean in the United States national discourse is usually minimized or dismissed by claims about their inferior status of economic dependency and political turmoil, despite these regions' historic economic and strategic geopolitical importance. Even in its territorial expansionist enterprise, the United States separated itself from Europe. In *Cultures of United States Imperialism*, Amy Kaplan and Donald Pease (1993) document the absence of empire in the study of US culture and conclude that US historiography has portrayed the nation as inherently anti-imperialist and has been reluctant to acknowledge that the country has engaged in imperialist practices. This paradigm of denial explains the exclusion of the many histories of continental and overseas expansion, of the conquest and resistance of the original populations and settlers of the West and the Southwest, and of the over 5 million US citizens, including Puerto Ricans, living in overseas colonial territories acquired from Spain in 1898. These prevailing standpoints in the historical narrative of the US nation achieve significant contemporary relevance if we consider the current national debates around multiculturalism, described by those who oppose it as producing a state of "culture wars," clearly indicating that any claims to the sharing of the US national identity that deviate from the dominant Anglo-Saxon narrative of the nation's history or from the mythical melting-pot, are considered disuniting, divisive, and essentially un-American.

Conventional historical accounts of the formative years of the United States tend to regard everything that preceded the establishment of the British 13 colonies as unimportant, paying little attention to other groups, such as Native Americans and Hispanics, who occupied North American territory long before the English settlers, and whose presence is interwoven into the historical fabric of the nation. The nineteenth-century westward territorial expansion of the United States from the original 13 colonies to the Pacific Coast and south to the Rio Grande and the Gulf Coast was the fulfillment of the nation's Manifest Destiny. But this confined view of US territorial expansion and the formative years of the nation tends to fragment or obscure the entire history of the past and its links to the present, leaving us with an impoverished understanding of how other groups, such as Latinos, have been and continue to be an integral part of this country's multicultural patrimony and have at different times played a perceptible role in the shaping of US history and society. Moreover, seeking to understand the larger meaning of the US Latino heritage allows us to recognize how the different parts of the American hemisphere are inexorably linked, more so than US and Latin American historical accounts have been willing to acknowledge. Not only must we begin to salvage these gaps in the construction of the United States' formative years as a nation, but also to acknowledge the complexity of the cultural interactions and amalgamations among indigenous populations, Spanish, British, and other European settlers, and African enslaved populations that took place in what is today US territory as well as throughout the Americas.

The increased population growth and visibility of US Latinos in recent decades and the work that is being produced by many Latino writers and scholars are leading us to pay more attention to the common denominators and the cultural bridges that have existed during various historical periods between the two Americas. Other non-Latino scholars have also suggested innovative ways of looking at the interconnections between the different parts of the hemisphere. For instance, Immanuel Wallerstein (1980), introduced the concept of "the extended Caribbean," suggesting the geographic linkages of the US South, the Caribbean islands, and the coastal areas of Central and South America all the way down to Brazil – areas where societies supported by enslaved labor and the agrosocial plantation system developed and thus share strong commonalities. More recently, the anthropologist Constance Sutton (1987) describes what she calls a "transnational sociocultural system" that allows Puerto Ricans and other Caribbean migrants to reconstitute their lives in New York City and affirm a separate cultural identity while maintaining strong interactions with their respective countries of origin. This process further creolizes Caribbean cultures and identities in both New York City and the countries of origin, challenging conventional notions of immigrant assimilation, and marking new possibilities in the struggles for social, cultural, and political empowerment of these marginal groups.

The consciousness-raising decades of the 1960s and 1970s, the civil rights and women's movements, and other struggles for social justice of the time allowed Chicanos and Puerto Ricans to join African and Native Americans in their efforts to revitalize and affirm their respective ethnic and racial identities. This was a movement of ethnic/racial minorities fighting the exclusionary practices of mainstream society and attempting to rid themselves of the negative self-images and stigma internalized from the racism and marginalization they had experienced and that denied them a collective positive identity. The results of the explosion in grassroots ethnic activism and organizing eventually reached the walls of the academy and African American, Chicano, Puerto Rican, and Native American ethnic studies and bilingual education programs began to proliferate across US colleges and universities.

For Latinos, one of the most worthwhile and promising outcomes of the ethnic revitalization movement is the *Recovering the US Hispanic Literary Heritage Project*, a ten-year scholarly undertaking directed by Professor Nicolás Kanellos at the University of Houston. During the last five years, the project has brought together around 20 Latino scholars searching for literary and historical writings by Hispanics from colonial times to the present in what is today the United States. One major aspect of the *Recovery Project* is the *US Hispanic Annotated Periodical Literature Project,* and the Center for Latino, Latin American, and Caribbean Studies (CELAC) at the State University of New York at Albany has joined the University of Houston and Colorado College in the major task of annotating and analyzing some of the over 1,000 periodicals already identified, which were published in the Hispanic communities throughout the United States since the early part of the nineteenth century.

We can only imagine what this process of recovery and (re)discovery represents for the Latino community since the project's full promise and impact will probably not be realized until many years from now. There is a plethora of information being generated that needs to be processed and analyzed, and community figures whose writings are being recovered and still need to be studied and contextualized. A noteworthy aspect of this whole recovery process is that many of the periodical publications are proving to be quite valuable in reconstructing a chronicle of the past and in providing glimpses into the everyday life of the diverse Latino communities at different historical periods. Of particular interest are the linkages that previous generations of US Latinos established among themselves or maintained with their diverse countries of origin. These periodicals are also facilitating our exploration of the relations and interconnections among diverse communities in US society at a particular time. One example that merits further study is the one represented by African American and Spanish Harlem during the 1920s and 1930s. This is the period when Black consciousness burgeoned into the cultural movement known as the Harlem Renaissance, a movement that coincides with the Afro Antillean and *négritude* cultural and literary movements in the Hispanic and French Caribbean, evidence of a strong continental PanAfrican consciousness during this period. Many notable figures of the Harlem Renaissance were, indeed, from the Caribbean – Marcus Garvey, Claude McKay, and Arthur Schomburg to mention a few – and these connections are awaiting further examination.

From the testimonial accounts of Puerto Rican *tabaqueros* (tobacco workers) Bernardo Vega and Jesús Colón, who migrated to the United States in 1916 and 1917 respectively, we have learned a great deal about the shared interethnic solidarities within the organized labor movement during the 1920s and 1930s, and about a community where intellectual pursuits often went hand in hand with sociopolitical activism, and prominent members of the intellectual elite stood side by side with members of the working class in their struggles for social justice. Weekly New York newspapers such as *Gráfico* (1927–31) *Pueblos hispanos* (1943–4), and *Liberación* (1946–9), confirm the continental, international, and Latino panethnic and anti-assimilation character of most of these publications, both in terms of their cultural vision reflected in many of the articles published, as well as their political goals. *Pueblos hispanos*, for example, describes itself as a progressive weekly at a time when the world was at war, that strived for: (1) the unification of all the Hispanic colonias in the United States to defeat Nazi-fascism and in solidarity with all democratic forces; (2) the defense of all the rights of Hispanic minorities; (3) combating prejudice against Hispanics based on race, color, or creed and the denunciation of prejudice against minorities. And if this discourse has a contemporary resonance, please note that it dates back to 1943. There are several other periodical publications, such as the *Revista de Artes y Letras* directed and owned by Josefina Silva de Cintrón from 1933 to 1945, which achieved international circulation and should be carefully examined from the perspective of women's concerns and the struggles of the time. These and many other periodicals injected a transnational dimension into the cultural life of the New York Latino community that clearly contradicts the image of the *barrios* as closed and hopeless spaces submerged in a "culture of poverty" and thus a "poverty of culture."

But nothing better illustrates the cultural and literary continuity of a Latino consciousness in the United States than the work being produced by Chicano, Puerto Rican, Cuban, Dominican, and other Latino writers and artists during the last few decades. Each major group has its own distinctive body of literature reflecting the interactions of their respective cultural worlds. These bodies of literature, written primarily in English, but frequently in Spanish or bilingually were, until recently, ignored by scholars of US and Latin American literatures alike. The language issue, compounded by the fact that these writings often have a working class character or that many books are published by small ethnic presses, further limit their diffusion and marketing, and hence their possibilities for critical acclaim.

Asunción Horno-Delgado, Eliana Ortega, and Nancy Saporta Sternback, in their book *Breaking Boundaries: Latina Writings and Critical Readings* (1989) underscore ways in which *latinismo* or a panLatino consciousness among Latina writers constitutes a unifying element in their works that incorporates elements of solidarity with other women's liberation movements in the United States, Latin America, and other parts of the Third World. Adopting the term "women of color" reflects a wider internationalist and humanitarian consciousness and a symbolic identification with the working class and other Third World women's struggles. The collections *This Bridge Called My Back* (1981), *Cuentos: Stories by Latinas* (1983), and *Compañeras: Latina Lesbians* (1987) were some of the pioneering efforts that attest to the emergence of a literary discourse based upon a cultural subjectivity of being a Latina, that recognizes the shared experiences both at an individual and panethnic level, but also transcends national origins in its spirit of solidarity and identification with other liberation movements of women and other groups oppressed because of class position, race, ethnicity, or sexual preference.

Anthropologist Ruth Behar in her two-volume edited collection of writings *Bridges to Cuba/Puentes a Cuba* (1994) juxtaposes the metaphors of "bridges," or points of connection, and "borders," or points of separation, between Cubans back on the island and in the diaspora. In doing so, she reveals the tensions, contradictions, and need for reconnecting to the roots, to an island community. Puerto Rican writer Luis Rafael Sánchez creates the metaphor of "la guagua aérea" (the airbus), that space where we find a nation floating or commuting between two ports. After all, as the author would say: "Nueva York sería la otra capital de Puerto Rico, si no lo fuera de toda Hispanoamérica" (p. 23) [New York would be the other capital of Puerto Rico if it were not already the capital of Spanish America].

More than any other group, Latino(a) writers and artists continue to span the distance between the Americas. They, as many other Third World peoples around the globe, are caught in a state of displacement that Angelika Bammer (1994) accurately describes as "one of the most formative experiences of our century" (p. xi) – a displacement produced by the physical dislocation from their native cultures experienced by (im)migrants, refugees, exiles, or by the colonizing experience. From that constant commuting – *el ir y venir* (the back and forth movement) of those from "here" and "there" (*los de aquí y los de allá*) – emerge the tensions, contradictions, and reconfigurations that influence and mold the construction of our contemporary Latino identities; identities marked by absence, loss, fragmentation, estrangement, reclaiming, and an inscribing presence. The words of the Cuban poet Lourdes Casal recreate what she sees as the unresolved nature of the process:

> That is why I will always remain on the margins,
> a stranger among the stones,
> even beneath the friendly sum of a summer's day,
> just as I will remain forever a foreigner,
> even when I return to the city of my childhood
> I carry this marginality, immune to all turning back,
> too *habanera* to be a *newyorquina*,
> too *newyorquina* to be
> – even to become again –
> anything else

(Lourdes Casal, "For Ana Veldford," p. 416)

The Puerto Rican voice of Sandra María Esteves captures the same sense of straddling between cultures and languages:

> Being Puertorriqueña
> Americana
> Born in the Bronx, not really jíbara
> Not really hablando bien
> But yet, not gringa either

(Sandra María Esteves, "Not neither," *Tropical Rains*)

Several Chicano writers and artists have introduced the notion of "border cultures" described by the writer and performing artist Guillermo Gómez-Peña in his artistic manifesto "The Border Is" (1993):

> Border culture means boycott, complot, ilegalidad, clandestinidad, contrabando, transgresión, desobediencia binacional . . .
>
> But it also means transcultural friendship and collaboration among races, sexes, and generations.

But it also means to practice creative appropriation, expropiation, and subversion of dominant cultural forms.

But it also means a multiplicity of voices away from the center, different geo-cultural relations among more culturally akin regions . . .

But it also means regresar, volver y partir: to return and depart once again . . .

But it also means a new terminology for new hybrid identities and métiers constantly metamorphosizing . . .

But it also means to look at the past and the future at the same time (pp. 43–4).

In her *Borderlands/La frontera: The New Mestiza* (1987), Chicana writer Gloria Anzaldúa adds a gender dimension to the oscillation between two worlds and claims an emerging new consciousness: "a new mestiza consciousness, *una conciencia de mujer*. It is a consciousness of the Borderlands" (p. 77):

Because I, a *mestiza*,
continually walk out of one culture
and into another,
because I am in all cultures at the same time
(Gloria Anzaldúa, "Una lucha de fronteras/A Struggle of Borders,"<br>*Borderlands/La frontera*, p. 77)

Yo soy un puente tendido
del mundo gabacho al del mojado
lo pasado me estirá pa' 'tras
y lo presente pa' 'delante.
Que la Virgen de Guadalupe me cuide
ay ay ay, soy mexicana de este lado

[I am an extended bridge
that links the white and wetback worlds
the past pulls me back
the present pushes me forward
May the Virgin of Guadalupe protect me
Ay, ay, ay I am Mexican from this side]
(Gloria Anzaldúa, "The Homeland, Aztlán," *Borderlands/La frontera,* p. 3*)*

Other Latino writers proclaim a new cultural synthesis that emerges from this cultural and linguistic straddling by affirming a new hybrid or syncretic identity that incorporates multiple forms of consciousness based on the multi, inter, intra, and crossconnections among the cultures shard and the multiple marginalities that arise from gender, racial, and class differences:

I am a child of the Americas
a light-skinned mestiza of the Caribbean
a child of many dispora, born into this continent at a crossroads.

I am not african. Africa is in me, but I cannot return.
I am not taína. Taíno is me, but there is no way back.

> I am not european. Europe lives in me, but I have no home there.
> I am new. History made me. My first language was spanglish.
> I was born at the crossroads
> and I am whole.
>
> (Aurora Levins Morales, "Child of the Americas," *Getting Home Alive*, p. 50)

All these crossroads languages also meet and Spanglish emerges as a creative force of hybrid interlinguality:

> assimilated? que assimilated,
> brother, yo soy asimilao,
>  asi mi la o sí es verdad
> tengo un lado asimilao,
>
> (Tato Laviera, "asimilao," *AmeRícan*, p. 54)

The North and the South converge creating a cultural meeting ground that challenges old cultural traditions and invents new ones; a place where class divisions and constructed borders between elite and popular cultural expression are constantly being transgressed. For the Nuyorican poet Tato Laviera it is all a matter of affirming new *Rican*figurations:

> we gave birth
> to a new generation
> AmeRícan salutes all folklores,
> european, indian, black, spanish,
> and anything else compatible . . .
>
> . . . AmeRícan defining myself my own way any way many
> ways Am e Rícan, with the big R and
> the accent on the í
>
> (Tato Laviera, "AmeRícan," *AmeRícan*, p. 94)

The voices of Latino writers are powerful examples of how geographic, cultural, and language borders are being transgressed, perhaps until they become meaningless or until the American continent ceases to be not just Anglo/European, not just white, not just the place where the subaltern "other" remains at the margins.

Martí's vision of a multicultural *Nuestra América* continues to have as much, if not more, relevance today than ever before. Whereas the sixteenth and seventeenth centuries have been characterized in the Western tradition as the Age of Discovery, it is the twentieth century where discovery has truly coalesced into integration and interdependence and is characterized by increasing closeness between peoples separated by what once were large physical distances. Now we find ourselves at a time when advances in technology, communication, and transportation have brought disparate communities closer together as information is made available virtually instantaneously and the advent of the Internet provides an avenue for uncensored news and communication. Moreover, the changing needs and demands of the economy that have accompanied these technological developments have had a fundamental impact on the division of labor at both the national and global level. Even in the more industrial societies, income inequality and polarization have resulted from, on the one hand, the draw of high-wage and high-skilled service-sector occupations, and on the other, a marginalized low-wage less educated labor force.

Latin America and the Caribbean have certainly not been immune to these global developments. On the contrary, the processes of structural adjustment, privatization, and liberalization that these countries have been subjected to in the last decade were made necessary because of the many economic inefficiencies that afflicted their economies, but at the same time have resulted in considerable hardship for large sectors of the population with only limited prospects for recovery and long-term prosperity. Where the private benefits of these economic processes have long found their way across national borders, we are now seeing that the social costs are also spreading far and wide.

Events in Chiapas provide a case in point. The rebels have managed to take their message, virtually unfiltered, beyond Mexico's borders. The instability and weakness in Mexico's political system have been impossible to hide. The lack of confidence has translated into an economic crisis that has been felt by Mexicans of all economic strata, but particularly those with the lowest levels of income. United States' holders of Mexican notes and bonds have demanded repayment of their investments while threatening to remove their financial capital from that country. President Clinton has responded by bypassing the US Congress and directly using funds destined for foreign exchange and balance of payments stabilization to provide the Mexican government with loans so that their repayment schedules can be met.

The US to Mexico loan guarantees have not come without conditions. Among these conditions are that the process of privatization and structural adjustment that began in the late 1980s is to continue and that the political system is to be opened. This has led the Zedillo government to engage in two contradictory policies: to clamp down on the insurgents in Chiapas and open the political system, chipping away at the dominance of his own Partido Revolucionario Institucional

(PRI). The economic hardship facing the Mexican people has been severe. Depreciation of the Mexican peso has reduced purchasing power and increased prices of imports, and ultimately, the prices of non-tradables and basic consumer goods. As expected, this crisis has resulted in an increase in immigration from Mexico to the United States, despite increased surveillance of the border area and a national mood against immigration, best exemplified by California's Proposition 187. In the 1990s (im)migrants have become the scapegoats for the ills of US society.

The current Mexican political and economic crisis is severe indeed and it provides but one example of the transcultural nature of movements of people, ideas, goods, entertainment, and information. Both Mexican and US societies are fundamentally affected and so are all countries of this hemisphere. The assimilationist's conception of the process has little basis in reality, if it ever did. Immigration has always represented transformation, both for the country of origin and the country of destination. What is different today is that the transformation is more immediate and profound. (Im)migrants are more knowledgeable about what to expect in the region of destination and they retain substantial ties to their countries of origin.

Similar examples can be found throughout the hemisphere. The dramatic increase in US (im)migration from Central America, the Dominican Republic, Haiti, Jamaica, and other islands of the Caribbean during the 1980s is a response to the political and economic marginalization of many people in these countries and the result of strategies of survival and the search for a better way of life. One could even argue that, based on the magnitude of the remittances which (im)migrants return to their countries of origin, the largest export from the Central American and Caribbean republics during the 1980s was people. The increase in US (im)migration from Latin America and the Caribbean during the 1980s is clearly linked to the declining standards of living in these countries during the "Lost Decade" and the changes provided by the family reunification provisions of the Immigration Law of 1965. Given the demographic characteristics of the recent (im)migrants, particularly their younger average age than the non-immigrant US population and the higher fertility rates among Latinos, the prospects for population growth among this group are considerable. These trends portend considerable demographic shifts in the nation and suggest that interethnic and interracial tensions will continue to be a growing concern.

A fundamental difference between (im)migration today and that at the turn of the century is that (im)migrants often retain considerable ties or interest in events occurring in their countries of origin. Instantaneous communication and improvements in transportation have much to do with this. Liberals and conservatives alike in the United States often decry the close ties between (im)migrants and their countries of origin as a reason for the lack of assimilation on the part of certain groups. The reality is that their objection is not truly aimed at (im)migration, for everyone but Native Americans can trace their roots to (im)migrants in this country, but rather to the fact that the "new immigrants" do not originate from traditional areas of European origin. Immigration has always been transformative – no different now than from the past. Those that push to restrict it simply worry that today's (im)migrants are transforming the society into something they find alien. It is a reflection of ignorance of alternative cultures more than an objection to (im)migration itself.

Resistance to (im)migration will continue at a fever pitch in the United States. It is clearly reflected in debates concerning multicultural and bilingual education and the dismantling of the safety net for those at the lower end of the income profile. The focal point will continue to be the border states of California, Florida, and Texas – precisely those states that registered large increases in (im)migrant and non-immigrant populations during the 1980s. The debate will be just as strident in those northeastern states that also received a heavy inflow of immigrants during the 1980s, and

where non-immigrant population growth is much slower. Latin America, the Caribbean, and Asia are now the primary areas of origin of these groups. If one were to rank the top 20 countries of birth among the foreign-born population in the United States, Mexico would rank first in 1990. According to Chiswick and Sullivan (1995), "Journalistic accounts of immigration occasionally lose sight of the fact that Mexico is a major source of *legal* immigrants. According to INS data, nearly one in every four legally admitted immigrants during the 1980s were from Mexico" (p. 222). Other Latin American and Caribbean countries ranked in the top 20 countries of birth among the foreign-born population in the United States in 1990 would be Cuba (number 4), El Salvador (number 12), Jamaica (number 14), the Dominican Republic (number 15), Colombia (number 18), and Guatemala (number 20). Although Puerto Rico is obviously not included in the INS data, given the number of Puerto Ricans born on the island and residing in the United States in 1990, Puerto Rico would rank second on the list, after Mexico. The "Latinization" or "Caribbeanization" of the (im)migrant stream brings on new challenges for the affirmation of cultural identity within an increasingly heterogeneous nation.

By revisiting the more than a century-old concept of *Nuestra América*, we hope to have shown the need to "reinvent" it by expanding the original meaning given to it by Martí and incorporating the cultural and historical realities and legacies bestowed upon us by those generations of Latinos who have forged their lives in the United States. The historical and cultural experience of US Latinos is forcing us to transcend the barriers imposed by national frontiers and by conventionally defined parameters about what constitutes Latin American or Caribbean cultural authenticity. In a postmodern world of increasing transnational connections, it is no longer tenable to talk about the concept of *Nuestra América* without, as we have suggested, including the Latino population in the United States. More than ever before, the two Americas intertwine, at a time when, paradoxically, some sectors of US society view with increasing disdain and hostility the presence of ethnic minorities and (im)migrants, wishing that a high wall be erected or a deep ditch be dug along the border, engaging in a polarizing discourse which appeals to deeply ingrained prejudices and fears, and hoping to reverse many of the modest gains of recent decades in the struggles against social, racial, and gender inequalities.

The decade of the 1990s brought the quincentennial commemoration of the encounter between the Old and New Worlds. In three more years, we approach the commemoration of the Cuban-Spanish-American War, which ended Spanish imperial domination in the Americas, but established the United States as the dominant power within the hemisphere. Rather than falling into the *fin de siècle* malaise or recriminations that were so predominant in the spanish and Latin American worlds a century ago, Latinos should take this opportunity to continue bridging the Americas, restoring the original hemispheric sense to the name America, producing emancipatory knowledge that recognizes our multiple cultural citizenships and alliances, and further promoting a liberating dialogue about the hemisphere, based not on one dominant country's exceptionalism, but on the many identities most of us share. Only when we tap into the multicultural and multiracial wealth of all the American nations will we move closer to achieving the human equality and dignity treasured by so many others before us.

# Bibliography

Acosta-Belén, Edna, and Sánchez Korrol, Virginia, (eds) (1993). *The Way it Was and Other Writings* by Jesús Colón. Houston: Arte Público Press.

Andreu Iglesias, César (ed.) (1977). *Memorias de Bernardo Vega*. Rio Piedras: Ediciones Huracán.

Anzaldúa, Gloria, (1987). *Borderlands/La frontera: The New Mestiza*. San Francisco: Spinters/Aunt Lute.

Bammer, Angelika. (1994). *Displacements: Cultural Identities in Question*. Bloomington: Indiana University Press.

Behar, Ruth (ed.) (1994). *Bridges to Cuba/Puentes a Cuba. Michigan Quarterly Review*, 33/3 and 33/4.

Casal, Lourdes. (1994). "For Ana Veldford" in *Bridges to Cuba/Puentes a Cuba*, ed. Ruth Behar. Michigan Quarterly Review 33/4: 416.

Chiswick, Barry R. and Sullivan, Teresa A. (1995). "The New Immigrants" in *State of the Union: America in the 1990s*, Vol. 2, ed. Reynolds Farley. New York: Russell Sage Foundation.

Colón, Jesús. (1982). *A Puerto Rican in New York and Other Sketches*. New York: International Publishers.

Esteves, Sandra María. (1984). *Tropical Rains*. New York: African Caribbean Poetry Theatre.

Foner, Phillip S. (ed.) (1977). *Our America by José Martí*. New York: Monthly Review Press.

Gómez, Alma, Moraga, Cherrie, and Romo-Cardona, Mariana, (eds) (1983). *Cuentos: Stories by Latinas*. New York: Kitchen Table Press.

Gómez-Peña, Guillermo. (1993). *Warrior for Gringostroika*. Saint Paul, MN: Graywolf Press.

Gutiérrez, Ramón, and Padilla, Genaro (eds) (1993). *Recovering the U.S. Hispanic Literary Heritage*. Houston: Arte Público Press.

Horno-Delgado, Asunción, Ortega, Eliana, and Scott, Nina M. (eds) (1989). *Breaking Boundaries: Latina Writings and Critical Readings*. Amherst: University of Massachusetts Press.

Kaplan, Amy, and Pease, Donald (eds) (1993). *Cultures of United States Imperialism*. Durham, NC: Duke University Press.

Laviera, Tato (1985). *AmeRícan*. Houston: Arte Público Press.

Levins Morales, Aurora, and Morales, Rosario (1986). *Getting Home Alive*. Ithaca, NY: Firebrand Books.

Moraga, Cherrie, and Anzaldúa, Gloria (eds). (1981). *This Bridge Called My Back*. New York: Kitchen Table Press.

Noble, David W. (1985). *The End of American History*. Minneapolis: University of Minnesota Press.

Ramos, Juanita (ed.) (1987). *Campañeras: Latina Lesbians*. New York: Latina Lesbian History Project.

Sánchez, Luis Rafael. (1994). *La guagua aérea*. Río Piedras: Editorial Cultural.

Sutton, Constance R., and Chaney, Elsa M. (eds) (1987). *Caribbean Life in New York City*. New York: Center for Migration Studies.

U.S. Bureau of the Census (1993). *Hispanic Americans Today*. Current Population Reports. P23–183. Washington, DC: Government Printing Office.

Wallerstein, Immanuel (1980). *The Modern World-System II*. New York: Academic Press.

# Encuentros y Encontronazos: Homeland in the Politics and Identity of the Cuban Diaspora

## María de los Angeles Torres

> . . . Nadie entendio: todos
> preferian su isla aparte,
> su mitad de verdad.
> . . . La sola construccion de la obra
> a todos ofendia.
> . . . Nadie quiere ceder pero tampoco nadie/puede
> obstruir: la obra avanza
> . . . Un pie aqui
> y otro alla.
> yo mismo el puente.
>
> *Jesus J. Barquet, "Un Puente Un Gran Puente"*

## I REVOLUTION, RUPTURE, AND EXILE: THE ORIGINS OF THE POSTREVOLUTIONARY CUBAN EXILE COMMUNITY

The relationship of Cuban exiles to their homeland after the 1959 revolution must be understood within a framework that analyzes United States and Cuban national security interests and how these influenced the formation of the politics of the community, and how, in turn, internal community dynamics evolved.[1] While the Cuban revolution was deeply rooted in the struggle to redefine a nation and institute a just social program, it also challenged United States hegemony in the Caribbean. This, in turn, had an impact on the post-World War II standoff between the Soviet Union and the United States – the cold war – and affected the movement of people out of the island, consequently the politics of émigré communities. Therefore, the broader framework of homeland politics – its organizational and ideological articulation – needs to be understood in this context. National security interests on both sides of the Florida

Straits have drawn the boundaries in which the dilemmas of race and class, immigrant and exile, the personal and the communal, have unfolded.

The postrevolutionary Cuban exile is a distinct political formation whose origin is fundamentally anchored in the foreign policy objectives of the United States government and internal policies of the Cuban state. Exiles provided the United States military with resources and ideological cannon fodder. Foreign policies aimed at overthrowing and discrediting the Cuban revolution were in part implemented through Cuban émigrés (see Arguelles). As long as Cuban émigrés were "exiles" and not a part of the United States, the administration could deny involvement in the military actions being taken against the revolution. By being "exiles," they provided "plausible deniability" to the CIA and to other governmental agencies involved in the planning and execution of the covert war against the Castro regime. In the process, these exiles institutionalized repressive methods of political participation – particularly those focused on

Cuba – within an evolving diaspora community in the United States.

Further, the flight of exiles to the United States also fulfilled the ideological functions of providing evidence that communism was a repressive system. After the 1959 Cuban revolution, United States policies politicized the process of immigration, setting up an unprecedented program of allowing private individuals to issue visa waivers to Cubans on the island. The CIA, State Department, and the Immigration and Naturalization Service (INS) collaborated in a program through which underground organizations were given authority to issue visa waivers to their members. According to congressional testimony provided by the director of the INS in the early sixties, over 600,000 visa waivers were issued from 1960 to 1962. In fact, one such program, the Peter Pan Operation, was aimed exclusively at bringing the children of the underground to the United States. Father Bryan Walsh, a Catholic priest, was in charge of issuing visa waivers for the children. Eventually, over 14,000 unaccompanied Cuban children were brought to the United States (see Torres, "Cold"). In effect, established immigration and security policies were circumvented. Aid packages and special privileges were also extended to Cuban exiles. The special treatment of Cuban exiles was predicated on the premise that the Cuban revolution would soon be toppled and exiles would return. In all, the extraordinary treatment of Cuban exiles fostered a distinct exile formation.

Cuban state policies contributed to this phenomenon. The Revolution itself had been a process broadly supported. The middle class in particular played a significant role not only in legitimating the rebellion, but also by participating in the underground. However, after the defeat of Batista, one organization, the 26 of July Movement headed by Fidel Castro, consolidated the revolutionary movement under its mandate. Many organizations and individuals opposed this centralization of power under one man. But critics were dealt with harshly. The death penalty, which had been abolished after the war of independence

from Spain, was applied frequently. Many who had supported the rebellion against Batista precisely because of the physical violence his regime employed became alienated from the new regime. Leaving the country became a political option that the new government defined as treason.

In reality, the large exodus benefited the emerging revolutionary government, providing it with a rallying point. Whether or not one stayed or left, and whether one supported or condemned those who left, became a litmus test of support for the revolution. In addition, externalizing opposition allowed the Cuban government to get rid of its dissidents in a fashion that essentially rendered them impotent to launch a legitimate challenge to a communist government that was increasingly relying on *nationalism* to consolidate its power. A force tied to one of the nation's historical enemies had no chance of mounting a popular claim against the island's government.[2]

The interaction of Cuban exiles with United States foreign policy objectives and domestic security policies in Cuba fueled the creation of a community abroad in exile. The close interaction of national security agencies within Cuba and the United States with the émigrés left a mark on the community's politics and identity. In this context, the relationship of Cuban exiles to their host and home countries acquired a political significance not normally ascribed to immigrant communities.

Exiles are not necessarily passive relative to events concerning their homeland, but generally speaking, they are also not the dominant actors in carving out strategic policies for either their host or home states. Émigré groups develop their own interests, which, at times, can be in harmony or in conflict with state interests; however, ultimately, host and home states have the upper hand.

## 2    HOMELAND RECONSIDERED

In 1961, the Cuban government decreed that in order to travel abroad, island residents had to receive an exit permit from the Ministry of the Interior. Failure to return to the island within 60 days was considered a "definitive abandonment." The same decree authorized the ministry to confiscate the property of the travelers. Furthermore, they could no longer return to the island – even for visits. In 1962, as a result of the October Missile Crisis, the United States prohibited travel to Cuba. In effect, travel to the island was forbidden by both home and host states.

Not being part of either the United States or Cuba, the exiles turned inward to define their identity. Cultural practices were ferociously defended. For instance, exiles expected their children to date with chaperons, following the same codes the parents had followed in Cuba. The insistence on maintaining their language eventually contributed to making Miami the first municipal government in the United States to provide services in English and Spanish. As their music and art evolved, it was permeated with nostalgia. In the early 1960s, painters such as Felix Ramos made a living recreating the pictures of lush and colorful "framboyanes" (tropical mimosa trees), which hung in the living rooms of Cuban families throughout the United States alongside the overreproduced iconographic photo of the *Malecon*, the Havana seawall. The desire to re-engage with the island was relegated to nostalgia because of the impossibility of returning. Consequently, Cuban exile culture became frozen in a version of the past, turning into *la cultura conjelada* (the frozen culture). Paradise had been lost forever to the "forces of evil." Prohibited from returning to the island, the first group of postrevolution émigrés turned nostalgia into a principle of constructing community and of defying the official Cuban position. Their "Cubanness" would not be taken away from them by the government.

As the years passed, exiles inevitably became concerned with their day-to-day existence in the United States. However, many still wanted to re-establish a relationship with the homeland. In the early 1970s, a debate began about whether Cuban exiles should hold a dialogue with the government that many of them had fled. Two groups led this

discussion: radical Catholics organized by the Instituto de Estudios Cubanos (Cuban Studies Institute),[3] and young exiles in search of identity and alternative politics. Lourdes Casal, a sociologist and poet, became the bridge between these groups.

The first group was composed mainly of academics who had fought against Batista and subsequently joined the anti-Castro opposition. They represented the radical wing of the Catholic Church. The second group consisted of people who had come to the United States when they were young and had been radicalized in the civil rights struggle and in the anti-Vietnam War movement. Radical Cuban exile politics unfolded in the context of this highly charged environment, while issues of equality and identity were at the core of the civil rights movement. The Vietnam War had placed United States foreign policy toward the Third World at the center of public debate. Bringing together these two issues was a logical outcome of the radicalization process undergone by some Cuban exiles. Two distinct groups of young radicals emerged around the publications *Joven Cuba* and *Areito*. *Joven Cuba (Young Cuba)*, published in New York, defined Cubans as a minority group and called for Cubans in the United States to join the struggles of other Latinos. Many of the members of this group had grown up outside of Miami and had confronted discrimination. Though their politics were oriented toward life in the United States, they also wanted to build bridges to the island. *Areito*, first published in Miami and later New York, held that Cubans should continue to view themselves as part of the island nation. Both groups included many middle-class Cubans who had come to the United States when they were young – many as children of the Peter Pan exodus – and were united by their desire to develop a relationship with their homeland.[4]

However, their desire was met by terrorism from extremist groups and stiff opposition from their parents. Generational conflict had been common in Cuban families. Adapting to a new culture had proven difficult, and Cuban families suffered cultural clashes typical of immigrant experiences. These clashes were particularly intense because they unfolded in the midst of a cultural revolution in the United States. In many ways, the social upheaval of the United States in the 1960s and 1970s legitimated young Cubans' struggle against parents, who seemingly had little to offer. In fact, they were caught in a very contradictory position: On the one hand, they wanted their children to follow "Cuban ways" but, on the other, they opposed their children's desire to return to Cuba, even for visits. The ensuing cultural and political confrontations with their parents contributed to radicalizing members of the younger generation. Curiously, the desire of the "bridge" generation (those born in Cuba and raised abroad)[5] to return to the homeland distinguished the Cuban experience from that of other immigrant groups: For Cuban exiles, "Americanization," instead of leading the children away from the homeland, provided the vehicle through which young people could conceive of the "return home."

The extreme bipolarity that characterized the debate about identity and politics made it difficult to explore the complexity of the exiles' dilemmas. On the rare occasions when young Cuban "exiles" were allowed to visit Cuba, some – especially artists and writers – began breaking through the artificial boundaries that dichotomized their identities. As new possibilities were explored, the definitive political polarization came into play, politicizing the cultural opening, and soon return to the homeland was seen in the community as an act of treason. In the Cuban exile community, even enjoying island music or art or the company of friends who lived in Cuba became an act of otherness, an act of betrayal.

The negative reaction came not only from the exile community: Cuban government officials were fearful that those returning for visits could be infiltrators or spies. The officials were also afraid of the impact that the visit could have on the Cuban population. But because of lobbying directed by young exiles at Cuban government officials at the United Nations and in other countries, throughout the 1970s the Cuban government allowed the visits of a number of selected Cuban exiles.

Only two or three individuals were allowed to travel at any one time – usually from different organizations. They were told by Cuban government officials not to tell anyone that they were Cubans. Finally, in 1977, the Cuban government granted the *Areito* group, which included along with the United States residents several exiles living in Spain, Mexico, and Venezuela, 55 visas.

The visit by the young Cubans of *Areito* to the island had a tremendous impact on the government and people of Cuba, who had not previously been willing to open communications with Cubans who had "abandoned" the revolution. Until then, Cubans on the island had lived with the myth that everyone who left was an enemy of the revolution. Just as Cubans in the United States had broken with the island, Cubans on the island had distanced themselves ideologically from those who had left. For instance, militants of the Cuban Communist Party were under strict orders not to even write to relatives in exile. Applications to study at the university contained questions about whether or not applicants had family in exile and whether or not they maintained contact with them. The void created in the absence of communication was filled with distorted images, a sense of profound loss, and no clear possibilities for recovering or rebuilding a relationship.

When the young people who had left – or had been taken out – returned, a sense of recovering something important for the nation permeated the welcome they received. The *Areito* group, traveling as the Antonio Maceo Brigade, was met with open arms and much emotion. The name of Antonio Maceo – the mulatto general of the war of independence – was chosen because "of our desire to maintain a continuity with the history of our homeland . . . our rebellion against the foreign decisions and against the historical circumstances which uprooted us from our homeland . . . and our protests against the blockade which impedes our need to get to know the Cuban reality" (*Areito*, Numero Especial, 1978, pp. 4–5). Above all, the brigade advocated the right of all exiles to travel to Cuba to become reacquainted with the new Cuba and define their relationship to the homeland.

The visit was covered on Cuban television stations with images of brigade members visiting relatives they had not seen for nearly 20 years, working with construction crews building apartments, touring the island, dancing and singing until dawn. They held meetings with high government officials, including Armando Hart, the minister of culture, who cried as he told the story of how his nephews, sons of a brother who had been tortured and killed by Batista's forces during the revolution, had been sent to the United States by their mother. At the meeting with Hart, Andres Gomez, a brigade member from Miami, asked if he and others could return to the island, not just for a visit, but to live. But the answer to the plea to allow repatriation finally came from Fidel Castro, who told the 55 young Cubans returning home that their country would be better served if they returned to their communities and worked there on behalf of the revolution.[6] In effect, they were denied the option of repatriation. If the children of Peter Pan had been used by the United States to show the world the desperation of parents living under communism, the brigade was charged by government leaders with the task of testifying to the horrors of capitalism and exile.

This initial group returned to the United States and decided to expand the Antonio Maceo Brigade.[7] Within a year of the first trip to Cuba, more than 300 young Cubans had signed up to join the second contingent of the brigade. They linked with organizations in the exile community, such as the Instituto de Estudios Cubanos, to call for a dialogue with the Cuban government. Both in Cuba and the United States, the myth of a monolithic Cuban exile community had been shattered. Furthermore, the Brigade's trip to Cuba paved the way for future dealings between the Cuban government and the Cuban communities abroad. But the process was not without conflict and violence, which all those who proposed building a relationship to Cuba encountered.

## 3   EL DIALOGO AND ITS AFTERMATH

In September 1978, Fidel Castro announced he would hold talks with the representatives of the Cuban communities abroad (see "Interview"). This "Dialogue" occurred for several reasons. Under President Jimmy Carter, there was a climate of détente between the United States and Cuba. The United States had lifted the travel ban to Cuba imposed as part of the blockade implemented in 1961. The Cuban government and the United States had traded "Interests Sections," indirect quasi embassies that operated through the governments of third countries, as a step toward re-establishing full diplomatic relations. Furthermore, there were Cubans abroad ready to talk to the Cuban government (see Casal).

But the changes in policy also fulfilled an ideological function for the Cuban government. Government officials saw this as a way of breaking the image of an exile Cuban community unwilling to recognize or sustain talks with the Cuban government.[8] The rapprochement initially gave the Cuban government an opportunity to demonstrate that not only were there deep divisions in the exile community regarding relations with the homeland but that the government's existence was recognized and thus legitimated by Cuban exiles willing to negotiate with its representatives. In addition, Cuban exiles advocating a dialogue with the Cuban government gave the Cuban state an inside political track to United States policy-makers – a voice from the community calling for normalization of relations.

The Dialogue was held in two sessions, one in November, which set the tone for the conversations, the other in December of 1978. The Dialogue brought 140 Cubans from abroad to Havana. The formal agenda – which had been agreed upon at the first meeting – included the release of political prisoners, permission to leave the island for these prisoners and for former political prisoners and their families, the reunification of divided families, and the right of Cubans living abroad to visit their relatives on the island. Unknown to most of the participants was the fact that these items had been discussed and agreed upon by the United States and the Cuban governments before the formal sessions with exiles (Smith, 1987: 161–3).

However, the Antonio Maceo Brigade presented the Cuban government with a more radical agenda than that which had been agreed upon by the overall group. This included the right of repatriation; the right to study in Cuba; the creation of an institute within the Cuban government to represent the interests of Cuban communities abroad; the opportunity to participate in social, professional, and even military organizations within Cuba; and the establishment of cultural and professional exchanges between Cubans on the island and those abroad (*Baraqua*, 1.1 [1979]: 2). In effect, the brigade had a more inclusive definition of *nation* than other participants in the negotiation.

The December 1978 talks resulted in agreements on the following: (1) the release of 3,000 political prisoners and permission for these prisoners and former prisoners and family members to emigrate, (2) permission for those with families in the United States to leave, and (3) permission for Cubans living abroad to visit the island.[9] At the time, these agreements were extraordinary. Prior to the Dialogue, not only had those who left been considered traitors, but there had been severe penalties imposed against those who had left without government permission. Persons simply applying for permission to leave Cuba automatically lost jobs and other benefits. The stigma for the remaining family members was not easy to overcome. Yet, in 1978, the leadership of the Cuban government negotiated an opening with Cubans who had left, including many who had participated in military actions against Cuba. This was a pivotal and historical point.

Implementing the Dialogue agreements proved to be more difficult than reaching them. The agreements on political prisoners had to be implemented with the full cooperation of the United States. The release of the prisoners proceeded as promised, but the processing of the visas to emigrate to the United States was very slow. Another agreement reached at the Dialogue meetings between the Cuban government and Cubans abroad resulted in the visit to Cuba by more than 120,000 Cubans in 1979. It became clear that while Cubans abroad had broken with the homeland's government, they were still interested in visiting their families and homeland (Azicri 1979: 4).

But much to the chagrin of organizers of the Dialogue and the groups that emerged during this period, Cuban visitors to Cuba often came back more embittered than they had been before going to the island. Many felt that the Cuban government was exploiting their desire to see their relatives by charging outrageous prices. At one time, the cost of a one-week visit from Miami was $1,500, even if the traveler stayed with relatives. Since the flight itself was very short, it became clear that the Cuban government viewed visits by Cuban exile relatives as a source of foreign exchange. Special stores were opened at which visitors could purchase for their relatives on the island consumer goods in short supply. In this way, the exile community acquired a new, perhaps cynical, function for the Cuban state – a bearer of hard currency. Contrary to the explicit hopes of those organizing the exchanges, the trips did not engender goodwill.

The effect of these visitors on the Cuban population was extensive as well. Many Cubans on the island objected to the uneven distribution of consumer products; those who did not have relatives in other countries could not buy the goods their neighbors obtained. (Even though high government and party officials had access to exclusive stores, these differences had not been very visible.) While there had been discontent before the 1979 visits, many observers blamed the visits by the exile community for the increase in numbers of people wanting to leave the country. This ultimately resulted in the dramatic exodus of more than 120,000 Cubans through the port of Mariel.

From 1977 to 1979, the exile community

was cast in a new role: Castro had urged people not to call it by the derogatory term *gusano* (worm) and instead suggested *comunidad* (community); colloquially, Cubans started using the term *mariposas* (butterflies), in the sense of transformed worms. But after 1979, the exile community returned to its previous label, "saboteur" of the revolution.

Still, the willingness of the United States and Cuban governments to negotiate during and after the Dialogue changed the political climate between the two countries and consequently opened a new political space in the Cuban exile community. United States Cuban organizations calling for normalizing relations between the two countries found that their demands were now more politically acceptable; organizations working toward re-establishing relations with the island flourished (Gomez, 1979: 7–9). The increased contact with Cuba also spurred professional and cultural interest among Cubans inside and outside of Cuba. For a time, the trend toward rapprochement became important beyond the youth sector, which had initially prompted it, although its articulation into a broader movement was tempered both by the political climate in Cuba and by terrorism within the exile community.

While a significant number of Cuban exiles welcomed the relaxation of relations with Cuba, groups who were still trying to overthrow the revolution felt more and more isolated. Their promises of invasion and return to the island, made relentlessly since the beginning of the revolution and partially financed through community fund-raising efforts, became less realistic and more desperate – and were recognized as such by most Cuban exiles. These groups reacted violently to the new developments. Their first attack was on the participants of the Dialogue. In 1979, Omega 7, one of the most active terrorist organizations, claimed credit for more than 20 bombings aimed at Dialogue participants' homes and businesses.

In spite of all this, the political legitimacy acquired by those calling for a rapprochement withe the revolution continued to shift the political middle ground in the Cuban com-

munity. Supporters of the Dialogue had successfully organized a base within the Cuban community. The demand to normalize relations with Cuba at least acknowledged that there was a government with which Cuban exiles had to negotiate. It also recognized that most Cuban "exiles" were in the United States to stay.

The political developments in the Cuban exile community were accompanied by parallel ideological currents. Especially significant was the emergence of another self-definition, which did not solely rely on the notion of exile. The concept of the *Cuban community* was used more frequently as people felt that they could visit their homeland. In some sectors, the definition also included a conception of Cuban émigrés as a minority group within the United States. Despite these changes, the organized political structures in both the host and home country continued to emphasize the *exilic* nature of the Cuban diaspora community.

## 4    NEW RUPTURES AND HARDENING POLICIES

In April 1980, Havana's apparent tranquility was shattered when a few Cubans killed a guard and entered the Peruvian Embassy in Miramar, an upscale Havana neighborhood. The Peruvian government refused to return the Cubans to their government. In retaliation, the Cuban government announced on radio that all those wanting to leave the country could do so through the Peruvian embassy. Within two days, more than 10,000 people had jammed the complex.

After weeks of tense negotiations, the Cuban government again invited relatives in the United States to come pick up their relatives, as they had in 1965. President Carter initially said that all would be welcomed with open arms. Thousands of boats started crossing the Florida Straits. Cubans from the island wishing to leave – including those in jails – applied for an exit permit. They were then placed on a boat at the port of Mariel.

In addition, the Cuban government reacted

violently toward those who wanted to leave. Through the Committees to Defend the Revolution, it organized *mitines de repudio* (meetings of repudiation) directed at those who were leaving. Leaving or staying once again became a litmus test to show loyalty to the revolution. These events provoked a profound crisis in Cuba and contributed to creating another layer of exiles. Over the next few months, 120,000 people left Cuba through the port of Mariel, hence their label, "The Marielitos." The immediate effect was to constrict the state's policies toward the community. The Cuban government was caught off guard by the number of people who wanted to leave the country. Someone had to be blamed, and since relations with Carter's government were not bad, the exile community became the convenient scapegoat.

The ideological crisis for the government was that by 1980, 21 years after the triumph of the revolution, the society supposedly had been purged of the ancien regime, and those who had stayed supposedly represented the new "man." Mariel showed that there were many bred in the revolution, and who had benefited from it, who were nevertheless disaffected. Mariel exemplified the Cuban government's incapacity to unite even the very people it had served best, the poor. The state had again failed to live up to its nationalist principles, which had been the moving force in the 1950s. In essence, the government pushed a significant sector of its population out of the geographic boundaries of the nation and officially denationalized it, claiming that "these" people, the lumpen and the *escoria* (scum), were not part of the nation. Another rupture was created between those staying and those leaving.

The exile community also faced a crisis. Before Mariel, common mythology characterized the Cuban exile community as mainly "white", conservative, and middle-class, as many of its members indeed were. The Mariel immigration was visibly more racially and economically diverse. It also injected into the community a significant number of intellectuals, writers, and artists who brought with them a more contemporary, albeit sometimes more complex and antagonistic, vision of Cuba. Their presence challenged the long-held assumption that the Cuban government had thwarted all cultural life. Furthermore, many, such as writer Reynaldo Arenas and painter Carlos Alfonso, did not adhere to the rigid sexual mores professed by "official" exile culture. Thus, a more fluid identity emerged at the margins of the established exile community.

After Mariel, both governments again restricted the movement of people between countries. The United States limited the number allowed to enter. The Cuban government limited the number of exiles allowed to visit their homeland. As a result, illegal means of obtaining re-entry permits for island visits and false visas to enter the United States proliferated. These activities became very lucrative for the various actors involved, including Cuban government officials, Cuban exiles, and officials in third countries such as Panama.

In November 1980, Ronald Reagan was elected president of the United States. The Republicans, who had worked closely with a group of conservative Cuban exiles, after the election helped form a lobbying group called the Cuban American National Foundation. Jorge Mas Canosa, a Miami contractor, became its chairman. By Reagan's second term, the foundation had become a powerful voice in Washington. In 1985, the Reagan administration, with the help of the foundation, succeeded in winning congressional approval to fund a radio program aimed at Cuba.[10] On May 20, 1985, Radio Martí went on the air. The Cuban government responded by canceling the only functioning agreement with the United States, 1984 immigration treaty. This treaty, set up to deal with the aftermath of Mariel, provided for an orderly procedure for the emigration of Cubans to the United States and the deportation to the island of Cubans found excludable. Furthermore, the Cuban government canceled the visits by all Cubans to the island, and included members of the Antonio Maceo Brigade in the ban.

In the fall of 1985, Cuban exiles organized

a meeting in New York to develop a strategy to protest these actions. By this time, the progressive coalition – which included the Cuban American Committee, El Circulo de Cultura Cubana, *Areito*, the Antonio Maceo Brigade, Casa de las Americas (a group of émigrés from the 1950s) and Marazul, the travel agency that chartered flights to Cuba – had lost political prestige in the community. The issue that they had defended, the right to return to their homeland without fear of reprisals from the right wing, was now being denied to them by the Cuban government (Perez-Stable, 1985: 5).

But the Cuban government did not respond to the pressure. There was no consensus in its ranks regarding what policy should be followed and which governmental agency should implement the policies toward the community abroad; this gave rise to intense bureaucratic warfare over policy control. The Communist Party had brought the Ministry of the Interior into the process, fearing that the Cuban exile right would use island visits to infiltrate the country. The ministry, which contains emigration and immigration services, is also in charge of the island's security forces. But those in the Communist Party's elite bureaucracy, such as the Department of the Americas, which oversaw foreign policy matters, argued that Havana's policy toward the exile community would have clear implications for Cuba's foreign policies, since most Cuban émigrés lived in the United States and the Cuban exile right wing was very active in foreign policy projects aimed at Cuba. Therefore, the foreign policy functionaries argued, they should be in charge of the policy. On the other hand, the policy also had tremendous domestic implications, as had been made clear by Mariel. The Communist Party ultimately defined that incident as a crisis of ideology; therefore, the policy also pertained to those who worked in the ideological arena, specifically in the Department of Ideological Orientation.

There was also no consensus in the Cuban government on how to handle the communities abroad. Hard-liners in the government did not want to have any relations with those who left. Because of their strength, they were successful in determining the terms in which the debate about the community abroad was couched. There was little room to advocate a new policy on humanitarian grounds; the positions were argued on political grounds. Those who had wanted greater communication with the exile community said that this would isolate the right wing of that community by demonstrating that Cubans abroad wanted to engage with their homeland, and this in turn would lessen the tensions between the community and the island; but they had little to show for their position. Ultimately, they were forced to justify their positions on economic grounds, that is, that foreign currency could be obtained from an opening to the community abroad.

After 1985, the Cuban government once again moved very cautiously to re-establish contact with the exile community. Family visits resumed but only under very specific conditions, mostly related to narrowly defined humanitarian concerns. For example, in order for a Cuban exile to receive a re-entry permit from the Cuban government, the person wishing to travel had to have a doctor in Cuba document that the close relative to be visited was seriously ill. One political consideration was reinstated as the relationship with exiles who advocated a normalization of relations with Havana was reconsidered, but this sector's credibility had been greatly damaged as a result of the way that events unfolded after the Dialogue.

In Cuba, the exile community again became a taboo topic. Cuban exiles disappeared from the Cuban press much as they had after the October Missile Crisis. Gone were the images of the Antonio Maceo Brigade that had filled the island's news screens of 1978, as were the stories of reunifying visits seen in Jesus Diaz's *55 Hermanos*. Instead, the theme of his mid-eighties film *Lejania* concerns the mother who returns to visit her "abandoned" son in Cuba – who in effect had not been allowed to leave with her because he was of military age – and how she tries to buy his affection with consumer products. At the end, he chooses to stay. The film, much like the island's public rhetoric, does not explore the exile side of the equation, nor does it provide a critical analysis of Cuban state policies.

## 5   THE END OF THE COLD WAR AND THE CALL FOR NATIONAL RECONCILIATION ON BOTH SIDES OF THE FLORIDA STRAITS

In 1987, the immigration treaty between the United States and Cuba was reinstated. As a result, Cuban citizens became eligible to apply for tourist visas. At first, the Cuban government allowed only persons 65 years of age or older to apply for these. The Cuban Communist Party announced that restrictions for island residents to travel abroad would be minimized. Throughout the next few years, the Cuban government progressively lowered the age of those allowed to leave the country, from 65 to 20. This dramatically increased the number of people allowed to travel abroad. The government also increased the number of Cuban exiles allowed to visit the island. As a result, contact among Cubans significantly increased, not only on the island but also in Miami.

One phenomenal and unexpected development was that Miami suddenly became a center for island visitors. At first, these visitors were treated as a rarity. They were bombarded with political questions: Were they members of the Communist Party, did they support Fidel? But little by little, politics gave way to other concerns and, as the walls came down, fear also subsided and the real stories of Cuba began to be told. People from the island also obtained a more realistic view of life in the United States, as they watched their relatives struggling with jobs and day-to-day existence. The sight of visitors from the island in Miami eventually became commonplace. In many ways, traveling in and out of the island lost its political connotations (Balmaseda, 1991: 1).

The more flexible travel policies were paralleled in other aspects of Cuban politics as well. By the end of the eighties, several human rights groups were operating on the island.[11] Some, like the Comisión de Derechos Humanos y Reconciliación Nacional, headed by Elizardo Sanchez, advocated a radical social democratic platform, which included a call for national reconciliation and a dialogue between the opposition, including the exile community, and the present Cuban government (see Hidalgo, 1994). Artistic production and debate flourished, and what became known as the "Generation of the 1980s" came of age.

But the momentum for political and economic changes came to an abrupt end when the Cuban political leadership became wary of the direction of the reform process in the Soviet Union. In part, their lack of enthusiasm may have reflected the deep political crisis brewing on the island, which erupted in the summer of 1989 and was to have serious consequences for the revolutionary leadership as well as the process of liberalization that had already been initiated.[12] Human rights activists who had been tolerated in the late 1980s became targets of repression.

Particularly threatening to the government were groups that had developed coherent political programs, with platforms that could be characterized as left of the regime. Many of these programs, such as the one promoted by Criterio Alternativo, in which Maria Elena Cruz Varela, a poet later jailed, participated, incorporated many of the unmet demands that had been made at the workplace conferences in the spring of 1990.[13] Interestingly, most of these platforms also called for a national dialogue and reconciliation among all Cubans, including those abroad. Those abroad were considered part of the nation; their exile, a political condition. In a reversal of the 1970s, when the government had taken the lead in calling for a dialogue, the opposition now led the debate.

Although more than 15 opposition groups were operating on the island at the beginning of 1990, their membership numbers remained low; but their political discourse gained ground among intellectuals. Their nationalist appeal found support among the vast numbers of the population who were increasingly excluded from the "New Cuba," which was being created for tourists and foreign capitalists. The government stepped up the arrests of leaders of the various groups and jail sentences were increased. Many of those detained were given the option of going either to jail or into exile. Concurrently, there was a renewed attack on those leaving as the "New Gusanos." Once again, attitudes toward the émigré community became an issue by which to measure loyalty to the government.

Events on the island had a ripple effect in Miami. In the spring of 1990, a powerful bomb exploded outside Miami's Museo de Arte Cubana Contemporanea, causing considerable damage to the building and to the artworks it held. The museo was one of the few organizations at the time willing to exhibit paintings produced by island-based artists. Its director, Ramón Cernuda, advocated revised United States–Cuba relations. Cernuda was also the United States-based spokesperson for the Cuban Commission on Human Rights and National Reconciliation, an island-based human rights group.

What was ironic about the targeting of Cernuda was that he, like other anti-Castro activists, advocated an end to totalitarianism in Cuba and to the one-man rule of Fidel Castro. Unlike many others, Cernuda believed that the best way to bring about political change in Cuba was not through confrontations with Castro but by ending United States economic and diplomatic hostility toward Cuba (see Cernuda, 1990). This put Cernuda at odds with Jorge Mas Canosa, president of the Cuban American National Foundation, and the Bush administration, which called for no dialogue, and it allied him with Cuban exiles supporting better relations between Cuba and the United States.

Clearly, a subtle yet very important realignment was occurring within the Cuban exile community. First, some groups within it were taking cues from opposition groups on the island, whose political agendas were more nationalist than those of past groups. Also, the groups abroad were advocating a more moderate agenda that called for a dialogue

with the Cuban government, allying themselves with organizations that had emerged in the 1970s and were calling for the same. Two currents of thought on how to relate to Cuba competed in the exile community: One was against dialogue; the other supported it.

Among those advocating dialogue, one set included groups with links to island-based human rights groups such as La Coordinadora de Derechos Humanos (the Human Rights Coordinator) and a Catholic group headed by Oswaldo Paya. These groups called for a political opening not only on the island but in Miami, too. The close relationship between groups abroad and the internal opposition of Cuba had a tremendous impact on the development of a much more contemporary political discourse in the Cuban exile community, which now looked for solutions to problems on both sides of the Florida Straits. In contrast to the traditional opposition, these groups recognized the importance of change coming from within the island. When the collapse of the USSR and the Eastern European socialist camp reopened the debate in the Cuban exile community about the future of Cuba and its relationship to the island, these groups took the lead.

In 1989, several organizations coalesced and formed the Plataforma Democratica (Democratic Platform). Its constituent groups, like traditional groups in the exile community, were militantly anti-Castro. Yet unlike the right, they advocated a political strategy that emphasized changes on the island and they were opposed to any United States-sponsored hostilities. This position placed these groups on the same side of the great dialogue divide as organizations more sympathetic to the Cuban government that also called for normalization of relations with the island. The distinction between these groups and the other pronormalization ones was that the former advocated an end to United States hostility as a means to help democratize the island, so that opposition groups then could flourish and participate. They hoped that if Castro did not have the threat of the United States with which to manipulate island politics, he would be forced to make political changes.

But since the goal of these organizations was precisely to hasten the democratization of the island and end Castro's one-man rule, they were looked upon with suspicion by Cuban government functionaries who did not heed the call for a national dialogue. Yet the coherence of the platform's political discourse and its emphasis on democracy and social justice on the island *and* in the exile community earned it popular political legitimacy on both sides of the Florida Straits. Its constituent groups got an extra boost when the Catholic Church on the island and in exile called for a national reconciliation and a dialogue.

Internationally, the Cuban government was also being pressured to talk to exiles, just as other groups – the Palestinians and Israelis, Koreans, the Salvadoreans – whose divisions had been fueled by the cold war were doing. Internally, as the economic crisis worsened, the pressure to resolve conflicts that hindered the economy increased as well. Therefore, the government felt that it at least had to publicly show that it was dealing with the exile/diasporic community. In the spring of 1994, it hosted a conference, "La nación y la emigración" (The Nation and Its Émigrés) (see Torres, "Setback," 1994). The obvious attempts to manipulate the event began early on, even with the naming of the conference. By choosing the neutral term *émigrés* over the term *exiles*, the organizers suppressed both the role of political oppression in the creation of its exile community and the notion of diaspora. Furthermore, decisions about the conference were made unilaterally. Key individuals in Cuba and in the exile community were not invited. Essential topics were excluded from the agenda. The production of images became more important than the substance. On the flight to Havana, for instance, those of us who were attending the conference were shown a videotape laced with nostalgic music about the upcoming event; it depicted where we would stay and meet, opinions of people on the street about the conference, and interviews with Monsignor Carlos Manuel de Cespedes and

Elizardo Sanchez, a leading human rights activist, both cautiously supporting the effort. Oddly, though they could be included on this Cuban television production (shown exclusively on the airplane), they were not invited to the conference.

At the conference, substantive discussion was discouraged. Participants had to write down their questions. A moderator chose which ones to pass on to the government officials on the podium. Furthermore, one participant's comments about how Cuban history had been forged by a spirit of inclusion and how Cuba needed to go beyond the exclusionary practices that had been imposed by a single authority for the last 35 years were met with hostility. There were no answers to radical suggestions that were made. For example, one was that family members on the island be permitted to use remittances for investments. This could be the vehicle through which exiles could play an important role in helping decentralize and bolster the economy. Questions and complaints were the thrust of the meetings. What did become evident was that Cubans from almost 30 countries around the world had similar problems with the Cuban government that could not always be explained away by invoking the United States blockade.

The backdrop to three days of meetings was the raging battle among different factions in Cuba, with its spillover effects in the exile community. These battles were not new. But now, added to the traditional actors in the bureaucracy that had been competing for control of the programs dealing with the community abroad was a group of Young Communist Party members whose former secretary general had just been named to head the Foreign Ministry. The stakes in this bureaucratic warfare had risen as well. Not only would the faction that gained control of the "community project" acquire power, information, and resources but it would also have access to remittances sent to Cuba by exiles. These had become the second largest source of gross national product, after tourism. Further, this particular policy could have profound consequences for the internal reordering of politics, economics, and ideology.

Not surprisingly, the conference ended in a fiasco. A private reception with Castro was videotaped without the consent of the participants. An edited version that seriously damaged the credibility of many of the reformers involved in the process was sold to the international press. The week before the conference, participants left for Havana through the Miami airport without any incidents, a sign that the intransigent forces of the exile were in decline. But this was exactly what those opposed to a reconciliation process in Cuba wanted to destroy: an exile more rational, more comprehensive, more inclusive than the Cuban government. Many suspected that the sale of the video was calculated to divide and resurrect the intransigent exile forces at the expense of (or to destroy) the broadening group of reformers in exile, as well as on the island, who could call for an end to the embargo as well as the democratization in both the community and the island. The hard-liners in the government did not want an opening toward the diasporan or the national community. These events put into question the strategy of "Dialogue" with government officials.

The subtleties of the debate about the "communities abroad" alluded to the United States. In the summer of 1994, in response to Castro's threat of encouraging rafters to leave the island, and under election pressure, President Bill Clinton changed a long-standing policy of accepting all Cubans who entered the United States. Fearful of the reaction of the exile community to his new immigration policy, Clinton issued regulations prohibiting the transfer of remittances to Cuba and restricting all travel to Cuba, except for reporters and travel licensed by the Treasury Department. Only researchers and extreme cases of humanitarian need were eligible to apply for travel permits. Ironically, the Clinton administration did exactly what hard-liners in the Cuban government had been advocating: it shut the doors between exiles and the island.

## 6 PROSPECTS FOR RECONCILIATION

Despite official policies on both sides of the Florida Straits, which discourage meaningful engagement, other factors may nevertheless contribute to a more positive re-engagement. In the early 1990s, Miami became home for a new wave of exiles: the children of the Cuban revolution. In the late 1980s, the Cuban government showed flexibility and permitted polemical exhibits to be shown. But hard-liners wanted the critics out of the island. Ironically, their request coincided with a reformist push to liberalize travel restrictions. The result was the exit of more than 4,000 Cuban intellectuals, musicians, and artists to Mexico, Spain, and other neutral "Third Spaces" (see Camara, 1994). But the fear that they would be deported back to the island led many to move to Miami, although reluctantly at first. Some, in fact, crossed the Rio Grande on the backs of "coyotes" (hired smugglers) whose passengers are normally more likely to be Mexico's poor than the revolution's cultural elite.

Unlike past waves of exiles who were dismissed as members of the ancien regime or outcasts of the new one, this one contains the revolution's own cultural elite, who criticize the government not for its leftist ideology but rather because it has betrayed its own nationalist and socialist principles. Many have studied at the Ministry of Culture's Art Institute, where students were encouraged to read the classics, not Soviet manuals; they have more analytical tools with which to *rethink the Nation.* In Miami, the city they were taught to hate and which was taught to hate them, new exiles are meeting the children of the 1960s exiles. Like their island counterparts, many Miami Cubans now also reject the dominant political culture of their community, including the prescribed ways each side is expected to deal with the other. The result is an intense exploration for new ways of rethinking Cuban identity, art, and politics.

This new synthesis became evident in a resurgence of cultural and academic activities in Miami. For instance, film festivals organized by Alejandro Ríos, until recently a television film critic in Cuba; experimental theater presentations by recent arrivals; publications in *El Miami Herald*, an independently run Spanish-language daily owned by the *Miami Herald*, and *Exito*, a weekly owned by the *Chicago Tribune*, and the recent arrival of critics such as Armando Correa have all contributed to bringing island culture closer to Miami. This phenomenon was exemplified in an important exhibit of visual arts called "Arte Cubana," which brought together works by 12 Cuban women from the island and others from abroad, which opened at Miami's Museo Cubano de Arte y Cultura in November 1993 (see Torres, "Dreaming").

In contrast, the island has been much slower in opening up to exiles. In 1994, for instance, only one Cuban exile, Natalia Raphael, was permitted to exhibit her work in Cuba – not in Havana but in Matanzas, whose cultural community sometimes avoids the capital's political battles and censures. Matanzas is also home to *Vigia*, a hand-assembled literary journal that has always included exiled writers. In contrast, in 1993, *Gaceta*, the publication of the Union of Writers and Artists, published a special section on Cuban-American writers in which it emphasized the differences between those who stayed and those who left. It also conveniently excluded discussion of the works of writers who have left most recently.

Furthermore, attempts to bring together intellectuals and artists from the island and abroad that include recent exiles have been resisted by government officials. In the 1994 Havana Biennal, the exhibit by Lourdes Portillos, a Mexican photographer, was initially cancelled because it contained photographs of recently exiled artists who had lived in Mexico. In addition, Abel Prieto, the president of the Union of Writers and Artists and a member of the Communist Party's Politburo, rejected a proposal by a Latin American Studies Association working group to participate in a conference in Miami on Cuban identity, because it was to include artists and intellectuals who had left the island in the early 1990s. In the spring of 1995, Prieto refused to provide exit permits to those island artists who had been invited to participate in a conference in Barcelona called "Cuba: la Isla Posible" (Cuba: The Possible Island) organized by Ivan de la Nuez, a leading cultural critic who had recently left. And government officials would not process requests by *Vigia* to invite "foreigners" (including Cuban exiles) to their tenth-year anniversary. Nor did they permit open participation in a conference on Cuban identity in June 1995, sponsored by the University of Havana and the Union of Writers and Artists. Finally, *Memorias de la posguerra*, an island-based newsletter that had published two issued and included articles by Cubans in and out of the island, was abruptly closed down by security agents. Unlike official publications, *Memorias* provided a different vision of those leaving. Its writers sought to engage in a reflective and critical discussion of not only their generation's exodus but also of the insular nature of the culture within, of the internal exile (see Bruguera).

Despite the official unwillingness to engage in a more open redefinition of Cuban culture to include diasporan production, informal debates about what constitutes "Cubanía" are ensuing across the Florida Straits. For instance, in the summer of 1993, copies of an article by Mirta Ojito published in the *Miami Herald* were circulating in Havana. In it, Ojito reported that most of Havana's artistic community could be found mingling with second-generation Cuban exiles at Friday night gallery openings and concluded that *Miami is more Cuban than the island itself.* Independent intellectuals found Ojito's argument overstated but admitted that Cuban culture on the island is in jeopardy. Since the fall of the USSR and East European socialism, the government caters to what was once unthinkable: foreign capitalists and tourists. The result is commercial entertainment for tourists that erodes the sense of nation brought about by the revolution. In their search for alternatives, island intellectuals are curious about the persistent sense of "Cubanía" in the exile community. But while many were willing to accept that Cuban culture could be created outside the national territory, they drew the line at literature written in a language other than Spanish. In response, Gaston Baquero, a Cuban poet who has resided in Spain since the early 1960s, has insisted that the literature written in exile is part of the national experience regardless of the language in which it is written. To make it available to Spanish speakers, Baquero suggests that it be translated into Spanish.

The result of the Cuban government's censorship of this topic is that it is being discussed primarily outside of Cuba. And not surprisingly, the discussion accompanies the emergence of a locus of cultural production in the very place that has been identified as the headquarters of the counterrevolution by the Cuban government: Miami. At first, many of the cultural debates in Miami and in other diasporan locations continued to reflect island debates. For instance, in the "Arte Cubana" exhibit at the Miami Museo, Quisqueya Hernandez's "Spiral," a series of sculptures and photographs consisting of a complex set of twists and turns – the visual representation of dialectics – in a unidimensional form suggests a critique of the way the Cuban leadership flattened the essence of Marxism. A similar message was found in her "Infinitas Formas de Transito," a long horizontal metal sculpture resembling an alphabet, in which all things are always in motion (or should be) – a message with symbolic meaning on both sides of the Florida Straits. Her work provided Miami a window through which to see intimate island debates and thus disturbed the prevailing notion of a static island. In turn, this forced Miami to rethink its own ideological parameters and its place in the future of the island. Later on, both Quisqueya and Consuelo Castañeda, another artist of the recent wave, began exploring issues of borders and language. Castañeda's recent work, exhibited in the spring of 1995, is entitled "On Becoming Bilingual." While her work could benefit from a more profound dialogue with other Latino artists who have been working on issues of transnational identity, it is reflective of a first attempt to engage with contemporary host country debates at the same time that it offers a critique of the narrowness of the island's official policy of denationalizing its recent exiles.

The immediate effect of having both generations in the same geographic space has been to shorten the distance between Miami and Havana. However short, this journey will not be easy, as Teresita Fernandez's one-room installation at the Museo intimates. In an almost completely white room, her unevenly sketched, stacked tiles fill the walls, creating an uncomfortable impression of being in an awkwardly familiar place, like a public rest room. A basin or urinal protrudes at waist level from a stained wall. Inside, a line of rotten-fruit-like sculptures intensify in color as they near the center. Fernandez, a Miami-born artist, wants her viewers to re-examine notions of familiar spaces and objects. She believes that each individual has the power to interpret his or her own life and questions any single authority to interpret history for all. While this empowers individuals, it also makes each one responsible for rethinking things taken for granted, a process that is always painful. This may even include the possibility of a harmonious reunion with those one has opposed.

Something new may be in the making as a generation that grew up across a divide discovers its other half. Artists, critics, and scholars of the various exile and diaspora generations are sharing experiences with each other in Miami. We now know that we listened to the same music – the Beatles, for instance, although here our parents said the Beatles were communists, while there their parents said they were imperialists. Some of us also read similar books and theorists – Marcuse, Habermas, and Gramsci – by authors accused of deviance or "communism" in Cuba or the United States. The island generation broke away from the power structure there, only to find it replicated in exile; we broke away from the exile power structure only to find its mirror image on the island. There is a common search, a similar disillusionment, a common political vision, and a shared generational experience across borders. This reunion of generations does not necessarily have a happy ending, but it has taken a first step toward gaining an understanding of differences, a necessary requirement of reconciliation.

## 7   THEORETICAL DEBATES: IN SEARCH OF NEW PARADIGMS

These encounters and mutual discoveries have contributed to theoretical debates about identity and politics in home and host countries, in the dominant culture and at the margins. In Cuba, the government has responded to the exodus of the cultural elite by trying not only to deterritorialize its members but also to denationalize them. Today, those who continue to leave are no longer betraying the revolution, but rather the nation: they are not called counter-revolutionaries, as in the early 1960s, but rather anti-Cuban (in political terms, "annexationists," and in sociological terms, "the assimilated"). Political dissenters are considered non-Cubans: exile is their punishment. The challenge posed to this exclusive definition of Cuban identity is, in part, the root of the preoccupation with not allowing culture outside geographic boundaries to be considered "Cuban." To accept that Cuban culture can be created outside its national borders is to admit that the nation has grown larger than the state boundaries permit. The state has lost control of the nation. Ironically, a country whose identity is precisely a product of cultural inclusiveness has little tolerance for political or ideological diversity.

In contrast, while the United States is a country with a political system that purports to be inclusive of all political ideologies, there is little tolerance of cultural diversity in the public sphere. Issues of identity are at the core of recent debates in the United States as well. The early nineties witnessed a resurgence of "race/cultural wars." The increased presence of "minorities" and immigrants in institutions that had previously excluded them signaled the end of "white" dominance, an event that has not been welcomed by all. The combina-

tion of competition and reaction has led to a rise in racism. This is accompanied by cultural assertion on the part of minorities fighting the demand that they assimilate into the dominant culture, since such integration is often accepted only if the minorities give up their identity.

Curiously, a similar theoretical limitation frames the debates about identity on the island and in the United States: is national identity defined by the geographic borders of a single nation-state? In the host country, immigrants' "ethnic" behavior at first becomes an exotic object of curiosity.[14] When the "strange" ethnic behavior persists, then immigrants are asked "Why don't you become American?" (See Rieff, 1993). And in the home country, Cuban exiles are asked "Why are you still Cuban?" But nation-states as the singular organizers of national identity, which demand either political or cultural homogeneity, may have outlived their usefulness in a world in which many of us for myriad reasons have crossed many borders and transformed both our home and host countries. Our own identities are now multiple, as are those of our sending and receiving societies. We live in a world in which capital, labor, images, and culture cross borders with great ease, and we are influenced and act upon some of the same elements. Added to this are the revolutions in communications and transportation that allow us to be in many places at the same time. The outcome is not a uniform, single identity, but rather a multilayered one. The negotiation of such identity, or politics, filtered through various contexts, is also more complex and demands a more genuinely pluralistic paradigm.

Political *and* cultural pluralism cannot exist without each other. There are considerable similarities in the structural mechanisms needed to impose either a single culture or a uniform political ideology. While not overt, there are repressive social and educational mechanisms in place in the United States to strip immigrants' children of a non-English language and to erase from their memory their heritage, just as there are national security mechanisms in place on the island to delegitimate opposing political ideas and to delete from the collective memory all dissidents, including those in exile.

Important questions emerge: Can states erase a person's nationality? Is there a distinction between the state and the nation(s)? In Cuba, the revolution blurred all distinction between society and the state, and between the state and the nation. As a result, *national identity had to find a context outside legal and political definitions.* Thus, culture and its definition became an important debate for Cubans inside and outside the country in the late 1980s (see de la Nuez, 1994). In the United States, ethnic communities are free to develop their own cultural and religious practices in the private arena but not necessarily in the public sphere. While the "ethnic" factor is crucial in United States elections, it is a means to mobilize votes, not a means to transform the public sphere. The hyphenation in United States politics is about "ethnics" becoming "American," not America becoming multiethnic.

At a time when the exile community is searching for a redefinition of identity that includes the homeland, those in Cuba searching for a new paradigm based on a nationalist vision are redefining the nation as well, in a way that often includes those who have left. As a result of the breakdown of official ideology in Cuba and the subsequent crisis of values, intellectuals on the island arrived at questions of identity by debating the future of the nation. In the diaspora, questions of identity have led intellectuals back to the nation. This crossroads provides an opportunity in which Cuban identity might shed the politicized dichotomy and the geographic distinctions imposed upon it.

The dichotomy does not always have to be antagonistic, and while nation-state may define these experiences as such, particularly in the case of feuding states, for societies and individuals this cross-fertilization can be a great source of strength. Home countries would be enriched if, instead of alienating those who emigrated, they worked to find a way to include them in the nation. There would be obvious benefits to the state. Most

Third World economies rely on remittances sent home by immigrants. Immigrants can also contribute a sense of identity that is often stronger outside than inside the nation. Plainly, immigrants can contribute to their home countries the political and social tools they have acquired in their struggles to maintain their ethnic identities. This can prove valuable to countries whose sense of identity is eroding as markets selling uniform cultural products sweep the globe. Immigrants also make valuable economic, political, and cultural contributions to their host countries.

Yet there are few *legal* and analytical constructs that enable people whose existence cuts across various nation-states to see and affirm the multiple sources of their transnational being. A framework is needed that welcomes the exploration of the multilayered identity that has been forced to evolve outside the confines of established rules and procedures. Like the theoretical debates ensuing in the Cuban exile community, art articulates a vision of transnational being. For example, Elizabeth Mesa-Gaido's multimedia installation in "Cubana" included a ship with severed masts above the hull; these masts could be viewed as tree trunks, because beneath the hull thick roots extended down and out. A video projected images of hands digging while the taped voices of her mother and relatives talked about their journey to the United States and their lives afterward. The ship signifies not one journey outward but moving in both directions; the roots are sunk in diaspora but nothing prevents their being interpreted as also rooted in the homeland. The installation legitimates the voices of women as valid participants in the discourse of identity.

An identity paradigm that embraces both home and host countries is also present in the works of writers such as Cristina García and in the work of artists such as Nereida Garcia-Ferraz, who paints colorful canvases that affirm her Cuban identity at the same time that they speak of the pain and explorations of her exile. Ironically, the fact that she lives in the United States has kept her from exhibiting on the island, while her visits to Cuba have resulted in her exclusion from important shows in the United States such as "Outside Cuba," the first retrospective work of Cuban exile art. Yet precisely because of her exile and many returns she has become a bridge connecting the various worlds in which "Cubanía" exists. Cristina García goes one step further in her novel *Dreaming in Cuban*, which ends with a letter from Celia, the grandmother who stays in Cuba, to her lover Gustavo, in which she says of Pilar, her granddaughter who eventually goes into exile: "She will remember everything" (p. 245). Exiles are given the role of remembering for the nation.

These broader conceptions of identity have also been present in various academic projects. The Instituto de Estudios Cubanos held a conference in the summer of 1994 in which over 40 years of Cuban intellectual history was represented, including people on the island and in the exile community. Only official academics from the island refused to participate because they would not sit at the same table with "dissidents." More recently, Ruth Behar and Juan Leon edited two issues of the *Michigan Quarterly* entitled "Bridges to Cuba" (33 3 and 4 [1994]), which contained a range of voices from not only the islander and the exile, but also from the official and the marginal.

A new vision of identity requires a new vision of power and organization across the borders of nation-states. Such a vision inevitably leads to an expansion of the boundaries of citizenship beyond any one single nation-state. But the extension of the vote to residents in the United States, or diasporan communities abroad, is not enough. Power itself needs to be redefined, not as a finite concept but rather as one that expands with an increasing number of participants. Debates about identity are intellectual spaces in which these other questions can be asked. For now, the critical perspective and the opportunities needed to construct a more inclusive vision of Cubanness are more visible in the exile community. Perhaps because diasporan communities have had to negotiate their identities in relation to various states and cultures, their experiences may be critical in developing new ways of thinking about

multiple identities in which nations – which are the soul, the imagination and artistic expression of actual communities – can survive, and states – the mechanisms that attempt to regulate these – are transformed. Despite the frustrated official "Dialogue," a more comprehensive reconciliation is occurring outside the established political mechanisms of Havana and Miami.

# Notes

The first part of the title of this article translates "Encounters and Clashes." An earlier version of this article was presented at the Latin American Studies Association's Convention in Atlanta, Georgia, in March 1994. The work was partially funded by LASA's Task Force on Scholarly Relations with a grant from the Ford Foundation. The epigraph translates:

> No one understood: everyone'd
> rather had their own separate island,
> their own half of the truth
>
> Just the construction of the work
> offended everyone.
> No one wanted to give in but neither can
> anyone obstruct: the work advances.
>
> One foot here
> another there:
> I myself am the bridge.
>     *(From "A Bridge A Great Bridge")*

1   For a more extensive review of the origins of the Cuban exile community, see Torres, "Politics," 1994.

2   For a discussion of exiles and home country government, see Shain, 1992, 23.

3   The first meeting of the Instituto de Estudios Cubanos was held in Washington, DC, in April 1969, and the papers presented were compiled in *Exilio: Revista de Humanidades*, 3 3–4 (1969).

4   The experiences of these two groups were later compiled by a group from *Areito* in a book, *Contra viento y marea.*

5   Gustavo Perez-Firmat explores the phenomenon of those who do not reconnect, calling this generation the one-and-a-halfers.

6    The brigade's trip had a profound impact on the island. The trip became the basis for a documentary by Jesus Diaz called *55 Hermanos*, which drew record crowds of viewers on the island. In it, young exiles tell of the horrors of living in the United States. People left the theaters crying. On subsequent trips, brigade members would be stopped on the streets and embraced. The testimonies were also published in a book by the same director, *Del exilio a la patria*.

7    To join the brigade, one had to have left Cuba because of parental decision, not participated in counter-revolutionary activities, be against the US economic blockade of the island, and support normalization of relations. *Areito* 4 3–4 (1978) is dedicated to the Antonio Maceo Brigade.

8    See the press conference given by Fidel Castro, First Dialogue, 21 Nov. 1978, reported in the Weekly News of ICAIC, Reel #894.

9    Acuerdos Oficiales de las Discusiones entre representantes del gobierno de Cuba y representatives de la comunidad cubana en el exterior, 7 de diciembre, 1978.

10   The Cuban American National Foundation was formed in 1980 with the help of Roger Fontaine, Latin American advisor to the National Security Council. Through high-level access to the Reagan administration and through a series of governmental grants, as well as directors' hefty financial contributions, the organization became one of the most powerful in the Cuban community.

11   The main figures who emerged out of this movement were Elizardo Sanchez, Gustavo Arcos, and Ricardo Boifill. Boifill left the country in the late 1980s. Arcos, who had been a member of the 26 of July Movement, Fidel Castro's original group, and who had participated in the attack of the Moncada Cuartel, the military actions that signaled the beginning of the armed movement against Batista, had broken away from Castro early on and had been jailed for most of the revolution. His group called for a return to the revolutionary principles of the 26 of July. Sanchez was a former mathematics professor at the University of Havana and a member of a group that had advocated Marxism in the 1960s.

12   That summer Cuban authorities shocked the nation by announcing the arrest of 14 officials from the Armed Forces and the Ministry of the Interior. The officers were accused of running drug operations. Among those arrested was Arnaldo Ochoa, a popular war hero and a Rambo-like figure in the Cuban military and a close associate of Castro's. After a summer of (edited) televised sentencing hearings, four of the accused were shot by a firing squad. There has been much speculation about the nature of this political crisis, but for a chronology of events, see Oppenheimer, 1992.

13   For instance, Criterio Alternativo, signed by many renowned writers and poets, outlined a political platform with the most popular demands that had been ignored by the Party Congress.

14   Joan Didion's *Miami* is an example of this trend.

# Bibliography

*Areito* (1978). Numero Especial, Spring.

Arguelles, Lourdes (1982). "Cuban Miami: The Roots, Development and Everyday Life of an Émigré Enclave in the National Security State." *Contemporary Marxism*, 5 (Summer), 27–44.

Azicri, Max (1979). "Un analisis pragmatico del Dialogo entre la Cuba del interior y del exterior." *Areito* 5/19–20: 4.

Balmaseda, Liz (1991). "Castro's Convertibles." *Miami Herald*, 14 Apr., gallery sec.: 1.

Baquero, Gaston (1993). "Literatura de cubanos en ingles." *El Miami Herald*, 19 de junio: 15a.

Barquet, Jesus (1993). *El libro de los puentes*. La Habana: Ediciones Extramuros, Colección La Ceiba.

Bruguera, Tania (1994). *Memoria de las posguerra*, 1 2 (Junio). La Habana, Cuba.

Camara, Madelin (1994). "Third Options: Beyond the Border." *Michigan Quarterly*, 33/4: 723–30.

Casal, Lourdes (1979). "Invitación al Dialogo." *Areito*, 6.

Cernuda, Ramon (1990). Personal interview, 30 June.

*Contra viento y marea* (1978). La Habana: Casa de las Americas.

de la Nuez, Ivan (1994). "Las dos Cubas," *Ajoblanco* (junio): 19–22.

Diaz, Jesus (1978). *Del exilio a la patria*. La Habana: UNEAC.

Didion, Joan (1987). *Miami*, New York: Simon.

Fernandez, Teresita (1993). Personal interview, Nov.

García, Cristina (1992). *Dreaming in Cuban.* New York: Knopf.

Gomez, Manolo (1979). "El exilio pide relaciones con Cuba." *Arieto,* 5/19–20: 7–9.

Hidalgo, Ariel (1994). *Disidencia: Segunda revolución cubana?* Miami: Ediciones Universales.

"Interview with President Fidel Castro." (1978). *Areito* 5/17: 5–8.

Ojito, Mirta (1993). "The Real Thing? Miami Has Become the Ultimate Cuban Place, More Cuban Than the Island Itself." *Miami Herald's Tropic,* 22 Aug.: 27.

Oppenheimer, Andres (1992). *The Final Hours of Fidel.* New York: Simon.

Perez-Firmat, Gustavo (1994). *Line on the Hyphen: The Cuban-American Way.* Austin: University of Texas.

Perez-Stable, Marifeli (1985). "Diversidad y política de Cubanos. *El Miami Herald,* 7 de octubre: 5.

Rieff, David (1993). *The Exile: Cuba in the Heart of Miami.* New York: Simon.

Shain, Yossi (1992). *Frontier of Loyalty: Political Exiles in the Age of Nation-States.* Middletown, CN: Wesleyan University Press.

Smith, Wayne (1987). *The Closest of Enemies: A Personal and Diplomatic History of the Castro Years.* New York: Norton.

Torres, María de los Angeles (1994). "The Cold War and the Politics of Refugee Children." Instituto de Estudios Cubanos Bi-annual Conference. Miami, June.

—— (1994). "The Politics of Cuban Émigrés in the United States," in *Handbook of Hispanic Cultures in the United States,* ed. Felix Padilla. Houston: Arte Publico Press, 133–50.

—— (1994). "A Setback for Reconciliation." *Miami Herald,* 1 May. Viewpoint sec.: 1.

# Aztlán, Borinquen, and Hispanic Nationalism in the United States

## J. Jorge Klor de Alva

*After eleven years of teaching at two universities in California, in 1982 I accepted an offer from the State University of New York at Albany. The shift to the East Coast introduced me to the complex world of Caribbean Latinos and the dramatic differences among the Hispanic cultures of the US. Immediately after my arrival I began to do research on and to write about these differences; one of my earliest efforts on the subject was the first draft of this essay. The text was presented in 1983 at the Latin American Studies Association meeting in Mexico City and the following year a second version was read at the annual meeting of the National Association of Chicano Studies held in Austin, Texas. Because of a long-time professional interest in Mesoamerican ethnohistory and Chicano intellectual history, prior to engaging in a reconsideration of the relevance of cultural nationalism among Latinos – the focus of the present article – I had already written several works concerned with the ideological uses of Aztlán made by Chicanos.[1] But through my Puerto Rican students and a summer of fieldwork in Puerto Rico (on the uses of music as a political tool), I discovered that Puerto Ricans had a concept analogous to the Aztlán of the Chicanos: Borinquen. This insight led me to write this essay. As something of a "period piece," I now present it as it was drafted in 1983 (with minor revisions), when the debate between cultural nationalism and historical materialism was still alive. Puerto Ricans were still new to me, and California was still fresh on my mind.[2]*

With a population of [17 to 20 million], Hispanics, if erroneously seen as one cultural unit, are the second largest ethnic group in the United States and have transformed this predominantly English-speaking country into the [fifth] largest Latino nation in the world. Given their phenomenal rate of growth, many demographers expect them to be the largest minority early in the next century.[3] Their high density in many areas has already forced local politicians to take unprecedented notice of Latino demands. At the same time, although their percentage of the total US population is relatively small [10 percent], their overwhelming concentration (63 percent) in the three critical states of New York, California, and Texas has given them a disproportionate national influence that presidential contenders are busily exploiting. With this potential thrust in mind, it is imperative that we come to grips with the fact that Hispanics have worked together very rarely on common political concerns and each group is appallingly ignorant of the others.[4] This essay is a contribution to the necessary dialogue demanded by the state of current Mexican/Chicano and Puerto Rican nationalism in the United States. It is a response to the critics of cultural nationalism as an organizing tool and it is a re-evaluation of the roles played by the two key symbolic expressions of Hispanic cultural nationalism during the 1960s and 1970s: Aztlán and Borinquen (the island of Puerto Rico).

It is clear from the 1980 census [and more recent demographic data][5] that the War on Poverty failed Latinos, who in the company of Blacks and Native Americans continue to be trapped, for the most part, at the bottom of the American working class. The economic and historical causes that have kept exploited, working-class Hispanics in the US from uniting in order to effectively advocate for the redress of their common grievances have been amply discussed in the relevant literature.[6] But one reason that is particularly salient for our discussion needs to be highlighted: Divisions within the working class have not been reduced by the exclusivist theoretical and cognitive approaches of the Latino leaders and scholars. This point is not novel, but it continues to be ignored by many. In short, while generally sharing a working-class origin, these leaders have frequently been divided, beyond regional and partisan concerns, by the tendency to view reality through too narrowly deterministic or idealist perspectives.

This epistemological or, more precisely, cognitive problem of interpretation is everywhere evident at both the level of practice among organizers and in the writings of the intellectuals.[7] Obviously, the results of this situation at the level of mobilization are disorganization and political ineffectiveness. At the theoretical level the problems are not always so evident, though the consequences, as reflected in divisiveness and organizational disarray, certainly are.

For the purposes of our study I will briefly describe two of the most important opposing positions. On one side are leaders with a humanist bent, often schooled in literature or fine arts, who tend to focus on cultural concerns while emphasizing the cultural autonomy of the individual. Their naïve cultural nationalism is ultimately too chauvinistic to promote the unification efforts needed to overcome the divisive forces of monopoly capitalism and the seductiveness of modern fragmenting individualism. On the other side are those primarily trained in the social sciences, whose research is delimited by a preoccupation with economic and political issues, and whose eyes are fixed on social structures and the work force. The radicals among them disparage the importance of culture and nationalism while focusing primarily on the significance of class. To be sure, this dichotomy is deceiving in its simplicity and has become trite through repetition. I bring it up once more only to point out the following: The studies on the history of the Chicano and Puerto Rican struggles of the last two decades [the 1960s and 1970s] have tended to confuse the shift in influence from one leadership sector to another for the progressive development of theory. That is, the loss of the vanguard position of early cultural nationalists and the subsequent rise to prominence of historical materialists and "socialists" have been interpreted primarily as an evolution in theoretical perspective while disregarding the possibility that what we have experienced may be "merely" a change in leadership.

The problem that attends this interpretation is not only the subsequent blunting of one of the most powerful tools for political organization (that is, cultural nationalism), but the unfortunate distancing of these two valuable and necessary camps.[8] While there have always been those who can bridge the gap[9] and although the boundary between the two groups is porous, the screen that separates the hard extremes is always present. To address the significance of this screen it is useful to undertake a comparative study of Chicano and Puerto Rican cultural nationalism and the attacks against its various forms; but before doing this, we must turn briefly to the questions raised, first, by the meaning of culture and, second, by the uses of nationalism.

## Culture

What is culture? The controversy triggered by this question is everywhere evident in the writings of Chicanos and Puerto Ricans. Except for those responses proffered by the more sophisticated (dialectical) scholars, the answers given tend to fall within one of two popular but simplistic categories: materialist or idealist. Both labels carry much politically significant semantic baggage, but in general the former suggests a materially determined basis for culture while the latter implies a certain autonomy for it.

Latino authors on the left agree that, in general, culture is class-based; that is, since the distinct classes reflect different material conditions they necessarily express themselves as different cultures.[10] The implications of this position are substantial: (1) Culture can be a tool for domination, if it is used to conceal reality, or liberation, if it helps to unmask the oppressor; and (2) culture is always changing, reflecting the transformations of the material base and the accompanying alterations resulting from the struggles between the classes.[11] Consequently, culture is not neutral. What counts as authentic culture is always a matter of class perspective; therefore, official and bourgeois claims concerning the supposed nonexistence of culture among Puerto Ricans or judgments about the "inferior" status of the culture of the ethnic communities in the US as opposed to the "high" cultures of the motherlands, say more about the class origins and political ideology of the commentators than about the nature of the object of their studies.[12]

On the other hand, when vulgar (uncritical) class-oriented perspectives are applied to the analysis of culture, "national" or "ethnographic" categories, delimited by adjectives like "Puerto Rican," "Mexican," "Anglo" (-American), "syncretic," or "pure," lose their descriptive relevance. In their place we find labels like "bourgeois," "imperialist," and "proletarian" used to describe the significant cultural groupings. This shift in the categories of analysis makes complex cultural distinctions more difficult to understand. It betrays, once again, the materialists' tendency to downgrade what are considered ideal (false?) constructs (for example, nation, ethnicity, or race). On the positive side, the search for the material bases of proletarian culture has led to an understanding of the false nature of some negative stereotypes. For instance, stereotypes that suggest the exploited masses are docile, inferior, or violent are either correctly assailed for being ahistorical and acritical or they have been identified as the result of the "colonized mentality" imposed by "imperialist" aggression.[13]

Unfortunately, the class-based categories of culture leave the question of identity up in the air. After all, being a proletarian is not quite the same thing as being a Chicano, although most Chicanos are proletarians. And while too much concern with identity "smacks of bourgeois individualism," the fact remains that the exclusive use of a class-based framework has done little to resolve the legitimate questions raised by the many Hispanics who suffer from being neither fish nor fowl, here or in their homeland. While I do not wish to suggest, as some have done, that "the most acute problem of the Puerto Rican in New York is that of the precariousness on which Puerto Rican identity is sustained,"[14] it is important to note that the issue of identity is critical both to the individual and to the task of political organization. Because materialists, as I have described them, assume culture is primarily determined by class, identity is likewise seen as the result of class membership.[15] The importance traditionally given to language, religion, and nationality (ethnic background) as determinants of identity is either denied or played down.[16]

Existentialist or optionalist postures that suggest the individual is the most critical force behind the formation of his or her identity are repeatedly assailed as idealist and lacking in historical perspective, since changes in identity are usually reduced by the critics to secondary responses following necessarily from the transformations in the material conditions. Paradoxically, although the role of personal choice as a psychological or social possibility is believed to be small, the political objective of the historical-materialist position depends precisely on the capacity of groups (necessarily made up of individuals) to overcome their oppression by *consciously* opting to struggle when the objective conditions promise success. This modern twist on the determinism versus free-will debate would be a trivial point, if Marxists and Existentialists had not continued debating it until the present, and if individual psychologies were not themselves even more complex than social structures.[17]

It makes sense that individuals cannot be fully aware of the multitude of forces acting to limit their options, particularly if their oppressors veil them, but to dismiss subjective preceptions as relatively insignificant is neither intellectually nor politically wise. However much material conditions set the stage for human action, it is individuals who must ultimately unravel the interpretations forced on them if they are to be mobilized to write their own social scripts. As a consequence, it sounds like an exaggeration when, for instance, an excellent scholar claims that with regard to the Caribbean peoples in New York today (or for that matter, with regard to Mexicans in Los Angeles) "we will never reach a comprehensive understanding of the implications of their presence here by asking particular individuals what they are doing in this city."[18] What particular individuals have to say on the subject is, in fact, absolutely necessary to know in order to reach a comprehensive understanding of the nonstructural reasons for migration. After all, not all those similarly situated migrate, even when theoretically they could be expected to do so. Why some do and some do not, when both "should" have, is not a question that can be answered without inquiring into the nature of real lives. The countless interviews of Mexican immigrants, common in border studies today, provide invaluable data that is as necessary to put the structural dimensions of Mexican migration into the proper context as the structural dimensions are critical to understanding these data.[19]

In effect, culture and identity are obviously circumscribed by historical and material limitations; nonetheless, people do not live out their lives as abstract categories. Their primary reality is their individual consciousness, however precarious it might be in comparison to the solidity of their identity through group membership. A survey of the history and fate of ethnic labels is enough to make clear the importance that personal assessments of identity have in determining group solidarity and class consciousness. Although it may be that for some "poco importa el nombre," the twentieth-century "dance" of ethnic designations suggests names matter to most.[20] Every label change, from Mexicano to Mexican American to Chicano, from Puertorriqueño to Hispano to Boricua or

Nuyorican, or from Latin American to Hispanic to Latino, has been the result not only of changes in the material conditions, but of a dialectic between personal responses and the new historical situations.[21] The struggle among both Chicanos and Puerto Ricans to create a consensus around mutually acceptable labels indicates the importance and complexity of addressing identity and culture as organizing tools in the process of community building.[22]

## Nationalism

Since "as a uniting force, nationalism is probably unparalleled in history,"[23] it is at the core of much of the political debate among both Chicanos and Puerto Ricans. This debate is suspended between two related poles: the link between class and nationalism, on one side, and the relation between culture and nationalism, on the other. Historical materialists emphasize the dependent nature of the former, while cultural nationalists stress the affinity of the latter. Once again, these two supposed extremes are opposed to each other only to draw out some salient distinctions pertinent to our study.

Nationalism as both an ideology and a material force can be either progressive or reactionary. In its progressive form it helps to clarify class contradictions, it leads the way to class solidarity, and it forms the catalyst by which subjective sentiments about exploitation can be transformed into social action. When the material conditions permit, progressive nationalism can result in socialism (which, barring imperialist forms of aggression, is ideally considered the authentic political expression of the state of the unexploited working class). Reactionary nationalism contributes to class oppression, is chauvinistic and divisive, leads to the idealization of the bourgeois state, and in its most extreme form results in fascism. The primacy of nationalism rests on the fact that "national consciousness often has been much more developed than class consciousness."[24] However, nationalism is not an autonomous force; it reflects class interests though it frequently cuts across them. This class-dependence has led some thinkers to argue that national struggle is class struggle (albeit of a distinctive form) or that nation and class do not contradict each other. Nonetheless, all agree that when overemphasized, nationalism not only negates class but serves to block the development of class consciousness.[25] Reduced to a nutshell, the above is representative of [1970s] Marxist Chicano and Puerto Rican thinking on the link between class and nationalism. Before we turn to a discussion of "the national question," a word on the relation between culture and nationalism would be useful.

To the extent that nationalism is class-based it cannot be stated categorically that it is defensive of culture. Class interests, especially in the age of transnational capital, often override nationalist sentiments, forcing so-called national culture to be demoted (by the promotion of foreign cultural elements) or destroyed (by denying its existence). Thus, nationalism is not always opposed to acculturation into a non-national culture. This is the case, for instance, in the Puerto Rico of Muñoz Marin and his followers, where cultural syncretism in the post-World War II period was promoted as official policy and arguments against the existence of Puerto Rican culture found official support. Furthermore, national culture in a class society is defined primarily by the cultural production of the dominant classes. Therefore, the merits of working-class culture are generally denied or attempts are made to empty them of their content by reducing "popular culture" to exotic or folkloric elements devoid of social significance.[26]

Except to the initiated, the relevance of nationalism to the study of ethnic minorities in the United States is not obvious. Laypersons naturally recognize nation and state as one, especially if they identify affirmatively with the latter. When ethnic concerns are considered "national" concerns what is usually meant is that they are widespread and in need of the federal government's attention. Ethnic groups are not assumed to be nations; thus nationalism is generally equated with patriotism and loyalty to the United States. On the other hand, some Chicano and Puerto Rican writers have claimed that their respective oppressed and unassimilated ethnic groups are nations that have been kept from being states solely by the political dominance and police powers of the US government.[27] Most authors, however, identify the Chicano and Puerto Rican peoples in the US not as nations, but as oppressed national minorities forming part of a multinational state.[28] This controversy is a domestic version of the international debate on the right of peoples who consider themselves nations to struggle for liberation from oppressive states and, therefore, to struggle for political self-determination. To understand this important debate, which is at the center of the conflicts between native peoples and colonizers everywhere in the world, we must ask three key questions: What is a nation? What is nationalism? And who has the right to self-determination? Technically, this highly charged polemic has been labeled "the national question."[29]

In the United States national questions arise primarily from two quarters: Native American assertions of autonomy and sovereignty, against the claims of the federal and state governments; and from racial minorities who usually feel themselves united by other forces beyond class solidarity, especially since racism and uneven development have always fostered intra-class divisions that very frequently are as pervasive as those between the classes. Now, a result of these various divisions has been the retardation of class unity based on class consciousness. Furthermore, "racial" minorities – minorities physically (or socioracially) color-coded and thus distinguished from European-origin minorities – are less assimilated than their white "ethnic" counterparts. Therefore, these racial groups possess extensive non-Anglo American cultural traits, frequently feel alienated from the political institutions of the US, participate disproportionately in working-class cultural activities, and have been kept at a substantial social distance from the white majority. This segregation under conditions of super-exploitation, coupled among some racial groups such as Latinos with the cultural re-inforcement provided by continuous immigration from the homeland, have made racial minorities politically and socioeconom-ically different from ethnic groups like the Irish, Polish, or Italian-Americans. The distinction goes beyond mere "patterned differentiation" to actual group "coherence and solidarity," reaching, although rarely, institutional completeness and therefore socioeconomic autonomy.[30] This situation of segregation and oppression is what creates the context for debate and action on the national question by way of conscious resistance to assimilation and advocacy (or, at times, violent struggle) on behalf of socioeconomic, political, and cultural rights. In effect, racial ethnic groups such as those composed of Chicanos and Puerto Ricans have many of the characteristics of nations, though as fragments themselves of other nations they are arguably more like national minorities than "real" nations.

Because the United States is a multi-national state, whose nations are not all unified by the same criteria, the relevance of this analysis is limited to the Puerto Rican and Chicano communities. Many of the members of these communities feel themselves alien-ated and aggrieved, and if one believes they are separate nations, they have a legitimate right to make nationalist claims. Con-sequently, among Chicano and Puerto Rican activists, national questions are ultimately questions of political strategy. Most Hispanics are members of the working class and there-fore the formation of class solidarity is one of their central political goals, but nationalism can be divisive so its use is often questioned. On the other hand, nationalism is the fore-most organizational tool. Yet its effective use is dependent on how one responds to the questions of strategy necessarily raised by struggles for national liberation. What should be the goal of national liberation: Political autonomy? Effective political representation through electoral strategies? Or should the demand for self-determination be primarily a call for cultural autonomy, with local control of schools and bilingual-bicultural education?

Chicano and Puerto Rican strategists are not in agreement as to what the right answers are. For those who do not apply mechanically Stalin's criteria for nationhood (common terri-tory, language, psychology, and economy) or who accept with a critical eye Lenin's theories on the subject, nationalism can mean many things. It can be political, economic, or cultural.[31] But to what extent it truly can be of one sort without implying another is a crucial question; even though here – as in the case of the question concerning the right to self-deter-mination – material, objective conditions, rather than theoretical expertise, ultimately determine the answer.[32]

## CULTURAL NATIONALISM

Cultural nationalism is a complicated concept subject to varying interpretations, some of which are mutually exclusive, and conse-quently the term is rarely defined when discussed. For at least one author, Tejano music is "the best example of Chicano cultural nationalism," for others it is at the center of racial identity and the political struggle for national liberation.[33] However defined, most writers correctly note that the romantic and parochial era of the cultural nationalist move-ment is now behind us, having been replaced by traditional or conservative ideologies, liberal concerns, or historical-materialist analyses. But because studies in the last cate-gory emphasize class, rather than race or culture, they are believed by progressive thinkers to be more likely to promote nation-alist objectives by clarifying the real contradictions in capitalism.[34]

However, the theoretical problem of race or racism has plagued progressive, class-oriented scholarship for some time. Like the national question (or the issue of gender), the question of race is nowhere adequately analyzed in the classic Marxist literature.[35] With minor exceptions, white radical scholars, if they discuss race at all, continue to treat it as either an epiphenomenal variable that will disappear when society becomes classless, or as a form of false consciousness whose net effect is to divide the working class.[36] This theoretical bias on the side of class and the accompanying downgrading of race is evident also among some Hispanics and others thoroughly acquainted with the complexities of racism.[37]

An understanding of the relation between class and race, critical for a comprehension of cultural nationalism, has come about slowly and primarily through the development of various theoretical models that have yielded the dependency, internal colonial, class segmentation, racial dualism, and world-system approaches.[38] The best synthesis of a theory that takes into consideration the roles of race and class in society is that articulated by Mario Barrera, who argues that Chicanos (read also: Puerto Ricans) are made up of an "ascriptive class segment" defined as,

> a portion of a class which is set off from the rest of the class by some readily identifiable and relatively stable characteristics of the persons assigned to that segment, such as race, ethnicity, or sex, where the relationship of the members to the means and process of production is affected by that demarcation.[39]

It must be added that since most Chicanos and Puerto Ricans are at the bottom of all classes, especially the working class, they form "subordinate" ascriptive class segments. This definition addresses only the socioeconomic placement of working-class Hispanics in the political economy of the United States. But as noted earlier, since both culture and nationalism are at least in part class-based, this principle can shed much light on Hispanic cultural nationalism. In particular, it limits the cultural content of this nationalism to the working-class version, and structurally explains its distinctions from other working-class cultures and Hispanic bourgeois cultures.

Puerto Rican and Chicano cultural nationalism were a response to both super-exploitation (white labor has not had a parallel movement recently) and racism. As Barrera and others have pointed out, racism has served as a sieve, limiting social integra-

tion to only the most acculturated sectors, and has maintained the overwhelming majority of Latinos economically marginalized. Not only does racism provide extra profits for capitalism, but since it also has made cultural assimilation a slow process for first and frequently second generation Hispanics, it has helped to preserve separate ethnic cultures while promoting the creation of new ethnic-proletarian cultural expressions.[40]

Capitalism, then, has profited from racism and, in turn, racism has made possible the socioeconomic segregation necessary to give specific cultural content to the resistance efforts of Chicanos and Puerto Ricans. These Latino class segments have remained in possession of old and have conceived new cultural elements that are at the same time responses to subordinate class conditions, to specific cultural origins, and to *individual* creative forces. Therefore, the sociocultural coherence of these groups is to a great extent the result of the racially based circumscription of their position in the productive process. This unity on the basis of racial-ethnic-class identity has the potential to be honed into sharp cultural instruments useful in a nationalist class struggle. In the 1960s the potential of these weapons was well enough appreciated by some observers that it led them to speculate that racism was no longer useful to the dominant class. The expenses resulting from the social chaos and violence produced by racial minorities rioting under the banner of cultural nationalism was believed by these scholars to no longer be worth the profits made through racist mechanisms of exploitation.[41]

Despite the inevitability of cultural nationalism, its utility as a tool for political organization, and its importance as a flint with which to spark social agitation, it has been criticized by Chicano and Puerto Rican leaders and intellectuals representing the whole spectrum of political ideology. The conservative responses to it are obvious and not germane to our study; the responses from the left, however, need comment. One criticism frequently leveled at early cultural nationalist artists, particularly poets, was that

they were too focused on existentialist preoc-
cupations. They were said to be too
subjective, individualistic, and neither class
nor revolution oriented since their solutions
were personal rather than social.[42] In effect,
this type of cultural nationalism was considered to be inspired by bourgeois rather than
proletarian concerns and the resulting lack of
proper political focus was severely assailed by
many. Puerto Rican critics noted in 1974 that,

> Unfortunately, we frequently find among
> these poets the same dangers that stand as a
> barrier between the cultural and the political
> life of the whole community: the strained
> rhetoric of narrow, short-lived cultural rebel-
> lion, the anarchistic flair and utopian
> constructions, and the formalistic and
> private airs that hover out of reach of the
> people . . . While it started in the cultural
> forefront of the political struggle, the . . .
> poetry as a whole has fallen behind . . . [and]
> has suffered from the lack of political direc-
> tion, which has left wide open the road to a
> modish aestheticism and willful bohemi-
> anism.[43]

Beyond the assaults on the self-centered
and politically ambiguous nature of the early
works of cultural nationalists, other related
complaints could be heard. I have already
mentioned the potentially negative effects
common to all forms of nationalism, especially chauvinistic divisiveness. However,
the naïve, romantic version popular among
early Hispanic cultural nationalists has been
reproved for having yielded results particular
to it that also exacerbated class schisms. First,
these cultural nationalists are said to have
placed too great an emphasis on race and
racism and thus obscured the real sources of
socioeconomic exploitation that victimize
Latinos along with other oppressed groups.[44]
Second, a tendency to reduce cultural poles to
two, Latino and Anglo, has been criticized for
having created a too rigid dichotomy that
suggested the following: a static vision of
culture, an absence of cultural elements
common to other groups that if recognized
could have been useful for community

building, and a lack of ethnic cross-fertilization that could lead to new shared forms of
resistance.[45] Third, because of the early
cultural nationalists' proneness to visualize
Chicano or Puerto Rican culture in an idealized fashion, accentuating its forms as unique,
it is argued that there was a proclivity to aim
at the preservation of culture rather than to
aspire to transform it into an efficient tool for
attacking capitalism by grounding this vision
in a class analysis.[46] Fourth, the early absorp-
tion with the search in Mexico and Puerto
Rico for the roots or essence of the culture and
personality of Chicanos and Puerto Ricans is
believed to have reduced the struggle for self-
determination to a mere ahistorical and
idealistic search for cultural identity. The
error here was that this not only suggested that
culture is static, but unwittingly disparaged
proletarian cultural forms by putting too
much stress on the cultural elements of the
ruling classes in the motherlands, who claim
for their "bourgeois" version of culture the
status of national culture.[47] Lastly, cultural
nationalists were believed to have at times
limited their demands to mere reforms,
stressing primarily the right to cultural
autonomy. To one scholar this latter "reformist thrust" was such a perversion of goals
that he declared: "Chicano cultural nationalism . . . is not a very important political
factor in and of itself."[48] Indeed, the cultural
pluralism frequently implied by old and
current cultural nationalists has been a
constant target for those opposed to its assimilationist assumptions, which argue that the
same economic and political structures can
serve as a base for dramatically different and
contradictory cultural expressions.[49]

With this brief survey completed, we can
now turn to the two most important symbolic
forms of cultural nationalism developed by
Latinos: Aztlán and Borinquen.

### Aztlán

Aztlán, the legendary point of origin of the
Aztecs, was believed by them to be located
somewhere to the north of their capital,

Mexico-Tenochtitlan.[50] For all the interest the notion of Aztlán has generated among both nonworking-class ethnohistorians in Mexico and primarily working-class-origin Chicanos, who identified it with the Southwest of the US, most Aztecs by the sixteenth century, shortly before and after the arrival of the Europeans, seemed generally indifferent to it. It seems that whatever orthodoxy existed on the subject was maintained only among those for whom the idea had political unity. In effect, Aztlán was a "class"-based symbol useful to the ruling elite as a part of their founding myth and charter of legitimacy; the nonprivileged sectors seemed to have derived little of value from this notion.[51]

Nonetheless, the appropriation from the elite lore of ancient Mexico of such a seminal emblematic device as Aztlán was the most brilliant political maneuver of the Chicano cultural nationalists. Nothing their critics have done has managed to surpass or equal this feat of organizational strategy. Under no other sign or concept, derived from the left, center, or right, were as many Chicanos mobilized and as much enthusiasm galvanized into political action – except for the concept of Chicanismo itself. For a movement hungry for symbols that could both distinguish it from other movements and unite it under one banner, Aztlán was perfect. So perfect, in fact, that almost two decades after it was unfurled it is still the single most distinguishing metaphor for Chicano activism. The term is ubiquitous, found in the strident political program called the *Plan Espiritual de Aztlán* and in the name of the most sober, scholarly Chicano journal, and it adorns the title of scores of poems, novels, paintings, and organizations, all of which display it both as a sign of their content and as a mark of their political ideology. Why?

It is well known that Aztlán, along with other symbols drawn from the mythology of the Aztecs, has been employed by Chicanos in many ways: in their search for a separate identity that can contrast with their Mexican heritage and Anglo environment; as a source of ethnic pride, by identifying with the well-known civilizations of ancient Mexico; and as

a flag capable of uniting the heterogeneous Mexican communities of the United States, which are composed of members of all social classes, are geographically dispersed and therefore have divergent historical experiences, and whose political ideologies extend from ultra-right to extreme left.[52] These Aztec motifs, along with others extracted from the Mexican Revolution of 1910, have also been resorted to as arms in the class struggle.[53] All of this hints at the material basis of the cultural nationalists' preoccupation with Aztlán and related concepts.

As stated earlier, Chicano cultural nationalism was a response to racism and exploitation. Its florescence was made possible, as was well known to its proponents, by the social and political crises in which the United States found itself in the 1960s. From its first popular expression in the *Plan Espiritual de Aztlán*, Aztlán, a concept derived from mythical geography and political history, was associated with the issues of poverty, land, sovereignty, and political organization. Though clearly not socialist in orientation, it was politically motivated. It was nourished by the California agricultural labor strike initiated by César Chávez in 1965; by the Alianza land grant movement spearheaded by Reies López Tijerina, who during 1966–7 attempted to reclaim parts of the Carson National Forest in New Mexico for the local Hispanic community; and by the urban movements in Colorado and, especially, California, where students were organizing boycotts, "blowouts," and strikes.[54] Of course, the context of the ideological and organizational hegemony of the cultural nationalists was broader.

In the United States, the Black struggle for civil rights, the urban insurrections, the peace movement against the tragic Vietnam War, the widespread appeal of the anticapitalism espoused by the Neo-Marxists and the New Left, the ascent of feminist radicalism, and the antimaterialist challenge of the counterculture of college-age "baby boomers" all made the moment ripe for Chicano political protest. The domestic economic expansion produced by the war economy also contributed by making both the government and the society more willing than usual to underwrite ethnic-directed programs aimed at pacifying the indignant communities and coopting their radical leadership. Many whites and most nonwhites believed, especially after Watergate in the early 1970s, that "America was systematically oppressive and immoral" and that "national confidence and self-respect were severely shaken" throughout.[55] It was a time for ethnic identities to be affirmed and aligned with the progressive sectors of the working class seeking to overcome their oppression. In the international scene, wars of liberation raged, students were rioting everywhere they could, and anti-Americanism was in full swing. In the midst of all these stimulations and opportunities for protest, the Chicano cultural nationalists were at the vanguard, particularly in the urban centers.

However romantic it may appear today, the *Plan Espiritual de Aztlán*, adopted by hundreds of young Chicanos and Chicanas during the 1969 Chicano Liberation Youth Conference in Denver, responded to the material conditions of the time and, although not class-based, it articulated a program for the "liberation" of a national minority. The national question concerning the political status of Chicanos was hypothetically resolved with the affirmation: "We are a Nation. We are a union of free pueblos. We are Aztlán." They advocated for "social, economic, cultural, and political independence" as "the only road to total liberation from oppression, exploitation, and racism." By focusing on nationalism, instead of class, they created the potentially most inclusive organizational base possible. They sought control of lands "rightfully" theirs, economic autonomy, community control of education, self-defense, cultural affirmation, and political power through electoral strength. This "Plan," which set the stage for the mobilization and unification of a whole generation of Chicano youth, formed the ideological background for the popularity of Aztlán as the key symbol of El Movimiento (the Chicano sociopolitical movement).

In spite of the critics, it was not self-centered or divisive in intent; nationalism, after all, was a point of departure, unity with others fighting US oppression and racism was a secondary, but important goal. It did not obscure socioeconomic issues, although it did underestimate the importance of class divisions. It sought to stimulate cultural creativity and did not hold a static view of culture; even though the full focus was on Chicano culture, and other working-class cultures were generally ignored, the "Plan" aimed at the transformation of elite, colonizing ideals and symbols through the production of a new "art that is appealing to our people *and relates to our revolutionary culture*." Thus it did not disparage proletarian culture while holding up a static version of elite Mexican culture as the model. It failed to develop a class analysis because it would not have been politically feasible at the time; unity, after all, had to precede everything else, especially since national consciousness was clearly more developed than class consciousness.[56]

The ideology surrounding Aztlán was only one aspect of Chicano cultural nationalism and it was primarily the product of only one sector of the community: the students. Turning to class analysis, much of the political confusion attributed to this ideology was the result of the race and class situation of the students that propagated it. Students, using the analysis of class structure by Erik Olin Wright, may be said to have "contradictory locations within class relations" and, therefore, "are not clear-cut members of the traditional classes, but occupy locations which are intermediate between two classes, in that they partake of some of the characteristics of both classes."[57] The political ambiguity resulting from this situation has already been analyzed;[58] in summary, students tended to be adventurist or reformist, failed to generate a mass movement, and though mostly of working-class origin, they were distanced from grass-roots elements. Furthermore, being more assimilated and assimilation-prone than the working-class Mexicans in the fields, restaurants, sweat-shops, or factories, the students were the group most concerned with questions of identity, ethnic affirmation, or radical (but alienating) nationalism. For the other sectors, less concerned with problems of identity or the need to underline their "Mexicanness" as a challenge to Anglo cultural domination, Aztlán and the indigenism it implied had little appeal.[59] While students were one of the most dynamic thrusts of the movement, they were destined to be replaced by the radical intellectuals (some of whom had been cultural nationalists), the working-class generated leadership, and the liberal bureaucrats spawned by the pacifying efforts of both the government and the private sector. The leftist theorists and working-class leaders had more clearly defined class-oriented goals, with the latter being more in touch with the oppression all rejected.

By 1973 the artists, students, and "lumpen" elements that had fostered cultural nationalism had lost the domestic and international historical contexts that had made widespread protest possible. Without that material base they were doomed to losing their hegemonic position to the reformist elements then in ascendancy and the socialist, historical-materialist theorists, whose intellectual acumen and radicalism, popular with the students, had caused to be turned over to them many of the new faculty positions created by the nationalist drive for Chicano studies programs. At that point cultural nationalism lost its support within the Chicano academic community and outside of it reformist elements were soon to put it aside as impractical, simplistic, and un-American. The momentum of the old cultural nationalism was thus deflected in nonpolitical directions before it could integrate a class-based analysis and a mature understanding of culture and race. With these advances it may have found a wider resonance within academia and among progressive Chicano activists, who would have welcomed its appealing organizational potential among Latinos and other working-class peoples.

Early Chicano cultural nationalism had its chauvinistic, individualistic, and ingenuous tendencies, but the specific ideology of Aztlán, espoused in the *Plan Espiritual de Aztlán*, was certainly liberationist. Despite its romantic utopianism and lack of a class

analysis, it was the clear result of the class contradictions being reflected through racism, with its accompanying segregation and oppression, and the resulting Chicano working-class culture. But it took individuals with vision and imagination to interpret, articulate, and clarify, through the discourse of art and myth, the objective bases of the class struggle in a way that would be intelligible to the community.[60] In a sense, Chicano working-class culture, located metaphorically by the nationalist in the mythical geography of Aztlán, was the scene, however brief, where the most significant and effective political battles were fought, unity was forged, and a common purpose recognized. Presently, with leftist intellectuals and radical activists marginalized from the centers of power in the communities and with the cultural nationalists on the defense, advocacy for structural change or social action gets very little attention. Thus it is primarily demography applied to the electoral process that promises the greatest hope for meaningful political power in the future. But mobilizing the community for effective political change is a difficult task. Old-style cultural nationalists did it once under very propitious conditions that no longer exist.[61] But today a revamped, class-based cultural nationalism, which includes the positive aspects present in the old, may be what is called for as a mechanism by which to mobilize people to register, identify their interests, and vote in accordance with them.

## Borinquen

Borinquen was the name given to the island of Puerto Rico by its original inhabitants. It is an island where all national questions are reduced to *the* national question: Is Puerto Rico a nation? Its continuous existence as a colony, from the Spanish defeat and destruction of its population until the present day, forms one of the two main determinants of its socioeconomic, political, and cultural reality. The other critical factor is the massive emigration that has resulted from its colonial status: Well over one third of all Puerto Ricans live in the United States.[62] Puerto Rico is a colony of the United States, and in an age of neo-colonialism and socialist revolutions this status is, at best, anachronistic. The significance of these facts is debated by all Puerto Ricans, on or off the island. No subject is more passionately discussed, affirmed, or attacked than that of the political status of Puerto Rico. Nothing is believed to oppress more, promise more, or affect more aspects of everyday life than a change of status. It is the master symbol of every shade of Puerto Rican political ideology.[63]

The colonial status of Puerto Rico makes the relation between Puerto Ricans and the United States very different from the one that exists between Mexicans and the United States. All Puerto Ricans are citizens of the United States; thus immigration laws and officers are not a concern for them as they are for Mexicans. The US presence is ubiquitous, affecting every institution on the island: From birth the islanders are intimately enmeshed in the political context of the US, from the postal service to the welfare system, from TV to the local naval bases. For all their class and culture-based similarities to Chicanos, Puerto Ricans in the United States are a unique Hispanic community.

Because of close air links with the island and the sharing of political experiences, the social, cultural, and political contacts between the mainland and island communities are extensive and intensive (though at times antagonistic), particularly when compared to those between US-born Chicanos and Mexicans in Mexico. Until the late 1970s boom in border and migration studies, most second-generation Chicanos had paid little attention to the contemporary political reality of Mexico. When the early Chicano cultural nationalists turned their eyes toward Mexico it was usually to survey the mythology of the indigenous population, to study the results of the Mexican American War, or to be inspired by the lessons of the Revolution of 1910. On the other hand, among Puerto Rican nationalists in the US (not to be confused with the followers of the Nationalist Party in Puerto Rico) the politics of Puerto Rico was/is *the* crit-ical issue. The very close ties between continent and island lead Puerto Rican leaders from New York to campaign in Puerto Rico and, in turn, island leaders regularly campaign in the United States.[64] It is not surprising, therefore, that the Young Lords, once the most militant, widespread Puerto Rican nationalist group in the United States, should have been so concerned with socialism and anti-imperialism since its early cultural nationalist phase.[65] For many Puerto Ricans their plight in the inner-city barrios was transparently connected to the political fate of Puerto Rico.

Since the 1898 Spanish American War, when Puerto Rico became a colony of the United States, the cultural identity of its inhabitants has been under siege. The extent of the resulting economic dependence that was imposed on the island has meant that no authentic national bourgeoisie capable of defending Puerto Rican culture has come into existence, and what could pass for such a sector has been pro-American in all but a token sense.[66] Ruling class culture in Puerto Rico, as is the case in capitalist societies everywhere, has been generally regarded as the national culture and consequently proletarian culture has been thoroughly discredited. Thus, except for the works of the leftist nationalists and socialists, working-class Puerto Ricans in the United States have had little from the island from which to draw in their efforts to assert a meaningful proletarian-oriented nationalism.[67] Their relatively small numbers, high concentration in a few large urban centers, and extensive exposure to US culture before arrival, make it even more difficult for Puerto Ricans, in contrast to Chicanos, to resist the pressure to assimilate culturally. The resulting weakened sociocultural matrix found in the United States, particularly for the second and third generations, makes personal and collective identity an even more critical issue than it is for Chicanos. Wherever resistance has been possible, a heightened consciousness of identity and extreme and sustained nationalism have been a defense against this cultural assault.

Notwithstanding the difficulties inherent in

relying on Puerto Rico for support, it was to Borinquen that the mainland Puerto Rican cultural nationalists of the late 1960s and early 1970s first turned. Their literary production and political ideology reflected a romantic, idealized vision of the island. Like the mythical Aztlán, Borinquen was transformed in the ethnic mythology of the times into a lost tropical paradise, "all pregnant with sweetness."[68] It was the repository of all cherished values, the wellspring of resistance, and the object of nostalgic remembrances. In poems, novels, paintings, and pronouncements, Borinquen, like Aztlán, was held up as the promised land of hope.[69] This search for roots was not limited to the improvisation of a fanciful contemporary island; it also devised a fabulous Borinquen, graced by peaceful Taino inhabitants living in an idyllic pre-Hispanic setting. This indigenist strain complemented a sentimental longing for the spiritually rich and quiet life of the bygone peasants, the legendary *jibaros*.[70]

These romantic myths were a call to action: Anglo-American imperialism was to be opposed by a nationalist cultural, social, and political program. And a pilgrimage to Borinquen to absorb the ancestral powers was a first step for many as they embarked on their resistance effort. Like first-generation Mexicans in the United States, numerous Puerto Rican migrants live with the dream of returning to the homeland, and many in fact do. But for the second generation this need to return became a part of the personal and collective search for a cultural shield with which to protect their identity. Many were disappointed with what they saw and experienced on their arrival: Borinquen was not the paradise they imagined and fellow Puerto Ricans did not always greet them like long-lost brothers and sisters.[71] Some disillusioned nationalist artists and political activists returned to their barrios in New York and elsewhere with a resolve to carry on their part of the class struggle at home, but they continued the battle for the independence of Puerto Rico.[72]

This shift signaled an important transformation in the politics and symbolism of activist Puerto Ricans in the US. Politically it implied a decrease in culture-based methods of organization and an increase in class-based techniques and aims: The Young Lords Party, for instance, became the Puerto Rican Revolutionary Workers Organization.[73] At the symbolic level the very real Borinquen, having failed to live up to its mythic image, was replaced by an emblematic Borinquen, one that was primarily "un estado de animo."[74] The metamorphosis of Borinquen, from an Edenic island in the Caribbean to a spiritual state within the heart of Puerto Ricans, parallels the transposition found in Rudolfo Anaya's *Heart of Aztlán*. In this novel the Chicano author creates an internal, psychological geography for Aztlán; this replaces its ancient mythical geography by a personal appropriation, but it also underlines the failure of the nation-building attempts of the stridently nationalistic *Plan Espiritual de Aztlán*.[75] Thus, before the mid-1970s the political organizational thrust of both of these symbols had lost its momentum: The cultural nationalists had gone from nation to notion, and in the process has lost their hegemonic position in their respective movements. But among mainland Puerto Rican cultural nationalists and socialists, concern with and agitation for the independence of the island continued to absorb their political energies.

Advocacy on behalf of the independence of Puerto Rico has a long history in the United States, dating at least to the nineteenth century. From the beginning of the modern diaspora, migrants had brought with them an ideology of nationalism and independence, and from the outset independence had both political and symbolic meanings. Puerto Ricans and non-Puerto Ricans in the 1930s showed their solidarity with the migrant community by expressing pro-independence sentiments. Many of those who arrived between the World Wars were socialists or supported the socialists' demands for independence; but even among those who did not, there was a constant interest in the political activities on the island and its status. However, after World War II, economic and political changes occurred in Puerto Rico that affected profoundly the political ideology of future emigrants. The postwar rise of a US-sponsored program (known as "Operation Bootstrap") focused on capital-intensive industrialization on the island, creating both the illusion of general prosperity and a very real increase in unemployment and dislocation as a consequence of the resulting uneven development. The socioeconomic transformation forced tens of thousands of displaced persons to emigrate to the United States, but the structural contradictions were veiled by the pro-American rhetoric of the new political administrations. Thus the emigrants translated their structurally constrained circumstances into subjective, personal motivations. Therefore, among the massive numbers of working-class migrants who arrived in the United States in the 1950s and early 1960s, few were committed to the independence of the island.[76]

Still, the drive for independence among activists in the US during the 1960s and 1970s, and to a great extent until the present, maintained the political and symbolic thrusts this crusade had for many of the early migrants. Before the 1950s the independence movement had always been symbolically important for the community-building efforts of the newly arrived. It was a nationalist banner under which most of the working class could unite in order to find the strength to resist and survive the racist and oppressive environment of the United States. The political end with regard to the island was, of course, its actual sovereign autonomy; however, after the 1950s this effort was attacked by many, particularly in Puerto Rico and among the conservative sectors in the United States. To most it seemed to be merely quixotic activism (particularly after the electoral defeats of the Independence Parties and the status plebiscites) or downright political and social thoughtlessness.[77] Although it soon began to represent a practically impossible goal for the near future, the pro-independence movement continued to be in the 1960s and 1970s an important *symbol* for uniting the nationalist elements in the US. And it was a superb tool for political organization on behalf of local barrio concerns.

Nonetheless, it did not overshadow, as one scholar has claimed,[78] the sociopolitical and economic goals of the early cultural nationalists; instead it helped to make mobilization for these goals possible.

Various early cultural nationalists, lacking a critical class analysis, naïvely tended to present the independence of Borinquen as a panacea guaranteed both to cure all the ills suffered by all Puerto Ricans and to unite them on the island. Progressive critics correctly assailed them for this, noting that even a socialist, autonomous Puerto Rico would neither solve the problems of Puerto Ricans in the US nor would it attract back to the island the masses of second- and third-generation English-speaking Puerto Ricans.[79] Still, unlike the early concept of Aztlán that has now run its politically useful course, pro-independence mobilization in the US continues to be a valuable symbolic weapon in the Puerto Rican "class struggle," both in the cultural and political planes.[80]

## Conclusion

Unlike what Chicano cultural nationalists did when they made the symbol of Aztlán represent the Southwest (which made sense because the Southwest was formerly Mexican), Puerto Rican nationalists on the mainland never transformed their communities into a symbolic Borinquen: Instead, their Borinquen remained anchored to the real island. Because the mainland Puerto Rican nationalists concerned themselves deeply with the political status of the island and because of their small number and close racial and residential proximity to the Black community, they integrated a materialist, class analysis into their work earlier and more extensively than happened among the more segregated and parochial Chicano nationalists. Consequently, after their disillusionment with the symbol of the mythical Borinquen, Puerto Ricans were able to transform it into a symbol of the real island's independence; that is, they replaced the symbolic Borinquen with pro-independence symbolism and activism. The shift from a deployment – for purposes of political organization – of romantic, naïve symbolic forms to a reliance on a very real fervor for independence gave Puerto Rican cultural nationalists a continuous public forum. Whether this forum can ultimately become an effective one for political organizing in the US depends on the fate of Puerto Rico, and the extent to which the interest in the island's independence can be transformed, through a class-based cultural nationalism, into an interest in pro-independentism electoral politics.

In the 1980s, liberals, the left, and progressive initiatives are under attack from the right and center. However, cultural nationalism – of the kind once found in the vanguard – could be a vibrant force for social change. But changed historic conditions demand different responses. Today a synthesis of old and class-based forms of Hispanic cultural nationalism may be the best mechanism for the successful channeling of the rising tides of Latinos toward political power and self-determination. But it remains to be seen whether today's Latino leaders can mobilize the communities as well as the cultural nationalists of the past. The call for a dialectical perspective on culture/nation and class is old, but this does not stop us from appealing to it again. We need leaders whose tactics are well grounded in the social sciences and whose strategies are informed by humanist concerns. In these times, more than ever in the recent past, much depends on this fusion of skills and interests.

## Notes

1   E.g., Klor de Alva, 1981, 1986.
2   Substantive revisions in the text or notes will be found within brackets.
3   [E.g., Moore and Pachon, 1985: 52, 199; Davis et al; 1988: 3.]
4   See Estades, 1978: 64, 73–7; Meyer Rogg and Santana Cooney, 1980: *passim*; and the obvious exception, *Revista Chicano-Riqueña*.

5   [For up-to-date data see Moore and Pachon, 1985; Brown, Oliver, and Klor de Alva, 1985; Acosta-Belén and Sjostrom, 1988.]
6   E.g., Acuña, 1981; Lopez, 1980.
7   On the former see, e.g., Garcia, 1978, Almaguer, 1978; on the latter see, e.g., Gómez-Quiñones, 1971, Gómez-Quiñones and Arroyo, 1976. Almaguer 1981: 459–63, Rios-Bustamante, 1978, *Centro Taller de Cultura*, 1976.
8   E.g., Gómez-Quiñones 1977: 3–5, 1978: *passim*, 1982: 75, 76; Muñoz, 1974: 120; Almaguer, 1981: 459–63; Mindiola, 1977: 179–85; *Centro Taller de Cultura*, 1976: *passim*; Estades, 1978: 45–52.
9   E.g., Limon, 1977; Flores, 1979; Sánchez, 1977, 1979.
10   E.g., Gómez-Quiñones, 1977: 6–7; Maldonado-Denis, 1976: 18; Ramirez, 1976: 109, 111, 114; Campos and Flores, 1979: 82, 143; Bonilla, 1980: 457; *Centro Taller de Cultura*, 1976: 2, 32–94; Muñoz 1974: 120.
11   Gómez-Quiñones, 1977: 7–8; Campos and Flores, 1979: 135; *Centro Taller de Cultura*, 1976: 64–8.
12   Campos and Flores, 1979: 131–43; Bonilla, 1980: 464; *Centro Taller de Cultura*, 1976: *passim*.
13   For examples of these critiques see Bonilla, 1980: 455–64; Barradas, 1980: 44; Seda Bonilla, 1974: 94–5; Vaca, 1967.
14   Seda Bonilla, 1972: 458.
15   Gómez-Quiñones, 1977: 10; Campos and Flores, 1979: 145.
16   Bonilla, 1973: 226, 1974: 68; Seda Bonilla, 1980: *passim*.
17   E.g., Novack, 1978.
18   Bonilla, 1974: 66.
19   E.g., Bustamante, 1981: 99.
20   Maldonado-Denis, 1976: 21; Gómez-Quiñones, 1977: 11.
21   Estades, 1978: 50; 73–5; Gómez-Quiñones, 1977: 11.
22   Barradas 1979: 48, 53; Barradas and Rodriguez, 1980: 14; Seda Bonilla, 1974: 96–7, 1977: 117.
23   Mindiola, 1977: 181.
24   Gómez-Quiñones, 1982: 75, 77, 80.
25   Gómez-Quiñones, 1982: 76, 79–80; Blaut, 1982: 22; Puerto Rican Socialist Party, 1974: 48; Pendás, 1976; Mindiola, 1977: 181.
26   For affirmations of this critique see Campos and Flores, 1979: 129–34; Ramirez, 1976: 113; *Centro Taller de Cultura*, 1976: 70.
27   E.g., August 29th Movement, 1976; Puerto

Rican Socialist Party, 1974: 47–64; Blaut, 1977: 35.

28    E.g., Rios-Bustamante, 1978; Muñoz, 1974: 122; Cervantes, 1977: 132; *The Rican*, 1974; and *Society and Culture*, 1976.

29    Gómez-Quiñones, 1982.

30    Peterson, 1982: 2.

31    Stalin, 1942; Lenin, 1968.

32    For a thorough review of this issue see Gómez-Quiñones, 1982.

33    Reyna, 1977: 191; *El Plan Espiritual de Aztlán*, 1972: 402–6.

34    *Centro Taller de Cultura*, 1976: 142; Muñoz, 1974: 120–1.

35    For a discussion of the problem see Barrera, 1979 [for a later study see Omi and Winant, 1986].

36    See Mindiola, 1977: 185; Almaguer 1975: 72, 93.

37    See the discussion in Blaut, 1977.

38    Bonilla and Girling, 1973; Barrera, Muñoz, and Ornelas, 1972; Almaguer, 1975, 1981; Garcia, 1975; Barrera, 1979; Montejano, 1981.

39    Barrera, 1979: 212.

40    Bonilla, 1973a: 227; Maldonado-Denis, 1976b: 19; Seda Bonilla, 1977: 109, 1974: 104; Ybarra-Frausto, 1982: *passim.*

41    See Barrera, 1979: 207.

42    E.g., Campos and Flores, 1979: 136–9; Klor de Alva, 1977: 20–4.

43    *Centro Taller de Cultura,* 1976: 146–8.

44    E.g., Muñoz, 1974: 120.

45    E.g., Ybarra-Frausto, 1978: 92; *Centro Taller de Cultura*, 1976: 8, 55–6; cf. Gómez-Quiñones, 1982: 15.

46    E.g., *Centro Taller de Cultura*, 1976: 48; Bonilla 1974: 69.

47    E.g., *Centro Taller de Cultura*, 1976: 58, 64–70, 186; Cervantes, 1977: 129; Campos and Flores, 1979: 131–5; Gómez-Quiñones, 1978: *passim*; Leal, 1977: 118–23.

48    Cervantes, 1977: 131.

49    E.g., Bonilla, 1973: 229, 1974: 68.

50    In general see Kirchhoff, 1961: 59–73; for its role among Chicanos see Klor de Alva, 1981: 28, [1986]; and Leal, 1981: 16–22.

51    E.g., Durán, 1967: 215–24; Chimalpahin, 1965a: 154 (for a Spanish version see Chimalpahin, 1965b: 123–5).

52    E.g., Elizondo, 1978: 24; Ortego y Gasca, 1979: 112; Ybarra-Frausto, 1979: 119; Leal, 1979: 28; Alurista, 1977: 49; Morales Blouin, 1979: 179–80; Lux and Vigil, 1979: 15; Macias, 1974: 143; Segade, 1973: 4–5.

53    [E.g., Klor de Alva, 1986.]

54    E.g., Matthiessen, 1969; López Tijerina, 1978; Gómez-Quiñones, 1978.

55    Gleason, 1982: 133–5.

56    See *Plan Espiritual de Aztlán*, 1972: 402–6; Gómez-Quiñones, 1978: 28, 32, 1982: 75.

57    In Barrera, 1979: 204.

58    Gómez-Quiñones, 1978; Muñoz, 1974.

59    See Gómez-Quiñones, 1977: 18.

60    E.g., Montoya, 1980: 126, 128–9; Alurista, 1980: 273–4, 276.

61    See Almaguer, 1978: 140–1.

62    *Puerto Ricans*, 1976: 4.

63    E.g., Bonilla, 1973: 224.

64    See Estades, 1978.

65    Estades, 1978: 45–51; Abramson, 1971; PRRWO, 1974: 70–9.

66    *Centro Taller de Cultura*, 1976: 72.

67    E.g., Campos and Flores, 1979; *Taller de Formación Política*, 1982.

68    Barradas, 1979: 51.

69    E.g., Barradas and Rodriguez, 1980: 16; Campos and Flores, 1979: 136; Barradas, 1979: 46–8, 1980: 45; for an opposing view see *Centro Taller de Cultura* 1976: 140.

70    Barradas, 1979: 50–1; Johnson, 1980: 110–23.

71    Merced Rosa, 1974: 57; Maldonado-Denis, 1976: 107; Seda Bonilla, 1974: 86, 1980: *passim*; López, 1976:4; Barradas, 1979: 52.

72    E.g., Barradas, 1979: 53; Estades, 1978: 50.

73    Flores et al., 1981; PRRWO, 1974: 76–8; Estades, 1978: 50.

74    Barradas, 1979: 54.

75    Anaya, 1976; Leal, 1981: 21–2.

76    See López, 1980; Quintero Rivera et al., 1981: *Taller de Formación Política*, 1982; Maldonado-Denis, 1976; Campos and Bonilla, 1982a; *Centro Taller de Migración*, 1975; Estades, 1978; History Task Force, 1979; Johnson, 1980.

77    E.g., Johnson, 1980: 127–60; Maldonado, 1983.

78    Estades, 1978: 78–9; Seda Bonilla, 1972: 455–6; cf. Silén, 1974: 19.

79    See López, 1976: 4–5; Ayala, 1974: 116.

80    E.g., Bonilla, 1980: 465.

# Bibliography

Abramson, Michael (ed.) (1971). *Palante: Young Lords Party*. New York: McGraw Hill.

Acosta-Belén, Edna, and Sjostrom, Barbara R. (eds)

(1988). *The Hispanic Experience in the United States*. New York: Praeger.

Acuña, Rodolfo (1981). *Occupied America: A History of Chicanos*. 2nd edn. New York: Harper and Row.

Almaguer, Tomás (1975). "Class, Race, and Chicano Oppression." *Socialist Revolution*, 5 (July–September): 71–99.

—— (1978). "Chicano Politics in the Present Period: Comment on Garcia." *Socialist Review*, 8 (July–October): 137–41.

—— (1981). "Interpreting Chicano History: The World-System Approach to Nineteenth-Century California." *Review*, 4 (Winter): 459–507.

Alurista (1977). "La estética indigena a través del Floricanto de Nezahualcóyotl." *Revista Chicano-Riqueña* 5, (Spring): 48–62.

Anaya, Rudolfo (1976). *Heart of Aztlán*. Berkeley, CA: Editorial Justa.

August Twenty-Ninth Movement (1976). *Fan the Flames: A Revolutionary Position on the Chicano National Question*. n.p.

Ayala, Dory (1974). "On the National Question." *The Rican: Journal of Contemporary Puerto Rican Thought*, 2: 114–16.

Barradas, Efrain (1979). "'De lejos en sueños verla. . .': Vision mitica de Puerto Rico en la poesia neoyorrican." *Revista Chicano-Riqueña*, 7 (Verano): 46–56.

—— (1980). "Puerto Rico acá, Puerto Rico allá." *Revista Chicano-Riqueña*, 8 (Primavera): 43–9.

Barradas, Efrain, and Rodriguez, Rafael, (1980). *Herejes y mitificadores: muestra de poesia puertorriqueña en los Estados Unidos*. Rio Piedras, P.R.: Ediciones Huracán.

Barrera, Mario (1979). *Race and Class in the Southwest: A Theory of Racial Inequality*. Notre Dame and London: University of Notre Dame Press.

Barrera, Mario, Muñoz, Carlos, and Ornelas, Charles (1972). "The Barrio as Internal Colony," in *People and Politics in Urban Society*, ed. Harlan Hahn. Los Angeles: Sage Publications.

Blaut, James (1977). "Are Puerto Ricans a National Minority?" *Monthly Review* (May): 35–55.

—— (1982). "Nationalism as an Autonomous Force." *Science and Society*, 46 (Spring): 1–23.

Bonilla, Frank (1974). "Puerto Ricans in the United States and Puerto Ricans in Puerto Rico." *The Rican: Journal of Contemporary Puerto Rican Thought*, 2: 65–9.

—— (1980). "Beyond Survival: Por que seguiremos siendo puertorriqueños," in *The*

Puerto Ricans*, ed. Adalberto López. Cambridge, MA: Schenkman.

Bonilla, Frank, and González, Emilio (1973). "New Knowing, New Practice: Puerto Rican Studies." In *Structures of Dependency*. Edited by Frank Bonilla and Robert Girling. Stanford, CA: Stanford Institute of Politics.

Bonilla, Frank, and Girling, Robert (eds) (1973). *Structures of Dependency*. Stanford, CA: Stanford Institute of Politics.

Brown, Lester B., Oliver, John, and Klor de Alva, J. Jorge, (eds) (1985). *Sociocultural and Service Issues in Working with Hispanic American Clients*. Albany, NY: Rockefeller College Press.

Bruce-Novoa, Juan (ed.) (1980). "Alurista," in *Chicano Authors: Inquiry by Interview*, Austin and London: University of Texas Press.

—— (1980). "Jose Montoya," in *Chicano Authors: Inquiry by Interview*. Austin and London: University of Texas Press.

Bustamante, Jorge A. (1981). "The Immigrant Worker: A Social Problem or a Human Resource," in *Mexican Immigrant Workers in the US*, ed. Antonio Rios-Bustamante. Los Angeles: Chicano Studies Research Center, U.C.L.A.

Campos, Ricardo, and Bonilla, Frank (1982). "Bootstraps and Enterprise Zones: The Underside of Late Capitalism in Puerto Rico and the United States." *Review*, 5 (Spring): 556–90.

Campos, Ricardo, and Flores, Juan (1979). "Migración y cultura nacional puertorriqueñas: perspectivas proletarias," in *Puerto Rico: Identidad Nacional y Clases Sociales (Coloquio de Princeton)*, ed. Angel G. Quintero Rivera et al. Rio Piedras PR: Ediciones Huracán.

*Centro Taller de Cultura* (1976). New York: Centro de Estudios Puertorriqueños, City University of New York.

Cervantes, Fred A. (1977). "Chicanos as a Post-Colonial Minority: Some Questions Concerning the Adequacy of the Paradigm of Internal Colonialism," in *Perspectivas en Chicano Studies*, ed. Reynaldo Flores Macias. Los Angeles: Chicano Studies Research Center, UCLA.

Chimalpahin Cuauhtlehuanitzin, Francisco de San Antón Muñoz (1965). *Die Relationen Chimalpahin's zur Geschichte Mexico's*, ed. Günter Zimmermann. Hamburg: Cram, de Gruyter.

—— (1965). *Relaciones originales de Chalco*

*Amaquemecan*, ed. and trans. S. Rendón. México: Fondo de Cultura Económica.

Cortes, F., Falcón, A., and Flores, J. (1976). "The Cultural Expression of Puerto Ricans in New York: A Theoretical Perspective and Critical Review." *Latin American Perspectives*, 3: 117–50.

Davis, Cary, Haub, Carl, and Willette, JoAnne L. (1988). "U.S. Hispanics: Changing the Face of America," in *The Hispanic Experience in the United States*, ed. Edna Acosta-Belén and Barbara R. Sjostrom. New York: Praeger.

Durán, Fray Diego (1967). *Historia de las Indias de Nueva España e Islas de la Tierra Firme*, ed. Angel Ma. Garibay. 2 vols. México: Editorial Purrua.

*El Plan Espiritual de Aztlán* (1972). In *Aztlán: An Anthology of Mexican American Literature*. Edited by Luis Valdez and Stan Steiner. New York: Vintage Books.

Elizondo, Sergio D. (1978). "Myth and Reality in Chicano Literature." *Latin American Literary Review*, 5 (Spring–Summer): 23–31.

Estades, Rosa (1978). *Patterns of Political Participation of Puerto Ricans in New York City*. Hato Rey: Editorial Universitaria.

Estrada, Leobardo (1982). "The Demographics of the Latino Vote." *El Mirlo*, 10 (Winter): 1–2, 11–12.

Flores, Juan, et al. (1981). "La Carreta Made a U-Turn: Puerto Rican Language and Culture in the United States." *Daedalus*, 110 (Spring): 193–217.

García, Mario (1975). "Racial Dualism in the El Paso Labor Market. 1880–1920." *Aztlán*, 6 (Summer):197–218.

García, Richard A. (1978). "The Chicano Movement and the Mexican American Community, 1972–1978: An Interpretative Essay." *Socialist Review*, 8 (July–October): 117–36.

Gleason, Philip (1982). "American Identity and Americanization," in *Concepts of Ethnicity*, ed. Stephan Thernstrom. Cambridge, MA: Belknap Press of Harvard University.

Gómez-Quiñones, Juan (1982). "Critique on the National Question, Self-Determination and Nationalism." *Latin American Perspectives*, 9 (Spring): 62–83.

—— (1978). *Mexican Students Por La Raza: The Chicano Student Movement in Southern California 1967-1977*. Santa Barbara: Editorial La Causa.

—— (1977). *On Culture*. Los Angeles: Chicano Studies Research Center, UCLA. (First published in *Revista Chicano-Ríqueña*, 5 [Spring]: 29–47.)

—— (1971). "Toward a Perspective on Chicano History." *Aztlán*, 2 (Fall): 1–49.

Gómez-Quiñones, Juan, and Leobardo Arroyo, Luis (1976). "On the State of Chicano History: Observations on Its Development, Interpretations, and Theory, 1970–1974." *Western Historical Quarterly*, 7 (April): 155–85.

History Task Force (Centro de Estudios Puertorriqueños) (1979). *Labor Migration Under Capitalism: The Puerto Rican Experience*. New York: Monthly Review Press.

Johnson, Roberta Ann (1980). *Puerto Rico: Commonwealth or Colony?* New York: Praeger.

Kirchhoff, Paul (1961). "¿Se puede localizar Aztlán?" *Anuario de Historia*, 1: 59–73.

Klor de Alva, J. Jorge (1986). "California Chicano Literature and Pre-Columbian Motifs: Foil and Fetish." *Confluencia: Revista Hispanica de Cultura y Literatura*, 1: 18–26.

—— (1981). "Aztlán," in *Dictionary of Mexican American History*, ed. Matt S. Meier and Feliciano Rivera. Westport, CN: Greenwood Press.

—— (1977). "Critique of National Character Versus Universality in Chicana Poetry." *De Colores Journal*, 3: 20–4.

Leal, Luis (1981). "In Search of Aztlán." *Denver Quarterly*, 16 (Fall): 16–22.

—— (1979). "Mexican American Literature: A Historical Perspective." In *Modern Chicano Writers*. Edited by Joseph Sommers and Tomas Ybarra-Frausto. Englewood Cliffs, NJ: Prentice-Hall.

—— (1977). "Octavio Paz and the Chicano." *Latin American Literary Review*, 10 (Spring–Summer): 115–23.

Lenin, V. I. (1968). *Selected Works*. 3 vols. New York: International Publishers.

Limón, José (1977). "El folklore y los mexicanos en los Estados Unidos: una perspectiva cultural marxista," in *La otra cara de México: el pueblo chicano*, ed. David R. Maciel. México: Ediciones "El Caballito."

López, Adalberto (1976). "The Puerto Rican Struggle in the U.S." *Sociedad y Cultura*, 1 (April): 4–7.

López, Adalberto (ed.) (1980). *The Puerto Ricans: Their History, Culture, and Society*. Cambridge, MA: Schenkman.

López Tijerina, Reies (1978). *Mi lucha por la tierra*. México: Fondo de Cultura Económica.

Lux, Guillermo, and Vigil, Maurilio E. (1979). "Return to Aztlán: The Chicano Rediscovers

His Indian Past," in *The Chicanos As We See Ourselves*, ed. Arnulfo D. Trejo. Tucson: University of Arizona Press.

Macias, Ysidro Ramon (1974). "Nuestros antepasados y el Movimiento." *Aztlán*, 5 (Spring and Fall): 143–53.

Maldonado, A.W. (1983). "Against Puerto Rican Statehood." *New York Times*, 22 January.

Maldonado-Denis, Manuel (1976). "El problema de la asimilación cultural." *Sociedad y Cultura*, 1 (April): 18–27.

—— (1980). *The Emigration Dialectic: Puerto Rico and the USA*. New York: International Publishers.

Matthiessen, Peter (1969). *Sal Si Puedes: César Chávez and the New American Revolution*. New York: Dell.

Merced Rosa, Florencio (1974). "One Nation, One Party." *The Rican: Journal of Contemporary Puerto Rican Thought*, 2: 49–64.

Meyer Rogg, Eleanor, and Santana Cooney, Rosemary (1980). *Adaptation and Adjustment of Cubans: West New York, New Jersey*. New York: Hispanic Research Center, Fordham University.

Mindiola, Tatcho (1977). "Marxism and the Chicano Movement: Preliminary Remarks." *Perspectivas en Chicano Studies*, ed. Reynaldo Flores Macias. Los Angeles: Chicano Studies Research Center, UCLA.

Montejano, David (1981). "Is Texas Bigger than the World-System? A Critique from a Provincial Point of View." *Review: Journal of the Fernand Braudel Center*, 4 (Winter): 597–628.

Moore, Joan, and Pachon, Harry (1985). *Hispanics in the United States*. Englewood Cliffs, NJ: Prentice-Hall.

Morales Blouin, Egla (1979). "Simbolos y motivos nahuas en la literatura chicana," in *The Identification and Analysis of Chicano Literature*, ed. Francisco Jimenez. New York: Bilingual Press.

Muñoz, Carlos, Jr. (1974). "The Politics of Protest and Chicano Liberation: A Case Study of Repression and Cooptation." *Aztlán* 5 (Spring and Fall): 119–41.

Novack, George (ed.) (1978). *Existentialism Versus Marxism: Conflicting Views on Humanism*. New York: Dell.

Omi, Michael, and Winant, Howard (1986). *Racial Formation in the United States: From the 1960s to the 1980s*. New York: Routledge and Kegan Paul.

Ortego y Gasca, Felipe de (1979). "An Introduction to Chicano Poetry," in *Modern Chicano Writers*, ed. Joseph Sommers and Tomas Ybarra-

Frausto. Englewood Cliffs, NJ: Prentice-Hall.

Pendas, Miguel (1976): *Chicano Liberation and Socialism*. New York: Pathfinder Press.

Petersen, William (1982). "Concepts of Ethnicity," in *Concepts of Ethnicity*, ed. Stephan Thernstrom. Cambridge, MA: Belknap Press of Harvard University.

PRRWO (Puerto Rican Revolutionary Workers Organization) (1974). "National Liberation of Puerto Rico and the Responsibilities of the U.S. Proletariat." *The Rican: Journal of Contemporary Puerto Rican Thought*, 2: 70–80.

Puerto Rican Socialist Party (1974). "The National Question." *The Rican: Journal of Contemporary Puerto Rican Thought*, 2: 47–8.

*Puerto Ricans in the Continental United States: An Uncertain Future* (1976). Washington, DC: US Commission on Civil Rights.

Quintero Rivera, Angel G., et al. (1981). *Puerto Rico: identidad nacional y clases sociales (Coloquio de Princeton)*. 2nd edn. Rio Piedras, PR: Ediciones Huracán.

Ramirez, Rafael L. (1976). "National Culture in Puerto Rico." *Latin American Perspectives*, 3: 109–16.

*Research Institute Recommendations*. August 10, 1979.

Reyna, José R. (1977). "Tejano Music as an Expression of Cultural Nationalism," in *Perspectivas en Chicano Studies*, ed. Reynaldo Flores Macias. Los Angeles: Chicano Studies Research Center. UCLA.

Rios-Bustamante, Antonio (1978). *Mexicans in the United States and the National Question: Current Polemics and Organizational Positions*. Santa Barbara, CA: Editorial La Causa.

Sánchez, Rosaura (1977). "The Chicana Labor Force," in *Essays on la Mujer*, ed. Rosaura Sánchez and Rosa Martinez Cruz. Los Angeles: Chicano Studies Research Center. UCLA.

Seda Bonilla, Eduardo (1980). *Requiem para una cultura*. 4th edn. Rio Piedras, PR: Ediciones Bayoan.

—— (1977). "Who is a Puerto Rican: Problems of Socio Cultural Identity in Puerto Rico." *Caribbean Studies*, 17 (April–July): 105–21.

—— (1974). "¿Qué somos: puertorriqueños, neorriqueños o nuyorriqueños?" *The Rican: Journal of Contemporary Puerto Rican Thought*, 2: 81–107.

—— (1972). "El problema de la identidad de los nuyorricans." *Revista de Ciencias Sociales*, 16 (Diciembre): 453–62.

Segade, Gustavo (1973). "Toward a Dialectic of

Chicano Literature." *Mester*, 4 (November): 4–5.

Silén, Angel Juan (1974). "Aspectos sobresalientes del problema nacional puertorriqueño y la nueva lucha de independencia." *The Rican: Journal of Contemporary Puerto Rican Thought*, 2: 14–20.

Stalin, Joseph (1942). *Marxism and the National Question*. New York: International Publishers.

Taller de formacion politica (1982). *La cuestion nacional: El Partido Nacionalista y el movimiento obrero puertorriqueño*: Rio Piedras, PR: Ediciones Huracán.

Vaca, Nick (1967). "Message to the People." *Mexican American Liberation Papers* (Berkeley, CA.)

Williams, Raymond (1967). "Culture and Civilization," in *The Encyclopedia of Philosophy*, New York: Macmillan.

Winick, Charles (1956). *Dictionary of Anthropology*, New York: Philosophical Library.

Ybarra-Frausto, Tomas (1982). "Califas: California Chicano Art and Its Social Background." Santa Cruz. CA. (Mimeographed.)

—— (1979). "Alurista's Poetics: The Oral, the Bilingual, the Pre-Columbian," in *Modern Chicano Writers*, ed. Joseph Sommers and Tomas Ybarra-Frausto. Englewood Cliffs, NJ: Prentice-Hall.

—— (1978). "The Chicano Movement and the Emergence of a Chicano Poetic Consciousness," in *New Directions in Chicano Scholarship*, ed. Ricardo Romo and Raymund Paredes. La Jolla. CA: University of California, San Diego (Chicano Studies Monograph Series).

# Chicano History:
# Transcending Cultural Models

## Gilbert G. González and Raúl Fernández

Mainstream US historians tend to ignore Chicano history, apparently considering it the domain of specialists.[1] But why should US social historians want to put aside issues as important as the social origins of pragmatism or the Civil War in Kansas and turn their attention to Mexican-American history? In part the answer has to be that it might help, along with other contemporary directions in cultural studies, to break down barriers to historical understanding among the various groups that comprise the United States. More specifically, such study would open up new areas of comparative research by adding to the proposition that "capitalism did not come to every region [of the US] at the same time nor on the same terms."[2] In this article, we are concerned with the second issue.

Important insights might be drawn by comparing the nineteenth-century evolution of economic forms in rural New England, the slave South, and the territories acquired from Mexico after 1836. At this time, such a comparison across the United States is still difficult because much Chicano historiography has built upon cultural and culture-conflict models focusing on race and nationality as the basis for social relations and, ultimately, for historical explanation. Clearly, in the post-1848 years in the newly acquired southwestern frontier, Anglo settlers frequently treated the Hispanic population much like they dealt with the native Indian population: as people without rights who were merely obstacles to the acquisition and exploitation of natural resources and land.

And, to be sure, the violence of the conquerors was often met with the resistance of the conquered.[3] But these cultural struggles and racial conflicts have become for many Chicano historians the principal basis for understanding Chicano history.

Culture-based explanations tend to minimize the role of economic factors, which are crucial in shaping social and cultural forms and very useful in drawing regional comparisons. Innovative scholarship by Rosalinda González, David Montejano, and Douglas Monroy moves away from culture-based models and toward an emphasis on economic power and processes.[4] The goal here is to advance and elaborate on some of these ideas about socioeconomic forms in a more systematic manner.[5]

We begin by critically analyzing approaches that describe the history of Chicano-Anglo relations as a story of cultural conflict and racism. Using Marxist taxonomies when appropriate, we seek to emphasize the *systemic* roots of conflict between pre-1848 Spanish-Mexican society and post-1848 Anglo-imposed social economy.[6] The history of the Southwest or, for that matter, the United States should not merely consist of a juxtaposition of cultural views – that is, the Chicano perspective, Anglo perspective, Asian perspective, women's perspective, and so forth. It should also examine the conflictive shared history of a prevalent economic organization of society. This approach can lead to a paradigm of complex and intertwined Anglo and

Chicano history, rather than one of separate perspectives.[7]

Historians who subscribe to the culture-based paradigm ground their perspectives in particular characterizations of pre-Anglo Spanish and subsequent Mexican societies in the Southwest. Some (for example, Albert Camarillo, Pedro Castillo, Richard Griswold del Castillo, Arnoldo De León, and Robert Rosenbaum) describe those societies as pastoral, communal, peasant, traditional, frontier, or hacienda. Other historians who place more emphasis on economic factors (for example, Juan Gómez-Quiñones, David Montejano, and Antonio Ríos-Bustamante) characterize this era as "early capitalist." All, however, agree that Anglo-American society is capitalist and all use their own characterizations of the period as points of departure for their inquiries. We hope to explore further the nature of these societies from the perspective of social and economic relations.

If the period that began in 1848 is viewed as one in which two distinct socioeconomic formations, one largely precapitalist and quasifeudal and the other predominantly capitalist, collide, the situation looks akin to the North–South conflict in the eastern United States. More than just a "rough and tumble," racially conscious Anglo society conquering and subduing quaint Mexican pastoralists, the conquest can be viewed also as one step in the economic (capitalist) transformation of the United States from east to west. In other words, as Montejano has pointed out, the Anglo conquest was also a capitalist conquest. Economic change took place on a par with cultural transformation.

In the second half of this article we demonstrate briefly how a perspective grounded in economic power and processes can also be applied to two other themes in Chicano history. The first is the significance of the nineteenth century for Chicano historiography. Some scholars, including Camarillo, Griswold del Castillo, Carlos Cortés, Gomez-Quiñones, and most recently Mario García, find the Anglo conquest of 1848 and the ensuing Spanish, Mexican, and Anglo conflict to be a historical watershed that initiated a continuous nineteenth- and twentieth-century Chicano experience. We challenge this assumed continuity. The second theme, and one we find equally problematic, is an emphasis on a common Chicano urban experience. Chicanos have been predominantly urban dwellers only since the 1940s, but scholars too often disregard the origins of socioeconomic structures that underlie the contemporary urban experience.

Our goal, then, is to develop a useful characterization of pre- and post-conquest societies. This approach, it is hoped, will help scholars to engage in a comparative analysis of US regional histories; encourage the study of the social, economic, and gender relations among Spanish, Mexican, and Anglo peoples of the American Southwest; and perhaps even contribute to moving Chicano history "from margin to center" in US history discourse.[8]

## THE CHARACTER OF SOUTHWESTERN SPANISH AND MEXICAN SOCIETY

The transition from Spanish and Mexican rule to US governance in the nineteenth century is critical to Chicano historiography. Most Chicano history scholars argue that the evolving relations between the Spanish-speaking and English-speaking peoples in the post-1848 era can be understood by studying the particular characteristics of these peoples, but they disagree about the characteristics themselves. Two definitions of Spanish/Mexican society have been offered most often. Albert Camarillo provides a succinct example of the first: "Once the subdivision of rancho and public lands had begun, the dominance of the emerging economic system of American capitalism in the once-Mexican region was a foregone conclusion. The process of land loss and displacement of the Mexican *pastoral economy* was fairly complete throughout the Southwest by the 1880s."[9] In a second view, which also emphasizes economic elements, Spanish/Mexican societies are seen as "early capitalist." Juan Gomez-Quiñones contends, for example, that the essence of Mexican society was an emerging capitalist order, a transition away from a formal, feudal social order.[10] A decade later David Montejano expressed a similar view: feudalism "is . . . a misleading description" of the pre-1848 Southwest and the Spanish-Mexican haciendas were "a form of early capitalism."[11]

Historians utilizing the first approach characterize Spanish/Mexican society less specifically than Anglo-American society. Vague terms – for example, traditional or pastoral – define the former; a more analytic one – namely, capitalism – the latter. The invading society is distinctly described as capitalist in economy, culture, institutions, and behavior. We would expect it either to conflict with opposing social forms or to merge with similar ones. However, the existing categorizations describe Spanish/Mexican society without regard to specific economic structure. We cannot examine a conflict between a society whose economy remains vaguely described (pastoral or traditional) and one with a specifically described (capitalist) economy.

Nor do the terms "pastoral," "communal," and "traditional" explain Spanish/Mexican society any more than the terms "technological" and "individualistic" explain Anglo society.[12] Analytic terms should not be used regarding Anglo-America without using the same degree of specificity when referring to Spanish/Mexican society. By default, this dichotomous mode of categorization leads toward a "culture conflict" model for interpreting the Anglo-Mexican encounter because a more sophisticated one based upon conflicting economic systems is unavailable.[13]

Historians using the second approach – defining the pre-1848 Southwest as "early capitalist" – cite as evidence the existence of wage labor[14] and the "capitalist" character of the hacienda or rancho. The problem with this evidence is that it is not altogether convincing. Several studies, for example, demonstrate the widespread presence of debt-peonage, hardly the stuff of free labor. Gilberto Hinojosa's study of Laredo, Texas,

reveals that "the indebted poor fled Laredo rather than submit to a peonage system which amounted to slavery. The frequency of calls for assistance in returning runaways suggests both the widespread use of peonage and the extensive escape from it."[15] Conversely, solid documentation for the prevalence of wage labor does not appear in the relevant literature. There is, for example, no entry for "wage labor" in the index of David J. Weber's Mexican Frontier, the most thorough study of the 1821–48 period.[16]

The descriptions of life in the Southwest prior to the Anglo conquest strongly suggest precapitalist (if not outright feudal) relations. California Indians, working as servants or laborers, were greatly exploited by the landowners and lived at the bottom of the class hierarchy. New Mexico consisted primarily of minifundia farming communities in which poverty-stricken subsistence villagers were forced into sharecropping and servitude by the latifundistas, the dominant economic, political, and social actors. The latifundistas used extra-economic coercion to exploit labor.

The idea that a Mexican "working class" existed before 1848 may arise from the appearance of monetary compensation for labor services. However, the existence of money payment does not, in itself, create a capitalist, free wage-labor system. Serfs and peasants at various times in precapitalist societies received monetary compensation. These labor forms generally were temporary, such as in periods of labor scarcity. The general practice was payment in kind or in labor services. Debt peonage, like money payment, can exist side-by-side with free peasantry, bound peasantry, and slavery.

Furthermore, a typical California rancho cannot be characterized as an "early capitalist" enterprise. None of the servants, laborers, or artisans working on the Mariano Vallejo, Bernardo Yorba, or Julian Chaves properties received a wage. Some were forced into labor through military raids. The Hacienda de los Yorbas (near present-day Santa Ana, California) was representative of the working California rancho:

The tradesmen and people employed about the [fifty-room] house were: Four wool-combers, two tanners, one butter and cheeseman who directed every day the milking of from fifty to sixty cows, one harness maker, two shoemakers, one jeweler, one plasterer, one carpenter, one mayordomo, two errand boys, one sheep herder, one cook, one baker, two washer-women, one woman to iron, four sewing women, one dressmaker, two gardeners, a schoolmaster, and a man to make the wine. . . . More than a hundred lesser employees were maintained on the ranch. The Indian peons lived in a little village of their own. . . . Ten steers a month were slaughtered to supply to hacienda.[17]

Generally, ranches and villages in California, New Mexico, and Texas provided for most of the needs of the residents, both laborers and landowners. They functioned largely as self-subsistence units. Although some of the products of the hacienda – primarily hides and tallow and, later, livestock – were exported, landholders used the proceeds to satisfy their taste for luxury, not to accumulate capital.[18] In New Mexico, small landowners and communal village farmers performed their own labor, had no servants, and often sharecropped for the larger owners. Within the large, small, and communal landholding system, labor remained relatively unspecialized. On the large landholdings, owners extracted wealth through the labor of their *peones*, in the communal villages, families eked out a marginal existence by their own labor and generally relied on payment in kind for labor services outside the village.

Those who see "early capitalism" as dominant in the Mexican Southwest claim that the pre-1848 and post-1848 Spanish borderlands societies differ not in quality but in quantity. From this perspective, linear change characterizes the historical process after 1848: a less developed, early capitalist Spanish south-western society merged with a higher stage of that same type of society characterized as US capitalist. This merger is considered a "modernization process."

Modernization theory, as applied in Chicano history, depends largely upon a view of the hacienda as a commercial institution and, therefore, capitalist.[19] There has been a long debate over the nature of the hacienda in Mexico and Latin America. The predominant attitude 25 years ago was that the hacienda was a feudal or quasifeudal institution. In the last two and a half decades, this approach, which was largely based upon Marxist approaches developed by François Chavalier and utilized by Woodrow Borah, came under strong attack from non-Marxists, particularly US scholars trained in a functionalist tradition. They substituted eclecticism and empirical historicism for Marxist concepts and methods.[20] The question of the nature of the hacienda became part of a larger debate over the character of Latin American society. In general, the non-Marxists shifted the crucial test for the character of the institution from the manner of extracting surplus labor at the hacienda (relations of production) to whether the products of that institution entered the world labor market (relations of exchange).

While these debates helped clarify concepts and approaches, they did not, in our estimation, undermine the evidence for the hacienda being an essentially non-capitalist enterprise. The influential Mexican historian Enrique Semo aptly described the economic essence of the hacienda by saying that it produced for the market during a period of world market booms and returned to being a self-sufficient enterprise during contractions of the world economy.[21] This prodigious feat is something a capitalist enterprise cannot do.[22] Furthermore, so far as social relations between laborers and owners of the haciendas are concerned, 25 years of detailed investigations have demonstrated that many forms of labor relations, besides debt peonage, could be found at the hacienda, including sharecropping, renting, service tenantry, and temporary wage labor. This is a far cry from a prevalence of capital/labor relations.[23]

Modernization theory, as well as "world-systems" theory, assumes that the essence of capitalism lies not in the social relations, property patterns, ideology, and political institutions of a society, but, rather, in the existence of commercial relations. Immanuel Wallerstein's world-systems approach has been justly criticized for making international commercial relations among countries the key to determining if a society were capitalist and for failing to address local, regional, and national influences on social structure.[24] Consequently, the claim that the Southwest was "early capitalist" stands upon the evidence of connections with international markets. If one accepts the "international trade equals capitalism" argument, then the possibility for historical analysis of specific economic forms collapses. Long-distance trade and production for distant markets exist in nearly all human societies. Is history, to paraphrase Marx, the record of only *one* socioeconomic form – capitalism? Modernization theory *ipso facto* obviates the question, "Was the Southwest in the Spanish/Mexican period precapitalist, quasifeudal, or capitalist?" In this view, the relations among Mission Indians, Pueblo Indians, Mexicans, Plains Indians, and Anglo-Americans are reduced to a relationship among different levels of capitalist society.

Despite differences in approach, most Chicano history scholars emphasize cultural conflict as the major theme in Chicano history. The first approach does this by default because conquering and conquered societies are defined in a way that precludes discussion of systemic economic conflict. In the second and significantly more complex approach, economic conflict is belittled by stipulating economic differences only of degree between the two societies. In our view, the use of vague economic categories has caused Chicano historians, almost by default, to emphasize conflict based upon cultural or racial models even as they sometimes mention economic factors and utilize Marxist rhetoric. Admittedly, every work in Chicano history cannot be wholly arranged into our scheme. A very important example is Ramón Gutiérrez's award-winning work on Spanish-Pueblo and gender relations in colonial New Mexico, which we cannot neatly place in the two groups above.[25] While Gutiérrez mentions the prevalence and, in fact, the increase of servile forms of labor in New Mexico toward the end of the eighteenth century, he focuses on gender systems and sexual practices as indicative of relations of domination and key to the construction, mediation, and defense of cultural identity. In his view, the Hispano-Anglo conflict can be seen primarily as a form of culture clash that can be explained without significant reference to systemic economic conflict.[26]

Our purpose is not to develop watertight classification schemes. Such an effort would be not only doomed from the start, given diversity within Chicano historiography, but also of limited value in and of itself. We now turn to drawing on currents present in some of these works to suggest that we think would be a stronger analytic framework for examining Chicano economic and social history.

## On relationships of production

Categories of political economy devised by Marx, with appropriate temporal and spatial specificity, reveal that pre-1848 Spanish-Mexican society derived from Spain's social structure in the New World. That is, the social heritage of the southwestern Spanish/Mexican era derived from hierarchical and inherited class relations characteristic of the Spanish social order.[27] This is not to say, however, that the pre-1848 New World social formations replicated Spanish social relations exactly and had no history of their own. The New World manifested numerous variations due to climate, topography, demography, and so forth, much as, in Spain itself, the large *dehesas* of Andalucia differed from the small peasant holdings of the Cantabrian range during the seventeenth and eighteenth centuries.

After the conquest of New Mexico, first the *encomiendas* and later the *repartimientos* formed the basis of colonial production. As an institution, the encomienda dates back to the colonization of Castile during the retreat of the Moors.[28] Its appearance in New Mexico reflects the traditional assignments granted to a Spanish conqueror – in this case, to some of Oñate's top soldiers – that included supervision of Indian subjects required to perform labor for the benefit of the *encomendero*.[29] Additionally, large land grants were given to the more prominent Spaniards. Through the encomiendas, the Pueblo villages contributed an annual tribute in kind to the leading colonists, usually consisting of maize and cotton blankets. In New Mexico, the tribute accruing from the encomienda did not amount to much. The repartimiento – or apportionment of coerced labor required from the Indian population living near an encomienda – was utilized to the fullest extent by the settlers living on ranches.[30]

Were these class distinctions softened by interaction and a reciprocal spirit?[31] In precapitalist societies, the need to cooperate against the forces of nature and the geographical isolation (and lack of transportation) encouraged a paternalism in which the lord cared for his vassals and serfs. This aspect of precapitalist society was reinforced by religious tenets that rationalized the lord/vassal relationship. From a romantic point of view, the nature of class relations in precapitalist societies can be favorably compared to the atomization and competitive mentality prevalent in a fully developed capitalist society. Social historical analysis, however, should look not only at the daily examples of benevolence or lack thereof, but also at a society's long-term development and at the opportunities of vassals to free themselves from coerced servitude. In precapitalist situations, then, "benevolence" may be viewed as an instrument for maintaining domination rather than as a characteristic of a virtuous older order.

Additional cases in point were the missions and ranchos of California. California missionaries confronted a different situation than those in New Mexico. In New Mexico, as in large parts of Mexico and South America, the Indian population was concentrated in relatively large native towns and villages where the missionaries took the faith to the residents. In California, where the Indians

were scattered in hundreds of small hamlets, the Spaniards brought many of them into specially created mission settlements and, despite some examples of "benevolence," subjected them to forced labor that resembled slavery in all but name.[32] That system came to an end in the 1830s with secularization and the rapid transformation of mission and other lands into privately held ranchos. The size and number of these ranchos and the social relations they engendered predominated for several decades. As already noted, the rancho in many ways resembled the medieval English manor in its self-sufficiency. Although there were exports of hides and tallow, those exports satisfied the luxury needs of the rancheros and did not lead to the accumulation of capital.

The absence of capitalism is also apparent in Arizona and Texas. Arizona was settled as early as 1696, when Father Eusebio Kino founded a number of missions including San Xavier del Bac, near present-day Tucson. By the end of his work, around 1712, 25 years of quiet were shattered by the discovery of silver in Arizona. After this brief mining boom, Arizona's economy was dominated by livestock production at the missions and the few haciendas. From the mid-eighteenth century onward, warring Indians made maintenance of this frontier next to impossible. With Mexican independence and the disappearance of the presidios, the area was abandoned from 1822 to 1862.[33]

The case of Texas was at once different and similar. The settlements were small and dispersed mostly around San Antonio, La Bahia, and Nacogdoches. The recent work by Gerald Poyo and Gilberto Hinojosa, while not focused on the issue at hand, provides what seems like a check list for the lack of capitalist characteristics: absence of laborers, lack of markets for products, backward agricultural technology, and local "elites" concentrating on raising cattle in an extensive manner, much like the Californios.[34] Montejano's detailed description of Texas border social relations supports a similar conclusion.[35] The population of Texas barely reached 4,000 at the end of the eighteenth century. In the lower

Rio Grande Valley (where the way of life was quite similar to that of early California), a "few large Mexican landowners lived an idle and lordly existence based on a system of peonage."[36] Already by 1830, Anglo-Americans outnumbered Mexicans by ten to one. They included some farmers, the harbingers of a new social system; many held slaves, planted cotton, and sold it. In Texas, then, two sets of relations – precapitalist and slavery – existed side by side.

## On relations of exchange

Commodity production – that is, organized production of goods for sale in the marketplace, a primary objective of the capitalist system – was nearly absent in the Mexican Southwest. To be sure, there were trade contacts with the outside. Despite centuries of isolation, the Spanish/Mexican Southwest maintained an array of commercial ties with surrounding economies, but this trade cannot be considered capitalistic.[37] As Douglas Monroy has observed about California, "the trade of the California coast in the early nineteenth century may well have been a part of the world market, but the territory was not capitalist – the market did not mediate between persons or things."[38]

In a conception of capitalism as a historically specific pattern of production, ownership of the means of production (in this case, land) separates the laborer from the capitalist. Labor power becomes a commodity which is purchased and utilized to produce other commodities. Commodity production on the basis of a wage-labor class constitutes the distinguishing feature of capitalism. Those scholars whom we are critiquing here use the term "capitalism," as Elizabeth-Fox Genovese has observed, "in a general, heuristic fashion to apply to concentration of wealth, participation in commerce, the presence of banks, and the quest for incomes."[39] Such use reflects ahistorical attributes of all or most economic activity and, therefore, tends to "conflate all historical experience."[40]

As in the case of some localities in classical antiquity and in medieval Western Europe, the intensification of commerce in the Southwest from 1831 to 1848 was not conducive to the development of local industry and manufacturing or to the growth of towns and handicraft industries.[41] One historian has noted that in New Mexico the landed oligarchy engaging in trade "became merchants as well as feudal lords."[42] Much of the revenue gained through trade was used to purchase luxury goods, manufactured items, and land. Consequently, the influx of revenue had little appreciable impact on the redistribution of land, division of labor, and technology in production. In fact, during the Mexican era, when trade expanded in New Mexico and California, class distinctions hardened, large land grants multiplied, and peonage increased.[43] Moreover, by 1846, foreigners dominated in artisan production, leading a contemporary to remark that, in spite of the high volume of trade in hide and tallow, "there are no capitalists in California."[44] It is difficult, if not impossible, to paint the rancheros as capitalists. Mariano Guadalupe Vallejo, the "proud oligarch of Sonoma,"[45] had his own private militia to guard his vast estate and 47 servants to tend to his wife and children.

## Periodization: The Key in the Nineteenth Century?

How was the pre-1848 socioeconomic formation in the Southwest finally broken? What was the social significance of the Mexican-American War? The answers to these questions are paradoxically both simple and complex: simple, in that within a few years, a different social organization of production prevailed in the southwestern economy; complex, in that (with regional and chronological differences) a variety of social mechanisms and individual agents simultaneously influenced this change. In some areas, it is clear that economic forces – specifically, differences in the methods governing the economic organization of production – were the principal determinants of social change. In other areas (or at other times), purely economic factors are obscured, and legal (and/or extra-economic) forms of coercion predominate. This situation is not surprising if the process is, as we assert, one of social revolution. It is certainly more difficult to identify and to ascertain the impact of social forces in an epoch of upheaval and rapid flux than in an era of stability.[46]

The notion that Chicano history begins with the conquest of 1848 is a common thread running through a majority of works in Chicano history.[47] Moreover, Chicano historians nearly unanimously emphasize a continuity of Chicano history from that point to the present, with cultural conflict between Anglos and Mexicans being the explanatory center of the discourse. Typically these same historians apply concepts that inadequately identify significant differences between nineteenth- and twentieth-century Chicano history, just as they tend to leave vague the nature of the economic conflict between conqueror and conquered in the mid-nineteenth century. On the other hand, a shared "cultural" trait – for example, being Spanish-surnamed or Spanish-speaking – provides prima facie evidence for continuity between the nineteenth and twentieth centuries.

The conquest of 1848 appears to be the key event that subordinated Mexicans and thus represents the beginning of Chicanos as a discrete population in the United States – the "Conquered Generation," in García's terms.[48] Later immigrants entered a society that had institutionalized the separate and subordinated status of Mexicans. This view is most clearly advanced by Albert Camarillo: "The history of the Chicano people as an ethnic minority in the United States was forged primarily from a set of nineteenth-century experiences."[49] "The key to reconstructing the history of Chicano society in Southern California," he continues, "is understanding the major developments of the half-century after the Mexican War."[50] He calls scholars' tendency to consider the nineteenth century fairly unimportant a "long-held but untenable" view. In sum, the nineteenth- and

twentieth-century Chicano experience seems fundamentally more continuous than discontinuous.[51] The "importance of the nineteenth century for understanding the twentieth-century Chicano experience" has emerged as "self-evident to historians," according to David J. Weber.[52] We question that assumption. The argument can be made for northern New Mexico, where twentieth-century Mexican immigration played a less significant role, and it may perhaps be extended to other subregions, but not persuasively to the region as a whole.

The question of when Chicano history begins is intertwined with another sharply debated issue: Do Chicanos constitute another immigrant ethnic group (similar to the Chinese, Japanese, Koreans, Germans, Jews, and others) or are they a "nationally" self-conscious, "conquered," indigenous population who were dispossessed of their land as were the American Indians? How are Chicanos similar to and different from other non-dominant peoples? Are Chicanos unique?[53]

The conventional view that the contemporary Chicano experience derives from social relations established after the 1848 conquest and that the nineteenth century is thus "key" to understanding Chicano history rests upon the assumption that today's Chicanos share certain characteristics with those of the past: possessors of a distinct culture and victims of racial prejudice that has led to life in segregated barrios, stereotyped behavior, violence, and subordinate social and occupational status. Camarillo and Griswold del Castillo, for example, see the barrios of today as originating in the conquest; De León contends that Mexican culture in the Southwest transcends the Mexican and Anglo-American periods; and Gómez-Quiñones argues that the history of the Chicano working class can be traced to the seventeenth century. Carlos Cortés summarizes the perspective: "Mexican Americans began as an annexed regional minority and continued so throughout the nineteenth century. They are still concentrated heavily in the Southwest."[54] Thus, the Chicanos' "conquered" legacy distinguishes them from other minorities such as the Chinese and Japanese (especially in the nineteenth century), and parallels the involuntary origins of African-Americans and American Indians.

If one focuses on issues of economic development, however, important differences emerge between the nineteenth and twentieth centuries. Our examination of the record suggests the existence of two separate epochs and populations in the history of Spanish-speakers in the Southwest,[55] a perspective that supports Almaguer's recent claim that "a major discontinuity exists between the nineteenth- and early twentieth-century Chicano experiences."[56] Of primary importance is the fact that, with the exception of New Mexico and southern Colorado, the small number of Mexicans annexed as a result of the conquest was inconsequential when compared to the much larger number of late nineteenth- and twentieth-century Mexican migrants to the region. Second, the parallels between the nineteenth-century Chicano experience and the experiences of other non-white minorities are striking. Mexicans suffered segregation, violence (such as lynching), and exploitation, but so too did the "non-conquered" Chinese, Japanese, Filipinos, and Asian Indians, among others.[57] Third, the massive economic transformations of the Southwest created a great demand for cheap, unskilled labor, which was met by unprecedented migration from Mexico beginning around the turn of the century.

Certainly, the pattern of regional development in the United States greatly affected Chicano history. The growth of southern California in particular became intimately related with demographic shifts in the Chicano population. The extraordinary development of the western half of the Southwest region – a result of mass migration – came with the growth of California agriculture and southern California industry, both of which would have been impossible without massive water projects.[58] Carey McWilliams noted economist Paul S. Taylor's trenchant 1927 observation: "Irrigation equals Mexicans."[59] Additionally, the recent regional development of the Southwest has depended on massive east-to-west US migration and on migrants from Asia, many of whom shared a common experience with those Mexican immigrants laboring for agribusiness.

There were frequent violent struggles between precapitalist Mexican and capitalist Anglo societies after 1848, but by 1900 they had faded as a new, integrated economic order arose. The 15,000 Mexican citizens living outside of New Mexico at the time of the conquest either accommodated to the new society or were overwhelmed by Mexican migrants. The conquered group lacked sufficient numbers to have a significant impact in the Anglo era. Moreover, once they had lost their lands by the late nineteenth century, they suffered further significant cultural disintegration. Except in New Mexico and southern Colorado, Mexican migrants introduced a completely new period in the history of the Spanish-speaking people in the Southwest, including Texas, where the break with Mexico had come earlier in 1836.[60]

Migration in the twentieth century altered the character of the southwestern Mexican community. By the 1920s, the Spanish-speaking population had grown dramatically, older settlements had expanded and many new ones had appeared, and Mexican labor had become of fundamental importance in economic development. There were other changes as well. Earlier Anglo-Mexican social relations had turned on the conflict between two distinct socioeconomic formations, while twentieth-century social relations centered upon the internal class conflicts inherent to corporate capitalism. The economic issues affecting Anglo-Mexican social relations had shifted from conflicting systems of production to class relations within the same system. Likewise, the political conflicts shifted from land issues in the nineteenth century to working-class concerns in the twentieth. As Montejano has demonstrated, these conflictive relations are expressed in the racial and ethnic dimensions of the contemporary Southwest.[61] The Mexican community, as we know it today, developed in this new atmosphere of corporate capitalism, a twentieth-century phenomenon.

We hope that a focus on these economic changes leads historians to reexamine Chicano history's dominant periodization to date, which assumes a fundamental continuity between the nineteenth and twentieth centuries. That "group history" view, based upon racial conflict and shared language, obscures broader and more fundamental themes based on economic transformations and their social consequences.

## THE URBAN EMPHASIS: A REAPPRAISAL

Besides calling for a rethinking of the periodization of Chicano history, we also suggest a reappraisal of the emphasis on the urban experiences of Chicanos. In a review of three major books on Chicano history by Albert Camarillo, Mario García, and Richard Griswold del Castillo, David J. Weber notes that "all three try to link their work to the mainstream of social and urban history while still focusing on the particularity of the Mexican American experience." Moreover, these scholars have "established the importance of the city as the crucible of change in Chicano society and culture, and have provided a valuable corrective to the notion of Chicanos as an essentially rural people."[62] Ricardo Romo, while acknowledging that "Chicanos have not always lived in urban areas," nonetheless contends that "since 1609, at least, when their Spanish-Mexican ancestors founded the pueblo of Santa Fe, they have contributed to and have been a part of the urbanization process in the Southwest." Griswold del Castillo concurs, adding that "[d]uring Spanish colonial times probably a larger proportion of the region's population lived in pueblos, towns, and cities than did the population in other areas of the United States."[63] Thus, historians have tended to view Chicano history since the Spanish era as a branch of urban history. An immediate problem with this view is that it labels as "urban" even small population centers, such

as Tucson in 1850. Such practice blurs the distinction between "urban" and "rural" to the point where it virtually disappears.

Another consideration here is that pre-1848 southwestern towns and pueblos can hardly be classed with contemporary industrial urban centers on the East Coast, the more so because precapitalist population centers differ significantly from cities and towns in a capitalistic social economy. Moreover, fully 70 percent of the southwestern population lived in rural areas at the turn of the century. It is doubtful that Chicanos were more urbanized at that time than the general population. As late as the 1930s, urban Chicanos made up only half of the Chicano population.[64] "Until the 1960s," states Martín Sánchez Jankowski, "Chicanos lived primarily in rural areas or were members of small or medium sized communities. During the 1960s and 1970s Chicanos became more urban."[65]

As a consequence of the emphasis upon so-called "urban" life, Chicano historiography has focused primarily on industrial, blue-collar labor and neglected rural and semiurban Chicano communities like the citrus-picker villages of southern California.[66] Carey McWilliams, one of the few historians to recognize the rural character of such communities, has observed: "This citrus belt complex of peoples, institutions, and relationships has no parallel in rural life in America and nothing quite like it exists elsewhere in California. It is neither town nor country, neither rural nor urban. It is a world of its own."[67]

Attention to the economic developments that engendered these communities would reveal, especially by the early 1900s when commodity production in large-scale agriculture, mining, and transportation was assuming economic predominance, a variety of community forms shaped by the industries that fostered them. Labor camps reflected the needs of railroad, mining, agricultural, stock-raising, lumbering, and other industrial enterprises. For example, Arizona mining towns, which employed considerable Mexican labor beginning in the late nineteenth century, differed in character from sharecropping communities of Texas, and from cities with a large commercial/industrial character like Los Angeles. Many communities existed only briefly, disappearing when a mine was exhausted, a track completed, or orchards subdivided. The Mexican community, affected by the demand for its labor power, settled according to the pattern of economic activity.

Rural citrus communities in southern California, as revealed in recent research by Gilbert G. González, tended to be permanent, remaining as barrios today in spite of the suburban sprawl that has engulfed them. This permanance reflected the citrus growers themselves, who were stable, year-round employers. Thus, some labor camps were clearly defined, permanent, stable, and well-structured Mexican villages. Such camps existed not only in the southern California citrus belt, but also in migrant agricultural areas (especially in sugar-beet fields), and in mining, railroad, and construction regions as well. On the other hand, those camps consisting of laborers under the contract system, which structured family labor in agriculture, were transitory and labor was unorganized (except in beet work).

Some camps were essentially company towns, owing their existence to a single company or grower association. *Colonias*, or barrios, in the copper towns of Arizona, the Goodyear cottontown of Litchfield, Arizona, the beet-fields of California and Colorado, the steel mills of Indiana, and the citrus-grower association camps of southern California were part of a larger pattern of company towns in the West, the Midwest, and the South. There were significant variations among these communities. For example, the sugar-beet company towns in Ventura County, California, had a decidedly different atmosphere than the towns of the South Platte Valley, Colorado. Even within southern California, the citrus company towns varied, some experiencing heavy-handed paternalistic intervention into daily life, others a hands-off policy by growers, and still others something in between.[68]

The great variety among camps led to significant differences in gender and family relations.[69] For example, employment and/or educational opportunities available to women and children varied with the organization of labor in particular enterprises. These, in turn, affected family, culture, and, ultimately, community. In the regions where family labor was widespread, the independence of women as economic actors was sharply curtailed in comparison to their urban counterparts. Where family labor was largely absent, as in the citrus industry, it was because such labor was of little significance in maintaining production. In the citrus industry, this permitted women to be widely employed in the packing houses where they earned wages equal to those of their male counterparts, the pickers. This distinguished female employment in citrus from that of migrant family labor in such activities as cotton production. Women packers developed a sense of self-worth based upon their individual labor and talents that was all but impossible for women who worked as part of a family unit. In the latter system, the male head of household nearly always received the wages directly from the employer or labor contractor. Thus, women engaged in family cotton-picking rarely received individual compensation for their labor. This pattern decidedly affected gender relations.

A measure of the wide distinction between the experience of women in cotton production and women in urban production appears when comparing the work of Ruth Allen to that of Vicky Ruiz. Allen's classic 1933 study of women in Texas cotton production noted that among Mexican women who did field work for hire, only a small percentage "received the income from their labor. In the case of the . . . married women the husbands received all the income." Among 110 women who worked in a family unit not one "reported that there was any arrangement to pay for her labor." Allen further states that

even when the woman is a hired [cotton] laborer, she has no individual economic existence. Her husband, father, or brother handles the financial affairs. She does not collect her own money; she does not know how much is paid for her services; she seldom knows how much cotton she picks a day or how many acres she chops. The wage paid is a family wage, and the family is distinctly patriarchal in its organization.[70]

Vicki Ruiz's study of California cannery and packing women of the 1930s and 1940s reported substantially different results. These women labored as individual wage-earners even if they generally received less than men for the same work. They developed a "cannery culture," a consciousness of common interests that fueled the movement towards unionization where ethnic women affected "every facet of decision making."[71]

Female citrus packers who received individual wages responded similarly. The packing house, declared one of them, offered "a greater opportunity for women" and provided "a sense of importance and purpose . . . I learned about my own rights." Furthermore, "it was better, a lot better than picking cotton . . . [which] was miserable. . . . [I]t was a step ahead . . . [and] we had a stable life."[72]

Educational opportunities also varied among the communities. In urban settings they were much greater than in the rural migrant settlements. Rural migrants were far less likely to attend school, or if attending at all, to attend only a portion of the school year. Statistics for Texas in 1945 indicate that only half of the Mexican children were enrolled in school. In part, this was due to a deliberate policy by boards of education to bar Mexican children, especially migrant children, from enrolling in school. In citrus towns, however, opportunities for education were greater due to the absence of family labor, and they were greater still in urban areas where fewer families were engaged in migratory work.[73]

Differences between rural and urban communities can also be detected in other areas, including the civil rights activities of the 1940s and as recently as the 1970s.[74] César Chávez, for example, left the Community Service Organization in the mid-1950s because the latter focused upon urban issues.

Chávez had dedicated himself to resolving the problems of rural Mexican communities, a decision with far-reaching and well-known effects on the history of farmworker unions and California agriculture. That urban and rural settlements differ is further underscored by their contrasting emphases on school reform during the 1960s and 1970s. Rural activists generally demanded integration, while urban activists turned toward separatism, community control of neighborhood schools, and bilingual education.[75]

Fortunately, the urban emphasis in Chicano historiography may be waning. For example, Sarah Deutsch's analysis of the transition from rural to urban life, Vicki Ruiz's incorporation of gender issues in her examination of women's organizations in the agriculture-based food-processing industry, Richard Griswold del Castillo and Richard García's biographical study of César Chávez, Robert Alvarez's study of Baja California migrating families, and Arnoldo De León's several works demonstrate that some communities do not fall into the urban pattern emphasized in the earlier literature.[76] Still, much remains to be done before we will have an adequate understanding of the complexity and enduring significance of Chicano community life.

We hope that the preceding pages have caused readers to think more deeply about the conventional wisdom that passes for much of Chicano history. Close attention to economic transformations questions the standard periodization of Chicano history and suggests that the nineteenth- and twentieth-century Spanish-speaking populations of the Southwest should be viewed as largely two different populations. And even within those populations, the nature of economic development has produced communities that vary significantly. Behind our approach lies the conviction that culture and economic life should not be kept in separate historical compartments. Moreover, our findings suggest that Chicano history should be viewed as something more than the distinct experience and contribution of one particular regional, ethnic group. Perhaps Chicano historians will also find value in the work of those southern historians who focus on capitalist development as a way of integrating the history of the South into the history of the entire nation. Chicano scholars might then take the first step in demonstrating that Chicano history is an integral component of American history. They might also be encouraged to advance efforts toward a multicultural history by distilling the common as well as the different experiences of cultural, ethnic, and gender groups. To paraphrase Cornel West, keen attention to economic structures can assist historians to contextualize cultural history.[77]

# Notes

1    Chicano historiography made impressive strides over the past twenty years. See, among others, the following studies: Pedro Castillo, "The Making of a Mexican Barrio: Los Angeles, 1980–1920" (Ph.D. dissertation, University of California, Santa Barbara, 1979); Albert Camarillo, *Chicanos in a Changing Society* (Cambridge, MA, 1979); Juan Gómez-Quiñones, "The Origins and Development of the Mexican Working Class in the United States: Laborers and Artisans North of the Río Bravo, 1600–1900," in Elsa C. Frost (ed.), *El trabajo y los trabajadores en la historia de México* (Tucson, AZ, 1979), 463–505; Richard Griswold del Castillo, *The Los Angeles Barrio, 1850–1890: A Social History* (Berkeley, CA, 1979); Mario García, *Desert Immigrants: The Mexicans of El Paso, 1880–1920* (New Haven, 1981) and García, *Mexican Americans: Leadership, Ideology, and Identity, 1930–1960* (New Haven, 1989); Robert J. Rosenbaum, *Mexicano Resistance in the Southwest* (Austin, TX, 1981); Rodolfo Acuña, *Occupied America: A History of Chicanos*, 2nd edn (New York, 1981); Ricardo Romo, *East Los Angeles: A History of a Barrio* (Austin, 1983); Richard Griswold del Castillo, *La Familia: Chicano Families in the Urban Southwest, 1848 to the Present* (Notre Dame, IN, 1984); Antonio Ríos-Bustamante, *Los Angeles: Pueblo and Region* (Los Angeles, 1985); David

Montejano, *Anglos and Mexicans in the Making of Texas, 1836–1986* (Austin, 1987); Vicki Ruiz, *Cannery Women, Cannery Lives: Mexican Women, Unionization and the California Food Processing Industry, 1930–1950* (Albuquerque, NM, 1987). See also Carlos Cortés, "Mexicans," in Stephan Thernstrom, Ann Orlov, and Oscar Handlin (eds), *Harvard Encyclopedia of American Ethnic Groups* (Cambridge, MA, 1980), 699; Arnoldo De León, *The Tejano Community 1836–1900* (Albuquerque, NM, 1982); Albert Camarillo, *Chicanos in California: A History of Mexican Americans in California* (San Francisco, 1984); John R. Chávez, *The Lost Land: The Chicano Image of the Southwest* (Albuquerque, NM, 1984); Arnoldo De León and Kenneth L. Stewart, *Tejanos and the Numbers Game: A Socio-Historical Interpretation from the Federal Censuses, 1850–1900* (Albuquerque, NM, 1989); Thomas E. Sheridan, *Los Tucsonenses: The Mexican Community in Tucson, 1854–1941* (Tucson, AZ, 1986).

2    Nan Elizabeth Woodruff, "The Transition to Capitalism in America," review of Christopher Clark, *The Roots of Rural Capitalism: Western Massachusetts, 1780–1860* (Ithaca, NY, 1990), in *Reviews in American History*, 20 (1992), 173.

3    See Pedro Castillo and Albert Camarillo (eds), *Furia y Muerte: Los Bandidos Chicanos* (Los Angeles, 1973); Rosenbaum, *Mexicano Resistance*, see also Acuña, *Occupied America, passim.*

4    Rosalinda González, "Distinctions in Western Women's Experience: Ethnicity, Class and Social Change," in Susan Armitage (ed.) *The Women's West* (Norman, OK, 1987), 237–52; Montejano, *Anglos and Mexicans*; Douglas Monroy, *Thrown among Strangers* (Berkeley, 1990). The question of the direction of Chicano history is the subject of several recent essays. See Alex Saragoza, "The Significance of Recent Chicano-Related Historical Writings: An Appraisal," *Ethnic Affairs*, I (1987), 24–62; Gerald E. Poyo and Gilberto M. Hinojosa, "Spanish Texas and Borderlands Historiography in Transition: Implications for U.S. History," *Journal of American History*, 75 (1988), 393–416; David J. Weber, "John Francis Bannon and the Historiography of the Spanish Borderlands," *Myth and the History of the Hispanic Southwest Essays* (Albuquerque, NM, 1988), 55–88; Tomás Almaguer, "Ideological Distortions in

Recent Chicano Historiography: The Internal Model and Chicano Historical Interpretation," *Aztlán* (1987), 7–27.

5   Generally speaking, Chicano historiography developed somewhat separately from the ongoing writing by Borderland scholars and focuses upon the later period. For a detailed evaluation of the vicissitudes and "sociology" of these fields of study, see David J. Weber, "John Francis Bannon and the Historiography of the Spanish Borderlands." See also José Cuello, "Beyond the 'Borderlands' Is the North of Colonial Mexico: A Latin-Americanist Perspective to the Study of the Mexican North and the United States Southwest," in Krityna P. Demaree (ed.), *Proceedings of the Pacific Coast Council on Latin American Studies*, 9 (1982), 1–24.

6   Howard Lamar, *The Far Southwest, 1848–1912: A Territorial History* (New Haven, 1966).

7   Rosalinda González provides several examples of integrating Chicana women's household labor and wage labor into the fabric of capitalism and agribusiness in the West. See her "The Chicana in Southwest Labor History, 1900–1975: A Preliminary Bibliographical Analysis," *Critical Perspectives of Third World America*, II (1984), 26–61; "Distinctions in Western Women's Experience: Ethnicity, Class and Social Change," in Armitage (ed.), *The Women's West*, 237–51; "Chicanas and Mexican Immigrant Families, 1920–1940: Women's Subordination and Family Exploitation," in Joan Jensen and Lois Scharff (eds), *Decades of Discontent* (Westport, CT, 1983), 59–84.

8   Bell Hooks, *Feminist Theory from Margin to Center* (Boston, 1985).

9   Albert Camarillo, "Chicanos in the American City," in Eugene E. García, Francisco A. Lomeli, and Isidro D. Ortiz (eds), *Chicano Studies: A Multidisciplinary Approach* (New York, 1984), 25.

10   He writes: "The economic formations within the Mexican communities of the greater Mexican North in the seventeenth and eighteenth centuries can be characterized as early-capitalist, a period of a variety of co-existing economic forms and practices, the predominant tendency being the transition to capitalism." See Juan Gómez-Quiñones, "Origins and Development of the Mexican Working Class," 464.

11   Montejano specifically rejects the views of the pre-1848 Southwest as a feudal or even a precapitalist (and merely pastoral) society. See Montejano, *Anglos and Mexicans*, 312–13.

12   Robert J. Rosenbaum carefully attempts to define Mexican society by applying the term "peasant." However, peasants were only one segment of Mexican society in the pre-1848 Southwest. The term is misleading in that it narrowly defines the class nature of Mexican society while at the same time providing too general an interpretive design. See Rosenbaum, *Mexicano Resistance*.

13   Others might argue that "nationalist" impulses led Chicano writers to emphasize a "them vs. us" attitude. See, for example, Saragoza, "Significance of Recent Chicano-Related Historical Writings," 27.

14   Gómez-Quiñones notes that the landless sector "worked for wages in principle; these were sometimes real, more often fictional. Wage labor worked alongside indentured labor and even slave labor." He also states that the "majority of landless mestizos were laborers or *medieros* (sharecroppers). Persons were paid in subsistence, shares, goods, and small wages." See Gómez-Quiñones, "Origins and Development of the Mexican Working Class," 481, 501.

15   Gilberto M. Hinojosa, *A Borderlands Town in Transition: Laredo, 1755–1870* (College Station, TX, 1983), 41. David Weber notes that in New Mexico the practice of debt peonage was widespread, even more so in the Mexican than in the Spanish period (Weber, *Mexican Frontier, 1821–1846* [Albuquerque, NM, 1982], 211–12). Cleland found the same in southern California, where the Indians were "the chief labor supply . . . They lived and worked under a form of peonage similar in some respects to that so long in effect in Mexico." (See Robert Glass Cleland, *The Cattle on a Thousand Hills* [San Marino, CA, 1951], 81.) Gomez-Quiñones elaborates: "As ranchos developed [Indians] were hired out to the rancheros for a fee to the missions to do similar work on the ranchos as for the missions. None or little payment went to the laborers . . . At most they received clothes, blankets, cheap trinkets and nearly always living quarters and food. Much of this they produced through their work." (See Gomez-Quiñones, "Origins and Development of the Mexican Working Class," 474.)

16   Antonio Ríos-Bustamante makes the most

cogent argument for capitalist development in the pre-Anglo Southwest, specifically, Albuquerque, New Mexico; however, his own data contradict his position. Bustamante found that 48.5 percent of the laborers were handicraftsmen and 23.8 percent were peasants; only 13.1 percent were day laborers. As he points out, even these day laborers often owned land and were "paid in produce." The description strongly resembles those of European villages at the height of the period generally known as feudalism. See Antonio J. Ríos-Bustamante. "New Mexico in the Eighteenth Century: Life, Labor and Trade in the Villa de San Felipe de Albuquerque, 1706–1790," *Aztlán,* 7 (1976), 357–89.

17  Cleland, *Cattle on a Thousand Hills,* 74. Señora Vallejo, wife of Don Mariano Guadalupe Vallejo, recalled that, in their northern California hacienda, each of her 16 children had a personal servant; she herself had two. In addition, 27 other women ground corn, served in the kitchen, washed clothes, sewed, and spun: a total of 45 servants in the master's house *ibid.,* 43). In New Mexico, the raiding party was employed to acquire servants from Navajos, Utes, or Apaches. Amado Chaves reminisced in 1927 that "many of the rich people who did not have the nerve to go into campaigns would buy Indian girls." Weber, *Mexican Frontier,* 212.

18  Lynn I. Perrigo, *Texas and Our Spanish Southwest* (Dallas, TX, 1960), 80–3.

19  Not all southwestern haciendas – or ranchos – meet this definition. Robert Glass Cleland compared the southern California ranchos with the English manor, noting that "each ranch was virtually a self-sustaining economic unit" (Cleland, *Cattle on a Thousand Hills,* 42–3). Sheridan notes that the haciendas in and around Tucson were "geared towards subsistence rather than commercial exploitation and expansion" (Sheridan, *Los Tucsonenses,* 14). Nancie L. González's study of New Mexico attests to the self-subsistence character of production in villages (although surplus was often traded): "The small northern Spanish villages were relatively isolated . . . from each other, and each one formed an almost self-sufficient unit, both in terms of economy and social structure" (Nancie L. González, *The Spanish-Americans of New Mexico* [Albuquerque, 1967], 38–9). Robert J. Rosenbaum corroborates the findings of Sheridan, Cleland, and González:

"Most mexicanos engaged in subsistence agriculture solidly rooted in the traditions and social relationships of their village or land grant . . . Producing a surplus for market was very low on their list of priorities." Rosenbaum, *Mexicano Resistance,* 11.

20  See Eric Van Young, "Mexican Rural History since Chevalier: The Historiography of the Colonial Hacienda," *Latin American Research Review,* 18 (1983), 12.

21  Enrique Semo, *Historia del Capitalismo en México: Los origines, 1521–1763* (México, 1973).

22  During periods of crisis, capitalist enterprises may, among other things, go bankrupt, close, disappear, get sold, or get absorbed, but they do not, chameleon-like, become self-sufficient English manors.

23  Van Young, "Mexican Rural History," 24. This situation is quite typical of precapitalist societies. Wage-labor, sharecropping, and other arrangements were known during Roman times.

24  The critiques are numerous, but see especially Eric Wolf, *Europe and the People without History* (Berkeley, CA, 1981) and Peter Worsley, *Three Worlds of Culture and World Development* (Chicago, 1984).

25  One of his principal aims, Gutiérrez explains, was not to be delimited by existing historiography but, rather, to initiate a "new dialogue." Ramón Gutiérrez, in a session devoted to his book, *When Jesus Came the Corn Mothers Went Away,* at the annual meeting of the Pacific Coast Branch of the American Historical Association, Corvallis, Oregon, Aug. 14, 1992.

26  Ramón Gutiérrez, *When Jesus Came, the Corn Mothers Went Away* (Stanford, CA, 1991), 325–27.

27  Perrigo, *Texas and Our Spanish Southwest,* 33–4, 44–5, 79–81.

28  Robert S. Chamberlain, *Castilian Background of the Repartimiento-Encomienda* (Washington, DC, 1939).

29  See James Lockhart, "Encomienda and Hacienda: The Evolution of the Great Estate in the Spanish Indies," *Hispanic American Historical Review,* 49 (1969), 411–29, for a discussion of the juridical, and the practical, relationship between encomiendas and land ownership.

30  George I. Sánchez, *Forgotten People: A Study of New Mexicans* (Albuquerque, NM, 1949), ch. 1.

31   Camarillo, *Chicanos in a Changing Society*, 12,
     13.
32   Varden Fuller, "The Supply of Agricultural
     Labor as a Factor in the Evolution of Farm
     Organization in California," in Senate
     Committee on Education and Labor, *Hearings
     on Agricultural Labor in California*, 67 Cong.
     (1940), part 54.
33   Odie R. Faulk, "The Presidio: Fortress or
     Farce?" *Journal of the West*, 8 (1969), 21–8. For
     a contrasting view, see James Officer, *Hispanic
     Arizona, 1536–1856* (Tucson, AZ, 1987).
34   Poyo and Hinojosa, "Spanish Texas and
     Borderlands."
35   According to Montejano:
         At the time of independence in 1836
         and annexation in 1848, one finds a
         landed Mexican elite, an ambitious
         Anglo mercantile clique, a class of
         independent but impoverished
         Mexican rancheros, and an indebted
         working class of Mexican peones. The
         new Anglo elite was generally
         Mexicanized and frequently intermar-
         ried or became compadres
         ("god-relatives") with landowning
         Mexican families. As one Texas
         scholar described the situation, the
         Anglo cattle barons established an
         "economic, social, and political
         feudalism" that was "natural" and not
         necessarily resented by those who
         submitted to it [O. Douglas Weeks.
         "The Texas-Mexican and the Politics
         of South Texas," *American Political
         Science Review*, 24 (1930), 610.]
         Annexation had merely changed the
         complexion of the landowning elite.
         (Montejano, *Anglos and Mexicans*, 8)
36   McWilliams, *North from Mexico*, 85.
37   Before the Spanish *entrada* into New Mexico
     during the 1600s, trade had already taken
     place among earlier groups of regional
     settlers. In his first expedition, Coronado
     observed the existence of commerce between
     the Plains Indians and the Pueblos. The Plains
     Indians, skillful tanners of buffalo and deer
     hides, exchanged these goods on a regular
     basis for Pueblo corn, cloth, and pottery.
38   Monroy, *Thrown among Strangers*, 101.
39   Elizabeth Fox-Genovese, *Within the Plantation
     Household* (Chapel Hill, NC, 1988), 53.
40   Ibid.
41   The development of commercial capital has
     been erroneously associated with unremitting

progress. Trade and commercial capital can
also make their appearance among economically undeveloped, nomadic peoples – as
evidenced by the Southwest before the
Spanish invasion. In the case of the
Southwest, manufacturing or industrial development did not occur as a direct result of
increased commercial activity. Weber makes
this specific observation in *Mexican Frontier*,
144.
42   Max Moorhead, cited in Weber, *Mexican
     Frontier*, 210.
43   Weber, *Mexican Frontier*, 209–12; Gutiérrez,
     *When Jesus Came*, 325–7.
44   Weber, *Mexican Frontier*, 146.
45   Ibid., 211.
46   One can identify two major contributors to
     historical change in the Southwest between
     1821 and 1880: the development of
     commodity circulation and the effects of
     usury capital. We have already discussed the
     development of commodity circulation as a
     weakening element. Usury capital as one
     example of a process that characterized the
     conflict between these two social economies is
     described in Raúl A. Fernández, *The United
     States-Mexico Border: A Politico-Economic Profile*
     (Notre Dame, IN, 1977).
47   Weber correctly points out that the bulk of
     Chicano history focuses on Mexican
     Americans in the border region since the
     Mexican-American War (Weber, "John
     Francis Bannon," 69). We note these impor-
     tant exceptions: Gutiérrez, *When Jesus Came*,
     Hinojosa, *Borderlands Town in Transition*; and
     Monroy, *Thrown among Strangers*.
48   García, *Desert Immigrants*. The fullest develop-
     ment of this notion is the "internal colony"
     model best represented in the works of soci-
     ologists Alfredo Mirandé, *The Chicano
     Experience: An Alternative Perspective* (Notre
     Dame, IN, 1985); Mario Barrera, *Race and
     Class in the Southwest: A Theory of Racial
     Inequality* (Notre Dame, IN, 1979); and
     Chávez, *The Lost Land*. For an early critique,
     see Gilbert G. González, "A Critique of the
     Internal Colony Model," *Latin American
     Perspectives*, 5 (1974), 154–61.
49   Camarillo, *Chicanos in a Changing Society*, 2.
50   Ibid., 3.
51   Saragoza, "The Significance of Recent
     Chicano-Related Historical Writings," 29.
52   David J. Weber, "The New Chicano Urban
     History," *History Teacher*, 16 (1983), 226.
53   Joan Moore and Harry Pachon argue that the

Spanish- and Mexican-origin population of the Southwest has a unique history. See their *Hispanics in the United States* (Engelwood Cliffs, NJ, 1985).

54   Carlos Cortés, "Mexicans," in Stephan Thernstrom, Ann Orlov, and Oscar Handlin (eds), *Harvard Encyclopedia of American Ethnic Groups* (Cambridge, MA, 1980), 699.

55   We note in passing that, in this age when terms of self-reference have acquired paramount importance, the term "Chicano" itself developed as a self-referent by working-class, immigrant Mexicans in the twentieth century (Camarillo, *Chicanos in a Changing Society*, x–xi). Also, old settlers and new arrivals considered each other to be culturally different.

56   Almaguer, "Ideological Distortions in Recent Chicano Historiography," 23.

57   We do not suggest that the experiences of these groups are identical. For example, the Asian experience was unique in that Asians were the only group to suffer total exclusion (1882 Chinese Exclusion Act, 1917 Barred Zone Act, and 1920 Immigration Act), as well as other legislative barriers imposed by American society. We argue, in contrast, that Chicano history has tended to examine the distinctiveness of the Chicano population at the expense of similarities it shares with other subordinated groups in the twentieth-century Southwest.

58   This growth cannot, of course, be limited to the utilization of the Colorado River. California's Central Valley and State Water projects and other western water projects are an integral part of the picture. Marc Reisner, *Cadillac Desert: The American West and Its Disappearing Water* (New York, 1986); Johannes Hemlun, *Water Development and Water Planning in the Southwestern United States* (Denmark, 1969); Charles W. Howe and K. William Easter, *Interbasin Transfers of Water* (Baltimore, MD, 1971); Norris Hundley, jr, *The Great Thirst: Californians and Water, 1770s–1900s* (Berkeley and Los Angeles, 1992).

59   McWilliams, *North from Mexico*, 162.

60   The argument for discontinuity is not new. Moses Rischin, "Continuity and Discontinuities in Spanish-Speaking California," in Charles Wollenberg (ed.), *Ethnic Conflict in California* (Los Angeles, 1970), 43–60, and Arthur F. Corwin, "Mexican-American History: An Assessment," *Pacific Historical Review*, 42 (1973), 270–3, made the argument nearly 20 years ago. Their views, however, were marred by an "assimilationist" approach. Chicano historians threw out the proverbial "baby with the bathwater" by ignoring their views in their entirety.

61   Montejano, *Anglos and Mexicans, passim.*

62   Weber, "The New Chicano History," 224.

63   Ricardo Romo, "The Urbanization of Southwestern Chicanos in the Early Twentieth Century," in Ricardo Romo and Raymund Paredes (eds), *New Directions in Chicano Scholarship* (La Jolla, CA, 1977), 183; Richard Griswold del Castillo, "Quantitative History in the American Southwest: A Survey and Critique," *Western Historical Quarterly*, 15 (1984), 408.

64   One extensive analysis of the 1910, 1920, and 1930 censuses found that, in 1930, "in the states west of the Mississippi, the average of the percent of Mexicans in urban communities, by states, is 36 percent" and, further, that the "distribution of Mexicans in western United States, in the principal region which they occupy, is largely rural." However, in the midwestern states (states east of the Mississippi), the Mexican community is largely urban, with 61 percent living in such areas. See Elizabeth Broadbent, "The Distribution of Mexican Population in the Unites States" (Ph.D. dissertation, University of Chicago, 1941), 61.

65   Martín Sánchez Jankowski, *City Bound Urban Life and Political Attitudes among Chicano Youth* (Albuquerque, NM, 1986), 4.

66   César Chávez and his rural union movement have been all but ignored by this urban history. Richard Griswold del Castillo and Richard García try to close the gap in *César Chávez: A Triumph of Spirit* (Norman, OK: 1995).

67   Carey McWilliams, *Southern California: An Island on the Land* (New York, 1946), 207.

68   The research of Gilbert González indicates that the citrus-picker community of southern California deviated significantly from the urban, blue-collar pattern. Many have viewed southern California barrios as parts of large, urban complexes. This may be true today, but it was not so during the height of the citrus industry. At about 1940, some 36,000 Mexican pickers and packers were employed by the 242 or so grower associations in California, principally in the southern part. About 75,000 to 100,000 Mexicans dwelled in

the camps, some of which had been in existence since 1910.

69   Nancy Hewitt presents a powerful argument for studying women within the context of the social and material circumstances of their communities in "Beyond the Search for Sisterhood: American Women's History in the 1980s," *Social History*, 10 (1985), 299–321.

70   Ruth Alice Allen, *Labor of Women in the Production of Cotton* (1933; Chicago, 1975), 231, 234.

71   Ruiz, *Cannery Women, Cannery Lives*, 39.

72   Interview with Julia Aguirre, Aug. 8, 1989, Placentia, California.

73   Gilbert G. González, *Chicano Education in the Era of Segregation* (Philadelphia, 1993) and Gilbert G. González *Labor and Community:* *Mexican Citrus Worker Communities in a Southern California County* (Champaign, IL, 1994).

74   Ernesto Galarza, "Program for Action," *Common Ground*, 10 (1949), 33.

75   Alan Exelbrod, "Chicano Education: In Swann's Way?" *Integrated Education*, 9 (1971), 28.

76   Sarah Deutsch, *No Separate Refuge: Culture, Class, and Gender on an Anglo-Hispanic Frontier in the American Southwest, 1880–1940* (New York, 1987); Robert Alvarez, *Familia: Migration and Adaptation in Baja and Alta California, 1800–1975* (Berkeley, CA, 1987).

77   Cornel West, "The Postmodern Crisis of the Black Intellectual," in Lawrence Grossberg et al. (eds), *Cultural Studies* (New York and London, 1992), 691.

# Mapping the Spanish Language along a Multiethnic and Multilingual Border

## Rosaura Sánchez

Amidst a new wave of neo-nativism and increased hostility against immigrants not only in the United States but throughout Europe – as evident in xenophobic fire bombings in Germany, "ethnic cleansing" in Yugoslavia, new French intentions to restrict immigration (Weiner, 1993), and proposed US Congressional bills for immigration reform – it is impossible to focus on the language of Latinos in the Southwestern border states without considering this worldwide phenomenon of ethnic intolerance and the marked trend toward demographic diversity in a country that is increasingly multiethnic and multilingual. "Control of the borders" is the latest cry of the political right, echoing recent published attacks against multiculturalism and calls for preserving a national identity based on northern European culture, all direct outgrowths of the present economic crisis and concern about the high rate of unemployment in this country, attributed by nativists to the growing presence of immigrants.

The Census Bureau estimates that by the year 2000 the US population will include 9 million immigrants who entered the country after 1986 and their descendants. It further estimates that by the year 2030, post-1986 immigrants and their descendants will number 32 million (Spencer, 1982; 1). Statistics on undocumented immigrants coming into the country during the last decade (Miller and Ostrow, 1993: A22) and detailed Census Bureau estimates of the hundreds of "foreign" languages spoken today

are daily and weekly fare in US newspapers. This type of information frightens anti-immigration nativists, despite assurances by those who downplay any political threat from the largest of the immigrant groups, the Latinos, by pointing to their political fragmentation (Shorris, 1992: 26).

The statistics, no doubt, can be variously interpreted. What cannot be denied is the growing language and ethnic diversity of the country, and especially of the US Southwest, underscored by the multiplicity of languages spoken. Spanish, Chinese, Tagalog, Vietnamese, Korean, German, Japanese, French, Italian, Portuguese, Farsi, Armenian, Cambodian, Laotian, Polish, Arabic, Hebrew, Russian; the languages of North India, Pakistan, and Bangladesh; and the other languages of Europe, southwestern Asia, and India are some of the major languages represented in this country today by thousands of speakers, even millions in some cases. Spanish, the main non-English language, is spoken by over 17 million (Quintanilla, 1993; E2). In particular, the states along the US–Mexican border can no longer be viewed as bilingual and bicultural, as language statistics for California clearly reveal. For very concrete historical reasons, the border states are pre-eminently multilingual, multiethnic, and multicultural.

The 1,933-mile border separating Mexico and the United States is a national boundary established, for the most part, in 1848 to separate two nation-states that epitomize the polarization of the world into center and periphery. Like any political boundary, the "border" between Mexico and the United States is historical and contingent, the result of hegemonic practices rather than a necessary, God-given, or natural partition. Since the early sixteenth century, Spanish cartographers had mapped the southern part of the United States, from Florida to Louisiana, and Texas and New Mexico. After explorations had led Hernán Cortés to Baja California, Francisco Vásquez de Coronado traveled to Arizona, up the Colorado River, and as far north as the southern boundary of Nebraska. During the same century, Juan Rodriguez Cabrillo explored the Pacific, sailing from Natividad (Colima) to San Diego and north to Monterey Bay and a bit beyond (Cleland, 1947: 1–15). Before then, of course, regional maps were configured orally and multilingually by the hundreds of native Indian tribes who often tied their spatial configurations to mythic interpretations of the landscape (Vallejo, 1875, vol. 1: 13–14). Early Spanish explorations led to a claim of the Southwest and Florida for Spain, and for close to 300 years the Southwest was considered the northernmost frontier of New Spain. Geological markers, like rivers, deserts, mountain chains, gulfs, and oceans, which today serve to divide and designate boundaries, were mere characteristics of the colonized territory. Geopolitics would, however, play a part in the territorial isolation of this northernmost area, as distance and inaccessibility (except by ship or arduous walking and riding) permitted only small Spanish, and later Mexican, settlements and allowed the region's eventual invasion by US settlers and troops.

Demography and geography do not, however, reveal the entire picture in view of colonial relations of production, which kept the Indian population either subservient to Spanish and Mexican settlers, despite their linguistic and cultural assimilation, or in a hostile position resisting the incursions of the colonists. Later, in the 1840s, the map of the Southwest would be redrawn according to the US policy of expansionism ("Manifest Destiny"). The political chaos in Mexico during the 1830s and 1840s, and Spain's failure to develop Mexico's economy before independence in 1822, would leave Mexicans weak and unable to resist the US invasion of their own capital. By the 1870s the Californio Mariano Guadalupe Vallejo could only look back and lament their loss of land, their loss of political and economic power as a conquered population, their proletarianization, and their linguistic oppression (Vallejo, 1875, vol. 5).

Political maps, however, are not synonymous with linguistic maps. They do not tell the entire story. In fact, Mexico's nineteenth-century lack of military, economic, and political power and its twentieth-century economic dependence have, perhaps ironically, only furthered the expansion of its geolinguistic power, for today, given large-scale immigration from Mexico, Mexico could be said to be demographically and linguistically reterritorializing the Southwest. The Latino population is fast becoming the largest minority population of the United States as well as the population with the lowest income and the highest rate of poverty (García and Montgomery, 1991: 7–8); it is expected to surpass the African American minority in size by the middle of the next century and to become the majority population in the state of California by the year 2040 (Miller and Ostrow, 1993: A22). This Latino population resides, of course, not only in the Southwest but throughout the United States; yet its marked concentration (about 63 percent in the US Southwest has led, particularly for Latinos of Mexican origin who recall their historical roots in the region, to the construction of the notion of the "border" states as the homeland.

The more recent reconfiguration of the linguistic and demographic map is a broader historical phenomenon, a product not only of the mass migration of Mexicans and nineteenth-century imperialism but of the postwar (1945–70) globalization of labor (Amin, 1992: 9) and subsequent social, economic, and political changes that have triggered the migration of Asian, Caribbean, and Latin American immigrants. The internationalization of capital – with its exportation of labor-intensive work as well as of technology from industrialized nations to developing nations – has not improved the economic situation in developing areas affected by the worldwide jobs slump. Thus, despite the relocation of industries to the Third World, current reports indicate that in light of labor-saving technological advancements that increase productivity with a smaller work force, Latin American and African unemployment rates have risen and led to increased international migration to industrialized nations (Havemann and Kempster, 1993). The case of Mexico is a clear example. The United Nations Fund for Population Activities (UNFPA) reports that Mexico now exports about 10 percent of its labor force to the United States. Domestic migration in Mexico has in turn further led to a concentration of its population primarily in urban areas. Mexico City is now listed by the UNFPA as the largest metropolitan area in the world with 20.2 million; by the year 2000 it is expected to continue as the largest in the world with a population of 25.6 million (Meisler, 1993, citing UN report).

The phenomenon of domestic and international migration is of course worldwide. The UNFPA estimates that there are now 100 million foreign immigrants in the world and millions moving within particular nations from rural to urban areas. This geographical and occupational migration relocates migrants in Western Europe, the United States, Japan, and the large urban centers of the Third World. Major cities of both industrial and developing nations, like Sao Paulo, Calcutta, Bombay, Beijing, Shanghai, Tokyo, Los Angeles, and Mexico City, as previously indicated, continue to grow at what can only be termed mind-boggling rates.

The situation of immigrant workers is not vastly improved by migrating, since unemployment rates are also high in the industrialized countries. Unemployment averaged 7.4 percent in the United States in 1992 and 10 percent in Western Europe (Havermann and Kempster, 1993), numbers that are expected to worsen during the next two years. Yet for these immigrants, both

documented and undocumented, low-wage employment in the service industries, agriculture, or secondary industries in the core countries is an improvement over unmitigated poverty back home. It is for this reason that international immigrants are estimated to send back a highly significant $66 billion to their home countries every year, "a total that makes these remittances second in value only to oil in world trade" (Meisler, 1993, citing UN report). As unemployment increases in the United States, however – an outcome of the relocation of major industries to Western Europe and Japan and labor-intensive industries to the Third World – and as social and health services for the unemployed are curtailed, a worsening scenario looms. This is clearly seen in increased homelessness, crime (especially drug addiction and dealing), and generalized and state violence in the ghettos and barrios of large urban sectors, areas where many of these ethnic/lingual minorities and recent immigrants are forced to reside due to economic circumstances. The growing polarization of society, with the wealthy getting wealthier and the poor getting poorer, and a drastically reduced middle class, has in turn catalyzed hostility against newcomers who serve as scapegoats for conditions produced by multinational capitalism. The aggression displayed of late by neo-Nazis in their violence against Turkish and North African immigrants in Germany is evident as well in the United States in racist violence against African Americans, Asians, and Latinos, especially against recent Mexican immigrants. The racist nativist hostility is, of course, not new in this country, which has a long history of racism against Chinese immigrants, Blacks, and Latinos. This century, for example, has seen cyclical media blitzkriegs against Mexican immigrants, beginning with reports promoting violence against the "zoot-suiters" of the 1940s; the deportation of "wetbacks" in the 1950s; and the raids and border violence against "Mexican illegals" throughout the 1970s, 1980s, and 1990s. Specifically, neo-nativists fomenting anti-immigrant hysteria today suggest that immigrants' presence is responsible for increased unemployment, rising crime, and a stagnant economy. To counter what they allege is the immigrant drain on county and state resources, neo-nativists propose that immigrants be denied access to basic human services (Cornelius, 1993). This hostility is evident in Congress as well, where Representative Romano L. Mazzoli (D-Kentucky), co-author of the 1986 Reform and Control Act, has proposed a constitutional amendment that "would revoke the sacrosanct right to citizenship for anyone born on American soil whose parents are here 'illegally'" (Miller and Ostrow, 1993: A1). Attorney General Janet Reno has called immigration the problem of the decade, while Senator Alan K. Simpson (R-Wyoming), the other co-author of the 1986 immigration bill, advocates more stringent measures to determine the credibility of claims of political persecution and has called for an identification card for all those who seek work. Even moderates like California Senator Dianne Feinstein have advocated tougher measures against undocumented immigrants (Miller and Ostrow, 1993), including the strengthening of the Border Patrol with monies raised by levying a one-dollar toll on everyone entering the country (Skelton, 1993), and repatriation of foreign national prisoners (Bunting and Miller, 1993: A18). The recent arrival of boatloads of undocumented Chinese and Haitian immigrants, as well as the increased focus on Middle Eastern immigrants as a consequence of the bombing of the New York City World Trade Center, have further fueled anti-immigrant sentiment in this country.

The immigration issue is dividing the heterogeneous Latino community as well. Some native and resident Latinos blame undocumented workers for high unemployment rates and a lack of public services in their communities, while others perceive the racism behind this selective anti-immigrant sentiment (Navarrete, 1992: M6; Bunting and Miller, 1993: A18). Proposals supporting the immigration of skilled and professional immigrants, submitted by some of California Governor Pete Wilson's appointees (Skelton, 1993), promise to provoke even more con-troversy in Latino and non-Latino communities alike.

Media emphasis on the presence and social cost of undocumented workers in this country has also led to the perception that all Latinos, especially those of Mexican origin, are "illegal" immigrants. Those decrying the social costs of undocumented immigration fail, of course, to recognize the $29 billion paid by Latinos in taxes in 1990 (Bunting and Miller, 1993: A18) as well as the contributions of this labor force in the face of extreme exploitation and oppression. Undocumented workers in rural areas, forced to live in huts, makeshift encampments, canyons, and excavated holes in ravines, arroyos, and hills (McDonnell, 1987: 1), have become a totally dispossessed and dehumanized labor force. In North San Diego County alone, more than 10,000 men, women, and children annually cross the border to care for children and clean houses, to harvest and plant, to prepare the soil and trim the trees in the county. They are characterized by constant geographical mobility between Mexico and the United States and often live in primitive conditions, ironically, only a short distance away from large suburban centers and affluent neighborhoods. It is only when undocumented workers are visible that the suburbanites become incensed and begin demanding their "removal." As only the latest wave of immigrants along the border, these Latino newcomers will inevitably settle here and assimilate to the regional culture.

Unlike earlier periods of immigration from Mexico, when hundreds and sometimes thousands of men came to work in the fields, on the railroads, and on the ranches of the Southwest, recent immigrants to the United States from Latin America, especially from Central America and Mexico, have included a good number of women. This too is a worldwide phenomenon. The UNFPA reports that nearly half of all the world's migrants are women, often on their own, who end up in the lowest-paying jobs, trapped in immigrant communities. They are more vulnerable to abuse and are also more likely to send money home (*Washington Post*, 1993: A24). This phenomenon is linguistically as well as socially significant. In the past, the majority of immigrants have been male and the preponderance of petitions for legalization of status has come from men (Passel, 1992: 21). From now on, the immigrant is just as likely to be a woman as a man. Linguistically, the shift will be relevant for language maintenance, for it is women who determine a child's mother tongue. Immigrant men, even when they marry and/or father children, are not generally the principal caretakers of children and thus do not often determine the language spoken in the home. In the case of Latino women, especially young, undocumented women, there is a likelihood that they will work as nannies in the homes of Anglos or other Latinos. Given the growing percentage of Latino women who work (now 51.4 percent), there is a good probability that the caretaker at home with the young Latino children is a monolingual Spanish-speaking woman, probably of Mexican or Central American origin.

Economic imbalances produced by multinational corporations in the periphery are not, of course, the sole stimulus for emigration. Economists have long noted that for every "push" there is also a "pull," that is, an attraction of the immigrant labor force by industries of the highly developed nations, as has been the case in the United States since the nineteenth century. But in addition to these economic immigrants, who in fact account for the majority of the cases of migration and include middle-class professional immigrants, there are also a number of political refugees requesting asylum in this and other countries of the world. The flow of political immigrants to the United States is closely tied to the numerous covert and overt military interventions by this country during the nineteenth and twentieth centuries (Mexico, the Philippines, Korea, Vietnam, Iran, Cambodia, Laos, Chile, Grenada, and Panama, for example), and to military coups carried out by US allies in Latin America during this century (Nicaragua, Uruguay, Argentina, Chile, Guatemala, Honduras, El Salvador, to name a few). Other political and economic refugees

have come to the United States from Eastern Europe, Cuba, Haiti, other parts of Latin America, various parts of Asia and Africa. Recent proposals by Senator Simpson and others would reduce the number of cases for asylum by an on-the-spot "expedited" inspection of arriving immigrants. Critics of this proposal point out that the measure would result in expelling a number of legitimate applicants for asylum. The antipolitical refugee proposal is clearly one more US government attempt to limit the number of undocumented immigrants from all over the world entering the country (Miller and Ostrow, 1993: A23), estimated by the UN to have been 7.4 million in the 1980s alone (Meisler, 1993: A4).

As a consequence of this migration, the United States continues to be a land of immigrants, but now, and increasingly, of Third World origin. For example, there are about 7 million Asians and Pacific Islanders in this country. The heterogeneous population of Asians, Pacific Islanders, and American Indians is projected to triple by the year 2040 (Spencer, 1982: 1). African Americans, now 28 million, are expected to increase by 50 percent by the year 2030 (Spencer, 1982: 1). The number of Latinos, a group including Mexicans, Puerto Ricans, Cubans, Central and South Americans, as well as Spaniards, is more difficult to determine, given the large number of undocumented immigrants, but Census Bureau reports indicate that there were 22,354,059 in 1990 (Garcia and Montgomery, 1991: 2). If we add an estimated 3 million undocumented workers to this statistic, there are now over 25 million Latinos in the United States. This population too is expected to double by the year 2030 but will in all probability exceed the projected 50 million by then. Together, Latinos, African Americans, and Asians may well constitute over half the population of the United States long before the year 2080, as predicted. In the long run demography and geography alone will not determine the future; they will merely form the background for the interaction of social and economic factors. Nevertheless, these changing geopolitical variables may contribute to the intensification of particular political contradictions, tensions, and organized struggles and the eventual alteration of property relations in this country or in this region of the world.

## THE BORDER

The construct of the "border," a trendy term within literary and cultural studies, has been used to refer to any number of boundaries within disparate semantic fields. Some critics tend to exalt and fetishize the border or "the borderlands" while others deny the very existence of a border between the two countries. The border is not some twilight zone or ideal space; it is a social space of concrete social practices constructed to designate a political boundary. It is, for that reason, a historical construct, a product of social and political relations used to demarcate hegemonic power, although in reality the power of the hegemonic nation-state is not confined by political and geographical boundaries but forces its way as far south as Tierra del Fuego. Global economic and political changes, rather than demographic or cultural idealizations of community, are, however, beginning to provide the illusion of nation-state borders under multinational and transnational capitalism (Miyoshi, 1993: 744). With the replacement of a national bourgeoisie by transnational capitalists, nation-states become increasingly irrelevant and their continuance questionable. Their primary reason for being, to protect a national economy, is now defunct (Miyoshi, 1993: 743). How, then, is the phenomenon of increased nationalism in Eastern Europe to be explained? It could, as Hobsbawm indicates, simply be residual, that is, "unfinished business" (Hobsbawm, 1992: 165), or analyzable, along with other world ethnic and religious antagonisms, as "neoethnicism" (Miyoshi, 1993: 744). Clearly, then, despite the decline of national "borders," there are social and political, ethnic and class boundaries that have not yet fallen. Far from being in decline, ethnicism is undergoing a global

revival, as is neo-racism (Miyoshi, 1993: 744; Balibar, 1991: 21).

In view of the North American Free Trade Agreement, which will further intensify the transnationalization of the Mexican economy, the border dividing Mexico and the United States could be said to be blurring, if not declining. With increased control of Mexico by transnational corporations, the notion of Mexico as a nation-state will become ever more debatable, reaching a point where the "border" as a national and economic boundary may become a residual construct of the past (Miyoshi, 1993: 744). But, as Brenner pointed out in his study of feudalism, neither trade relations and economic conditions nor even demography can explain economic development (Brenner, 1990: 25). Because transnational capitalism is simply the latest phase of capitalist development, relations between corporations and the labor force in the periphery will not be significantly affected. Racial and ethnic boundaries will likewise not disappear as long as transnational corporations are in need of a cheap labor force in the Third World for their labor-intensive industries, despite the fact that, as under neo-colonialism, the local or regional ethnic elite will serve the needs of the corporation. Real changes will have to come, not at the level of nation-states, but at the level of relations of production. And it is here that ethnicism and collectivities identified by national origin and language loyalty could have a new role to play in the social dynamic. Already labor organizers working with those Mexicanos/Chicanos displaced in California by industries relocating to Mexico – like Yolanda Navarro of the Watsonville Teamster Local 912, for example – have begun contacting and attempting to organize Mexican workers in relocated Green Giant industries in Irapuato, Mexico (Cockburn, 1993).

Although moving toward a future "borderless" transnational world, today the sense of a national "bordered" community persists. When Mexicans refer to *el otro lado* (the other side), the line may be discursive and even invisible in some areas, a mere line in the desert, but the demarcation persists because the social boundary, ever more racial/ethnic and linguistic than national, is real and material. It can prove deadly and violent, as for those to whom access into the "American closure" is forbidden but who attempt to cross the "line," the fence, the desert, or the river without discursive authorization have found. To borrow from Lefebvre, the border is both a *field of action* (an area marked by particular political and social relations) and a *basis for action* (the produced space within which state power enables these relations) (Lefebvre, 1991: 191). The US-Mexican border is the edge of the periphery, marked by a string of multinational industries relocated on Mexican soil from Tijuana to Matamoros in order to make use of and exploit cheap Mexican labor and, on this side, by the extensive use of cheap undocumented Mexican labor principally in the agricultural and flower fields of San Diego County. The border is also the margin of the center, that is, of the superpower; it is a strategic area that enables state power to make commercial concessions that benefit capitalist interests. In the future only that state power that is useful for transnational corporations will survive as a supranational entity, as a global police force doing the bidding of transnational corporations.

The border, although produced and controlled by state power and contradictorily configured as both center and periphery, is also a fuzzy area, an ambiguous ideological field capable of generating counter action. In many ways the situation is paradoxical, for in organizing and regulating space in a particular way, the state simultaneously creates spaces of divergence with its own productive capacity and underscores ethnic/racial and linguistic boundaries, which are in most cases class boundaries as well. Although bounded cultural spaces are prone to fall within the control of the established order despite the illusion of being counter spaces (Lefebvre, 1991: 383), (for example, spaces of leisure [Lefebvre, 1991: 385] or spaces for those producing linguistically diverse media, literature, art, and music), these closures do momentarily give rise to marginal cultural

production that is not immediately subsumed or appropriated by hegemonic cultural apparatuses. For this reason, and however momentary, borders can be said to be as much spaces of domination as of counterculture, that is, counter spaces or heterotopias (Foucault, 1986; Lefebvre, 1991: 383). In California, the border, with its large mass of Mexican immigrants involved in farm labor, gave rise to Chicano agit-prop theater during the United Farm Workers' drives to organize farmworkers in the 1960s and 1970s (Kanellos, 1983: 38). Once mainstreamed, Luis Valdez's production took an entirely different direction.

This brings us back to the issue of borders as social spaces. As historical constructions and configurations, they are always reconfigurable, even erasable. This spatial historicity itself calls for a reconsideration of the notion of the border.

Geographically, the US border region can be viewed at its greatest as the border states or even as the former Mexican Southwest, including Colorado and Nevada. At its most limited, the border is a space with a radius of 10 to 20 miles around the nation-state boundary. Figuratively, however, the "border" could be said to be a social space contiguous to the national boundary and extending as far as the nearest urban or metropolitan site where the immigrant population from Mexico is concentrated. San Diego, California, is, for example, given the city's lack of industrial diversity, a mere point of transition for most Mexican immigrants headed for Los Angeles. In Texas the local border, especially the Valley, is an area of Mexican concentration where Chicanos/Mexicanos represent over 90 percent of the county and city population. But new immigrants generally move beyond this poverty-stricken area and head for Houston, San Antonio, Dallas, or Chicago, metropolitan areas where work is available. The border could thus be viewed as extending to the closest metropolitan site of immigrant concentration. It would follow then that the "border" extends at least 200 miles north from the Rio Grande, Tijuana (Baja California), Nogales

(Sonora), or Juárez (Chihuahua). This social space is, however, as previously indicated, quite diverse and demographically heterogeneous.

The border states are thus not simply bilingual and bicultural but multiethnic and multilingual. In fact the border of both nation-states is multinational and multicultural, for in addition to its various native and more recently arrived indigenous populations from Oaxaca, the Mexican border area (as a result of the displacement of farm workers and farmers by agribusiness linked to US interests, the construction of *maquiladoras* [the US assembly shops along the border], and rising unemployment and inflation) has in the last 30 years attracted mass migration from the interior, as evident in the demographic explosion of border towns and cities like Tijuana, now numbering about 2 million people, which far outnumbers San Diego. In addition to the domestic Mexican migration, there is also a history of German, Russian, and Chinese immigrants during the nineteenth and twentieth centuries, as well as the migration of Spanish political refugees during the 1930s, and scattered Anglo and Jewish immigrants, all residing among its largely Mexican mestizo population. Ethnic heterogeneity is, however, greater in the United States, as I previously noted. The diversity in the Southwest is especially evident in the Los Angeles Unified School District, where 80 languages other than English are spoken by 44 percent of the 641,000 students (Quintanilla, 1993: E2).

Of course, multilingual diversity within this area does not preclude the dominance on both sides of the border of particular classes, ethnic groups, and a particular language. Nevertheless, the dominance of English on the US side of the border is subject to sociospatial contingencies. Within particular US urban areas, Spanish, Korean, or Chinese, for example, may be the dominant language, especially in communities and areas of large immigrant concentration, like the Texas Valley, the Imperial Valley of California, and cities like San Antonio, Los Angeles, or San Francisco. Los Angeles County, for example, claims the largest Mexican, Armenian, Korean, Filipino, Salvadoran, and Guatemalan communities outside their respective home nations and the largest Japanese, Iranian, and Cambodian populations in the United States (Quintanilla, 1993: E2). For this reason, in given ethnic zones, oral and written communication can occur primarily in the minority language. In the greater Los Angeles area, for example, there are three Spanish-language television stations, several Spanish-language radio stations, several Spanish-language newspapers, many Spanish-language bookstores, video-rental stores, record/tape/compact disc shops, and movie theaters, as well as numerous other commercial establishments in which Spanish is the dominant or only language spoken. Other language communities have some of these same services. Quintanilla reports that there are broadcasts in 17 foreign languages on KCSI-TV, not including Spanish, and that 50 foreign-language newspapers are published in Los Angeles county as well (1993: E2).

What was once termed a situation of diglossia is clearly now a situation of heteroglossia, with a multiplicity of languages occupying the same space. On Alvarado Street in Los Angeles between Echo Park and MacArthur Park, and often within the same block, one can find commercial establishments catering to several ethnic populations and advertising their wares in Spanish, Korean, Chinese, and English. In the case of ethnic restaurants or small grocery stores, there may be a diversity of customers. The same cannot be said for other establishments (like *El Million Dollar* theater in downtown Los Angeles, for example), which cater to a particular ethnic clientele (in this case a distinctly Latino audience). Behind the surface of heteroglossia lies a multiplicity of cultural and lingual monotopias, often spatially contained within segregated social sites, but more often fragmented and scattered within larger spatial confines.

The cultural and linguistic diversity evident along this border zone has led to estimates of California as the first Third World state in the United States in the near future, with the

Latino population as the majority population in the state by the year 2040 (Miller and Ostrow, 1993: A22). Current statistics indicating over 17 million speakers of Spanish in the United States place almost a third of them in California. The state as a whole, with a population of 29.7 million, has 8.6 million non-English speakers who speak 230 non-English languages (Quintanilla, 1993: E2). Unfortunately, most of the Native American languages spoken in California before 1846 are now extinct; only 30 of some 100 native languages previously used in the area are still spoken and only by a handful of American Indians (Feldman, 1993: A3). More important, the state's multiethnic diversity attests to its status as a border state not only to Mexico but to the entire Pacific Rim, as evidenced in its large Asian immigrant population. In a way, the cycle of immigration from Asia to the Americas that began over 20,000 years ago continues today across the Pacific. In a sense, too, their descendants, the mestizos and Indians of Latin America, are reversing the direction and moving north again rather than south.

## LANGUAGE IN A MULTILINGUAL SPACE

What role can language play in this social space of multidiversity? Language itself can be viewed abstractly, as an ideal grammar, or sociolinguistically and sociospatially, as a network of discourses. Along the border there are several networks in operation, not all equally powerful, not all hegemonic, not all dominant within particular social spaces, not all equal in social and cultural exchanges. Because these networks are socially produced, they operate hierarchically at the zone of intersection of a multiplicity of political, economic, and cultural relations. Discourses are the product of particular social relations clustering within given social spaces. Each discourse can thus be described in terms of layered social relations. In a world of contradictions, disparities, violence, and conflict, particular sociospatial configurations are the

underpinnings for particular discourses and for the dominance or subordination of particular networks. It is these social, collectively produced discourses that interpellate individuals and serve to construct identities.

A common language has always played a role in what Hobsbawm calls proto-nationalist movements as it serves to identify speakers as members of a supralocal language community. For Hobsbawm, who sees nationalism as a product of the modern state, proto-nationalist movements arise prior to the formation of a state although states are also capable of mobilizing already existing ethnic, linguistic, or religious attachments (1992: 46). Language can serve to connect individuals who have no necessary relation with a particular state (p. 47), especially if it is a "print" language (Anderson, 1987) or the language of mass media. Societies with an elite or literary language can, through print, construct the notion of community and create an identity in relation to a collectivity or "imagined community." Today radio and television can have a similar impact. Identity is, thus, not a given, not an essence determined by biology or heredity, but a discursively constructed identification. This construction is generated by an ensemble of relations, all discursively articulated in varying overdetermined patterns within particular social spaces.

Print languages that generate a sense of community are often minority or elite languages, as was the case in Peru and Paraguay in the nineteenth century after independence, since the majority of the population spoke indigenous languages, not Spanish. Nevertheless Spanish became the official language of these countries and not until much later, the latter half of the twentieth century, did modernization and the need for a skilled labor force lead to the implementation of bilingual education and a recognition of the utility of these indigenous languages as teaching tools for *castellanización*, that is, Spanish language assimilation and literacy of indigenous populations throughout Latin America. Language loyalty or monolingualism is thus not a necessary ingredient for the formation of a nation-state. For example, the multiplicity of languages within Mexico did not impede the creation of a Mexican state, nor has the wide use of Quechua subsequently led to the creation of separate Peruvian states. The same could be said of Guatemala or Ecuador or any other multilingual state in the world. As Hobsbawm indicates, "languages multiply with states, not the other way around" (1992: 63).

Language loyalty may not in itself be the critical criteria determining collective identity but it is undoubtedly a strategic element allowing for popular cultural identification and may in fact further buttress national identity, although not necessarily. As previously indicated, the language policy of a particular nation-state does not necessarily reflect the linguistic makeup of the majority of the population; the "national" language may in fact be a minority language, even the language of the colonizer, as was often the case in African nations after independence. But in some cases language may serve as a rallying strategy and prove to be useful to a nationalist movement. In Ireland, for example, the fact that the construct of language loyalty was a strategic move and nothing more became evident when state policy and efforts supporting the use of the Irish language were unable to overturn a century-old switch to English, the language of the hegemonic power in the region. Language loss of Irish had been initiated long before and is even said to have been completed as early as 1851 (Macnamara, 1975: 65). Despite nineteenth-century language-revival movements, and the creation of the Gaelic League in 1893 to "de-Anglicize Ireland," nationalist writings were not expressed in Irish but in English (pp. 67–8). The language revivalist movement did, however, play a part in fomenting political awareness; in fact the leaders of the revolutionary movement to gain Irish independence were all members of the Gaelic League (p. 68). Language, however, was also seen as a divisive element, contributing to the civil war with Northern Ireland since the northern Presbyterians' ancestors had never spoken Irish (pp. 68–9). With the establishment of the Irish Free State in 1922, Irish and English were both declared official languages of Ireland and efforts were made to promote the Irish language in schools and colleges. Despite all these efforts, which were especially supported by the Irish middle class, by 1971 only 3 percent of the population spoke Irish (pp. 65; 87), although 76 percent of the population, as indicated in a national survey in 1964, did favor the teaching of Irish as a second language (p. 83). The case of Ireland is especially interesting because identity was not linked exclusively to language but rather to a series of elements including language, territory, religion, literature, a history of struggle against England, and later to the creation of a nation-state. The loss or undermining of one element, language, did not weaken this sense of an "imagined community." Interest in promoting a "national" language may be set aside after independence by leaders of nationalist movements driven by goals of modernization of the newly formed state through use of the formerly imposed colonial language; the choice is always strategic and political. In fact, fragmentation within linguistic groups is common and has never determined national allegiances, with speakers of a common language often preferring to secede from or to form part of, say, Uruguay rather than of Argentina.

The Irish example is relevant for the variety of elements that come into play, including territory, religion, language, history, and economics. Economic dependence has determined language choice, despite nationalism. The choice, however, as previously indicated, was not recent and affected 3.5 million people, not including the Irish abroad and in Northern Ireland. In the case of the Latino population in the United States, the scope of the issue expands markedly, for Spanish is the home language of over 17 million and, more important, it is itself a world language spoken by over 265 million people (*Britannica Book of the Year*, 1993: 778–82).

As in the case of Ireland, there are historical claims to this once Mexican territory and linguistic, religious, and cultural ties. It is equally important to consider the multiethnic configuration of the border today and the fact that the transnational migration of Latinos to this same area is similar to the diaspora of many national minorities throughout the world (Gilroy, 1987: 155). Diaspora brought on by conquest, migration, and colonization has scattered common language speakers throughout the world and allowed for new concentrations in distant lands as linguistic and ethnic minorities and, consequently, for the formation of organized collectivities, especially in cases in which linguistic and ethnic/racial barriers exclude the newcomers from integrating fully as members of the host country. The diaspora of Mexicans, Central Americans, South Americans, Cubans, Puerto Ricans, and Spaniards has likewise led to their relocation within the United States and allowed for the construction of a new Latino ethnicity; but one perhaps should speak of a proto-ethnicism, with language at its core, because the collectivity, while sharing a common linguistic base, is still highly fragmented by national origin, generation, and class.

The Latino community in the United States is, as previously indicated and as the Census Bureau makes clear, multinational, multiethnic, and multiracial and includes mestizos, indigenous people (Native Americans), Blacks, mulattos, *criollos* (Whites), and Asians. But Latinos are not a synthesis of races; they are no mystical *raza cósmica*, nor can they be essentially defined in any way. Latinos are a heterogeneous population, politically fragmented, but united by a history of conquest and colonialism, a history of proletarianization and disempowerment in this country and, to a large extent, by a common language, Spanish. Ethnic identity for the Latino population is thus a matter of national origin and language, rather than a matter of race or *mestizaje*. As Hobsbawm observes, "the crucial base of an ethnic group as a form of social organization is cultural rather than biological" (1992: 63). This multiethnic, multiracial diversity has not, however, eliminated the racism internal to the Latino group, with light-skinned Latinos, for example, often disdainful of or condescending toward dark-skinned Latinos, nor has it led to eliminating class

distinctions. It has, however, served to enable the construction of an identity that transcends these differences, if only at a discursive level.

Identifying as a Latino today means consciousness of a greater Spanish-speaking collectivity that transcends national boundaries. This awareness comes with time, separation from other countrymen, and with increased contact with other Latinos; often it takes a generation to become aware of the larger community and to identify with other Latinos. The first generation generally identifies on the basis of national or regional origin and, in the case of Mexicans, often on the basis of attachment to a particular Mexican state, city, or town. Until two decades ago it was easy for the majority Latino population of Mexican origin to identify strictly on the basis of national origin (as Chicanos, Mexican Americans, or Mexicanos) rather than on the basis of the larger ethnic collectivity (as Latinos), given their superiority in numbers and concentration as the sole Latino minority in some areas of the Southwest. That situation, however, has undergone a marked shift, as previously indicated. In areas where a diversity of Latin Americans reside, the term "Latino" is and has been the preferred identity of all, as is evident in the California Bay Area or in Chicago or has been a supplementary identity, after that of national origin, deployed strategically when a supranational notion of collectivity is sought.

When and if the Spanish language should no longer be the language of over half of the Latino population, the construct of identity would not necessarily change. In the particular case of Chicanos, the loss of the Spanish language has not obliterated identity on the basis of national origin, at least for first- and second-generation persons of Mexican origin, who continue to identify themselves ethnically as Chicanos, Mexicanos, or Mexican Americans even after becoming English dominant or English monolinguals. An overall language shift, however, appears highly unlikely. Given the large percentage of first-generation Latinos in this country, Spanish will not fade from the linguistic map any time soon. For this reason, Spanish will continue to figure as one of the ensemble of factors and relations that determine identity within the Latino population in the Southwest.

However Latinos may choose to identify themselves, the dominant society, through the Census Bureau and the media, has already chosen to call this group "Hispanics," a Eurocentric term rejected by many Latinos. And fragmented though Latinos may be by national origin, class, and generation, the media has succeeded in representing them as one collectivity by using the terms "Hispanic" or "Latino." This constructed public consensus has in turn led many Latinos to become aware of the collectivity and accept these labels without hesitation, in so doing affirming the notion of an "imagined" community (Anderson, 1987). The sheer numbers of Latinos are also having an impact, gaining for this population an increased visibility. This demographic growth has not gone unnoticed by marketing experts who are fully aware of the aggregate Latino household income, which has increased significantly since 1982 and totals, according to 1990 Census Bureau reports, $173 billion. Although this income represents only about 5 percent of the US total income figure of $3.5 trillion, it is still a sizable market share (García and Montgomery, 1991: 5) not often taken into account when immigrants are accused of consuming a considerable amount in educational, medical, and correctional services (Bunting and Miller, 1993: A18). It is as consumers of commodities and services that the collectivity has been linguistically and culturally addressed by advertisers. In so doing, however, these companies have – perhaps unwittingly – strengthened an identification with ethnicity through mass media, although one must at the same time realize that being "ethnic" has been depoliticized to a large extent in this country.

If, as Hobsbawm indicates (1992: 191), ethnicism rather than nationalism will flourish in the future within a supranational framework, then one can conjecture that the Southwest may well become the staging area from which transnational corporations will produce and issue supranational policies affecting the Pacific Rim. The multilingual diversity of the population may give rise to a society on the model of Hong Kong, with multiethnic technocrats and managers. The greater part of the multiethnic population, however, will not form part of this elite. The role to be played by ethnicism in this type of stratified society is unclear, but it could be politicized and serve to organize individuals along international ethnic/race and class lines. This type of multiethnic struggle will call for a common language and it is probable that, in addition to Japanese and English, Spanish will play a major role not only in conducting the affairs of the transnational corporations but in countering the transnationals themselves at an international level as well.

As in the case of Ireland, more immediate economic and political factors will undoubtedly write the story of language choice for the Latino minority, at least for now. But what will happen during the twenty-first century when Latinos will be the majority population in particular regions and states and over half of the Latino population will be first or second generation and still, in great measure, Spanish dominant? Undoubtedly third- and fourth-generation Latinos will by then be English dominant or, most probably, English monolinguals, especially in the case of middle-class families, but not necessarily in the large urban barrios and ghettoes that are expected to burgeon. Over 90 percent of the Latino population now resides in metropolitan areas (Word, 1989: 66), although there are already plans to relocate and disperse this population. In the future, according to Henry G. Cisneros, a former Secretary of Housing and Urban Development, the push will be to move minorities from the inner cities to the suburbs through the construction of public housing outside the metropolitan area (DeParle, 1993: A8). The sociospatial configuration of about 60 million Latinos in the United States by the year 2060 and their economic and political power will determine the survival of Spanish and even its status as the first or second language of this region.

Language loyalty, like culture in general or even ethnicity, may ultimately be irrelevant in political movements, but for now it is an obvious element that can be tapped for identity and even be crucial in setting the stage for social organization of any type; in fact, language, culture, and ethnicity/race are strategic for struggle because they are often the tools used by hegemonic forces to oppress, exploit, and divide populations. As Chatterjee points out (1985: 15), ethnicity is often the basis for exclusion even in cultural production; it can, for example, play a role in hegemonic patterns of funding scientific research, the assignment of research priorities, and the selection of problems for investigation. The relation between ethnicity/national origin and language became an issue during the civil rights movement. In court cases concerning the rights of language minority students, one significant outcome was the 1974 Supreme Court *Lau vs. Nichols* decision (Keller and Van Hooft, 1981; Avila and Godoy, 1979) concluding that discrimination on the basis of language was in fact discrimination on the basis of national origin. More recent cases of workers charging racial and linguistic discrimination in the workplace have based their charges on findings that English-only policies in the workplace are forbidden by federal law. As Reginal Welch, communication director for the Equal Employment Opportunity Commission in Washington, DC, explains: "An individual's first language is part of his national heritage and forbidding him to speak that language is discrimination based on national origin" (O'Donnell, 1993).

In fact, language oppression is nothing more than racism, for, as Balibar indicates, the new racism is a *differentialist racism* based on cultural differences, that is, on language, descent, and tradition as well as on race (Balibar, 1991: 21, 61). This neo-racism often disguises itself and focuses not on race or ethnicity but on maintaining social boundaries and differences by pointing out "the harmfulness of abolishing frontiers, the incompatibility of life-styles and traditions" (p. 21). These are segregationist tactics manipulated by dominant races or groups to establish closures and exclude particular

ethnic/racial populations. But what is equally clear is that the group suffering racist policies often retaliates by deploying difference itself as a basis for political struggle. As political scientists and theorists like E. San Juan (1989), Cornel West (1988), and Mario Barrera (1979) have noted, in this country race and class must be necessarily considered jointly in any analysis of working-class minority populations, particularly in view of the institutional racialization (Balibar, 1991: 210) of particular occupational sectors, including service industries, manual labor, and farm work, within which the majority of ethnic minority workers can be found. Latino men, for example, are more likely to be employed in operator, fabricator, and laborer occupations (29 percent) and in service occupations (54 percent) than non-Latino men (del Pinal and DeNavas, 1989: 4). Latino women are more likely to be employed in service industries (26 percent), in technical, sales, and administrative support (40 percent), and in positions as operators, fabricators, and laborers (14 percent) than non-Latino women (García and Montgomery, 1991: 3). These are all low-paying jobs that offer little stability and carry implications at the level of housing segregation and educational attainment. Ironically, this racialization of low-wage occupations has also contributed to the maintenance of Spanish within these particular employment domains, just as low income and high poverty levels maintain Latinos within barrios, for often it is only in these inner city communities that low-income housing is available. Difference, especially the linguistic difference, is maintained through the construction of barriers and the creation of closures that guarantee exclusion; yet it is in turn that very difference that can serve as a basis for identification and political struggle.

A more blatant expression of intolerance for ethnic/racial and linguistic differences is evident in the English-only movement pushed by the US English organization. The leaders of this organization, which has long pushed to make English the national language of this country, and to eliminate bilingual education, bilingual ballots, and other multilingual services for non-English-speaking residents have also been prominent in FAIR (Federation for American Immigration Reform), a racist anti-immigration organization (Trombley, 1986). The group's success in making English the official state language in several states in the union provides a good indication of the country's intolerance for minority culture (Trombley, 1986), despite the efforts of academics to promote multiculturalism.

In the face of linguistic oppression and intolerance for minority languages, speakers of these languages often respond in one of two ways: (a) they submit to the proposal that English should be the only public language and accept the proposition that bilingualism creates divisiveness while assimilation and English monolingualism increase the possibility of socioeconomic success, or (b) they observe the unemployment, homelessness, and destitution of poor Whites and English-speaking minorities, reject any Anglocentric attempt to impose an official language and a Eurocentric notion of culture, and resist language loss, even while promoting the acquisition of English by supporting the use of minority languages and strengthening the development of minority student cognitive skills in their native language. The long-term maintenance of a minority language is contingent upon a number of social, economic, and political factors, but human agency – that is, collective agency and the pressure brought to bear by it on social policy – undoubtedly plays a part as well, as has previously been suggested.

## LANGUAGE MAINTENANCE AND SHIFT

The Latino community, as noted, includes both rural and urban members, temporary and permanent residents, documented and undocumented immigrants, employed and unemployed individuals, professionals as well as manual laborers and operatives, metropolitan and suburban dwellers, the young and the old, and is not only multinational but multi-

generational with a continual presence of first-generation immigrants. All of these differences contribute both to the strengthening of language loyalty and the use of the minority language as well as to the fragmentation of the Latino population. Whatever strengthens linguistic contact, that is, interaction of Latinos with other Spanish speakers, works toward language maintenance. Ethnicity, poverty, low income, and gender are all factors that segregate collectivities and as a result reinforce linguistic differences, that is, maintenance of the native immigrant language. By the same token, whatever fragments the Latino community and diminishes interaction among Latinos works against language maintenance and in turn facilitates language shift. Class differences, for example, play a role in fragmenting the Latino community. Professionals, for the most part, have little to do with nonprofessionals, whether fellow countrymen or other Latinos, unless it is to hire them as maids, gardeners, nannies, and other manual workers. Professionals often live in predominantly Anglo areas and have little or no contact with other Latinos. National and regional origin also divides the population, with social interaction often being limited to activities with fellow countrymen.

Generation, however, is a double-edged variable. It is a significant factor in determining ethnic and linguistic contact, for incoming immigrants tend to form insular communities by settling close to family, countrymen, and friends in particular barrios. A study by Aída Hurtado and others offers interesting insights into the generational makeup of the Latino population in California. Hurtado estimates that 65 percent of Latinos in California in 1989 were first-generation residents, 23.0 percent were second generation and 12.0 percent were third generation (cited in *UC Latino Student Eligibility*, 1993). A large number of first-generation immigrants clustering in metropolitan communities on the basis of national or regional origin guarantees a strong Spanish-dominant Latino presence. Nationwide, first-generation immigrants are said to represent half of the growth in the Latino population from 1980 (16 million) to 1990 (22.3 million) (del Pinal and DeNavas, 1989: 1). If the generational distribution of one decade is reproduced during the next 50 years as expected and given the rapid pace of growth of the Latino population ("about 5 times as fast as the rate experienced by the non-Hispanic population" [del Pinal and DeNavas, 1989: 1]), there will continue to be a substantial Spanish-speaking population in the Southwest and in the country, as marketing experts have already recognized.

Generational differences, however, can also serve to fragment the Latino population, for long-time residents or Latinos born in this country who are English dominant or monolingual often have little or no interaction with newcomers, except in smaller cities and rural areas of the Southwest, where, given smaller segregated enclaves, there is often much interaction between Chicano/Mexicano townspeople and newly arrived immigrants, documented and undocumented. A generational difference is evident in the schools where the student population not only divides racially (Whites, Blacks, and Latinos) but also generationally, with Chicanos (second-, third-, or fourth-generation Latinos) and Mexicanos (first generation) often at odds. Along the US-Mexican border, upper-class Mexicans who cross the border to attend local high schools clash with working-class Chicanos. But the opposite is also evident, with Chicanos disdaining the non-English-speaking, recently arrived, working-class Mexicans. In the latter case, these tensions are not long-lasting because of what I will call *achicanamiento*, that is, acculturation to the local Chicano culture. Newly immigrated children from Mexico or other parts of Latin America who live in the barrios and attend local community schools rapidly adopt the dress, hair style, and ways of the local children and teenagers. They join gangs and other groups. Divisions occur subsequently on the basis of turf and gang allegiances rather than strictly on the basis of generation or national origin. Linguistically, of course, they begin to code-switch, mixing Spanish and English in their speech. The process of code-switching is

an international phenomenon and can lead to adopting the style as a mark of "difference" or to the eventual loss of the minority language. By the time first- or second-generation, working-class, Latino students enroll in colleges and universities, they are all in a similar linguistic and social situation, as Latino student protests at the University of California at Davis demonstrated in 1989–90. They are now "Chicanos," because their lived experience in the United States is that of working-class Chicanos, whether originally from Mexico, El Salvador, Guatemala, Argentina, Colombia, Puerto Rico, or Cuba. Like their Chicano counterparts, they have had little or no formal training in Spanish. English is their dominant school language, but Spanish is – whatever the variety – their home language.

Among Latinos, generational differences became markedly clear after the 1992 Los Angeles uprisings in response to the first court decision in the Rodney King beating case. Chicanos like Rubén Navarrete, author of *A Darker Shade of Crimson*, aware that at least half of the arrested looters were Latinos, tried to distance themselves as third-generation "Mexican Americans" from newly arrived immigrants, declaring that "the ethnic link between the two groups [i.e., Central Americans and Chicanos] is thin – no more pronounced than the one joining dark-skinned African-Americans with dark-skinned Haitians denied entry into the United States" (Navarrete, 1992: M6). Black leaders like Jesse Jackson and other human-rights activists who have protested President Clinton's policy of forcible return of Haitians refugees, unlike Navarrete, recognize the many faces of racism and ally to counter it. In a post-uprising column published in the *Los Angeles Times*, Navarrete indicates that he feels economically and "culturally" threatened by Latinos and suggests with FAIR that "Mexican Americans" are opposed to "excessive immigration" (Navarrete, 1992: M6). In this particular case, generation, class, and political orientation all intersect to produce a Latino voice that reproduces the hysteria of the political right, as so often has been the case with other Latino columnists, like Richard Rodríguez, published by mainstream media. Fortunately, for every Navarrete there are many second- and third-generation Chicanos/Latinos who argue against nativist racist proposals to curb immigration selectively and who identify with working-class Latinos from Mexico, Central America, and South America.

Linguistic acculturation of second- and third-generation immigrants is common, as is language shift among first-generation children, but this shift is definitely not a given nor ever a fully completed process. Language shift depends upon several social factors that contribute to or impede inter-lingual contact and access to means for the acquisition of the English language. The shortage of funds for adult education programs offering English-as-a-second-language courses, for example, limits accessibility to the dominant language, especially for young and older adults; moreover, residence in a Latino barrio, as previously indicated, can reinforce language maintenance, especially in the case of adults. In a recent study by Alejandro Portes of 5,000 students who are the children of Cuban, Haitian, Filipino, Mexican, and Vietnamese immigrants, a high percentage of all students surveyed indicated that their knowledge of English was good or very good, but only the Latino children had a high percentage who had a good command of their parents' native language. Just over half of the children of Vietnamese immigrants said they preferred English to their parents' language, while fewer than half (44 percent) of the children of Mexican immigrants said the same. This maintenance of the parents' language correlated well with their perception of discrimination, that is, their sense of being different and ill-treated because of that difference. Mexican and Haitian children were also less willing to kowtow to the interviewers by praising this land as the best in the world, revealing thereby a sense of identity not entirely determined by hegemonic discourses. Portes concludes that these immigrant children are "well on their way to being fluent English speakers, even, one could argue, on

the way to monolingualism" and that "it is the parents' language, not English, that is endangered" (Sontag, 1993: A6). The study also allows for a different reading of the data, for language shift is contingent upon a number of factors and identification with another nationality, ethnicity, race, or class in the face of discrimination and rejection can play a role in language solidarity and trigger an individual's desire to maintain his/her immigrant parents' language.

Language maintenance and shift have also been affected by the institution of bilingual education programs in schools with large concentrations of limited-English speakers. These programs, established in the 1970s primarily to facilitate the transition from the minority language to English, have long been the target of the political right, despite the increased educational attainment of students enrolled in such programs, as attested in the case of the Calexico School District in California. In a 1993 report issued by the Little Hoover Commission, the California Department of Education is criticized for teaching immigrant children their native language rather than teaching them to speak English (Chávez, 1993: A19). This type of misrepresentation and attack has been widespread for three decades and demonstrates a failure to recognize the linguistic and cognitive needs of immigrant children, who, as revealed in recent studies by the US Department of Education, continue to need bilingual instruction. According to its report, there were 5.4 million Latino children aged 5 to 17 in US schools in 1992. An additional 2.4 million Latino children are expected to attend US schools within the next five years (Tomás Rivera Center, 1993: 1). Although these Latino children constitute 32 percent of the students in this country, only 10 percent of the teachers are Latino. In the area of educational attainment, Latinos have the lowest ratios of completed education in comparison to Whites, Blacks, and other races. The Census Bureau indicates that only 50 percent of Latino adults have completed high school, 22 percent have completed one or more years of college, and 10 percent have completed four or more years of college (Kominski and Adams, 1991: 4).

This shortage of Latino teachers correlates highly with the dwindling numbers of Latino students in colleges and universities. A recent report issued by the University of California Latino Eligibility Task Force reveals that only 4 percent of Latino high school graduates in California are fully eligible for admission to the university. In a state where the number of Latino students was 1,200,000 in 1985 – expected to reach 2,300,000 in 1995 and 3,100,000 by 2005 (UC Latino Student Eligibility, 1993: 8) – enrollment of Latino students at the University of California has in fact been declining – from 2,991 in 1989 to 2,218 in 1992 (p. 24). A number of factors have contributed to the decline, including the rising cost of a college education, the low-income status of Latino students, and the weak academic preparation provided by barrio and ghetto schools.

What has been increasing, however, is the violence in the barrios and the incarceration of Latino youth. Statistics indicate that "today's entering Latino kindergartner is as likely to go to jail as meet the admission standards of the state universities" (Acuña, 1990: B7). In his review of Duane Campbell's book *Choosing Democracy*, Acuña indicates that by the year 2000 inmates in California prisons may exceed 300,000 and of those it is likely that 50 percent will be Latino (Acuña, 1990: B7). Unemployment, poverty, and lack of recreational outlets have also contributed to teenagers' gang affiliation and to drug abuse and dealing, often the easiest way to make money. The problem of violence in Latino communities is now at a critical level. As the Latino population increases it will need to regain control of its own urban space and improve its educational attainment level if it is not to self-destruct or end up being the poor, laboring, and lumpen *majority* ruled by a White minority, as in South Africa. Here too Spanish could play a role if the large, first-generation, Spanish-speaking population is to be organized and academically prepared for employment, school/college, and political struggle.

Language loyalty and the actual use of Spanish may vary from Latino family to family as correlated to generation, age, residence, occupation, and education, although linguistic trends are in fact set at the community level. The fact that studies focusing on Spanish language use have generally depended on interview-surveys that provide attitudinal information or self-assessment of language use and maintenance (see Sontag, 1993) has not allowed for indications on the actual proficiency of the surveyed population in one or both languages nor of actual language use in a variety of domains. An insider's view of Spanish language use would, however, reveal that these functions vary not only in terms of social space and sociospatial practices, but also in terms of power relations. It is an ensemble of social relations and situational factors like audience, speech acts, social functions, and domain, as well as generation, age, class, national origin, and even mood, which determine language choice and language variety or register. Thus, given various possible combinations of these factors, within any given social site, we may find intimate/familial, informal and formal varieties of language intersecting. In other words, no social site is limited to one variety, nor do divisions of social space in terms of private and public really hold, since the private and public always overlap. Likewise formal and informal, intimate and familiar spaces also intersect, giving rise to continuous shifting between varieties and sometimes between languages.

No set pattern of language use can be established to describe the current diversity of Latino families. All that can be said, following Glyn Lewis, is that there is a great deal of dynamic bilingualism in the border states and beyond. This dynamic or changing bilingualism is triggered by social and/or geographical mobility and signals a beginning shift in language function from one language to another (Lewis, 1972; Sánchez, 1983). Once the overlapping is widespread, with both languages competing for particular functions within particular social sites (a case of transitional bilingualism), then inevitably one of the languages will come to dominate and displace the other. A more stable bilingualism would guarantee that particular functions within particular social sites and practices were the domain of one of the languages while others were the domain of the other. This balanced bilingualism is, of course, a theoretical construct rather than a reality within a rapidly changing world. For many Chicanos, especially second- and third-generation persons who move beyond the barrio, English is now their sole language, despite some passive competence in their parents' language. But for those Chicanos who stay in the barrios or in the rural areas, generation is not the determining factor at all. The situation is complex, particularly in light of the continued presence of first-generation Spanish-speakers. Predictions of language shift for second- and third-generation speakers have often been based on an assessment of a minority language within an English-dominant society. What will happen when the minority community becomes the majority in the state of California and in particular regions of the Southwest is another matter; given two supranational languages (English and Spanish), the choice will be political, economic, and cultural.

## LANGUAGE AND CULTURE

Language and culture are not, of course, synonymous. In fact, language is sometimes said to be the carrier of culture although clearly more than one culture can share the same language, as is evident in comparing a former colonial power, for example, Spain, and a former colony, such as any one of the Latin American countries. Culture is not nation-specific, as there is generally a variety of cultures within any one country, but for purposes of example, one can point to marked differences between cultural practices in, say, Ecuador and Spain. Aspects of one culture may be shared by more than one language as well, as is evident in the internationalization of particular aspects of American jet-setter culture shared by the bourgeoisie of the Western world, whether English, French, German, Dutch, Spanish, Swedish, Danish, or Portuguese. The same is true for Latin America, as indicated, for example, by Carlos Monsiváis (1984), who has written on the North-Americanization of bourgeois culture in Mexico City.

Culture is both material and discursive. It is the sum of cultural production and cultural (i.e., economic, social, political) practices of a community, including a collectivity's way of life on the basis of structural positioning and its patterns of housing, clothing, eating, working, and leisure; but culture is also a construct, a discursive construction of the history, social practices, traditions, and identity of a collectivity. This cognitive mapping is especially evident in cultural production, be it in literature, music, film, or other signifying practices through which a collectivity makes sense of its social space (Jameson, 1991). The fact that culture is an ideological construction allows as well for inventions or retrieval of residual culture, often made necessary by particular histories of language suppression, cultural oppression, or proto-nationalism. Smith, for example, in discussing "invented traditions," notes that the Scots invented the tradition of tartan and kilt in the mid-eighteenth century (Smith, 1991: 177). Seamus Deane notes that when late nineteenth-century England, seeking to revive its national identity, determined to supplement the national character with the Celtic element, it gave the Irish the opportunity to modify the Celt into Gael and to use this identity as the basis for constructing their radical difference and a movement for liberation. Thus their very Celtic nationalism was in part produced by the colonial power that suppressed it (Deane, 1990: 11–13). Culture and descent thus appear to be highlighted in areas on the verge of losing their language in order to heighten ethnic or national identity. These two examples are interesting for their similarities with Southwest experiences. In this country, attempts to bolster national identity through a multiethnic supplementarity have recently called for a recognition of multinational and multiethnic roots evident in a series of televised films on early Jewish, Italian, and Chinese immigrants; African slavery and forced migration; the Mafia; the westward movement of White and Black settlers; and Japanese displacement to relocation camps during World War II. To a degree, this media recognition is meant to disarm ethnicism through appropriation and selective rendering of ethnic experiences. The Latino experience, on the other hand, has not been as visible on television but has been in Southwest schools, where the inclusion of units on a historical Spanish and Mexican past have served to affirm Chicano/Latino ties to the territory and to mark historical changes. Students whose parents were deprived of knowledge of their past are today being made aware, at least minimally, of their ethnic roots and the imperialist policies that led to US expansionism and the appropriation of half of the Mexican state in 1846–7.

The relation between language and culture is thus intimate but one does not imply the other. Nationalism or ethnicism may in fact call for stressing one or the other, or both. In the Southwest there is no "Spanish" culture, only a diversity of Latino cultures, but language has been linked to culture at every level, especially within cultural production. Despite what writers like Richard Rodríguez have said in ignorance (perhaps because he himself never developed a network of Spanish discourses in both private and public spheres [Rodríguez 1981]), Spanish has been, since the sixteenth century, both a private and a public language in the Southwest. Before 1846 (1836 in Texas) Spanish was of course the official and dominant language of the Spanish and later Mexican Southwest. After the US invasion, Spanish continued to be the language of the conquered population and the language of most of their oral and written cultural production, especially in the areas of music, poetry, narrative, and theater. The testimonials of the Californios interviewed by Hubert H. Bancroft for his historiographical project, for example, are all in Spanish. The early literature, poetry and romantic novels produced in New Mexico after 1846, is also in Spanish (Leal, 1985). Kanellos (1983) and

Miguélez (1983) have traced the history of Spanish and Mexican theater in the Southwest from the sixteenth century to the twentieth century and have documented the various Mexican troupes and special theaters constructed for various Spanish-language traveling theater companies.

In the nineteenth century, as in the twentieth, Spanish as a "print" language (Anderson, 1987) was most in evidence in the regional Spanish-language newspapers, like *El Bejareño* (San Antonio), *La Gaceta, La Crónica, Alta California,* and *El Nuevo Mundo* (San Francisco), *El Cronista del Valle* (Brownsville), *El Hispano Americano* (Las Vegas, New Mexico), *La Gaceta* (Santa Barbara, California), or *El Correo de Laredo* (Laredo) all of which attest to the formal and public function of the Spanish language in the Southwest even after invasion (Tatum, 1981: 58; Rodríguez, 1983: 208). By the twentieth century each major city of the Southwest had at least one Spanish-language newspaper. Chief among them are *La Prensa* (San Antonio), *La Opinión* (Los Angeles), *El Tucsonense* (Tucson), and *La Crónica* and *El Demócrata Fronterizo* (Laredo). In areas where there was no Spanish-language publication, Spanish-language columns would often be included on a regular basis in English-language newspapers. Border cities also had access to Mexican newspapers. Tatum estimates that between 1848 and 1958 about 400 Spanish-language newspapers appeared (Tatum, 1981: 58). The circulation of Spanish-language newspapers has increased notably so that in 1987 Los Angeles had three daily newspapers: *La Opinión,* with a circulation of about 72,000; *Noticias del Mundo,* with between 35,000 and 50,000 readers; and *El Diario,* with a circulation of 40,000 (Rosenstiel, 1987). The three newspapers combined offered advertisers over 150,000 readers each day.

Spanish has had a long-standing place as the language of radio. The decade of the 1930s would bring the creation of two powerful Mexican radio stations, XEQ and XEW, which could be heard as far away as California and Texas, allowing the population of

Mexican origin in the United States at least an evening (when reception of the airwaves was more likely) of Spanish-language music, newscasts, comedy hours, mysteries, romantic radio plays, and variety shows (Ybarra-Frausto, 1983). During this same period, the production of the Mexican film industry featuring Mexico's most famous screen stars (Pedro Infante, Jorge Negrete, Gloria Marín, Pedro Armendáriz, María Félix, Emilio Tuero, Dolores del Rio, Carlos López Moctezuma, and many others) reached Latino movie houses in the Southwest, where a faithful clientele lined up every weekend to see Spanish-language films. Now, of course, these and hundreds of other films produced since that golden era are available at local video stores specializing in Spanish-language music (cassettes and compact discs) and Latin American and Spanish videos, along with a wide range of more current video fare.

The advent of television and the availability of video-cassette recorders led to the closing of many of these Spanish-language movie houses, except in the larger cities where theaters like El Million Dollar in Los Angeles serve as much for film showings as for live musical variety shows. It is, however, Spanish-language television, available locally and via cable, that has served to create an "imagined" national Latino community, in a way that Spanish-language theater, newspapers, magazines, or radio never did, for these stations have created a nationwide network of viewers heretofore unimaginable. It is now possible to transmit the same message in Spanish to millions of viewers in New York, Seattle, Chicago, Miami, El Paso, San Benito, San Francisco, and San Diego, as well as Guadalajara, Caracas, and Madrid. Only Spanish-language radio, with its steady stream of popular Latin American hits, rivals the outreach capacity of television, but only in a limited sense, for radio stations do not generally transmit beyond a few hundred miles. Only radio stations based along the Mexican border, although transmitting out of the United States, have the capacity of reaching the entire Southwest, Northwest, and western part of Mexico. Night radio programs often serve for the transmission of messages from Mexican nationals in the United States to family members in various parts of the Mexican republic; other times family members in Mexico resort to the use of these airwaves to search for and contact their relatives in the United States, especially during times of family crisis.

Local radio stations serve as an important network uniting immediate communities and barrios. These Spanish-language stations did not exist in the 1920s and 1930s, for then only limited blocs of time sold to brokers were made available for Spanish programming. In 1979, Gutiérrez and Schement estimated a total of 41 Spanish-language radio stations in the Southwest. Already in 1973 there were over 250 radio stations airing some Spanish-language programming in the United States, but by 1978 there were over 600, with 100 of these broadcasting almost entirely in Spanish (Gutiérrez and Schement, 1979: 5). The number of Spanish-language radio stations has undoubtedly increased significantly since then, as has the number of listeners. In Los Angeles, with seven Spanish stations in 1991 (Puig, 1991: 9), it is, as previously indicated, a Spanish-language station, KLAX-FM, that has the largest audience of any radio station in the city (Quintanilla, 1993: E2). Local Spanish-language stations in the United States serve an important function beyond advertising goods and services; they too create a sense of community and belonging in the process of transmitting not only news broadcasts, popular music, and radio soaps, but also public service announcements and calls for assistance to earthquake or hurricane victims in Latin America (Puig, 1991: 89). Because these Spanish-language stations cater primarily to the largest Latino group, the Chicanos/Mexicanos (Puig, 1991: 9), they not only provide an "imagined" interlocutor to Latinos suffering from isolation, but they acculturate Latinos to the regional Mexican culture. Latinos residing in border towns have had Mexican radio stations available for a longer period of time.

These Spanish-language radio stations appeal primarily to new immigrants and older

Latino adults since Latino teenagers and young adults are more likely to listen to English-language stations. In fact, popular dance music and golden oldie stations in Los Angeles have a large Latino audience (Puig, 1991: 89). For this reason, in an effort to attract Latino listeners in the 18–34-year-old Latino age group, some stations, like KLVE-FM in Los Angeles, offer selections by more contemporary artists: rock in Spanish and the music of well-known US stars who record in both Spanish and English (Puig, 1991: 89). Far from fearing total acculturation of the young and language loss, managers of these Spanish-language stations indicate that as teenagers mature and become aware of their ethnicity, they return to the radio stations favored by their parents (Puig, 1991: 89). These monolingual Spanish stations also predict a growing bilingual media, with bilingual DJs who code-switch, common on Texas radio stations, for example, and even Spanish-language talk-radio, which already exists in Miami (Puig, 1990:90).

The power of Spanish-language media has, of course, been recognized by marketing experts, and there is ample proof of massive Spanish-language advertising of products previously advertised only in English. This advertising is not limited to television, radio, and newspaper ads, for there are now billboards and busboards in Spanish throughout Latino communities, as well as Spanish-language newspaper inserts and flyers. More important, the products, the commodities themselves, now often offer bilingual instructions on use or preparation. Public spaces – like bus stations, train stations, and post offices – also offer instructions in Spanish, as do numerous business and public centers, telephone operators, public signs, and traffic signs. Utility bills are often bilingual as well. The proliferation of printed Spanish has changed dramatically in the last 20 years. Even the California state lottery offers Spanish-language oral and printed instructions at every computerized Lotto stand. The impact of the Latino community on the market goes beyond language, as is evident in the availability of consumer goods targeted for this group but now consumed by the general public. Products previously only available in Latino stores, such as frozen Mexican food (burritos, tacos, tamales, enchiladas, etc.), canned menudo, salsa, canned refried beans, corn husks and cornmeal dough (masa), tamales, corn and flour tortillas, Mexican sweet bread, religious candles, various fruits and vegetables, and piñatas, are now available in most supermarkets. Even Planter's Peanuts has now come out with a spicy peanut assortment previously found only in Mexican and Chinese stores. Consumerism, like tourism, has finally allowed the market to discover a Mexican past and present.

Despite the proliferation of the printed word in Spanish advertising, the publishing of Latino research and creative works in Spanish continues to be problematic. The few token apertures in mainstream presses are all in English. The same is true for film-making, with limited exceptions. Minority publishers are also moving toward English-language publication almost exclusively. Today, for example, a fast screening of the catalog of Arte Público Press, the most influential Latino press in this country today, reveals that out of 176 titles, only 20 are works in Spanish (1993: 54–6). Clearly, professional and educated Latinos, especially those who are not first-generation scholars or writers, are now writing in English. Perhaps it is important to recall that only about 10 percent of Latinos complete four or more years of college, compared with 22.3 percent of the non-Latino population (García and Montgomery, 1991: 2; Kominski and Adams, 1991: 3). The educational attainment rates differ substantially by Latino origin, however, with only 6.2 percent of those of Mexican origin completing four years of college and more, compared with 18.5 percent of those of Cuban origin. What is clear, however, is that the intellectual Latino elite who write in English have little to say to the Spanish-speaking Latino immigrant or to the working-class Latino in the barrios and ghettos of metropolitan areas. These writers are producing for mainstream English-speaking

America, and for other college-educated assimilated Latinos. Tapping the 22 percent of Latinos who move beyond high school and the 51.3 percent who graduate from high school (Kominski and Adams, 1991: 3) as potential readers or viewers would enable writers to bridge the widening gap between Latino culture producers and the general Latino population. Only Spanish-language publications can target the majority of Latinos in the United States today, but this market is being served by Mexican rather than Latino publishers.

## CONCLUSION

Latinos are a diverse population, multinational in origin and multiethnic. The Spanish presently spoken in the border states reflects this multinational diversity. Today the entire linguistic map of Latin America and Spain, all the posited dialectal zones (Canfield, 1981; Cárdenas, 1970) can be found in the Southwest where, on the basis of intonation, morphology, pronunciation, and vocabulary, one can place Peninsular, Chilean, Argentine, Cuban, Puerto Rican, Salvadoran, Guatemalan, Peruvian, Ecuadorian, Colombian, Mexican, and Chicano varieties in schools, supermarkets, colleges, and universities; on city buses and trains; at workplaces; and in beauty salons, department stores, and large retail stores. The multiple varieties spoken within each nation-state have migrated north, producing a linguistic state of flux; only time will reveal which elements from which varieties survive in the Southwest. Undoubtedly, given the number of Mexican immigrants and their historical and kinship ties to long-time residents of the Southwest, the Mexican Spanish varieties will dominate the linguistic map.

Its relation to English is clear for the moment. Spanish is a minority language, subordinate to the dominant language and in danger of being displaced as the home and community language of second- and third-generation Latinos. Its future is not as clear, given the rapid demographic, economic and political changes already evident today and in gestation for the next century. Will economic interests prevail, as in the case of Ireland, and lead to mass language shift or will mass immigration and a growing Latino population shift the balance in the direction of Spanish? Will the decline of nation-states and the creation of supranational entities lead to an Anglicization of the entire continent? Surely Nicolás Guillén's worst nightmare cannot lie ahead. No more comforting is the thought of a Spanish-speaking Latino population at the service of transnational corporations in the management of the Latin American continent. More likely is the prospect of a multiethnic, multilingual supranation in which English, Spanish, Japanese, and Chinese become the world languages of the Pacific Rim. The future billions of Chinese will not likely allow their languages to be suppressed.

History teaches us that 700 years of Arab domination of the Spanish peninsula did not eradicate the Latin languages introduced a thousand years before 711 A.D. by the Roman invaders. But the earlier Iberian languages did all disappear after the Roman invasion, leaving only a trace of their presence in the names of rivers, mountains, and towns, except of course in the case of the Basque language, Euskera. This language, the origin of which is unknown, survived for one simple reason: the unwillingness of Basques to acculturate and their isolation in the mountainous area where they could preserve their language and culture for centuries, until industrialization brought mass migration of workers into the Basque region. At that point Euskera was on the verge of disappearing. Nationalist interests, however, and the death of the fascist dictator Francisco Franco, have allowed for a revitalization of the language and its introduction into the educational system. This committed language policy faces an uphill battle, however, for as in the case of Ireland, relatively few speakers of Euskera remain.

The invasion of the Southwest by English speakers took place only 150 years ago and now the mass migration into the region of millions of speakers of the Spanish language is opening the doors to an ethnic and language revival. Will a stable bilingualism ensue or will millions of Latinos come to speak English and only English? The dynamic bilingualism now in operation forecasts language shift, but linguistic assessments are tentative and prognostications risky. In the end, language choice will be a political as well as an economic decision. In fact, language loyalty may turn out to be the strategy needed to overcome the collectivity's fragmentation. Language, ethnicity, and class are all variables that will need to be deployed for political action if the multiethnic population of the border states is to effectively address and change social conditions that create and foster unemployment, poverty, homelessness, drug abuse, and intra- and inter-group violence in the twenty-first century.

# Bibliography

Acuña, Rodolfo (1990). "California Commentary: Life Behind Bars Is No Way to Build Character." *Los Angeles Times*, February 12: B7.

Amin, Samir (1992). *Empire of Chaos*. New York: Monthly Review Press.

Anderson, Benedict (1987). *Imagined Communities*. London: Verso.

Arte Público Press Catalog (1993). Houston, TX: Arte Público Press.

Avila, Joaquín Guadalupe, and Godoy, Ramona (1979). "Bilingual/Bicultural Education and the Law," in *Language Development in a Bilingual Setting*, ed. Eugen J. Briere. Los Angeles: National Dissemination and Assessment Center.

Balibar, Étienne (1991). "Racism and Nationalism," in *Race, Nation, Class: Ambiguous Identities*, ed. Étienne Balibar and Immanuel Wallerstein. London: Verso.

Barrera, Mario (1979). *Race and Class in the Southwest: A Theory of Racial Inequality*. Notre Dame, IN: University of Notre Dame Press.

Brenner, Robert, (1990). "Agrarian Class Structure and Economic Development in Pre-Industrial Europe," in *The Brenner Debate*, ed. T. H. Aston and C. H. E. Philpin. Cambridge: Cambridge University Press.

Bunting, Glenn F., and Miller, Alan C. (1993). "Feinstein Raises Immigration Profile." *Los Angeles Times*, July 18: A3, A18.

Canfield, D. Lincoln (1981). *Spanish Pronunciation in the Americas*. Chicago: University of Chicago Press.

Cárdenas, Daniel (1970). *Dominant Spanish Dialects Spoken in the United States*. Arlington, VA: Center for Applied Linguistics.

Chatterjee, Partha (1985). *Nationalist Thought and the Colonial World: A Derivative Discourse*. London: Zed.

Chávez, Stephanie (1993). "Panel Assails State's Bilingual Education." *Los Angeles Times* July 10: A19.

Cleland, Robert Glass (1947). *From Wilderness to Empire: A History of California, 1542–1900*. New York: Alfred A. Knopf.

Cockburn, Alexander (1993). "When Jobs Go South – a True Parable." *Los Angeles Times*, July 27: B7.

Cornelius, Wayne A. (1993). "Neo-nativists Feed on Myopic Fears." *Los Angeles Times*, Opinion Section, July 12: B7.

Deane, Seamus (1990). "Introduction," in *Nationalism, Colonialism and Literature*, ed. Terry Eagleton, Fredric Jameson, and Edward W. Said. Minneapolis: University of Minnesota Press.

DeParle, Jason (1993). "Housing Secretary Carves Out Role as a Lonely Clarion Against Racism." *New York Times*, July 8: A8.

Feldman, Paul (1993). "Breathing New life into Dying Languages." *Los Angeles Times*, July 12: A3.

Foucault, Michel (1986). "Of Other Spaces." *Diacritics*, 16/1: 22–7.

García, Jesús M., and Montgomery, Patricia A. (1991). See US Census Bureau.

Gilroy, Paul (1987). *There Ain't No Black in the Union Jack*. London: Hutchinson.

Gutiérrez, Felix F., and Reina Schement, Jorge (1979). *Spanish-Language Radio in the Southwestern United States*. Mexican American Studies Monograph No. 5. Austin: University of Texas.

Havemann, Joel, and Kempster, Norman (1993). "The Case of the Disappearing Worker: What's Gone Wrong?" *Los Angeles Times*, World Report, July 6: 1, 4.

Hobsbawm, E. J. (1992). *Nations and Nationalism since 1780*. Cambridge: Cambridge University Press.

Hurtado, Aída, et al. (1992). *Redefining California: Latino Social Engagement in a Multicultural*

*Society.* Los Angeles: UCLA Chicano Studies Research Center.

Jameson, Fredric (1991). *Postmodernism, or, The Cultural Logic of Late Capitalism.* Durham, NC: Duke University Press.

Kanellos, Nicolás (1983). "Two Centuries of Hispanic Theater in the Southwest," in *Mexican American Theater: Then and Now,* ed. Nicolás Kanellos. Houston, TX: Arte Público Press.

Keller, Gary D., and Van Hooft, Karen S. (1982). "A Chronology of Bilingualism and Bilingual Education in the U.S." in *Bilingual Education for Hispanic Students in the United States,* ed. Joshua Fishman and Gary D. Keller. New York: Teachers College Press.

Kominski, Robert, and Adams, Andrea (1991). See US Census Bureau.

Leal, Luis (1985). *Aztlán y México: Perfiles literarios e históricos.* Binghamton, NY: Bilingual Review Press.

Lefebvre, Henri (1991). *The Production of Space.* Cambridge: Blackwell.

Lewis, E. Glyn (1972). *Multilingualism in the Soviet Union.* The Hague: Mouton.

McDonnell, Patrick (1987). "North County's Farm Worker Camps: Third World Squalor Amid Affluence." *Los Angeles Times,* August 17: part II, pp. 1–3.

Macnamara, John (1975) "Success and Failures in the Movement for the Restoration of Irish," in *Can Language Be Planned?* ed. Joan Rubin and Bjorn H. H. Jernudd. Honolulu: University of Hawaii Press.

Meisler, Stanley, (1993). "Migration Viewed as 'Human Crisis'." *Los Angeles Times,* July 7: A4.

Miguélez, Armando, (1983). "El Teatro Carmen (1915–1923): Centro del Arte Escénico Hispano en Tucson," in *Mexican American Theater: Then and Now,* ed. Nicolás Kanellos. Houston, TX: Arte Público Press.

Miller, Alan C., and Ostrow, Ronald J. (1993). "Immigration Policy Failures Invite Overhaul." *Los Angeles Times,* July 11: A1, A22–A23.

Miyoshi, Masao, (1993). "A Borderless World? From Colonialism to Transnationalism and the Decline of the Nation-State." *Critical Inquiry,* 19 (Summer): 725–51.

Monsiváis, Carlos (1984). "Cultura urbana y creación intelectual," in *Cultura y creación intelectual en América Latina,* ed. Pablo González Casanova. Mexico City: Siglo XXI.

Navarette, Rubén. (1992). "Should Latinos Support Curbs on Immigration?" *Los Angeles Times* July 5: M1, M6.

O'Donnell, Santiago (1993). "Two D.C. Officers Say Speaking Spanish Got Them Reprimanded." *Washington Post,* June 11: B3.

Passel, Jeffrey S (1992). "Demographic Profile." *NACLA* 26, no. 2 (September): 21.

del Pinal, Jorge H., and DeNavas, Carmen (1989). See US Census Bureau.

Puig, Claudia (1991). "Off the Charts." *Los Angeles Times,* Calendar Section, April 7: 9, 89, 90.

Quintanilla, Michael (1993). "They Don't Understand." *Los Angeles Times,* July 5: E1, E2.

Rodríguez, Juan (1983). "Notas sobre la evolución de la prosa de ficción," in *A través de la frontera,* ed. Ida Rodríguez Prampolini. Mexico City: Instituto de Investigaciones Estéticas, UNAM.

Rodríguez, Richard (1981). *Hunger of Memory.* Boston: David R. Godine.

Rosenstiel, Thomas B. (1987). "L.A. Papers Speak a New Language." *Los Angeles Times,* November 9: A1, A19.

San Juan, E. (1989). "Problems in the Marxist Project of Theorizing Race." *Rethinking Marxism,* 2/2: 58–80.

Sánchez, Rosaura (1983). *Chicano Discourse: Sociohistoric Perspectives.* Rowley, MA: Newbury House.

Shorris, Earl (1992). "Latinos: The Complexity of Identity." *NACLA* 26 2 (September): 19–26.

Skelton, George (1993). "Feinstein Takes Immigration Out of Closet." *Los Angeles Times,* July 12: A3.

Smith, Anthony D. (1991). *The Ethnic Origins of Nations.* Cambridge: Blackwell.

Sontag, Deborah (1993). "A Fervent 'No' to Assimilation in New America." *New York Times,* June 29: A6.

Spencer, Gregory (1982). See US Census Bureau.

Tatum, Charles (1981). "Some Examples of Chicano Prose Fiction of the Nineteenth and Early Twentieth Centuries." *Revista Chicano-Riqueña,* 9/1: 58–67.

Tomás Rivera Center: Project Update (1993). "Reshaping Teacher Education in the Southwest." (January): 1–3.

Trombley, William (1986). "Prop. 63 Roots Traced to Small Michigan City." *Los Angeles Times,* October 20: part I, pp. 3, 20–1.

US Census Bureau (1982). *Projections of the Population of the United States by Age, Sex and Race: 1988 to 2080,* by Gregory Spencer. Current Population Reports. Series P-25, no. 1018.

—— (1989). *The Hispanic Population in the United States: March 1989*, by Jorge H. del Pinal and Carmen DeNavas. Current Population Reports. Series P-20, no. 444.

—— (1989). *Population Estimates by Race and Hispanic Origin for States, Metropolitan Areas, and Selected Counties: 1980 to 1985*, by David L. Word. Current Population Reports. Series P-25, no. 1040-RD-1.

—— (1991). *Educational Attainment in the United States: March 1991 and 1990*, by Robert Kominski and Andrea Adams. Current Population Reports. Series P-20, no. 462.

—— (1991). *The Hispanic Population in the United States: March 1991*, by Jesús M. García and Patricia A. Montgomery. Current Population Reports. Series P-20, no. 455.

—— (1992). *1990 Census of Population. General Population Characteristics. Arizona.* 1990 CP-1-4. Issued May 1992.

—— (1992). *1990 Census of Population. General Population Characteristics. California.* 1990 CP-1-6. Issued July 1992.

—— (1992). *1990 Census of Population. General Population Characteristics. Metropolitan Areas.* 1990 CP-1-1B. Issued November 1992.

—— (1992). *1990 Census of Population. General Population Characteristics. New Mexico.* 1990 CP-1-33. Issued May 1992.

—— (1992). *1990 Census of Population. General Population Characteristics. Texas.* 1990 CP-1-45. Section 1 of 2. Issued June 1992.

*UC Latino Student Eligibility and Participation in the University of California* (1993). Santa Cruz: University of California Latino Eligibility Task Force, March.

Vallejo, Mariano Guadalupe (1875). "Recuerdos históricos y personales tocantes a la Alta California." Vols 1 and 5. University of California, Berkeley, Bancroft Library manuscript.

*Washington Post* (1993). "Migration Across Borders, to Cities Nears Crisis, U. N. Says." July 7: A1, A24.

Weiner, Tim (1993). "On These Shores, Immigrants Find a New Wave of Hostility." *New York Times*, June 13: sec. 4, p. 1.

West, Cornel (1988). "Marxist Theory and the Specificity of Afro-American Oppression," in *Marxism and the Interpretation of Culture*, ed. Cary Nelson and Lawrence Grossberg. Chicago: University of Illinois Press.

Word, David L. (1989). See US Census Bureau.

Ybarra-Frausto, Tomás (1983). "La Chata Noloesca: Figura del Donaire," in *Mexican American Theater: Then and Now*, ed. Nicolás Kanellos. Houston, TX: Arte Público Press.

# Part II

## *Cultural Politics and Border Zones: Recasting Racialized Relations*

# The Politics of Biculturalism: Culture and Difference in the Formation of *Warriors for Gringostroika* and *The New Mestizas*

## *Antonia Darder*

There is a whisper within you that reminds me of who I am . . .
> *Guillermo Gomez-Peña (1993)*

The dormant areas of consciousness are being activated, awakened.
> *Gloria Anzaldúa (1987)*

The yearning to remember who we are is a subject that is rarely discussed in the realms of traditional academic discourse. It is not easily measured or observed by the standard quantification of scientific inquiry, nor is it easily detected in the qualitative dimensions of focus groups and ethnographic research methods. It is a deeply-rooted quality, obscured by layers upon layers of human efforts to survive the impact of historical amnesia induced by the dominant policies and practices of advanced capitalism and postmodern culture.

For these reasons, efforts to articulate a conclusive politics of biculturalism is a highly complex and messy endeavor. Yet it is significant to note that even the naming of such a phenomenon clearly is linked to an experience of listening to "the whisper within" and giving voice to an unspoken, yet ever-present memory of difference – "dormant areas of consciousness" that must be awakened. This view is readily supported by the fact that despite countless studies and writings about people of color by white researchers, none name or engage the experience of two-world-ness or double consciousness. It was not until scholars of color, such as Du Bois (1903), Fanon (1952), Valentine (1971), Ramirez and Casteñeda (1974), Solis (1980), Rashid (1981), Redhorse (1981), de Anda (1984), Buriel

(1984), and others began to posit specific theoretical frameworks grounded in their own community histories and cultural knowledge that notions of biculturalism began to appear in the discourse of the social sciences and historical studies. These scholars of color during the last thirty years have made significant contributions to an understanding of biculturalism. As a consequence, there has been a slowly, but consistently, emerging body of work that has attempted to give voice to a variety of explanations of bicultural processes and identities. These efforts, to a greater or lesser degree, have discussed the societal and psychological impact of living between two world views. In more recent years, a new wave of critical scholars of color (Darder, 1991: Akinyela, 1992: Millán, 1993; and Romay, 1993) in different disciplines have also begun to address the notion of biculturalism in their work.

## TOWARD A CRITICAL THEORY OF BICULTURALISM

The story never stops beginning or ending. It appears headless and bottomless for it is built on differences.
> *Trinh Minh-ha (1989: 2)*

Within a critical theoretical tradition, biculturalism must be understood as a contested terrain of difference. It is upon this highly complex and ambiguous ground that subordinate groups create both a private and public space in which to forge battle with the faces of oppression, while flying high their banners of cultural self-determination. Biculturalism as a critical perspective acknowledges openly and engages forthrightly the significance of power relations in structuring and prescribing societal definitions of truth, rules of normalcy, and notions of legitimacy which often defy and denigrate the cultural existence and lived experiences of subordinate groups.

The story of where, when, and how biculturation processes and identities begin, move, and end is generally a difficult one to recount, given the historical and contextual dimensions which shape the particular survival requirements of different groups at any given moment in their histories. This is to say that each subordinate group grapples with the effects of cultural imperialism according to the manner in which geographical, political, social, and economic forces shape and influence the efforts of members of a group to resist, oppose, negotiate, or even accept passive or voluntary assimilation into the dominant group.

Further, given the wide-reaching effects of advanced capitalism and a deeply rooted tradition of cultural oppression and domination in the United States, African Americans, Chicanos, Puerto Ricans, Native Americans, Asians, and other subordinate cultural groups for the most part exist in a hybridized state. This is to say that their histories of forced interaction with the dominant culture have required consistent forms of adaptional behaviors which have, in many instances, eroded, restructured, and reconstructed the language system, cultural beliefs, and social traditions of these groups.

Michael Omi and Howard Winant (1983a) argue that throughout most of the history of the United States, the discourses of subordinate cultures received very little political legitimacy. "However democratic the United States may have been in other respects, with respect to racial [and cultural] minorities it may be characterized as having been to varying degrees despotic for much of its history" (p. 55). Given a collective history of social marginalization, exploitation, cultural invasion, powerlessness, and systematic violence,[1] all subordinate cultures in this country currently experience an advanced state of hybridization. Understanding this phenomenon requires that we acknowledge the deep historical consequences of being driven out of the dominant political space and relegated to a subordinate position. Black, indigenous, and mestizo communities across the United States evolved over the last 400 years through their efforts to survive conditions of oppression, develop alternative structures, and resist annihilation of cultural knowledge and traditions.[2]

It cannot be denied that patterns of cultural, economic, and political oppression have been repeated in the international arena wherever European colonizers and their descendants have appropriated the land and resources of indigenous populations. Usurping the people's natural resources, destroying their economic and agricultural self-sufficiency, placing the children in foreign educational environments, devaluing the language community, and interfering with the generational transmission of spiritual knowledge are all common strategies of cultural imperialism. As such, every subordinate cultural group in the United States, to one extent or another, has been required to contend with the destructive impact of all or some of these strategies. Most insidious are the established relationships of domination and dependency which, despite ongoing and persistent group efforts to resist cultural oppression, further complicate the struggle to affirm the cultural integrity and self-determination of subordinate cultural groups.

## RETHINKING ETHNICITY AND THE FORMATION OF IDENTITY

> We will not remain the same. Either we re-make ourselves or we will be remade by others.
>
> *Gonzalo Santos (1992: 24)*

In many respects, biculturalism entails an ongoing process of identity recovery, construction, and reconstruction driven by collective efforts of subordinate cultural groups to build community solidarity, engage tensions surrounding nationality differences, revitalize the boundaries of subordinate cultures, and redefine the meaning of cultural identity within the current social context (Nagel, 1994). Further, this phenomenon is influenced by the persistent efforts of those who have been historically marginalized to establish a sense of place from which to struggle against relations of domination. Along the same lines, Stuart Hall (1990a) argues that a notion of ethnicity is required in order to truly engage the relationship between identity and difference.

> There is no way, it seems to me, in which people of the world can act, can speak, can create, can come in from the margins and talk, can begin to reflect on their own experience unless they come from some place, they come from some history, they inherit certain cultural traditions. What we've learned about the theory of enunciation is that there's no enunciation without positionality. You have to position yourself somewhere in order to say anything at all . . . the relation that peoples of the world now have to their own past is, of course, part of the discovery of their own ethnicity. They need to honor the hidden histories from which they come. They need to understand the languages which they've been taught not to speak. They need to understand and revalue the traditions and inheritances of cultural expression and creativity. And in that sense, the past is not only a position from which to speak, but it is also an

absolutely necessary resource in what one has to say. (p. 19)

Hall's use of the term *ethnicity* provides us with a framework upon which to rethink the analytical value of ethnicity with respect to biculturalism, particularly as it relates to identity formation. This requires a dialectical reading of ethnicity[3] that, first of all, retrieves the category from the political opportunism and academic domain of neo-conservatives, and secondly, challenges the failure of critical scholars to conceptualize the liberatory dimensions of this category in more fully class-specific terms. Thus, a critical definition of ethnicity is one that engages, in both concept and articulation, a politics of difference and class specificity within the context of a changing economy and postmodern world.

## ON ESSENTIALISM

> I can voice my ideas without hesitation or fear because I am speaking, finally, about myself.
>
> *June Jordon (1992: 189)*

In conventional critical debates about culture, there is generally a tremendous uneasiness when there is any effort made to seriously explore notions of cultural consciousness and the merits of knowledge that is rooted in the lived cultural experience of marginalized communities.[4] Often this uneasiness seems to stem most directly from an overarching commitment to protect Western assumptions of individualism, objectivity, and universal truth which deceptively conceal institutionalized structures of entitlement and privilege embedded in critiques of identity politics that, intentionally or unintentionally, function as "the new chic way to silence . . . marginal groups" (hooks, 1994: 83). And though it is true that cultural groups are not entities that exist apart from individuals, neither are they just arbitrary classifications of individuals by attributes which are external to or accidental to their cultural identities.

Group meanings partially constitute people's identities in terms of the cultural forms, social situations, and history that group members know as theirs, because their meanings have been either forced upon them or forged by them or both. Groups are real not as substances, but as forms of social relations . . . A person's sense of history, affinity, and separateness, even the person's mode of reasoning, evaluation, and expressing feelings, are constituted partly by her or his group affinities. (Young, 1990: 44–5)

Along with the traditional academic anxiety over obliterating the individual as subject are the overzealous denouncements of essentialism whenever scholars of color attempt to grapple with those actual experiences of cultural identity rooted in social and material conditions of racialized relations – experiences that, more often than not, reinforce a strong sense of cultural consciousness and solidarity among members of subordinate cultural communities. There is an expectation that they abdicate the power of their experience, without concern for the fact that "only the powerful can insist on a neat separation between the thought and reality . . . a separation that serves them well" (Sampson, 1993: 1227).

It is not surprising then to note that often critiques of essentialism embody the mistaken dichotomous notion that inquiry focused on subordinate life experiences automatically precludes recognition of in-group differences and cultural change, and amounts to nothing more than the act of reducing culture to a theory of reifying collectivity. As a consequence, scholars of color whose research engages cultural questions in their own communities are often marginalized by the "enlightened" mainstream of their disciplines, while those who are deemed more "open-minded" by Eurocentric standards are permitted to play freely in the arena of intellectual thought.

At this point, it is imperative to stress that I am not suggesting that subjective interpretations of lived experience alone can suffice in the struggle to overcome and transform structural conditions of domination, whether in theory or practice. And further, it cannot be denied that claims to exclusive "authority" derived solely from lived experience can be misused to silence and undermine the possibility of dialogue. Yet, despite these possible dangers, we must find the manner to incorporate in our intellectual work those ways of knowing that are rooted in experience. Hooks (1994) addresses eloquently this idea in the following passage from her essay *Essentialism and Experience.*

Though opposed to any essentialist practice that constructs identity in a monolithic, exclusionary way, I do not want to relinquish the power of experience as a standpoint on which to base analysis or formulate theory. For example, I am disturbed when all the courses in black history or literature at some colleges and universities are solely taught by white people, not because I think that they cannot know these realities but that they know them differently. Truthfully, if I had been given the opportunity to study African American critical thought from a progressive black professor instead of the progressive white woman with whom I studied . . . I would have chosen the black person. Although I learned a great deal from this white woman professor, I sincerely believe that I would have learned even more from a progressive black professor, because this individual would have brought to the class that unique mixture of experiential and analytical ways of knowing – this is, a privileged standpoint. It cannot be acquired through books or even distanced observation and study of a particular reality. To me this privileged standpoint does not emerge from "the authority of experience" but rather from the passion of experience, the passion of remembrance. (p. 90)

## CULTURAL CONSCIOUSNESS AND DECOLONIZATION

> Whereas the colonized usually has only a choice between retraction of his being and a frenzied attempt at identification with the colonizer, the [decolonized] has brought into existence a new, positive, efficient personality, whose richness is provided . . . by his certainty that he embodies a decisive moment of [cultural] consciousness.
>
> *Frantz Fanon (1964: 103)*

It is impossible to arrive at an emancipatory politics of biculturalism without questions of cultural consciousness and knowledge derived from lived experience receiving a rightful place within critical discourses on culture and difference. Likewise, the reality of subordinate groups cannot be sufficiently grasped without a foundational understanding of culture as an epistemological process that is shaped by a complex dialectical relationship of social systems of beliefs and practices which constantly moves members between the dynamic tension of cultural preservation and cultural change. This is to say that no culture (particularly within the Western postmodern context of advanced capitalism) exists as a fixed, static, or absolute entity, since culture, and hence cultural identity, is a relationally constituted phenomenon, activated and produced through constant social negotiation between others and one's own integration in the daily life and history of the community (Epstein, 1987). "It is something that happens over time, that is never absolutely stable, that is subject to the play of history and the play of difference" (Hall, 1990a: 15).

Nevertheless, forms of cultural consciousness, grounded in collective memories of historical events, language, social traditions, and community life, exist. This collective experience of affinity that emerges from such forms of cultural knowledge is often echoed in historical discursive accounts of African Americans, Latinos, Native Americans, and Asian Americans in this country. For example, it is not unusual for a person who identifies ethnically with the Latin American cultural experience to readily discuss the differences in affinity experienced when immersed within a Spanish-speaking versus an English-speaking context. This experience of affinity is a powerful connecting and perpetuating force in the lives of members of subordinate cultural groups – a force so strong that it continues to play a significant role in supporting a politics of identity, resistance, self-determination, and cultural nationalism among members of historically disenfranchised cultural communities worldwide.

In light of this, it is no wonder that all strategies of colonial oppression, to one extent or another, function to interfere with cultural community beliefs and practices that foster cultural integrity and cohesion among colonized subjects (Fanon, 1964). This process of cultural subjugation continues within the current so-called post-colonial era. This is readily evident in a multitude of economic, political, legal, educational, and religious institutional policies and practices in the United States aimed at furthering the assimilation process of subordinate groups. More specifically, we see it at work today in the forging of trade agreements that solidify the labor market's exploitation of workers of color, English-only initiatives to interfere with the advancement of bilingualism, covert and overt educational strategies that support cultural domination, laws to prevent particular religious activities of groups who exist outside Judeo-Christian traditions, the current inflammatory politics of immigration control as evidenced in California's passage of Proposition 187, and the worldwide commodification of subordinate cultural forms as multinational profit ventures.

There can be no question that biculturalism in the United States has evolved from a set of conscious and unconscious adaptational strategies to preserve significant dimensions of cultural knowledge and collective identity, adapt to changing material conditions, and resist institutional forms of psychological and physical violence (Young, 1991). In many respects, the bicultural process reflects what Frantz Fanon (1963) describes as a process of decolonization where "the meeting of two forces, opposed to each other by their very nature, which in fact owe their originality to the sort of substantiation which results from and is nourished by [the political and economic context of domination]." Biculturalism can then best be understood as incorporating the complex multilayered realities that shape a people's cultural and material struggle for survival. It is a phenomenon that "is born of violent struggle, consciousness raising, and the reconstruction of identities" (West, 1993: 15), and one that is most intensely felt within those subordinate cultural contexts that most greatly differ from the established social beliefs, expectations, and norms of the dominant group. As such, subordinate communities continue to be stigmatized by both external and internalized perceptions of inferiority and deficit, whereby their members are, for the most part, viewed as inadequately prepared or socially unfit to enter mainstream American life.

## GROWING POVERTY AND THE EVASION OF CLASS

[P]olitical [economic] questions are disguised as cultural ones, and as such become insoluble.

*Antonio Gramsci (1971: 149)*

At this juncture, it must be stressed that the dominant culture and its fabrication of the American middle-class mainstream is clearly driven by the political economy of advanced capitalism, with its overwhelming emphasis on the interests of the marketplace and its "tendency to homogenize rather than diversify human experience" (Wood, 1994: 28). Even more important is the recognition that postmodern mechanisms of cultural domination in the United States and abroad are most directly linked to the domination of multinational firms and new international divisions of labor. The impact of these rapidly changing and deepening economic and class relations serves to perpetuate the embroilment of subordinate cultural communities in a fierce struggle for economic survival with fewer and

fewer possibilities of self-sufficiency. And despite the growing number of professionals of color and the glossy image portrayal of their success, the majority of American institutions, with their accompanying resources, continue to be overwhelmingly controlled by a cadre of elite white males who are, slowly but steadily, being joined by their female counterparts. The consequences have resulted in an actual decrease in the proportional wealth and resources of communities of color over the last 30 years (Children's Defense Fund, 1994).[5] This widening economic gap is directly linked to what Xavier Gorostiaga (1993) characterizes as the "dominant fact of our age – growing poverty" (p. 4). In his analysis of a 1992 United Nations report, he explains:

[T]hroughout the world the last decade has been characterized by the rise of inequality between the rich and the poor . . . In 1989 the richest fifth controlled 82.7 percent of the revenue; 81.2 percent of the world trade; 94.6 percent of commercial loans; 80.6 percent of internal savings and 80.5 percent of investment. If in terms of distribution the panorama is untenable, it is equally so regarding resources: The rich countries possess approximately one-fifth of the world population but consume 70 percent of world energy, 75 percent of the metals, 85 percent of the timber, and 60 percent of the food. Such a pattern of development . . . is only viable in the degree to which the extreme inequality is maintained, as otherwise the world resources would be exhausted. Therefore, *inequality is not a distortion of the system. It is a systematic prerequisite for growth and permanence of the present system.* (p. 4, author's emphasis)

It is the tendency to ignore or overlook this "systematic prerequisite" of capitalism in discussions of culture, difference, and identity politics in the United States that motivates Ellen Meiksins Wood (1994) to question why "having recognized the complexities, diversities, and multiple oppressions in the so-called postmodern world, we can't also recognize that capitalism is not only dominant but massively present in every aspect of our lives and in all our 'identities'" (p. 28). Wood's critique rightfully challenges class-blind notions of cultural identity and argues that identity politics decontextualized from material conditions only limit and narrow the impact of such discourse upon the deep structures of economic inequality. Further, the absence of class discourse in the politics of marginalized communities in no way lessens the exigencies of class struggle. In fact, "since the discourse of justice is intimately tied to class, ethnicity, race, and gender, the absence of one of its most salient components – class" (Aronowitz, 1992: 59) foredooms the transcultural solidarity required to effectively address the plight of economically dispossessed people, not only in this country but around the world. Stanley Aronowitz (1992), in his writings on working-class identity,[6] sheds light on this issue.

> The American evasion of class is not universal. We have no trouble speaking of ourselves as a "middle class" society or, indeed, endowing the economically and politically powerful with the rights and privileges of rule. American ideology identifies the middle class with power and, in its global reach, has attempted to incorporate manual workers into this family. The anomaly of the large and growing working poor, some of whom are hungry, others homeless and, indeed, the increasing insecurity suffered not only by industrial workers but also professional and clerical employees in the service sector, make some uneasy but have, until recently, failed to faze the ongoing celebration. Or, to be more accurate, class issues are given other names: crime, especially drugs; teenage pregnancy and suicide; homelessness and hunger; chronic "regional" unemployment that is grasped as an exception to an otherwise healthy national economy. (p. 71)

## THE MEDIA AND IDEOLOGICAL DISTORTIONS OF DIFFERENCE

> Mass media in the United States exploit . . . representations of race and racialized contact in various ways daily: angry black folks doing violence, somebody – usually a young black man – dying.
>
> *bell hooks (1990: 173)*

It is impossible to fully grasp the social formation of ideological distortions about class, "race," and gender in the postmodern world if we ignore the overwhelming impact of today's accelerated media and communications technology. Through its captivating influence on "mental production" and its false presentation of democratic cultural differentiation, the media increasingly gives shape to new forms of postmodern repression while sustaining common-sense approval for its capitalist representations. Within the structured relationships between the media and the ideas it extends forth to the public, its ideological function is deceptively concealed. Hall and his colleagues (1978) explain this relationship in terms of Marx's basic proposal that "the ruling ideas of any age are the ideas of its ruling class."

> [The] dominance of the "ruling idea" operates primarily because, in addition to its ownership and control of the means of production, this class also owns and controls the means of "mental production." In producing their definition of social reality and the place of "ordinary people" within it, they construct a particular image of society which represents particular class interests of all members of society; this class's definition of the social world provides the basic rationale for those institutions which protect and reproduce their "way of life." This control of mental resources ensures that theirs are the most powerful and "universal" of the available definitions of the social world. Their universality ensures that they are shared to some degree by the subordinate classes [and cultures] of the society. (p. 59)

The media, with its highly centralized and almost monolithic structure, provides an essential link between the ruling ideology of the dominant culture and the society at large (Winston, 1982). In a society such as the United States where most of the people do not have any direct access to or power over the bulk of decisions that affect their lives, the media plays a powerful legitimating role in the social production of mass consensus. And although it may be argued that the power of the media is not absolute, in that there frequently exist counter-ideologies and definitions which challenge its legitimacy by way of dissident voices.

> many emergent counter-definers however have no access to the defining process at all . . . [for] if they do not play within the rules of the game, counter-spokesmen [sic] run the risk of being defined out of the debate (because they have broken the rules of reasonable opposition) . . . Groups which have not secured even this limited measure of access are regularly and systematically stigmatized, in their absence, as "extreme," their actions systematically deauthenticated by being labelled as "irrational." (Hall et al., 1978: 64)

## OPPOSITIONAL CONSCIOUSNESS

> This means locating the structural causes of unnecessary forms of social misery, depicting the plight and predicaments of demoralized and depoliticized citizens caught in market-driven cycles of therapeutic release . . . and projecting alternative visions, analyses, and actions that proceed from particularities and arrive at moral and political connectedness.
>
> *Cornel West (1992: 35)*

It is against such a backdrop of societal contradictions and mainstream cultural complexities that subordinate cultural groups must endeavor to rethink past strategies for cultural survival that now prove ineffective and to discover new ground upon which to carry out political projects of resistance and negotiation. This also includes the need to forge a new consciousness of opposition, in light of assimilationist postmodern rhetoric and right-wing conservative backlash.[7]

In the face of wide social and economic inequalities, biculturalism as a political construct must move beyond simple notions of individual psychological theories of identity, liberal paradigms of pluralism, and unproblematic notions of two distinct cultural world views interacting. Instead a genealogy of biculturalism must be theoretically grounded in the historical intricacies of social formations that emerge from the collision between dominant/subordinate cultural, political, and economic relations of power which function to determine the limits and boundaries of institutional life in this country. Given the hegemonic nature of American institutions, marginalized communities must develop the ability to negotiate and navigate through the current social complexities and co-opting nature of postmodern conditions of cultural domination. This requires a mode of oppositional consciousness that depends on the ability to read actual situations of power and to choose and adopt tactics of resistance that are best suited to push against the different forms of power configurations that shape actual experiences of injustice and inequality. Chela Sandoval (1991), in her work on US Third World feminism and oppositional consciousness, describes this as a "differential mode of oppositional consciousness" which provides members of subordinate groups with

> enough strength to confidently commit to a well-defined structure of identity . . . enough flexibility to self-consciously transform that identity according to the requisites of another oppositional ideological tactic, if readings of power's formation require it; enough grace to recognize alliances with others committed to egalitarian social relations and race, gender, and class justice, when their readings of power call for alternative oppositional stands. (p. 15)

In historical struggles against cultural oppression, bicultural communities have oftentimes joined together, albeit not always smoothly or easily, to oppose practices of social injustice directed against those groups in the United States who have been perceived consistently as unentitled to a rightful place within the mainstream. These coalitions and movement organizations have generally been primarily founded upon bicultural affinities of struggle rooted in the shared historical opposition of African Americans, Latinos, Asians, and Native Americans to cultural, class, and gender subordination. As the "nature" of post-modern social oppression presents itself in a more highly sophisticated, differentiated, and confusing manner, there is a greater necessity for members of subordinate groups to incorporate a differential mode of oppositional consciousness in order to build expanding alliances of struggle. Such alliances can serve as vehicles by which to more effectively identify and challenge actual relations of power at work and to select more effective modes of intervention that are directed toward actualizing an alternative vision of both institutional and community life.

## RACIALIZATION AND NOTIONS OF DIFFERENCE

[W]here cultural difference is represented as natural and immutable, then it has all the qualities signified by the notion of biological difference, with the result that the distinction between racism and nationalism seems to have been dissolved.

*Robert Miles (1993: 100)*

As discussed earlier, expressions of bicultural affinity among members of subordinate cultural groups are generally linked to experiences of difference and the role that difference plays in the social construction of both dominant and subordinate attitudes, beliefs, and practices in the United States. This is particularly at play when both dominant and subordinate groups struggle to challenge racism and the problematic inherent in

notions of "race relations"; for the manner in which these notions are commonly used, more often than not, implies "an acceptance of the existence of biological differences between human beings, differences which express the existence of distinct, self-producing groups" (Miles, 1993: 2). Robert Miles (1993), in his most recent book, *Racism After Race Relations*, challenges this racialization of groups by arguing that all forms of racism "are always mediated by and through other structures and social relations, the most important of which are class relations and the political reality of the nation state" (pp. 12–13). Therefore as relations of economic domination intensify worldwide, subordinate cultural groups must not fall into the trap of defining cultural differences as a "race problem" or a "race struggle." Instead what must be confronted is

the problem of racism, a problem which requires us to map and explain a particular instance of exclusion, simultaneously in its specificity and in its articulation with a multiplicity of other forms of exclusion. Hence, we can now confront the fundamental issues concerning the character and consequences of inequality reproduced by and in contemporary capitalist social formations, freed from a paradigm which finds an explanation for that inequality within the alleged "nature" of supposedly discrete populations rather than within historical and so humanly constituted social relations. (Miles, 1993: 23)

From this vantage point, we must also understand notions of "race identity and difference" as politically formed rather than embedded in the color of the skin or a given nature (Hall, 1990a, 1990b). In other words, to identify as Black or Chicano is not so much a question of color as it is a question of cultural, historical, and political differences. Hence, to conceptualize accurately the social construction of bicultural identity formation requires an understanding of the process of racialization. In other words, the theoretical foundation of a politics of biculturalism challenges the "common sense" discourse of "race" and problematizes its utility as an analytical category. This summons a bold analytical transition from the politics of "race" to recognizing the centrality of racism and racialization in the interpretation of exclusionary practices.

## LIFE ON THE BORDER

> The prohibited and forbidden are its inhabitants. Los atravesados live here: The squint-eyed, the perverse, the queer, the troublesome, the mongrel, the mulatto, the half-breed; in short, those who cross over, pass over, or go through the confines of the "normal."
>
> *Gloria Anzaldúa (1987: 3)*

The transcultural dimensions of biculturalism must then be situated within a continually changing process of cultural identity formation, as much as within complex human negotiations for social and material survival. The place where these processes and negotiations evolve and shift, construct and reconstruct, is what Homi Bhabha (1990) terms "the third space." It is also in his discussions of the third space that Bhabha engages the "process of hybridity." Hybridity here does not represent a relativist notion of culture, but instead challenges the global structures of domination which shape the lives of subordinate groups and creates a space for new formations of cultural identity to take hold. "This process of hybridity gives rise to something different, something new and unrecognizable, a new area of negotiation of meaning and representation" (p. 211).

It is then this "process of hybridity" that constitutes one of the central characteristic of border existence where the border itself becomes a political terrain of struggle and self-determination. Lawrence Grossberg (1993) expounds on the nature of this "in-between" place by engaging the work of Gloria Anzaldúa, *Borderlands/La Frontera: The New Mestiza.*

Here the subaltern are different from the identities on either side of the border, but they are not simply the fragments of both. The subaltern exists as different from either alternative in the place between colonizer and the (imagined) precolonial subject or, in Gloria Anzaldúa's borderland, between the Mexican and the American: "A borderland is a vague and undetermined place created by the emotional residue of an unnatural boundary . . . People who inhabit both realities . . . are forced to live in the interface between the two." . . . Anzaldúa describes the third space as "a shock culture, a border culture, a third culture, a closed country." (p. 97)

In the safety of the "third space," notions of bicultural identity are constructed, deconstructed, and reconstructed anew, all while negotiating the tension of ongoing interactions with social and material conditions of subordination. This suggests "a form of border crossing which signals forms of transgression in which existing borders forged in domination can be challenged and redefined" (Giroux, 1992: 28). In short it is a "transborder" experience of identity that "is involved in constantly struggling to emerge from the bottom-up" (Santos, 1992: 16).

In many respects at its very core, this "bottom-up" act of challenging and redefining reflects an effective strategy of cultural survival that Trinh Minh-ha (1992) terms "displacing."

> Displacing is a way of surviving. It is an impossible truthful story of living in-between regimens of truth. The responsibility involved in this motley in-between living is a highly creative one; the displacer proceeds by increasingly introducing difference into repetition. By questioning over and over again what is taken for granted as self-evident, by reminding oneself and the others of the unchangeability of change itself. Disturbing thereby one's own thinking habits, dissipating what has become familiar and clichéd, and participating in the changing of received values – the transformation (without master) of the selves

through one's self . . . Strategies of displacement defy the world of compartmentalization and the system of dependence it engenders, while filling the shifting space of creation with a passion named wonder. (pp. 332–3).

The meaning and complexity of this culture of hybridity, transgressing nature, and bottom-up displacement that shapes and enlivens a critical politics of biculturalism is fiercely echoed in the border culture manifesto of Guillermo Gomez-Peña's *Warrior for Gringostroika.*

> Border culture means boycott, complot, ilegalidad, clandestinidad, contrabando, transgresión, desobediencia, binacional; en otros [sic] palabras, to smuggle dangerous poetry and utopian visions from one culture to another, desde alla, hasta aca. But it also means to maintain one's dignity outside the law. But it also means hybrid art forms for new content-in-gestation . . . to be fluid in English, Spanish, Spanlish, and Ingeñol, 'cause Spanglish is the language of border diplomacy . . . But is [sic] also means transcultural friendships and collaborations among races, sexes, and generations. But it also means to practice creative appropriation, expropriation, and subversion of dominant cultural forms . . . a multiplicity of voices away from the center . . . to return and depart once again . . . a new terminology for new hybrid identities. (p. 43)

## BICULTURAL RE-PRESENTATIONS AND A SOLIDARITY OF DIFFERENCE

The insidious colonial tendencies we have internalized – and that express themselves in sadistic competition for money and attention, political cannibalism, and moral distrust – must be overcome. We must realize that we are not each other's enemies and that the true enemy is currently enjoying our divisiveness.

*Guillermo Gomez-Peña (1993: 62)*

The bicultural re-presentations of Gomez-Peña and Anzaldúa, as the *warrior of gringostroika* and the *new mestiza,* unmistakably emerge from the passion of experience, the power of reflection, and the courage to act. From these examples, we can glimpse at the face of revolutionary commitment – a grounded commitment to struggle against any and all forms of theory or practice that imprison our minds and incarcerate our hearts. Collectively these bicultural re-presentations call forth not only themes of opposition to dominant structures and cultural forms that impede the humanity and liberation of subordinate subjects, but also signal new ways of perceiving our dialectical capacities to transform the social and material conditions of our communities. It is through their vibrant discourses of simultaneous deconstruction and reconstruction, undoing and redoing, embracing and releasing, that we find the hidden seeds of self-determination and catch glimpses of the possibilities awaiting us, possibilities that are given birth through our courage to transgress the antiquated "sacred cows" of profit and privilege, and that join us together in a solidarity of difference – a solidarity that is ever mindful of the manner in which

> Institutionalized rejection of difference is an absolute necessity in a profit economy which needs outsiders as surplus people. As members of such an economy, we have all been programmed to respond to the human differences between us with fear and loathing and to handle that difference in one of three ways: ignore it, and if that is not possible, copy it if we think it is dominant, or destroy it if we think it is subordinate. But we have no patterns for relating across human difference as equals. As a result, those differences have been misnamed and misused in the service of separation and confusion. (Lorde, 1992: 281–2).

Audre Lorde's words strongly reflect one of the most important questions we must openly acknowledge and consistently address in our efforts to establish a solidarity of difference.

How do we move across a multiplicity of subjectivities rooted in both material conditions and diverse orientations that historically shape our world views? For example, so often we hear people, even within bicultural communities, bemoan the "loss of community." Yet, if the truth be told, a return to the good old days of such an imagined community actually would require returning to a simpler, unproblematic vision of community – a vision that, in fact, was often theorized in monolithic and solely essentialist terms and enacted through exclusionary practices that precluded the full participation of women, poor and working-class people, gays, lesbians, and those perceived as "racially" inferior.

As critical beings we must consistently recognize the dangers of falling into the hidden traps of both absolutely exclusionary (assimilationist) and relativistically inclusive (liberal pluralist) theories and practices. A solidarity of difference instead challenges us to actively struggle across human differences within the ever-present dialectical tension of inclusionary/exclusionary personal and institutional realities and needs. For the purpose is not to obscure or obliterate differences or diminish and destroy cultural self-determination in the search for "common values"; rather, our greatest challenge is to negotiate the ongoing construction and reconstruction of relations of power and material conditions that both affirm and challenge our partialities in the interest of cultural and economic democracy, social justice, human rights, and revolutionary love.

# Notes

1    See Iris Marion Young's (1991) text *Justice and the Politics of Difference* for an excellent critical analysis of the sociopolitical contexts that shape the histories of subordinate cultural groups in the United States.

2    Although there no longer exist cultural groups in the United States untouched by the dominant artifacts, structures, and economic relations of power, the beginning stages of this hybridization process can be observed in indigenous cultures that exist in remote regions of the world. One such example is the culture of the Q'eros in Peru. The Q'eros are the remaining community of people in the Peruvian highlands who are the direct descendants of the Inca. To flee the violent rampage of the conquistadors in the 1500s and to protect their way of life, the Q'eros fled into the Andes, living virtually in isolation for 500 years. It is only recently that the Q'eros have begun to have some contact with the West. Government projects to assimilate the Q'eros into the mainstream of Peruvian life have taken the form of setting up farm collectives and Spanish-language educational programs for the children. As the Q'eros begin to have greater contact with the West, it is expected that a way of life conserved for hundreds of years will undergo dramatic reconstruction, if not be lost altogether. This is already evident in those members of Q'eros who have moved into the cities, only to face harsh conditions of poverty and very few opportunities for a better life amidst the Peruvian mainstream (Cohen, 1993).

3    For a more extensive and thought-provoking discussion of ethnicity, see "Ethnicity: Identity and Difference" and "Cultural Identity and Diaspora" by Stuart Hall (1990a, 1990b); and Stanley Aronowitz's (1992) *The Politics of Identity*.

4    See chapter 6, "Essentialism and Experience," in *Teaching to Transgress* by bell hooks (1994) for an incisive discussion and critique of Diana Fuss's *Essentially Speaking: Feminism, Nature, and Difference*, particularly with respect to the manner in which Fuss problematizes student voices that she characterizes as speaking from the "authority of experience."

5    According to the Children's Defense Fund yearbook, *The State of America's Children*: In 1992, more children lived in poverty than in any year since 1965; the share of family income received by the poorest one-fifth of families shrank to 4.4 percent in 1992, while the share going to the richest one-fifth reached 44.6 percent. In *Who We Are: A Portrait of America*, among other income inequities Roberts (1993) shows that despite an increase in total Black families who earn more than $50,000 (from 7 percent to 15 percent), the total number of Black families earning under $5,000 has risen from 8 percent

in 1967 to 12 percent in 1990. Edward Luttwak (1993) bemoans the "Third-Worldization" of America in his book *The Endangered American Dream*. He writes: "America's slide toward Third World conditions is even now being prepared by the sheer force of demography: the proportion of poor Americans is increasing, the concentration of wealth in the hands of the richest one percent is also increasing, and the proportion of Americans in between who have enough wealth and income to claim genuine middle-class status is therefore in decline" (p. 153). Luttwak also provides the following figures: Between 1979 and 1990, the number of workers below the poverty line nearly doubled, from 7.8 million to 14.4 million; the combined net worth of the richest 1 percent was greater than the total net worth of the bottom 89.9 percent of all American families, at $5.2 trillion.

6    For an eloquent discussion of the history of working-class identity see *The Politics of Identity: Class, Culture, Social Movements*, a text by Stanley Aronowitz (1992).

7    Michel Omi and Howard Winant (1983b) in their essay "By the Rivers of Babylon: Race in the United States (Part II)," provide an informative and useful discussion of the New Right's "programmatic attempts to limit the political gains of the minority movement (and its successors) by reinterpreting their meanings." In their work, the authors outline several of the major currents in the rearticulation process which have fueled the right-wing conservative backlash in the United States.

# Bibliography

Akinyela, M. (1992). "Critical Africentricity and the politics of culture." *Wazo Weusi (Think Black)* (Fall). Fresno, CA: California State University.

Anzaldúa, G. (1987). *Borderlands/La frontera: The New Mestiza*. San Francisco: Aunt Lute.

Aronowitz, S. (1992). *The politics of identity: Class, Culture, Social Movements*. New York: Routledge.

Bhabha, H. (1990). "The third space," in J. Rutherford (ed.), *Identity, Community, Culture Difference*. London: Lawrence and Wishart.

Buriel, R. (1984). "Integration with traditional Mexican-American culture and sociocultural adjustment," in J. Martinez (ed.), *Chicano Psychology*, 2nd edn. New York: Academic Press.

Children's Defense Fund (1994). *The State of America's Children Yearbook*. Washington, DC.

Cohen, J. (1993). *Q'eros: The Shape of Survival*. New York: Mystic Fire Video.

Darder, A. (1991). *Culture and Power in the Classroom: A Theory for a Critical Bicultural Pedagogy*. New York: Bergin and Garvey.

de Anda, D. (1984). "Bicultural socialization: Factors affecting the minority experience," *Social Work*, 2: 101–7.

Du Bois, W.E.B. (1903). *The Souls of Black Folk*. Chicago: A. C. McClurg.

Epstein, S. (1987). "Gay politics, ethnic identity: The limits of social constructionism," *Socialist Review*, 17 (May–August), 9–54.

Fanon, F. (1964). *Toward the African Revolution*. New York: Grove.

—— (1963). *The Wretched of the Earth*. New York: Grove.

—— (1952). *Black Skin, White Masks*. New York: Grove.

Giroux, H. (1992). *Border Crossings*. New York: Routledge.

Gomez-Peña, G. (1993). *Warrior for Gringostroika*. Saint Paul, MN: Graywolf Press.

Gorostiaga, X. (1993). "Is the answer in the South?" Paper presented at the international seminar on *First World Ethics and Third World Economics: Christian responsibility in a world of plenty and poverty*, Sigtunn, Sweden.

Gramsci, A. (1971). *Selections from Prison Notebooks*. New York: International Publishers.

Grossberg, L. (1993). "Cultural studies and/in New Worlds," in C. McCarthy and W. Crichlow (eds), *Race, Identity, and Representation in Education*. New York: Routledge.

Hall, S. (1990a). "Ethnicity: Identity and difference." *Radical America*, 13/4: 9–20.

—— (1990b). "Cultural identity and diaspora," in J. Rutherford (ed.), *Identity, Community, Culture, Difference*. London: Lawrence and Wishart.

Hall, S., et al. (1978). *Policing the Crisis*. London: Macmillan.

hooks, b. (1994). *Teaching to Transgress*. New York: Routledge.

—— (1990). *Yearnings*. Boston: South End Press.

Jordon, J. (1992). *Technical Difficulties*. New York: Vintage Books.

Lorde, A. (1992). "Age, race, class and sex: Women redefining difference," in R. Ferguson et al. (eds), *Out There: Marginalization and*

*Contemporary Culture.* New York: New Museum of Contemporary Art.

Luttwak, E. (1993). *The Endangered American Dream.* New York: Simon and Schuster.

Miles, J. (1993). *Racism after Race Relations.* London: Routledge.

Millán, D. (1993). "The Chicano collective bicultural consciousness: Identity and the politics of race," in A. Darder (ed.), *Bicultural Studies in Education: The Struggle for Educational Justice.* Claremont, CA: Institute for Education in Transformation/Claremont Graduate School.

Minh-ha, T. (1992). "Cotton and iron," in R. Ferguson et al. (eds), *Out There: Marginalization and Contemporary Culture.* New York: New Museum of Contemporary Art.

—— (1989). *Woman Native Other.* Indianapolis: Indiana University Press.

Nagel, J. (1994). "Constructing ethnicity: Creating and recreating ethnic identity and culture." *Social Problems,* 41/1 (February); 152–76.

Omi, M. and Winant, H. (1983a). "By the rivers of Babylon: Race in the United States" (Part I). *Socialist Review,* 13/5: 31–65.

—— (1983b). "By the rivers of Babylon: Race in the United States" (Part II). *Socialist Review,* 13/6: 35–68.

Ramirez, M. and Castañeda, A. (1974). *Cultural Democracy: Bicognitive Development and Education.* New York: Longman.

Rashid, H. (1981). "Early childhood education as a cultural transition for African American children." *Educational Research Quarterly,* 6/3: 55–63.

Redhorse, J., et al. (1981). "Family behavior of urban American Indians," in R. Dana (ed.), *Human Services for Cultural Minorities.* Baltimore, MD: University Park Press.

Roberts, S. (1993). *Who We Are: A Portrait of America.* New York: Random House.

Romay, E. (1993). "Policy implications for the United States through Mexican immigration bilingual teachers' experiences of bilingual-bicultural education: A participatory research process." Ph.D. dissertation, University of San Francisco.

Sampson, E. (1993). "Identity politics: Challenges to psychology's understanding," *American Psychologist,* 48/12 (December): 1219–30.

Sandoval, C. (1991). "U.S. third world feminism: The theory and method of oppositional consciousness in postmodern world," *Genders* (Spring): 1–24.

Santos, G. (1992). "Somos RUNAFRIBES? The Future of Latino ethnicity in the Americas." *National Association of Chicano Studies Annual Conference Proceedings.*

Solis, A. (1980). "Theory of biculturality." *Calmeccac de Atzlán en Los,* 2: 36–41.

Valentine, C. (1971). "Deficit, difference, and bicultural models of Afro-American behavior." *Harvard Educational Review,* 42: 137–57.

West, C. (1993). *Race Matters.* Boston: Beacon Press.

—— (1992). "The new politics of difference," in R. Ferguson et al. (eds), *Out There: Marginalization and Contemporary Culture.* New York: New Museum of Contemporary Art.

Winston, M. (1982). "Racial consciousness and the evolution of mass communications in the United States." *Daedalus,* 8: 171–82.

Wood, E. M. (1994). "Identity crisis," *In These Times* (June 13): 28–9.

Young, I. M. (1990). *Justice and the Politics of Difference.* Princeton, NJ: Princeton University Press.

# Beyond the Rainbow:
# Mapping the Discourse on Puerto Ricans and "Race"

## Roberto P. Rodriguez-Morazzani

Prefabricated Negroes are sketched on sheets of paper and superimposed upon the Negro Community; then when somebody thrusts his head through the page and yells, 'watch out there, Jack, there're people living under here,' they are shocked and indignant.

*Ralph Ellison[1]*

Over the past three decades there has emerged a body of writing, relatively small when compared with that addressing other issues, which attempts to explore the question of "race" as it pertains to Puerto Ricans. What follows is a preliminary critical analysis of some of the more significant statements on Puerto Ricans and racial identity for this period.[2] It is intended to engage two general theoretical pursuits. The first consists of analyzing the history of *racial formation*, that is, the transformation over time of what counts as "race," the obtaining of racial membership, and the overarching material and discursive forces that produce these effects and meanings. The second concern focuses on racial subjectification and subjection: how social agents are defined or define themselves as racial subjects, and what sort of social subjection this entails both for the racially formed (*racialized*) and racially forming (*racializing*) producers.

"Race" is understood here as a socially constructed category with no basis in empirical sciences such as biology. Yet, it should be stated that "race," while socially constructed and constituting an ontologically empty and metaphysical concept, is real insofar as identities are constituted based on "race" as an *ontologically grounded* category. Hence, the paradox of "race" as a social construct and as something that has real, indeed monstrous,

effects. For while "race" might be a fiction, it is a fiction that informs and organizes the actions of people and the structures of power. For this reason it is important to historicize and deconstruct the racial discourses on which notions of "race" are maintained. In this connection it is also important to point out that the concept of "race" is not universal, not even in Western history. In fact, the concept of "race" can be traced historically.[3]

Such concerns replace the problems of empirical testing of racial attitudes, which had guided much earlier thinking and aptitudes with analyses of the body of discourse concerning Puerto Ricans and "race"/racism. They seek to surmount the irresolvable difficulties of objectively measuring an attitude measurement by means of analyzing the discourse about racially constituted bodies and subjects. Here discourse serves as an analytical category connected to the production of material practices. These displacements also mark a shift in the rules of analytic engagement, from the passive distance of objective social science to active commitment in resisting the particular racisms of given historical moments. The present article identifies these distinct moments in the discourse on Puerto Ricans and "race"/racism since the 1960s. I speak here of "moments" rather than periods, since while these discourses can be marked off chronologically, there is also considerable temporal overlap. In the case of the discourse on Puerto Ricans and "race," dominant, contestatory and emergent models coexist.

There are two main parts to this article. The first seeks to review some of the main discourses and counter-discourses on Puerto Ricans and "race." The second part examines the tenets of the "third movement" of the 1960s and 1970s, and the current dominant discourse on Puerto Ricans and "race" in the United States, focusing on what has become the main intervention on the subject, the theory of the "rainbow people."

## FIRST MOMENT: RACE AS SOCIOPATHOLOGY

Much of the literature written on Puerto Ricans and race has been generated by North American anthropologists, social scientists, journalists, and policy-makers. For the most part, this literature represents a continuation of earlier formulations of "ethnic" relations literature. Books written in the 1960s, such as *Beyond The Melting Pot* by Nathan Glazer and Daniel Patrick Moynihan[4] and *La Vida* (1965) by Oscar Lewis[5] established a paradigm within the social sciences and political arenas for looking at Puerto Ricans and the question of ethnicity and race. These studies have remained hegemonic in the discourses on the subject to this day.[6] Especially influential is Lewis' culture of poverty thesis, which has lost none of its discursive power despite its being critiqued throughout the first half of the 1970s. (The ethnic relations literature has its counterpart within the historical writing on immigration to the United States. Oscar Handlin's *The Newcomers: Negroes and Puerto Ricans in a Changing Metropolis*[7] is the best-known example of this genre.)

These anthropological, sociological, and historical writings were concerned to analyze what was seen as the anomalous case of the Puerto Rican. Puerto Ricans were described as deficient at a number of levels which could be explained as the result of sociocultural pathologies. In "blame the victim" fashion,

Puerto Rican poverty and social stigmatization were explained as a result of Puerto Rican dysfunction. Puerto Ricans were seen as morally lacking, prone to violence, undisciplined, present-oriented, devoid of a work ethic, oversexed, etc. This sociopathology was the key to understanding and addressing the failure of Puerto Ricans to assimilate into the "mainstream" of American society, as had been the case with "other ethnic groups," such as Irish, Italian, Jewish, and other hyphenated Americans. In short, Puerto Ricans constituted a problem.[8] An important paradox of the liberal social science literature is that "race" is elided in favor of the notion of ethnicity. Such a deployment veils the racist "common sense" that informs the analysis of poverty and powerlessness among Puerto Ricans and other racialized groups.[9] This writing also tended to be ahistorical, as Puerto Ricans were continuously described as recent or new "immigrants," concealing the fact of a measurable Puerto Rican presence since the turn of the century, and their status as US citizens. There was also a marked tendency to ignore the colonial relationship between the US and Puerto Rico as being in any way related to the condition of Puerto Ricans in the US.

This body of writing, addressing what was conceived as the "Puerto Rican problem," promoted strategies that would aid in transforming the dysfunctional aspects of Puerto Rican "community" life. It is important to note that the above literature was authored by individual scholars with decidedly liberal credentials. Moreover, the social context for the strategies proposed by these writers coincided with the second expansion of the US semi-welfare, funded by the War on Poverty program. These programs were the response to demands being placed upon the state by emergent social movements, the most central at this time being the traditional civil rights movement, and their liberal allies. The mid-1960s also saw, in addition to transformations in the African American movement, the birth of movements, including a radical Puerto Rican movement that drew from a number of political and intellectual currents.

Before engaging these writings and their context(s), it is necessary to comment on the Puerto Rican diasporic experience as it relates to race, particularly the relationship between Puerto Ricans and African Americans in New York City. The experience of Arturo Alfonso Schomburg and his times claim our attention, since that experience demonstrates a need to problematize binary thinking on "race" and identity.

## DIASPORIC EXCHANGES: EXPANDING THE "BLACK ATLANTIC"

It is important to note here that the social movements generated by the African American people in the United States was, and remains, significant for the Puerto Rican diasporic experience. The process of racialization Puerto Ricans underwent was not totally unlike that of African Americans, especially in the post-Second World War era. From the late 1940s on, African Americans migrated in large numbers from the agrarian south to the industrial belt of the Northeast and Midwest. Puerto Ricans similarly settled in cities such as New York, Trenton, Philadelphia, and Chicago. Both groups experienced unemployment, housing discrimination, police brutality, racial violence, and racial devaluation via academic and popular portrayals.[10] In this context it is very suggestive that much of the literature of the 1960s and 1970s in the social sciences concerning Puerto Ricans compares and contrasts their situation with that of African Americans.[11] The propensity for such linking could lead anyone unfamiliar with the existence of the two different groups to view them as one, or as a hyphenated signifier, i.e., African American-Puerto Rican. In short, the perceived position of the two peoples vis-à-vis civil society and the state were similar.

While it is traditional to think of different groups as hermetically sealed, social interaction includes exchange, borrowing, and transformation. It is a process that can be observed even by the casual observer. The social position of African Americans and

Puerto Ricans resulted in a sociocultural and ideopolitical complex of exchanges and transformations not easily reduced to their individual parts. Certainly one can isolate certain ideological currents originating among the African American people, which Puerto Ricans employed for understanding their situation in the US. But much of the development of African American thought on these matters was itself generated by the broader experience of appropriation and transformation within the African diaspora.[12]

The actual lived history of interaction between African American and Puerto Ricans in the US has not been seriously explored by scholars. Puerto Rican writers have also tended to be reluctant to explore this experience.[13] The few references lack historical depth and are typically impressionistic.[14] Also, they more often than not pose the relationship between African Americans and Puerto Ricans as either oppositional or united.[15] Again, a complex and constantly changing relationship is understood rigidly and ahistorically. The appropriation by both African Americans and Puerto Ricans of the legacy of Arturo Alfonso Schomburg (1874–1938) richly illustrates this complexity.

Arturo Alfonso Schomburg's biography encompasses the history of Puerto Rico, the Puerto Rican diasporic community of political exiles in New York at the turn of the century, and the history of Black scholarship and culture.[16] To identify him as a political activist, bibliophile, collector, librarian, and figure of the Harlem Renaissance is only to begin to describe this complex individual. What interests us here is that there has been a tendency for Schomburg to be identified simply as an African American by African Americans, and simply as Puerto Rican by Puerto Ricans. In truth, at different stages in his life, Schomburg defined himself both as Puerto Rican and as Black. As he became more involved in collecting and documenting the African presence in Europe and the Americas, and as he became active in Harlem's political and cultural life, he began to use the English translation of his name – Arthur A. Schomburg instead of Arturo Alfonso Schomburg.

However, late in his life he began again to use the Spanish spelling of his name. Schomburg's identification with blackness on the one hand and a Puerto Rican national identity[17] on the other intimates an interaction between the need for social agency and the sociopolitical vehicles for its realization. Moreover, it illustrates processes of racialization at work over time in the US from the turn of the century to the 1940s.

In looking at the biography of Schomburg it becomes clear that what is required is a historically informed analysis, which, rather than reifying genealogies of either group, grasps the shifting terrain of sociocultural interaction in all of its manifestations. For example, an examination of the life of Jesús Colón, a member of the American Communist Party, a journalist, and a fighter for social justice, would provide us with another set of complexities with respect to how "race" was experienced by a Black Puerto Rican in the period before and after the Second World War. In the course of Colón's being simultaneously Puerto Rican, Black, Red, and diasporic? An analysis of his writings on racial discrimination and his active efforts to foster Black–Puerto Rican unity within the context of the twists and turns of Communist Party policy on what was known as the "Negro Question" would add greatly to our knowledge on the question of "race," leftist political culture, and the efforts of Puerto Ricans to exercise human agency.[18] Another example is the biography of a friend and political comrade of Colón, Bernardo Vega. In his memoirs Vega describes himself as "white, a peasant from the highlands (a *jíbaro*)."[19] What did whiteness mean for a Puerto Rican migrating to the US in the first decades of this century? How did his claim to whiteness affect his ability to move within the labor movement, the Socialist Party, and the Puerto Rican community as compared to Jesús Colón? How would this whiteness compare with Cuban immigrants who claimed white identities during this period?[20]

These are two examples that speak to us from the past through their writing. But the many different lives of individual Puerto Ricans who cannot speak to us, and in particular the lives of the many Puerto Rican women who migrated, would in all likelihood present us with even more nuanced understandings of the racialization process as Puerto Ricans experienced it before the Second World War. Racialization is also a gendered process. These types of explorations would lay the basis for a richly textured comprehension of how political cultures evolve and of the limitations of binary thinking in accounting for convergences and divergences among and between African Americans and Puerto Ricans. The existence of individuals from both worlds who exist at the different borders and intersections blur the hard and fast lines of demarcation.

During the postwar era, the profound socioeconomic and ideopolitical transformations which took place would also result in a rearticulation of "race." The way in which a Puerto Rican might understand and articulate a racial identity would reflect these transformations. For example, the way in which Schomburg or Colón might view "race" would be somewhat different that Black Puerto Ricans such as Antonia Pantoja and Piri Thomas or Pablo "Yoruba" Guzmán, who represent different post-1945 generational experiences.[21]

## SECOND MOMENT: COUNTERING THE DOMINANT DISCOURSE

By the late sixties there emerged a "counter-discourse" articulated by Puerto Ricans, both within the academy and in various public spheres that sought to critique conservative and liberal discourses on Puerto Ricans. This response was generated by Puerto Ricans active within the many social movements of the period. The most radical impulse on the question of race came from the independence and left-wing sectors of the movements which emerged in the late 1960s and early 1970s. Deeply influenced by different radical intellectual traditions and by different political cultures, both those past and those being created, the question of "race" as it applied to

Puerto Rico and the diasporic Puerto Rican communities in the United States was explored. Below we will look at some of the more significant statements that emerged both from Puerto Rico and the US. The influences shaping the discourses under consideration in what we refer to here as the "Second Moment" differ in several respects, though I would argue that they should be grouped together because of their common referent to colonial domination and the eliding of "race" in the nationalist project, as well as their common commitment to an alternative political project.

It is significant that much of the thinking on the question of "race" and Puerto Rican identity was articulated not in systematic academic fashion, but rather in political tracts, manifestos, organizational platforms, and newspaper articles; also, in the debates and discussions that took place among countless individuals in everyday life. That is to say, the debate took place outside of the dominant state ideological apparatuses.[22] This is not to argue that the dominant logics of capitalist modernity in the US were overcome, but rather to suggest that the possibility existed for doing so since what had heretofore been invisible was now being brought into focus.

In reviewing some of the writing of this period it is evident that a key document was Juan Angel Silén's *Hacia una visión positiva del puertorriqueño*,[23] which was translated into English as *We, the Puerto Rican People: A Story of Oppression and Resistance*.[24] Interestingly, Silén did not address the question of Puerto Rican racial identity. Instead, the question of colonialism and the struggle for nationhood are the central coordinates by which Puerto Rican identity is constructed. Following in the tradition of Puerto Rican nationalism, Silén asserts that "*lo nacional*" is the framework for understanding Puerto Ricanness. He believes that the extent to which "race" is an issue, it is one generated by external factors such as Spanish colonialism and US imperialism. Despite his criticism of the literature produced by Creole elites on the "docile Puerto Rican," from the nineteenth century to René Marqués' writings of the 1960s, the question

of "race" is not broached in any significant manner.[25] This silence, together with other omissions, will prove significant for the Puerto Rican nationalist project of the 1970s.

In his article "The Prejudice of Having no Prejudice in Puerto Rico,"[26] sociologist Samuel Betances influentially addressed the question of Puerto Ricans and "race." Here he addresses the subject of "race" and racism among Puerto Ricans, and challenges the "myth that Puerto Rico is a kind of human relations paradise where racism is nonexistent." Published in the Chicago-based pro-independence journal *The Rican*, Betances' article received mixed responses from various audiences.[27] One response was that Betances was not accurate in his assessment because his historical reflection on and analysis of Puerto Rican society was largely the result of the context in which he was writing. The context was that of the US and the discourse on "race" and racism generated by the struggle of African Americans and other racialized groups in the United States. Therefore, "race" and racism was something that had to be contended with in the US, not in Puerto Rico. But this assertion made by critics of Betances was never substantiated. Rather, it rested on two propositions: first, the myth of a non-racial order achieved through racial miscegenation (*mestizaje*); second, the transposition of a paradigm on "race" operative within the context of the United States, but not Puerto Rico. However, for many who read the article, and especially for black Puerto Ricans and others who had reflected on the racism which they had experienced and witnessed within the Puerto Rican diaspora and in Puerto Rico, the article was a confirmation of a lived experience.

In the mid-1970s there were other attempts to address the question of Puerto Ricans and "race" in Puerto Rico, most notably the work of Isabelo Zenón Cruz. The publication in 1974–5 of his *Narciso descubre su trasero: el negro en la cultura puertorriqueña* represents an important benchmark in the ideopolitical culture of Puerto Rico with regards to "race."[28] In this book, the traditional silence within the independence movement in particular, and the left in general, on the question of "race" and racism was broached in polemical fashion. Zenón's book provoked debate among the pro-independence left intelligentsia and political activists and the island's traditional political and cultural elite. The pages of newspapers such as the Puerto Rican Socialist Party's *Claridad*, as well as the daily press such as *El Nuevo Día* and *El Mundo*, debated the contents of the book and what constitute "race relations" in Puerto Rican society.[29] Unlike the response to Betances' article in *The Rican*, it was much more difficult to dismiss Zenón Cruz as an "outsider," since he was not part of the Puerto Rican diaspora. Indeed, his position as an academic and black Puerto Rican within Puerto Rico did not permit such facile dismissal. However, despite criticism by Betances and Zenón Cruz, the myth of the human relations paradise in Puerto Rico remained hegemonic. The social irreverence of Zenón Cruz became in many circles an excuse for ignoring his criticism. To date there has been little serious engagement with this book. However, among black Puerto Ricans and among those who reflected on the question of "race" and racism in Puerto Rico, *Narcisso descubre su trasero* was received with varying degrees of enthusiasm. Many described reading the book as the most significant work on race they had read. Professor Magali Roy Fequere remarks, "For my part, I had never read anything like it. The book forever changed the way I would view Puerto Rican literature and culture." So despite the relatively silent responses, Zenón Cruz's work provided a small opening for looking at the issue of "race" and racism in Puerto Rico.[30]

In the late 1970s and early 1980s several works appeared that reflected both the current trends within intellectual discourse and the fortunes and contradictions of the social movements and political culture(s) of Puerto Ricans in Puerto Rico and the United States. This period marks the decline of the anti-systemic movements that emerged during the 1960s and 1970s. The independence movement and the left began a decline in strength and influence, from which it would not recover. By the first half of the eighties

most of the political organizations that made up the organized Puerto Rican left had fragmented or ceased to exist altogether.

During this period three works stand out as the most significant with respect to "race" and Puerto Rican identity. One of the works, authored by the writer José Luis González, created a great deal of controversy and debate within the independence movement left, the literary intelligentsia, and a broad range of cultural elites in the island, reminiscent of the response to Zenón Cruz's book five years earlier. *El país de cuatro pisos* addressed the question of race/identity within the framework of the "national question."[31] The privileging of the African in the historical process of the making of Puerto Rican identity/nationality proved the most provocative dimension of his thesis. According to González: "It is by now a commonplace to assert that this culture has three historical roots: the Taino Indian, the African, and the Spanish. What isn't however a commonplace – in fact just the opposite – is to say that of these three roots the one that is most important, for economic and social – and hence cultural – reasons, is the African."[32]

Once again, the polemics greeting this work went to great pains to argue that Puerto Rico is a country not divided by "race," and that what existed was a people who were basically Hispanic in heritage and culture. The status of the African and the indigenous people, the Taino, in the making of the Puerto Rican nation was subordinate to its European component. Puerto Ricans, while a racially "mixed" or "mulatto" people, were culturally European.[33]

Another important statement made during the 1970s was Angela Jorge's "The Black Puerto Rican Woman in Contemporary American Society," which appeared in an anthology on Puerto Rican women.[34] Here was a rare attempt to look at the way in which "race" intersects with gender in the case of Puerto Rican women. The question of racism, both within the Puerto Rican community and in the US, and its impact on black Puerto Rican women are explored via Jorge's personal observations and reflections as a black Puerto Rican woman. The psychological stress resulting from the denial of blackness is highlighted by Jorge; the social and sexual dimensions of black female devaluation is also reflected upon.

Unlike previous attempts to grapple with the question of race and racism among Puerto Ricans, the position of the author as a black Puerto Rican woman assumes a central place. It is seen as important to conveying the first-hand experience of the social and psychological impact of "race"/racism within Puerto Rican society, the diasporic community, and the US. Jorge also addresses how relations between Puerto Rican men and women and among other groups are structured by race, as the possible choices for intimate relations are racially circumscribed.

The reception to this article among Puerto Ricans in the US varied. The public "washing of dirty laundry" made some very uncomfortable. It was argued that racism was an external problem and that any attempt to discuss it was destructive for Puerto Rican unity. Others, notably black Puerto Rican women, received the article as a breath of fresh air. However, for the most part, the piece was met with a stony silence. In Puerto Rico the reception of the article was, to say the least, extremely limited, as the article was not included in the Spanish language version of the book published on the Island.

Another important work appearing a year after Jorge's article is Juan Flores' *Insularismo e ideología burguesa.*[35] This book critiqued an essentialized Eurocentric version of Puerto Rican identity, articulated most forcefully in the 1930s by Antonio S. Pedreira in his classic statement on the subject, *Insularismo* (1934). In this book Pedreira's Hispanic conceptualization of Puerto Rican cultural identity, his denigration of Black people as constituting an inferior "race," and his racial determinism as the central organizing principle in his writing are critiqued by Flores from within a Marxist tradition.

The responses to Flores' book were somewhat different than those which greeted previous attempts to criticize racial hierarchy and Hispanophile conceptualizations of Puerto Rican culture and society. The book won the Cuban Primio de Ensayo de Casa de las Américas in January 1979, and it was published in Spanish by Ediciones Huracán that same year. However, despite the enthusiasm on the part of the Cubans, in Puerto Rico the book does not appear to have had the same impact that the work of Zenón Cruz or José Luis González had generated.[36]

## Reflecting on the second moment

The literature produced during this second moment of discursive production represented a genuine advance over the literature on Puerto Ricans and "race" generated by the US mainstream academic and policy institutions. "Race" and racism was directly confronted and named, breaking the polite silence imposed by hegemonic ideopolitical and sociocultural forces. The existence of racism in Puerto Rican society, the role of the African in Puerto Rican history and culture, the gendered dimension of Puerto Rican racial experience, and the ideological roots of Eurocentrism in the Puerto Rican context were brought into sharp relief. The central coordinate of ethnicity was abandoned in favor of the differing notions of *lo nacional.* Puerto Ricans writing in the US sought to connect with Puerto Rico as part of a strategy to overcome the discourse on ethnic groups that marked Puerto Ricans as a "minority" and as pathological. These counter-hegemonic ideological currents resonated within the US-based independence movement and other anti-systemic and reformist movements that Puerto Ricans created and participated in. The writings of different currents within Marxism and Third World revolutionary currents, together with the theoretical and political statements elaborated by the Black Power movements, formed an important part of the discourse of the period for Puerto Ricans in the diaspora.

In Puerto Rico the different sectors of the independence left generated its own ideological matrix from some of the same sources that informed Puerto Ricans in the US in addition to ideopolitical traditions of the nationalist movements from previous decades. The question of "race" and racism proves difficult and problematic within the context of an anti-colonial struggle based on a nationalist imaginary that denied or subordinated the significance of the African, and denied or subordinated the question of racism as it existed within Puerto Rican society.

## THIRD MOMENT: OBFUSCATING RACIAL FORMATION AND SIGNIFICATION

Since the 1980s, the efforts of Puerto Ricans to analyze "race" has tended to occur within traditional "objective" social sciences and are not linked in any significant way with the social movements of recent decades. Most contemporary writing eschews the polemical style and the sense of political commitment typical of the literature generated by the social movements of the 1960s and 1970s, and much of it is produced by individuals located within the US academy.

The writings of Clara Rodríguez on Puerto Ricans and ethnic/racial identity have come to dominate the way in which the subject is treated.[37] In this work we can see a return to some of the elements of the ethnic/race paradigm elaborated in the 1960s, combined with elements of the "counter-hegemonic" discourses elaborated in opposition to mainstream conceptualizations. This eclectic approach can most clearly be seen in Rodríguez's book *Puerto Ricans Born in the U.S.A.*, in particular the chapter "The Rainbow People," which has become the most cited text on the subject since its appearance in 1989.[38]

### The "Rainbow People" thesis

In reviewing this recent work on Puerto Ricans and race one is struck by the fact that its basic propositions harken back to earlier formulations. In 1974, Clara E. Rodríguez published what was to be the first of several attempts to address the question of Puerto Rican ethnic and racial identity in the United States. In "Puerto Ricans: Between Black and White," Rodríguez presents a thesis which will remain central to her late arguments:

> Perhaps the primary point of contrast is that, in Puerto Rico, racial identification is subordinate to cultural identification, while in the U.S., racial identification, to a large extent, determines cultural identification. Thus when asked the divisive question, "What are you?" Puerto Ricans of all colors and ancestry answer, "Puerto Rican," while most New Yorkers answer, Black, Jewish, or perhaps, "of Italian descent." This is not to say that Puerto Ricans feel no racial identification, but rather that cultural identification supersedes it.[39]

This argument is repeated, nearly verbatim, 15 years later in "The Rainbow People" when she states the following:

> Perhaps the primary point of contrast was that, in Puerto Rico, racial identification was subordinate to cultural identification, while in the United States, racial identification, to a large extent, determined cultural identification. Thus Puerto Ricans were first Puerto Rican, then *blanco/a* (white), *moreno/a* (dark), and so on, while Americans were first white or black, then Italian, Irish, West Indian, or whatever. This is not to say that Puerto Ricans did not have a racial identification, but rather that cultural identification superseded it.[40]

For Puerto Ricans, then, "racial identification was subordinate to cultural identification," and for other groups "racial identification, to a large extent, determined cultural identification." It bears mentioning that Rodríguez is not the only author who asserts the primacy of cultural over racial identification. In 1974, sociologist John F. Longres, Jr published an article titled "Racism and Its Effects on Puerto Rican Continentals"[41] in which he asserts: "In Puerto Rico, the primary source of self-identity is culture or class, not color. Unlike the United States, subgroup identities do not involve considerations of color."[42]

A problem with this formulation is that "cultural identification" is never clearly defined. Is "cultural identification" a reference to an "ethnic" or national identification? Do Puerto Ricans at all times and in all places identify culturally or "ethnically" before identifying racially? It seems rather, that there can be a great deal of variation in the self-identification of a single Puerto Rican, including more than one racial or "cultural" identification. Puerto Ricans in the US have historically had a number of different racial identifications, which result from the racial formation that takes place in diasporic conditions linked to colonialism. It is important to note that the mass migration which racialized the migrants was undertaken by the darker peoples of the global South.

### The census as measure of racial identification: mis-measuring Puerto Ricans and/or "race"

The work of Clara Rodríguez is marked by a reliance upon classificatory schemas. The categories employed by the US Census for Puerto Ricans and the analysis of Puerto Rican responses to this classificatory schema is the central empirical basis for her analysis of Puerto Rican racial self-identification. There are a number of problems with this approach.

First, the conceptual basis for the categorization of human beings in the census is accepted with little reservation. There is no thought given to the origins of classificatory schemes or their functions historically or in the present. The classifying of "natural types" and the typologies of "natural races" emerged simultaneously in what Michel Foucault called the Classical epistime.[43] [44]

A further problem is the way in which Rodríguez sees the responses by Puerto Ricans to census categories as signifying racial ambivalence. She does not explore how Puerto Ricans may understand the classifica-

tions provided by the census and how they are framed within a system of signification. A certain common-sense understanding as to the responses given by Puerto Ricans is operative in this analysis. In other words, the results are taken to speak for themselves. Rodríguez concedes that there may need to be a greater refinement of the census, or any other instrument used for classifying or measuring self-identification. However, the possibility that the very act of identification constitutes a problem is never acknowledged.

### Negotiating the medical/scientific discourse

Puerto Ricans have negotiated the racialization process inherent in the diaspora experience in a variety of ways over time. One of the common ways in which this is done is by deployment of a national identity in an effort to escape identification as black or as non-white. The identification as Puerto Rican first, which the "rainbow people" thesis presents as evidence for the primacy of "cultural identification," is not itself racially neutral. The negation of racial identification, while potentially representing resistance, relies on an identification that is itself racially constituted. The Puerto Rican nation, as we noted above, has been represented as both white and male. Conversely, in the global context in which national identification occurs, Puerto Rican nationality is identified by the globally hegemonic as non-white. The attempt to deploy a national identity as a shield against racialization collapses on two fronts. Evidence of this is the continued identification of Puerto Ricans as non-white, e.g., as "spics" or as Black – in other words, the dark Other – by state ideological apparatuses and in the mass media.[45] At another level the resistance to racial identification is itself based on the acceptance of a racializing logic. This resistance does not undermine racial signification; rather, "race" or blackness is a quality of the "otro Other." The identification of a person as Puerto Rican may serve as a means of identifying that person as non-black, not as a way of identifying as non-white. The hierarchical normative value of "whiteness" is not questioned, much less undermined in this negotiation of identity. Another instance in which Puerto Ricans have contested racialization on its own terms has been in response to the racialized discourse on hygiene.

The racist inscription of impurity, uncleanliness, and disease onto the bodies of the colonial dark Other can be observed historically and in contemporary life. Puerto Ricans have been depicted as insects, carriers of tuberculosis and AIDS, creators of dirty slums, etc. Much of this discourse has its origins in the medical professions as they evolved during the nineteenth century and their linkage to the colonial enterprise. The history of immigration offers a clear example of the nexus of medical science, racialization and state power. Alan M. Kraunt makes the following observation:

> The reciprocal influence of immigration and public health in the United States stands at a busy cultural and social intersection, where at least four significant themes converge to shape the relationship. The first theme is the relationship among health, disease, and nativism, those prejudices and policies that express opposition to the foreign-born. The medicalization of preexisting nativist prejudices occurs when the justification for excluding members of a particular group includes charges that they constitute a health menace and may endanger their hosts. While some members of an immigrant group may or may not have a contagious disease that can cause others to become sick, the entire group is stigmatized by medical nativism, each newcomer being reduced from " a whole and useful person to a tainted, discounted one," because of association with disease in the mind of the native-born. Thus there is a fear of contamination from the foreign-born.[46]

The discourse which this produced on Puerto Ricans and hygiene is part of a medicalized vision of racial Otherness. At the level of everyday popular racist discourse Puerto Ricans and other groups have been described as "dirty spics," "greasy Porto Ricans," etc. Puerto Ricans often respond by claiming hygienic practices as inherent to Puerto Rican culture. "We are clean. White people are the dirty ones. Have you ever been in a white person's house? It's so dirty . . . *parece que nunca limpian!*," are some common assertions. Some representations of the Puerto Rican home attest to a near fetishistic preoccupation with cleanliness and hygiene. In the play "Las Ventanas" by Roberto Rodríguez Suárez, which depicts life in a poor Puerto Rican neighborhood in New York City, one of the characters remarks on the obsessive cleanliness of another character and how the dominant racist culture identifies and devalues Puerto Ricans:

> *Alejandra*: ( . . . ) Miren al Goyo limpiando la calle, pa' que los gringos no digan que los "espiques" somos unos puercos . . . Usted no sabe lo que tenemos que pasar aquí, don Juan. Dicen que somos basura, que las mujeres son toas unas putas, que los hombres son tos mirihuaneros y cortadores de cara . . . Y dicen que la venérea está regá por toa la cuidad proque y que la trajeron los puertorriqueños. Y en un anuncio de la tienda Kassay, de esos que salen en los periódicos, decía que había llegado el producto pa' matar cucarachas puertorriqueñas.[47]

This preoccupation with hygiene is not a simple response to medicalized racial signification and its popular deployments in the US. Dating from the later part of the nineteenth century in Puerto Rico, a discourse on cleanliness and hygiene evolved in the multiple social struggles that took place between the popular classes and the Creole and colonial elites. Central to many of these struggles was the battle over public space between Black domestic workers and urban administrators. When the Spanish authorities launched campaigns in the name of improving public hygiene, their actual goals were the regulation of public space and the control of domestic workers, many of whom were Black women.[48] One can see an intensification of such campaigns following the US invasion of 1898. The US colonization of Puerto Rico involved the implantation of a new regime. Part of this process meant seeing the colonized as pathological and diseased colonial body, requiring the implementation of social hygiene technologies.[49] Therefore, Puerto Ricans who migrated had already been subjected to a medically sanctioned racial discourse in Puerto Rico.

The "rainbow people" thesis does not view such negotiations as a discursive continuum on "race" and the body, but rather as evidence of the incompatibility of racial paradigms between Puerto Rico's racial order and that of the US. Thus it is claimed that since the racial hierarchies in Puerto Rico and the United States have been historically constituted differently, Puerto Ricans would experience a "clash" when confronted with US society: "Given the experiences Puerto Ricans brought with them, and given the US racial context they entered, there was bound to be a clash as the North American system was superimposed on the rainbow people."[50] The main issue for Rodríguez is the misunderstanding of race that Puerto Ricans bring with them to that of the United States, which she identifies as infinitely harsher than that which operates in Puerto Rico in particular, the Caribbean and Latin America generally. The notion of "clash" also implies a psychological dimension resulting from encountering a different racial paradigm which results in a "perceptual dissonance."[51]

As evidence of this difference, she asserts that unlike the United States, which is multiethnic and biracial, Puerto Rico is a culturally homogeneous, racially integrated society:

> Although not without strong class differences, the society in Puerto Rico is basically culturally homogeneous and racially integrated. This contrasts with the more biracial, multiethnic society that has historically existed in the United States. While in the United States ethnic-racial minorities have traditionally been segregated, in Puerto Rico, Blacks were not a distinguishable ethnic group. This is not to say Blacks were

evenly distributed throughout the social structure, for there is still debate on this issue. Nor is it to say that Blacks in Puerto Rico were treated in all regards exactly as Whites. But in terms of housing, institutional treatment, political rights, government policy, and cultural identification, it appears that black, white and tan Puerto Ricans were not treated differently.[52]

Professor Rodríguez qualifies her statement a few pages later:

> These descriptions of differing racial ambiances in New York and Puerto Rico should not be taken to mean that Puerto Rico is the ideal racial environment. Indeed, some authors argue that 'Puerto Ricans seem to have developed a Creole ethos tolerant of the mulatto group . . . but scornful of the black sector' (Duany, 1985: 30; see also Zenón Cruz, 1975; Longres, 1974: 68 ff.). Betances (1972) argues that the general lack of concern with racial issues on the island constitutes for some 'the prejudice of no prejudice.' He argues that claiming that there is not prejudice may in itself be a prejudicial act. But, 'if racism can be seen in term of degree, then obviously there is much less racism in Puerto Rico than in the United States' (Longres, 1974: 68). This was the situation from which Puerto Ricans came.[53]

These two statements would seem to be at odds with each other, though the relative brevity of the second proposition on "prejudice" in Puerto Rico seems to support the contention that racism in Puerto Rico does not exist. Or rather, while racism in the Puerto Rican context may exist, the issue is one of degree. How should this contradiction be understood? Above all, Rodríguez seems to want to have her cake and eat it too. Racism as a concealed fact in Puerto Rican society is acknowledged but simultaneously subordinated in significance to that of racism in the US.

The larger implications of the "rainbow people" notion for US sociology are suggested in Rodríguez's assertion that "the irony was that Puerto Ricans represented the ideal of the American melting pot ideology – a culturally unified, racially integrated people."[54] Similarly Longres Jr claims that Puerto Ricans are "a culturally homogeneous and racially integrated and mixed group."[55] Here we see the redeployment of a long-standing myth concerning the ways in which "race" and racism are experienced by Puerto Ricans in Puerto Rico. The putative absence of hard and fast racial discrimination and racial violence is equated with a softer and more benign racial order. Puerto Rico's racial order, although not perfect since Blacks are not at all treated the same as Whites, is nevertheless superior, since institutionalized racism and cultural belonging are not significant questions within Puerto Rican society. Indeed if Americans could learn from the case of Puerto Rico, Glazer and Moynihan's "melting pot" could become a reality in the US.

### Overlooking race in contemporary Puerto Rico

Another dimension to the "rainbow people" thesis is that it does not concern itself with the present state of affairs with respect to race in Puerto Rico. The few references to Puerto Rico and "race" are not recent ones, and one has the impression that it is not a significant issue in contemporary Puerto Rico. However, an observation that does not comply with the imposed silence on "race" in Puerto Rican politics or culture might draw quite different conclusions.

The statehood party's cynical support for such a class and race marked musical form as "Plena"; the continued existence of blackface comedy on Puerto Rican television; the conflict throughout the 1980s between youth who defined themselves according to musical preference, the *cocolos* favoring *salsa* and Latin-Caribbean music generally, and the *rockeros* favoring rock and roll and US popular music generally; the racist jokes and discrimination against Dominican immigrants on the island; and more recently, the controversies over rap music are only some of the more glaring

instances in which "race" remains salient in Puerto Rican society.[56] Recently Kelvin Santiago-Valles has analyzed the convergence of poverty, "race," and criminalization, arguing that as social polarization increases and "law and order" is demanded by a broad spectrum of the island's political class and by the colonial state, the racialization of the spaces in which illegal activities occurs is intensified. Within Puerto Rican society crime and criminal activity is increasingly imagined as that which is committed by non-whites.[57]

Thus, insofar as "race" is a problem in Puerto Rico today, it is a problem for Black Puerto Ricans. Understood in another way, blackness is a problem. The Creole dream of *blanqueamiento* (whitening) or *mejorando la raza* (improving the race) is hampered by the continued existence of the Other Puerto Rican – that is, *el Puertorriqueño negro*. The presence of Black Puerto Ricans and the history of racial formation in Puerto Rico will continue to frustrate the Creole racialist fantasy of exorcising the African dimension of Puerto Rican identity.

### Racial formation in the US: undermining the "one drop rule"

As for its view of the US, the "rainbow people" thesis relies on the formula of the "one drop rule" – "one drop of black blood makes you black." Yet, the racialization of Irish, Italian and Jewish immigrants who were identified as non-white Others was not based on the one drop rule but rather directly related to racialization processes linked to power and domination on both sides of the Atlantic. Similarly, the attempt to establish the corollary "Over there one drop of blood makes you black. Here [in Puerto Rico], one drop of white blood makes you white" becomes untenable.[58]

It is clear that the "rainbow people" thesis is not informed by an awareness of the actual histories of racial formation either in Puerto Rico or the US. Furthermore, it does not seek to problematize these racial constructions.

This allows for Puerto Ricans, and other groups who are defined as racial others, to be defined against a normative and naturalized whiteness. Whiteness is never questioned or interrogated, rather it is the non-disclosed dominant identity. The dependence on the ethnic paradigm elaborated by American pluralists in the construction of the "rainbow people" thesis is obvious in the description of the US racial order. For Clara Rodríguez, there is a repression of ethnicity rooted in a fear of Otherness: "the fear of 'difference' has been a central, recurring phenomenon."[59] In fact US history is conceived of as "ethnic" history with European immigrants experiencing an ethnic whiteness.[60] Here Rodríguez, while claiming distance from the earlier formulations on Puerto Ricans as an ethnic group, subscribes to an ethnic group model in order to understand social hierarchy in the United States.

In Rodríguez's writing the terms "ethnic" or "ethnicity" are employed as signifying a distinct identity separate from any notion of "race." On other occasions this distinction is not at all clear. Puerto Ricans are viewed as both an ethnic group and as a racial group. Such imprecision in defining and employing concepts and categories makes for a murky picture of the Puerto Ricans' subordinate insertion into US society. It would appear that the failure of Puerto Ricans to achieve integration and upward mobility, as explained by the "rainbow people" thesis, is the result of the contradiction between the ethnic group model for advancement and the problem posed by race. Puerto Ricans, at once claimed as an "ethnic" group and as a "mixed" racial group, find difficulty advancing in accordance with the ethnic group model since the system of racial ordering precludes advancement for non-whites.

However, a number of questions arise once this duality is asserted. How accurate is it to claim that Puerto Ricans are an ethnic group, given that the history of Puerto Rican migration to the US does not resemble that of European immigrants, which is what the ethnic relations model is based on? Moreover, the explanatory strength of the ethnic model falters when the actual history of European migration is critically examined. In fact, contrary to Rodríguez's assertion, racial hierarchies in Puerto Rico are actually less fluid than previously imagined. In addition, US racialization processes appear less static than simplistic Black–White dichotomies allow for. Very suggestive for re-examining the history of European immigration and claims on white American national identity is the notion of "inbetweenness" and "not-yet-white," which Orsi and Roediger employ in examining the racial histories of Italian and Irish immigrants in the US.[61] In the case of Puerto Ricans and other racialized groups the actual relations of power between the sending country and the US must be explored and compared. As E. San Juan Jr argues:

> Concrete investigation of various historical conjunctures is needed to answer how the reproduction of social relations operate through race insofar as capitalism, for example, articulates classes in distinct ways at each level (economic, political, ideological) of the social formation. In effect, the schematics of race and its use to ascribe values, allocate resources, and legitimize the social position/status of racially defined populations (in short, racism) centrally affect the constitution of the fractions of black, Asian, or Hispanic labor as a class.[62]

In this context it should also be pointed out that while colonialism is mentioned in an earlier section of *Puerto Ricans Born in the U.S.A.*, it does not figure in the section on "race" as at all significant in the process of racial formation or signification. Does the fact that Puerto Ricans are colonial migrants determine their insertion into the US system of racial hierarchy? Obviously not, if one is employing the ethnic model, which does not recognize colonialism as part of the structuring of discursive and material power in Western capitalist democracies such as the US.[63] The ethnic model, as elaborated by Gunnar Myrdal in 1944, and traditional American structural-functionalist sociology, which informs Professor Rodríguez's analysis of "race" in the US, eschews relations of power as determinant.[64]

By obfuscating and distorting the history of racial hierarchy in Puerto Rico the "rainbow people" thesis confuses the different ways by which Puerto Ricans experience the different racializing processes inherent in the migratory process over time. In the same measure, the thesis also minimizes the complexity of racial formations in the US, ignoring how racial hierarchies have been historically constituted and structurally mediated. Instead, two static and historically inaccurate narratives on "race" in Puerto Rico and the US result in a culture clash whichever way they turn. Yet, does moving between racial formations entail a "clash," with its implied psychological dimensions? Or should we instead conceptualize the conflict involved with Puerto Rican self-identification as occurring within a shifting terrain of racial signification, which is then negotiated on differing terms by Puerto Ricans with heterogeneous racial identities, class positions, sexualities etc.?

### What's in a metaphor?

The "rainbow people," a metaphor intended to signify diversity and inclusion, actually works to deny hierarchy based on race. To say "rainbow people" conjures images of not only white, black, or "tan," but also green, purple, and orange, etc. Therefore the rainbow contains colors that have no correspondence with the sociopolitical construction of "race." These other colors do not have the sociocultural or political salience of "race" and help form a discourse that seeks to evade "race" as evidencing relations of power and subordination.

### At the end of the "rainbow"

The "rainbow people" thesis thus represents a turn away from the critical counter-discourses initiated in the 1970s. Reliance on an ethnic paradigm for explaining the social advancement of groups and its empiricist and neopositivist methodological approach link it to the first moment, that is, to the mainstream conceptualizations articulated during the 1960s by liberal and neoliberal academics and public policy analysts. In addition, the mere numeration of social statistics and the mention of colonialism do not add up to a radical critique of imperialism or of a racialized capitalist hierarchy. Moreover, the coincidence of this discourse on "race" in Puerto Rico with that of the Creole mythology of racial harmony also brings it in line with the continuing conspiracy of silence in the Island.

That Puerto Ricans encounter a differently constituted racial field when they migrate to the US is logically consistent. However, this movement, and the racialization inherent in it, must be rigorously examined and analyzed. That Puerto Ricans are not easily contained within the classificatory schemes established in the US by the census or by other state or private agencies is not evidence of an undermining of US racial hierarchy or systems of signification. As long as the concept of "race" remains unchallenged there is no possibility of challenging racial signification. The conceptualizing of Puerto Ricans as a "rainbow people," somehow standing between "black/white," elides what "blackness" or "whiteness" means for Puerto Ricans in the US or in Puerto Rico. Given the concealed, hegemonic status of "whiteness" there is no deconstruction of how "race" is invented – "blackness" becomes the heart of the problem of "race relations."[65] Notions of being "tan" or *café con leche* (coffee and milk) explains little of what it means to be a "racially mixed" Puerto Rican, since the meaning of what is contained or excluded in the "mix" is again obscured.

At the end of the "rainbow," we do not find a theorization which can capture the complexities of Puerto Rican racial formation and signification. The problem of "difference," and "race" has been theorized in an ahistorical and reductionist fashion, which has resulted in a failure to visualize how Puerto Ricans re-articulate what constitutes "race" through such supposed difference. This re-articulation demands a renewed intellectual vision that goes beyond linear and binary thinking, and relies on the functionalist and empiricist methodology that has dominated social theory in the US.

## A FOURTH MOMENT?

Since the mid-1980s in there has begun to emerge a new discourse on "race" and racism. The work of Stuart Hall, Omi and Winant, Alexander Saxton, David Roediger, Theo Goldberg, E. San Juan Jr, Theodore Allen, and Anne McClintock has begun, from different perspectives, to analyze the socially constructed nature of "race" through sociohistorical, textual, and philosophical treatments. Much of the impulse for this new theorization has come from different intellectual traditions, e.g., Marxism, structuralism, postmodernism, post-colonial theory, etc. Similarly a number of Puerto Rican intellectuals drawing from these intellectual currents have begun to address the question of Puerto Rican racial identity. This new body of work shares with the above-mentioned authors a concern with how "race" is socially constructed and rooting this process in a rigorous reconstruction of historical and structural processes. Coloniality, imperialism, and other forces of domination and subjugation are central to this reconstruction, as is the critical examination of the conceptual tools and categories employed in this undertaking. In addition to the above intellectual project(s) there are also a number of academics and students who eclectically draw from the works of the different moments mapped in this article, but in the final instance tend toward the formulations identified in the "rainbow people" conceptualization.

The existence of these two different intellectual trajectories will make for an increasingly complex and contested ideopolitical terrain in the years to come. The debates that will emanate between these, and perhaps other, tendencies point toward a new moment in the discourse on Puerto Ricans and "race." This new moment promises to be both an advance over earlier formulations and revealing of other problematic issues and themes.

## Notes

1  Ralph Ellison, *Shadow and Act* (New York: Random House, 1964), p. 123.

2  Of course, there have been earlier efforts, both in Puerto Rico and the United States, to address the issue of Puerto Ricans and "race." I hope to analyze this earlier body of writing in the future. Some examples of this literature include José Celso Barbosa, *Problemas de Razas* (San Juan, Puerto Rico: Imprenta Venezuela, 1937); Tomás Blanco, *Prejuicio Racial en Puerto Rico* (San Juan, Bibliotecà de Autores Puertorriqueños, 1942); Charles Rogler, "The Morality of Race Mixing in Puerto Rico," *Social Forces*, 25, (October, 1946); Joseph P. Fitzpatrick, "Attitude of Puerto Ricans Toward Color," *American Catholic Sociological Review*, 20/3 (1959); and Edwardo Seda Bonilla, "Social Structure and Race Relations," *Social Forces*, 40/2 (December 1961).

3  Ivan Hannaford, *Race: The History of an Idea in the West* (Baltimore, MD: Johns Hopkins University Press, 1995).

4  Nathan Glazer and Daniel Patrick Moynihan, *Beyond the Melting Pot*, 2nd edn (Cambridge MA: MIT Press, 1970). The first edition of *Beyond the Melting Pot* received the Anisfield-Wolf Award in Race Relations. Like *La Vida, Beyond the Melting Pot* has become part of the established canon within the liberal tradition in the social sciences.

5  Oscar Lewis, *La Vida: A Puerto Rican Family in the Culture of Poverty – San Juan and New York* (New York: Vintage Books, 1966). A runaway bestseller, *La Vida* won the National Book Award for nonfiction in 1967. Lewis' work is perhaps the most cited study of Puerto Ricans in traditional social sciences.

6  In the tradition of Oscar Lewis see Philippe Bourgois, *In Search of Respect: Selling Crack in El Barrio* (Cambridge: Cambridge University Press, 1995). For a critical review of Bourgois see Adam Shatz, "Among the Dispossessed," *Nation* (December 25, 1995), pp. 836–9.

7  Oscar Handlin, *The Newcomers: Negroes and Puerto Ricans in a Changing Metropolis*

(Cambridge, MA: Harvard University Press, 1959).

8    The viewing of Puerto Ricans as a problem follows a tradition within US social science which views the very existence of different racial/ethnic groups as itself constituting a problem. The mere presence of diverse groups is seen as giving rise to conflict generated by cultural difference. For a representative statement, see T.J. Woofter, *Races and Ethnic Groups in American Life* (New York and London: McGraw-Hill, 1933).

9    For a critique of the ethnic paradigm on "race" see Hermon George, Jr, *American Race Relations Theory: A Review of Four Models* (Lanham, NY and London: University Press of America, 1984), pp. 1–48.

10   Andrés Torres, *Between Melting Pot and Mosaic: African Americans and Puerto Ricans in the New York Political Economy* (Philadelphia: Temple University Press, 1995).

11   Today there is a tendency on the part of much of the writings on Puerto Ricans to contrast and compare this experience to that of other Hispanics/Latinos, ignoring the historical relationship with African Americans and other members of the Caribbean/African diaspora. This has tended to blur the similarities between African Americans and Puerto Ricans on a number of levels.

12   The African diaspora is not represented by a straight line from Africa to the US, but rather encompasses the African continent, Europe, the Americas, and the complex world of the Caribbean. In *The Black Atlantic: Modernity and Double Consciousness* (Cambridge, MA: Harvard University Press, 1993), Paul Gilroy has referred to the field of meaning created out of this diaspora as the Black Atlantic. Puerto Rico, together with Cuba and the Dominican Republic, is part of the world which Gilroy has begun to "re-imagine," although his limited knowledge of the Spanish-speaking Caribbean has tended to obscure his efforts. A consideration of this syncretic culture, described by Alejo Carpentier as Baroque, would enhance and further complicate Gilroy's Black Atlantic. For a work which presents the complexity of the Caribbean world in iconoclastic and suggestive ways, see Antonio Benítez-Rojo, *The Repeating Island: The Caribbean and the Postmodern Perspective* (Durham, NC and London: Duke University Press, 1992). On Alejo Carpentier's notion of the Baroque, see

Roberto González Echevarría, *Alejo Carpentier: The Pilgrim At Home* (Austin, TX: University of Texas Press, 1990).

13   Histories of the Puerto Rican communities in New York City and Chicago have inexplicably declined to examine this question. See Virginia Sánchez-Korrol, *From Colonia to Community: The History of Puerto Ricans in New York City*, 2nd edn (Berkeley: University of California Press, 1994); and Félix M. Padilla, *Puerto Rican Chicago* (Notre Dame, IN: University of Notre Dame Press, 1987). However, one can find a few journalistic pieces that attempt to explore this relationship. See Barbara Omolade and Angelo Falcón "Black/Latino Politics . . . Black/Latino Communities," *Puerto Rico Libre* (Summer, 1985), pp. 18–23.

14   In the introduction to Allon Schoener (ed.), *Harlem On My Mind: Cultural Capital of Black America*, (New York: Random House, 1968), p. 4, the argument is made that in their relations with Puerto Ricans, "Blacks are left with only three choices – fight them, ignore them or welcome them." The author betrays an incredible ignorance of the contact between African Americans and Puerto Ricans. In addition, such options never present themselves in such neat terms or as options at all. Rather, contact between groups is mediated by historical forces, structural arrangements, and the agency of different collectivities and individuals.

15   For a representative example of the perspective that African American and Puerto Rican relations are antagonistic and inevitably competitive, see Julio Morales, *Puerto Rican Poverty and Migration: We Just Had to Try Elsewhere* (New York: Praeger, 1986), pp. 45–61. More recently this framework has been extended by liberal analysts looking at the relations between African Americans and Latinos in general. See Jack Miles, "Blacks vs. Browns," *Atlantic Monthly* (October, 1992), pp. 51–60, and Jerry Yaffe, "Prospects and Barriers to Successful Latino and African-American Coalitions," *Harvard Journal of Hispanic Policy*, 8 (1994–5), pp. 61–86.

16   For accounts of the life of Schomburg, see Victoria Ortiz, "Arturo A. Schomburg: A Biographical Essay" in *The Legacy of Arthur A. Schomburg: A Celebration of the Past, A Vision for the Future* (New York: New York Public Library, 1986); and Elinor Des Verney Sinnette, *Arthur Alfonso Schomburg: Black*

*Bibliophile and Collector* (Detroit: New York Public Library and Wayne State University Press, 1989).

17 This national identity is further complicated if we contextualize it within the ambiance of Black nationalism in Harlem. Many of the Black activists before the Second World War were immigrants from English-speaking Caribbean countries. Pan-Africanism was articulated by intellectuals from the Caribbean who had immigrated to New York City. With the decline of the nineteenth-century *independentista* movement in Puerto Rico, the most vibrant political movement in New York City was that of labor, which was connected with Socialist and Communist parties and the Black nationalist movements. The best known of the latter is the movement led by Marcus Garvey. This was, in part, the ideopolitical context in which Schomburg, a Black Puerto Rican concerned with documenting the African contribution to world history, found himself. The Caribbean connection in the emergence of Pan-Africanism is probably not irrelevant for understanding his turn, together with the Hispanophilic and Eurocentric racism in Puerto Rican society and in diaspora. Moreover, Schomburg, a believer in the notion of an intellectual-class leadership, or "talented tenth," possessed class aspirations that could not be realized within the small Puerto Rican community made up mostly of workers.

18 While a number of interesting studies have appeared on the role of African Americans within the Communist Party and the its role within the Black community, there has not been any major exploration of the Puerto Rican presence within the party or of its activities within Puerto Rican communities such as Harlem's East Harlem. For treatment of the Communist Party's relation with African Americans see Mark Naison, *Communists in Harlem During the Depression* (Chicago: University of Illinois Press, 1983); Robin D. G. Kelly, *Hammer and Hoe: Alabama Communists During the Great Depression* (Chapel Hill, NC, and London: University of North Carolina Press, 1990); and Earl Ofari Hutchinson, *Blacks and Reds, Race and Class in Conflict 1919–19909* (East Lansing: Michigan State University, 1995).

19 César Andreu Iglesias (ed.), *Memoirs of Bernardo Vega: A Contribution To The History Of*

*The Puerto Rican Community in New York* (New York and London: Monthly Review Press, 1984), p. 3. In the Spanish-language original, Vega's text explicitly links "whiteness" to a masculine national identity: "Jíbaro de la montaña, era blanco, y en mi rostro había un matiz de cera, característico de los hombres del corazón de nuestra patria." César Andreu Iglesias (ed.), *Memorias de Bernardo Vega* (Rio Piedras, Ediciones Huracán, 1977), p. 37.

20 For an interesting memoir on being a white Cuban growing up in Ybor City in the 1930s see Ferdie Pacheco, *Ybor City Chronicles: A Memoir* (Gainesville: University Press of Florida, 1994), pp. 1–26.

21 Antonia Pantoja migrated to the US in the postwar era and was a key member of the generation of the 1950s and 1960s known as the "Young Turks." Piri Thomas is best known for his coming-of-age autobiography *Down These Mean Streets*, published in 1967 by Vintage Books. For an interesting reading of this work relevant to the above discussion, see Marta S. Sanchez, "Revisiting Binaries of Race and Gender: Piri Thomas' *Down These Mean Streets* and the Construction of the Puerto Rican Ethnic Nationalist Subject," 1996 (unpublished paper). Pablo "Yoruba" Guzmán was a leader of the Young Lords Party in New York City during the late 1960s and early 1970s. In his own account of his political education, Guzmán credits the political movement of the African American people as having a major impact on his life. See Pablo Guzmán, "The Young Lords Legacy: A Personal Account" *Critica*, no. 11–12 (April–May 1995), p. 1.

22 See Louis Althusser, "Ideology and Ideological State Apparatuses" in Louis Althusser, *Lenin And Philosophy And Other Essays*, (New York and London: Monthly Review Press, 1971), pp. 127–86.

23 Juan Angel Silén, *Hàcia una visión positiva del puertorriqueño* (Rio Piedras, PR: Editorial Edil, 1970).

24 Juan Angel Silén, *We, the Puerto Rican People: A Story of Oppression and Resistance*, trans. Cedric Belfrage, (New York and London: Monthly Review Press, 1971).

25 Ibid., pp. 36–45.

26 Samuel Betances, "The Prejudice of Having No Prejudice in Puerto Rico: Parts I and II," in *the Rican* (Winter 1972 and Spring 1973) pp. 41–55, 22–37.

27 This assessment is based on discussions with

a number of activists and intellectuals active during the period. There did not appear to be much response to the article in writing at the time. However, it has been one of the most frequently quoted articles on the subject.

28   Isabelo Zenón Cruz, *Narciso descubre su trasero: el negro en la cultura Puertorriqueña* (Humacao, PR: Editorial Furidi, 1974).

29   Juán Antonio Corretjer, "El libro de Isabelo Zenón," *El Nuevo Dia* (February 14, 1975), p. 21; Ernesto Reques, "¡Negro no, incierto!" *Claridad* (February 28, 1975), p. 14; Wilfredo Mattos Cintrón, "Racismo e ideologia," *Poder Estudiantial* (February 19–March 5, 1975), p. 9; Cesar Andreu Iglesias, "El Narciso de Zenón," *Avance* (February 17, 1995), p. 17; Mariano Muñoz Hernández, "Racismo e imperialismo en Puerto Rico," *Claridad, En Rojo* (May 1, 1995), p. 11; Juan Cepero, "¿Negro Puertorriqueño o Puertorriqueño Negro?", *El Mundo* (March 23, 1975), p. 10; Juan Silén, "Una critica y una contra-critica," *Claridad* (Marzo 27, 1995), p. 17; Luis P. Ruiz Cepero, "Los negros Boricuas," *El Nuevo Dia* (April 25, 1975), p. 23; Manuel Maldonado Denis, "El descubrimiento de Zenón," *Claridad, En Rojo* (May 24, 1975), p. 7; Jorge María Ruscalleda Bercedóniz, "Carta a Isabelo Zenón," *Claridada, En Rojo* (July 5, 1975), p. 7; Amelía Agostini de del Río, "Impresiones sobre *Narciso descubre su trasero*," *El Nuevo Dia* (October 4, 1975), p. 16; Efraín Barradas, "Narciso descubre su trasero (El negro en la cultura Puertorriqueña)" in *Sin Nombre* (July/September, 1975), 6/1, pp. 73–5; Enrique A. Laguerré, "Identidad Puertorriqueña", *El Mundo* (Noviembre 6, 1975), p. 7A; and José Luis González, "Antes y despues de Zenón," *Claridad, En Rojo* (August 16, 1976), pp. 4–5.

30   The work of Zenón Cruz was less known among Puerto Rican left activists in the US. Betances' article seems to have been the best-known account on race and Puerto Rico in the US.

31   José Luis González, *El pais de cuatro pisos y otros ensayos* (Rio Piedras: Huracan, 1980).

32   José Luis González, *Puerto Rico: The Four Storeyed Country and Other Essays* (Princeton and New York: Markus Wiener, 1993), p. 9.

33   Manuel Méndez Ballester, "Un ataque brutal" *El Nuevo Dia* (May 12, 1980), p. 21; José Luis Méndez, "La arquitectura intelectual de *El País de cuatro pisos*" *Claridad* (April 22, 1982), p. 16 and April 29, p. 23 and Manuel

Maldonado Denis, "En torno a *El país de cuatro pisos*," *Casa de las Américas*, 135 (November–December) pp. 151–9. For a sympathetic and appreciative critique see Juan Flores, "The Puerto Rico that José Luis González Built," in *Divided Borders: Essays on Puerto Rican Identity* (Houston, TX: Arte Público Press, 1993), pp. 61–70.

34   Angela Jorge, "the Black Puerto Rican Woman in Contemporary American Society," in Edna Acosta-Belen (ed.), *The Puerto Rican Woman: Perspectives on Culture, History and Society* (New York: Praeger, 1979).

35   Juan Flores, *Insularismo e ideologia burguesa* (La Habana: Casa de las Américas, 1980 and Rio Piedras: Ediciones Huracán, 1980).

36   Ramon de Armas, "Insularismo a la luz de hoy," *Casa de las Américas*, 20, no. 117 (November–December, 1979).

37   See Clara E. Rodríguez, "Puerto Ricans: Between Black and White," in Clara E. Rodríguez, Virginia Sanchez Korrol, and José Oscar Alers (eds), *The Puerto Rican Struggle: Essays on Survival in the U.S.* (Maplewood, NJ: Waterfront Press, 1980) pp. 20–30 (paper originally published in *New York Affairs*, 1/4, pp. 92–101); Clara Rodríguez, "Racial Identification among Puerto Ricans in New York," *Hispanic Journal of Behavioral Sciences*, 12/4., pp. 366–79; Clara E. Rodríguez, "Race, Culture, and Latino 'Otherness' in the 1980 Census," *Social Science Quarterly*, 73, pp. 930–7; Clara E. Rodríguez "Challenging Racial Hegemony: Puerto Ricans in the United States," in Steven Gregory and Rodger Sanjek (eds), *Race* (New Brunswick, NJ: Rutgers University Press, 1994), pp. 131–45; Clara E. Rodríguez et al., "Latino Racial Identity: in the Eye of the Beholder?", *Latino Studies Journal*, 2/3, (1991), pp. 33–48; and Clara Rodríguez and Hector Cordero-Guzman "Placing Race in Context," *Ethnic and Racial Studies*, 15/4 (October, 1992), pp. 523–42.

38   Clara Rodríguez, *Puerto Ricans Born in the USA* (Boston: Unwin Hyman, 1989), pp. 49–84.

39   Clara E. Rodríguez, "Puerto Ricans: Between Black and White," p. 21.

40   Clara E. Rodríguez, "The Rainbow People," in Clara E. Rodríguez, *Puerto Ricans Born in the USA*, p. 52.

41   John F. Longres, Jr., "Racism and Its Effects on Puerto Rican Continentals," *Social Casework* (February, 1974), pp. 67–75.

42   Ibid., p. 69.

43    Michel Foucault, *The Order of Things: An Archaeology of the Human Sciences* (New York: Vintage Books, 1970); Michel Foucault, *The Archaeology of Knowledge* (New York: Pantheon Books, 1972); and Michel Foucault, *The History of Sexuality* (New York: Vintage Books, 1978).

44    Arguing via Foucault, both Cornel West and David Theo Goldberg have attempted genealogies of modern racism – meaning here not contemporary racism so much as the racism of modernism – that link the Western fetishistic practices of classification, the forming of tables, and the consequent primacy of the visible with the creation of metaphysical and moral hierarchies between racialized hierarchies of human beings. Given this genesis, the concepts of race and racial difference emerge as that which is visible, classifiable, and morally salient. Hence, the utilization of classificatory schemas that are founded on a racialist logic. These schemas emerged as capitalist modernity expanded, and they reproduce, at least discursively, the same racial typologies.

45    See Richie Pérez, "From Assimilation to Annihilation: Puerto Rican Images in U.S. Films," *Centro*, 2/8, pp. 8–27; Blanca Vázquez, "Puerto Ricans and the Media: A Personal Statement," *Centro*, 3/1, pp. 4–15, and Alberto Sandoval Sánchez "West Side Story: A Puerto Rican Reading of "America," *Jump Cut*, 39 (1994), pp. 59–66.

46    Alan M. Kraunt, *Silent Travelers: Germs, Genes, and the "Immigrant Menace"* (New York: Basic Books, 1994), pp. 2–3.

47    "Alejandra: ( . . . ) Look at Goyo cleaning the street, so the gringos don't say that the 'spics' are pigs . . . You don't know what we have to go through here don Juan. The say that we're garbage, that the women are whores, that the men are marijuana smokers and face cutters . . . And they say VD has been spread throughout the city because Puerto Ricans brought it with them. And there is an announcement at the Kassay store, those that come out in the newspapers, it said that the product had arrived to kill Puerto Rican cockroaches." Roberto Rodriguez Suárez, *Las Ventanas* (San Juan: Instituto de Cultura Puertorriqueña, 1969) p. 204.

48    Felix V. Matos-Rodríguez, "Street Vendors, Pedlars, Shop-Owners and Domestics: Some Aspects of Women's Economic Roles in Nineteenth-Century San Juan, Puerto Rico (1820–1870)," in Verene Shepherd, Bridget Brereton, and Barbara Bailey (eds), *Engendering History: Caribbean Women in Historical Perspective* (New York: St. Martin's Press, 1995), pp. 176–93, and Yvette Rodríguez, "Las mujeres y la higiene: la construcción de 'lo social' en San Juan, 1880–1920," unpublished paper, 1995.

49    Kelvin Santiago-Valles, "On the Historical Links Between Coloniality, the Violent Production of the "Native" Body, and the manufacture of Pathology," in *Centro*, 7/1, (Winter 94–5/Spring 95), pp. 108–18.

50    Clara E. Rodríguez, "Rainbow People," p. 56.

51    Rodríguez approvingly quotes Longres, who asserts that "the experience of being seen in a way different from the way you see yourself, particularly as it pertains to race, is clearly an unsettling experience. Indeed it has often been maintained that for the migrating Puerto Rican, the experience of racial reclassification, and its attendant racism, 'frequently undermines the sense of autonomy and initiative . . . and leaves a residue of self-doubt and inadequacy.'" Clara E. Rodríguez, Ibid., p. 76. There is no question that racialization involves psychological dimensions. The work of Frantz Fanon has clearly demonstrated this. However, two questions should be posed. First, what is the nature of this psychological impact? Second, what is the psychological impact of racism on Puerto Ricans in Puerto Rico? With respect to the first question Rodríguez offers very little by way of an explanation or analysis. With respect to the second, her understanding of racism in Puerto Rico precludes this question, as we shall see later on. Thankfully, Rodríguez does not reiterate Longres' position that: "Upon arrival, Puerto Ricans find that they are viewed as a racially mixed group, which for most Puerto Ricans, means that they have been labeled black. Given the Puerto Rican orientation to color, psychological processes, although having their roots in prejudices on the island, are compounded and become destructive to mental health." Longres, "Racism and Its Effects on Puerto Rican Continentals," p. 71.

52    Clara E. Rodríguez, "Rainbow People," p. 54.

53    Ibid., p. 56.

54    Ibid., p. 49.

55    John F. Longres, Jr, "Racism and Its Effects on Puerto Rican Continentals," p. 67.

56    See the documentary by Ana María García,

*Cocolos y Roqueros*, 1994; Palmire N. Ríos, "Acercamiento al Conflicto Dominicano-Boricua," *Centro*, 4/2, pp. 44–9; and Raquel Z. Rivera, "Rap Music in Puerto Rico: Mass Consumption or Social Resistance?" *Centro*, 5/1 (Winter 1992–3), pp. 52–65.

57   Kelvin Santiago-Valles, "Vigilando, administrando y patrullando a negros y trigueños: del cuerpo del delito al delito de los cuerpos en la crisis del Puerto Rico urbano contemporáneo," *Bordes*, no. 2, pp. 28–42.

59   Clara E. Rodríguez, "Rainbow People," p. 50.

60   Ibid., p. 50.

61   Robert Orsi and David Roediger, *Towards the Abolition of Whiteness* (New York and London: Verso, 1994), pp. 181–98.

62   E. San Juan, Jr, *Racial Formations/Critical Transformations: Articulations of Power in Ethnic and Racial Studies in the United States* (New Jersey and London: Humanities Press, 1992), pp. 47–8.

63   For a recent book in the tradition of the ethnic model, which attempts, following the "rainbow people" thesis, to situate Puerto Ricans together with other groups as ethnics, see Judith Goode and Jo Anne Schneider, *Reshaping Ethnic and Racial Relations in Philadelphia: Immigrants in a Divided City* (Philadelphia: Temple University Press, 1994).

64   Gunnar Myrdal, *An American Dilemma* (New York: Harper, 1944). For a critique of this work, see Robert Blauner, *Racial Oppression in America* (New York: Harper and Row, 1972).

65   For an interesting attempt to map the invention of the white race in the US see Theodore W. Allen, *The Invention of the White Race* (New York and London: Verso, 1994).

# Chicana Artists:
# Exploring *Nepantla, el Lugar de la Frontera*

## *Gloria Anzaldúa*

I stop before the dismembered body of *la diosa de la luna*, Coyolxauhqui, daughter of Coatlicue. The warrior goddess' eyes are closed, she has bells on her cheeks, and her head is in the form of a snail design. She was decapitated by her brother, Huitzilopochtle, the Left-Handed Hummingbird. Her bones jut from their sockets. I stare at the huge round stone of *la diosa*. She seems to be pushing at the restraining orb of the moon. Though I sense a latent whirlwind of energy, I also sense a timeless stillness – one patiently waiting to explode into activity.

Here before my eyes, on the opening day of the "Aztec: The World of Moctezuma" exhibition at the Denver Museum of Natural History, is the culture of *nuestros antepasados indígenas*. I ask myself, What does it mean to me *esta jotita*, this queer Chicana, this *mexicatejana* to enter a museum and look at indigenous objects that were once used by my ancestors? Will I find my historical Indian identity here at this museum among the ancient artifacts and their *mestisaje lineage*?

As I pull out a pad to take notes on the clay, stone, jade, bone, feather, straw, and cloth artifacts, I am disconcerted with the knowledge that I am passively consuming and appropriating an indigenous culture. I arrive at the serpentine base of a reconstructed 16-foot temple where the Aztecs flung down human sacrifices, leaving bloodied steps. Around me I hear the censorious, culturally ignorant words of the Whites who, while horrified by the bloodthirsty Aztecs, gape in vicarious wonder and voraciously consume the exoticized images. Though I too am a gaping consumer, I feel that these artworks are part of my legacy – my appropriation differs from the misappropriation by "outsiders."

I am again struck by how much Chicana artists and writers feel the impact of ancient Mexican art forms, foods, and customs. *Sus símbolos y metáforas todavía viven en la gente chicana/mexicana*. This sense of connection and community compels Chicana writers/artists to delve into, sift through, and rework native imagery. We consistently reflect back these images in revitalized and modernized versions in theater, film, performance art, painting, dance, sculpture, and literature. *La negación sistemática de la cultura mexicana-chicana en los Estados Unidos impide su desarrollo haciéndolo este un acto de colonización*. As a people who have been stripped of our history, language, identity and pride, we attempt again and again to find what we have lost by imaginatively digging into our cultural roots and making art out of our findings.

I recall Yolanda López' *Portrait of the Artist as the Virgin of Guadalupe* (1978), which depicts a Chicana/*mexicana* woman emerging and running from the oval halo of rays that looks to me like thorns, with the mantle of the tradiional *virgen* in one hand and a serpent in the other. She wears running shoes, has short hair, and her legs are bare and look powerful – a very dykey-looking woman. *Portrait* represents the cultural rebirth of the Chicana struggling to free herself from oppressive gender roles.[1]

I remember visiting Chicana *tejana* artist Santa Barraza in her Austin studio in the mid-1970s and talking about the merger and appropriation of cultural symbols and techniques by artists in search of their spiritual and cultural roots. As I walked around her studio, I was amazed at the vivid *Virgen de Guadalupe* iconography on her walls and on the drawings strewn on tables and shelves.

*La gente chicana tiene tres madres.* All three are mediators: *Guadalupe*, the virgin mother who has not abandoned us, *la Chingada (Malinche)*, the raped mother whom we have abandoned, and *la Llorona*, the mother who seeks her lost children and is a combination of the other two. *Guadalupe* has been used by the Church to mete out institutionalized oppression: to placate the Indians and *mexicanos* and Chicanos. In part, the true identity of all three has been subverted – *Guadalupe* to make us docile and enduring, *la Chingada* to make us ashamed of our Indian side, and *la Llorona* to make us long-suffering people. This obscuring has encouraged the *virgen/puta* dichotomy. The three *madres* are cultural figures that Chicana writers and artists "reread" in our works.

Now, 16 years later, Barraza is focusing on interpretations of Pre-Columbian codices as a reclamation of cultural and historical mestiza identity. Her "codices" are edged with *milagros* and *ex votos*.[2] Using the folk-art format, Barraza is now painting tin testimonials known as *retablos*. These are traditional popular miracle paintings on metal, a medium introduced to colonial Mexico by the Spaniards. One of her devotional *retablos* is of *la Malinche*, made with *maguey*. (The *maguey* cactus is Barraza's symbol of rebirth.) Like that of many Chicana artists, her work, she says, explores indigenous Mexican "symbols and myths in a historical and contemporary context as a mechanism of resistance to oppression and assimilation."[3]

I wonder about the genesis of *el arte de la frontera*. Border art remembers its roots – sacred and folk art are often still one and the same. I recall the *nichos* (niches or recessed areas) and *retablos* that I had recently seen in several galleries and museums. The *retablos* are placed inside open boxes made of wood, tin, or cardboard. The *cajitas* contain three-dimensional figures such as *la virgen*, photos of ancestors, candles, and sprigs of herbs tied together. They are actually tiny installations. I make mine out of cigar boxes or vegetable crates that I find discarded on the street before garbage pickups. The *retablos* range from the strictly traditional to modern, more abstract forms. Santa Barraza, Yolanda López, Marcia Gómez, Carmen Lomas Garza and other Chicana artists connect their art to everyday life, instilling both with political, sacred and aesthetic values. *Haciendo tortillas* becomes a sacred ritual in literary, visual, and performance arts.[4]

Border art, in critiquing old, traditional, and erroneous representations of the Mexico–United States border, attempts to represent the "real world" *de la gente* going about their daily lives. But it renders that world and its people in more than mere surface slices of life. If one looks beyond the tangible, one sees a connection to the spirit world, to the underworld, and to other realities. In the "old world," art was/is functional and sacred as well as aesthetic. When folk and fine art separated, the *metate* (a flat porous volcanic stone with rolling pin used to make corn tortillas) and the *huipil* (a Guatemalan blouse) were put in museums by Western curators of art.[5]

I come to a glass case where the skeleton of a jaguar with a stone in its open mouth nestles on cloth. The stone represents the heart. My thoughts trace the jaguar's spiritual and religious symbolism from its Olmec origins to present-day jaguar masks worn by people who no longer know that the jaguar was connected to rain, who no longer remember that Tlaloc and the jaguar and the serpent and rain are tightly intertwined.[6] Through the centuries a culture touches and influences another, passing on its metaphors and its gods before it dies. (Metaphors *are* gods.) The new culture adopts, modifies, and enriches these images, and it, in turn, passes them on changed. The process is repeated until the original meanings of images are pushed into the unconscious. What surfaces are images more significant to the prevailing culture and era. The artist on some level, however, still connects to that unconscious reservoir of meaning, connects to that *nepantla* state of transition between time periods, and the border between cultures.

*Nepantla* is the Nahuatl word for an in-between state, that uncertain terrain one crosses when moving from one place to another, when changing from one class, race, or gender position to another, when traveling from the present identity into a new identity. The Mexican immigrant at the moment of crossing the barbed-wire fence into the hostile "paradise" of *el norte*, the United States, is caught in a state of *nepantla*. Others who find themselves in this bewildering transitional space may be those people caught in the midst of denying their projected/assumed heterosexual identity and coming out, presenting and voicing their lesbian, gay, bi-, or transsexual selves. Crossing class lines – especially from working class to middle classness and privilege – can be just as disorienting. The marginalized, starving Chicana artist who suddenly finds her work exhibited in mainstream museums, or being sold for thousands of dollars in prestigious galleries, as well as the once-neglected writer whose work is on every professor's syllabus for a time inhabit *nepantla*. For women artists, *nepantla* is a constant state; dislocation is the norm. Chicana artists are engaged in "reading" that *nepantla*, that border.

I think of the borderlands as Jorge Luis Borges' *Aleph*, the one spot on earth which contains all other places within it. All people in it, whether natives or immigrants, colored or white, queer or heterosexual, from this side of the border or *del otro lado*, are *personas del lugar*, local people – all of whom relate to the border and to *nepantla* in different ways.

The border is a historical and metaphorical site, *un sitio ocupado*, an occupied borderland where individual artists and collaborating groups transform space, and the two home territories, Mexico and the United States, become one. Border art deals with shifting identities, border crossings, and hybridism.

But there are other borders besides the actual Mexico/US *frontera*. Chilean-born artist Juan Davila's *Wuthering Heights* (1990) oil painting depicts Juanito Leguna, a half-caste, mixed breed transvestite. Juanito's body is a simulacrum parading as the phallic mother with hairy chest and hanging tits.[7] Another Latino artist, Rafael Barajas (who signs his work as "El Fisgón"), has a mixed-media piece entitled *Pero eso si . . . soy muy macho* (1989). It shows a Mexican male wearing the proverbial sombrero taking a siesta against the traditional cactus, tequila bottle on the ground, gunbelt hanging from a nopal branch. But the leg sticking out from beneath the sarape-like mantle is wearing a high-heeled shoe, pantyhose, and a garter belt. It suggests another kind of border crossing – gender-bending.[8]

According to anthropologist Edward Hall, early in life we become oriented to space in a way that is tied to survival and sanity. When we become disoriented from that sense of space we fall in danger of becoming psychotic.[9] I question this – to be disoriented in space is the "normal" way of being for us mestizas living in the borderlands. It is the sane way of coping with the accelerated pace of this complex, interdependent, and multicultural planet. To be disoriented in space is to be *en nepantla*, to experience bouts of disassociation of identity, identity breakdowns and buildups. The border is in a constant *nepantla* state, and it is an analog of the planet.

This is why the border is a persistent metaphor in *el arte de la frontera*, an art that deals with such themes as identity, border crossings, and hybrid imagery. The Mexico–United States border is a site where many different cultures "touch" each other and the permeable, flexible, and ambiguous shifting grounds lend themselves to hybrid images. The border is the locus of resistance, of rupture, of implosion and explosion, and of putting together the fragments and creating a new assemblage. Border artists *cambian el punto de referencia*. By disrupting the neat separations between cultures, they create a culture mix, *una mestizada* in their artworks. Each artist locates herself in this border *"lugar"* and tears apart then rebuilds the "place" itself. "Imagenes de la Frontera" was the title of the Centro Cultural Tijuana's June 1992 exhibition.[10] Malaquís Montoya's Frontera Series and Irene Pérez' Dos Mundos monoprint are examples of the multi-subjectivity, split-subjectivity, and refusal-to-be-split themes of the border artist creating a counter-art.

The *nepantla* state is the natural habitat of women artists, most specifically for the mestiza border artists who partake of the traditions of two or more worlds and who may be binational. They thus create a new artistic space – a border mestizo culture. Beware of *el romance del mestizaje*, I hear myself saying silently. *Puede ser una ficción.* But I and other writers/artists of *la frontera* have invested ourselves in it. *Mestizaje*, not Chicanismo, is the reality of our lives. *Mestizaje* is at the heart of our art. We bleed in *mestizaje*, we eat and sweat and cry in *mestizaje*. But the Chicana is inside the mestiza.

There are many obstacles and dangers in crossing into *nepantla*. Popular culture and the dominant art institutions threaten border artists from the outside with appropriation. "Outsiders" jump on the border artists' bandwagon and work their territory. The present unparalleled economic depression in the arts gutted by government funding cutbacks threatens *los artistas de la frontera*. Sponsoring corporations that judge projects by "family values" criteria force multicultural artists to hang tough and brave out financial and professional instability.

I walk into the Aztec Museum shop and see feathers, paper flowers, and ceramic statues of fertility goddesses selling for ten times what they sell for in Mexico. Border art is becoming trendy in these neo-colonial times that encourage art tourism and pop-culture rip-offs. Of course, there is nothing new about colonizing, commercializing, and consuming the art of ethnic people (and of queer writers and artists) except that now it is being misappropriated by pop culture. Diversity is being sold on TV, billboards, fashion runways, department-store windows, and, yes, airport corridors and "regional" stores where you can take home a jar of Tex-Mex *picante* sauce along with Navaho artist R. C. Gorman's "Saguaro" or Robert Arnold's "Chili Dog," and drink a margarita at Rosie's Cantina.

I touch the armadillo pendant hanging from my neck and think, *frontera* artists have to grow protective shells. We enter the silence, go inward, attend to feelings and to that inner *cenote*, the creative reservoir where earth, female, and water energies merge. We surrender to the rhythm and the grace of our artworks. Through our artworks we cross the border into other subjective levels of awareness, shift into different and new terrains of *mestizaje*. Some of us have a highly developed *facultad* and many intuit what lies ahead. Yet the political climate does not allow us to withdraw completely. In fact, border artists are engaged artists. Most of us are politically active in our communities. If disconnected from *la gente*, border artists would wither in isolation. The community feeds our spirits and the responses from our "readers" inspire us to continue struggling with our art and aesthetic interventions that subvert cultural genocide. Border art challenges and subverts the imperialism of the United Sates, and combats assimilation by either the United States or Mexico, yet it acknowledges its affinities to both cultures.[11]

"Chicana" artist, "border" artist. These are adjectives labeling identities. Labeling creates expectations. White poets don't write "white" in front of their names, nor are they referred to as white by others. Is "border" artist just another label that strips legitimacy from the artist, signaling that she is inferior to the adjectiveless artist, a label designating that she is only capable of handling ethnic, folk, and regional subjects and art forms? Yet the dominant culture consumes, swallows whole the ethnic artist, sucks out her vitality, and then spits out the hollow husk along with its labels (such as Hispanic). The dominant culture shapes the ethnic artist's identity if she does not scream loud enough and fight long enough to name herself. Until we live in a society where all people are more or less equal, we need these labels to resist the pressure to assimilate.

Artistic ideas that have been incubating and developing at their own speed have come into their season – now is the time of border art. Border *arte* is an art that supersedes the pictorial. It depicts both the soul *del artista* and the soul *del pueblo*. It deals with who tells the stories and what stories and histories are told. I call this form of visual narrative *autohistoria*. This form goes beyond the traditional self-portrait or autobiography; in telling the writer/artist's personal story, it also includes the artist's cultural history. The *retablos* I make are not just representations of myself, they are representations of Chicana culture. *El arte de la frontera* is community and academically based – many Chicana artists have M.A.s and Ph.D.s and hold precarious teaching positions on the fringes of universities. They are over-worked, overlooked, passed over for tenure, and denied the support they deserve. To make, exhibit, and sell their artwork, and to survive, *los artistas* have had to band together collectively.[12]

I cross the exhibit room. Codices hang on the walls. I stare at the hieroglyphics. The ways of a people, their history and culture put on paper beaten from maguey leaves. Faint traces of red, blue, and black ink left by their artists, writers, and scholars. The past is hanging behind glass. We, the viewers in the present, walk around and around the glass-boxed past. I wonder who I used to be, I wonder who I am. The border artist constantly reinvents herself. Through art she is able to reread, reinterpret, re-envision and reconstruct her culture's present as well as its past. This capacity to construct meaning and culture privileges the artist. As cultural icons for her ethnic communities, she is highly visible.

But there are drawbacks to having artistic and cultural power – the relentless pressure to produce, being put in the position of representing her entire *pueblo* and carrying all the ethnic culture's baggage on her *espalda* while trying to survive in a gringo world. Power and the seeking of greater power may create a self-centered ego or a fake public image, one the artist thinks will make her acceptable to her audience. It may encourage self-serving

hustling – all artists have to sell themselves in order to get grants, get published, secure exhibit spaces, and get good reviews. But for some, the hustling outdoes the art-making.

The Chicana border writer/artist has finally come to market. The problem now is how to resist corporate culture while asking for and securing its patronage; how to get the dollars without resorting to "mainstreaming" the work. Is the border artist complicit in the appropriation of her art by the dominant art dealers? And if so, does this constitute a self-imposed imperialism? The artist, in making *plata* from the sale of her sculpture, "makes it." Money means power. The access to privilege that comes with the bucks and the recognition can turn the artist on her ear in a *nepantla* spin.

Finally, I find myself before the reconstructed statue of the newly unearthed *el dios murciélago*, the bat god with his big ears, fangs, and protruding tongue representing the vampire bat associated with night, blood sacrifice, and death. I make an instantaneous association of the bat man with the stage of border artists – the dark cave of creativity where they hang upside down, turning the self upside down in order to see from another point of view, one that brings a new state of understanding. Or it may mean transposing the former self onto a new one – the death of the old self and the old ways, breaking down former notions of who you are. Night fear, *susto*, when every button is pushed. The border person constantly moves through that birth canal, *nepantla*. If you stay too long in *nepantla* you are in danger of being blocked, resulting in a breech birth or being stillborn.

I wonder what meaning this bat figure will have for other Chicanas, what artistic symbol they will make of it and what political struggle it will represent. Perhaps the *murciélago* questions the viewer's unconscious collective and personal identity and its ties to her ancestors, *los muertos*. In border art there is always the specter of death in the background. Often *las calaveras* (skeletons and skulls) take a prominent position – and not just on *el día de los muertos* (November 2). *De la tierra nacemos,* from earth we are born, *a la tierra regresaremos*, to earth we shall return, *a dar lo que ella nos dió*, to give back to her what she has given. Yes, I say to myself, the earth eats the dead, *la tierra se come los muertos.*

I walk out of the Aztec exhibit hall. It is September 28, *mi cumpleaños.* I seek out the table with the computer, key in my birthdate and there on the screen is my Aztec birth year and ritual day name: 8 Rabbit, 12 Skull. In that culture I would have been named Matlactli Omome Mizuitzli. I stick my chart under the rotating rubber stamps, press down, pull it out and stare at the imprint of the rabbit (symbol of fear and of running scared) pictograph and then of the skull (night, blood sacrifice, and death). Very appropriate symbols in my life, I mutter. It's so *raza. ¿y qué?*

I ask myself, What direction will *el arte fronterizo* take in the future? The multi-subjectivity and split-subjectivity of the border artist creating various counter arts will continue, but with a parallel movement where a polarized us/them, insiders/outsiders culture clash is not the main struggle, where a refusal to be split will be a given. We are both *nos* (us) and *otras* (others) – *nos/otras.*

My mind reviews image after image. Something about who and what I am and the 200 "artifacts" I have just seen does not feel right. I pull out my "birth chart." Yes, cultural roots are important, *but I was not born at Tenochitlán in the ancient past nor in an Aztec village in modern times. I was born and live in that in-between space, nepantla, the borderlands.* Hay muchas razas *running in my veins,* mescladas dentro de mi, otras culturas *that my body lives in and out of.* Mi cuerpo vive dentro y fuera de otras culturas *and a white man who constantly whispers inside my skull. For me, being Chicana is not enough. It is only one of my multiple identities. Along with other* border gente, *it is at this site and time,* en este tiempo y lugar *where and when, I create my identity* con mi arte.

## Notes

I thank Dianna Williamson and Clarisa Rojas, my literary assistants, for their invaluable and incisive critical comments, and Deidre McFadyen.

1   See Amalia Mesa-Bains, "*El Mundo Femenino:* Chicana Artists of the Movement – A Commentary on Development and Production," in Richard Griswold Del Castillo, Teresa McKenna, and Yvonne Yarbo Bejarano (eds), *CARA, Chicano Art: Resistance and Affirmation* (Los Angeles: Wight Gallery, University of California, 1991).

2   See Luz María and Ellen J. Stekert's untitled art catalog essay in *Santa Barraza*, March 8–April 11, 1992, La Raza/Galería Posada, Sacramento, CA.

3   Quoted in Jennifer Heath's "Women Artists of Color Share World of Struggle," *Sunday Camera*, March 8, 1992, p. 9C.

4   See Carmen Lomas Garza's children's bilingual book, *Family Pictures/Cuadros de familia* (San Francisco: Children's Book Press, 1990), in particular "*Camas para sonar/*Beds for Dreaming."

5   The Maya huipiles are large rectangular blouses which describe the Maya cosmos. They portray the world as a diamond. The four sides of the diamond represent the boundaries of space and time; the smaller diamonds at each corner, the cardinal points. The weaver maps the heavens and underworld.

6   Roberta H. Markman and Peter T. Markman (eds), *Masks of the Spirit: Image and Metaphor in Mesoamerica* (Berkeley: University of California Press, 1989).

7   See Guy Brett, *Transcontinental: An Investigation of Reality* (London: Verso, 1990).

8   See *ex profeso, recuento de afinidades colectiva plástica contemporánea: imágenes: gay-lésbicaséroticas* put together by Circulo Cultural Gay in Mexico City and exhibited at Museuo Universitario del Chope during Gay Cultural Week, June 14–23, 1989.

9   The exact quote is: "We have an internalization of fixed space learned early in life. One's orientation in space is tied to survival and sanity. To be disoriented in space is to be psychotic." See Edward T. Hall and Mildred Reed Hall, "The Sounds of Silence," in James P. Spradley and David W. McCurdy (eds), *Conformity and Conflict: Readings in Cultural Anthropology* (Boston: Little, Brown, 1987).

10   The exhibition was part of Festival Internacional de la Raza '92. The artworks were produced in the Silkscreen Studios of Self Help Graphics, Los Angeles, and in the studios of Strike Editions in Austin, Texas. Self Help Graphics and the Galería Sin Fronteras, Austin, Texas organized the exhibitions.

11   Among the alternative galleries and art centers that combat assimilation are the Guadalupe Cultural Arts Center in San Antonio, Mexic-Arte Museum and Sin Fronteras Gallery in Austin, Texas, and the Mission Cultural Center in San Francisco.

12   For a discussion of Chicano posters, almanacs, calendars, and cartoons that join "images and texts to depict community issues as well as historical and cultural themes," and that metaphorically link Chicano struggles for self-determination with the Mexican Revolution, and establish "a cultural and visual continuum across borders," see Tomás Ybarra-Fausto's "Gráfica/Urban Iconography" in *Chicano Expressions: A New View in American Art, April 14–July 31, 1986* (New York: INTAR Latin American Gallery, 1986), pp. 21–4.

# The Shock of the New

## Rubén Martinez

*"La noche que Chicago se murió . . ."*

The boots. Smooth, black, brushed-leather boots. Snakeskin boots. Cheap white vinyl boots. Sharp-toed boots. Tassled boots. Hundreds of boots shuffling, kicking, twirling. lick forward, twirl at the knee, kick back, twirl at the knee . . . *fast*, across the dance floor. Boots belonging to boys and girls. The boys in jeans and crisp white shirts,or in T-shirts with the names of their dance crews in graffiti-style lettering – "La Herradura," "Vaqueros Norteños," "Casimira." The girls in jeans too, or short shorts, silver nylons, and blouses sequined and sparkling. The boys with their mustaches, lots of mustaches. The girls made up, some modestly, others *chola*-heavy. And the hats, the all-important *tejana*, the Texas-style Stetson, preferably black, tugged down low over the eyes. A sea of hats across the dance floor, bobbing up and down, along with the shoulders, the chests, the breasts, the hips, the knees and the boots that kick forward, twirl at the knee, kick back, kick fast, kick-twirl-kick-shuffle to the beat: ump-pa-bum, um-pa-bum, um-pa-bum.

It's Friday night at Mi Hacienda in La Puente, and I'm witnessing the resurgence of the American cowboy and cowgirl: the brown-skinned and black-eyed *vaqueros y vaqueritas.* The new American cowboys and cowgirls are mostly from Mexico and have been here only a few years. But there are Salvadoran *vaqueros,* too. And second-generation Chicana *vaqueritas.* Most are in their late teens and early twenties, dancing to the *quebradita* beat of Banda Toro, a brass-heavy Mexican outfit in matching uniforms of embroidered shirts, boots and, of course, black *tejanas.*

*"La noche que Chicago se murió . . ."*

"The night Chicago died." The melody brings back memories of the seventies: A group called Paper Lace hit it big with this song about gangsters in Chicago. And here it is in 1994, in Spanish, set to the polka-ish, tinny, fast *quebradita* sound that the *vaqueros y vaqueritas* live for. "*Arriba Michoacán!*" cries out Toro's lead singer between songs, a salutation to the natives of that Mexican State. A cheer sounds, hats are raised. "*Arriba Jalisco!*" More cheers, more hats. "*Arriba Zacatecas!*" Hey, that's me! Well, sort of. My grandmother was born in a small town of that Mexican state. If I had a hat, I'd wave it.

To say that there is Latino pride in La Puente tonight would be an understatement. It's more like a cultural revolution. We're Mexican, speak Spanish, dance *quebradita*, and are damn proud of it.

And therein lies the revolution. The *quebra-dita* fad began here, though its roots are obviously south of the border. Historians and ethnomusicologists agree this is the first instance in which a Mexican popular music – in this case from nineteenth-century Sinaloa – has been revived and commercialized in the United States, then shipped back to the Old Country. In Mexico, *quebradita* is just starting to catch on, about two years after the scene took off here.

To Steven Loza, a professor of ethnomusi-cology at UCLA, the *quebradita* scene is about establishing a sense of Latino independence – in the North. "People are saying that we don't have to look like Prince or Madonna," he says. "We can wear our boots and hats. The *vaquero* style is important as a symbol. When a Mexican puts on that suit, just like when in the old days you put on a zoot suit, you can walk into that club and be proud that you're a Mexican."

All of which begs many questions that relate to California's most volatile and polarizing political topic: immigration. Why is it that Mexicans both recently arrived and American-born are proclaiming themselves Mexican on *this* side of the border? Are Mexicans and other Latino immigrants overturning America's cherished rites of assimilation, proclaiming themselves an independent cultural Other within the United States? And why now? Is it mere coincidence that the *quebradita* craze was born roughly at the same time that politicians began staking out positions against the presence of immigrants – especially the illegal immigrants – in our midst?

Most observers think that questions of "why so much pride" and "why now" merit a simple answer: "It's almost like a response, a backlash, if you want to call it, against the anti-immigrant rhetoric," says Loza. The question of the creation of a non-assimilated Other is a little more complex.

*Quebradita* is but one of many signs that the city of Los Angeles is undergoing a radical transformation. Latino Los Angeles hovers at more than 40 percent of the population – a plurality heading toward a majority. Historians and demographers refer to this percentage, which includes newcomers and several generations of the American-born, as a "critical mass," an agent of change.

This is not just a matter of numbers. The fact that Mexico and Central America, the immigrants' Old Countries, are just across the border is equally important. Latin culture, as well as people, travel across that border daily. Unlike other US immigrants, Latinos can touch their roots with ease. And, of course, the city itself shares those roots.

"Latinos are not like the old European immigrants, nor like a racial minority. What we have is something fundamentally different," says David Hayes-Bautista, director of the Alta California Policy Research Center, an independent think tank studying Latino issues. Latinos in LA, he adds, are their "own civil society, almost equivalent in size to the state of Minnesota."

Put it this way, then: While Governor Pete Wilson, Senator Barbara Boxer and Dianne Feinstein, and many other pols in the state rant about the "immigration problem," the more pertinent issue might be this: When will they learn to dance the *quebradita?*

This transformation has set the city on edge. White suburban dwellers grit their teeth at seeing vendors or day laborers on street corners in the San Fernando Valley. African Americans in South-Central LA watch black neighborhoods turn brown, and worry over competition for jobs. The fear, anger, and frustration among non-immigrant LA transcends racial and class lines.

But transformation and its discontents work both ways. Latino culture, too, is being remade. Indeed, some would argue that the *quebradita* craze is merely a nostalgic yearning in a culture that will inescapably be changed now that it has crossed the border. Then there's the feeling on the part of most immigrants that they are being unfairly blamed for California's economic woes. The "new" LA–Mexicans, and Central Americans who've arrived in the past decade, Chicanos who've been here for generations, working-class teens and doctoral candidates at Caltech, business people and domestic workers, the elite and the welfare recipients, legal and illegal – is as uncertain, and fearful, about this transformation as the old LA.

But tonight the new LA is not fearful or uncertain or contemplating a hostile reconquest of the Southwest. Tonight the new LA is dancing up a storm in La Puente, remember?

There is Griselda Mariscal, 20, a native of LA whose mother was born in Guadalajara and whose father hails from Tepic. She is here, with her ivory-toned *botines* (boots); her loose blue jeans held up by a braided piece of leather work called a *cinto piteado* and her *pañuelo* (bandanna) of green, white, and red, the colors of the Mexican flag, that announces "Nayarit," her father's home state. Her date, a shy *vaquero*, tucks his thumbs into the corners of his jeans pockets. His Stetson is pulled down low. Very cool.

"*Quebradita* is a way of showing you can be all into your culture," says Mariscal, who, when she's not out dancing, crams for midterms and finals at Occidental College, where she is a third-year history major. "To me, it's a way of holding your head up high. It says that I am in college because of the strength of my culture, because of the sacrifice of *mis papás, mis abuelitos.*" Mariscal grew up near Belmont High School, where, she says, "there were no white people." The first Anglo institution she encountered was Occidental College, with a student population of 1,650, of which 60 percent are Anglo. "I didn't know anything about being a Chicana until then," she says. She joined the militant Chicano student organization MEChA (Movimiento Estudiantil Chicano de Aztlán), and promptly declared herself Mexicana: "I hated the gringos." A trip to Mexico brought her disillusionment, however. "They called me a *güerita*" – an American-looking girl. And whenever an English word crept into her otherwise flawless Spanish, she'd get more grief: You don't belong here. You're from *el otro lado*, the other side of the border. "It took me a trip to Mexico to realize that I had something in common with the gringo."

Then she heard about *quebradita*. Now it was her Chicano friends who questioned her for being so retrograde. "They'd see me in my *botines* and ask me where my horse was." But she persisted. Gradually, the *quebradita* fever spread to more of her Chicano friends. Today, Mariscal doesn't see herself as a pure Mexicana. But she still doesn't see herself completely as an American either.

On stage, Banda Toro is tearing into a *popurrí* of songs: Suddenly, the umpah-bum gives way to a rock'n'roll backbeat and the thousand pairs of boots are trying out some version of the twist. We are not in Mexico, nor in Aztlán, the mythical Chicano nation separate from white America. But we're not quite in the United States, either. We're in Los Angeles.

In the 1920s, the Martinez-Del Rio duo was among the musical acts that played LA's Mexican theaters. They sang *corrido* tales from the Revolution and other dramas of the day.

Juan Martínez and Margarita Del Río were my grandparents. They came north, riding their generation's wave of migration, and stayed, settling in the Silver Lake hills along with the Russians, Irish, Asians, and Italians of the old LA. They loved America, even when America deported hundreds of thousands of their compatriots back to Mexico during the Great Depression.

They were spared that fate by landing a job at a popular Anglo nightclub Downtown, where they were paid very well for their talents. They would look at the poor Mexicans in East LA and say to themselves: "They just don't have what it takes."

Curiously, my grandparents never completely assimilated. They spoke enough English for the essentials – to make a bank deposit, to meet and greet in their gigs at the nightclub. (For the tougher transactions, they relied on their only child, my father, who was born here and had a thorough American education and spoke English without an accent.) But they were also as American as could be: Their ambition to succeed led them to close the door on their Mexican past. They returned only for brief visits; they became US citizens; their home was this country. The irony, of course, is that they were only able to declare America their home by playing Mexican folk music to the Anglo elites of their day.

My mother, a native of El Salvador, remembers her arrival to this country in the late fifties. It began with a 12-hour flight on a Pan American bimotor. At dawn, the plane set down in San Francisco. She recalls an idyllic sight: the Golden Gate bridge gleaming and the waters of the bay dappled by the silver light bursting over the green hills of Berkeley. America.

America for her was freedom from the constraints of a conservative family in the Old Country. It was also the fulfillment of a dream that her mother had had in the forties. "She used to talk about America as a place where women could wear pants and work," she says, the words coming out slow and thick with nostalgia. But when she speaks of her years of studying English, getting her first job, meeting her future husband, raising her children, going back to school, and finally, getting her license in family counseling, the voice lightens, quickens. It's the classic American story, but, of course, there was a price to be paid.

"I ached inside, especially those first few years," she says. "I missed my family so much." It was more than family. It was a way of life, a way of seeing the world. It was growing up in one world, abandoning it for another, and growing up all over again with a whole new set of values and beliefs.

My father strikes a more ambivalent note. "I can see things from both sides," he says. On the one hand, he's famous for referring to the recently arrived immigrants, just as his parents did, as *chusma* (rabble). But then he'll talk about the white survivalist types who are arming themselves to the teeth in anticipation of LA's next riot. "Sure, I get angry when they talk about the Mexicans this, Mexicans that," he says. "I feel like they're the ones who would have looked at my parents and made fun of them for the way they spoke English." A visible hurt tightens the muscles of his face.

But my father protests when I mention his parents' lack of assimilation. "They never learned English well, but they spent all those years with the Americans, paying their bills, living in Silver Lake." He is saying that assimilation is as much an economic rite of passage as a cultural one. And he is, of course, right.

We were an American family, assimilated, middle-class. We spoke English, except for my mother's terms of endearment like *m'hijo* (my son). And there was her heavy accent, which my brother, sister, and I made fun of. My Mexican grandparents were mysterious figures from far-off lands, their voices even thicker with the accent of another time and place. They could only half understand their grandchildren. Isolated in their world, they waited for death while living in memory, satisfied that they'd done the right thing by ensuring their children and grandchildren a better life in the United States.

But I became the cultural revisionist in my family. I have been obsessed, for the better part of my adult life, with questions of cultural identity and its relation to the history of the city. In my 31 years, I have played the role of an accentless, perfectly assimilated American kid. But I've also betrayed my parents' and grandparents' ideals of assimilation. I have returned to the Old Countries; I have on occasion proclaimed myself separate from Anglo American culture; I've been known to warn Anglos that they just might be the ones who are going to get deported – back to Europe – when I hear them talking about deporting my Latin American brothers and sisters.

I have also dreamed of a California in which a historical wound hundreds of years old might be healed: a reconciliation between North and South, the Catholic and the Protestant, the First and Third Worlds. I've come to admit that rock'n'roll is as important to my spiritual well-being as *la Virgen de Guadalupe*. I will always be the outsider in Latin America. I also oftentimes feel like an outcast in the United States. The only place I could be at home is in the new – the almost new – Los Angeles.

The transformation of LA is not without precedent. After the Mexican-American War of 1846–8, the signing of the Treaty of Guadalupe Hidalgo and the US annexation of the Southwest, Anglos overran Los Angeles, displacing the native Mexican "Californio" population. Along with WASPy descendants of the early Americans came more immigrants – Chinese, Italians, French, Irish. Then during the Mexican Revolution that began in 1910, hundreds of thousands of refugees crossed the border and reasserted the Latino identity of Los Angeles.

The years of the first Cultural Revolution here, the mid-1800s, were tumultuous ones. The radically different sensibilities clashed violently, but sometimes they melded seamlessly, too. Many of the Chinese merchants of the Old Plaza, near today's Olvera Street, were fluent in Spanish (as are many of today's Korean merchants). Some of the old *rancheros* intermarried with Italians. At the city's centennial celebration in 1881, booster speeches were shouted out in English, Spanish, and French.

Nevertheless, LA's primitive multicultural experiment was short-lived. Lynchings of Chinese and Mexicans weren't unheard of. The "Californio" *rancheros* saw their lands usurped, sometimes legally, sometimes not. By the late 1880s, the new dominant culture had just about wiped out LA's old Mexican downtown. A Catholic Mexican town became yet another modern Protestant town of the American Southwest. Even the Latino influx during the Mexican Revolution couldn't tip the demographic balance away from the Anglo mainstream. In this century, migrants from the American South and Midwest made the biggest mark on LA, until recently, when that distinction went to the foreign-born. (Latinos make up the vast majority of newcomers but Asians are also a significant percentage; From 1980 to 1990, their numbers in the city nearly doubled, to 10.6 percent of the population.)

All over the Southwest, pitched battles between the Anglo and Mexican conceptions of city life were fought after the Mexican-American War and well into this century. Historian William Estrada, who teaches Chicano studies at Cal State Northridge, notes that each city resolved the conflict in different ways. San Antonio, he says, "integrated its Mexican past." It is still visible in that town's *pueblo*-like buildings. In other cities, such as Albuquerque and San Diego, the Americans of the nineteenth century were "successful in erasing historical memory." LA, Estrada says, falls somewhere in between. "Downtown LA has Pershing Square and Bunker Hill, but it also still has the Old Plaza."

And now, when people talk about immigration problems, they are talking about what kind of city they want LA to be. Will it be a city of the North or the South? Should it have vendors hawking mangoes and papayas on the sidewalk? (The proponents are mostly Latino and the opponents nearly all Anglo. The City Council has sided, narrowly, with the vendors.) Should it speak English only? (Whatever English-only laws remain on the books, the fact remains

that LA is a city of dozens and dozens of languages. Studies have found that most Latinos in the US are bilingual, and many, especially young Mexican-Americans, prefer to use Spanish.)

Demographers like David Hayes-Bautista don't see these culture wars as a win–lose proposition. For him, the Latin American concept of *mestizaje*, the mixing of European and indigenous cultures that gave rise to a third culture, is applicable to LA. "The real melting pot occurred in Latin America," he says. "Anglo-Protestantism doesn't allow for half-breeds; Latino Catholic culture does. [Through immigration] we are continuing the mestizo tradition and fulfilling the promise of a real US melting pot. We're the rest of the American story. What we're seeing in LA is the emergence of a truly American identity for the twenty-first century."

The newest of the new Angelenos try on the consonants and vowels of their future in a classroom at Evans Community Adult School in Downtown. "Good morning, how are you?" says ESL teacher Sylvia Martinez, much too bouncy, loud, and cheerful for a Monday morning at 7:30.

"Faahine, how are juuuu?" the class responds in unison, 40 or so voices – men and women, teens to middle-aged people, Mexicans, Central Americans, and a sprinkling of South Americans.

'The al-pha-bet," Martinez says. "The ahl-fa-beh," the class repeats.

"The al-pha-be*ttt.*"

"The ahl-fa-be*hhttt.*"

"A, B, C, D . . ."

Martinez prowls up and down between the rows of seats, tapping out a rhythm on the floor with a long wooden pointer.

"Where are you from?" Martinez asks, enunciating every syllable, making a show of tongue, lips, and teeth.

"Where ahhre juuuu frohhm?" Loose vowels, soft consonants.

"Ireland," Martinez says. "Irish," says the chorus. "Peru." "Peruvian." "Vietnam." "Vietnamese." "El Salvador." "Salvadoran," they say, noticeably louder.

I ask Yolanda Franco, who, in her thirties, is one of the older women in the classroom, what English sounds like to her. "*¡Fabuloso!*" she says, with all the immigrant hope in the world showing through her smile. English is her ticket to success. She's come north alone; a daughter waits in Mexico for her to gain a toehold here so that they can be reunited. Right now, Franco works as a housekeeper. But it's only a matter of time, she says. Just some more consonants, pronouns, and practice stand between her and a better life.

Franco may be embracing transformation, but English and the American Way aren't all that *fabuloso* for Yesica Remedios, 18. She was born here, but she moved to Guadalajara at the age of 2 and only six months ago came north for the first time. "I have to learn English," she says, because most of the texts in children's psychology, her career choice, are in English. "But I don't like it here," she insists. "There's more freedom in Mexico. You can go out at night, stroll through the plazas without giving it a second thought. But here! The gangs! *Este no es mi país*. (This is not my country.)"

What does the future hold for the students at Evans, most of whom have been in the United States for less than a year? Will Franco continue to believe life is *fabuloso*? Will Remedios be seduced by America?

To find some answers, I visit the South Gate Women's Clinic, where a dozen or so Latinas who have gathered at random speak of their hopes and fears. They sit before me, many wearing sweatshirts and tennis shoes, the uniform of the Latina working class. Not one wears makeup, and most have deep, dark circles under their eyes. These are the women who sew in garment factories, clean up office buildings late at night, sell fruit or trinkets on the street. Most have been here several years and have done their time in crowded classrooms learning basic English. And many of them have begun to wonder whether they made the right decision in coming north.

"Once you're here, you become something different," says Norma, in her twenties and a native of Michoacán (all the women gave their first names only, since most are undocu-

mented). "The family changes. The children don't have the same respect for their parents."

Nods of agreement around the table. "You have to work and leave them alone all day," says Rosario, who is Guatemalan. "It's the way of life in this country. I've never seen gang members in my homeland."

You can't discipline your children here, the mothers complain. "Here, the parents fear the children." Who knows, with all those laws on the books here, maybe a spanking could constitute child abuse, they say. But, Rosario insists, people aren't going to go back home. "No matter how bad off we are here, it's worse in one's own country."

Others aren't so sure. Hermila, from Guadalajara, is thinking of saving up some more money and then heading home. She talks about being looked at funny because she's brown, short, and poor, about all the factories where bosses have tried to have their way with her. "I'll work a little longer and get out of here. Wilson can do whatever he wants," she says. More nodding of heads.

The mention of Governor Wilson's name draws the most passion from the group. "Pete Wilson is a jerk," Rosario pronounces to much laughter. "We come here to work!" says Idelisa, another Guadalajara native, protesting Wilson's portrayal of some immigrants as welfare spongers. "Wilson thinks he can solve the problems, but he's just going to create more," says Rosario.

Despite her talk of going home, Hermila acknowledges, "You can at least eat here. You can still get ahead. *Querer es poder.*" (It's a popular saying in Mexico, and it sounds like it comes straight out of a California motivational seminar: "If you want it, you can get it.")

And so the conversation goes, back and forth. Half the time, it's we've had it, we're leaving. But inevitably the dream is resurrected: We're going to make it here. It's a well-known Latino trait: to be *terco*, stubborn, to stake one's pride on doing what others say can't be done, especially when the odds are stacked against you.

The old and the new seem to face off daily in LA. The Anglos say that bilingual education is bad; Latinos take pride in retaining their Spanish. The Anglos say that immigrants should assimilate: Latinos retaliate with *quebradita.* The Anglos say the immigrants are a drain on the economy; the undocumented immigrants start marching on City Hall. The gulf widens.

Nowhere is this more apparent than on college campuses, where Latino students are now more militant than at any other time since the Chicano movement of the late sixties and early seventies. That generation started out with an ultra-nationalist, separatist philosophy, but most of the activists eventually wound up working within the (white) Establishment. Many of today's young Chicanos look upon the old activists as sellouts, even the region's most progressive Latino pols, up to and including County Supervisor Gloria Molina. For the new generation, activism and Aztlán, the mythical Chicano land of milk and honey, separate from white America, are viable again.

Today, however, there isn't just one "movement." There are several. Where Latino students of the sixties were mostly Mexican American and identified with MEChA, today there are also LASA (Latin American Students Association) and ALAS (Association of Latin American Students) for foreign-born Latinos who don't identify themselves as Chicano, and making an even narrower distinction, CASA (Central American Student Association).

I sit in on a CASA meeting at Occidental College in the Coons Boardroom, a corporate-style meeting hall for campus organizations. Lining the walls are portraits of gray-haired white men, the college's founders. In the swivel chairs sit the future power-brokers of the city, brown-skinned children of Guatemalans, Salvadorans, Nicaraguans, Panamanians – wearing backward baseball caps, checkered flannel shirts, Doc Martens. The look is part grunge, part hip-hop, part university whiz-kid square.

There has been plenty of controversy surrounding CASA. "When we formed [last September], there were a lot of criticisms," says CASA president Melvin Cañas, a 21-

year-old premed student majoring in sociology. "People were saying, 'You're going to divide the community, make a weaker front.' But the reason we formed was to learn our culture, not to fight Chicanos for political power on campus. It was to not lose our identity."

"A lot of gringos think that we're Mexicans," says William Vela, a 21-year-old Guatemalan psych major. "CASA formed to let the community know that there are other Latinos as well."

Such divergence – on many fronts – is apparent throughout LA's Latino community. The issue of immigration itself, especially illegal immigration, divides many Latinos. A *Los Angeles Times* poll last September showed that 75 percent of California Latinos view illegal immigration as either a major or moderate problem, and 43 percent have the same response to *legal* immigration. Two-thirds said charging a toll at the border to increase surveillance was a good idea. (Whites agreed on all counts, only more so – 92 percent, 43 percent, and 75 percent respectively.)

But for the vanguard of the new LA – activists like the students at Occidental and their counterparts at campuses across Southern California – what divides the Latino community is not nearly as important as what unites it. When it comes to the hottest of the hot-button immigration issues, Latinos close ranks. More than 60 percent reject Governor Wilson's proposals to deny citizenship to children born of undocumented parents and to cut off illegal immigrants' health and education services. And despite evidence of Latino hostility toward illegal immigration, 60 percent believe that any crackdown on illegal immigration will lead to increased discrimination.

There are other issues that unite the new LA as well, issues that CASA, ALAS, and LASA might call the "real" immigrant problem. The economy, for instance. The new LA may be most successful at redefining cultural assimilation, but as my father pointed out, any assimilation is about decent wages and jobs. Once, immigrant pushcart vendors could open up a store; factory workers were union members with health benefits, pension plans, and middle-class wages. Now, most of these economic routes upward are closed, and not only to immigrants.

In Los Angeles, Latino per capita income is only about 45 percent of the city average; nearly a quarter of Latino families live in poverty. The problem is that the jobs Latinos hold are concentrated in low-wage service and non-union manufacturing sectors. "In the past, people could enter the middle class much quicker," says Rodolfo Acuña, a professor of Chicano studies at Cal State Northridge. "You were socialized by your work place, and could afford to move out and were assimilated. There's been an elimination of those steppingstone jobs."

Another troubling issue is voting. Mexican political scientist Jorge G. Castañeda and others warn of an "electoral apartheid" in California because its Latino immigrant population – a majority of which is legal – has yet to flex much political muscle. This is attributed to its disproportionately young median age, the fact that many legal residents are not yet citizens, and finally, because many are not registered to vote. "In effect, a small, privileged minority is determining the fate of a largely poor, non-voting majority," writes Castañeda in *The California–Mexico Connection*, a collection of essays published last year.

It must be, then, the broadest possible interpretation of *mestizaje*, not separatism, that the new LA will need to assert in the face of such challenges. Castañeda says that one solution is for the white electorate to exercise enlightened self-interest and join with voting Latinos to increase, rather than decrease, social services to immigrants. The newcomers, after all, are the future of the city and the state.

For every separatist slogan, then, there is countervailing evidence of *mestizaje*. In the boardroom at Occidental, the CASA students might complain about the "white man," but they conduct their meetings in English. And who should show up here – because, she says, she thinks she has things in common with her brothers and sisters from throughout Latin America – but Mexicana-Chicana-Americana-*vaquerita* Griselda Mariscal.

I am surrounded by the old LA – Pasadena, actually, old Pasadena, monied Pasadena. The front yard of the house I've been invited to speak at is, literally, a 100-yard golf course. The Chardonnay sparkles in the smoggy afternoon sunlight. It is a fund-raiser for an exclusive artists' colony in Northern California where I had been in residence. I am to speak on – what else? – LA's new immigrant culture. Here we go again.

I sip some Chardonnay and debate silently what tack I'll take this time. Should I try the sensitive multicultural routine, disarming them by listening sympathetically and replying to the inevitable fear in measured tones? Should I become the cultural guerrilla, threatening a violent takeover if demands of social and economic equal opportunity aren't met? Or how about the Jesus-at-the-temple variation, throwing each and every bottle of Chardonnay through the mansion's beautiful wood-framed windows?

I pick the California Idealist approach.

There is a plaque at Olvera Street, I tell them, that lists the names of the 44 *pobladores* who arrived here in 1781 and founded the city of El Pueblo de la Reina de Los Angeles Sobre el Río de Porciúncula. Do they know what the ethnic makeup of that group was? The majority were Black or mulatto. The next-largest group was *mestizo*. There were Indians from Mexico. And there were a couple of Spaniards. Los Angeles, I say, has always held out the promise of multiculturalism.

I get polite applause at the end of the talk, and a few liberals – the kind who assume I lived a nightmarish childhood in the barrio and made it out against the odds – ask sympathetic questions. But later, as I'm making my way back to the appetizers, I am cornered by an agitated group, the conservatives who were afraid to voice their un-PC opinions before the larger crowd. They hurl questions at me: Isn't bilingual education failing to educate Latino children? Don't you think that there should be more birth control in your community? Don't you understand that the economy just can't handle any more immigrants? Doesn't the United States have a right to regulate its borders?

I try to maintain my composure. And then a tall, white-haired man in white slacks and snappy summer shirt tells me: "You're just trying to make yourself out to be a victim so I'll feel guilty. But I'm not guilty of anything. Your problems are not my responsibility."

The guerrilla in me explodes.

I can't remember what I said. But what I should have said is this: In a sense, we're all victims of this crazy time we live in.We are reaping the fruit of hundreds of years of a great and violent history. A history of American optimism and greed. A history of Latin American solidarity and victimization. Racism, and, yes, reverse racism. I would like to meet you as an equal, on the border. Right smack between our two worlds; right here, in Los Angeles.

You must accept that the Latinos of California aren't going anywhere, I should have told him. We have always been here and we are here to stay. You must stop thinking and acting with the arrogance of a culture that sees itself as *the* arbiter of life in the city: Your culture will become less and less dominant.

And I must accept that you aren't going anywhere, either. That your culture runs through my veins, that the immigrant that crosses the border leaves behind one world to enter a new one.

You must allow yourself to be transformed, even as we are being and have been transformed. It is a process that is at the heart of America's democratic identity. Resisting this change is to resist history itself – and the consequences could be disastrous.

Triqui-triqui. It means "trick or treat." It is Halloween, and I am on Sunset Boulevard in Echo Park. The sidewalks are choked with hundreds of costumed children and their parents, aunts, uncles, and grandparents. Nearly all are Mexican and Central American.

I stand in front of a *panadería* whose storefront windows display not only all the typical sugary breads, but also blow-up pumpkins,

cobwebs, and huge black widow spiders dangling over the kids' heads. *Triqui-triqui.*

A slightly tipsy father with a blurry pirate's mustache penciled on his upper lip trains his videocam on the scene. "Isn't it great?" he says. "It's so beautiful, Halloween."

At the counter, Marisela de la Rosa, who's been here only two years from Mexico City, smiles at a 5-year-old ninja warrior and drops candy into his plastic pumpkin basket. "But it's not like back home," she says wistfully, recalling *el Dia de los Muertos,* the Day of the Dead, which is celebrated in Mexico on November 1 and 2. The holiday isn't a Mexican Halloween, it's a *mestizo* blend of pre-Columbian and Catholic rituals. "We go to the cemetery with flowers and offerings to the dead, their favorite food and drink. All the family gathers together and we clean off the grave. We prepare *moles* and *ponches.*" Halloween, she says, is more about "just having fun."

And fun is what people are having tonight. A sea of costumes on Sunset: Superman, Wonder Woman, ninjas, Ninja Turtles, little devils with red capes and pitchforks, gypsies, little angels with golden wings and magic wands. Looks like the battle between Halloween and the Day of the Dead is over and done. *Triqui-triqui.*

But this is LA. I stop by a Mexican restaurant on Sunset Boulevard in Echo Park and watch a parade of kids walk up to Candelaria Reyes, who with her folkloric waitress outfit, her plumpness, and her sweet demeanor reminds me of every Latino grandmother I've ever met. "Yes, Halloween is fun," she says, dropping candies in the succession of bags and buckets the kids hold up to her, acknowledging every one of them with a "*m'hijito*" or "*m'hijita*". But, Candelaria says, that doesn't mean we have to lose our traditions. "In my house, we celebrate the Day of the Dead *and* Halloween. We have our *nacimiento* at Christmas. We go to church all Easter Week. We celebrate Mexican Independence. And the Fourth of July. We have to respect this country's traditions, too, become good citizens."

The wisdom of a grandmother, I think to

myself. After 35 years in this country, Candelaria Reyes has brokered a treaty between the factions that have been at war ever since the Treaty of Guadalupe Hidalgo was signed in 1848.

When I walk back out onto Sunset Boulevard, I see the scene with different eyes. I watch families, the big Latino families participating in a ritual as American as Jason and "Friday the 13th," but with the communal spirit of a Sunday gathering in a small-town plaza south of the border. It is Halloween and Day of the Dead all at once. It is the new Los Angeles.

# Our Next Race Question
# The Uneasiness between Blacks and Latinos

## Jorge Klor de Alva, Earl Shorris, and Cornel West

The angry and confused discourse about American race relations that followed the O. J. Simpson trial may have been passionate, but it blindly assumed (as if the year were 1963 or 1861) that the only major axis of racial division in America was Black–White. Strangely ignored in the media backwash was the incipient tension between the country's largest historical minority, Blacks, and its largest future one, Latinos.

In 15 years, Latinos (known to the US Census as Hispanics) will outnumber Blacks, as they already do in 21 states. Each group constitutes an ever greater percentage of the total population; each is large enough to swing a presidential election. But do they vote with or against each other, and do they hold the same views of a white America that they have different reasons to distrust?

Knowing that questions of power and ethnicity are no longer black-and-white, *Harper's Magazine* invited three observers – a Black, a Latino, and a White moderator – to open the debate.

EARL SHORRIS: To begin, would you both answer one question with a yes or no, no more than that? Cornel, are you a black man?

CORNEL WEST: Yes.

SHORRIS: Jorge, do you think Cornel is a black man?

JORGE KLOR DE ALVA: No, for now.

SHORRIS: Apparently we have something to talk about. Jorge, can you tell me why you say, "No, for now?"

KLOR DE ALVA: To identify someone as black, Latino, or anything else, one has to appeal to a tradition of naming and categorizing in which a question like that can make sense – and be answered with a yes or a no. In the United States, where unambiguous, color-coded identities are the rule, Cornel is clearly a black man. Traveling someplace else, perhaps in Africa, Cornel would not necessarily be identified as black. He might be seen as someone of mixed African descent, but that's different from being identified as black. Cornel is only black within a certain reductionist context. And that context, where color is made to represent not so much the hue of one's skin as a set of denigrated experiences – and where these experiences are applied to everyone who ever had an African ancestor – is one I consider to be extremely negative.

WEST: I think when I say I am a black man, I'm saying first that I am a modern person, because black itself is a modern construct, a construct put forward during a particular moment in time to fit a specific set of circumstances. Implicit in that category of "black man" is American white supremacy, African slavery, and then a very rich culture that responds to these conditions at the level of style, mannerism, orientation, experimentation, improvisation, syncopation – all of those elements that have gone into making a new people, namely black people.

A hundred years ago I would have said

that I was a "colored man." But I would still have been modern, I'd still have been New World African, I'd still have been dealing with white supremacy, and I would still have been falling back on a very rich culture of resistance, a culture that tried to preserve black sanity and spiritual health in the face of white hatred and job ceilings. I think Jorge and I agree that we're dealing with constructs. And I think we agree in our objections to essentialist conceptions of race, to the idea that differences are innate and outside of history.

KLOR DE ALVA: What advantage has it been, Cornel, for blacks to identify themselves as blacks?

WEST: For one, that identification was imposed. We were perceived as a separate people – enslaved, Jim Crowed, and segregated. To be viewed as a separate people requires coming to terms with that separateness. This category "black" was simply a response to that imposition of being a separate people, and also a building on one's own history, going back to Africa, yes, but especially here in the United States. So when I say, for example, that jazz is a creation of black people, I'm saying that it's a creation of modern people, New World African people. And we've come up with various categories, including black, as a way of affirming ourselves as agents, as subjects in history who create, initiate, and so forth. So in that sense there have actually been some real benefits.

KLOR DE ALVA: When the Europeans arrived in Mexico, they confronted people whose level of social organization was not unlike that of the Romans. Before millions died from newly introduced diseases, the Europeans called them *naturales,* or "natural people." Afterwards the survivors came to be called "Indians," a term the natives did not use until the nineteenth century, preferring to identify themselves by their tribal group. And to the extent that they were able to do that, they managed to maintain a degree of cultural integrity as separate groups. When that ended, they were all seen as despised Indians.

The general label only helped to promote their denigration. Now, I agree that group designations help build a sense of community, but as free and enslaved Africans took on the general labels that oppressed them, they also helped to legitimize their being identified as one irredeemable people. In the United States this unwillingness to challenge what has come to be known as the one-drop rule – wherein anyone who ever had an African ancestor, however remote, is identifiable only as black – has strengthened the hand of those who seek to trap them, and other so-called people of color, in a social basement with no exit ladder.

WEST: When we talk about identity, it's really important to define it. Identity has to do with protection, association, and recognition. People identify themselves in certain ways in order to protect their bodies, their labor, their communities, their way of life; in order to be associated with people who ascribe value to them, who take them seriously, who respect them; and for purposes of recognition, to be acknowledged, to feel as if one actually belongs to a group, a clan, a tribe, a community. So that any time we talk about the identity of a particular group over time and space, we have to be very specific about what the credible options are for them at any given moment.

There have been some black people in America who fundamentally believed that they were wholehearted, full-fledged Americans. They have been mistaken. They tried to pursue that option – Boom! Jim Crow hit them. They tried to press that option – Boom! Vanilla suburbs didn't allow them in. So they had to then revise and recast their conception of themselves in terms of protection, association, and recognition. Because they weren't being protected by the police and the courts. They weren't welcome in association. Oftentimes they were not welcome in white suburbs.

And they weren't being recognized. Their talents and capacities were debased, devalued, and degraded. "Black" was the term many chose. Okay, that's fine, we can argue about that. But what are the other options? "Human being?" Yes, we ought to be human beings, but we know that's too abstract and too vague. We need human communities on the ground, not simply at the level of the ideal.

KLOR DE ALVA: Nobody is born black. People are born with different pigmentation, people are born with different physical characteristics, no question about that. But you have to learn to be black. That's what I mean by constructedness.

WEST: But are people born human? Is "human" itself constructed, as a category?

KLOR DE ALVA: Certainly as a category, as a social, as a scientific category, of course it's a construct. The species could have been identified in some other fashion. Since Columbus' landfall you had very extensive debates as to whether indigenous peoples in the Americas were human, like Europeans, or not. The priest Montesinos posed that question to the Spanish colonists in 1511, and Las Casas, a fellow priest, and the theologian Sepúlveda debated the issue at mid-century before Emperor Charles V.

WEST: You see, this historical process of naming is part of the legacy not just of white supremacy but of class supremacy. Tolstoy didn't believe his peasants were actually human until after he underwent conversion. And he realized, "My God, I used to think they were animals, now they're human beings, I have a different life and a new set of lenses with which to view it." So it is with any talk about blackness. It's associated with subhumanness, and therefore when we talk about constructed terms like "black" or "peasant" or "human," it means that the whole thing's up for grabs in terms of constructedness. And if that's so, then all we have left is history.

KLOR DE ALVA: All identities are up for grabs. But Black intellectuals in the United States, unlike Latino intellectuals in the United States, have an enormous media space within which to shape the politics of naming and to affect the symbols and meanings associated with certain terms. Thus, practically overnight, they convinced the media that they were an ethnic group and shifted over to the model of African-American, hyphenated American, as opposed to being named by color. Knowing what we know about the negative aspects of naming, it would be better for all of us, regardless of color, if those who consider themselves, and are seen as, black intellectuals were to stop participating in the insidious one-drop-rule game of identifying themselves as black.

WEST: If you're saying that we are, for the most part, biological and cultural hybrids, I think you're certainly right. But at the same time there's a danger in calling for an end to a certain history if we're unable to provide other options. Now, because I speak first and foremost as a human being, a radical Democrat, and a Christian, I would be willing to use damn near any term if it helped to eliminate poverty and provide adequate health care and child care and a job with a living wage, some control at the workplace, and some redistribution of wealth downward. At that point, you can call all black people colored. That's fine with me.

SHORRIS: Are you saying that you're willing to disappear?

WEST: Well, I would never disappear, because whatever name we would come up with, we're still going to have the blues and John Coltrane and Sarah Vaughan and all those who come out of this particular history. And simply because we change the name wouldn't mean that we would disappear.

KLOR DE ALVA: I think that's the wrong emphasis. I think what has happened is that much of the cultural diversity that Cornel mentions has, in fact, disappeared behind this veil that has transformed everybody with one drop of African blood into black. That reductionism has been a much more powerful mechanism for causing diversity to disappear.

WEST: Well, what do you mean by disappearance at this point?

KLOR DE ALVA: Let me answer your question from a slightly different perspective. We have, in the United States, two mechanisms at play in the construction of collective identities. One is to identify folks from a cultural perspective. The other is to identify them from a racial perspective. Now, with the exception of black-white relations, the racial perspective is not the critical one for most folks. The cultural perspective was, at one time, very sharply drawn, including the religious line between Catholics and Protestants, Jews and Protestants, Jews and Catholics, Jews and Christians. But in the course of the twentieth century, we have seen in the United States a phenomenon that we do not see anyplace else in the world – the capacity to blur the differences between these cultural groups, to construct them in such a way that they became insignificant and to fuse them into a new group called whites, which didn't exist before.

WEST: Yes, but whiteness was already in place. I mean, part of the tragedy of American civilization is precisely the degree to which the stability and continuity of American democracy has been predicated on a construct of whiteness that includes the subordination of black people, so that European cultural diversity could disappear into American whiteness while black folk remain subordinated.

KLOR DE ALVA: But everything, even whiteness, must be constructed and is therefore subject to change.

WEST: Categories are constructed. Scars and bruises are felt with human bodies, some of which end up in coffins. Death is not a construct. And so, when we're talking about constructs having concrete consequences that produce scars and bruises, these consequences are not constructed, they're felt. They're very real. Now, in light of that, I would want to accent the strengths of the history of black resistance. One of the reasons why black people are so integral a part of American civilization is because black people have raised a lot of hell. That's very important, especially in a

society in which power and pressure decide who receives visibility. By raising hell I mean organization, mobilization, chaos-producing capacity, as in rebellion. That's a very important point. Why is it important? It's important for me because what's at stake is the quality of American civilization, whether it actually survives as a plausible idea.

That's why a discourse on race is never just a discourse on race. Richard Wright used to say that the Negro is America's metaphor. It means you can't talk about one without talking about the nature of the other. And one of the reasons we don't like to talk about race, especially as it relates to black folk, is because we're forced to raise all the fundamental questions about what it means to be an American, what it means to be a part of American democracy. Those are exhausting and challenging questions.

The best of the black intellectual and political tradition has always raised the problem of evil in its concrete forms in America. People like Frederick Douglass, Martin Luther King, and Ella Baker never focused solely on black suffering. They used black suffering as a springboard to raise issues of various other forms of injustice, suffering, and so forth, that relate to other groups – black, brown, white workers, right across the board, you see. During the eighties, the major opposition to right-wing Reaganism was what? Jesse Jackson's campaigns. Opening up to workers, gay brothers, lesbian sisters, right across the board. Black suffering was a springboard. Why? Because a question of evil sits at the heart of the American moral dilemma. With the stark exception of its great artists – Melville, Faulkner, Elizabeth Bishop, Coltrane, Toni Morrison – American society prefers to deny the existence of its own evil. Black folk historically have reminded people of the prevailing state of denial.

SHORRIS: We've just demonstrated one of the tenets of this conversation. That is, we have discussed almost exclusively the question of blacks in this society. But we started out saying we could have a black-brown dialogue. Why does that happen? And not only in the media. Why did it happen here, among us?

KLOR DE ALVA: Part of the answer, as Cornel was pointing out, is that blacks are the central metaphor for otherness and oppression in the United States. Secondly, in part I take your question, when focused on Latinos, to mean, Don't Latinos have their own situation that also needs to be described if not in the same terms, then at least in terms that are supplementary?

I'm not sure. The answer goes to the very core of the difference between Latinos and blacks and between Cornel and myself: I am trying to argue against the utility of the concept of race. Why? Because I don't think that's the dominant construct we need to address in order to resolve the many problems at hand. Cornel wants to construct it in the language of the United States, and I say we need a different kind of language. Do you know why, Earl? Because we're in the United States and blacks are Americans. They're Anglos.

WEST: Excuse me?

KLOR DE ALVA: They're Anglos of a different color, but they're Anglos. Why? Because the critical distinction here for Latinos is not race, it's culture.

WEST: Speaking English and being part of American culture?

KLOR DE ALVA: Blacks are more Anglo than most Anglos because, unlike most Anglos, they can't directly identify themselves with a nation-state outside of the United States. They are trapped in America. However unjust and painful, their experiences are wholly made in America.

WEST: But that doesn't make me an Anglo. If I'm trapped on the underside of America, that doesn't mean that somehow I'm an Anglo.

KLOR DE ALVA: Poor whites similarly trapped on the underside of America are also Anglos. Latinos are in a totally different situation, unable to be captured by the government in the "five food groups" of racial classification of Americans. The Commerce Department didn't know what to do with Latinos; the census-takers didn't know what to do with Latinos; the government didn't know what to do with Latinos, and so they said, "Latinos can be of any race." That puts Latinos, in a totally different situation. They are, in fact, homologous with the totality of the United States. That is, like Americans, Latinos can be of any race. What distinguishes them from all other Americans is culture, not race. That's where I'm going when I say that Cornel is an Anglo. You can be a Latino and look like Cornel. You can be a Latino and look like you, Earl, or like me. And so, among Latinos, there's no surprise in my saying that Cornel is an Anglo.

WEST: But it seems to me that "Anglo" is the wrong word.

KLOR DE ALVA: Hey, I didn't make it up, Cornel.

WEST: "Anglo" implies a set of privileges. It implies a certain cultural formation.

KLOR DE ALVA: I'm trying to identify here how Chicanos see "Anglos."

WEST: But I want to try and convince those Latino brothers and sisters not to think of black folk as Anglos. That's just wrong. Now, they can say that we're English-speaking moderns in the United States who have yet to be fully treated as Americans. That's fine.

KLOR DE ALVA: My friend, Cornel, I was speaking of one of the more benign Latino names for blacks.

WEST: Let's hear some of the less benign then, brother.

KLOR DE ALVA: Do you think of Latinos as white?

WEST: I think of them as brothers and sisters, as human beings, but in terms of culture, I think of them as a particular group of voluntary immigrants who entered America and had to encounter this thoroughly absurd system of classification of positively charged whiteness, negatively charged blackness. And they don't fit either one: they're not white, they're not black.

SHORRIS: What are they?

WEST: I see them primarily as people of color, as brown people who have to deal with their blackness-whiteness.

SHORRIS: So you see them in racial terms.

WEST: Well, no, it's more cultural.

SHORRIS: But you said "brown."

WEST: No, it's more cultural. Brown, for me, is more associated with culture than race.

SHORRIS: But you choose a word that describes color.

WEST: Right. To say "Spanish-speaking" would be a bit too vague, because you've got a lot of brothers and sisters from Guatemala who don't speak Spanish. They speak an indigenous language.

KLOR DE ALVA: You have a lot of Latinos who aren't brown.

WEST: But they're not treated as whites, and "brown" is simply a signifier of that differential treatment. Even if a Latino brother or sister has supposedly white skin, he or she is still Latino in the eyes of the white privileged, you see. But they're not treated as black. They're not niggers. They're not the bottom of the heap, you see. So they're not niggers, they're not white, what are they? I say brown, but signifying culture more than color. Mexicans, Cubans, Puerto Ricans, Dominicans, El Salvadorans all have very, very distinctive histories. When you talk about black, that becomes a kind of benchmark, because you've got these continuous generations, and you've got very common experiences.

Now, of course, blackness comprises a concealed heterogeneity. You've got West Indians, you've got Ethiopians. My wife is Ethiopian. Her experience is closer to browns'. She came here because she wanted to. She was trying to get out from under a tyrannical, Communist regime in Ethiopia. She's glad to be in a place where she can breathe freely, not have to hide. I say, "I'm glad you're here, but don't allow that one side of America to blind you to my side."

So I've got to take her, you know, almost like Virgil in Dante's *Divine Comedy*, through all of this other side of America so that she can see the nightmare as well as the dream. But as an Ethiopian, she came for the dream and did a good job of achieving it.

KLOR DE ALVA: So you are participating in the same process as the other Americans, other Anglos – to use that complicated term – that same song and dance of transforming her into a highly racialized American black.

WEST: It wasn't me. It was the first American who called her "nigger." That's when she started the process of Americanization and racialization. She turned around and said, "What is a nigger?"

KLOR DE ALVA: And you're the one who explained it.

SHORRIS: How do you see yourself, Jorge?

KLOR DE ALVA: I'm an American citizen. What are you, Cornel?

WEST: I am a black man trying to be an American citizen.

KLOR DE ALVA: I'm an American citizen trying to get rid of as many categories as possible that classify people in ways that make it easy for them to be oppressed, isolated, marginalized. Of course, I'm a Chicano, I'm a Mexican-American. But for me to identify myself that way is not much help. More helpful is my actually working to resolve the problems of poor folks in the United States.

If I were black, I would heighten the importance of citizenship. Why? Because every time we've seen huge numbers of immigrants enter the United States, the people most devastated by their arrival, in terms of being relegated to an even lower rung on the employment ladder, have been blacks.

SHORRIS: Are you defining "black" and "Latino" as "poor"?

KLOR DE ALVA: No, no. I'm not defining them that way at all.

WEST: What's fascinating about this issue of race is the degree to which, in the American mind, black people are associated with instability, chaos, disorder – the very things that America always runs from. In addition, we are associated with hypersexuality, transgressive criminal activity – all of the various stereotypes and images.

SHORRIS: We all know LBJ's comment about affirmative action. He said that it's the right thing to do but that it will destroy the Democratic Party. There certainly is every likelihood that it has destroyed the Democratic Party as it's traditionally been understood, that the Democratic Party's base in the South has disappeared, that the white South now votes Republican and many blacks don't vote at all. What does this mean about America and the likelihood of any kind of affirmative action, or any program for social justice, succeeding, either for blacks or for Latinos?

KLOR DE ALVA: No matter what kind of policy you set in place, there has to be something in it for everybody or the policy is not going to last very long. And I'm not even going to get into the issue that affirmative action has been essentially an African-American thing, not a Latino thing.

WEST: But who have the major beneficiaries been? White women. And rightly so. More of them have been up against the patriarchy than black and brown people have been up against racism.

KLOR DE ALVA: If you're right that white women are the main beneficiaries, and if I'm right that African-Americans were meant to be the primary beneficiaries, then we have to ask if affirmative action is an effective strategy for the resolution of the Latinos' problems. And has the failure of class organization been due primarily to the racial divisions in the society? If so, then race is a lamentable category for any kind of progressive organization, and we need an alternative to affirmative action. I would remove the government from participation in the naming game and its divisive racializing of identities.

WEST: To the degree to which the Democractic Party cuts against a strong white supremacist grain in America and identifies with black people unequivocally, it will be destroyed. That's essentially what the Republican strategy has been since 1968. The question then becomes, How do we talk about these issues of class while also recognizing that any silence with respect to the de facto white supremacy results in institutions that ought to be changed because they have little moral content to them? If you're going to have a spineless, milquetoast Democratic Party that can't say a word against racism, it doesn't deserve to exist anyway.

KLOR DE ALVA: Affirmative action has had the capacity to create a black middle class. Many of these folks also have been the dominant group in the civil rights arena and in other human rights areas. The net effect has been to create a layer, essentially of African-Americans, within the public sphere that has been very difficult for Latinos to penetrate and make their complaints known.

WEST: That's true, and I think it's wrong. But at the same time, blacks are more likely to register protests than Latinos are. That's what I mean by raising hell, you see. Black people are more likely to raise hell than brown people.

KLOR DE ALVA: But having been blocked from the public sector, I am concerned that Latinos turning to the private one will buy deeply into US concepts of race and will be even less willing than Anglos to employ blacks. So for me, any new social or public policy must begin with dismantling the language of race.

WEST: It's important not to conflate overcoming racial barriers with dismantling racial language. I'm all for the former; I'm not so sure about the latter, because it ignores or minimizes the history of racism. Most of human history is a history of oligarchs, unaccountable elites, manipulating anger, rage, setting working people against one another to enable those elites to maintain their position. That's why democracies are so rare in human history.

SHORRIS: Let me ask you a question about oligarchies. There are wealthy blacks, middle-class blacks, and many poor blacks. There are wealthy browns, middle-class browns, many poor browns. Are we talking about two groups or six? Are we talking about economic self-interest being greater than any kind of cultural or racial self-interest?

WEST: There is always going to be self-interest operating. The question is: How does it relate to the common good and contribute to the production, distribution, and consumption of goods and services so that there's some relative equality? Now, the six groups that you're talking about have to do with class divisions within brown and black America. The class divisions are there. And they're going to increase, there's no doubt about that. We're going to see more conservatives in black America, more conservatives in brown America, because the country in general is tilting in that direction and it's nice to be on the bandwagon. Even though we claim to be with the underdog, it's very American to want to be with the winners. So as those class divisions escalate, you're gong to get class envy and class hatred within brown America as well as within black America. One of the purposes of a black–brown dialogue is to head of precisely these kinds of hatreds and various forms of bigotry.

KLOR DE ALVA: At the level of the working class, we're seeing a great deal of cooperation, but as you move up the economic scale you have progressively more turf wars – how many slots blacks get for this, how many slots Latinos get for that. Once you get to mayors of towns or cities, you have Latinos who aren't going to do terribly much for the black community or, if they're black, not very much for the Latino community. Hence my emphasis on a solution that addresses economics rather than race.

WEST: We do have some data in terms of voting behavior when it comes to brown–black contrast. Ninety percent of whoever votes in the black community still votes Democratic, right? Cubans, a million Cubans in America, vote for Republicans. We have 2.8 million Puerto Ricans. They vote for Democratic roughly 60–40. We have 17.1 million Mexicans. They vote,

the majority, for the Democratic Party. Black Americans tilt much more toward the Democratic Party than any other group, à la LBJ's idea: It's going to destroy this party, all these black folk over here. You see, once you get that racial divide, you can promote white anxieties and white fears, and you can use that for all it's worth. And the Republicans are going to use that into the twenty-first century. There's no doubt about it.

KLOR DE ALVA: Cornel, you're going back to the question of this evil empire.

WEST: No, it's not evil. It's a civilization in which there is a problem of evil.

KLOR DE ALVA: All civilizations have a problem with evil.

WEST: But some – like the United States – are in sustained denial even as they view themselves as the embodiment of good.

KLOR DE ALVA: I don't agree with that. I would say that one of the significant ideological possibilities, a door that's always open in the United States – and it goes back to that old contrast between Mexico and the United States – is that the United States has an epic vision, a vision of good against evil. Latinos supposedly have a tragic vision – a conflict between two goods. But in the United States, evil is always right there, and its defeat, like its creation, can therefore be imagined. Cornel, you represent evil if you take off your three-piece suit and walk out into the street at three o'clock in the morning.

WEST: Brother, I represent evil now, as a savage in a suit. Because this is black skin, what we started with. So I don't need to take off my suit. But the difference is this: The tragic view – of Unamuno or Melville or Faulkner or Morrison or Coltrane – is a much more morally mature view of what it is to be human. The triumphant view of good over evil, which is Manichaean, is sophomoric, childish. It has been dominant in America because our civilization is so spoiled.

KLOR DE ALVA: I would like to agree with you were it not for the fact that the tragic vision is also a kind of Hamlet vision. It makes it very difficult to move, to overcome evil.

WEST: But better Hamlet than Captain Ahab in *Moby-Dick*. And that's precisely what Melville was getting at – this tremendous voluntaristic view of the world in which a will to power, based on an absolute conception of good over evil, allows one to lead toward what? Nihilism, self-destruction. I'd go with Hamlet any day.

KLOR DE ALVA: Not me, not at the price of indecision and paralysis.

WEST: Now, Martin Luther King was neither Hamlet nor Captain Ahab, you see. King was something else. King actually comes out of a black tradition with a profound sense of the tragic. When he has Mahalia Jackson sing "Precious Lord," that's not triumphalism. That is the deepest sense of the tragic nature of this civilization, the same tragic sense at work in the spirituals and the blues and jazz. King was not in any way a triumphalist. The great King insight is that because he rejects triumphalism he knows that the evil is not simply external, that it's in him. He knew that there was white supremacy in him. That's what allowed him to love Bull Connor even as he opposed Connor's white supremacy. That's the great Christian insight.

KLOR DE ALVA: I agree with you. The evil is here in the United States, but it can be challenged.

SHORRIS: Cornel, what do you most worry about in the future?

WEST: I think my fundamental concern is the disintegration of American civilization as black people become more and more insulated, isolated, targeted, and hence subjected to the most brutal authoritarian rule in the name of democracy. And that's exactly where we're headed, so it's not just a fear.

KLOR DE ALVA: I would say that what you've described for America would be true of just about any nation I know, particularly any multicultural nation. It's not something that's unique to the United States. My biggest fear, as this nation moves into an inevitable browning, or hybridization, is that there will be a very powerful minority, overwhelmingly composed of Euro-Americans, who will see themselves in significant danger as a consequence of the way democracy works: winner take all. And they will begin to renege on some of the basic principles that created the United States and made it what it is.

SHORRIS: We've been talking about conflicts. Let's stipulate, unless you disagree, that the advantage to the people in power of keeping those at the bottom at each other's throats is enormous. That's the case in all societies. So we have blacks and browns, for the most part, at the bottom. And they are frequently at each other's throats. They're fighting over immigration, fighting over jobs, and so on. A group of young people comes to you and says, "Tell us how to make alliances, give us a set of rules for creating alliances between blacks and browns." What would you answer?

WEST: I'd appeal to various examples. Look at Ernesto Cortés and the Industrial Areas Foundation in Texas or the Harlem Initiatives Together in New York City, which have been able to pull off black–brown alliances of great strength, the "breaking bread" events of the Democratic Socialists of America. Or I'd talk about Mark Ridley-Thomas in South-Central Los Angeles and look at the ways in which he speaks with power about brown suffering as a black city councilman, the way in which he's able to build within his own organization a kind of black–brown dialogue. Because what you really see then is not just a set of principles or rules but some momentum at work.

SHORRIS: But how do you do that? What's the first step?

WEST: Well, it depends on what particular action you want to highlight. You could, say, look at the movement around environmental racism, where you have a whole host of black–brown alliances. With Proposition 187 you had a black–brown alliance among progressives fighting against the conservatives who happened to be white, black, and brown. In the trade-union movement, look at 1199, the health-care workers union, here in New York City. You've got brown Dennis Rivera at the top, you've got black Gerry Hudson third in charge, running things. That's a very significant coordinated leadership of probably the most important trade union in the largest city in the nation. So it depends on the particular issue. I think it's issue by issue in light of a broad vision.

SHORRIS: What is the broad vision?

WEST: Democracy, substantive radical democracy in which you actually are highlighting the empowering of everyday people in the workplace and the voting booth so that they can live lives of decency and dignity. That's a deeply democratic sensibility. And I think that sensibility can be found in both the black and brown communities.

KLOR DE ALVA: Unless there's a dramatic shift in ideology, linkages between people who are identified as belonging to opposing camps will last only for the moment, like the graffiti I saw during the LA riots: "Crips. Bloods. Mexicans. Together. Forever. Tonite [sic]," and then next to that, "LAPD" crossed out and "187"

underneath. That is, the alliances will work only as long as there's a common enemy, in this case the LAPD, whose death the graffiti advocated by the term "187," which refers here to the California Criminal Code for homicide.

As long as we don't have a fundamental transformation in ideology, those are the kinds of alliances we will have, and they will be short-lived and not lead, ultimately, to terribly much. Clearly, the progressive forces within the United States must be able to forge ideological changes that would permit lasting linkages. At the core of that effort lies the capacity to address common suffering, regardless of color or culture. And that cannot be done unless common suffering, as the reason for linkages across all lines, is highlighted in place of the very tenuous alliances between groups that identify themselves by race or culture.

SHORRIS: Let's see if anything happened in this conversation. Cornel, are you a black man?

WEST: Hell yes.

SHORRIS: Jorge, is he a black man?

KLOR DE ALVA: Of course not.

# Part III

*Critical Discourses on Gender, Sexuality, and Power*

# Chicana Feminisms: Their Political Context and Contemporary Expressions

## Denise A. Segura[1] and Beatriz M. Pesquera

> Because I, a *mestiza*,
> continually walk out of one culture
> and into another,
> because I am in all cultures at the same time,
> *alma entre dos mundos, tres, cuatro,*
> *me zumba la cabeza con lo contradictorio.*
> *Estoy norteada por todas las voces que me hablan*
> *simultaneamente.*[2]
>
> Gloria Anzaldua (1987: 77)

Chicanas,[3] women of Mexican heritage in the United States, are bilingual, bicultural women of color who weave diverse paths through multiple social terrains. Chicana feminists strive to maintain racial-ethnic unity while contesting patriarchal domination. This struggle poses many contradictions: "Estoy norteada por todas las voces que me hablan simultaneamente [I am guideless for the many voices that speak to me simultaneously]."

This essay explores historical and contemporary expressions of Chicana feminisms.[4] We begin with a brief profile of Chicanas. We follow this with an exploration of the political context of Chicana feminisms. Then, we profile three Chicana feminist organizations that embody various aspects of the Chicana movement. We conclude with a discussion of contemporary Chicana feminist perspectives.

## WHO ARE CHICANAS?

Chicanas' membership in a historically subordinated racial-ethnic group, their concentration among the poor and working class, and their gender have resulted in a situation of "triple oppression" (Segura, 1986; Apodaca, 1986; Mirande and Enriquez,

1979). As Mexicans, Chicanas have been treated as "second-class citizens" since their incorporation into the United States in 1848 (Acuña, 1981; US Commission on Civil Rights, 1972). Historically, they have encountered racial-ethnic and gender discrimination, limiting their access to education, jobs, and political participation. They are overrepresented among the poor and lower working classes. Concurrently, Chicanas have maintained a distinct Chicano/Mexican culture (Garcia, 1982; Keefe and Padilla, 1987).

A profile of Chicana education, employment, earnings, and income reveals key differences by gender and race-ethnicity that place them in disadvantageous situations vis-à-vis the majority white population. In 1992, approximately 14 million people of Mexican heritage lived in the United States. They were 63.6 percent of the US Hispanic population (US Bureau of the Census, 1992: Table 1).[5] Chicano families have a substantially lower median income ($23,019 in 1990) than non-Hispanic white families ($39,240 in 1991). Moreover, in 1992 over one-quarter (27.4 percent) of Chicano families lived below the poverty line, compared to 7.1 percent of non-Hispanic white families (US Bureau of the Census, 1992: Table 4).

Chicanas' employment experiences inform their political consciousness or sense of themselves as racial-ethnic women. In 1992 the Chicana labor force participation rate was at 51.6 percent for persons 16 and over, which is slightly lower than the 58 percent rate of non-Hispanic white women but substantially lower than that of either non-Hispanic white men (74.6 percent) or Chicano men (80 percent) (US Bureau of the Census, 1992: Table 2). Their 1992 unemployment rate was higher (10.5 percent) than that of non-Hispanic white women (5.4 percent), but lower than that of Chicano men (12.4 percent). These differences reflect several phenomena: high fertility among young Chicanas, lower levels of education, inadequate affordable child care, and employment in relatively unstable or seasonal jobs. Like all women, Chicanas tend to work in administrative support (clerical) jobs. But only 14 percent of Chicanas, compared to 29.7 percent of non-Hispanic white women, work in managerial or professional occupations (US Bureau of the Census, 1992: Table 2). In this regard Chicanas appear more similar to Chicano men, of whom 9.3 percent worked as managers or professionals. Far more Chicanas (16.2 percent) than non-Hispanic white women (6.5 percent) worked in low-paying, often unstable jobs as operators, fabricators, and laborers (14.9 percent and 7.5 percent respectively). At the same time, 29.2 percent of Chicano men worked in these jobs. The median 1991 earnings of all full-time Chicana workers was $15,637. This was substantially lower than that of Chicano men ($18,156), non-Hispanic white women ($21,098), and non-Hispanic white men ($31,161) (US Bureau of the Census, 1991: Table 2). This brief comparison demonstrates how the intersection of gender and race-ethnicity negatively affects Chicana employment and earnings. This unique set of circumstances informs a distinct Chicana perspective, a world view that guides their assessment of the relevancy of social reforms or movements, including American feminism.

## THE POLITICAL CONTEXT FOR CHICANA FEMINISMS

Contemporary Chicana feminism emerged during the turbulent social movements of the 1960s and early 1970s that challenged existing power relations on the basis of race-ethnicity and gender/sexuality. The "second wave" of the American women's movement called into question patriarchal relations – systemic male domination and female subordination. Social movements by people of color, including the Chicano movement, opposed the structuring of power and privilege on the basis of race-ethnicity. Central to these movements was a critique of power relations in social institutions and the prevailing cultural ideologies that justified them. However, each differed in their focus (women, the Chicano community), their understanding of oppression, overall ideological orientations, and political programs to eliminate social inequality.

Many Chicanas perceived that their realities did not readily "fit" into the perspectives and programs of either social movement. Chicanas' needs and aspirations for liberation were typically ignored, subsumed, or trivialized within both the American women's movement and the Chicano movement. Chicana feminists took exception to the framing of oppression based primarily on gender. In addition, they criticized the reformist character espoused by many prominent mainstream feminist groups such as NOW and *Ms.* magazine. By *reformist* they meant a focus on incorporating women into existing, highly stratified socioeconomic structures (e.g., women accessing male domains) as opposed to changing race-ethnic, class, and gender relations in these structures. Chicanas perceived this reformism as inadequate in that it would not change all forms of social inequality (Del Castillo, 1971; Nieto-Gomez, 1973, 1974; Martinez, 1972; Flores, 1973).

In October 1970, at the "Women's Workshop" of the Mexican American Issues Conference, Chicana participants identified the absence of organizations that met their needs as a serious obstacle to their empowerment. To address this issue, a resolution was passed to establish a Chicana-centered organization, Comision Femenil Mexicana Nacional, Inc. Part of the resolution stated:

The efforts and work of Chicana/Mexicana women in the Chicano Movement is generally obscured because women are not accepted as community leaders either by the Chicano Movement or by the Anglo establishment (Comision Femenil Mexicana Nacional, Inc., 1986)

The Chicana movement developed during the late 1960s and early 1970s. Chicanas formed numerous groups at the grass-roots level and on college campuses. They also developed state and national organizations. Some of these groups published newspapers, pamphlets, and magazines. Hijas de Cuauhtemoc arose at California State University, Long Beach, and published a newspaper with the same title. With women from other campuses and community groups, they published *Encuentro Femenil.* Comision Femenil Mexicana Nacional, Inc., formed in Los Angeles, California, in 1970 and published the magazine *Regeneracion.* At the national level, MANA (Mexican American Women's National Association) formed in 1974 in Washington, DC. Many pamphlets and other magazines were also published during this time by various groups and Chicana activists (e.g., Martha Cotera's *Diosa y Hembra* and *The Chicana Feminist*). Others published articles on Chicanas in student newspapers and leftist publications of the period (e.g., Marta Vidal in *International Socialist Review*; Magdalena Mora in *Sin Fronteras*). Few articles appeared in mainstream feminist outlets (e.g., *Ms.* magazine).

For their organizations and publications, Chicanas often adopted names rooted in a revolutionary heritage from Mexico. Hijas de Cuauhtemoc, for example, was a women's organization founded in 1910 in Mexico City that opposed the Diaz dictatorship (Macias, 1982). *Regeneracion* was the official journal of the Partido Liberal Mexicano, a progressive Mexican political party (Macias 1982). These

quintessential images of revolutionary struggle provided Chicanas with one way to frame their local agendas within a larger critique of race, class, and gender domination.

Chicanas sought various ways to reconcile their critique of male domination within the Chicano community to the Chicano movement agenda. Unwilling to be dismissed as political actors, Chicanas formed caucuses within Chicano movement organizations, formed Chicana women's groups, and organized conferences on *la mujer* (women). They argued that these groups were necessary in order for women to develop their political consciousness free from male centered ideas and influences.

Although Chicana women's groups were exclusively female, they were viewed as essential parts of the "larger" Chicano movement. Adelaida del Castillo, editor of *Encuentro Femenil,* a Chicana feminist journal, articulated this perspective in 1974:

We're not a separatist movement, that would be suicidal. We as Chicanas and Chicanos are oppressed. We're not going to ally ourselves to white feminists who are part of the oppressor. I mean, that would be a contradiction. It also hurts when Chicano men don't recognize the need for this specialization which is called "Chicana Feminism."

Chicanas focused on expanding the boundaries of the Chicano movement and argued that their activities were for *la Raza* (the people), with a special emphasis in *la mujer.* Fashioning the discourse in this manner, Chicanas, as many women have done throughout history, gave formal recognition to patriarchal contours while eroding its base through underground subversive separatism. These activities did not, however, go unchallenged, given the powerful ideological hegemony of Chicano cultural nationalism.

The term *Chicano* arose as the symbolic representation of the struggle for self-determination and betterment of the Chicano community (Chicano Coordinating Committee on Higher Education, 1969; Alvarez,

1971; Acuña, 1981). Chicano cultural nationalist ideology locates Chicano oppression in the colonial domination of Mexican Americans following the annexation of northern Mexico by the United States after the US–Mexico War of 1846–8, which limited Chicano access to education, employment, and political participation (Almaguer, 1971; Barrera, Muñoz, and Ornelas, 1972; Blauner, 1972; Estrada, Garcia, Macias, and Maldonado 1981). Ideologically, cultural differences between Anglos and Mexicans were used to legitimate racial inequality (e.g., Mexicans were viewed as intellectually and culturally inferior) (Blauner, 1972; Takaki, 1979; Montejano, 1987). One example is the popularity of using a "cultural deficiency" framework to explain an array of characteristics (e.g., lower levels of education, higher unemployment rates) as part of an ethnic or cultural tradition. Such a framework depicts Mexican American culture as lagging behind American culture in developing behaviors and attitudes conducive to achievement (Baca Zinn, 1979, 1980, 1982).

Within a cultural nationalist ideology that celebrated Chicanos' cultural heritage from Mexico and their indigenous roots, *la familia, la Virgen de Guadalupe* (the patron saint of Mexico), and *la Adelita* (women who fought during the 1910 Mexican Revolution and nurtured the troops) symbolized ethnic pride and resistance. Concurrently, these cultural symbols recognized both women's importance within the confines of their traditional roles and insurgent activities in social change. Chicanas were exalted as self-sacrificing mothers (*la madre*) and as caretaker-fighters in revolutionary struggle (*la Adelita*).

Chicano movement groups often organized around the ideal of *la familia.*[6] A high value was placed on family solidarity, with individual desires subsumed to the collective good. Critiques of gender relations in the family, the Chicano community, and movement groups met with hostility. Cynthia Orozco asserts, "When Chicanas raised the issue of male domination, both the community and its intellectual arm, Chicano Studies, put down the ideology of feminism

and put feminists in their place" (1986: 12). Feminists, in contrast, argued that the struggle against male domination was central to the overall Chicano movement for liberation. Anna Nieto-Gomez, one of the most prolific Chicana feminist writers of the late 1960s and early 1970s, proclaimed:

> What is a Chicana feminist? I am a Chicana feminist. I make that statement very proudly, although there is a lot of intimidation in our community and in the society in general against people who define themselves as Chicana feminists. It sounds like a contradictory statement, a *Malinche*[7] statement – if you are a Chicana you're on one side, if you're a feminist, you must be on the other side. They say you can't stand on both sides – which is a bunch of bull. (Nieto-Gomez, 1974)

Chicanas who departed from the nationalist political stance were labeled *vendidas* (sellouts), *agabachadas* (white identified), or *Malinche* (betrayer/collaborator) (Lopez, 1977; Nieto-Gomez, 1973, 1974). Labeling was a tool of repression against Chicanas who advocated a feminist position. Martha Cotera points out that the label *feminist* was also a social control mechanism:

> We didn't say we were feminist. It was the men who said that. They said, "Aha! Feminista!" and that was a good enough reason for not listening to some of the most active women in the community. (1977: 31)

Such social and political sanctions were meant to discourage women from articulating a feminist standpoint.

In the Chicano community, the labels *vendida, agabachada, Malinche,* and *feminista* denoted cultural betrayal and assimilation into non-Chicano values and lifestyle. These labels accused Chicanas of acting "like white women" – a disloyal act to *la cultura* and community politics anchored in a cultural nationalist sense of racial-ethnic unity. Moreover, these charges implied that Chicanas' critiques of gender relations were anti-family, anti-men, and pro-Anglo. Within this formulation, feminism is irrelevant at best; at worst it is divisive of the "greater" Chicano struggle.

The antagonism toward American feminism of this period can be understood in light of the antithetical characterizations of "the family" in both movements. The American women's movement argued that the subordination of women within the patriarchal family is a primary form of oppression. Furthermore, feminist critiques of patriarchal relations often identified men as the enemy. Both formulations (the family as a locus of female oppression and the specter of men as the enemy) stood in direct opposition to the cultural nationalist ideology that eulogized the traditional role of women in the family, the Chicano family as an agent of resistance, and *carnalismo* (brotherhood of *La Raza*).

In light of the political milieu of the 1960s and 1970s, it is not surprising that many Chicanas felt ambivalence toward American feminism. They tended to perceive the women's movement predominantly white, middle-class leadership as largely unable or unwilling to articulate a vision of women's empowerment sensitive to race-ethnic and class differences (Cotera, 1980). During this period, few Anglo or Chicana feminists moved to build coalitions between both communities of women (Del Castillo, 1974; Martinez, 1972; Nieto, 1974; Cotera, 1973; Flores, 1973; Gonzalez, 1977). Chicanas questioned the feminist call to "sisterhood," arguing that unity based on only the subordination of women overlooked the historical race-ethnic, class, and cultural antagonisms between women. They opposed American feminist writings that equated sexism with racism as ahistorical, inasmuch as gender and race are not analogous systems of oppression (Nieto-Gomez, 1973; Apodaca, 1986). Chicanas expressed skepticism that eliminating sexual oppression would end class and race-ethnic inequality. Instead, they argued that feminism was irrelevant to Chicanas until it addressed race-ethnic and class concerns. Chicanas doubted, however, that such an inte-

grative approach would emerge in light of racism and "maternal chauvinism" among women's movement activists, as Anna Nieto-Gomez states:

> Chicanas, having to deal with racism in the feminist movement and sensing that Anglo women believe they can solve the problems of minority women, have tried to circumvent this maternal chauvinism. (1973: 46)

Concern with what Nieto-Gomez termed *maternal chauvinism*,[8] or the idea that white feminists can comprehend, analyze, and devise the best solutions to Chicanas' concerns, reverberates throughout the writings of early Chicana feminists.

Chicanas also decried the articulation of feminist concerns and proposals for solutions to gender inequality that omitted them and other women of color. Reviews of key feminist writings of the late 1960s and early 1970s by Chicana feminists such as Martha Cotera (1977, 1980) and Alma Garcia (1989) confirm the accuracy of this perception. In the rare instances Chicanas were included within feminist writings, their experiences tended to be cast in ways that reinforced cultural stereotypes of them as women who "did not want to be liberated" (Longeaux y Vasquez, 1970). Most often, however, Chicanas have been silent objects within feminist writings – neither included nor excluded by name. Thus, Chicanas in this period concluded they were not "equal" sisters in the struggle against gender oppression.

## CHICANA FEMINIST ORGANIZATIONS

A theme that spans the past decade is the framing of Chicana feminisms in the collective struggles of the Chicano community. Chicanas at various levels of society, class locations, sexual preferences, and political perspectives share a collective identity as Mexican women but diverge on how best to address the historical inequality of Chicanas. At the state and national levels, Comision Femenil Mexicana Nacional, Inc., and

MANA have continued their organizational efforts to empower Chicanas. However, as in the past, most work is done by numerous small and localized groups on college campuses, in community-based organizations, and workplaces.

## Comision Femenil Mexicana Nacional, Inc.

Founded in 1970, Comision is the largest Chicana organization and includes 23 chapters nationwide, with the majority in California. Francisca Flores, a founder of Comision, stated in 1971:

> The time has come to quit quibbling and start mingling with other women. A movement of Mexican women such as has never been seen before. That is what we are going after. No more will anyone say to us . . . you are not organized . . . [her spacing; there is no missing text] there is no national organization to represent women from the migrant farms to the tall urban centers in the cities. There will not be an agency which will not know of our existence. (Flores, 1971: 7)

Comision promotes Chicana leadership in education, employment, economic development, community, and electoral politics. In the Los Angeles area (the area with the highest concentration of Mexicans in the United States), Comision currently runs numerous social-service delivery programs, including the Chicana Service Action Center, which provides job training; Casa Victoria, a community-based alternative to Chicana juvenile incarceration; and Centro de Niños, a bilingual/bicultural child development center geared to the needs of the working poor. They publish a newsletter, hold annual conferences, and participate in national and international women's conferences. Comision works with such organizations as Planned Parenthood Foundation and local and state agencies to promote health and reproductive rights for Chicana/Latina women. The

following quote from the *1985–6 Annual Report* embodies Comision's spirit:

> Student, mother, wife, professional, farmworker, homemaker, single parent, it doesn't matter. *Comision Femenil Mexicana Nacional, Inc.* is there for all Latinas to take, to hold, to embrace, to learn, to share, to advocate, but most of all, it is a vehicle for change for Latinas in the United States. (1986: 6)

## Mexican American Women's National Association

The Mexican American Women's National Association (MANA) was founded in Washington, DC, in October 1974, "when Mexican American women of different political, educational, professional and geographic backgrounds met to discuss the need for a self-identifying organization which would focus on the concerns of the more than five million Chicanas in the United States" (Mexican American Women's National Association, 1982). Since its inception, MANA has been "striving for parity between Chicanas and Chicanos as they continue their joint struggle for equality . . . creating a national awareness of the presence and concerns of Chicanas and the active sharing of its Mexican American heritage" (Mexican American Women's National Association, 1982).

In practice, MANA supports efforts to strengthen families while advocating for equal rights for women. MANA supported the passage of the Equal Rights Amendment (ERA). Moreover, MANA has collaborated with the Women's Legal Defense Fund, the National Organization for Women, the National Council of La Raza, Mexican American Legal Defense and Educational Fund, and other national Chicano/Latino and women's organizations to advocate for programs that benefit women of color. MANA prepares position papers on areas of concern to the organization (e.g., reproductive rights, the ERA) to attempt to publicize Chicanas' perspectives on these issues.

MANA's collaborative efforts with other feminist groups are not undertaken without tension. For example, at a major five-hour pro-choice "Mobilization for Women," organized by NOW on November 12, 1989, at the Lincoln Memorial, Irma Maldonado, president of MANA, was the only Latina invited to speak. As time passed, the rally's organizers tried to scratch her from the scroll of invited speakers to "speed up" the event (*Hispanic Link Weekly Report*, 1989).

Several MANA chapters run Hermanitas Programs (Little Sisters), which link MANA members to teenage Chicanas/Latinas to nurture leadership and self-esteem among these young women (Mexican American Women's National Association, 1990). In 1984 MANA founded a national scholarship program to help support high-achieving Latinas in higher education. Currently, MANA's Washington, DC, chapter operates the Economic Equity Project, which is funded by the Ford Foundation, to research and develop issue papers on the economic plight of Hispanic women for dissemination to policy-makers and Hispanic organizations at the state, local, and federal levels (Mexican American Women's National Association, 1991). MANA organizes and conducts annual training conferences to develop leadership among the members and promote a greater awareness of Chicana/Latino heritages. MANA publishes a newsletter that helps provide information on national issues and programs to members.

### Mujeres Activas en Letras y Cambio Social

In California, Chicanos/Latinos comprise approximately one-quarter of the state's population, yet Chicanas constitute less than 2 percent of the faculty of the prestigious, nine-campus, University of California system. In 1983 Chicana faculty and graduate students from northern California founded Mujeres Activas en Letras y Cambio Social (Women Active in Higher Education and Social Change) (MALCS) in Berkeley. MALCS is dedicated to the recruitment and retention of Chicanas/Latinas in higher education. The organization is particularly interested in supporting collaborative ventures that can challenge institutional racism, sexism, and homophobism.

Adaljiza Sosa Riddel, the first chair of MALCS, describes its purpose as

> empowerment of *mujeres* as *mujeres* is what MALCS is all about. Our empowerment efforts are in the realm of ideas, values, analysis, and the translation of those ideas from our minds and hearts onto acts of lasting benefit, writings, creative acts, and, we fervently hope, structural change. Our efforts are aimed directly at bridging the gap between the academic environment within which we work and the communities from whence we came and in which we live. We want to improve the quality of life for us all, but especially for the overwhelming majority of Chicanas who have little economic, academic, cultural, or political power over their own lives. (Mujeres Activas en Letras y Cambio Social, 1989)

Most MALCS organizers had been active in the insurgent feminist politics situated within the Chicano movement. Although critical of the American women's movement and feminist theories for their inattention to the intersection of race, class, *and* gender/sexuality, many critiqued patriarchal relations. MALCS works toward the support, education, and dissemination of Chicana issues. As one MALCS member states:

> Chicana scholarship is going to impact the intellectual world and also the work at the practical level to help the 95 percent of our sisters who are not at the university and aren't going to be unless we make it happen. So, Chicana scholarship has to reach out and push the intellectual boundaries and reach back to its roots – the community.

Chicanas' efforts to promote research on their community have sometimes met with considerable resistance and, at other times, have been subjected to indifference. As one response to this problem, MALCS published a Working Paper Series cosponsored by the Chicano Studies Program and Women's Resource and Research Center at the University of California, Davis. In 1992 the Working Paper Series gave way to a yearly anthology of Chicana scholarly writings.

To combat the marginalization of Chicana studies within traditional disciplines and Chicano studies as well as women's studies, MALCS institutionalizes alternative avenues and "safe spaces" to develop intellectually and continue the tradition of political dissent. One mechanism to accomplish this is through the annual Chicana/Latina Summer Research Institute, where Chicanas/Latinas from various institutions (academic and nonacademic) come together to network, share information, offer support, and re-energize. The 1991 "Statement" from the MALCS Conference organizers in Laredo, Texas, states:

> The MALCS Institute is one of the few places Chicanas can come together without the influences of male and/or Anglo consciousness or opinion. For most Chicanas, this is the only place to come together. While some charge that this is separatist, the MALCS reply is not one of apology. This is our space. The dynamics of this Chicana space are worth guarding, even in the face of criticism from those we respect and work with in our home institutions. It is our sincere hope that the critics outside MALCS will understand the above position and respect the reasons this space has been created. (*MALCS Annual Research Institute Program*, 1991).

MALCS is committed to the development of Chicana feminist discourse that validates, nurtures, and empowers Chicanas. Chicana feminists in MALCS insist on posing Chicana questions grounded in the objective conditions of the Chicano community (e.g., poverty, rising rates of households headed by women, immigration, lack of educational equity, cultural suppres-

sion, etc.). This kind of intensive inquiry is best accomplished in an autonomous space that is Chicana-centered. MALCS allies itself with groups within the academy and the larger community that share similar interests and concerns (e.g., employment rights, reproductive and health care rights, immigrant rights). Alliances with women's studies and women's centers vary across campuses. The intellectual work that MALCS members are responsible for, however, is facilitated by their relative autonomy and the creation of a Chicana intellectual community within the academy.

## CONTEMPORARY CHICANA FEMINISMS

Chicanas, like other women in our society, vary in their level of knowledge and attitudes regarding feminism. Chicanas' feminisms are mediated by their social locations (e.g., region, education, immigrant status, employment, and social class) and life experiences. Chicanas are concerned with female empowerment and social change to better their lives.

Rosario Torres Raines conducted a study in 1985 of 185 middle-class Chicana mothers and daughters and 130 Anglo mothers and daughters in south Texas. She found considerable support for (what she terms) "materially relevant related issues emcompassed within the agenda of the American women's movement," particularly equal employment rights, day care, and the ERA. Her study also found less support for abortion among Chicanas than Anglo women because it was conceptualized as a family issue. Torres Raines argues that the high level of support for "materially-based issues" provides one potential base for feminist unity. However, different beliefs concerning the role of women in the family and the "sacred" nature of *la familia* can be a source of tension among women.

Similar to Chicanas in the Torres Raines study, a 1990 study of feminism among Chicana white-collar workers (Pesquera and Segura, 1993) showed they supported such issues as training opportunities, equal pay, and affirmative action. Their support for these issues was not just gender-based but stemmed from their awareness of the unique social vulnerability of Mexicans in the United States. They believed that "Mexicans do not share equally in the good life" and cited institutional discrimination in education and employment as key barriers to social equality. They spoke poignantly of their own struggles and those of their families to make it through high schools where their abilities were often questioned and undermined by insensitive curriculums and inadequate counseling. By and large Chicanas reject individualistic explanations for the persistent low social status of Mexicans in this society and advocate group solutions such as bilingual education and family health care to be able to bring healthy children into the world.

Chicana white-collar workers demonstrated strong support for reproductive rights. They felt warmly toward feminism, and over half felt comfortable calling themselves "feminists." Although many of the women had advocated for Chicana and Chicano rights, few felt comfortable with the idea of joining a feminist organization.

Women in this study familiar with the women's movement tended to feel that it has tried to empower *all* women. One clerical worker stated:

> At the beginning, I felt it was more for white women, trying to get equal pay for equal work, at the material level. But now, I feel that it's more inclusive of all cultures, of all women.

While many women believed they benefited from the women's movement's agendas, they also argued that the movement has not advocated specifically for Chicana/Latina women:

> I think they categorize [the movement] as all women. What they don't realize is that there are real barriers that Latinas have additionally to being a woman. I've never heard the minority thrust at all.

The sentiments by Chicana white-collar workers regarding the women's movement and Chicana concerns resemble those articulated in the previous decades by Chicana activists. That is, Chicanas want feminists to listen to their concerns and incorporate them into women's movement agendas.

A 1988 study of 101 Chicanas/Latinas in MALCS (Segura and Pesquera, 1992) explored their attitudes toward the women's movement, the Chicano movement, and Chicana feminism. Similar to the Chicana white-collar workers, the majority of MALCS Chicanas supported features of American feminism, especially the struggle for gender equality. By and large, MALCS Chicanas refer to themselves as "Chicana feminists" and see themselves as distinct from other feminist traditions. Since they also feel that American feminism has not been sensitive to important race-ethnic or class concerns of Chicana/Latina women, they tend not to join mainstream feminist groups such as NOW.

MALCS Chicana feminist expressions revolve around the principles of collectivity and insurgent analysis but differ in their strategies for social change. Of the women who called themselves Chicana feminists, 62 discussed what this meant. From their descriptions of Chicana feminism, the following typology was developed: *Chicana Liberal Feminism, Chicana Cultural Nationalist Feminism,* and *Chicana Insurgent Feminism.* Each category is grounded in the material condition of the Chicano people and highlights different aspects of Chicana feminism. Each encompasses diverse ways of interpreting oppression and advocating strategies for social change.

The Chicanas within the liberal feminist tradition espoused an "equal rights" approach. They advocate strategies that empower Chicanas, ranging from personal support to policy initiatives and affirmative action. They feel that Chicana subordination can be redressed through institutional reforms that bring Chicanas into the political and social mainstream.

Chicana cultural nationalist feminism describes the attitudes of women who identify as feminists but are committed to a cultural nationalist ideology. They believe that change in gender relations should be accomplished without destroying traditional cultural values. For example, one 41-year-old Chicana graduate student wrote:

> I want for myself and for other women the opportunities to grow, and develop in any area I choose. I want to do this while upholding the values (cultural, moral) that come from my being a part of the great family of Chicanos.

Reminiscent of the slogan popularized during the Chicano movement (that all Chicanos are members of the same family – la gran familia de la raza), Chicana cultural nationalism articulates a feminist vision anchored in the ideology of la familia. While advocating feminism, this perspective retains allegiance to cultural nationalism that glorifies Chicano culture. Chicana cultural nationalism, however, downplays how cultural traditions often uphold patriarchy. It ignores the difficulty of reconciling a critique of gender relations within the Chicano community with the preservation of Chicano culture.

Other women, in the tradition of insurgent feminism, argue that "real liberation" for Chicanas is not possible without a radical restructuring of society. They seek to expose unequal and exploitative relations of power and privilege in our society and champion revolutionary change to end all forms of oppression. They want more than "special emphasis" on la mujer, arguing that the liberation of the community can be accomplished only with the elimination of gender/sexuality oppression. For example, one MALCS member stated:

> I believe that the impact of sexism, racism and elitisms, when combined result in more intensely exploitative, oppressive and controlling situations than when these conditions exist independently of one another. The status and quality of life of the Chicano community as a whole can only improve/change when that of women within

that community changes/improves. Any revolutionary change must include a change in relationships between men and women.

This woman, like the majority of MALCS Chicanas, views political activism as a critical component of Chicana feminisms. Political activism in this context ranges from fighting for the educational rights of Chicanos to marching in the streets for family health care as well as reproductive rights to creating safe spaces (such as MALCS) that foster the development of intellectual frameworks grounded in Chicanas' lived experiences.

## CONCLUSION

Chicana feminist expressions are rooted in their diverse social locations. Across the span of history, political ideologies, and organizational strategies, Chicana feminists struggle to eradicate all forms of social inequality. This struggle is anchored within the social and political struggles of the Chicano/Latino community at large. Chicana feminist organizations, whether at the grass-roots, state, national, or academic level, advocate Chicana empowerment. Although Chicanas credit the American women's movement for their efforts to eradicate gender inequality, they are critical of its exclusionary practices and reluctance to address the contradictions posed by race-ethnicity and class. Rather, Chicana feminists seek ways to better their community and maintain their ethnic identity. Their actions and words echo what Chicana feminist Martha Cotera stated in 1977:

> There has always been feminism in our ranks and there will continue to be so as long as Chicanas live and breathe in the movement, but we must see to it that we specify philosophical directions and that our feminist directions will be our own and coherent with our Raza's goals in cultural areas which are ours. Chicanas will direct their own destiny. (Cotera, 1977: 13)

# Notes

1   Author's names are listed randomly. Our research has been supported by grants from the academic senates of the University of California at Davis and at Santa Barbara. Dr Pesquera acknowledges the support of a Humanist-in-Residence Rockefeller Fellowship at the University of Arizona, Tucson, and Dr Segura acknowledges the support of a Ford Foundation Postdoctoral Fellowship at the University of California, Los Angeles.

2   The English-language translation for the second half of the quote is "my soul between two, three, four worlds, my head spins with contradiction. I am guideless for the many voices that speak to me simultaneously." The term *mestiza* refers to a woman of mixed blood – typically the mixture of the Indian and the Spanish. We thank Dr Francisco Lomili, Professor of Spanish and Portuguese at the University of California, Santa Barbara, for his help in translating this passage. We also note his concern that English does not convey the full meaning of the metaphoric *norteada* (lost, seeking guidance [as if] by the North Star to find the way).

3   The terms *Chicana* and *Chicano*, respectively, refer to a woman and to a man of Mexican descent residing in the United States without distinguishing immigrant status. *Chicano* also refers generically to the category of persons (male and female) who claim Mexican heritage (e.g., the Chicano community). These labels offer an alternative to the more common ethnic identifiers *Mexican* and *Mexican American*. Other terms associated with people of Mexican descent include *Hispanic* and *Latino*. Both of these terms typically include Spaniards and a variety of ethnic groups who were colonized at one time by Spain. Readers interested in the history and significance of different labels used by the Mexican origin population are referred to Portes and Truelove (1987: 359–85), Garcia (1981: 88–98), and Peñalosa (1970: 1–12).

4   We use the plural *feminisms* to underscore how there is no one universally accepted understanding of Chicana oppression and empowerment.

5   Most of the data in this publication were collected by the Bureau of the Census in the March 1992 supplement to the Current Population Survey. Hispanic origin was determined by a question asking for self-identification of a person's origin or descent. Race is determined by a separate question. "Hispanics" normally include persons of any race. This is the first CPS report to separate persons who are white but not of Hispanic origin. Persons of Mexican, Puerto Rican, Cuban, Central and South American, and other Hispanic origins are also shown. However, the social and economic characteristics provided are not given separately by sex for all groups.

6   The intertwined notions of *familia* and *community* as integral to different types of Chicano political activism are discussed in Muñoz and Barrera (1982: 101–19), Gonzalez (1982: 146–9), Segura and Pesquera (1992: 69–92), and Pardo (1990: 1–7).

7   In Mexican culture, the word *Malinche* has become synonymous with *betrayal*. The word is rooted in the conquest of Mexico by the Spaniards. *Malinche* was applied to Malintzin, an Indian woman who was given to the Conquistador Hernan Cortes by a tribe antagonistic to the powerful Aztecs. Cortes called her Doña Marina. In later years, Doña Marina/Malintzin became vilified as a collaborator with the Spaniards who facilitated the downfall of the Indian way of life (as opposed to the incompetence of the male leadership of the Aztecs) and was called "Malinche." This image was resurrected in the days of the early Chicano movement and used to discourage Chicana feminists from critiquing sexism in the Chicano community. Chicana feminists have been actively re-examining the pejorative image of Malinche and reclaiming her as "Malintzin," a strong, creative woman who challenged the boundaries of her life and that of other Indian women. For additional information on this topic, we advise readers to consult Del Castillo (1977: 124–49) and Alarcon (1983: 182–90).

8   Nieto-Gomez' use of the term *maternal* can be regarded as a metaphor for *paternal*. Specifically, she critiques the notion that one group (e.g., "woman") is most capable of solving social problems. Essentially, she is charging white women with paternal behaviors but gendering her critique, hence the word *maternal*.

# Bibliography

Acuña, Rodolfo (1981). *Occupied America: A History of Chicanos*, 2nd edn. New York: Harper and Row.

Alarcon, Norma (1983). "Chicana's Feminist Literature: A Re-Vision Through Malintzin/or Malintzin: Putting Flesh Back on the Object," in *This Bridge Called My Back: Writing by Radical Women of Color*, 2nd edn. ed. Cherrie Moraga and Gloria Anzaldua. New York: Kitchen Table, Women of Color Press, 182–90.

Almaguer, Tómas (1971). "Toward the Study of Chicano Colonialism." *Aztlán, Chicano Journal of the Social Sciences and Arts*, 2: 7–22.

Alvarez, Rodolfo (1971). "The Unique Psycho-Historical Experience of the Mexican American." *Social Science Quarterly*, 52: 15–29.

Apodaca, Maria Linda (1986). "A Double Edge Sword: Hispanas and Liberal Feminism." *Critica, a Journal of Critical Essays*, 1 (Fall): 96–114.

Baca Zinn, Maxine (1979). "Chicano Family Research: Conceptual Distortions and Alternative Directions." *Journal of Ethnic Studies*, 7: 59–71.

—— (1980). "Employment and Education of Mexican-American Women: The Interplay of Modernity and Ethnicity in Eight Families." *Harvard Educational Review*, 50/1 (February): 47–62.

—— (1982). "Mexican-American Women in the Social Sciences." *Signs: Journal of Women in Culture and Society*, 8: 259–72.

Barrera, Mario, Muñoz, Carlos, and Ornelas, Charles (1972). "The Barrio as an Internal Colony," in *People and Politics in Urban Society, Urban Affairs Annual Review*, vol. 6, ed. Harlan H. Hahn. Beverly Hills, CA: Sage Publications, pp. 465–99.

Blauner, Robert (1972). *Racial Oppression in America*. New York: Harper and Row.

Chicano Coordinating Committee on Higher Education (1969). *El Plan de Santa Barbara: A Chicano Plan for Higher Education*. Santa Barbara, CA: La Causa Publications.

Comision Femenil Mexicana Nacional, Inc. (1986). *1985–86 Annual Report*. Los Angeles, CA: Comision Femenil Mexicana Nacional, Inc.

Cotera, Martha P. (1973). "Mexicano Feminism." *Magazin*, 1: 30–2.

—— (1977). *The Chicana Feminist*. Austin, TX:

Information Systems Development.

—— (1980). "Feminism: The Chicana and Anglo Versions, A Historical Analysis," in *Twice a Minority: Mexican American Women*, ed. Margarita Melville, St Louis, MO: C. V. Mosby, pp. 217–34.

Del Castillo, Adelaida R. (1974) "La Vision Chicana." *La Gente*, 8: 3–4.

—— (1977). "Malintzin Tenepal: A Preliminary Look into a New Perspective," in *Essays on la Mujer*, ed. Rosaura Sánchez and Rose Martinez Cruz. Los Angeles: University of California, Los Angeles, Chicano Studies Center Publications, pp. 124–49.

Estrada, Leobardo F., Garcia, F. Chris, Flores Macias, Reynaldo, and Maldonado, Lionel (1981). "Chicanos in the United States: A History of Exploitation and Resistance." *Daedalus*, 110: 103–31.

Flores, Francisca (1971). "Comision Femenil Mexicana," *Regeneracion* 2: 6–7.

—— (1973). "Equality." *Regeneracion*, 2: 4–5.

Garcia, Alma M. (1989). "The Development of Chicana Feminist Discourse, 1970–1980." *Gender and Society*, 3 (June): 217–38.

Garcia, John A. (1981). " 'Yo Soy Mexicano . . .': Self-Identity and Socio-Demographic Correlates." *Social Science Quarterly*, 62 (March): 88–98.

—— (1982). "Ethnicity and Chicanos: Measurement of Ethnic Identification, Identity, and Consciousness." *Hispanic Journal of Behavioral Sciences*, 4: 295–314.

Gonzalez, Cesar A. (1982). "La Familia de Joaquin Chinas." *De Colores, Journal of Chicano Expression and Thought*, 2: 146–9.

Gonzalez, Sylvia (1977). "The White Feminist Movement: The Chicana Perspective." *Social Science Journal*, 14: 67–76.

*Hispanic Link Weekly Report*, November 27, 1989.

Keefe, Susan E., and Padilla, Amado M. (1987) *Chicano Ethnicity*. Albuquerque: University of New Mexico Press.

Longeaux y Vasquez, Enriqueta (1970). "The Mexican-American Woman," in *Sisterhood Is Powerful*, ed. Robin Morgan. New York: Vintage, pp. 379–84.

Lopez, Sonia A. (1977). "The Role of the Chicana Within the Student Movement," in *Essays on La Mujer*, ed. Rosaura Sánchez and Rosa Martinez Cruz. Los Angeles: Chicano Studies Center Publications.

Macias, Anna (1982). *Against All Odds*. Westport, CT: Greenwood Press.

Martinez, Elizabeth (1972). "La Chicana," in *Third*

*World Women.* San Francisco, CA: Third World Communications, pp. 130–2.

Mexican American Women's National Association (MANA) [Newsletter]. Fall 1991, Spring 1990, 1982. Washington, DC: MANA.

Mirande, Alfredo, and Enriquez, Evangelina (1979). *La Chicana.* Chicago: University of Chicago Press.

Montejano, David (1987). *Anglos and Mexicans in the Making of Texas, 1836–1986.* Austin: University of Texas Press.

Mujeres Activas en Letras y Cambio Social (1989). *Noticiera de MALCS* [Newsletter] (Winter). Davis: Chicano Studies Program, University of California, Davis.

Muñoz, Carlos, Jr, and Barrera, Mario (1982). "La Raza Unida Party and the Chicano Student Movement in California." *Social Science Journal,* 19/2 (April): 101–19.

Nieto, Consuelo (1974). "Chicanas and the Women's Rights Movements." *Civil Rights Digest,* 4 (Spring): 38–42.

Nieto-Gomez, Anna (1973). "La Femenista." *Encuentro Femenil* 1: 34–47.

—— (1974). "Chicana Feminism." *Encuentro Femenil,* 1: 3–5.

Orozco, Cynthia (1986). "Sexism in Chicano Studies and the Community," in *Chicana Voices: Intersections of Class, Race, and Gender,* ed. Teresa Cordova, Norma Cantu, Gilberto Cardenas, Juan Garcia, and Christine M. Sierra. National Association for Chicano Studies, Conference Proceedings. Austin: Center for Mexican American Studies, University of Texas, Austin, pp. 11–18.

Pardo, Mary (1990). "Mexican American Women Grassroots Community Activists: (Mothers of East Los Angeles)." *Frontiers, A Journal of Women's Studies,* 11: 1–7.

Peñalosa, Fernando (1970). "Toward an Operational Definition of the Mexican American." *Aztlán, Chicano Journal of the Social Sciences and Arts,* 1: 1–12.

Pesquera, Beatriz M., and Segura, Denise A. (1993). "There Is No Going Back: Chicanas and Feminism," in *Critical Issues in Chicana Studies: Temas Criticos en Estudios Chicanas,* edited by Norma Alarcon, R. Castro, M. Melville, E. Perez, Tey D. Rebolledo, C. Sierra, and A. Sosa Riddell. Berkeley, CA: Third Woman Press, 1993.

Portes, Alejandro, and Truelove, Cynthia (1987). "Making Sense of Diversity: Recent Research on Hispanic Minorities in the United States." *Annual Review of Sociology,* 13: 359–85.

Segura, Denise A. (1986). "Chicanas and Triple Oppression," in *Chicana Voices: Intersections of Class, Race, and Gender,* ed. Teresa Cordova, Norma Cantu, Gilberto Cardenas, Juan Garcia, and Christine M. Sierra. National Association for Chicano Studies, Conference Proceedings. Austin: Center for Mexican American Studies, University of Texas, Austin, pp. 47–65.

Segura, Denise A., and Pesquera, Beatriz M. (1992). "Beyond Indifference and Antipathy: The Chicana Movement and Chicana Feminist Discourse." *Aztlán, International Journal of Chicano Studies Research,* 19: 69–92.

Takaki, Ronald T. (1979). *Iron Cages: Race and Culture in Nineteenth Century America.* New York: Alfred A. Knopf.

U.S. Bureau of the Census (1992). "The Hispanic Population in the United States: March 1992." *Current Population Reports,* Series P-20, no. 465. Washington, DC: US Government Printing Office.

U.S. Commission on Civil Rights (1972). *Education for Mexican Americans: The Excluded Student.* Report III: Mexican American Education Study. Washington, DC: US Government Printing Office.

# Crazy Wisdom:
# Memories of a Cuban Queer

## Lourdes Arguelles

I'd like to first tell you a story and then try to explain briefly its relevance for queers who, like me, are often personally misunderstood, theoretically excluded, and, more important, perceived as somewhat crazy. The story marks the first of my many encounters with people who have shown me the world through different lenses, until things became somewhat clearer – including gender, sexuality, and oppression. This story is undergirded by a vision different from those that govern mainstream lesbian certainties and uncertainties, a vision which draws from the teachings of many "crazy beings" and which still greatly upsets my conventional mind and the part of my being which continues to be absorbed in the lesbian fashions of the times.

The story begins in the city and period of my early youth, La Habana, Cuba, in the late fifties. It revolves around Teresa, who was for many girls of my generation a cultural heroine and for many other Cubans a trickster, a spiritual eccentric of sorts, a prostitute, and a fraud. Teresa, in turn, saw herself quite differently and might have described the story I am about to tell you as the tale of a *mulatta tortillera* who simply lived, laughed, and loved.

Teresa was thought to be the descendant of a family of unattached women deeply engaged in the exploration of Afro-Cuban and European traditions of spirituality and social protest such as Santería, Freemasonry, Espiritismo, and popular Catholicism. Teresa, however, always refused to validate the theo-ries of her origin, and in a society and era consumed by a passion for genealogy, she never claimed any particular heritage.

I was barely 13 when I found this enigmatic *entendida* (the preferred name by which Cuban and Cuban-American lesbians refer to each other), and she was well into her fifties, avidly practicing what was perceived to be a dangerous magical/spiritual craft while passionately engaged with a woman named Mercedes. Teresa was inseparable from Mercedes, her young, white, and wealthy apprentice, to whom she claimed to have been married in many other lives. Teresa lived in a mansion on the outskirts of La Habana, where her life seemed premised on the display of "crazy-wise" behaviors designed to break every racial, sexual, religious, and class taboo that one could hold onto in a society gripped by American neocolonial terror and consumerism and by Spanish colonial religion and prejudice.

No description of Teresa would be complete without mention of the fact that her house had served as a haven for urban *guerrilleros* as well as for the sick and the poor. Ironically, she routinely entertained members of the political establishment. When asked about this seemingly contradictory behavior, Teresa would shrug and, to everyone's consternation, say things like, "Oh, they are prick and balls underneath it all. And the women, all receptacles."

My first glimpses into Teresa's life came by way of a rumor, a joke, a melody that Tata, my milk mother, would hum throughout the day, saying that Teresa had composed it. Gradually, as my attraction to Teresa and her world grew, I began to spend hours watching from a nearby corner the comings and goings on her veranda. On each of the many days when I waited and watched, I could see Teresa with her legs spread wide apart sitting on an old rocker, her strong hands caressing Mercedes' long black hair, talking, singing, preaching, and laughing while smoking big thick cigars. I remember her powerful body covered by a simple white robe and her head by a red turban. She wore no jewelry or makeup, and I often wondered if one day she would do away with her robe and her turban.

At first, in the early stages of my voyeurism, I would stand staring at seemingly well-to-do white strangers to the island who paid homage to Teresa while dancing with each other and with "negros Ba-kongos" (blacks from an African ethnic group in Cuba) amid the rapturous sound of the sacred African double-headed bata drums, as Teresa and Mercedes handed plates of food to an endless parade of beggars, some of whom would be asked to join in the dancing. The gaudy images of Afro-Caribbean deities, trans-sexed and gender-blended gods and goddesses, of a veiled picture which I was told represented Death, and of the bulging, sweat-ridden, black, brown, and white bodies of men, women, and in-betweens pressed against each other often followed me to my dreams.

Each day Teresa and Mercedes seemed different. At times Teresa looked like Mercedes and Mercedes looked like Teresa. Sometimes Teresa looked like someone I knew but could not quite place. Sometimes Mercedes' face looked quite masculine, as if she had begun to grow a mustache, but at other times her face was made up in stereotypical *criollo* feminine fashion. Occasionally when I watched them I had the impression that in some strange way they were fused.

Eventually I moved a bit closer to the house in the hope of immersing myself more deeply in the mysteries of the play on the veranda. I even dared to hope that one day I would peer behind Death's veil.

Earlier I had begun to feel my mind and my heart emptying out my bourgeois, adolescent, racial and sexual assumptions, which were increasingly threatened by the continuing revolutionary war. But it was when I watched Teresa's veranda that I suddenly felt for the first time in my life fully awake and aware of the delusional nature of all the important structures and assumptions that made my world. I also felt poised to enter into those other realities in which Teresa seemed so comfortable. I intuited that life as she lived it, at the edge, afforded ways of existence unavailable to those who, like me, seemed stuck in the glue of social convention.

Months passed during which Teresa's crazy world continued to fuel my dream life. But the revolution of economy and society which began in 1959 changed all that: One day Teresa and Mercedes left abruptly for an unknown destination and their house stood empty. The following day it was taken over by several destitute families. I continued to stand near the abandoned veranda, guiltily wishing it all back. But Teresa's world had vanished.

Tata took pity on me and shared some of the teachings about life, death, and love she felt she had received on the days when she had been asked to join in the dancing on the veranda. She said that Death had taken everything away as He takes all that lives. Eventually I too left for one of many exiles, and Tata died soon thereafter.

The potential implications and the uses of crazy wisdom teachers and teachings for lesbian life and community are many and complex. I will attempt to explain a few of the implications which seem pertinent in this historical era and which have to do with trans-biographical and spirit-based relationships, autonomy versus fusion in relationships, social hierarchy, difference, and change.

Some queers like me come from or have sought social and cultural circumstances in which independent teachers like Teresa, whom some call "crazy wisdom masters," are "on the loose." Their lives constantly challenge conventional wisdoms and ordinary morality, eccentrically assisting in the process of understanding the play and transience of psychohistorical structures and conventions rooted in history and in the psyches of individuals. Such eccentric teachings seem to empty the body and mind of crippling biographical and cultural baggage as a necessary prerequisite to the development of understandings which may lie outside ordinary human judgment, free of cultural blinders.

The first assumption that left my mind as I watched Teresa's veranda was the notion of partnership in life as based only on romantic love, rational considerations, or initial sexual chemistry. Teresa and Mercedes opened for me the possibility of relationships based on the perception of a trans-biographical experience or shared spirituality. As a young girl, I witnessed Teresa and Mercedes in their relationship by becoming a part of their world, listening to their conversations, and observing their interactions. Such relationships appear to be inordinately joyful and creative and seem to endure in the face of numerous problems. They involve ways of relating that run contrary to Western notions of intimacy.

The most relevant implications for contemporary lesbians seem to revolve around issues of how these types of relationships can become vehicles to transmute problems and pain as well as instruments of joy and pleasure. When lesbian relationships can be predicated on the understanding that the psyches of the lovers are not limited to postnatal biography and that existence cannot be reduced to the material, the tangible, and the measurable, habits of perception tend to be activated and reinforced that can lead to viewing problems and hurts as challenging stages in the development of consciousness. Such couples see this spiritual development as occurring across many lifetimes and at many levels. Pressure to resolve issues in the here and now therefore is not as intense. Though partners in these relationships may struggle to neutralize painful events and, in some cases, to dramatically change the course of their lives, their struggles may not be based on a sense of individual entitlement to feel specific emotions, to enjoy specific material conditions, or to control given situations. The demands of everyday life appear to weigh less heavily in relationships based on the perception that the ties that join the lovers will survive crises, changes in social circumstances, conflict, distance, or age. Boredom and the incessant quest for novelty, and hence an ever-widening search for new partners, seems less likely among these couples. There is a depth and resilience to these relationships, as well as a special evolving erotic pleasure that emerges from spirit-based purpose and trans-biographical links between partners, which is difficult to explain but easy to recognize.

In later years my recollections of Teresa and Mercedes allowed me to question the current convention of assessing the health of a relationship by measuring the autonomy of each of the partners. Woven into the poetry of Teresa's songs and played out on her veranda were images of the blending of two strong women, the union of thoughts and feelings, the absence of boundaries. Fusion in relationships became a viable and acceptable possibility for me, as had spirit-oriented and trans-biographical unions.

The lack of boundaries between self and other of women who have been involved in controlling or abusive relationships has made many lesbians fearful of voluntarily relinquishing boundaries in relationships, keeping them from viewing "fused" lovers as models and preventing them from understanding the pleasures involved in fusion between two strong women. This closing off to experiences of fusion may be contributing to making our lesbian communities into sites where autonomy and individualism are seen as the only acceptable options in relationships. Some lesbian writers take an even more extreme view that individualism within a relationship is not a realistic or acceptable option, proposing that total noncommitment is the only way to preserve a sense of freedom and adventure. Crazy wisdom teachings remind us that autonomy and fusion are not mutually exclusive. Teresa and Mercedes were both autonomous individuals, yet they also achieved fusion in their relationship.

Another assumption that died for me as I

watched Teresa's veranda was that social hierarchy or difference creates unsurmountable obstacles to compassionate action. On the veranda social and racial hierarchies and differences, rather than being flattened, ignored, or denounced, were systematically inverted, through continuous sharing, or used to illustrate an alternative reality, to create complementary polarities, and to afford protection from ordinary morality. This became possible due to a crazy wisdom not only capable of perceiving the interconnectedness and underlying sameness of all beings and the transitoriness of social positioning but capable of accepting the shadow, or dark side, of each being. Teresa was willing to act compassionately toward *guerrilleros*, beggars, and establishment politicians alike, precisely on the basis of their perceived shadow. The recognition and acceptance of the shadow parts of each being and of social groups seem to be necessary prerequisites for the building of compassionate communities and coalitions. Lesbian psychologies and sociologies seem to me to be essentially psychologies and sociologies of the "light" side of being, and tend to be unable to accept the tensions between the light and the shadow in each of us and in our communities. The emphasis on the good, the positive, and the elimination of the bad (an understandable response to society's pathologizing and vilification of same-sex eroticism and relationships) continues to lead dangerously to the systematic disowning of unacceptable thoughts and actions and their projections onto others "out there." One example is the denial or concealment of battering within lesbian relationships and the implicit projection of the image of the batterer onto the "other," which is male. Shadow negotiation, recognizing and integrating the dark sides of our multiple individual and collective selves, remains a critical task.

In Teresa's house gender-blending and sexual role-play as people danced to the rhythm of primal sounds seemed to derive part of their charge from racial and class differences and perceived hierarchies. The presence of the wealthy and the powerful combined with the presence of feared African deities provided protection from conventional sanctions. The combined power of class status and spirituality guarded against police intervention. The public erotic union between the less affluent, aging, gender-blended *mulatta* teacher, Teresa, whose power derived from the creative appropriation of hybrid magical practices, and the white and wealthy student, Mercedes, whose condition as an apprentice was determined by her youth as well as by her whiteness and wealth, is as illustrative of erotic charge as of the suspension of social judgment. In that context, age conveyed power.

Other assumptions that might have dissolved in the power of Teresa's magic did not, and linger with me still, at least in remnants. The process of reflecting and writing has brought them into sharper focus. In recollecting Teresa's dismissal of the importance of origins and genealogy in herself, I am made aware of the salience of origins and backgrounds in my own and others' expressions of ourselves. Whatever our internal makeup, our outward expressions of ourselves are often designed for the purpose of "fitting in" to one or more categories. Teresa's lack of concern for fit into any sociocultural, spiritual, or even genealogical norms continues to challenge my searches for identity, community, and security. Further, the memory of her disdain for "fitting in" keeps alive for me the archetype of the lesbian as a stranger, a misfit, one who is homeless, mysterious, unpredictable, and barren. For me this balances the increasing "ladyfication" of our lesbian communities, with their penchant for ordinariness, procreation, and conventionality. The celebration of spaces free from political and social dogmas where we can love and dance in our difference seems of the essence for well-being and free flow within our stratified and conflicted communities.

I might also have reconsidered the illusion that anyone could, or should attempt to, change the world permanently. Teresa's fullest expression of self had nothing to do with attempting to alter the world or anyone in it. She lived and loved, danced and taught, and understood the delusional nature of "reality" sufficiently to know the folly of choosing to conform to it or trying to reshape it. When the dance that I was privileged to observe came to a close, Teresa and Mercedes moved on to find new music. To keep dancing, on or off the veranda, as various political or psychological generations seek the spotlight may be just the kind of crazy-wise behavior that could benefit lesbians of all colors, classes, ages, and abilities.

On some days the veiled picture on Teresa's veranda which I was told represented Death comes to mind. As I look back, and the sounds of bata drums pierce the soundless isolation of my suburban exile, I begin to suspect that there was not one image of Death, but many. I imagine Teresa and Mercedes each day selecting a different image to put behind the veil, a fitting recognition of the impermanence of gender, sexuality, class, ability, and race, and of life itself. I also suspect that these experiences of crazy wisdom may be a necessary component of the consciousness needed to make lesbian life and community unafraid of its own shadows and richer in fantasy and festivity, as much as in love and compassion, amid a forever-changing dark/light world.

# Teatro Viva! Latino Performance and the Politics of AIDS in Los Angeles

## David Román

The patriarch of a dysfunctional Latino family living in the barrio is scandalized that his son has brought home the neighborhood's two cross-dressers. "My son's a homo!" he cries waving a pistol. The cross-dressers retaliate by biting the man's arm and announcing that they both have SIDA [AIDS]. The father, horrified of contagion, shoots. This scene appears as a segment of "Doña Flora's Family" one of the eleven skits in *SOS* written, directed, and performed by Culture Clash, an immensely popular Latino comedy theater troupe. Such a pathological, melodramatic, indeed ridiculous scene provides an entrance to an essay that will begin to locate the discourses by and about Latino gay men in contemporary US theater, discuss the ways that AIDS is imagined and/or experienced in Latino communities, and offer a cultural practice that addresses both (homo)sexuality and AIDS. My aim here is to provide a critical methodology that at once contextualizes various contemporary Latino performances that discuss AIDS and chronicles the important and often neglected work of Latino gay men in the theater.[1]

*SOS* premiered in the summer of 1992 at the Japanese American Cultural and Community Center (JACCC) in the heart of Little Tokyo in downtown Los Angeles as part of the Celebrate California Series which promotes "multicultural diversity through the arts."[2] Tickets for the three-day run including an added matinee at the 800-seat capacity theater immediately sold out. Upon arriving at JACCC, it became clear that Culture

Clash's appearance was much more than a night at the theater for most of the Latinos in attendance. Parents brought along their children. Long-standing community leaders were present alongside Chicano youth involved in street activist politics. For all appearances, it seemed a family affair; an in-house Latino assemblage but with an open invitation addressed to all people disturbed by the recent events in Los Angeles.[3] After all, we were gathering in Little Tokyo not East Los Angeles. The idea of Culture Clash at JACCC seemed to be the type of gesture necessary to continue the "healing" of Los Angeles; a bicultural occasion where two communities– the Asian American and the Latino – could begin to understand each other a little better, in this case through the theater. In the statement printed in the performance program, Culture Clash foregrounds the political nature of their work: "How can we ignore the quincentennial, the Rodney King case, AIDS, the NEA censorship and the election of yet another Republican? Time for an 'SOS', a signal of distress."

Culture Clash further called attention to the political potential of the event by offering their Saturday night performance as a fundraiser for the Latino activist organization PODER, the Pro-Active Organization Dedicated to the Empowerment of Raza. "Comedy for these urgent times," the *SOS* publicity promo promised; and "necessary funds for the needs of the Latino community of Los Angeles," PODER activists told us before the performance. Given the multitude of problems facing Latinos in Los Angeles – deportation, economic exploitation, gang warfare, inadequate health care – such an evening held the possibility of offering at least some relief for those able to afford the ten-dollar tickets. In "SOS Rap," an early and particularly effective scene, one of the performers catalogs a litany of these social ills repeatedly returning to the hard refrain, "todo tiene que cambiar" [everything must change]. In *SOS*, as in all of their work, Culture Clash sets out to denaturalize Anglo superiority and reclaim Latino culture and history from the perspective of *La Raza*. Their primary method to achieve this goal is through humor, parody, and social satire.

Throughout *SOS*, Culture Clash proceeded to critique many of the institutions and hegemonic processes that oppress Chicanos and Latinos, but as the scene in Doña Flora's family demonstrates, they fell short of imagining Latino gays and lesbians as part of the social utopia posited in their performance. Imagined gays were attacked in one scene, raped in another ("American Me Tail")[4] and lesbians, as usual, were not to be found. AIDS was presented as a threat posed by gays and women to unsettle the family and *la raza*. In another scene, "Angel's Flight," one of the performers positioned underneath a tapestry of La Virgen de Guadalupe explains to the men in the audience that they must use condoms to protect themselves from AIDS. But as the iconography of the scene too obviously suggests, men invoke the madonna to protect them from the whore. Women in Chicano culture, as Cherrie Moraga has argued, are continually placed within this rigid madonna/whore binary system (Moraga, Almaguer). In a gesture which immediately recalled Panamanian artist and activist Rubén Blades' appearance in the PBS video *AIDS: Changing the Rules* where Blades, talking directly to straight men, put a condom on a banana, the performer in "Angel's Flight" places a condom on an ear of corn. Douglas Crimp's complaint against the condom and the banana scene of 1987 still rings true today: "evidently condoms have now become too closely associated with gay men for straight men to talk straight about them" (Crimp, 1987: 255). In their efforts to preserve *la raza* from the oppression of centuries of Anglo domination, Culture Clash imagines in *SOS* a Chicano social usurpation. Their new LA, however, fails to address the social networks – including the theater – that oppress many Latinos outside the subject position of the straight Chicano male. If the performance, by nature of its stage venue at JACCC, is to some degree an attempt to form coalitions with other people of color, the ideal spectator is still assumed to be a heterosexual male.

In many ways, Culture Clash's performances can be best understood as participating in a long history of Chicano and Latino theater practices and conventions originating in the United States as early as the 1840s. According to Latino theater historian Nicolás Kanellos, this theatrical tradition has demonstrated "the ability [of Latinos] to create art even under the most trying of circumstances, social and cultural cohesiveness and national pride in the face of race and class pressures, [and] cultural continuity and adaptability in a foreign land" (Kanellos, 1990: xv). Culture Clash comes out of a theatrical trajectory that recalls both the energy of the Mexican carpa [traveling circuses] of the 1890s and the political activism of El Teatro Campesino in the 1960s.

Much of the work of Culture Clash bears the influence of Luis Valdez, founder of El Teatro Campesino, who believed that the theater should play a vital role in the awakening of the Chicano social consciousness. Like Valdez, Culture Clash insists that the theater must remain oppositional to the exploitative practices of the dominant Anglo culture. And like El Teatro Campesino, Culture Clash posits a type of cultural nationalism with all of its inherent contradictions and problems. If, on the one hand, cultural nationalism fosters a sense of cultural pride, it also conflates all Chicano experience into a unified Chicano subject. In short, by failing to account for the differences among Latinos, Culture Clash inadvertently performs the very limits of the identity politics they invoke.[5]

Chicana feminist cultural critic Yvonne

Yarbro-Bejarano has written on the female subject in Chicano theater and the ways by which the representational systems of Chicano theater privilege heterosexual men. Yarbro-Bejarano argues that it is precisely the operations of cultural nationalism in Chicano theater that have led to the uncritical "reinscription of the heterosexual hierarchization of male/female relationships" (Yarbro-Bejarano, 1990: 132). Yarbro-Bejarano's work on demystifying the conventions of Chicano theater not only exposes the sexist ideology normalized in the materials of production, but also serves as a critical model to interrogate its homophobic tendencies as well.

Starting in the late 1970s, Chicanas in the theater began organizing and networking, resulting in all-women *teatros* and a series of plays that explored women's issues. Moreover, after years of struggle, Chicanas have gained entry in traditionally male-centered venues and collectives. Chicana lesbian playwright Cherríe Moraga, for example, presents the strongest critique of patriarchal and heterosexist attitudes.[6] Her plays, as Yarbro-Bejarano argues, demonstrate how female sexuality is constructed and contained within the mythical model of La Malinche, Cortés' supposed mistress and translator. La Malinche serves as a "signifier of betrayal, through which the historical experience of domination is spoken in the language of sexuality" (Yarbro-Bejarano, 1990: 135). The insistence of the *chingón/chingada* dynamic (fucker/fucked; active/passive) remains perhaps the most prevalent sociosexual system in Chicano and Latino culture. Emerging from the experience of colonization, the *chingón/chingada* dynamic locks women into subordinate roles, inscribes inflexible definitions of masculinity and femininity, and on a larger scale, becomes the surveillance test of true nationalism. Whoever is penetrated, in other words, is immediately interpreted by dominant Latino culture as passive. Passivity, within this system, is understood to mean open to sexual betrayal and, therefore, a threat to the nation.

The scenes in *SOS* where anal rape is staged as male humiliation and punishment, for example, in "American Me Tail," or where homosexuality – as an identity – is introduced only to be annihilated in "Doña Flora's Family," signal as much to this kind of cultural nationalism where the assertion of male power mitigates male anxiety regarding the loss of power in a culture of domination, as they do to the homophobic and sexist enterprise that constructs passivity as threatening and degrading. Rather than deconstructing the *chingón/chingada* polarization, Culture Clash participates in the continual reinscription of a binary sociosexual system that insists on fixed gender roles and rigid socially constructed meanings for sex acts. Chicano power, as staged by Culture Clash in *SOS*, remains in the hands of impenetrable men who exercise their privilege in continual displays of phallic domination; a socio-masturbatory flaunting meant to eroticize these representations of power in an unending exhibition of seduction.

Despite the fact that Chicana and Latina feminists have gone to great lengths to critique the representations of women in the theater, many plays continue to offer problematic if not degrading depictions of women. (The women actors who have appeared in Culture Clash's three productions *The Mission, Bowl of Beings*, and *SOS* never speak.) And yet the fact that more plays by Latinas are included in national theater festivals and that feminist concerns are beginning to be voiced in conventional theater forums offers a good indication of their success.[7] While women in various areas of the theater have slowly gained some degree of recognition, Latino gay male playwrights have historically been denied a place on the stage. One exception, as Yarbro-Bejarano notes, was Edgar Poma's play about a Chicano gay man coming out to his family. Poma's *Reunion*, produced in 1981, "broke a fifteen year silence on homosexuality within the Chicano theater movement" (Yarbro-Bejarano, 1990: 145). Yarbro-Bejarano's explanation of the play's reception is worth quoting in full:

> [*Reunion*] was performed to large community audiences at the Cultural Center in the heart

of San Francisco's Mission District. Performances were followed by lengthy, lively discussions. The exclusion of a performance of this play during the TENAZ [National Teatros de Aztlán] Eleventh Festival in the Fall of 1981 revealed the depth of resistance to considering the Chicano theater movement an appropriate vehicle for the exploration of questions of sexuality. This attitude was further demonstrated during the Festival by the virtual boycott of a workshop on *Reunion* and the heated arguments by Latin-Americans and Chicanos alike against a resolution condemning sexism and homophobia during the general assembly. Dialogue has recently been reopened within the Chicano community by a production of *Reunion* in June 1986 in Tucson Arizona by Teatro Chicano, a member group of TENAZ headed by a woman, Sylviana Wood. (p. 145)

The problems encountered with productions of *Reunion* are typical of the resistance to gay issues in contemporary Chicano and Latino cultural discourse. Performances that foreground the perspective of gay men – as was the case with women previously – are viewed as incongruent with the larger political movement. Gay issues, as in most communities of color, are often understood by the reigning heterosexist ideology of cultural nationalism to be symptomatic of white domination. For Latinos, since Catholicism rules as the religion of the majority and the church remains an infallible institution, homosexuality is knowable only as unnatural and therefore unacceptable. The combined rhetoric of cultural nationalism and Catholic dogma eradicates any identity based on homosexuality.

Even among straight activists and cultural theorists who work out of the Chicano movement, homosexuality is not an issue comfortably discussed. In the recent groundbreaking anthology *Criticism in the Borderlands: Studies in Chicano Literature, Culture, and Ideology*, for example, the editors – two of the leading Chicano critics in the

United States – announce that their project "should offer an important cultural perspective absent to an international scholarly community" (p. 7). Essays address a broad sampling of issues but not one of the 15 essays is authored by a self-identified gay or lesbian. Moreover, the few essays that discuss gay and lesbian writers fail to address the ways in which sexuality informs both their work and its reception.[8] This process of neglect inevitably produces a normalized conception of heterosexuality – or heterosexism – that is never critically challenged; homosexuality remains taboo.

Current counter-hegemonic critical interventions such as *Criticism in the Borderlands*, which set forth the agenda for the issues open to discussion for cultural theorists, refuse to provide a forum for gay and lesbian concerns. AIDS, moreover, is never mentioned in the essays, an unconscionable omission given that Latinos – and heterosexual Latinos in particular – constitute one of the largest growing groups of people affected by HIV and AIDS. By the end of 1991, for example, Latinos accounted for a total of 10,276 – or 28 percent – of the cumulative AIDS cases in New York City alone. Thirty-three percent of the cumulative AIDS cases in New York City among women were Latinas, 27 percent of cases among men were Latino. Injection drug use continues to be the leading mode of HIV transmission: Latino men at 54 percent, Latinas at 60 percent (Maldonado, 1992: 13). Nationally, according to the Centers for Disease Control, Latinos accounted for 16.5 percent of people diagnosed with AIDS. While the majority of Latinos with AIDS continues to be gay or bisexual men, women and injection drug users represent an increasing proportion of AIDS cases.[9]

In the introduction to their anthology, Hector Calderón and José David Saldívar write: "*Criticism in the Borderlands* is an invitation, we hope, for readers – (Pan-)Americanists, cultural studies critics, feminists, historians, and anti-racists – to remap the borderlands of theory and theorists" (p. 7). But if, as Calderón and Saldívar argue, studies of US culture that fail to consider the centuries of Mexican-mestizo presence "will of necessity be incomplete," (p. 7) they will need to recognize that studies that fail to incorporate a critical analysis of sexuality or the affects of AIDS in Chicano and/or Latino cultures will be not merely "incomplete" but, as Eve Sedgwick succinctly states, "damaged" (Sedgwick, 1990: 1).

There is no question in my mind that the work of Culture Clash and the individual and collective work of the cultural theorists in *Criticism in the Borderlands* are necessary, indeed welcome, interventions in an Anglo culture of domination and exploitation. However, these same sites of intervention – theater and theory – must also be interrogated in such a way that denaturalizes the assumptions and destabilizes the privileges set forth in each. Cultural theorists and activists need to recognize and counter the racist and homophobic practices that oppress all Latinos. If the diverse and heterogeneous Latino populations in the United States are to successfully fight AIDS in their communities, "todo" – not just Anglo domination – "tiene que cambiar."

The groundwork for an interrogation of AIDS in the Latino population was set in February 1988, when various Latinos – gay, bisexual, and straight; health-care providers, activists, and educators – met in Los Angeles for a National Strategy Symposium on Latinos and AIDS. This symposium, the first ever of its kind, was held in order to discuss and actualize a national AIDS policy and programmatic agenda specific to the needs of Latinos. As Lourdes Arguelles writes in the preface to the published proceedings of the conference, the HIV/AIDS epidemic in communities of color in the United States remained largely misunderstood, even by as late a date as 1987: "These misunderstandings, coupled with well-known historical factors having to do with the relative political powerlessness of the various communities in question, were leading to policy and programming decisions which were less than optimal in controlling the epidemic and in servicing those people of color infected" (*Latinos and AIDS*, 1989: vii). AIDS challenges Latino communities already burdened with an excess of morbidity and morality, with inadequate resources including access to education and health care, who suffer language oppression and a discriminatory US legal system of deportation, and who all the while maintain stigmatizing views of sexual acts and intravenous drug use. The conference in LA set out to implement methods to counter these burdens but it also set out to empower community-based Latino AIDS projects, which for the most part, have not received adequate funding.

But perhaps the most significant accomplishment of the conference was the increased visibility and communal commitment of Latinos fighting AIDS – nationally and locally. Up until this time, most of the existing programs aimed at educating and informing the Latino community have had their sources outside the Latino community or have been headed by persons unfamiliar with Latino culture, its bicultural process, and the social, spiritual, and economic realities of the Latino community. The result has been inappropriate and inadequate educational materials and programs; inattentive, if not racist, disregard for indigenous or alternative health-care beliefs and practices; and the exclusion of Latinos and other people of color, including women, from clinical drug trials. The leadership demonstrated at the 1988 conference was as effective at forming an AIDS coalition among Latinos as ACT UP (AIDS Coalition To Unleash Power) had proven in 1987. The proliferation of AIDS organizations specific to communities of color such as the Minority AIDS Project, Milagros, and Cara a Cara, to name only a few, have helped enormously in the fight against AIDS, despite the continual struggle to maintain adequate funding for their programs and services. While many of these organizations work with clients who are gay or bisexual, services specific to gay men of color remain horrifyingly underfunded, given the grave statistics of AIDS cases among gay men of color. Moreover, in Latino communities, gay or bisexual men must confront a relentlessly homophobic ideology. As Latina AIDS activist Alice Villalobos explained in 1990: "one of the most difficult and heartbreaking aspects of [Latino gay or bisexual men with HIV or AIDS] is that they are usually forced to live within the homophobic Latino/a community because of poverty and oppression. Not only are they rejected by their own people, but they also have to deal with a white, Anglo culture that categorizes them as second class citizens merely because of the color of their skin" (p. 10). Villalobos writes as a member of ACT UP/Los Angeles in a newsletter that at the time was informing and educating primarily non-Latinos about the issues facing Latino gay men with AIDS in Los Angeles County. Such work is intense and often highly volatile. Los Angeles County includes the largest Latino population in the United States. Non-Latino AIDS activists and straight Latinos must both be educated continually about the specific experiences of gay or bisexual Latinos. Latino gay men fighting AIDS must find support from two very different and often opposing communities. "White AIDS agencies aren't sensitized about monolingual, non-documented seropositives who fear being deported," explains Juan Ledesma, former director of the East LA AIDS Hotline and now with AIDS Health Care Foundation. Arturo Olivias, former executive director of Cara a Cara Latino AIDS Project adds, "My community doesn't acknowledge that there's such a thing as a Latino man who has sex with men" (Sadownick, 1989: 14). Latino gay men have realized that the fight against AIDS is interrelated with a continuing struggle against racism, classism, and homophobia, the very issues that have enabled AIDS to infiltrate communities of color so extensively in the first place.

In Los Angeles, one of the most successful areas where Latino gays and lesbians have been able to counter the pervasive ideologies that facilitate the spread of AIDS among gay male Latinos has been through performance and the arts. In part this success is due to VIVA! a gay and lesbian arts organization founded in 1988 that serves both as a support network for local Latino/a artists and

a coalition advocating for Latino/a gay, lesbian, and AIDS visibility in other venues. Doug Sadownick reports, for example, that when Highways Performance Space in Santa Monica first opened in 1988, the inaugural events staged – a Cinco de Mayo marathon put on the Border Arts Workshop – were assailed by VIVA! for failing to discuss gay and lesbian issues. One month later, VIVA! was angered again when Highways sponsored a lesbian and gay performance festival that lacked Latino/a representation. After VIVA! brought attention to the issue, Latinos were added to the schedule. Highways has since proven to be one of the most visible locations for Latino/a gay and lesbian artists, thanks to its multicommunity-based structure and the intervention of VIVA! members. Like other gays and lesbians of color, politicized Latinos find that in order to insure that their concerns be addressed they must consciously work within and around various hegemonic systems.

Latino gays and lesbians in theater perform their art and activism from the multiple positionalities that inform their Latino gay/lesbian identities. Their performances enact the "oppositional consciousness" that Chicana lesbian Chela Sandoval has theorized as a tactic utilized by marginalized people to resist hegemonic inscription: "The differential mode of oppositional consciousness depends upon the ability to read the current situation of power and of self-consciously choosing and adopting the ideological form best suited to push against its configurations, a survival skill well known to oppressed peoples" (Sandoval, 1991: 16). Sandoval argues against a political identity reduced to a single or fixed perception by dominant culture and the identity politics engendered by such configurations. Rather, oppositional consciousness accommodates a tactical privileging of one component of identity without disturbing the notion of identity as a dynamic process. While Sandoval writes specifically within the context of US Third World feminism, oppositional consciousness, as she explains, "is also a form of resistance well utilized among subordinated subjects under various conditions of domination and subordination" (p. 16).[10] As I hope to make clear, Latino gay performers can be best understood in light of Sandoval's theory. Moreover, as Sandoval's theory begins to suggest, one of the benefits of the differential mode of oppositional consciousness is the possibility of forging links with others experiencing social marginality. With Sandoval's theory in mind, I will argue how in one localized (albeit enormous) social space – Los Angeles – counter-hegemonic coalitions based on what I identify as a "politics of affinity" are materializing through performance. I draw my examples from the performances of Latino gay and lesbian artists working in Los Angeles, in particular Luis Alfaro's solo and collaborative works. These Latino performers offer a much-needed voice in the work of what Antonio Gramsci has called the "historical bloc of organic intellectuals," the counter-hegemonic practices of subordinate groups working as a coalition or "bloc" against existing power relations. In this sense, these performers participate in the process that George Lipsitz has outlined in his insightful reading of popular music in East Los Angeles. If, as Lipsitz argues, the music of Chicanos "reflects a quite conscious cultural politics that seek inclusion in the American mainstream by transforming it" (p. 159), Latino gay performers must also work against the grain of the Latino heterosexist mainstream in order to dismantle it as well. Latino gay performers often must maneuver between Latino conventions on the one hand and dominant white gay traditions on the other. In terms of the theater, their work may involve an interreferential allusion to the already parodic and satirical models of Culture Clash, thus furthering and enhancing the intertextual dialogues within Latino theater, or it may suggest an affinity with politicized white gay male performers in Southern California such as Tim Miller or Michael Kearns, all the while expressing the oppositional consciousness first articulated by Third World US feminists.

Such a varied and deliberate tactic goes one step further than the bifocality that Lipsitz argues for popular music in East Los Angeles. Lipsitz reads the cultural performances of

Chicano musicians through anthropologist Michael M. J. Fischer's concept of bifocality or reciprocity of perspectives. Bifocality, Lipsitz writes, is a process of self-respect: "prevented from defining themselves because of pervasive discrimination and prejudice, but unwilling to leave the work of definition to others [Chicano musicians], adopted a bifocal perspective that acknowledged but did not accept the majority culture's image of Chicanos" (p. 154). Sandoval's theory of oppositional consciousness provides the basis for the explication of how Latino gay performers moreover must adjust through a *multi*focality in order to resist the stereotypes imposed by dominant heterosexist ideologies. This multifocal perspective is keenly attuned to the multiple sites of their discrimination stemming from their ethnicity, sexuality, class background, HIV status, or gender.

Luis Alfaro's performance work is a case in point. In his solo piece, *Downtown*, Alfaro – a Chicano playwright, performer, and community activist – performs various characters who live in the Pico-Union district, the heavily populated and impoverished Latino neighborhood in downtown Los Angeles where he grew up.[11] *Downtown* is a nonlinear montage of multicharacter monologue, movement, autobiography, and sound. In *Downtown*, Alfaro investigates the rhythms of his neighborhood, reconfiguring Los Angeles from his working-class Latino background and his gay identity. Alfaro scrutinizes Los Angeles by laying bare the glorification of the city and the glamorization of its people fabricated by Hollywood and offered for mass consumption by the entertainment industry. He provides snapshots of his neighborhood and family – from skyscrapers and alleys, undocumented workers, and the 18th Street Gang, to local junkies and his Tia Ofelia, Tita, and Romie – that suggest the formation of his politicized identity. But rather than offering a historical chronicle of his own political trajectory, Alfaro stages these stories as unrelated vignettes linked only as indelible memories of a vast urban and psychic landscape.

No comfortable claims are made for and about a Latino gay male identity in *Downtown*;

instead Alfaro stages the multiple and often contradictory configurations that construct the possibility for the oppositional consciousness that emerges from a self-conscious and self-articulated Latino gay male perspective. Like Culture Clash, Alfaro draws from Latino culture, but he diffuses the centrality of his ethnicity by cultivating a deliberately gay perspective. From his marginality he offers a cultural politics that foregrounds both his ethnicity and sexuality, depending on his point of emphasis, and in the process destabilizes the privileged status of either.

*Downtown* begins with Alfaro situated against a scrim onto which drive-by film shots of downtown Los Angeles street corners are projected; Petula Clark's classic pop hymn "Downtown" provides the soundtrack. The interplay between Petula Clark's escapist view of urban life and the harsh black and white images of Downtown LA sets the tone for Alfaro's bittersweet relationship to the city. Alfaro first positions himself as part of this landscape by joining the nameless pedestrians projected upon the scrim. He then breaks the illusion by stepping out of the image to speak of the experience. Alfaro at once invokes the crisis of modernity – Walter Benjamin's reading of Baudelaire being "jostled by the crowd" – and the oral tradition of the epic poet composing and reciting the myths of an era. Such lofty posturing – *flâneur* and bard – is given a camp poignancy and a postmodern twist with Petula Clark's resounding, "you can forget all your troubles, forget all your cares, so go downtown" refrain. Alfaro's man about town – Latino, gay, and poor – can't escape the omnipresence of the pop culture that infuses the neighborhood. In his performance Alfaro will manipulate such realities by appropriation, commenting all the while on both the process of creating art and on the equally trying challenge of fashioning an identity.

With the ominous and always scrutinizing sounds and lights of a police helicopter hovering over the neighborhood in the background, Alfaro begins his first monologue "On a Street Corner" with reminiscences of formative occasions from his childhood. He offers headlines:

A woman got slugged.
A man got slapped.
A clown threw toys.
A drunk staggered.
An earthquake shook.[12]

which are then further abbreviated to simple gestures first spoken and then performed on his own body: "A Slap. A Slug. A Shove. A Kick. A Kiss." Initially sounding like non sequiturs, these masochistic gestures will be recontextualized throughout the performance and serve as the leitmotifs of the piece, physical reminders of the battles Latinos face daily. While the LAPD surveillance helicopters patrol the neighborhood, a plastic rotating Virgin Mary doll from Tijuana surveys the Alfaro household – "she would turn and bless all sides of the room." The Virgin Mary doll becomes a symbol of kinship, a token from the homeland that comforts and detracts from the urban hardships of downtown LA, the reminder of the family mantra ingrained in the young boy's consciousness: "You see, blood is thicker than water, family is greater than friends and the Virgin Mary watches over all of us." At one point, 10-year-old Luis offers the doll to his ailing Tia Ofelia, who has breast cancer, in order to drive away *La Bruja Maldita* who was "slowly eating at her insides." When the boy innocently asks to see her chest, Tia Ofelia slaps him so hard on the face that even he could feel *La Bruja Maldita* eating away at his heart. Soon after his Tia dies and is buried, the Crips firebomb the 18th Street Gang living underneath her old apartment. Rummaging through the charred remains of the apartment building, he finds what's left of the rotating Virgin Mary, now useless and empty of its meaning.

Alfaro tells the story of the Virgin Mary in order to call into question the cultural belief systems of his Latino and Catholic family. This scene offers a poignant and deeply affectionate send-up of the assumptions impoverished Latinos maintain in order to endure the hardships of everyday life – inadequate health care, gang warfare, and an LAPD that essentially quarantines their neighborhoods through its aggressive surveillance.

Alfaro, while critical of this system of exploitation vis-à-vis the church and the state, cannot deny the power of its influence. He ends this section with the familiar iconography of the neighborhood, expanding the connotations of his background to accommodate his emerging sexual identification:

> When I was eighteen, I met this guy with a rotating Virgin Mary. He bought it in Mexico, so, of course, I fell in love. His skin was white. He ate broccoli and spoke like actors on a T.V. series. It was my first love and like the *Bruja Maldita*, he pounded on my heart. He taught me many things; how to kiss like the French, lick an earlobe and dance in the dark. He was every Brady Bunch/Partridge Family episode rolled into one. He gave me his shirt and I told him about the fields in Delano, picking cherries one summer and my summer in Mexico. Once my grandmother sent me a crate of grapes. We took off our clothes, smashed them all over our bodies and ate them off each other. When he left, the *Bruja Maldita's* hand replaced his in my heart and she pounded on me. And she laughed like Mexican mothers at a clothes line. And I covered my tears with a smile that was like the veils at Immaculate Conception. But my sorrow was so strong that relatives near by would say *"Ay Mijo*, don't you see? Blood is thicker than water, family is greater than friends, and the Virgin Mary watches over all of us." (Blackout).

The conflicting interpretations of the signification of the iconography – for the Latino the Virgin Mary as a sign of kinship, for the white man a sign of kitsch; for nonwhites the Brady Bunch (incredibly) as a sign of normalized family structures, for whites a banal popular entertainment – sets off the imbalance that will eventually bring back the pounding of the *Bruja Maldita* against the young man's heart. In "Virgin Mary" Alfaro demonstrates the forces that shape the construction of his Latino gay male identity. The performer, over a decade later, offers this construction to his audience in order to demonstrate the tensions

that give shape to his desire – "A Slap, A Shrug, A Kiss." The scene ends without resolution, only with the melancholy recognition of his desire and its problematic reception in two conflicting social fields of power; the kinship systems of his Latino family and of an imagined gay community.[13]

In subsequent scenes, Alfaro includes Eric Bogosian-like portraits of various characters from the neighborhood that extend beyond his immediate family. He inhabits the voices and movements of Latinos in the barrio, people he encounters on the street that give him a sense of himself and who inform the performance of the desperate economic conditions of the neighborhood. In these scenes, he foregrounds different aspects of the urban Latino experience and gives voice to the underrepresented thousands who populate LA's downtown. While these portraits contribute to the overall social milieu of *Downtown*, their main purpose is both psychological and interreferential. Alfaro locates the soul of the persona offering it to the audience as his point of connection with the neighborhood; these are moments of both epiphany and affinity. In "Lupe," for example, Alfaro opens by describing his venture through the sweatshops where undocumented Latina women labor for less than minimum wage working 12-hour shifts on a six-day week. He spots Lupe who has a face "brown like my father's" and who "paid a *coyote* $150 to smuggle her across the border." He shifts from his performance persona to the voice of Lupe. To mark the transition he puts on a dress. We meet Lupe as she's about to go out on the town on a Saturday night. Lupe's downtown – full of cumbias, *Bohemias*, and street-corner lunatics – begins as a temporary refuge from the buzz of the sewing machines of the sweatshop. With her boyfriend she finds romance, but the promise of downtown – "you can forget all your troubles, forget all your cares, so go downtown" – is haunted by the distant sound of the machines "singing to me to come down to the other side of downtown and punch in, punch in, punch in." With fingers bleeding, sirens sounding, and the helicopter always overhead, Lupe fights to hang on to the romance of the city and the bargain of the border. Alfaro ends this portrait with her resounding, albeit temporary, triumph: "Tonite they can all be on fire. Because tonight there is no job. Tonite there is no stitch. No needle, no fabric, no pattern, no nothing. Because tonite is Saturday nite and my dress is too tight and my name is Lupe (Blackout)."

The "Lupe" section concludes with Alfaro still in character. The identification process of the Latino gay man with the young undocumented worker suggests an intercultural affinity that recognizes both class oppression and gender specificity. Alfaro's performance of Lupe is staged neither as the omniscient privilege of the creative agent's insight which escapes the character nor as "classic" drag, where the male temporarily puts on a dress in an imagined transgression which by the end only reinforces gender binarism.[14] Instead, Alfaro's performance of Lupe reveals more about his own persona and his choices of affinity. Lupe's oppression and her defiance are interrelated to his own. Such is the tactic of performative oppositional consciousness. In "Lupe" Alfaro plays against preconceived notions of drag as gay performance in order to highlight the experiences shared by Latinos in the barrio. His performance can be interpreted as a political tactic to challenge the alienation of the oppressed by demonstrating the affinities between and among people living in the city. The multifocalities of the performer and the character – the specificity of class, gender, sexuality, and ethnicity – joined in performance enact the coalition-building necessary to counter hegemonic configurations that insist on the conflation of differences.

In "Federal Building," Alfaro describes his involvement in the 1 March 1990 artist chain-gang protest regarding censorship and the crisis at the National Endowment for the Arts. Over 70 artists and their supporters marched from the County Museum of Art to the downtown Federal Building where civil disobedience turned into performance pieces staged en route. Artists dressed as criminals carried huge images of banned artists and engaged spectators read quotations about freedom of speech. Guerrilla theater vignettes, bilingual performances and press conferences, and an extended parable involving a debate between the Spirit of Freedom of Speech and a fundamentalist from North Carolina contributed to the militant defense of artistic freedom which resulted in 27 arrests.

For Alfaro the Federal Building – "the big beautiful marble structure on Los Angeles Street" – is an emblem of his relationship with the city that dates back to his early years when his father would drive the family by the halls of justice "looking for distant Mexican relatives with phony passports ready for a life in Our Lady Queen of the Angels." Like the helicopter that opens and closes *Downtown*, the Federal Building is omnipresent: always visible and always threatening to reveal its power. Like the rotating Virgin Mary doll, the building is a symbol of surveillance: "We have a long history together this *ruca* and I. She has watched me grow up and play on her steps. Watched me low ride in front of her. Watched me spit at her face at an Immigration demonstration that I don't understand but comprehend enough to know that my dad can go back anytime, just never when he wants to." The personal context of the building resurfaces for Alfaro when he returns to protest with artists and members of ACT UP/L.A. shouting in both English and Spanish such chants as "Art is not a Crime," "Alto a la Censura," and "AIDS Funding Now." Unlike some of the other protestors, Alfaro has been here before. The downtown Federal Building has always been for him a microcosmic icon of his relationship with the city, a place where the notion of home shifts to and from a sense of belonging or displacement. The specific circumstances articulated in the first half of "Federal Building," where long-standing Latino issues such as immigration and deportation were introduced as evidence of nationalist muscle, now resurface as HIV issues with the discriminatory policies and procedures of the INS. And while the performer's ethnicity was the initial political identity foregrounded, by this point in

"Federal Building" Alfaro's political tactic is to foreground his sexuality. By the end of this section, however, Alfaro demonstrates how both facets of his identity – sexuality and ethnicity – are enmeshed in his desire for, and denial by, the downtown Federal Building and the home that it has symbolically represented:

I didn't get arrested because my government wants to control the content of art, or because a Republican congressman from Orange County thinks AIDS activists are a "dying breed." I got arrested because [former] Mayor Sam Yorty told me we were all the mayor. Because a black and white can stop you anywhere, anytime, for whatever reason. Because big marble buildings stare down with a *chale* stare. Because I've never owned anything in my life – much less a city. (Blackout.)

In "Federal Building" Alfaro demonstrates how AIDS issues for people of color cannot be viewed without an analysis of race and class. Although he joins the others in the spirit and mission of the protest, his personal investment in the Federal Building extends beyond the specifics of the moment and involves the complex contextual history of his relation to Los Angeles as a Latino gay man. And yet, Alfaro's arrest *does* result from his protest against censorship and AIDS bigotry and not this personal backdrop. The arresting officer who "puts handcuffs on me while hundreds of people blow whistles and yell shame, shame, shame" has no idea of why Alfaro is there, only that he is "trespassing on government property." The personal agenda articulated in performance is unavailable to "the man in the helmet and plastic gloves." For the arresting officer Alfaro is only one more protestor. But for the spectator, manipulated by the performative tactics of oppositional consciousness, Alfaro's political identity as a Latino gay man is quite specific though by no means static. The oppositional consciousness model that forms the basis of this performance – the continual dynamic shift in focus from Latino to gay, for example – at its most successful,

unsettles the audience's own capacity to conflate differences. Instead, the operative dynamic of oppositional consciousness in Alfaro's performance suggests the possible affinities between performer and audience while simultaneously forcing the spectators to consider the specificity of their own subject-positions.

Alfaro's tactic to perform the links between oppressions also points to the possible counter-hegemonic responses to oppression. In "Federal Building" Alfaro demonstrates how his multifocal identity and politics of oppositional consciousness work in the best interests of coalition movements. The demonstrators all chant various causes and concerns – anticensorship, AIDS, queer visibility and rights – in both English and Spanish. That Alfaro's performance in "Federal Building" is then about a performance, or more specifically an activist performance, suggests the deeply interdependent nature of his politics and his art. In reclaiming and recontextualizing downtown Los Angeles, Alfaro participates in the counter-hegemonic practice of both self-individualization and community formation. *Downtown* ends with Alfaro reciting (and enacting through gesture) a litany of epiphanic moments that encapsulate the characters introduced throughout the performance; each moment is prefaced by "one strong shove":

One strong shove and the LAPD lets me know who is in charge . . .
One strong shove and my fingers are bleeding . . .
One strong shove and the sound of a helicopter or ambulance in the middle of the night lets me know I'm alive.
One strong shove and a helicopter light has found me in downtown.
(Alfaro gestures shoves in silence. Blackout.)

Caught once again in the glare of surveillance, Alfaro disappears into the darkness of the stage. The theater then becomes the site of refuge; a place where identity can be explored or contested, created and shared.[15] His work is, as Jan Breslauer explains in describing Los Angeles performance art, "a theater of liberation" (p. 95).

As with other gay male playwrights or performers of color, AIDS issues in *Downtown* are thoroughly connected with the prevailing issues of class and race bias.[16] AIDS is experienced as one component in a complex system of exploitation and oppression. Through performance Alfaro stages affinities across boundaries of racial and gender difference in order to foreground the "historical bloc" necessary to intervene in the hegemonic scripts of dominant culture. While the material within Alfaro's performances displays many of Sandoval's ideas, the productions of his performance begin to materialize Sandoval's theory toward a cogent model for political praxis.

*Downtown* is usually produced as a solo artist evening, although Alfaro has performed it in various group shows ranging from David Schweizer's full-scale production of three solo performance pieces, *True Lies*,[17] to stripped-down versions at Chicano or gay and lesbian art festivals in the Los Angeles area. In these settings, Alfaro's work is received as either the gay piece or the Latino piece, or in the case of the LATC production, the gay and Latino piece. From this perspective, Alfaro's performance risks the appropriation of mainstream production where the work is interpreted either as an exercise in multiculturalism and thus carrying the burden of representation, or where his presence is singled out as the spectacle of difference normalizing the assumptions inherent in the other performances staged.[18] Such risks are worth taking, however, given the design of *Downtown* which allows Alfaro to contextualize difference *and* point toward a politics of affinity.

In his collaborations with other gay and lesbian performers, Alfaro continues to articulate a politics of oppositional consciousness. In *Queer Rites*, for example, Alfaro performs with two white lesbian feminists, Robin Podolsky and Sandra Golvin, and with Doug Sadownick, a Jewish gay male performer.[19] Given that it is already understood that the four performers in *Queer Rites* are queer, it is left up to the four of them to establish points of difference and points of connection. Alfaro, as the only person of color, foregrounds his ethnicity. Sadownick in turn highlights his Jewish identity and Golvin and Podolsky focus on their gender and class. Many issues are addressed throughout the performance including a woman's right to choose, coming out, censorship, AIDS, and anti-semitism, and overall the effect here is to demonstrate how these issues are all interrelated. *Queer Rites* celebrates difference while demonstrating the effects of coalition building and dialogue between seemingly disparate communities. *Queer Rites* was performed in the summer of 1991 first at Highways and then at Celebration Theatre in West Hollywood.

The same weekend that Culture Clash premiered *SOS* in downtown Los Angeles, Alfaro joined two other Los Angeles-based Latino performers, Monica Palacios and Alberto "Beto" Araiza, to premiere their collaboration *Deep in the Crotch of My Latino Psyche* at the Fourth Annual Gay and Lesbian Performance Festival at Highways. Palacios, self-described "Latin Lezbo Comic" with a solo show of the same name, is a veteran of both comedy clubs and alternative performance venues. Her work is specific to her experience as a Chicana lesbian and continually and hilariously refutes the rigid sexual scripts expected of all women in Latino culture. Araiza – a multitalented actor, playwright, and director – has toured his solo show *Meat My Beat* throughout North America and Europe. *Meat My Beat* chronicles Araiza's travels through urban gay male culture and concludes with a powerful and deeply disturbing response to his own experiences of living with HIV. Together with Alfaro in *Deep in the Crotch of My Latino Psyche* they begin to negotiate through performance a Latino gay and lesbian politics.

In scenarios that vary from stand-up, melodrama, satire, and personal testimony, the three performers set out to critique institutions in both Latino and mainstream gay communities. As "Latino homos without a home" in either community they take to the stage to carve out a niche and claim their rights. They contest a monolithic perception of the Latino gay experience by underlining the vast differences among them, from their own performance styles to their HIV status. *Deep in the Crotch of My Latino Psyche* closely resembles *SOS* in style; short skits that may involve all three performers, solos, or combinations of two. But unlike Culture Clash, these performers insist on rupturing the gender binarism of the *chingón/chingada* polarity and critiquing Latino homophobia and the silence around AIDS.

*Deep in the Crotch of My Latino Psyche*, as its title indicates, is a humorous and sexy exploration of Latino lesbian and gay sexuality.[20] The performance, however, also seriously engages a number of political issues, most notably through Araiza's two sections on AIDS and HIV in the Latino community, "HIVato" and "Safos," and Palacios' solo "Tom Boy Piece" about her coming out process. Alfaro offers a number of solos including a lyrical AIDS memorial, "Where are my heros? Where are my saints?" In "Isolation" – the most effective piece of the performance – the three actors, with only their upper torsos lit, sit on stools and face the audience as an ominous voice-over interrogates them at length about their personal lives. The performers must raise their hand in silence to answer the interviewer's questions which range in tone and intensity from "Have you ever lied about your nationality?" and "Have you lost a lover to AIDS?" to "Do you prefer flour to corn tortillas?" and "Have you ever put on make-up while driving your car?" By the end of this scene, composed of nearly 50 questions, spectators – whether Latino or non-Latino, gay or non-gay – cannot possibly consider Latino gay and lesbian sexuality within a comfortable categorization. Latino gay identities are presented as dynamic and contradictory. The material production of performance stripped down here to its most basic demystifies the performance process and facilitates the effective representation of both the silence around homosexuality in Latino culture and the real and living bodies of Latino/a queers. The interactions among

these very different Latino performers in *Deep in the Crotch of My Latino Psyche* demonstrates Sandoval's idea that "self-conscious agents of differential consciousness recognize one another as allies, country women and men of the same psychic terrain" (p. 15).

Alfaro, Araiza, and Palacios, three of the driving forces behind *VIVA!*, have collaborated on various "behind the scenes" efforts to gain visibility for Latino gays and lesbians. *Deep in the Crotch of My Latino Psyche* is but one of the many tactics that demonstrate the inseparable nature of their art and activism. Perhaps their most impressive collaboration so far has been the AIDS Intervention Theater project *Teatro VIVA!*, an AIDS outreach program that provides bilingual prevention information in both traditional (community centers and theaters) and non-traditional sites (parks, bars, community fairs and bazaars, art galleries and private homes). Funded with a $50,000 grant from the United States Conference of Mayors, *Teatro VIVA!* presents short skits on such HIV/AIDS issues as transmission, prevention, safer sex negotiation skills, popular misconceptions about AIDS, daily considerations of people with HIV and AIDS, and local community resources. The main component of the program was its bilingual mobile *teatro* presentations, performed in agit-prop minimalistic style, to allow for flexibility in response to the varying aspects of each venue. These performances were then followed by a question-and-answer period which allowed for more detailed discussions about AIDS. Ariaza, the project director for the first grant, reports that over 5,000 individuals – including nearly 2,000 self-identified gay and bisexual Latinos – viewed the *Teatro VIVA!* AIDS Outreach Project. Forty presentations were given within Los Angeles County between July 1991 and April 1992. Such interventions demonstrate that Latino gay men can begin to unsettle the muscle of cultural nationalism and homophobia that have combined with other social factors to render Latino gay men powerless. Latina lesbians have already proven their power by organizing first and foremost as Latina lesbians and by forming coalitions with other women who respect the issues specific to their survival. With the supportive and reciprocal alliances between Latina lesbians and Latino gay men available through *VIVA!* the possibilities for future political work seem endless. The proven success of *Teatro VIVA!*, while localized within the confines of Los Angeles County to help combat AIDS among Latino gay and bisexual men, hints that the political landscape is changing. *Teatro VIVA!* has been refunded for 1993 by the County of Los Angeles AIDS Program Office with Palacios and Alfaro now serving as codirectors.

The theater, of course, is only one of the many sites of contestation in the fight against AIDS and performance only one of the many means possible to counter AIDS and its insidious mystifications in dominant culture. But performance, as I have argued elsewhere, holds the capacity to articulate resistance and generate necessary social change.[21] The work of Alfaro, Palacios, and Araiza – individually and in collaboration, in the theater and on the streets – provides one model for Latinos and our supporters to engage at once in the tactics of oppositional consciousness and in the coalition-building available through an affinity politics. The name *Teatro VIVA!* translates in the most pragmatic and descriptive sense as "VIVA's theater," the theater component of the Latino gay and lesbian arts organization *VIVA!* However, I employ *teatro viva* here in the literal sense of "theater" and the imperative modality of the present subjunctive of the verb "to live"; to convey quite simply, an acclamation of desire for theater and life.

## Notes

This essay was written in the summer of 1992 with support from the Graduate School at University of Washington-Seattle. I'd like to thank the many friends who helped shape my ideas throughout the writing process: Yvonne Yarbro-Bejarano, Dorinne Kondo, Luis Alfaro, Beto Araiza, Brian Freeman, Tim Miller, Susana Chávez-Silverman, Douglas Swenson, and, in the final stages of revision for publication, Douglas Crimp. Thanks are also due to the two anonymous readers for Duke University Press who, along with the editors of this anthology, provided useful commentary. Versions of this paper were presented at the "Gender, Sexuality, and the State in a Hispanic/Latino Context" conference at the University of California Berkeley and at the "AIDS Appropriations: Cultural Studies Perspectives" conference at Rice University. Questions and comments from these audiences have enabled me to clarify specific points. This essay is for my parents.

1   Readers who are unfamiliar with the extensive bibliography on AIDS and cultural representations should begin with the foundational works by Crimp, Crimp with Rolston, Patton, and Watney. I want to stress that there are necessary distinctions between AIDS-phobia, homophobia, and misogyny; that these same discrete and dynamic terms, however, are often conflated in people's understandings and responses to AIDS; and that the practice of viewing the terms as interchangeable, in this case when discussing AIDS, is itself symptomatic of the very conditions that the terms describe.

2   Press release.

3   Including not only the Rodney King verdict and the riots that resulted,but also the racist rhetoric that characterized much of the popular media's coverage of these events. For artists' responses to the LA riots see the special edition of *High Performance* "The Verdict and the Violence," Summer 1992.

4   "American Me Tail" is a clever take-off on *American Me*, a 1992 film about Latino prisoners and *An American Tale*, a Disney Studios animated film. The core of the skit involves the power relations within competing factions in a prison negotiated, predictably enough, through male rape.

5   Perhaps the most obvious failure of identity politics in the performance emerges from the interchangeable Chicano/Latino terminology. Chicano refers to a very specific set of political identifications among Mexican Americans; Latino, like Chicano, is a term of self-identification that differentiates from the

more official and imposed term "Hispanic." See Alonso and Koreck for a detailed account of these terms in relation to AIDS.

6   See, for instance, her trilogy of plays – *Giving Up the Ghost*, *Shadow of a Man*, and *Heroes and Saints*, along with Yarbro-Bejarano's discussion of them.

7   At the biannual Latino Festival Theater held in the South Bronx in 1990, for example, El Teatro de la Esperanza presented one of the best received plays of the festival, Josefina Lopez's *Real Women Have Curves*. For more information on the festival see Arratia's discussion in *Drama Review*. Also in 1990, the University of California at Irvine held "The Representation of Otherness in Chicano and Latin American Theater and Film" conference in *Theater Journal*. Not all women, of course, are able – or for that matter willing – to see their work staged in these forums. For all-women performance venues, festivals, and conferences, see Yarbro-Bejarano's essays. For discussions of more recent Latino theater festivals, see the writings of Ed Morales. For an overview of Chicano theater, see the invaluable work of Jorge Huerta.

8   For an insightful critique of *Criticism in the Borderlands* written from the perspective of a Chicana lesbian, see González.

9   See Alonso and Koreck, "Silences: 'Hispanics,' AIDS, and Sexual Practices."

10  Yvonne Yarbro-Bejarano has already demonstrated how Sandoval's theory of oppositional consciousness provides fresh insight for critical formations in theories of difference and gay and lesbian studies; see her contribution to *Professions of Desire* and her article on Anzaldúa's *Borderlands*.

11  For an in-depth discussion of Los Angeles Latinos and poverty, see Mike Davis, *City of Quartz*. In "The Hammer and the Rock," a chilling chapter on inner-city social conditions, Davis explains how "poverty is increasing faster among Los Angeles Latinos, especially youth, than any other urban group in the United States" (p. 315).

12  All quotes are from the author's unpublished performance text.

13  For an excellent discussion of kinship and conflict as it pertains to lesbians and gay men, see Kath Weston.

14  On "classic" drag, see chapter 1 of Sue Ellen Case's *Feminism and Theater*. But see also Marjorie Garber, *Vested Interests: Cross-dressing and Cultural Anxiety* for a different reading of

cross-dressing and for a more extensive bibliography.

15  On the idea of theater and political identities as related to people of color, see Dorinne Kondo; as related to gay men in response to AIDS, see my "Performing All Our Lives."

16  See my essay "*Fierce Love* and Fierce Response" for a discussion of Pomo Afro Homos and some of these same issues.

17  Alfaro's *Downtown* was performed as *Pico-Union* on a bill with Chloe Webb's *Walkin' the Walls* and Rocco Sisto's rendition of Dario Fo's *The Tale of the Tiger*. *True Lies* was performed at the Los Angeles Theater Center from 25 July to 8 September 1991.

18  Most of the reviews of *True Lies* for example, while favorable of *Pico-Union*, describe in detail Alfaro's sexuality and ethnicity – some even to the extent that they talk about his physical appearance – without going into any discussion of either of the two white performers' sexuality or ethnic background, let alone their physical traits.

19  Unfortunately *Queer Rites* was not reviewed in any great detail. Rachel Kaplan writes, however, a very descriptive review of their individual performances in "A Queer Exchange" at San Francisco's 1800 Square Feet. These performances developed into the collaborative *Queer Rites*. See Kaplan for a more in-depth analysis of this work.

20  Their promotional slogan: "Comedy, Drama, Pathos and Piñatas!" further accentuated the humor.

21  "Performing All Our Lives."

# Bibliography

Alfaro, Luis. *Downtown* (1990). Performed at Highways Performance Space in Santa Monica, CA. 30 November, 1–2, 7–9 December.

Alfaro, Luis, Araiza, Alberto, and Palacios, Monica (1992). *Deep in the Crotch of My Latino Psyche*. Performed at Highways Performance Space, 9–11 and 14–16 July.

Almaguer, Tomás (1991). "Chicano Men: A Cartography of Homosexual Identity and Behavior." *differences*, 3: 75–100.

Alonso, Ana Maria, and Koreck, Maria Teresa (1989). "Silences: 'Hispanics,' AIDS and Sexual Practices." *differences* 1: 101–24.

Arratia, Euridice (1991). "Teatro Festival: The Latino Festival Theater." *Drama Review*, 35: 176–82.

Breslauer, Jan (1992). "California Performance." *Performing Arts Journal*, 41: 87–96.

Calderón, Hector, and Saldivar, José David (1991). *Criticism in the Borderlands: Studies in Literature, Culture, and Ideology*. Durham, NC: Duke University Press.

Case, Sue-Ellen (1988). *Feminism and Theater*. New York: Routledge.

Crimp, Douglas (1987). "How to Have Promiscuity During an Epidemic." *AIDS: Cultural Analysis/Cultural Activism*, ed. Douglas Crimp. Cambridge, MA: MIT Press.

Crimp, Douglas, with Rolston, Adam (1990). *AIDS Demographics*. Seattle: Bay Press.

Culture Clash (1992). *SOS*. Performed at the Japan American Theater, Los Angeles. 9–11 July.

Davis, Mike (1990). *City of Quartz: Excavating the Future in Los Angeles*. London: Verso.

Garber, Marjorie (1991). *Vested Interests: Cross-dressing and Cultural Anxiety*. New York: Routledge.

González, Deena J. (1991). "Masquerades: Viewing the New Chicana Lesbian Anthologies." *Outlook*, 15: 80–3.

Huerta, Jorge (1993). "Professionalizing Teatro: An Overview of Chicano Theater During the 'Decade of the Hispanic.'" *Theater Forum*, 3: 54–9.

Kanellos, Nicolás (1990). *A History of Hispanic Theater in the United States: Origins to 1940*. Austin: University of Texas Press.

Kaplan, Rachel (1991). Review of *A Queer Exchange. San Francisco Bay Times* (March): 50.

Kondo, Dorinne (1991). "The Narrative Production of 'Home,' Community and Political Identity in Asian American Theater." Paper delivered at the 1991 American Anthropological Association Conference.

Lipsitz, George (1990). *Time Passages: Collective Memory and American Popular Culture*. Minneapolis: University of Minnesota Press.

Maldonado, Miguelina (1992). "On the Out Side: Latinos and Clinical Trials" *SIDAhora*, 11: 13.

Martinez-Maza, Otoniel, Shin, Diana M., and Banks, Helen F. (1989). *Latinos and AIDS: A National Strategy Symposium*. Los Angeles: Center for Interdisciplinary Research in Immunology and Disease (CIRID).

Moraga, Cherrie (1983). *Loving in the War Years*. Boston: South End Press.

Morales, Ed. (1992). "Shadowing Valdez." *American Theater*, 97: 14–19.

—— (1993) "Welcome to Aztlán" *American Theater*, 103: 38–40.

—— (1993) "Those Who Can Act: 'Cultural Workers' at TeatroFestival." *Village Voice*, 3 August: 95–6.

Patton, Cindy (1990). *Inventing AIDS*. New York: Routledge.

Román, David (1993). "*Fierce Love* and Fierce Response: Intervening in the Cultural Politics of Race, Sexuality, and AIDS." *Critical Essays: Gay and Lesbian Writers of Color*, ed. Emmanuel S. Nelson. New York: Haworth Press.

—— (1992). "Performing All Our Lives: AIDS, Performance, Community." *Critical Theory and Performance*, ed. Janelle Reinelt and Joseph Roach. Ann Arbor: University of Michigan Press.

Sadownick, Doug. (1989). "Family Among Strangers: Crossing the Borders in Gay L.A." *LA Weekly*, 23–29 June: 12–20.

Sandoval, Chela (1991). "U.S. Third World Feminism: The Theory and Method of Oppositional Consciousness in the Postmodern World." *Genders*, 10: 1–24.

Sedgwick, Eve Kosofsky (1990). *Epistemology of the Closet*. Berkeley: University of California Press.

Taylor, Diana (1991). Review of *The Representation of Otherness in Chicano and Latin American Theater and Film Conference* at UC-Irvine, 18–20 October 1990. *Theater Journal*, 43: 377–9.

Villalobos, Alice (1990). "AIDS and the Latino/a Community." *ACT UP/Los Angeles Newsletter*, 5: 10.

Watney, Simon (1989). *Policing Desire: Pornography, AIDS, and the Media*. 2nd edn. Minneapolis: University of Minnesota Press.

Weston, Kath (1991). *Families We Choose: Lesbians, Gays, Kinship*. New York: Columbia University Press.

Yarbro-Bejarano, Yvonne (1990). "The Female Subject in Chicano Theater," in *Performing Feminisms: Feminist Critical Theory and Theater*, ed. Sue-Ellen Case. Baltimore: Johns Hopkins University Press.

—— (0000) "Expanding the Categories of Race in Lesbian and Gay Studies," in *Professions of Desire: Lesbian and Gay Studies in Literature*, ed. George E. Haggerty and Bonnie Zimmerman. New York: MLA Publications.

—— (1993). "Cherrie Moraga's *Shadow of a Man*: Touching the Wound in Order to Heal," in *Acting Out: Feminist Performances*, ed. Lynda

Hart and Peggy Phelan. Ann Arbor: University of Michigan Press.

—— (1986). "Cherrie Moraga's *Giving Up The Ghost*: The Representation of Female Desire." *Third Woman*, 3/1–2: 113–20.

—— (1994). "Gloria Anzaldua's *Borderlands/La frontera*: Cultural Studies, 'Difference,' and the Non Unitary Subject." *Cultural Critique* (Fall): 5–28.

# The Latin Phallus

## Ilán Stavans

Somos el duelo a muerte que se acerca fatal.

*Julia de Burgos*

I envision a brief volume, a history of Latin sexuality through the figure of the phallus, not unlike Michel Foucault and René Magritte's *Ceci n'est pas une pipe*: a compendium of its capricious ups and down, ins and outs, from the Argentine Pampa to the Rio Grande and the Caribbean. An essay in representation, it would begin with the intimidating genitalia of the sovereigns of courage, Hernán Cortés, Francisco Pizarro, and Spanish explorers like Hernando de Soto and Cabeza de Vaca. It would make abundant display of the often graphic art of the gay awakening of the early seventies, shameless in its depiction of the male organ. And it would conclude, perhaps, with the ribbing of feminists. Here, for instance, is a poem by Cherríe Moraga, for one of its last pages:

> there is a man in my life
> pale-man born infant
> pliable flesh his body remains
> a remote possibility
>
> in secret it may know many things
> glossy newsprint female thighs
> spread eagle wings
> in his flying imagination
>
> soft shoe
> he did the soft shoe
> in the arch that separated the living
> from dining room
> miller trombone still turns his heel
> and daughter barefoot and never pregnant
> around and around and around

> soft-tip
> penis head he had
> a soft-tipped penis that peeked out
> accidentally one kitchen cold morning
> between zipper stuck and boxer shorts
> fresh pressed heat lining those tender white-
> meat loins
>
> wife at the ironing board:
> "what are you doing, jim, what are you
> doing?"
> he nervously stuffed the little bird back
>
> it looked like Peloncito
> the bald-headed little name
> of my abuelita's pajarito

Let me map the ambitions of my little book by starting at the beginning. The Iberian knights that crossed the Atlantic, unlike their Puritan counterparts in the British colonies, were fortune-driven bachelors. They did not come to settle down. As Cortés wrote to Charles V in his *Cartas de Relación*, the first conquistadors were trash: rough, uneducated people from lowly origins. Their mission was to expand the territorial and symbolic powers of the Spanish crown; their ambition in the new continent was to find gold and pleasure. And pleasure they took in the bare-breasted Indian women, whom they raped at will and then abandoned. A violent eroticism was a fundamental element in the colonization of the Hispanic world, from Macchu Picchu to Chichén Itzá and Uxmal. The primal scene of the clash with the Spaniards is a still-unhealed rape: the phallus, as well as gunpowder, was a crucial weapon used to subdue. Machismo as a cultural style endlessly rehearses this humiliating episode in the history of the Americas, imitating the violent swagger of the Spanish conquerors. (This, despite the Indian legends that Cortés was the owner of a tiny, ridiculous penis.)

The hypocrisy of the church played a role as well. Although the priesthood bore witness to the rapacious sexuality of the Spanish soldiery, *fingieron demencia*: they pretended to be elsewhere. Simultaneously, they reproduced the medieval hierarchy of the sexes that prevailed in Europe: man as lord and master, woman as servant and reproductive machine. In his insightful book *Demons in the Convent*, the journalist and anthropologist Fernando Benítez eloquently described how the church in the seventeenth century established an atmosphere of repressed eroticism. The archbishop of Mexico City, Aguiar y Seijas, a demonic man who walked with crutches and nourished a thousand phobias, *detested* women: They were not allowed in his presence. If, in a convent or monastery, a nun walked in front of him, he would *ipso facto* cover his eyes. Only men were worthy of his sight – men and Christ. In the religious paraphernalia of the Caribbean, Mexico, and South America, Jesus and the many saints appear almost totally unclothed, covering only their private parts with what in Spanish is known as *taparrabo*; whereas the Vírgen de Guadalupe, the Vírgen de la Caridad, the Vírgen del Cobre, and a thousand other incarnations of the Virgin Mary are fully dressed.

In a milieu where eroticism reigns, my volume on the Latin phallus is obviously far from original. In Oscar Hijuelos's Pulitzer Prize-winning novel *The Mambo Kings Play Songs of Love* (1989), the male organ plays a crucial, obsessive role. The narrative is a sideboard of sexual roles in the Hispanic world. Nestor and Cesar Castillo, Cuban expatriates and musicians in New York City, personify Don Quixote and Sancho Panza: One is an outgoing idealist, the other an introverted materialist. Throughout Nestor's erotic adventures, Hijuelos refers to the penis as *la*

*cosa*: the thing. Its power is hypnotic, totemic even: When men call on women to undo their trousers, women reach down without looking to unfasten their lover's buttons. The novel's libidinal voyeurism even extends to incestual scenes, like the one in which Delores, Hijuelos' female protagonist, finds herself in touch with her father's sexuality.

In imitation of her mother in Havana, Delores would cook for her father, making do with what she could find at the market in those days of war rationing. One night she wanted to surprise him. After he had taken to his bed, she made some caramel-glazed *flan*, cooked up a pot of good coffee, and happily made her way down the narrow hallway with a tray of the quivering *flan*. Pushing open the door, she found her father asleep, naked, and in a state of extreme sexual arousal. Terrified and unable to move, she pretended that he was a statue, though his chest heaved and his lips stirred, as if conversing in a dream . . . He with his suffering face, it, his penis, enormous . . . The funny thing was that, despite her fear, Delores wanted to pick up his thing and pull it like a lever; she wanted to lie down beside him and put her hand down there, releasing him from pain. She wanted him to wake up; she didn't want him to wake up. In that moment, which she would always remember, she felt her soul blacken as if she had just committed a terrible sin and condemned herself to the darkest room in hell. She expected to turn around and find the devil himself standing beside her, a smile on his sooty face, saying, "Welcome to America."

For a culture as steeped in sexuality as our own, it is strange that the substance of our masculine identity remains a forbidden topic. We are terrified of exposing the labyrinthine paths of our unexplained desire, of engaging in what the Mexican essayist and poet Octavio Paz once called "the shameful art of *abrirse*" – opening up and losing control, admitting our insecurities, allowing ourselves to be exposed, unprotected, unsafe. We are not Puritans; our bodies are not the problem. It is the complicated, ambiguous pathways of our desire that are too painful to bear. We have adopted the armature of our Spanish conquerors: Hispanic men are machos, dominating figures, rulers, conquistadors – and also, closeted homosexuals. In *The Labyrinth of Solitude*, Paz has been one of the lonely few to criticize male sexuality:

> The macho commits . . . unforeseen acts that produce confusion, horror and destruction. He opens the world; in doing so, he rips and tears it, and this violence provokes a great, sinister laugh. And in its own way, it is just: it re-established the equilibrium and puts things in their place, by reducing them to dust, to misery, to nothingness.

Unlike men, Hispanic women are indeed forced to open up. And they are made to pay for their openness: they are often accused of impurity and adulteration, sinfulness and infidelity. We inhabitants of the Americas live in a nest of complementing stereotypes: on one side, flamboyant women, provocative, well-built, sensual, lascivious, with indomitable, even bestial nerve and intensity; on the other, macho men. Both seemingly revolve around the phallus, an object of intense adoration, the symbol of absolute power and satisfaction. It is the source of the macho's self-assurance and control, sexual and psychological, and the envy of the Hispanic woman. Our names for the penis are legion; besides the *parajito* of Cherríe Moraga's boxer-short reverie, it goes by *cornamusa, embutido, flauta, fusta, garrote, lanza, másta, miembro viril, pelón, peloncito, pene, pinga, plántano, príapo, pudendo, tesoro, tolete, tranca, verga,* and *zurriago,* among many others.

Where to begin describing the multiple ramifications of the adoration of the phallus among Hispanics? In the Caribbean, mothers rub a male baby's penis to relax him, to force him out of a tantrum. In Mexico the *charros* (*guasos* in Chile, *gauchos* in Argentina) are legendary rural outlaws, independent and lonely men. Their masculine adventures, clashes with corrupt landowners and politicos, live on through border ballads, known in the

US-Mexican border as *corridos,* and *payadores,* a type of South American minstrel who accompanies himself with a guitar. (The fantastic no-budget film *El Mariachi* is a revision of this cultural myth.) The Latin man and his penis are at the center of the Hispanic universe. Ironically, more than one rebellious Hispanic artist, including Andres Serrano, has equated the Latin penis to the crucifix. Which helps understand what is perhaps the greatest contradiction in Hispanic male sexuality: our machismo, according to the dictionary an exaggerated sense of masculinity stressing such attributes as courage, virility, and domination. Take bullfighting, an errotic event like no other, supremely parodied in Pedro Almodóvar's film *Matador.* Where else can the male strike such provocative sexual poses? Carlos Fuentes described the sport in his book *The Buried Mirror.* "The effrontery of the suit of lights, its tight-hugging breeches, the flaunting of the male sexual organ, the importance given to the buttocks, the obviously seductive and self-appraising stride, the lust for blood and sensation – the bullfight authorizes this incredible arrogance and sexual exhibitionism." Essentially bestial, the *corrida de toros* is a quasi-religious ceremony unifying beauty, sex, and death. The young bullfighter, an idol, is asked to face with grace and stamina the dark forces of nature symbolized in the bull. His sword is a phallic instrument. A renaissance knight modeled after Amadís de Gaula or Tirant Lo Blanc and parodied by Don Quixote, he will first subdue and then kill. *Viva el macho!* Blood will be spilled and ecstasies will arrive when the animal lies dead, at which point the bullfighter will take his hat off before a beautiful lady and smile. Man will prevail, the phallus remains all-powerful, and the conqueror will be showered with red flowers.

The Hispanic family encourages a familiar double standard. Few societies prize female virginity with the conviction that we do. But while virginity is a prerequisite for a woman's safe arrival at the wedding canopy, men are encouraged to fool around, to test the waters, to partake of the pleasures of the flesh. Virgins are *mujerers buenas*: pure, ready to sacrifice their body for the sacred love of a man. Prostitutes, on the other hand, are hedonistic goddesses, *mujeres malas*, safeguards of the male psyche. Like most of my friends, I lost my virginity to a prostitute at the age of 13. An older acquaintance was responsible for arranging the "date," when a small group of us would meet an experienced harlot at a whorehouse. It goes without saying that none of the girls in my class were similarly "tutored": They would most likely become women in the arms of someone they loved, or thought they loved. But love, or even the slightest degree of attraction, were not involved in our venture. Losing our virginity was actually a dual mission: to ejaculate inside the hooker, and then, more importantly, to tell of the entire adventure afterwards. The telling, the story of the *matador* defeating his bull, the conqueror's display of power, was more crucial than the carnal sensation itself. I still remember the dusty art deco furniture and the blank expression of the woman. She was there to make me a man, to help me become an accepted member of society. Did we talk? She asked me to undress straightaway and proceeded to caress me. I was extremely nervous. What if I were unable to prove myself? The whole ceremony lasted 20 minutes, perhaps less. Afterward I concocted a predictable cover, announcing to my friends that the prostitute had been amazed at my prowess, that I had made her *very* happy, that she had been shocked at my chastity.

We told tall tales to compensate for the paucity of our accomplishments. After all, a prostitute is an easy triumph. Even consensual sex is an unworthy challenge for the aspiring macho. Courting women with serenades and flowers, seducing them, undressing and then fucking them, *chingar*, only to turn them out: That's the Hispanic male's hidden dream. *Chingar* signifies the ambiguous excess of macho sexuality. Octavio Paz's exploration of the sense of the term concludes that the idea denotes a kind of failure: The active form means to rape, subdue, control, dominate. *Chingar* is what a macho does to women, what the Iberian soldiers did to the native Indian population, what corrupt politicos do to their electorate. And the irreplaceable weapon in the art of *chingar*, the key to the Hispanic worldview, is *el pito*, the phallus.

Not long ago, while writing on the Chicano movement of the late sixties, I came across the extraordinary figure of Oscar "Zeta" Acosta, defender of the dispossessed. Born in 1936 in El Paso, Texas, Acosta became a lawyer and activist, well acquainted with César Chávez, Rodolfo "Corky" Gonzalez, and other political leaders of the era. An admirer of Henry Miller and Jack Kerouac, and a close friend of Hunter S. Thompson, whom he accompanied in his travel to Las Vegas (Acosta is the 300-pound Samoan of *Fear and Looting in Las Vegas*), Acosta wrote a couple of intriguing novels about the civil rights upheaval in the Southwest, *The Autobiography of a Brown Buffalo*, published in 1972, and *The Revolt of the Cockroach People*, which appeared a year later. Both volumes detail a man's rite of passage from adolescence to boastful machismo. A cover photograph by Annie Leibovitz showed Acosta as a Tennessee Williams type, a perfectly insecure macho with flexed muscles and spiritual desperation in his eyes: He is in an undershirt and stylish suit pants, fat, the lines in his forehead quite pronounced. He is 39 years old and looks a bit worn out. Besides this picture, nothing is certain about him, except, perhaps, the fact that in the early seventies he went to Mazatlán, a resort area and port on Mexico's Pacific coast, and disappeared without a trace.

The moral of Acosta can be used to understand what lies behind the ostentation and bravado of the macho: a deep-seated inferiority complex. The size and strength of the penis is the index of masculine value, as well as the passport to glorious erotic adventure. Inevitably, then, it is also a boundless source of anxiety.

Acosta is an emblem of the insecure Hispanic male. His machismo could not hide his confusion and lack of self-esteem. He spent his life thinking his penis was too small, which, in his words, automatically turned him into a fag. "Frugality and competition were my parents' lot," he writes, describing his and his brother's sexual education. "The truth of it was [they] conspired to make men out of two innocent Mexican boys. It seems that the sole purpose of childhood was to train boys how to be men. Not men of the future, but *now*. We had to get up early, run home from school, work on weekends, holidays and during vacations, all for the purpose of being men. We were supposed to talk like *un hombre*, walk like a man, act like a man, and think like a man." But Acosta's apprenticeship in masculinity was undermined by the embarrassment of his tiny phallus. He perceived himself as a freak, a virile metastasis.

> If it hadn't been for my fatness, I'd probably have been able to do those fancy assed jack-knifes and swandives as well as the rest of you. But my mother had me convinced I was obese, ugly as a pig and without any redeeming qualities whatsoever. How then could I run around with just my jockey shorts? V-8's don't hide fat, you know. That's why I finally started wearing boxers. But by then it was too late. Everyone knew I had the smallest prick in the world. With the girls watching and giggling, the guys used to sing my private song to the tune of "Little Bo Peep" . . . "Oh, where, oh where can my little boy be? Oh, where, oh where can he be? He's so chubby, *pansón*, that he can't move along. Oh, where, oh where can he be?"

Acosta is a unique figure among male Chicano novelists, in that his bitter, honest reflections do nothing to enhance his machismo.

> I lost most of my religion the same night I learned about sex from old Vernon. When I saw the white, foamy suds come from under his foreskin, I thought he had wounded himself from yanking on it too hard with those huge farmer hands of his. And when I saw his green eyes fall back into his head, I thought he was having some sort of seizure like I'd seen Toto the village idiot have out in his father's fig orchard after he fucked a chicken.

I didn't much like the sounds of romance the first time I saw jizz. I knew that Vernon was as tough as they came. Nothing frightened or threatened him. He'd cuss right in front of John Hazard, our fag Boy Scout leader as well as Miss Anderson [our teacher]. But when I heard him OOOh and AAAh as the soap suds spit at his chest while we lay on our backs inside the pup tent, I wondered for a second if sex wasn't actually for sissies. I tried to follow his example, but nothing would come out. With him cheering me on, saying, "Harder, man. Pull on that son of a bitch. Faster, faster!" it just made matters worse. The thing went limp before the soap suds came out.

He advised me to try it more often. "Don't worry, man. It'll grow if you work on it."

Taboos die hard, if they ever do. After emigrating to the United States in 1985, my identity changed in drastic ways. I ceased to be Mexican and became Hispanic, and my attitude toward homosexuals underwent a metamorphosis. Still, that transformation took time. Even as homosexuals entered my peer group, and became my friends, I was uneasy. At times I wondered whether having homosexual friends would make others doubt my sexual identity. Though I've never had an intimate encounter with another man, I have often wondered what I would feel, how I would respond to a kiss. As José Ortega y Gasset said: *Yo soy yo y mi circunstancia*, I am the embodiment of my culture.

My father had taught me to show affection in public. When departing, he would kiss me without inhibition. But as I became an adolescent, I heard my friends whisper. Was I secretly a deviant? To be a Hispanic man was to hide one's emotions, to keep silent when it came to expressing your heart. We are supposed to swallow our pain and never cry *como una niña* like girls. Keep a straight face, suck it up – *sé muy macho*. Many Hispanic adolescents still find role models in the confident and aggressively reserved stars of the Golden Age of Mexican film, black-and-white celebrities like Pedro Armendáriz, Jorge Negrete, and Pedro Infante, Hispanic analogues of James Dean and John Wayne. These figures were classic macho: ultra-masculine Emiliano Zapata mustaches, closely-cropped dark hair, a mysterious Mona Lisa smile, thin, well-built bodies, and an unconquerable pride symbolized by the ubiquitous pistol. Vulnerability means cowardice. Deformity was not only evidence of weakness but a sign of unreadiness to face the tough world. In spite of his verbal bravura, Cantinflas, the Charlie Chaplin of Spanish-language films like *Ahí está el detalle*, was anti-macho: poorly dressed, bad-mouthed, short, unhandsome, without a gun and hence probably possessed of a tiny phallus.

Among Hispanics, homosexuals are the target of well nigh insurmountable animosity. If the Latin phallus is adored in heterosexual relations, it is perceived as wild, diabolic, and uncontrollable for homosexuals. Reinaldo Arenas, the raw Cuban novelist who died of AIDS in New York City in 1990, argued that Latin society comprises five classes of homosexual: the *dog-collar gay*, boisterous and out, constantly being arrested at baths and beaches; the *common gay*, who is sure of his sexual identity but who never takes risks, save to attend a film festival or write an occasional poem; the *closeted gay*, a man with a wife and children and a public profile, who is reduced to sneaking off to the baths without his wedding ring; the *royal*, a man whose closeness to politicians and people of power allows him to be open about his sexual identity, to lead a "scandalous" life, while still holding public office; and finally the *macho*, whose cocksure bravado is intended to fend off questions about his sexual identity. It goes without saying that most gay men are forced to assume the less public personas.

In his second book, *Days of Obligation*, Richard Rodriguez includes an essay, "Late Victorians," about his own homosexuality and AIDS. He ponders the impact of the epidemic. "We have become accustomed to figures disappearing from our landscape. Does this not lead us to interrogate the landscape?" Very few in the Hispanic world have dared to address the subject: Hispanic gays

remain a target of mockery and derision, forced to live on the fringes of society. To be gay is to be a freak, mentally ill, the sort of abnormality José Guadalupe Posada, the celebrated turn-of-the-century Mexican lampooner, often portrayed in his sarcastic cartoons: a creature with legs instead of arms, a dog with four eyes. And yet, homosexuality, a topic few are willing to address in public, is the counterpoint that defines our collective identity. Despite the stigma, homosexuals have been a ubiquitous presence in the Hispanic world, a constant from the Cuban sugar mill to the colonial *misión*, from Fidel Castro's cabinet to the literary intelligentsia. And, like St Augustine's attitude toward the Jews, the established approach toward them follows the maxim: Don't destroy them, let them bear witness of the lawless paths of male eroticism. They are the other side of Hispanic sexuality: a shadow one refuses to acknowledge – a "they" that is really an "us." Again, the language betrays us: the panoptic array of terms for homosexual includes *adamado, adelito, afeminado, ahembrado, amaricado, amujerado, barbalindo, carininfo, cazolero, cocinilla, enerve, gay, homosexual, invertido, lindo, maría, marica, mariposa, ninfo, pisaverde, puto, repipí, sodomita, volteado, zape*, to name only a few.

I recall an occasion in which one of my Mexican publishers, the Colombian director of the extraordinarily powerful house Editorial Planeta, sat with me and a gay friend of mine from Venezuela. In a disgusting display of macho pyrotechnics, the man talked for the better part of an hour about the size of his penis. His shtick was full of degrading references to homosexuals, whom he described variously as kinky, depraved, and perverted. The presence of a self-identified "queer writer" at the table only stimulated his attack. He suggested that the United States was the greatest nation on earth, but that sexual abnormality would ultimately force its decline. Days later my Venezuelan colleague told me that the publisher had made a (successful) pass at him that very night. They shared a hotel room. This sort of attitude isn't uncommon. The Hispanic macho goes out of his way to keep appearances, to exalt his virility, but he often fails. Sooner or later, his glorious masculinity will be shared in bed with another man.

In the Mexico of the seventies in which I grew up, common sense had it that machos were the unchaste victims of an unsurpassed inferiority complex. Unchaste victims – impure, yes, but sympathetic characters, and commanding figures. Homosexuals, on the other hand, were considered oversensitive, vulnerable, mentally imbalanced, unproven in the art of daily survival. At school, the boys were constantly made to test their muscular strength. Girls were allowed to cry, to express their emotions, while we *men* were told to remain silent. If to open up was a sign of feminine weakness, to penetrate, *meter,* meant superiority. Sex – fucking – is how we prove our active, male, self, subduing our passive, female, half. Physical appearance was fundamental to this regime: Obesity and limping were deviations from the norm, and hence effeminate characterstics.

Who is gay among us? It's a secret. We simply don't want to talk about it. Although a few essays have been written about Jorge Luis Borges' repressed homosexuality, the topic is evaded in Emir Rodríguez Monegal's 1978 biography. Borges lived most of his life with his mother and married twice: once, briefly, in his forties, and then to María Kodama a few months before his death in 1986, in order to turn her into the sole head of his estate. His writing is remarkable for its lack of sexuality. When his stories do verge on the intimate, they portray only rape or molestation. Still, the matter is hushed up, the details of a life subordinated to the dense lyricism of an *oeuvre.* Undoubtedly concern for the master's reputation can explain some large part of the silence.

Take the case of John Rechy, whose 1963 novel *City of Night,* a book about hustlers, whores, drugs, and urban criminality, garnered him accolades and a reputation as one of the most promising Chicano writers of his generation. Shortly thereafter Rechy's book was categorized as a "gay novel," a

stigma that tarred the book for Hispanic readers in the United States. It is only recently, since the onset of the North American gay rights movement, that Rechy's achievement has been reevaluated. And then there's Julio Cortázar, the celebrated Argentinean novelist and short-story writer responsible for *Hopscotch.* In 1983, at the peak of his fame and just a year before his tragic death, he made a trip to Cuba and then New York, there to address the United Nations about the *desaparecidos* in South America. Cortázar was alone, and lonely, as a strange sickness began taking over his body. He lost his appetite, became thinner, became susceptible to colds. After his divorce from Aurora Bernardez some 15 years previously, he had been involved with a number of women and men, although he tried desperately to keep his homosexual encounters secret. In the depths of his solitude, he told Luis Harss, he began to lose confidence in his own writing. A symbol of liberation for many Hispanics, Cortázar had probably contracted AIDS. He died in Paris, on February 12, 1984, when the epidemic was still largely unrecognized, its details elusive to scientists and never openly discussed. A number of Cortázar tales deal with homosexuality and lesbianism, including "Blow-Up," "The Ferry, or Another Trip to Venice," and "At Your Service." The last, the story of an elderly servant woman working as a dog-sitter in a wealthy Parisian home, moved a Cortázar specialist to ask him about his own homosexuality. He answered quite impersonally, with a lengthy dissertation on the general subject, a history of homosexuality from the open love of the Greeks to the present-day climate of ostracism and homophobia. "The attitude toward [it]," he suggested, "needs to be a very broad and open one, because the day in which homosexuals don't feel like . . . persecuted animals . . . they'll assume a much more normal way of life and fulfill themselves erotically and sexually without harming anyone and by being happy as much as possible as homosexual males and females." He concluded by applauding the more tolerant atmosphere of select North American and European societies. One might assume that the profound questions of sexuality and repression broached in this discussion would have had severe, productive repercussions in the critical work on one of the giants of Latin American literature. But Cortázar's gay life, like Borges', remains a forbidden issue.

Since the sixties, gay artists in Latin America have worked to put Latin homosexuality on the map. They have devised strategies to name the unnameable and map a symbolic picture of our collective erotic fears. The Argentine Manuel Mujica Láinez's 1962 novel *Bomarzo*, for instance, equates the male organ, and homosexuality in general, with the monstrous. Thanks to him and to many others (José Ceballos Maldonado, José Donoso, Carlos Arcidiácono, Reinaldo Arenas, José Lezama Lima, Richard Rodriguez, Manuel Puig, Virgilio Piñera, Severo Sarduy, Xavier Villaurrutia, Luis Zapata, and Fernando Vallejo), a small window of vulnerability has been created, a space for the interrogation of suffocating, monolithic sex roles. The most significant of these, to my mind, are Puig, Arenas, and José Lezama Lima. *Kiss of the Spider Woman*, Puig's most celebrated work, directed for the screen by Héctor Babenco, portrayed a forced male relationship in a unspecified prison in Latin America. The film made waves from Ciudad Juárez to the Argentine Pampa with its startling conclusion, a kiss between a macho Marxist revolutionary and a gay man, and the suggestion that the characters complemented each other.

Puig is one of the principal characters in the long history of homophobia and gay bashing in the Hispanic world. In the early seventies the committee for the prestigious Seix Barral award in Spain selected his first novel, which the film-maker Néstor Almendros and novelist Juan Goytisolo openly endorsed. But the publisher rejected the recommendation of the selection committee because of Puig's sexual orientation. He was similarly stigmatized in his native country, where the Peronists banned his work, calling it "pornographic propaganda."

Puig died in his mid-fifties in 1990, in Cuernavaca, Mexico, during a bizarre (and suspicious) gall-bladder operation. Was it AIDS? Puig chose to keep silent about his impending demise. At the time I was preparing a special issue of the *Review of Contemporary Fiction* about his *oeuvre* and had been in contact with him. I last saw him at a public reading at the 92nd Street Y a few months before his death; he looked thin but energetic. There was no mention of an illness. Of course, having been burned so many times before, it was unlikely that he would open up now. Two years after Puig's death, Jaime Manrique, the Colombian author of *Latin Moon in Manhattan* and a close friend of Puig, reconstructed the gay subtext of Puig's life in a moving reminiscence. "Manuel Puig: The Writer as Diva," for *Christopher Street*. After considering the possibility of Puig opening up, *abrirse*, in public, Manrique concluded that whatever honors Puig could still hope for were infinitely more secure with his personal secrets kept hidden. In the end, he had moved back to Cuernavaca with his beloved mother, spending the last months of his life "busy building his first and last home in this world," a fortress closed to strangers, filled with Hollywood memorabilia. Puig's death is emblematic of the fate of the Hispanic gay.

Puig's work was remarkably tame, at least with regard to the representation of the Latin penis; he feared the persecution of the Argentine military, and only ever depicted its image in a short section in the novel *Blood of Required Love*. Like most gays in the Hispanic world, Puig was trapped between his sexual preference and the prejudices of the larger society. And yet, what is distinctive about him and the literary generation that came of age in the wake of the sixties is the desublimation of the phallus. Puig and other gay writers began a process of *apertura*: they have named names, celebrated and mocked Latin masculinity and the omnipresent phallus.

Reinaldo Arenas is probably the best-known openly gay writer from Latin America. His writings explore Latin sexuality and the phallus with eloquence. His final years, prior to his suicide – years marked by extreme fits of depression, a chronic and abrasive pneumonia, paranoia, and increasing misanthropy – saw him complete a surrealist novel, an autobiography, the completion of the last two installments of the *Pentagonía*, a five-volume novelization of the "secret history of Cuba." *Before Night Falls*, the autobiography, is destined to become a classic. It traces Arenas' birth in Holguín in 1943 as well as his rural childhood; his difficult transition to Havana; his friendships with Virgilio Piñero, José Lezama Lima, Lydia Cabrera, and other important Cuban artists and intellectuals; his "youthful loyalty" to Castro's socialist regime and his subsequent disenchantment with the revolution; his betrayal by a family member; the persecution, "re-education," and imprisonment he suffered in Havana's infamous El Morro prison because of his homosexuality; his participation in the 1980 Mariel boat-lift and his bondage experiences in Florida and Manhattan.

Dictated to a tape-recorder and then transcribed by friends, *Before Night Falls* is one of the most incendiary, sexually liberating texts ever to come from Latin America. Published posthumously in 1990, shortly after the long-suffering author committed suicide in his New York City apartment, it appeared in English in 1993. Its confessional style and courageous depiction of homosexual life make it a remarkable and haunting book. Its impact in the Spanish-speaking world, including Spain (where it appeared under the prestigious Tusquets imprint), has been enormous. "I think I always had a huge sexual appetite," writes Arenas. "Not only mares, sows, hens, or turkeys, but almost all animals were objects of my sexual passion, including dogs. There was one particular dog who gave me great pleasure. I would hide with him behind the garden tended by my aunts, and would make him suck my cock. The dog got used to it and in time would do it freely."

Guillermo Cabrera Infante, a fellow Cuban, summed up Arenas' career in an obituary published in *El País*: "Three passions ruled the life and death of Reinaldo Arenas: literature (not as game, but as a consuming fire), passive sex, and active politics. Of the three, the dominant passion was, evidently, sex. Not only in his life, but in his work. He was a chronicler of a country ruled not by the already impotent Fidel Castro, but by sex . . . Blessed with a raw talent that almost reaches genius in his posthumous book, he lived a life whose beginning and end were indeed the same: from the start, one long, sustained sexual act." And indeed, Arenas repeatedly described his sexual intercourse with animals, family members, children, old people, friends, lovers, and strangers. The volume ends with a personal letter, written shortly before Arenas' death, in which he bids farewell to friends and enemies. "Due to my delicate state of health and to the horrible emotional depression it causes me not to be able to continue writing and struggling for the freedom of Cuba, I am ending my life," Arenas writes. "Persons near to me are not in any way responsible for my decision. There is only one person to hold accountable: Fidel Castro."

The autobiography details his multifarious sexual encounters. He recalls the fashion in which he was abused by his grandfather, his close attachment to his mother, a woman who left Cuba early on in the child's life to make money for the family by working in Florida. What's remarkable is the fact that the book comes out of the Spanish-speaking world, where erotic confessions are few, and seldom related to politics.

> In [Cuba], I think, it is a rare man who has not had sexual relations with another man. Physical desire overpowers whatever feelings of machismo our fathers take upon themselves to instill in us. An example of this is my uncle Rigoberto, the oldest of my uncles, a married, serious man. Sometimes I would go to town with him. I was just about eight years old and we would ride on the same saddle. As soon as we were both on the saddle, he would begin to have an erection. Perhaps in some way my uncle did not want this to happen, but he could not help it. He would put me in place, lift me up and set my butt on his penis, and during that ride, which would take an hour or so, I was bounding on

that huge penis, riding, as it were, on two animals at the same time. I think eventually Rigoberto would ejaculate. The same thing happened on the way back from town. Both of us, of course, acted as if we were not aware of what was happening. He would whistle or breathe hard while the horse trotted on. When he got back, Carolina, his wife, would welcome him with open arms and a kiss. At that moment we were all very happy.

Arenas' other major work, the *Pentagonía* quintet, is similarly obsessive about sex and politics. Though the text has fascinated critics for some time, it continues to scare lay readers. An exercise in literary experimentation modeled after the French *nouveau roman*, the first three volumes, *Singing from the Well, The Palace of the White Skunks*, and *Farewell to the Sea*, display a fractured narrative and convoluted plot that often make them appear impenetrable. *The Assault*, the fifth installment, is the most accessible. A compelling exercise in science fiction, it is structured as a tribute to Orwell's *1984* and Kafka's *The Castle*. It is narrated by a government torturer, a leader of the so-called Anti-Perversion Brigade, who spends his days visiting concentration camps and prisons looking for the sexual criminals to annihilate. The book's nightmarish landscape is a futuristic Caribbean island deliberately similar to Cuba under Castro's dictatorship. At the heart of the book is the torturer's search for his mother, whom he glimpses from afar but seems unable to approach. He is passionate and inscrutable in his hatred for her, ready to undertake any action that might lead to her destruction. The book opens: "The last time I saw my mother, she was out behind the National People's Lumber Cooperative gathering sticks." Approaching her, the narrator thinks to himself: "This is my chance; I knew I could not waste a second. I ran straight for her, and I would have killed her, too, but the old bitch must have an eye where her asshole ought to be, because before I could get to her and knock her down and kill her, that old woman whirled around to meet me." With macabre echoes of Luis Buñuel, the allegory

is not difficult to decipher: Pages into the book, the reader comes to understand that the torturer's mother is Castro himself. As the search for her continues in various "Servo-Perimeters" of the land, Arenas prepares us for a colossal encounter, savage and profane. In the final scene, Arenas' protagonist fearlessly employs his penis one last time: He fucks and then kills his lover, whose identity is dual: his own mother, whom he describes as a cow and the Resident, as Fidel Castro himself.

With my member throbbingly erect, and my hands on my hips, I stand before her, looking at her. My hatred and my revulsion and my arousal are now beyond words to describe. And then the great cow, naked and horrible, white and stinking, plays her last card; the sly bitch, crossing her ragged claws over her monstrous breasts, looks at me with tears in her eyes and she says *Son.* That is all I can bear to hear. All the derision, all the harassment, all the fear and frustration and blackmail and mockery and contempt that that word contains – it slaps me in the face, and I am stung. My erection swells to enormous proportions, and I begin to step toward her, my phallus aimed dead for its mark, that fetid, stinking hole. And I thrust. As she is penetrated, she gives a long, horrible shriek, and then she collapses. I sense my triumph – I come, and I feel the furious pleasure of discharging myself in her. Howling, she explodes in a blast of bolts, washers, screws, pieces of shrapnel-like tin, gasoline, smoke, semen, shit, and steams of motor oil. Then, at the very instant of my climax, and of her final howl, a sound never heard before washes across the square below us . . . While the crowd goes on moving through the city, hunting down and destroying to the accompaniment of the music of its own enraged whispering, I tuck the limp mass of my phallus (now at last spent and flaccid) into my overalls. Wearily, I make my way unnoticed through the noise and the riot (the crowd in a frenzy of destruction, like children, crying *The Resident is dead, the beast at last is dead!*), and I come to the wall of the city. I walk down to the shore. And I lie down in the sand.

It is the singular achievement of the gay Cuban writer Lezama Lima to have provided an accounting of the Latin phallus equal to its inflated importance in the Hispanic world. Lezama Lima (1912–76) was the author of *Paradiso*, published in 1966, a book hailed by Julio Cortázar and others as a masterpiece. It was a remarkable text: In the words of the critic Gerald Martin, the text rendered "both classical and Catholic imagery, lovingly but also scandalously, achieving the remarkable double coup of offending both the Catholic Church and the Cuban Revolution through its approach to eroticism in general and homosexuality in particular." Chapter VIII details the promiscuous sexual adventures of young casanovas Farraluque and Leregas. Leregas' penis, which would swiftly grow from the length of a thimble to "the length of the forearm of a manual laborer," becomes legendary among his classmates:

> Unlike Farraluque's, Leregas's sexual organ did not reproduce his face, but his whole body. In his sexual adventures his phallus did not seem to penetrate but to embrace the other body. Eroticism by compression, like a bear cub squeezing a chestnut, that was how his first moans began. The teacher was monotonously reciting the text, and most of his pupils, fifty or sixty in all, were seated facing him, but on the left, to take advantage of a niche-like space, there were two benches lined up at right angles to the rest of the class. Leregas was sitting at the end of the first bench. Since the teacher's platform was about a foot high, only the face of his phallic colossus was visible to him. With calm indifference, Leregas would bring out his penis and testicles, and like a wind eddy that turns into a sand column, at a touch it became a challenge of exceptional size. His row and the rest of the students peered past the teacher's desk to view that tenacious candle, ready to burst out of its highly polished, blood-filled helmet. The class did not blink and its silence deepened, making the

lecturer think that the pupils were morosely following the thread of his discursive expression, a spiritless exercise during which the whole class was attracted by the dry phallic splendor of the bumpkin bear club. When Leregas's member began to deflate, the coughs began, the nervous laughter, the touching of elbows to free themselves from the stupefaction they had experienced. "If you don't keep still, I'm going to send some students out of the room," the little teacher said, vexed at the sudden change from rapt attention to a progressive swirling uproar.

The chapter becomes increasingly daunting as the florid prose continues.

> An adolescent with such a thunderous generative attribute was bound to suffer a frightful fate according to the dictates of the Pythian. The spectators in the classroom noted that in referring to the Gulf's currents the teacher would extend his arm in a curve to caress the algaed coasts, the corals, and anemones of the Caribbean. That morning, Leregas's phallic dolmen had gathered those motionless pilgrims around the god terminus as it revealed its priapic extremes, but there was no mockery or rotting smirk. To enhance his sexual tension, he put two octavo books on his member, and they moved like tortoises shot up by the expansive force of a fumarole. It was the reproduction of the Hindu myth about the origin of the world.

The phallus remains an all-consuming image for Hispanic society, whether as the absent, animating presence in the *repressive* culture of machismo or the furtive purpose of the *repressed* culture of homosexuality. It is the representation of masculine desire, a fantastic projection of guilt, shame, and power. Hyperactive bravura and suppressed longing are its twin modalities.

Like its subject, my little text on the Latin phallus has swelled to gargantuan proportions. I now envision an open book, steeped in the infinite richness of reality, a Borgesian volume of volumes incorporating every detail of every life of every man and woman in the

Hispanic world, alive and dead – the record of every innocent or incestuous look, every masturbatory fantasy, every kiss, every coitus since 1492 and perhaps even before. The book is already in us and outside us, simultaneously real and imaginary, fatal and prophetic, *abierto* and *cerrado*. As a civilization, we *are* such a history – a living compendium of our baroque sexual behaviors. From Bernal Díaz del Castillo's chronical of the subjugation of Tenochtitlán to Mario Vargas Llosa's novella *In Praise of the Stepmother*, from Carlos Fuentes' climax in *Christopher Unborn* to José Donoso's *The Obscene Bird of Night* and his untranslated erotic novel *La misteriosa desaparición de la Marquesita de Loira*, from Lope de Vega's Golden Age *comedies* to Sor Juana Inés de La Cruz's superb baroque poetry and Cherríe Moraga's *peloncito*, the tortuous history of our sexuality is the story of the Latin phallus. In a continent where tyranny remains an eternal ghost and democracy (the open society, *la sociedad abierta*) an elusive dream, the phallus is an unmerciful dictator, the totemic figure of our longing.

# Part IV

*Labor and Politics in a Global Economy: The Latino Metropolis*

# Rank and File: Historical Perspectives on Latino/a Workers in the US

## Zaragosa Vargas

## INTRODUCTION

Within the next ten years, 35 million immigrants will be added to the United States population. Most of the immigrants will come from Mexico, Central America, the Caribbean, Columbia, and Venezuela, countries whose total population growth is projected to double to 340 million by the year 2010. Owing to unemployment and under-employment, a direct consequence of the key role the United States plays in the emergence of a global economy, these people in search of work will make their way northward to the United States. Within the next half-century America's population growth will be spurred primarily by Third World immigration and racial minority births. Latinos, as America's fastest growing population, will contribute to this dramatic population increase. Scholars estimate that over 25 million Latinos currently live in the United States. Due to continuing immigration and relatively higher birth rates than the general US population, Latinos will soon surpass African Americans as the nation's largest minority group.[1]

The history of Latino workers – Mexican Americans, Puerto Ricans, Cubans, and the recent immigrants from Central America, Latin America, and the Spanish-speaking Caribbean – forms part of the larger history of America's ethnically and racially diverse working classes. Segments of the Latino work force have been present since the nineteenth century as the result of United States capitalist expansion into the American Southwest, Mexico, the Caribbean, and Latin America.

Latino workers are a significant and growing section of the American working classes. Projected to grow by about 60 percent by the end of this decade, the Spanish-speaking workforce will comprise about 27 percent of America's overall labor force. These percentages do not include the more than 3 million Puerto Ricans on the island of Puerto Rico who are US citizens. The feminization of labor, a national and international trend, has brought large numbers of Latina women into the semi-skilled and unskilled employment sectors of the United States. Within the next eight years Latina workers will outnumber their Anglo female counterparts as production workers.[2]

The growth of America's Latino population in the last ten years, which includes the rapidly growing numbers of legal and un-documented Latino immigrants in the United States, is taking place within the context of economic englobalization. Global economic integration has restructured the US. The restructuring of the US economy is characterized by the following: the rapid growth and expansion of subcontracting, sweatshops, and industrial homework; the downgrading of job skills; the rise of high technology industries that employ low-wage production workers; and the rapid growth of the service sector. The majority of Latino workers have been incorporated into the low-wage industrial manufacturing and service sectors and into farm labor where they form the main work force. Recently arrived Latino immigrant workers are concentrated in hotel and restaurant work, retail food stores, and food processing factories. Latino workers are the workers most exposed to the ravages from the restructuring of the American economy and therefore are persistently plagued by such ills as high unemployment rates and a lack of job security. Though Latinos represent a broad range of working experiences, they undergo a process of proletarianization exacerbated by race. Along with African Americans, Latinos occupy the lowest rungs of a segmented labor market that has been produced by the racism of employers, unions, and US foreign policy in Mexico, Central and Latin America, and the Spanish-speaking Caribbean. The dynamic of racial and ethnic discrimination has largely determined the history of Latino workers in the United States.[3]

The attention of research scholars to labor migration, racial and ethnic relations, and American working-class history makes the study of Latino workers timely. While contemporary Latino workers have been the focus of public policy experts, their experiences and work lives have essentially been ignored by labor historians. In contrast to the rich studies available on the contributions of working women and African Americans to the American labor movement, the history of Latino workers remains relatively unknown. The following examines several key elements that underscore the current Latino worker experience. These are: the effects of deindustrialization on Latino job loss in industrial manufacturing through a case study of the US auto industry; the potential impact of the North American Free Trade Agreement on Latino workers; the contributions and participation of Latinos in the labor movement and their relationship to organized labor; and the present situation of Latino workers, in light of the ongoing immigration from the Spanish-speaking countries of the Third World.

## LATINO WORKERS AND DEINDUSTRIALIZATION

As it did for blacks, the 1960s civil rights movement raised the expectations and hopes of Latino workers for increased job and wage opportunity and workplace equality. Despite persistent discrimination, Latino wage workers continued to reduce the income gap. Throughout the 1950s and 1960s, the sustained increases in the productivity of American industrial workers paid for their annual increases in real wages. Union contracts improved the standard of living for America's workers as a form of business unionism that relied less on confrontation gained prominence. Persistent racial discrimination, however, prevented rank-and-file Latinos, blacks, and women from reaching wage parity with their white male counterparts. Local union affiliates excluded minorities and women from membership or did not fully address issues of racial and gender equality in the call for democratic working-class solidarity. By the 1970s the downward shift of the American economy was beginning to undermine the vaulted status of America's workers. The increases in wages, offset by an upsurge in the cost of living, was occurring during a downturn in the profitability of American corporations. For the nation's auto makers, this precipitous decline conincided with the large-scale assault by the Japanese to gain control of the world car market.[4] Auto workers reponded to the loss of their livelihood and status by staging wildcat strikes, but this worker insurgency was checked by the 1974–75 recession, the nation's worst economic crisis since the Great Depression era. Unemployment among factory workers climbed to nearly 14 percent but was twice this percentage for Latinos and other blue-collar minorities who were often the first workers let go. The recession ushered in a new economic order, one that would have severe and long-lasting implications for America's heretofore privileged wage workers. Next, deindustrialization led to the massive displacement of auto workers. Latino auto workers would lose their recently won middle-class status through plant closures, downsizing, and consecutive wage concessions.[5]

By the early 1970s the US had become part of an internationally integrated economy.

This globalization led to deindustrialization and the shift to a service economy and ushered in dramatic and unprecedented changes in the American labor force. Low growth coupled with inflation and fueled by a world debt undermined America's position as a world economic power. Moreover, Europe and Japan, emerging from the economic devastation of World War II, effectively began competing with the United States worldwide and with the US domestically for economic markets. The "Great U-Turn" of the American economy – corporate restructuring with government backing – had begun. This profound economic transformation of global dimensions would mark the downfall of unions and the rise of the present two-tier society of haves and most nots.[6]

Before the mid-1960s, US car production was organized on a national basis and was in essence safe from imports. This changed when the creation of the European Common Market and the signing of the Canada–US Auto Pact drew the American auto industry into an integrated global one.[7] Several factors underscored the "Great U-Turn" of the US auto industrial sector. Car production facilities that were dispersed in the South and West did not produce the profits projected by the car-makers as automobile production declined by one-third. After 1979, the US auto industry was forced to respond and adjust to the rise of Japan as a major world producer and exporter of automobiles. This seriously imperiled the earnings of America's workers, one-sixth of whom worked in auto-related industries. American auto workers were next hit by the deep recession in the early 1980s that signaled an extraordinary decline in the American standard of living. Latino auto workers in the Northeast, the Midwest, and the West Coast felt the full brunt of this recession, losing forever the hard-won prosperity they had enjoyed for two generations as highly paid industrial workers. In Detroit, unemployment reached 15 percent but it was over 26 percent for Detroit's minorities as dozens of auto-related shops closed or moved out of the Motor City. More than 100,000 Detroiters were thrown out of work, some

with more than 15 years of seniority, and without any hope of regaining their jobs. International competition and an economic downturn, along with ill-judged corporate management and financial decisions, thus led to the extensive restructuring and reorganization of American auto manufacturing in the 1980s and 1990s. These factors would further undermine the economic prosperity and protection of American workers.[8]

Japanese assembly and component plants, or "transplants," and the rise of highly productive and cost-efficient Far East industrial manufacturing had a significant impact on the American car industry. Corporate America's response was to set trade limitations on Japanese imports and force the Japanese companies to build transplants in this country. A rise in Japanese-bashing that catered to a unique brand of racist American patriotism rounded out this strategy. To increase worker productivity, enhance product quality, and reduce costs, the nation's auto-makers resorted to low-cost parts suppliers and producers of "entry level" vehicles in the Far East. Auto companies closed dozens of plants, made large investments in new plants and modernized existing plants. This strategy became known as the "weeding of the gardens." In California, Latinos were among the more than 11,000 auto workers who lost their jobs when Ford closed its Pico Rivera plant and GM closed its Southgate and Fremont plants in the early 1980s.[9]

The plant closures and the work rationing schemes, often undertaken with the co-operation of conciliatory union officials, became an effective means for disciplining labor. American workers had to accept major wage and benefit concessions and new, autocratic shopfloor work rules or else risk losing their jobs. A hostile anti-worker era was ushered in by the Reagan administration, that was clearly evidenced by the president's handling of the PATCO strike. Along with high unemployment, the disassembly of 50 years of social legislation, and the neutralization and weakening of pro-worker government programs such as OSHA and the National Labor Relations Board, Ronald

Reagan's anti-labor policies greatly undermined the well-being of American workers. Latinos, blacks, and women were especially impacted by the mean-spirited Reagan policies.[10]

The situation for America's auto workers in the late 1970s and early 1980s was complicated by wage concession bargaining inaugurated by the 1979 Chrysler–UAW negotiations. It was a portent of what was to unfold for other segments of the American working class as concessionary bargaining eventually spread from the industrial sector to the private service sector and then to public city and state service employment. Chrysler auto workers were told that if they were to save their company from impending bankruptcy and secure the guarantee of a $3.5 billion bail-out by Congress, they would have to accept both huge layoffs and massive wage and benefit concessions totaling almost a half billion dollars. Under imminent threat of plant closings and the financial demise of their employer besieged Chrysler auto workers in 1981 and 1982 made additional "give-backs" to the auto company. The deceptive ploy worked.[11]

Despite its miraculous turn-around, the auto industry had 127,000 fewer auto workers and the auto-makers threatened more layoffs through plant closings. The trade-off of concessions for employment and long-range income security for the remaining workers took hold across the country. This was evidenced by the noble campaign waged by GM Latino, Black, and Anglo auto workers in Van Nuys, California, to keep their doomed plant open. Interpreted at first as temporary setbacks, changes in wage-setting and in work rules would mark the remainder of the 1980s for America's auto workers. The exploitive "team work" concept and "quality circle" came into vogue and were utilized by management to change how workers perceived their own position in production. However, because of racism and gender discrimination, Latinos, Blacks, and women had little say in the workings of this supposedly egalitarian measure. Workers had to accept management's bottom line imperative

as a creed for shop floor behavior.[12]

Adding to the woes of the American auto worker in the early 1980s was a rapid increase in the export of Mexican-assembled automobiles to this country. Mexico was reappraised as a source of low-cost, entry-level vehicles for US auto-makers that had abandoned their East Asian strategy because of quickly rising wages and the threat of labor disturbances by Asian workers. By the end of the 1980s, American auto-makers had supplemented existing engine plants in Mexico with stamping and plastic body parts plants. In the 1990s, Mexico will be the site for significant car market growth; largely through the implementation of the North American Free Trade Agreement, the Mexican car market will expand from 600,000 vehicles in 1994 to over 2 million vehicles by the year 2010.[13]

The new spatial divisions of labor in American auto industry have been disastrous for auto workers. These spatial divisions have been brought about through regional disinvestment strategies and new manufacturing methods that have led to the reintegration of existing regional auto production clusers, and the development of new clusters in northern Mexico – all integrated into a continental and global system of trade.[14]

For Latinos, blue-collar employment, that previously provided middle-class income and status for America's workers, was dramatically reduced by deindustrialization and the recomposition of the American labor force. For instance, the decline of the American steel industry markedly affected Chicano steelworkers and their families in Chicago and elsewhere in the Great Lakes region. As this industry collapsed so did Latino neighborhoods. Few of these Spanish-speaking worker communities escaped the impact of unemployment. In Detriot between 1979 and 1984, over half the Chicano blue-collar workers employed in the city's industries lost their jobs, resulting in the economic ghettoizing of Latinos into low-wage, service-sector employment and the deterioration of their communities. Nationwide, unemployment for Latino workers stood at nearly 14 percent in 1982 and was 9 per cent five years later.

Latinos, along with Blacks, were late arrivals to industrial employment and were subjected to discrimination that limited job mobility. Their shift out of traditional factory employment was much slower than their white counterparts. Concentrated in declining heavy manufacturing centers like Chicago, Gary, Detroit, the northeastern and Sunbelt regions like Los Angeles County, Latinos not only inherited high rates of joblessness but blighted blue-collar communities. As with Latino steel-workers and auto workers, Puerto Rican workers in northeastern cities were significantly affected by the decline of the goods-producing industries.[15]

The postwar Puerto Rican migration to the northeast region coincided with the era's severe decline in manufacturing jobs. New York City experienced the sharpest drop in manufacturing jobs, from over 1 million in 1950 to about 380,000 by 1987. Puerto Rican workers in the clothing industry suffered the greatest job loss as dozens of apparel firms either relocated to lower-cost regions in the United States or moved abroad. Job displacement among New York City Puerto Ricans occurred as immigration increased from Asia and Latin America. This generated job competition between Puerto Ricans and the new immigrants, a scene that would be played out again and again in other regions of the United States. Local employers took advantage of the tight job market by exploiting the huge worker surplus of Latino and Asian immigrant workers through low-paying jobs and bad working conditions typical of the sweatshop environment. Moreover, racial discrimination remains an obstacle to job access by Puerto Ricans. Puerto Rican workers not only experience anti-Latino discrimination but anti-Black discrimination as well. Also, the lack of educational and occupational skills hinders Puerto Ricans from competing for the new jobs created in the urban centers of the Northeast.[16]

## LATINO WORKERS IN THE PRESENT ERA.

The massive transformation of the American economy has redefined work as we near the next century. The increasing bifurcation of society throughout the world is accompanied by a new segmentation of the labor force. Since 1982, part-time hirings and temporary employment in the United States have increased ten times faster than overall employment which has grown by less than 20 percent. For instance, of the nearly 2 million jobs created in the current economic recovery, 526,000 or 28 percent came from temporary-help agencies. Temporary, contract, and part-time workers now comprise one-tenth of the US workforce. By the year 2000, half of all American workers will be classified as involuntary "part-timers." Increasingly, a disproportionately high percentage of Latinos will be trapped within this second-tier labor market and be burdened with high poverty rates. A similar fate has befallen larger segments of the Anglo working population.[17]

Latinos, Blacks, and women are replacing white native-born males as the mainstay of the US labor force. About 2.3 million Latinos have entered the work force since 1980 and represent one-fifth of the total increase in the nation's jobs. Racial discrimination and lack of English proficiency beleaguer Latino workers in contrast to their increasing importance in the labor market. Employers take advantage of these Latino workers' lack of formal education and weak command of English. Most receive minimum wages and sometimes substandard wages for the arduous and dreary work they perform.[18]

The polarization of the job market has resulted in Latinos being confined to low-wage and low-skill occupations such as construction work, manual labor, and service-sector jobs as domestics, and as hotel and restaurant workers. Tens of thousands who are undocumented work as day laborers, in sweatshops, or predominate in the illegal underground economies. There is an absence of union protection and, to avoid government guidelines and the provision of worker benefits, these workers are paid in cash. Latinos have consequently experienced the greatest declines in real wage incomes and some of the biggest increases in poverty rates within the United States. From 1973 to 1990, for example, the incomes for Latino families headed by a parent under 30 years of age declined 20 percent. The poverty rates for the youngest Latino families in these years rose 44 percent. In the present period, the overall poverty rate for Latinos is 29 percent. Many Latino men over 25 years old are three times as likely as in 1979 to earn poverty wages. The dismal working and living conditions for tens of thousands of Latino workers in urban centers like Houston, Texas, and farming communities like those in Arizona resemble those in the Third World. Many of these working-class households are headed by Latinas who endure the double burden of racial and gender oppression.[19]

Because of class, ethnic, and racial constraints, Latinas historically have had high labor force participation rates in such low-wage jobs as garment work and domestic-service jobs. Regarding the latter, although Latina women prefer domestic service because it offers flexible work schedules, autonomy, and other benefits, private household work has become more institutionalized like other more formal jobs.[20] In the contemporary era, Latinas are a prominent part of the recomposition of the US labor force. The expanding immigrant workforce in the United States that augments the nation's restructured and service-oriented economy, is an indirect result of the emergence of transnational corporations in Third World countries. Indeed, the availability of femal labor worldwide has particularly influenced the shift from manufacturing to service-sector employment. Since the mid-1970s there has been a 70 percent rise in the Latina female work force in the United States. Latinas, however, occupy the bottom ranks of the wage labor force. In 1979, over 18 percent of Latina hourly workers earned poverty-level wages. Ten years later, this percentage had risen to over 31 percent. The intense competition between Latina women and Asian immigrant women for low-wage jobs has lead to the exploitation of both groups by employers through expansion of sub-minimum wage sweatshops and illegal homework. In addition, the relocation of American industries abroad displaced some Latina women from their jobs, such as Puerto Rican apparel workers and Chicanas once employed at the GM-Van Nuys plant in California. Chicana and Mexicana frozen food workers in Watsonville likewise lost their jobs when their employer relocated to Mexico. Most of these Latina workers who lost their jobs have reappeared in other sectors of the low-wage service economy. Their fellow Mexicana workers across the border share a worse fate.[21]

Mainly through the exploitation of low-wage Mexican women, the American, Japanese, and Korean companies located along the 2,000 mile long US-Mexican border has made it one of the world's most rapidly developing regions. Young Mexicana women make up 85 percent of the half million *maquiladora* workers, a labor force that is projected to swell to 3 million workers by the year 2000 as more and more multinational firms like Ford, RCA, and Zenith set up factories along the border. General Motors already has 30 such plants employing 30,000 workers. As noted, during the 1980s Mexico emerged as the world producer of labor-intensive auto parts that now includes engines and assembled automobiles. American companies were lured to Mexico by an abundant and cheap labor force. The investment in Mexico by the US car companies is leading to the integration of Mexico as both a production site and market for automobiles, but it will have long-range repercussions for the welfare of Latino workers. The newly ratified North American Free Trade Agreement, along with Mexico's ongoing economic crisis, assures a further fall in their meager standard of living.[22]

## LATINO WORKERS AND THE NAFTA

The North American Free Trade Agreement had brought Mexico and Canada into the deregulated arena of the US economy. This means cheaper access to natural resources, energy sources, and most important the bonanza of Mexico's economically depressed work force of nearly 30 million people. For American workers, free trade will mean job loss, the reduction of community tax revenues as companies relocate to Mexico, and the degradation of the environment particularly along the border now known as America's new "Love Canal." The worldwide search by the transnationals for low-wage labor, natural resources, weakly enforced or nonexistent environmental laws, and large tax breaks will no doubt be affected by the General Agreement on Tariffs and Trade or GATT, passed by Congress. NAFTA will eliminate more of the existing requirements on content, US sourcing of components, and other conditions that have averted the transfer of jobs to the border runaway shops. The combination of Japanese and European technology and a highly productive low-wage Mexican workforce will leave American workers at a disadvantage and could lead some corporations to demand lower wages. Free trade might create another reordering of the US labor force. American workers will witness: the continued outflow of low-skill jobs to their southern neighbor; only short gains of high-skill jobs from US exports to Mexico; and the continued influx of Mexican workers into the low-skill industrial and service sectors, where they will enter into prolonged competition with and inevitably displace large numbers of American workers for these jobs.[23]

NAFTA is a response to the formation of powerful economic blocs in Europe and Asia. The 12 nations of the European community agreed to end all trade and investment barriers, thus creating a single European market. Meanwhile, Japanese companies began moving their production to lower-wage nations in East Asia. NAFTA was pushed on the fast track by former President George Bush to beat the Europeans in creating the world's largest industrial power and market. NAFTA manifests the idea of "harmonization," that is, over time the laws, taxes, social programs, and regulations of the US, Canada, and Mexico will be brought in line with one another. However, the principle of harmonization conceals other motives; it will be used by American corporations to end social programs, labor laws, and any environmental protection that they consider constitute "unfair trade practices."[24]

Tens of thousands of American workers will undergo job loss to Mexico where extremely low hourly wages range from $1.85 for Mexican manufacturing to $0.50 or less for *maquiladora* workers. These wages are the equivalent of hourly wages for American industrial workers in 1955. Young women comprise the vast majority of this army of *maquila* workers employed in garment and electronics plants.[25] Free trade will not create manufacturing jobs in this country but instead will eliminate them. In the first five years, NAFTA will generate about 316,000 new jobs. During the same time, however, 145,000 jobs will be lost as the direct result of NAFTA. The net increase of jobs created by free trade therefore will be 170,000, yet most of this job gain has already taken place. In contrast, total loss of manufacturing jobs from NAFTA in service industries like telecommunications, financial services, and transportation are estimated at 500,000. Also, as previously noted, free trade will further weaken the economic base of many US regions and local communities and there will be a decrease in the growth of service jobs. These facts refute the contention by pro-NAFTA spokespersons that American workers will see higher wages as the result of free trade. In past times, imports have usually meant job loss and wage reductions for US workers that bring about their immiseration. Through NAFTA, 70 percent of the nation's labor force will experience an average wage loss of $1,000 per worker.[26]

Labor analysts note that NAFTA will have an impact on Latino workers in the United States, including garment and electronic workers along the US border, in Chicago, and the Northeast. Latinos comprise 24 and 7 percent respectively of all workers in these two employment sectors. Chicana and Mexicana food-processing workers in the

West, who represent 12 percent of the region's food processing industry work force, and Chicano and Mexicano farm workers will lose their jobs to increased fruit and vegetable imports from Mexico. Latino workers in the furniture, cement, steel, and auto industries similarly will undergo job loss.[27]

NAFTA will not be the much heralded panacea to reduce immigration from Mexico. Like the *maquiladora* agreement made in the mid-1960s, free trade will attract Mexican workers to the border region. Mexicans employed in the runaway shops, 90 percent owned by US multinational corporations, will be unable to support their families on the horribly low wages nor endure for long the substandard health and safety conditions in the *maquilas* and therefore will cross into the United States. The continued influx of undocumented Mexican workers will increase the racial bashing of Latinos and lead rampant discrimination against this minority group. This racial backlash to widespread unemployment, overcrowded communities, and the drain on social services was evidenced in California by the "Save Our State" initiative.[28]

## LATINO WORKERS AND UNIONS

Latino workers have high participation rates in unions. Approximately 1.5 million Latino workers belong to the AFL-CIO, representing 10 percent of the national federation's total membership. Notwithstanding the large and growing union membership of the Latino rank and file, the AFL-CIO continues to exclude Latinos, other minorities, and women from its executive council. Despite the indifference of union leaders, discrimination, and language barriers faced by recent immigrants, Latinos are the second largest minority group in the ranks of unionized labor. By the mid-1980s, nearly one-fourth of Latinos belonged to unions, a membership rate that was slightly below that of Blacks, but equal to Anglos. Unions with large Latino memberships like the ILGWU and the UAW have sought to organize Latino and Asian workers, including undocumented workers. Latino workers have

taken the initiative to organize among themselves by forming new unions like FLOC and COTA. These initiatives were undertaken in response to employer assaults, to a failing economy, and in light of the recomposition of the US labor force that reflects the nation's restructured and service-oriented economy where employment is increasing.[29]

The changing structure of the US economy in the 1970s contributed to the declining levels of unionization as the highly unionized industrial sectors of auto, chemical, rubber, and steel eroded. As noted, the American labor movement in the 1980s was hit hard by the hostile anti-unionism of the Reagan administration and management's unfair labor practices. However, the demise of union support has also been the product of corporate relocation schemes designed to fragment and sidestep unionization.[30]

By the end of the 1980s Latino union membership had dropped, reflecting the overall decline in unionization rates 12 percent by 1990. For Latinos, this was offset by the large increase in the total size of the Latino workforce, most of which was employed by non-union companies in service-sector employment. Union membership also declined for Latinas as the decade of the eighties closed. Despite lower union membership rates than Latino males, Latina women had higher union membership rates than Anglo women (about 17 percent versus 13 percent), though lower than Black women (almost 23 percent). A positive side to the influx of Latina women into the workforce is their growing participation in labor organizations. Union organizing drives by Latinas, strengthened by family and kinship networks, was demonstrated by striking Chicanas and Mexicanas in Globe, Arizona, and by Watsonville cannery workers. Mexicans employed in the border runaway shops are actively organizing, as are Salvadoran women domestic workers in Washington, DC. Despite the rise in racism and immigrant-bashing in the wake of California's anti-immigrant Proposition 187, Latina luxury-hotel workers in northern California are organizing against ill-treatment on the job and low wages.[31]

As with all organized and unorganized workers, Latinos have been the victims of unfair labor practices. They have suffered from employer attempts to lower wages by creating two-tier wage structures, demanding wage concessions and benefit give-backs; hiring part-timers, temporary help, home-workers, and the sub-contracting of work to other firms or to those overseas. While aiding employers, government inaction on behalf of labor has weakened the power of workers. Unfair labor practices and government spending cuts have drastically reduced unemployment compensation and public-service employment that provides employment for many Latinos, like the health-care workers of Los Angeles County and workers elsewhere.[32]

In the past five years Latino workers, drawing on a long tradition of struggle and using well-developed organizing strategies, are playing a prominent role in the growing resistance to the employer offensive. Latino, Asian, and Portuguese hotel workers in Boston fought back concessions; the 1990 Justice for Janitors victory in Los Angeles, led by the progressive Service Employees International Union Local 399; the strike by Latina high-tech workers in Sunnyvale, California; and the recent strike by Latino immigrant carpenters in southern California, demonstrate that immigrant workers will organize if they believe they can hold onto their jobs. Last April, the UFW launched a major organizing campaign to rebuild the union to its membership levels of 100,000 achieved in the 1970s. Over 30,000 farm-workers and their supporters marched from Delano, California to the state capitol in Sacramento. At issue are wages, job security, benefits, and protection against toxic work-place conditions. Through the mobilization committee of the Multiracial Alliance, the mostly Central American and Mexican immigrant membership of SEIU Local 399 are waging a movement for democratic reform and greater worker participation within the local union. Indeed, Latino workers, both citizens and recent immigrants, are leading the re-emergence of rank-and-file unionism in

America, a fact acknowledged by many employers, union leaders, and labor experts. According to labor journalist Kim Moody: "Far from undermining US labor, Latino workers are on the front lines fighting to defend them.!"[33]

## LATINO WORKERS AND THE IMMIGRATION INFLUX

Except for the relatively prosperous World War II years and overall improvement during the 1960s, wage and job disparity has increased for Latinos. From 1973 to 1987, the standard of living of Latinos dropped an average of 9 percent, and their poverty rates rose three times higher than their Anglo counterparts. Latino unemployment is one and a half times the national average. The present crisis ushered in by the globalization of the American economy has been detrimental to the livelihood of Latino workers. As noted, those in the Northeast and Midwest fell victim to the decline of manufacturing, while Latinos in the Southwest more and more will be affected by the continuing restructuring and integration of this region with Mexico. Because of global crisis, immigrants from Mexico, Central and South America, and the Caribbean will continue to come to the United States.[34]

More than 20 percent of Latino immigrants arrived in the United States within the last 15 years. The largest immigration of Latinos has been from Central America, South America, and the Spanish-speaking Caribbean. By 1988, one out of every nine Latinos in the US were from these Spanish-speaking countries. One-fourth of the Latino immigrants are from the Dominican Republic. Unemployment, political discord, and the escalation of violence by *narco traficos* [drug traffickers] underscored this migration from Central and South America.[35] For instance, United States foreign-policy decisions in the 1980s displaced nearly 2 million Central Americans from their homelands. The political violence made this region one of Latin America's poorest, resulting in the migration of nearly a quarter million Central Americans to the United States to seek political and economic refuge. Partly because of its self-interest and its catering to American corporate investors, US organized labor has contributed to the surging tide of Latino immigrants from this region by undermining militant unionism through the AFL-CIO-sponsored Institute for Free Labor Development.[36] Over 10 percent of El Salvador's 5 million people now live in the United States, along with significant numbers of Nicaraguans and Guatemalans. The Central American migration consists mainly of young males, though they have been joined by an increasing number of females. The immigrants from Central America work in manufacturing, construction, and food retailing. Like Mexicans, a large number of the Central Americans are undocumented and live and work under threat of deportation.[37]

Economic and demographic trends in Mexico and the United States will undoubtedly increase the flow of workers moving northward. A huge foreign debt and high birth rate have produced a 50 percent underemployment rate in Mexico. In the early 1980s, Mexico experienced its worst economic crisis since the Great Depression. To pay off its debt, the Mexican government lowered the living standards of its people and increased manufacturing exports by 300 percent. The wages of Mexico's industrial workers are nearly half the levels of 1982, and for Mexican workers as a whole their wages have dropped by two-thirds below 1982 levels. Each year 1 million young people enter the Mexican job market, which is growing four times as fast as its American counterpart. While the Mexican economy recently created half a million new jobs (80 percent are *maquiladora* jobs), 1 million jobs were lost due to the destruction of Mexico's old industrialized sector and the privatization of state enterprises.[38] Meanwhile, the privatization of *ejido* lands has already had profound repercussions in the coutryside, affirmed by the recent rebellion in Chiapas. Passage of NAFTA has also undermined Mexican agribusiness' ability to compete with foreign grain exports from the United States and Canada. Demographers predict that by the year 2000 perhaps 15 million Mexicans will be displaced from their lands. Given these realities, not even the creation of 1 million jobs each year over the next eight years will curb unemployment and poverty in Mexico.[39] Meanwhile, family, friends, and large Spanish-speaking communities in the US will continue to attract thousands of Mexican migrants. Also, the more than 2 million undocumented Mexican aliens who qualified for amnesty in 1987 met the residency requirement to become naturalized US citizens in 1994. As they become new American citizens, they will petition to bring spouses, parents, and children to the United States.[40]

## CONCLUSION

The efforts by Latino workers to correct economic and social ills take place at a time of retrenchment, when America is moving backward in achieving full participation by racial minorities. Since the 1960s the majority of Latino workers have experienced a sharp drop in stable job opportunities, the weakening of union protection, and the decline of their earning power. Latino industrial workers succumbed to the troubled times of deindustrialization. Racism continues to work against Latino workers; it has channeled them into the secondary sector of a racially segmented labor market. As Stanley Aronowitz has reminded us, racism "arises on the soil of competition among laborers, especially in the wake of technological change and uncertainty about economic stability." Latina workers also face gender discrimination. The restructuring of the US economy will continue to undermine the job prospects of unskilled workers and thereby their future economic well-being.[41]

The Latino population is changing the complexity of America, but this change is accompanied by considerable debate because it is occurring as living standards keep falling for most wage-earning Americans. A third of all Latinos are immigrants and another 40 to

45 percent are the children of immigrants. Large numbers of Latino immigrant newcomers have already undergone proletarianizing in their home countries. They are also familiar with the US labor market because family and kinship networks help them obtain jobs. Latino workers will soon make up 10 percent of the US labor force.[42]

There has been an increase in arrests of undocumented workers. In 1990, these arrests rose above 1 million for the first time since 1987. Undocumented immigrants are a boon for agribusiness and increasingly for the industrial and service sectors of the American economy because these fearful workers are easily exploited. For example, in the Los Angeles garment industry, 41 percent of undocumented Mexican women receive less than the legal minimum wage.[43] Yet Latinos continue to wage resistance against their exploitation in the workplace, NAFTA, and the current wave of immigrant-bashing. Ignored for the most part by organized labor, Latino workers will seek support from within their own ranks by creating and forming alternative labor movements. For example, through the newly emerging community-based "Workers Centers" Latino workers are organizing in the agricultural, garment, restaurant, and commercial food-processing sectors. The *Associación de Trabajadores Latinos* [Latino Workers Association], *Union de Trabajadores Agricolas Fronterizos* [UTAF], *La Mujer Obrera* [Woman Worker] and other community-based worker centers stress worker empowerment through unionization to fight against worker abuse, anti-immigrant sentiment, and discrimination.[44] The strong racial-ethnic identity attached to Latino working-class consciousness will spur these minority workers to gain recognition and acceptance as Latinos and as important members of the American working classes. With Blacks and women, Latinos will continue the struggle to achieve equal rights in the workplace and within the unions.

# Notes

1   Leon F. Bouvier and Robert W. Gardner, "Immigration to the US: The Unfinished Story," *Population Bulletin*, 41 (November, 1986), pp. 18–26; Saskia Sassen, "Why Migration?," *Report on the Americas*, 26 (July 1992), p. 15; Manning Marable, "Beyond Racial Identity Politics: Towards a Liberation Theory for Multicultural Democracy," *Race and Class*, 35 (1993), p. 124.

2   Sassen, "Why Migration?," p. 17; Gregory DeFreitas, *Inequality at Work: Hispanics in the US Labor Force* (New York: Oxford University Press, 1991), pp. 3–4; Kim Moody, *An Injury to All: The Decline of American Unionism* (New York: Verso Books, 1987), p. 282.

3   Sassen, "Why Migration?," pp. 17–18; DeFreitas, *Inequality at Work*, pp. 4–6.

4   Moody, *An Injury to All*, pp. 72–5; Martin Conroy et al., *Latinos in a Changing US Economy: Comparative Perspectives on the Labor Market since 1939* (Inter-University Program for Latino Research, 1990), p. 4; J. Holmes, "The Continental Integration of the North American Automobile Industry: From the Auto Pact to the NAFTA and Beyond," *Environment and Planning*, A24 (January 1992), pp. 99–100.

5   Moody, *An Injury to All*, pp. 87–92.

6   Ibid., pp. 95–6. See also Bennett Harrison and Barry Bluestone, *The Great U-Turn: Corporate Restructuring and the Polarizing of America* (New York: Basic Books, 1988), especially chapters 1 and 2.

7   During this initial reorganization and expansion, low-wage rates in Canada lured a large share of labor-intensive work – final assembly and production of labor intensive parts. The production of body stamping, engines, and drive-train components remained concentrated in the US. Holmes, "Continental Integration," pp. 96–7.

8   Jeanie Wylie, *Poletown: Community Betrayed* (Urbana: University of Illinois Press, 1989) pp. 29–32; J. Holmes and A. Rusonik, "The Break-up of an International Labour Union: Uneven Development in the North American Auto Industry and the Schism in the UAW," *Environment and Planning*, A 23 (January 1991), p. 18; Holmes, "Continental Integration," pp. 99–101.

9   Wylie, *Poletown*, pp. 31–2; Holmes and Rusonik, "The Break-up of an International

Labour Union," p. 18; Holmes, "Continental Integration," pp. 91–101; Moody, *An Injury to All*, pp. 99–101; Eric Mann, *Taking on General Motors: A Case Study of the UAW Campaign to Keep GM Van Nuys Open* (Center for Research and Education, Institute of Industrial Relations, University of California Los Angeles, 1987), pp. 97–8.

10    Gordon L. Clark, *Unions and Communities Under Siege: American Communities and the Crisis of Organized Labor* (Cambridge: Cambridge University Press, 1989), p. 67; *Moody, An Injury to All*, pp. 177–8.

11    Moody, *An Injury to All* pp. 154–5; Holmes and Rusonik, "The Break-up of an International Labour Union," pp. 20–3. That the traditional relationship between management and labor was breached was evidenced by the UAW agreement to a profit-sharing scheme and for UAW President Douglas Fraser to sit on the Chrysler Board of Directors. On the heels of the Chrysler concessions and in the depth of the 1982–3 recession, both GM and Ford demanded and received $1 and $3 billion respectively in concessions in the form of a wage and benefit freeze and the introduction of new forms of work organization in all plants. With almost half of Ford's 160,000 hourly workers and GM's 340,000 hourly workers on layoff, the UAW once again had no other recourse but to abide by the concessions. The auto industry again became profitable, reporting earnings of $6.1 billion in 1983 and $3.2 billion in the first quarter of 1984. Profit-sharing payments for GM and Ford auto workers totaled a trifling $640 and $440 respectively. Holmes and Rusonik, "The Break-up of an International Labour Union," pp. 24–5.

12    Holmes and Rusonik, "The Break-up of an International Labour Union," pp. 26 and 31; Moody, *An Injury to All*, p. 189.

13    Moody, *An Injury to All*, pp. 113–16.

14    Ibid., p. 117.

15    David Bensman and Roberta Lynch, *Rusted Dreams: Hard Times in a Steel Community* (Berkeley: University of California Press, 1987), pp. 101–2; Richard A. Navarro, "Structural Changes in the Midwest Economy and the Hispanic Labor Force: Trends, Future Prospects, and Needs," unpublished paper. East Lansing: Michigan State University, 1987, pp. 8–9; DeFreitas, *Inequality at Work*, pp. 45–6.

16    DeFreitas, *Inequality at Work*, pp. 140 and 142.

17    Lawrence Mishel and Jared Bernstein, "The Joyless Recovery," *Dissent*, 41 (Winter 1994), pp. 137–8; Marable, "Beyond Racial Identity Politics," p. 128; Mike Davis, "Armageddon at The Emerald City," *Nation*, 259 (July 11, 1994), p. 48. Presently, the largest private employer in America is Manpower Inc., the world's biggest temporary employment agency, with 560,000 workers. Marable, "Beyond Racial Identity Politics," p. 128.

18    Fernando Torres-Gil, "The Latinization of a Multigenerational Population: Hispanics in an Aging Society," *Daedalus*, 115 (Winter 1986), pp. 328, 332–3; William Serrin, "The Myth of the 'New York': A Great American Job Machine?" *Nation*, 249 (September 18, 1989), p. 272; Mike Davis, *Prisoners of the American Dream: Politics and Economy in the History of the US Working Class* (New York: Verso Books, 1986), p. 227; DeFreitas, *Inequality at Work*, pp. 45–6; Hector L. Delgado, *New Immigrants, Old Unions: Organizing Undocumented Workers in Los Angeles* (Philadelphia: Temple University Press, 1993), p. 150.

19    Conroy et al., *Latinos in a Changing US Economy*, pp. 10–13; Moody, *An Injury to All*, p. 7; Marable, "Beyond Racial Identity Politics," p. 124; Mary Hollens, "The Changing Face: Latino Workers in the United States" (Detroit: Labor Notes, 1993), p. 1; Delgado, *New Immigrants, Old Unions*, p. 150.

20    On Chicana domestic workers in Colorado, see Mary Romero, *Maid in the USA*. (New York: Routledge, Chapman, and Hall, 1993). For a discussion of the formalization of private household work, see Carole Turbin, "Domestic Service Revisited: Private Household Workers and Employers in a Shifting Economic Environment," *International Labor and Working-Class History*, 47 (Spring 1995), p. 99.

21    Alice Kessler Harris, *Out to Work: A History of Wage-Earning Women in the United States* (New York: Oxford University Press, 1982), p. 128; DeFreitas, *Inequality at Work*, pp. 140, 143–4, 188; Hollens, "The Changing Face," pp. 2–3; Delgado, *New Immigrants, Old Unions*, p. 150; Sassen, "Why Migration?," p. 17.

22    Oscar J. Martinez, *Troublesome Border* (Tucson: University of Arizona Press, 1988), pp. 126–8; Rachael Kamel, "'This is How it Starts': Women *Maquila* Workers in Mexico," *Labor Research Review*, 11 (Fall 1987),

pp. 17–18; Susan Kern and Tim Dunn, "Mexico's Economic Crisis Spawns Wildcate Strikes in Maquiladora Plants," *Labor Notes*, no. 194 (May 1995), p. 16. Indeed, Mexican engine plants achieve levels of efficiency, labor productivity and quality comparable to US plants. With a planned capacity of 3.5 million engines, Mexico is the world's major source for auto engines. Holmes, "Continental Integration," pp. 111–12.

23  Jeff Faux, "The NAFTA Illusion," *Challenge*, 36 (July–August 1993), p. 4; Kim Moody, "If NAFTA Don't Get You . . . Then the GATT Will," *Labor Notes*, no. 179 (February 1994), p. 12; David E. Simcox, "Immigration and Free Trade with Mexico: Protecting American Workers Against Double Jeopardy," *Population and Environment: A Journal of Interdisciplinary Studies*, 14 (November 1992), pp. 167–8.

24  Kim Moody and Mary McGinn, *Unions and Free Trade: Solidarity vs. Competition* (Detriot a Labor Notes Book, 1992), pp. 3–6.

25  Ibid., pp. 8–11; Hollens, "The Changing Face," p. 5.

26  Kim Moody and Mary McGinn, *Unions and Free Trade*, pp. 22–3; Kim Moody, "The Free Trade Deal: How Will It Affect Trucking, Auto, and Communications," *Labor Notes, no. 163* (October 1992), p. 8; Faux, "The NAFTA Illusion," pp. 4–6.

27  Moody and McGinn, *Unions and Free Trade*, pp. 23–5; Hollens, "The Changing Face," p. 5; Moody, "The Free Trade Deal," p. 8.

28  *Los Angeles Times*, September 25, 1994.

29  Camille Colatosi, "Latino Official Protest Exclusion from AFL-CIO Executive Council," *Labor Notes, no. 130* (January 1990), pp. 1 and 14; Clark, *Unions and Communities Under Siege*, pp. 4–6.

30  Clark, *Unions and Communities Under Siege*, pp. 4–6; Delgado, *New Immigrants, Old Unions* p. 9.

30  Clark, *Unions and Communities Under Siege*, pp. 4–6; Delgado, *New Immigrants, Old Unions*, p. 9.

31  Rachael Kamel, "'This is How it Starts'," p. 26; Ruth Neddleman, "A World in Transition: Women and Economic Change," *Labor Studies Journal, 10* (Winter 1986), pp. 211, 221–7; DeFreitas, *Inequality at Work*, p. 84; Moody, *An Injury to All*, pp. 283, 285–6; Hollens, "The Changing Face," p. 7; Delgado, *New Immigrants, Old Unions*, p. 8; Nathan Newman, "Immigrant Hotel Workers Fight for Justice," *Labor Notes, no. 197* (August 1995), pp. 8–9.

32  DeFreitas, *Inequality at Work*, p. 85; *Los Angeles Times*, September 18, 1995, pp. A1, A12.

33  Moody and McGinn, *Unions and Free Trade*, p. 41; "Immigrants Unite in Silicon Valley," *Labor Notes, no. 167* (February 1993), p. 9; David Bacon, "Immigrant Carpenters Battle Contractors and the 'Migra'," *Labor Notes, no. 195* (June 1995), p. 2, 14; Sue Johnson, "Farm Workers' March Kicks Off New Organizing," *Labor Notes, no. 183* (June 1994), pp. 5–6; "What? The Members Want to Run the Union?" *Labor Notes, no. 197* (August 1995), pp. 3–4; *Los Angeles Times*, August 8, 1995, B3; Moody, *An Injury to All*, pp. 287–8.

34  Moody, *An Injury to All*, p. 253–4; Hollens, "The Changing Face," p. 5.

35  Moody and McGinn, *Unions and Free Trade*, pp. 39–41; Hollens, "The Changing Face," p. 5. The majority of Colombians had first migrated within South America, mainly to Venezuela and Ecuador. Typical of the new Latino immigrant workers, both Dominicans and Colombians migrate from urban centers, are highly educated, and left skilled jobs in their home countries. Moody and McGinn, *Unions and Free Trade*, pp. 42 and 43.

36  Delgado, *New Immigrants, Old Unions*, pp. 148–9; Danile Cantor and Juliet Schor, *Tunnel Vision: Labor, the World Economy, and Central America* (Boston: South End Press, 1987), pp. 41–8. This section is based on Elizabeth G. Ferris, *The Central American Refugees* (Westport, CT: Praeger, 1987), chapters 2 and 7.

37  Delgado, *New Immigrants, Old Unions*, pp. 75–6. Many of these Central American immigrant workers are educated and have previous professional, technical, or white-collar occupational experience in their homelands. Ibid.; DeFreitas, *Inequality at Work*, pp. 44–5.

38  DeFreitas, *Inequality at Work*, pp. 44–5.

39  Ibid., p.256; Faux, "The NAFTA Illusion," p. 6, Moody and McGinn, *Unions and Free Trade*, pp. 30–2; Mary McGinn, "Why Mexican Peasant Farmers Rebelled Against Free Trade Pact," *Labor Notes, no. 179* (February 1994), p. 14. From 1982 to 1990 Mexico's economy grew by an average of only 1 percent a year while its population was growing by 22 percent in the same period. Beaten down by inflation, unemployment, and wage stagnation, average incomes of

Mexican workers fell by more than a third in the 1980s. Moreover, Mexico's labor force grew 3 percent annually in the 1980s, adding nearly a million job seekers. Because of the large number of births in the 1970s and declines in infant mortality, 1 million workers a year will swell the Mexican labor force in the 1990s. Simcox, "Immigration and Free Trade with Mexico," pp. 161–2.

40   Simcox, "Immigration and Free with Mexico," p. 163.

41   Stanley Aronowitz, *False Promises: The Shaping of American Working Class Consciousness* (New York: McGraw-Hill, 1974), p. 186; DeFreitas, *Inequality at Work*, pp. 254–7; Torres-Gil, "The Latinization of a Multigenerational Population," p. 336.

42   Torres-Gil, "The Latinization of a Multigenerational Population," pp. 344–5; Delgado, *New Immigrants, Old Unions*, p. 150.

43   Kitty Calavita, *Inside the State: The Bracero Program, Immigration, and the I.N.S.* (New York: Routledge, Chapman and Hall, 1992), p. 167. The Human Rights Commission in San Francisco found one garment sweatshop in which undocumented workers had not been paid for eight months and had lodged no complaints. So valuable is this cheap labor that the Chambers of Commerce of US border cities throughout the decade of the seventies advertised its availability in an attempt to lure industry to the area. Exploitation of sweatshop workers remains endemic. Ibid.

44   Mary Hollens, "Worker Centers: Organizing in Both the Workplace and Community," *Labor Notes, no 186* (September 1994), pp. 8–9; Cahti Tactaquin, "What Rights for the Undocumented?," *Report on the Americas, 26* (July 1992), p. 27.

# Latinos in a "Post-Industrial" Disorder

## Victor Valle and Rodolfo D. Torres

## POLITICS IN A CHANGING CITY

Finding those snap shots that reveal the sweat and blood of immigrant workers in a changing economy obscured by such terms as "post-industrial" or "post-modern" has become a crucial challenge for academics, activists, and enterprising journalists. Sometimes the desired revelatory image, or frozen time surface, reveals far more than was initially intended. This appears to be the case in a recent investigative series published in the *Los Angeles Times* on Latino immigrant workers in Los Angeles County's manufacturing work-places, which begins with three anecdotes of post-industrial Sinclairian death and misery: "One woman was doused head to toe with boiling oil when a machine that laminates menus exploded; a man drowned in a glue vat, and another was struck in the head by a 50-pound chunk of flying metal while tooling a chrome wheel. Some were electrocuted; several were crushed by hydraulic presses or pulled into the gears of other powerful machines."[1]

The final image, which comes straight out of a postmodern "Modern Times," adds a final note of irony to the grim tally: of the 43 workplace fatalities reported during a recent four-year period, 29 were Latino. The math is chilling, especially when placed in demographic context: "Latinos make up 36% of Los Angeles County's over-all labor force. They represent 44% of those in manufacturing, according to census figures. But they accounted for 67% of workers who lost their lives in manufacturing-related accidents between 1988 and 1992, an examination of coroner's records shows."

David Freed, the *Times* staff writer, justifiably focuses on the causes of Latino workplace deaths and injuries: regulatory neglect, lack of medical coverage, and greedy or indifferent employers who tolerate unsafe working conditions or an ill-trained work-force. These facts are the sort of information that have led some on the left to a nostalgia for union organizing in the good old days of high-wage, high-benefit, mass-production manufacturing.

Yet Freed's impressive reporting does an incomplete job of identifying solutions, none of which focus on developing strategies by which the Latino community might reshape the landscape where it works and lives. Instead, the articles focus their attention on suggesting ways for making the status quo work better than it does: greater regulatory oversight and employer accountability, as well as better worker education.

But there's another story hidden behind all the numbers, one that points to a host of strategic opportunities for Latino political community organizers. These opportunities are suggested by the following contrast between raw numbers and the material conditions in which worker deaths and injuries occur. First, Latinos account for nearly half of Los Angeles County's manufacturing work-force, although they comprise only about a third of its population. Second, the deaths and injuries are taking place in so-called global factories.

The convergence of these realities demands

a reconsideration of the meaning of so-called ethnic workers and their role in the new global economy. The nation's largest manufacturing center is about to become completely Latinized, a dramatic transformation that has only recently received glib commentary. Part of the underestimation of the role of Latino workers stems from a tendency to view them as a marginalized sector of the labor force. Another reason is the failure to come to grips with the socioeconomic consequences of a post-industrial society.

Two intentions – one descriptive, the other strategic – underlie our study. Of the two, however, this study places the greatest emphasis upon the search for a conceptual language that explains the consequences of the reorganization of industrial production for the global economy. As such, this study can be understood as a first step toward the discovery of an epistemology for labor and community organizers in a restructuring economy. Today poor and working communities find themselves in a frustrating struggle to identify and name their enemies and allies. Yet concepts of class struggle refined during past industrial regimes no longer explain the emerging world of work and money they seek to influence. Something has changed. For many community, labor, and political groups, changing conditions have outpaced the language of social and political rewards that had once sustained the illusion of an expanding middle class. One of the clearest expressions of this profound moment of incongruity reveals itself in the way many social scientists, labor organizers, and political activists have either underestimated or ignored the emergence of a majority Latino working class in the greater Los Angeles area, still the nation's largest manufacturing center in spite of recessions and the elimination of tens of thousands of defense-related jobs.

It's not hard to see why the strategic opportunities hidden in the midst of plant closings, riots, and earthquakes have gone unnoticed. Finding meaning in so much pain must seem the highest form of impertinence. But these conditions themselves can't be blamed for blinding social scientists, community activists, and political leaders from the important work of re-evaluating the Latino community's role in a emerging post-industrial economy. Other factors have contributed to this inattention.

Most social, economic, and political events within the Latino community are framed in the language of economic marginalization or soical pathology. Latino poverty and social inequality, it is assumed, reflect an inability to contribute to, or participate in, the mainstream of economic life. Latino powerlessness and poverty are also described as the results of a social pathology attributed to racial discrimination. Freed's articles, though well researched and well intentioned, nevertheless perpetuate this image of Latino victimization. Many labor leaders and sympathizers inflamed by anti-immigrant rhetoric portray Latinos as both victims and villains. Their status as undocumented workers not only exposes them to exploitation, they are also blamed for lowering wages and undermining the overall bargaining power and social benefits of unionized employees. Each characterization, though based on a partial truth, negates or obscures the changing status of the Latino community and the strategic opportunities that flow from that change. This paper, therefore, proposes to develop a conceptual language by which academics and activists can identify new strategic opportunities. The creation of a fully developed strategy, however, will be left for another day, as it goes well beyond the scope of this study. Strategic opportunities will instead be presented to illustrate the viability of the conceptual categories of description put forth in this study.

No matter the scale, global economies must still function in local landscapes. Moreover, global enterprises seek comparative advantages provided by the ability of local governments to transfer social wealth into the hands of private capital. Thus, capital's globalizing reach becomes most vulnerable when it encounters democratic initiatives that emerge from local landscapes. Unfortunately, however, the social and economic transformations needed to facilitate the economies of global efficiency have progressively reduced the control of local communities over their own political institutions. In the name of catch-phrases such as government "privatization" and "running government like a business," communities have allowed capital to appropriate more and more of local government's economic planning and regulatory functions. Capital's increasing co-optation of local government in the name of efficiency has been calculated to appeal to the anti-big-government, anti-tax sentiments of suburban middle-class voters. Often capital has persuaded suburbanites that handing over the functions of government would help eliminate the social welfare programs they so resent paying for. Paradoxically, capital's success at cloaking the economic planning and resource allocation functions of local government from public scutiny has enabled it to speed up economic restructuring, which has in turn hastened the Latinization of the Southland's working class. The demographic reconstitution of the working class is also occurring in other major US industrial cities. Thus, the creation of "stealth government" and the emergence of a majority Latino working class must be understood as merely different aspects of a single process of landscape creation and destruction. As a result, any effort to make local government more accountable and democratic must factor in the Latino community as both a voting and, more important, a working population upon which Southern California's present and future economic regime is being built. No fatalistic appeals to "Blade Runner" city or yearning for the good old days will change the present-day configuration of economic and labor forces.

Rather, efforts must be made to come to terms with material conditions of economic restructuring by developing a method of identifying strategic opportunities for enhancing community participation in the formulation of micro-industrial and micro-economic policies for the Latino community in East Los Angeles. Hopefully, the discovery of such a descriptive-conceptual language will lay the foundations upon which the Eastside's Latino community may develop strategies and tactics for redirecting and reducing the most damaging aspects of economic restructuring.

## CONSTRUCTING POLITICAL SPACE: TOWARD A LANGUAGE OF CITIES AND WORK

The concept of "landscape" advanced in this study borrows from Sharon Zukin's recent writings.[2] The novelty of her work stems from the way she expands the meaning of landscape beyond the geographical. For her, human landscapes are constructed from the dynamic linkages between a totality of socioeconomic, cultural, and political spaces. Existing social and political institutions and the changing material conditions of the marketplace, she argues, shape a landscape's spatial dimensions. "In a narrow sense, landscape represents the architecture of social class, gender, and race relations imposed by powerful institutions. In a broader sense, however, it connotes the entire panorama that we see: both the landscape of the powerful cathedrals, factories, and skyscrapers and the subordinate, resistant, or expressive vernacular of the powerless village chapels, shantytowns, and tenements."[3]

Zukin's multidimensional approach to landscape reading provides useful analytic categories for describing the architecture, organization, and loci of power in the Greater Eastside. Her approach also provides a method of narrating the Eastside's construction in time by focusing upon the dialectics of capital accumulation and the formation of local political institutions. Explicit in this economic-political dialectic is our representation of the Eastside as a contested terrain where its actors – indigenous or outside capital, indigenous social classes, and local political bureaucracies – vie for stategic advantages.

The spatial convergence of capital, politics, and class, Zukin argues, can be portrayed as a dialectic of places. The marketplace, the industrial park, and the suburban neighborhood are defined by their distinct roles as places of production or consumption. According to Zukin, these roles take on a revealing character in the transition to a post-industrial society. "Those places that remain part of a production economy, where men and women produce a physical product for a living, are losers. To the extent they do survive in a service economy, they lack income and prestige, and owe their souls to bankers and politicians. By contrast, those places that thrive are connected to real estate development, financial exchanges, and entertainment – the business of moving money and people where consumer pleasures hide the reins of concentrated economic control."[4]

The dialectics of place acquire distinct spatial expressions in late twentieth-century, post-industrial cities. Zukin and others have shown that the spatial expansion of urban landscapes proceeds along centrifugal force lines, perpetually moving outward beyond the fringes of previous periods of industrial and suburban development. Eventually, the older urban landscape is left behind to atrophy as each succeeding growth ring moves the benefits of capital further from the original urban core.[5]

At first reading, Zukin's dialectic of places does not appear to favor the Greater Eastside, since Latino barrios are often depicted in popular and academic literature as places of residence for a marginalized pool of surplus labor. Though applicable to certain East Coast Latino barrios, such broad generalizations do not readily apply to the Greater Eastside. Moreover, such simplistic generalizations should be resisted lest they blind us to perceiving the strategic advantages present in specific landscapes. Zukin, for example, recounts several cases where politically and economically marginalized communities have effectively organized to reverse, or at least moderate, the more noxious effects of post-industrial transformation. Therefore, rather than view Latino barrios in the context of an imploding inner city, we contend that the spatial expansion of the Greater Eastside flows directly from the centripetal forces that

have created the post-industrial city. In other words, the Eastside's shape and size are a direct consequence of its transformation from a collection of semi-rural "edge suburbs" to an interdependent network of newer and maturing near-in cities and suburbs. Our description of the Greater Eastside as a clustering of post-industrial edge suburbs contradicts the conventional view of the barrio as politically and economically marginalized territory. Therefore, rather than search the Greater Eastside's landscape for metaphors of Third-World marginalization, we view it as a functional totality. Seen from the ground, the Greater Eastside appears as a random patchwork of uneven developments marked off by freeways, concrete-lined rivers, rail lines, and land-fills, the Hopewell-like monuments of a throw-away consumer civilization. However, seen from the air, or on the demographer's map, the seemingly convoluted patterning of the landscape reveals its structure, which takes on the shape of a growing multi-celled organism. Socially and economically differentiated Latino suburban cells, manufacturing zones, and commercial districts radiate eastward from the organism's nucleus, which is just beyond the city's old urban core. Arterial freeways link the old core to the expanding edge, facilitating the circulation of goods, people, and information. At the organism's amorphous edges, privileged suburban cells encroach upon places created by older forms of capital accumulation. The newer suburbs wedded to globalized capital are rewarded with more hospitable landscapes, while those wedded to obsolete modes of production lose control of the ability to re-create their neighborhoods.

The Greater Eastside was, and continues to be, shaped by the destructive and creative energies unleashed in the competition between older and newer forms of capital accumulation. Whether post-industrial transformation is seen as the result of a shift toward a service economy, or as the most recent expression of the continued economic supremacy of industrial manufacturing, is not our concern in this article. We are more interested in deciphering those strategic features of the landscape that marginalized communities might exploit in their struggles for economic justice and political empowerment.

Unfortunately, our narration cannot suggest every landscape nuance since the documentary details needed for recounting Southern California's social history are at best fragmentary. The resulting dearth of narrative detail has undermined recent social histories, which have ignored or misconstrued the Latino community's landscape-building role. Yet, despite such narrative gaps, enough of a plot line can be salvaged from available sources to retrace the Greater Eastside's sociospatial construction. Rodolfo F. Acuña maintains that the creation of the Eastside's seminal urban Latino core resulted from an economic exodus. As had happened during the Gold Rush, massive white American immigration during the late nineteenth century again overwhelmed the local Mexican population, most of which lived downtown west of the Los Angeles River in an area known as "Sonora town."[6] Later, by the 1920s, the downtown Anglo elite's rise to economic dominance led by Harry Chandler's *Los Angeles Times* further accelerated the Mexican community's eastward flight. The driving force behind the displacement of Mexicans was "soaring property values and skyrocketing rents," which the Chandler growth strategy had ignited.[7] By 1929, more than 30,000 Mexicans had crossed the river, and settled in Belvedere Gardens, a planned housing development built over farmlands. At the same time, other Mexicans escaped downtown to establish residential suburbs in El Hoyo Maravilla, Montebello, and points beyond. Prior to their exodus from downtown, the Mexicans of Sonora town had served as a surplus labor pool for local industries. They continued in this role after the exodus as the cluster of Eastside Mexican communities began to coalesce and industry moved east of the river to take advantage of cheaper property values. Although the Mexican industrial labor force was in its majority composed of unskilled "pick-and-shovel" laborers, a micro-middle class, consisting of small merchants and

professionals, also settled in the new Eastside suburbs.[8]

The origin of an urbanized Mexican labor force is a subtlety often lost to non-Latino scholars, who tend to start their studies of urban labor history with the Mexican and Central American migration of the 1970s and 1980s. The fact is, Latino migration, both external and internal, has played a cyclical role in the social history of Los Angeles, beginning with the diaspora caused by the Mexican Revolution of 1910.

The urban Latino core east of the Los Angeles River may thus be viewed as an organic demographic unit from which other Latino satellite communities would grow, cell by suburban cell. It is important to stress here that this growth was accelerated by a process of uneven economic development. The creation of dozens of new municipalities encouraged the fragmentation of former farmlands into a patchwork of residential and industrial places. A key factor in this process of economic gerrymandering was a municipality's ability to create, or protect, its strategic economic assets. Those portions of the Greater Eastside that could neither capture nor create strategic advantages became dependent upon economically dynamic neighbors.

After World War II, the Mexican population continued its gradual drift east and southeast until reaching the boundaries of an industrial landscape dominated by heavy and light industry, and the mostly white working-class suburbs upon which these industries depended.[9] The decline of unionized, mass-production, automotive and steel industries in towns such as Maywood and Bell set in motion the rapid emigration of its white workforce from southeastern suburbs in the late 1950s and early 1960s. Eastsiders quickly filled this void. By the late 1970s, it became clear that the expanding Eastside would displace the formerly white southeast while filling in the interstitial spaces left between such older Mexican enclaves as El Monte, La Puente, and Santa Fe Springs.

Thus, the Greater Eastside is not merely an aggregate of Spanish-surnamed residents, but a network of neighborhoods, commercial strips, and, above all, suburban manufacturing zones linked by the day-to-day reality of work. These linkages, or pairings, express relationships between suburbs, or landscapes of rest and consumption and places of industrial production that typify the Greater Eastside's spatial organization.

## CONSTRUCTING THE GREATER EASTSIDE

Two interconnected transformations – the spread of the post-Fordist industrial development east and southeast areas of downtown, and the accompanying cycles of suburbanization at the edges of the Los Angeles urban core – were greatly shaped by capital's virtual monopoly over Los Angeles County land-use policies. "The way the suburban system works," wrote Bill Boyarsky, is summed up in the gold letters engraved on one wall of the hall where the Los Angeles County Supervisors sit during their meetings. It reads, "THIS COUNTY IS FOUNDED ON FREE ENTERPRISE. CHERISH AND PRESERVE IT." In areas with large amounts of undeveloped land, such as suburbia, free enterprise means the sale and development of land. County officials have traditionally encouraged and subsidized this business, even though it is often destructive to the suburbanite's way of life.[10]

As with other forms of suburban government, Los Angeles County gave its elected representatives the power to run their districts like personal fiefdoms. An individual supervisor, for example, could direct the expenditure of discretionary funds in the home district. The local political pork barrel was especially visible to suburban residents since it was used to reward or punish neighborhoods by granting or denying such county-funded improvements as street renovations, new library branches, or regional parks. A rapidly declining tax base has since curtailed the redistributive largesse of individual supervisors. Even so, these powers, even when not encumbered by federally mandated programs or tax revolts, paled when compared to a supervisor's ability to privatize land-use policies. The various functions of economic government were privatized through the cozy practice of appointing friends or political patrons to the county regional planning commission and other policy-making panels.

It was not at all unusual for the regional planning commission to allow wealthy property owners and developers to buy zoning exemptions with generous campaign contributions. Not surprisingly, the supervisor's power to appoint or remove commissioners reinforced their roles as magnets for campaign contributions. "Incumbent supervisors collected 91% of the campaign contributions given to supervisorial candidates from 1981 to 1986," wrote J. Morgan Kousser, a Caltech professor of history, in a recent report.[11] Only 2 percent of these contributions went to the challengers, added Kousser. Because supervisors rarely face viable challengers, they can amass huge war chests to advance their own political interests, or those of their contributors.[12]

The practice of giving private investors a strong say over land-use policy has tended to outlive the life of any individual project. Over time, capital's cumulative effects shaped both suburban landscapes and the organization of economic government. The Los Angeles County Regional Planning Commission perfectly illustrates this pattern of privatized government, but it was not an isolated case. All local government agencies charged with managing public resources such as redevelopment funds, water, air quality, or transportation funds have been privatized to some degree.

This appropriation of economic functions was paid for with a seemingly endless flow of campaign contributions. Money given to supervisors by powerful real-estate and industrial developers not only smoothed the way for county-financed storm drains, sheriff's substations, and myriad capital-attracting inducements, it also facilitated the creation of more than 30 cities east of downtown, each one reserving the right to sell its functions of economic government to the highest bidder. Blurring the political-economic boundaries between the public and private sectors thus produced its own ironic legacies. After the Watts Riot in 1965, the white middle and upper class fled to new edge suburbs to escape growing minority communities, and a corrupt, unresponsive Los Angeles city government. Upon arriving in suburbia, however, they encountered a county bureaucracy that made City Hall look virtuous by comparison.[13]

The seeds of cyclical middle-class exodus were sown in political-economic arrangements, which reached their clearest expression during the post-World War II succession of real-estate and industrial booms that swallowed up the county's remaining reserves of developable raw land. The county's eastern region was especially hard hit by the dual onslaught of post-Fordist suburbanization and industrialization. It was not at all uncommon for cities in and near the Greater Eastside to hand over land planning to private developers, who then proceeded to design whole suburbs, industrial parks, and cities to their specifications.[14]

Here too, capital's appropriation of the land-planning process transformed the structure and organization of local government. The most crucial of these transformations was the integrated legal, economic, and political rationale that led to the creation of what is euphemistically called the "single-use industrial city." These cities, populated with businesses instead of people, should be viewed as the equivalent of the post-Fordist center of flexible manufacturing. The degree of flexibility varied from city to city. Some, because they were held back by larger voting constituencies, did not privatize the functions of economic government as thoroughly as other cities lacking the encumbrance of a voting citizenry.

Still, despite the economic differences and antagonisms among competing cities, a high degree of political coordination emerged between the various functions of intra-city and regional economic government. Such a system of informal and formal intergovern-mental cooperation, whether achieved through backroom deal-making or through umbrella organizations, such as the Southern California Association of Government, was designed to protect the political-legal apparatus, which permitted the growth of flexible economic government.

Today, some Greater Eastside flexible cities, such as Vernon, resemble the *maquiladoras* deployed along Mexico's northern border, while others, such as Santa Fe Springs, are prosperous Latino middle-class enclaves sustained by post-Fordist manufacturing. Whatever the forms, however, the Greater Eastside's landscape is dominated by the county's most concentrated collection of such municipalities. The traits shared by flexible burgs such as the City of Industry, the City of Commerce, Santa Fe Springs, Irwindale, Azusa, and Vernon can be summarized as follows:

> It is our thesis that to correctly understand . . . the City of Industry, one must conceive of Industry's basic municipal purpose as one of becoming as much like a private industrial developer as possible, while retaining full municipal powers to raise taxes, [to] use the power available to all cities.[15]

Among the functions of economic government most coveted by capital are a municipality's authority to expropriate private property, draw municipal boundaries, and subcontract private firms to provide public services. These powers are typically deployed in the following sequence.

First, single-use cities eliminate the inconvenience of citizen rule by carving out city boundaries that exclude voters and, more important, include vital economic assets, such as rail lines, freeway access, or mineral rights. Second, liberal municipal incorporation laws allow single-use cities to contract private firms to provide public services, a technically legal arrangement that often leads to the creation of private monopolies hired to provide public services formerly dispensed by the city. Third, loosely written redevelopment laws permit single-use cities to condemn almost any property, including virgin farmlands, as urban blight. When used in combination, these functions of economic government free capital to transfer awesome sums of public capital into private hands, and, as a result, offer numerous opportunities for municipal corruption.

Redevelopment thus has diverted millions of property tax dollars to Greater Eastside economic government, money that would have otherwise gone to the county's general fund. Although this form of economic development arguably flows from redevelopment, its pay-offs all tilt toward the state's vast industrial and real estate development infrastructure. To date, taxpayers have had little success in renegotiating the way redevelopment benefits are distributed. The combined might of the redevelopment lobby, California's equivalent of the military-industrial complex had, until very recently, persuaded state and local government to divert to it an ever-increasing stream of tax dollars. Ironically, this diversion of public capital continued even as voters staged taxpayer revolts that diminished local government's ability to provide basic services.

Despite such massive transfers of public capital into private development, the Greater Eastside's landscape is anything but monolithic. The county's former expanses of raw land, the sheer scale of development, the uneven distribution of economic assets to local governments, and the diversity of economic interests resulted in anarchic development. The creation of the Greater Eastside's fragmented and unequal landscape can be expressed in the following spatial-temporal terms: The remnants of older forms of capital accumulation remained closer to the urban core, while newer, more flexible forms of capital sprouted on the periphery. The district's southeastern and western extremes illustrate these disparities between newer and older industrial landscape especially well.

A 1992 survey of two-digit SIC categories for 21 Greater Eastside cities shows that manufacturers there employed a total of 125,518 workers.[16] The largest employers of the 21-city group were firms producing trans-portation equipment (SIC 37), employing 14.8 percent of the total workforce. The next highest categories were the related industries of fabricated metal products (SIC 34), at 13.7 percent, and industrial and commercial machinery (SIC 35), at 10.1 percent. Food and other products (SIC 20) employed 10.7 percent of the manufacturers surveyed. Northrop Aircraft in Pico Rivera accounted for 66 percent of the 18,568 employed in the transportation category. But this pattern of highly concentrated employment was the exception, not the rule. As is typical of industries organized upon the flexible model of production, most Greater Eastside manufacturers in the 21-city group surveyed employed fewer than 100 employees.[17]

The data, although not conclusive, generally support Scott and Paul's thesis that flexible specialty craft industries have fueled the active resurgence of manufacturing in Southern California.[18] Nor does our survey contradict Scott and Paul's claim that Latinos, Asians, and women form the backbone of the specialty craft industries, with especially heavy Latino and female participation in apparel, furniture, and leather manufacturing. Our data, however, do suggest that the range of specialty craft industries employing Latinos is significantly broader than Scott and Paul acknowledge, with sizable numbers of Latinos employed in the metal-related industries, which accounted 23.8 percent of the jobs in the Eastside's 21-city group. Los Angeles business economist Joel Kotkin claims this number is significant: Metal-related manufacturing pays $500 to $700 per week, compared to garment-making jobs, which pay between $250 and $300 per week.[19]

Without further microeconomic surveys, however, the task of determining the number of Eastsiders employed by its resident manufacturers remains problematic. But given the high spatial correlation of Latino employment and residence patterns, one may expect such socioeconomic indicators as income and property value to reflect the uneven spatial deployment of flexible manufacturing in the Greater Eastside. Far from making any conclusive claims, the following narratives must thus be read as an initial attempt to uncover the Eastside's sociospatial organization, and, thus, its strategic power points.

## THE OCTOPUS REVISITED

Vernon's pliable government has facilitated the creative destruction of its landscape by facilitating each transformation of industrial production. In its most recent industrial role, Vernon has become a platform for post-Fordist, craft specialty industries. The flight of auto, tire, and steel-related mass production industries and jobs during the 1960s and 1970s were largely replaced in the 1980s by low-wage apparel, food, and furniture industries. Newer flexible industries, together with the older ensemble of low-wage foundry, meat packing, and metal plating shops, effectively pushed wages and benefits downward.

Mike Davis cites redevelopment records which show that 96 percent of

> Vernon's 48,000 workers earn incomes so low that they would qualify for public housing assistance. . . . At least 58 percent of this largely unorganized work force fall into the official "very low income" category, making less than half the county median a dramatic downturn from the area's union-wage norms twenty years ago.[20]

Declining wages and benefits in Vernon were mirrored throughout the region. Scott and Paul write that average manufacturing wage levels in Southern California fell 10.4 percent between 1970 and 1982, compared to a nationwide decline of 2.9 percent for the same period.[21] Meanwhile, the unions of Los Angeles County registered a 35.5 percent drop in membership between 1970 and 1983, compared to a 37.2 percent drop registered nationwide.[22] But even as new craft specialty manufacturers relocated in Vernon, others decided to leave. In the 1980s, apparel and furniture manufacturers left the country in search of Mexican and Asian workers willing to accept even lower wages.

If Vernon provided the prototype for the single-use industrial city, then the City of Industry, with its larger-than-life name, ranks as its most ambitious incarnation. A single-use city founded in 1957, its industrial infrastructure was post-Fordist, and thus a prime location for both low- and high-tech flexible industries. The city's shrewd exploitation of the redevelopment process and manipulation of county land-use laws flooded it with massive transfusions of public and private capital. It achieved this goal at taxpayers' expense. During the mid-1980s, Industry repeatedly ran up California's highest municipal debts.

The city, built over once-cheap South San Gabriel Valley farm land, stands apart from Vernon for other reasons. It embodies the nation's most potent example of a ghost government. The 14-square-mile municipality got its dragon-like-shape from the rail lines, freeways, and ground-water reserves included within its boundaries, and from the exclusion of its mostly working-class Latino population. Home to more than 1,500 businesses and a daytime commuter workforce of more than 65,000, the city houses slightly more than 600 people.[23] But only 200 or so of its residents are registered to vote. A quick analysis of the city's voter registration records reveals that Industry's voters are connected as blood relations, close friends, employees, or employers to each member of city government. As a result, since the city's council members and mayors are almost never opposed, they routinely win elections by margins of 59 to 0.[24] The Greater Eastside, which suffers the consequences of chronically underfunded schools and social services, can be seen as the county's black hole of redevelopment, and the City of Industry as its dollar-swallowing supernova.

More than $186.2 million, or 51.7 percent of 1989–90 property increments, were diverted to 64 redevelopment projects now operating in the Greater Eastside's First Supervisorial District. By contrast, only $25 million, or 6.9 percent of that year's tax increments, were diverted to 20 projects in the Second District, a political jurisdiction that includes South and South Central Los

Angeles.[25] The contrast is especially striking when viewed within the context of the LA riots. But this transfer of public capital represents only part of the redevelopment equation, since its aim is also to attract millions of dollars of private capital to a specific location.

During the mid and late 1980s, Industry held the distinction of having the state's most indebted redevelopment agency. Today, however, this city of not much more than 630 residents owns a debt second only to the Los Angeles' Community Redevelopment Agency. In fiscal year 1989–90, Industry's redevelopment projects racked up a debt of $1.22 billion, and tax increments totaling 4.7 million, compared to the CRA's debt of $1.72 billion, and tax increments totaling more than $101 million.[26]

Despite all the public and private capital swallowed up by Industry, it did give something back – about 55,000 manufacturing jobs plus another 6,000 service-sector jobs. Payroll data compiled in 1990 by the Stanford Research Institute for the Industry Manufacturers Council in 1990 reported an average salary of slightly more than $20,000.[27] The salary average reflects in Industry's mix of manufacturing jobs, newer plants, and the living standards of Industry's workforce.

Our research suggests that Industry's largest employers are in fabricated metals products (SIC 34), with 18.4 percent of the city's manufacturing workforce. The average company in this group employed 113 workers, showing the predominance of flexibly organized firms. This manufacturing group takes on greater weight when contrasted with related industries. Manufacturers in the machinery, except the electrical category (SIC 35) employed almost 9 percent of Industry's workforce. These two related categories (SIC's 34 and 35) employed 27.2 percent of Industry's workforce, and, as a group, represented the kind of value-added manufacturing that has traditionally paid higher wages than the food or apparel industries. The second-largest employer group was food and other products (SIC 20), with 13.2 percent of the city's workforce. The average

company in this group employed 216 workers, with the largest employing 672 workers. The next largest of Industry's employer groups were in the high technology categories. Transportation equipment category (SIC 37) employed 11.3 percent of Industry's workforce, and electric and electronic equipment (SIC 36), employed 7.39 percent. Together, these employment groups known for paying higher wages accounted for 18.69 percent of the city's workforce.

The contrast with Vernon's workforce is dramatic. Vernon's largest employer group was food and other products (SIC 20), which employed 34 percent of its workforce. Its second largest employer group was apparel and other textile products (SIC 23), employing 22 percent of its workforce, compared to 0.12 percent in Industry. The city's third largest employer group was primary metals (SIC 33), with 13.5 percent, which in Vernon's case often means dirtier and more dangerous foundry and bronze-casting jobs.

In typical Greater Eastside fashion, Industry's employment data is mirrored in La Puente's residential landscape. In La Puente, a city of more than 37,000 residents, 86 percent of them Latino, the median family income was $33,273 in 1989, slightly below the national mean, compared to $23,819 in Bell Gardens, the bedroom suburb to industrial Vernon.[28]

But Industry gives back more than relatively higher paying jobs. It's an especially influential political benefactor. The members of Industry's powerful Industry Manufacturers Council gave more than $130,000 to three state legislators during a 10-year period ending in April 1984. During the same time period, council members contributed more than $95,000 to five Republican political action committees, and more than $90,000 to former First District Supervisor Peter F. Schabarum. In 1983, the city paid more than $30,400 – more than any city in Los Angeles County except Los Angeles itself – to hire former Assembly Speaker Robert Moretti as its lobbyist.[29] Recently, Schabarum drew from his traditional base of political support in cities such as Industry to launch his own political initiatives. In 1990, he directed that more than $440,000 of his own campaign funds be spent on passing Proposition 140, the initiative limiting incumbent terms in Sacramento. Campaign records show that the funds, transferred through loans he later forgave, served as seed money to qualify the initiative, which he helped draft, and to raise another $1 million in contributions. Remarkably, Schabarum did this while diverting more than $52,000 to his favorite conservative candidates and causes.[30]

Supervisor Gloria Molina, elected to a First District that preserves much of Schabarum's former industrial base, has by now discovered just how generous her district can be. City and county campaign records show that she raised more than $801,000 in 1991, the year she won the supervisor's seat, a 73.6 percent increase over 1987 fund-raising levels of $461,609, her most profitable fund-raising year as a Los Angeles City Councilwoman. The same records show that 95.2 percent of the contributions to her supervisorial campaign were in excess of $100, a clear indication of the presence of big money, much of it from new corporate contributors.

## TOWARD A STRATEGIC AGENDA

Two weeks before the April–May 1992 riots, during an off-the-record dinner gathering with local Latino journalists, Los Angeles County Supervisor Gloria Molina candidly responded to one reporter's comment that local African American political leaders were continuing to deny Latinos their fare share of the city's political and economic pie.

Molina said she understood the reporter's frustration. Local African American political leadership had become a prime obstacle to continued Latino political and economic empowerment. Sooner or later, she promised, there would have to be a summit in which leaders like herself would oblige her African American counterparts to face up to the political consequences of demographic reality: Latinos are ready to accept the rewards of being the county's new majority. Her comments were well received. Molina correctly sensed the growing dissatisfaction with the way African American leaders in Los Angeles have used race to define "minority" struggles for social and political justice. The weeks following the riots would render these frustrations visible. Other Latino community leaders, some elected, others not, would repeat in public what Molina had said in private.

These Latino leaders now insist that because their constituencies have grown in numbers, they deserve a proportionate share of government power. Sound fair? Not to African American leaders, who argue that their constituencies are entitled to a larger share of government to compensate for past injustices. The riots only exacerbated these competing claims. The escalating rhetoric surrounding job competition in the rebuilding of South Central Los Angeles signifies the quandary in which Latino political leadership now finds itself: Although they perceive themselves as agents of progressive change, they continue to ply the old politics of racial entitlement. Politics, for these Latino leaders, is nothing more than a zero-sum, race-reductionist game. Consequently, their failure to face up to this contradiction has distracted them from taking inventory of the political and economic power that is already within reach, and it perpetuates the image of Latinos as victims.

Taking stock of the Greater Eastside's economic and political landscape does not mean that Latino elected officials should drop their demands for more responsive and inclusive government. It merely requires that these leaders put this aspect of political representation in its proper context. Seeking improved social services, for example, for their Latino constituents represents only one avenue of political empowerment. Unfortunately, this redistributive aspect of local government is becoming less and less important, as continuing budget shortfalls so painfully reveal. Local government has fewer and fewer discretionary funds to spend on alleviating social ills.

Economic government is another matter. Of the two branches, it is now, and will continue to be, the more dynamic, wealth-creating arena for making public policy. That's why Latino leaders simply can't afford to continue to express their frustrations in ways that reinforce a status quo predicated upon a system of race-based power sharing, while ignoring the opportunities that come with understanding the functions of economic government. Yet that's precisely what they do in seeing government as a banquet at which the guests are served according to how loudly they proclaim their appetites.

Margit Mayer argues that the flexiblized world of post-Fordist manufacturing that has resulted from the increasing globalization of capital has fundamentally changed the faces of local politics and urban spaces:

> So-called world cities as well as formerly peripheral cities and regions are becoming direct players in the world economy . . . The changing division of labor, together with the disengagement of most federal governments from certain domestic programs, has conferred new challenges on the regional and local level and upgraded local politics everywhere. In this heightened interurban and interstate competition for growth industries, state funding, skilled workers, and consumer dollars, cities have come to emphasize, exploit, and even produce local specificities and assets. Their planners and politicians confront the task of tailoring conditions to create an environment in which profitable enterprises can flourish.[31]

In Eastside cities such as Industry and Santa Fe Springs, the political economy of place is clearly dominant. Here, aggressive chamber organizations vie for new investment by advertising their respective access to freeways, sea and airports, universities, and a trained and exploitable workforce. Only a handful of local functionaries, most of them unelected and with ties to capital, decide how the Greater Eastside's collection of ghost governments will affect the lives of millions of taxpayers and voters. Unfortunately, this feature of economic government isn't unique to the Greater Eastside. Increasingly, major questions of industrial policy are being decided piecemeal by such local bureaucracies as the Metropolitan Water District, the California Coastal Commission, the State Agricultural Commission, the county's Regional Planning Commission, and the Southern California Air Quality Management District.

But the hegemony of economic government is far from absolute. The tendency to externalize the efficiencies of production continues to pressure capital to seek markets and production locations that offer real or perceived economic advantages. Mayer argues that the competition between emerging post-Fordist cities and industries has thus created new political space for communities historically disconnected from directing the functions of economic government. As competition among cities and regions intensifies, and localities find their financial resources curtailed as a result of national austerity politics, local and regional political bodies must adopt new roles. First, local and regional government must create landscapes that foster flexible forms of economic growth. Second, local and regional government must create new forms of economic government to support and regulate post-Fordist industries. To be effective, such new forms of economic government must also have the power to cut across the traditional administrative lines, so as to create a regional coherence that the new flexible manufacturers and services enterprises cannot produce on their own.[32]

The evolution toward new forms of overarching economic government offers local communities, ethnic or otherwise, several avenues for political organizing in a post-Fordist era. Local community groups can organize themselves to shape the formation of new forms of economic government. Groups such as the Mothers of East LA have demonstrated the viability of this approach, albeit defensively, by shutting down noxious plants and prisons. Local communities can challenge existing forms of economic government to make its policy-making and planning functions more democratic. That's why the Greater Eastside's concentration of ghost governments can become an asset instead of a liability – all of these agencies are within easy driving distance, which makes them vulnerable to old-fashioned political pressure.

Latino-elected leadership, when taken as a whole, already represents every inch of the Greater Eastside's political landscape. Even if no new Latinos were elected to office, the present cast of elected officials already hold enough political authority to begin a grass-roots dialogue on a micro-industrial policy for the Greater Eastside. Initiating such a wide-ranging discussion could begin with local hearings, or by convening conferences on micro-industrial policy. Eventually, these dialogues could lead to the creation of a post-Fordist governmental entity charged with implementing micro-industrial policy for the Greater Eastside. If proved successful in the Eastside, the model could be emulated by other communities cut off from the local economic government.

We maintain that the economic forces that have transformed the Greater Eastside into one of the nation's most dynamic industrial landscapes require a rethinking of Latino political and economic life. Future policy research on the Latino political and economic condition must, therefore, be recast in a more rigorous analytical and theoretical framework. To date, research on the political economy of Latino communities has been mired in the unquestioned categories of "race relations." As a result, preconceived notions of what constitutes a Latino "barrio" have prevented many from perceiving the actual Latino political and economic landscape. Such a lack of theoretical imagination has, in turn, led many to reproduce the outdated categories of political analysis on subjects such as political redistricting and post-riot economic development. Unable to advance an independent policy discourse, Latino scholars, and community and elected leaders, have been drawn into no-win debates with African American communities on the distribution of economic revitalization funds.

An analysis of the dialectics of landscape can help reveal the locations of actual and potential political power. Arriving at this understanding requires Latino leadership to map emerging forms of new technologies and identify the changing organization of work in post-industrial Los Angeles. Performing this task should prepare Latino leaders to discuss the possibilities of democratic economic reform with consumers, labor, and the business community. Whether such dialogue can be realized remains to be seen, but the benefits could be enormous – a more democratic and prosperous Latino community.

# Notes

1    David Freed, "Few Safeguards Protect Workers from Poisons," *Los Angeles Times*, September 6, 1993, p. 1.

2    Sharon Zukin, *Landscapes of Power: From Detroit to Disney World*. (Berkeley: University of California Press, 1991).

3    Ibid., p. 16.

4    Ibid., p. 5.

5    Joel Garreau, *Edge City: Life on the New Frontier* (New York: Doubleday, 1991).

6    Rodolfo Acuña, *Community under Siege: A Chronicle of Chicanos East of the Los Angeles River, 1945–1975*, Chicano Studies Research Center Publications, Monograph no. 11, University of California Los Angeles, pp. 7–10.

7    Ibid., pp. 10–11.

8    Ibid., pp. 10–13.

9    Mike Davis, "The Empty Quarter," in David Reid (ed), *In Sex, Death, and God in L.A.*, (New York: Pantheon Books, 1992), pp. 56–8.

10    Bill and Nancy Boyarsky, *Background Politics*, (Los Angeles: J.P. Tarcher, 1974), p. 52.

11    Valle and Torres, "The Economic Landscape of the Greater Eastside: Latino Politics in 'Post-Industrial' Los Angeles," *Prism*, 1/1 (Fall 1993).

12    Ibid.

13    Boyarsky, pp. 62–70.

14    Mike Davis, *City of Quartz* (London and New York: Verso, 1990), pp. 165–9.

15    Don Morian and Victor Valle, "City of Industry: It Has Clout Where It Counts – in

the State Capital," *Los Angeles Times*, April 15, 1984.

16  The following analysis of SIC categories in the First District was based on the data-base compiled in the *Southern California Business Directory and Buyers Guide 1992*, which lists the number of employees, year established, payroll information, type of business, plant size, annual revenue, business description, as well as primary and secondary SIC codes. Company officials claim that the database collected a 60 percent sampling of manufacturing businesses in California. These data, however, must be placed in proper context, since the 21-city group for which SIC were analyzed accounts for only 53 percent of the district's total population. Further analysis of district-wide data is needed; however, other studies provide some partial answers. Scott and Paul, for example, estimate that more than 96,000 workers are employed by apparel and other textile manufacturers, almost all of which are located within the First District's boundaries. By contrast, only 2.95 percent, or 3,713 jobs, fell under SIC 23 (apparel and other textile products) in the First District's 21-city group, a figure that suggests a lack of sampling redundancy.

17  Ibid.

18  A.J. Scott and A.S. Paul, *Industrial Development in Southern California 1970–1987* (New York: Pantheon Books, 1992).

19  Interview with Joel Kotkin, May 1992.

20  Davis, "Empty Quarter," p. 60.

21  Scott and Paul, p. 205.

22  Ibid.

23  Morian and Valle.

24  Ibid.

25  Our analysis of tax increment diversions was made by calculating the total number of city- and county-run redevelopment projects within each of the five supervisorial districts. The actual increment figures were taken from the Office of the State Controller, *Annual Report 1989–1990 Financial Transactions Concerning Community Redevelopment Agencies of California* (Los Angeles: Division of Local Government Fiscal Affairs, 1991), pp. 296–340.

26  Ibid., pp. 313, 323.

27  The Industry Manufactures Council, *City of Industry Factbook* (City of Industry, 1990), p. 6.

28  Shawn Hubler, "South L.A. Poverty Rate Worse in 1965," *Los Angeles Times*, May 11, 1992.

29  Valle.

30  Valle and Torres.

31  Magit Mayer, "Politics in the Post-Fordist City," *Socialist Review*, 21/1 (1991), pp. 105–24.

32  Ibid., p. 113.

# What's Yellow and White and Has Land All Around It?
# Appropriating Place in Puerto Rican *Barrios*

## Luis Aponte-Parés

Jaran's face filled with joyful pride as he showed us photos of the latest party held at his *casita*, his "little house." He recalled building it with his family and neighbors on 142nd Street and St Ann's Avenue in the South Bronx some years back, and how they christened it with that evocative name, *Villa Puerto Rico*.[1] Looking through those recent photos, he told us of the many times Villa Puerto Rico had served the neighborhood as a place for celebrations and get-togethers of all kinds: birthday parties, Puerto Rican Day Parade ceremonies, Thanksgiving dinners, block association meetings, political rallies, etc. Like the many memorable events, their *casita* itself is a source of pride and memory – it articulates and validates their Puerto Rican identity in space.

At its name suggests, Villa Puerto Rico embodies, in emblematic ways, the endurance of Puerto Rican culture in the New York setting, and the strength of Jaran and his neighbors in appropriating and conferring meaning to the environment by building alternative landscapes on the devastated urban milieu. On 142nd Street, and throughout the South Bronx, East Harlem, *El Barrio*, the Lower East Side, *Loisaida*, and Brooklyn, *casitas* stand as cogent metaphors of place and culture.

Villa Puerto Rico and scores of other *casitas* built around the City belong to a family of balloon-frame wooden structures – shacks, bungalows or cottages – generally identified with Third World vernacular architecture

(King, 1991). Built on stilts with land all around, frequently with a vegetable garden, you can identify them by their corrugated metal gable roofs, windows openings with shutters, bright colors, and ample verandas so favored by Caribbean architecture. This architecture took shape during the nineteenth century, when increased trade between the islands and the US led to exchanges of people and their cultures, bringing about the transformation and modernization of the islands' traditional and/or vernacular architecture[2] (Newel Lewis, 1983; Segre, 1985; Berthelot and Gaumé, 1982; Aponte-Parés, 1990).

*Casitas* built in New York are specific to Puerto Rico and are generally located in neighborhoods with extreme poverty that witnessed massive population displacement in the past three decades. In these neighborhoods large tracts of empty land are surrounded by abandoned tenements and ubiquitous "towers in the Park" enclaves, legacies of government housing paradigms, perhaps envisioned as instruments to "eradicate the most vocal and visible pockets of nonwhite inner-city life" (Boddy, 1992: 134), that have been so successful in fracturing the city.

## THE LEGACY OF THE 1970S

Today, terms like Cyber-City, Exurbia, Theme Parks, Fortress City, Informational City, Analogous City, Virtual City, City of Quartz, Exopolis, Megalopolis, and Landscapes/Architecture of Despair, to name a few, are formulations attempting to describe and possibly explain the way changing economic, political and cultural forces of the global economy are being articulated in the American city. These forces have been manifested as profound transformations of the urban landscape during the second half of the twentieth century, namely: suburbanization; class- and ethnic-specific segregation of residential districts with the poor and people of color isolated in distressed neighborhoods, while the wealthy converge in well-appointed and protected enclaves; the privatization and subsequent loss of public space with the concomitant exclusion of the poor and people of color; and the increased employment of "stage set" concocted environments, or "theme park" architecture and urban design solutions to revitalize cities (Sorkin, 1993).

## Displacement and replacement

Jaran's smile thus betrays the deeper role and complex meaning that these humble structures have assumed in the lives of his fellow Puerto Ricans in New York City. With the relocation of industrial jobs from New York to other parts of the world and its transformation from an industrial to a post-industrial city, significant numbers of displaced industrial workers and their families, many of them Puerto Ricans and African Americans, were not integrated into the new economy. As a consequence there have been sharp increases in their poverty rates, decreased labor force participation, increased dependence on transfer payments, and an overall decline in their standard of living[3] (Rosenberg, 1987).

The inability of the new economy to fully incorporate these displaced workers, and the added pressures exerted by the influx of new immigrants, has led growing numbers of New Yorkers to work in the "informal," "floating," illegal, or underground/street economy, language closely associated with Third World countries rather than with the Metropolis (Friedmann and Wolff, 1982; Sassen, 1991).

Testimony of which is the increased presence of street vendors, illegal sweatshops, and an assortment of unregulated jobs accompanied by squatters, cardboard condos or "Bushvilles", and *casitas*, the new alternative informal urban landscapes of the post-industrial city.

These transformations have led to sharper contrasts in the daily living of New Yorkers with concomitant class- and ethnic-specific divergence in the quality of life among certain city neighborhoods, perhaps greater than ever before. Another result is a unique American form of urban apartheid: "fortress cities" brutally divided into "fortified cells of affluence" and "places of terror" where police battle the criminalized poor (Davis, 1992: 155; Harris, 1992). In addition, as class polarization and segregation increase, inequality in how different populations choose where to build and appropriate space – the underlying framework to their identity as people in a neighborhood as a fundamental human activity, has increased too.

Paradoxically, in "Cyber-City," the city ostensibly with no material spatial needs, the "virtual" electronic city of computers, modems, and electronic highways linking together any place in the globe, the need for meaningful and precious places validating cultural identities in space may have increased, as witnessed by the presence of *casitas*. They are built by the disenfranchised urban poor living in landscapes of pollution, joblessness, and violence, increasingly invisible to the rest of society, and representing the underside of the "triad imagery of post-industrial landscapes like silicon valley, i.e., ecology, leisure, and 'liveability'" (Zukin, 1991:17). Predictably, they are the same people who are unable to "buy" manufactured landscapes like Battery Park City; be connected to the virtual reality of cyberspace; or who are left out of the information circuits/highways, representing "lag-times – temporary breaks in the imaginary matrix" – of the new city (Boyer, 1992: 118; Oulette, 1993).

Market forces have brought desolation and despair to the inner city, rendering the urban fabric into residual and discontinuous fragments attended by a loss of memory and identity, producing a lumpen geography of capital (Walker, 1978), "reserved" neighborhoods with arrested development potential analogous to the industrial reserve of workers. Here, the decaying industrial city retains its most striking contradictions, clearly examples of urban dystopias dividing the city between the "citadel and the ghetto" (Friedmann and Wolff, 1982: 325).

Conversely, others live in places like Battery Park City(adel), a class-driven "scenographic reassembly of urban components" (Boddy, 1992: 131), an inaccessible protected enclave, or "yuppified urban village" (Davis, 1992: 164), built for a select number of whites – the newly emerging minority in an increasingly non-white city. The Citadel houses the World Financial Center, home to the Winter Garden, a shopping mall decorated with out-of-climate palm trees playing the role of a figurative center; a privatized indoor urban plaza, where architectural space has been theatrically manipulated to perhaps achieve some of the density and bustle of a downtown; a "fantasy urbanism, devoid of the city's most negative aspect" (Crawford, 1992: 22), i.e., the weather, traffic, and the homeless; and where people of color are mostly seen serving the tables and providing security. Puerto Ricans and other Latinos, people of color, and other poor and working people are increasingly banned from these "analogous cities" by the use of urban design schemes that segregated urban landscapes, while abandoning the street by enclosing urban amenities in new suburb-in-the-city solutions for living, working, and shopping (Boddy, 1992), thus sharply partitioning the city between "landscapes of power and (landscapes) of devastation" (Zukin, 1991: 5).

## LANDSCAPES OF DESPAIR: URBAN DYSTOPIAS[4]

During the past two decades, massive urban dislocation impacted many neighborhoods across the city with the loss of hundreds of thousands of homes, at times at a rate of 3,274 units a month, thus changing the character of many neighborhoods, while annihilating others[5] (Stegman, 1988). Declining numbers of ethnic minorities[6] and poor and working-class households in some Manhattan districts evidence their displacement from select neighborhoods enjoying renewed investment value under the emerging economic logic of New York as a "control center of the global economy," a World City, (Friedmann and Wolff, 1982: 319) with Manhattan as its center. But not all neighborhoods have fared equally in the center-periphery relationship of land values between Manhattan and the outer boroughs. At the core, neighborhoods in Manhattan like El Barrio, East Harlem, lost close to one third of its built environment, while others, like Loisaida, in the Lower East Side, long the home of the working poor, became attractive for reinvestment. Neighborhoods like Loisaida experienced gentrification articulated by a "frontier motif," i.e., neighborhoods where "hostile landscapes are regenerated, cleansed, reinfused with middle-class sensibility" and where the new "settlers," brave pioneers, go to "where no (white) man has gone before" (Smith, 1992: 70). In the outer boroughs, the "periphery," some former middle-class neighborhoods in the Bronx or Brooklyn, for example, became residual or surplus with diminished value to the financial hub, with others perhaps becoming new or reconfigured "borderlands," places of arrival for new immigrants: high-density ethnic enclaves bursting with energy, at times resembling bazaars, and with the dynamism of a Third World Metropolis like New Delhi, Mexico City, or Sao Paulo.

The losses, of course, were not only of buildings and people, but of primary "life spaces," areas people occupied in which their "dreams were made, and their lives unfolded" (Friedmann and Wolff, 1982: 326). These losses signaled the detachment of a people from their most recent history, their memories, sus memorias, rendering them invisible, and making them guest visitors to the neighborhoods they were forcibly relocated to. It also represents the loss of place, the break from the regulated formal urban landscape of the modern city produced when its residents were relocated to the secluded and highly segregated "projects," monumental prisons where poor workers and displaced people are warehoused, or to the unchartered, unregulated, unpredictable informal city, the city of squatters, shanties and "Bushvilles."[7] The decline and loss of institutions, *bodegas*, churches, social centers, schools, friends and neighbors led to a collective need to play an active role in rearranging the environment, and thereby restoring the community's sense of well-being.

## CASITAS: ARCHITECTURE OF RESISTANCE

It was to address these needs that Jaran and others like him and their families chose to take an active role in reshaping landscapes of despair into landscapes of hope: transforming fragmented and discontinuous urban landscapes into "cultural forms with continuity," rich in values, and bringing forth a sense of "attachment" – a feeling of "congruence of culture and landscape" – while perhaps providing them a sense of regional identity (Riley, 1992: 17). Key to this attachment is the ability to take possession of the environment simultaneously through physical orientation and through a more profound identification.

> When an action takes place, the place where the action occurs becomes meaningful, in the sense of expressing the possibility of the very occurrence. What happens does not partake in a spatial structure, but is also linked with a system of values and meanings, and thus acquires character and symbolic importance. (Norberg-Schultz, 1988: 31)]

Of course, in our times, and for Puerto Ricans, African Americans, and other urban poor, mapping of the urban landscape by building "life spaces," and taking possession of the environment and assigning meaning to it by "building communities" is a decidedly different experience from that of earlier times,

or by others in a more fortunate economic position, or that of people who see place as investment and real estate. But Jaran and other founders of *casitas* can hardly boast of the means to build model communities: Their will to reshape is tempered by meager resources and their recent history. Their language is thus limited to one of circumscribed impact, where holding ground, turf, *rescatar*, takes on the primary role, a true architecture of resistance subverting the traditional city. Thus the *casita*, like the ubiquitous Puerto Rican flag, becomes a vehicle through which their builders articulate and defend their national identity, their *imagined community* (Anderson, 1991), their innate essence determining who they are in the urban milieu.

## THE PUERTO RICAN EXPERIENCE: FROM BODEGAS TO CASITAS

The urban narrative of Puerto Ricans in the US has been marked by pain, discord, and a diaspora that, unlike that of Chicanos and other Latinos, reflects the dual condition of colonial citizens with no ostensible borders to cross, while adapting to a foreign culture.[8] Although the story of Puerto Ricans in the US dates back to the nineteenth century (Sánchez-Korrol, 1994), their place in the urban narratives of US cities is not fully understood. Since their arrival in New York City earlier in the century, Puerto Ricans have defied severe housing problems and involuntary resettlement, with displacement being the most disruptive and significant of them (Sánchez, 1986). For over half a century since their "great arrival" in the 1940s and 1950s, Puerto Ricans slowly gave shape, character, and meaning to many "life spaces" in places like Bellevue, Chelsea, Lincoln Square, or Hells Kitchen. But by the 1960s Puerto Ricans began to lose the tenuous control over their environment they had gained earlier during their resettlement from the island (Andreu Iglesias, 1984; Colón, 1961). During the 1950s and through the nadir of the fiscal crisis of 1975, urban renewal and the private market intersected, thereby accelerating displacement, and inducing a "process of loss, rupture, and deterritorialization" (Gómez-Peña, 1993: 20) of a whole community. "Building community" became less an act of settling and shaping neighborhoods into ethnic enclaves and more like a resettlement process of a people being expelled from place to place, by the relocation officers of City agencies, unscrupulous landlords, or the heat from the last fire (Aponte-Parés, 1988). A disrupted historical and environmental narrative, and loss of memory[9] resulted from this removal of buildings and people. Puerto Rican displacement meant the "erasure" of images recording their cultural presence in the City, and of the contributions Latinos had made to the built environment in New York as well as personal narratives – the houses of our memories.

With names like *Villa Puerto Rico, El Jaragual, Añoranzas de mi Patria, Rincón Criollo*, to name a few, *casita* builders introduce and defend the possibility of place, both physical and metaphorical. For in addition to reoccupying abandoned and misused territory, the practice of building *casitas* imparts identity to the urban landscape by rescuing images, *rescatando imágenes*, by alluding to the power of other places everybody recognizes, feels good about, and can identify with. "The house as word, as being basic to our values: space for our solitudes, refuge of remembrance, shield for disillusion" (Abad, 1992: 48).

Building *casitas* is an act of reterritorialization that affirms the power of culture in space while offering resistance to further de-territorialization by appropriating place in the urban environment. *Casitas* symbolically link the viewer to the values and meanings evoked, and "cross the borders of dreams and friendships" (Gómez-Peña, 1993), or, in the words of Said, is an act that asserts "belonging in and to a place, a people, a heritage" affirming the home created by a community of language.

*Casitas* become places to displaced people, new "urban bedouins" (Davis, 1992: 164) removed from other places. Perhaps they also become new *invented traditions* (Hobsbawm and Ranger, 1992), new segregated "public arenas" for the Other to congregate and cele-

brate self-identity in a city where their invisibility in the public discourse renders many of them non-personae, at best, or personae-non-grata, at worst, and where unifying and inclusive images of the urban narrative seem to be fading daily.

Puerto Rican migration patterns, furthermore, have been fundamental to the development of *casitas*. As one account has it,

> a permanent and restless traffic, a massive circulation of workers without fixed abodes or occupations, between Puerto Rico and a growing number of regional concentrations scattered throughout the U.S. Around the relatively stable core of each Puerto Rican community gravitate groups of fresh arrivals and contingents newly poised for departure. (Bonilla and Campos, 1981: 133)

Unlike immigrants of yesteryear, and as "colonial citizens," Puerto Ricans circulate freely between two spaces: colony and metropolis; thus circumventing or destroying traditional barriers associated with borders or *fronteras*. This condition has provided several consequent generations ongoing contact with "fresh" images of the *otra patria*, the "other country or homeland" provided fluidity in exchanging people, as well as culture and images.

> On the airbus . . . Puerto Ricans who are there but dream of being here . . . Puerto Ricans who are permanently installed in the wander-go-round between here and there and who must therefore informalize the trip, making it no more than a hop on a bus, though airborne, that floats over the creek to which the Atlantic Ocean has been reduced by the Puerto Ricans. A crossing over the Atlantic made simpler so as to return, go, return once more, a return fervently and loudly applauded whenever the airbus lands anew. (Sánchez, 1992)

Events in New York can instantly affect events in the island, as well as island happenings being able to impact what happens in a *Nueva York Barrio*, an experience articulated by Luis

Rafael Sánchez in *La Guagua Aérea*, the "air bus," where boundaries are continuously crossed and transformed, created and erased; where time is disordered – the before and after confuse their sequential logic – a "journey (that) goes not only from South to North, (but) from Spanish to English" (Gómez-Peña, 1993: 16); and where the commuting airplane becomes an agent linking contiguous social realities: Puerto Rico and *Nueva York* – thus East Harlem and *La Perla*, a shanty town in San Juan, become adjacent and culturally closer than East Harlem and Battery Park City.

This continuity/discontinuity and fluidity/rupture of space of the emerging Global Economy and its attendant World City, the city of discontinuity, chaos, and polarization, intersects the new economic structure, suggesting a functional and new spatial integration among cities, where traditional boundaries between Third World cities and the city in the Metropolis become ambiguous. Hence, *casita* builders, when introducing the *casita* language to *Nueva York*, do more than just provide places for the local neighborhood; they also release a new urban language, a Caribbean vernacular, to many the language of Third World *favelas*, squatters, shanties, *arrabales*, or *villas miserias*.[10]

To the outside world, the abiding message of the *casita* is one of shelter, a squatter's metaphor many find disturbing, particularly in the increasing presence of the wandering homeless in the most advanced and richest urban center in the world (Brown, 1993). The presence of *casitas* signals that the visual discourse of *favelas, arrabales, comunidades marginadas* – the destitute slums ringing the periphery of Third World cities – has its place in the urban vocabulary of the "developed" world alongside concocted theme parks, the places for the rich, the "dreamscapes of visual consumption" (Zukin, 1992). They also become "conquered space," where the "separation of the Puerto Rican Diaspora is defeated" (Abad, 1992). Behind their quaintness and charm, there is something ominous about the presence of *casitas* on the streets of New York City, something threatening to many, who may otherwise live in relative security.

Whether they instill fear or "joyful pride," *casitas* provide a new fascination to the visual texture of the New York landscape: a language that breaks with traditional cultural models usually associated with European-derived architectural and urban forms and reweaves the otherwise ordinary modern industrial city with what many would consider "traditional" or premodern cultural images, images made possible by the spaces created in the new emerging "borderlands" of the postmodern city.

## CASITAS AND THE PUERTO RICAN DIASPORA

As we approach the end of the twentieth century accelerated migration of people of Hispanic origins to the US and the cultural impact they are having represent opportunities to be explored. The resulting diaspora of the millions of Puerto Ricans, Cubans, Mexicans, Dominicans, and others presents challenges that must be addressed. However and wherever this diaspora is constructed and interconnects (most likely in the many urban centers of the US like New York, Los Angeles, Miami, and Chicago), it will be a difficult and arduous process, and one that will be opposed by many. As Gómez-Peña puts it, the contemporary Latin American experience in the United States, framed by diaspora, economic despair, police harassment, cultural exclusion, and aesthetic misunderstanding, is of epic dimensions (Gómez-Peña, 1993: 16).

In an island-nation like Puerto Rico, which just "celebrated" 500 years of colonialism, a new century/millennium brings forth the "identity issue" to a new and higher level of complexity. More than one third of all Puerto Ricans live outside of Puerto Rico. New York is home to the largest urban concentration of Puerto Ricans anywhere, followed by San Juan, Chicago, and possibly Ponce. Increasingly, Puerto Rican immigrants from earlier periods return to the island to retire. Many are not Spanish-dominant and their children require SSL (Spanish as a Second Language) in the school system.

Circular migration continually exchanges people and refreshes cultural images. Thus, *casitas* continue to be summoned by Puerto Ricans, in both the island and New York, as metaphors of places past. In the island, their rebirth may have been ignited by economic and cultural forces. Responding to worsening and divergent economic conditions, for example, lumber companies repackaged the balloon-frame wooden house as additions to the homes of economically strapped urban dwellers, and to the small group benefiting from these changes and who could afford them for their leisure, as second homes or *casas de campo* nostalgic references to yesterday's *quintas*.[11]

This occurrence has brought peculiar typologies across island *urbanizaciones* as well as in poor rural areas, where *casitas* are built atop flat-roofed concrete tract housing. To those who can afford the second home in a micro farm in exurbia in the interior of what has become an almost totally urban island, the *casita* brings them closer to their identity as *Puertorriqueños* in a rapidly changing world and island. To the others who recall them in New York, *casitas* grant their builders, like Jaran, the power of place and culture, in a city that has yet to offer many of them acceptance and place for their identity, the sense they belong and are accepted.

> Give yourself a lift at this departure wherein the tropical aesthetic wants to strew starry rain over the city, over the Babel of spik talk. Travel in this mechanical rainbow where we can look and see New York! New York! through the sliding curtain. We bear the North as if the South did not exist when we return to repopulate the island, to decorate the island with whatchmacallits and the latest gadgets or ultra postmodern floral arrangements for ma's divine altar in Las Piedras. (Abad, 1992: 51)

## Notes

1   Building *casitas* is a collective effor of neighbors in different neighborhoods in New York City. Since recording of *casitas* began some ten years ago, many have been destroyed due to fire, or direct actions of the City of New York fearing they would be generalized as squatters' settlements. Villa Puerto Rico, one of the oldest *casitas* in the South Bronx, was rebuilt in 1991. *Casita Culture*, a video produced by Kathy Hukum for the Smithsonian Institution, records the building of Villa Puerto Rico.

2   The term "vernacular architecture" tends to oversimplify complex and different cultural expressions of a society. In Puerto Rico, like elsewhere, the transformation of a pre-Columbian habitat to a vernacular took different routes. Each was colored by a number of factors, including location and geography, i.e., rural vs. urban, coast vs. mountain; the economic/class status of the inhabitant; the colony/Metropolis relationship; and the development level of the Metropolis, i.e., technology, commercial/market relationships to other metropolises, etc. In the longer version of this work we look at the transformation of the Taino hut into the *casita*, a particular expression of Puerto Rican popular dwelling most common among the working classes and the poor.

The balloon-frame was invented in the early part of the nineteenth century in Chicago. Although Puerto Rico did not have direct trade with the United States during that period, the technology reached the island soon after, possibly during the second half of the nineteenth century. As elsewhere in the Third World, this wood technology had an everlasting impact on the vernacular architecture of each region. In the Caribbean each island vernacular was impacted differently, reflecting primarily the influence the Colonial Metropolis had on each, as well as the degree of economic development the island had reached by the nineteenth century.

3   In 1987 it was estimated that over 25% of all New Yorkers were poor; however, among Hispanics and African Americans the rate was 31.9% and 42.9% respectively. Poverty was also geographically uneven. In 1986,

while 25.8% of all renter households lived below the Federal poverty or near-poverty levels, in the Bronx, they represented 44.8%, 36.8% in Brooklyn, 20.5% in Queens, and 27.1% in Staten Island. (Source: *Housing Vacancy Report*, Michael Stegman, Department of Housing Preservation and Development, April 1988).

4    Dystopia is a hypothetical place, state, or situation in which conditions and the quality of life are dreadful. It is used here to infer an "inverted Utopia," or an anti-Utopia, where the most negative elements of urban living are concentrated.

5    See, for example, data by City Planning on the loss of population in New York. Places where the loss was greatest were those where Latinos and other non-whites lived.

6    During the past three decades, Puerto Ricans, African Americans, and other minorities have been displaced from key districts in the City to others of lesser economic value. Nevertheless, new arrivals, other Blacks from the Caribbean, and other Caribbean Latinos, i.e., from the Dominican Republic, and Asian/Asian Pacific peoples have repopulated other middle-class districts in the City.

7    There has been a small community of shanties in the Lower East Side for over five years. Margaret Morton, in her work, has identified the community as "Bushville." The name implies that the community emerged as a result of the Bush years in the White House. "Bushville" is used here in a similar manner to "Hooverville."

8    In 1993 the Museum of the City of New York, in collaboration with City Lore, published as short bulletin/catalogue titled "The New Immigrant" celebrating the multicultural heritage of the City for an exhibit called "Welcome to your Second Home," a look at the "new immigrants." The bulletin contains several articles on the different immigrant groups that have arrived to New York City in the recent past, and on the front page there is a photo with the caption "Playing dominos at a *casita* in East Harlem." The bulletin also contains a short article with another photo of another *casita* in the South Bronx. It is unfortunate that prestigious institutions like the Museum and City Lore still see Puerto Ricans as outsiders and not as American citizens.

9    As is true for other people of color, the contributions made by Puerto Ricans to the built environment has not been studied. In fact, for the new majority of New Yorkers – people of color and immigrants – the built environment of New York City has no apparent relationship to their history, i.e., they are guests in someone else's city. Except for a recent attempt by New York City's Landmarks Commission to begin to recognize important places in the South Bronx, Queens, and in Harlem, the City's preservation efforts have concentrated on the History of European descendants. Even those buildings being preserved in the Bronx have little association with the history of Puerto Ricans in the City.

10    During the month of August 1993, the City of New York destroyed a shanty, a.k.a. the Hill, which had been featured in the front page of the March 28, 1993, Sunday *New York Times Magazine*. The author wrote a letter to the editor criticizing the article's voyeur-like viewpoint and the lack of professional commitment of the article's writer, who made no effort to protect those she was featuring. In fact, the cover photo depicted a shack built years earlier by a couple of homeless Puerto Ricans living under the Brooklyn Bridge, which was demolished by the City shortly after the publication of the *Times* article.

11    During a 1991 visit to Puerto Rico, the author encountered an interesting and revealing occurrence. In the middle of the Plaza de Cabo Rojo, a very old town on Puerto Rico's southern coast, townspeople had placed an "authentic" vintage 1930 *casita*. A group of women seated on park benches nearby explained that there had just been a town festival celebrating Puerto Rican culture, and that when they were searching for a "universal symbol" of Puerto Rican culture, the *casita* won by acclamation. They found and rebuilt one in the middle of the *Plaza*.

# Bibliography

Abad, Celedonio (1992). "El Espacio Conquistado" in Museo del Barrio catalogue *La Casa de Todos Nosotros* for exhibit by artist Antonio Martorell. New York City.

Anderson, Benedict (1991). *Imagined Communities, Reflections on the Origin and Spread of Nationalism.* London: Verso.

Andreu Iglesias, César (1984). *Memoirs of Bernardo Vega. A Contribution to the History of the Puerto Rican Community in New York,* trans. Juan Flores. New York: Monthly Review Press.

Aponte-Parés, Luis (1990). "Casas y Bohios: Territorial Development and Urban Growth in XIX Century Puerto Rico," Ph.D. dissertation, Columbia University, New York.

—— (1988). "Housing and Puerto Ricans: In Search of Community," paper presented at New York City Project Conference of the Institute for Puerto Rican Policy, New York.

—— (1991). "What's Yellow and White and Has Land All Around it?," presentation made at People of Color in Architecture Conference, School of Architecture, Yale University, New Haven, Connecticut.

Berthelot, Jack, and Martine, Gaumé (1982). *Kaz Antiyé. Jan Moun Ka Rété. Caribbean Popular Dwelling.* Editions Perspectives Créoles, Point-à-Pitre, pp. 97–110.

Boddy, Trevor (1992). "Underground and Overhead: Building the Analogous City," in Michael Sorkin (ed.), *Variations on a Theme Park: The New American City and the End of Public Space.* New York: Noonday Press.

Bonilla, Frank and Campos, Ricardo (1981). "A Wealth of Poor: Puerto Ricans in the New Economic Order." *Daedalus,* 110: 133–76.

Boyer, Christine M. (1992). "The Imaginary Real World." *Assemblage,* 18: 115–27.

Brown, Patricia L. (1993). "The Architecture of Those Called Homeless." *Sunday New York Times,* March 28.

Colón, Jesus (1982). *A Puerto Rican in New York and Other Sketches.* New York: International Publishers.

Crawford, Margaret (1992). "The World in a Shopping Mall," in M. Sorkin (ed.), *Variations on a Theme Park.* New York: Noonday Press.

Davis, Mike (1992). "Fortress Los Angeles: The Militarization of Urban Space." in M. Sorkin, (ed.), *Variations on a Theme Park.* New York: Noonday Press.

Friedmann, John, and Wolff, Goetz (1992). "World City formation: an agenda for research and action," *International Journal of Urban and Regional Research,* 6/3 (Sept.): 309–44.

Gómez-Peña, Guillermo (1993). *Warrior for Gringostroika.* Minnesota: Graywolf Press.

Harris, Richard (1992). "The Geography of Employment and Residence in New York

since 1950," in John Mollenkopf and Manuel Castells, (eds), *Dual City: Restructuring New York.* New York: Sage.

Hobsbawm, Eric, and Ranger, Terence (1992). *The Invention of Tradition.* New York: Cambridge University Press.

King, Anthony D. (1991). *Urbanism, Colonialism, and the World Economy Cultural and Spatial Foundations of the World Urban System.* London: Routledge.

Newel Lewis, John (1983). *Ajoupa, Architecture of the Caribbean, Trinidad's Heritage.* Trinidad: J. Newel Lewis.

Norberg Schultz, Christian (1988). *Architecture, Meaning and Place.* New York: Rizzoli.

Oulette, Saurie (1993). "Information Age Lock out." *Utne Reader* (September/October).

Riley, Robert B. (1992). "Attachment to the Ordinary Landscape," in Irwin Altman and Setha M. Loe (eds) *Place Management* New York: Plenum Press

Rosenberg, Terry J. (1987). *Poverty in New York City: 1985–1990.* New York Community Service Society.

Sánchez, José R (1986). "Residual Work and Residual Shelter: Housing Puerto Rican Labor in New York City from World War II to 1983," in Rachel G Bratt, Chester Hartman, and Ann Meyerson (eds), *Critical Perspectives on Housing.* Philadelphia: Temple University Press.

Sánchez, Luis Rafael (1992). *La Guagua Aérea,* trans. Diana L. Velez. Museo del Barrio catalogue for exhibit, *La Casa de Todos Nosotros* by Antonio Martorell, New York City.

Sánchez-Korrol, Virginia (1994). *From Colonia to Community. The History of Puerto Ricans in New York City.* Berkeley: University of California Press.

Sassen, Saskia (1992). "The Informal Economy," in J. Mollenkopf and M. Castells, (eds), *Dual City.* New York: Sage.

Segre, Roberto (1985). "Continuidad y Renovacion de las Tradiciones Vernaculas en el Ambiente Caribeño Contemporane," in *Anales del Caribe,* 4/5, 1984–5. Centro de Estudios del Caribe, Casa de las Americas. El Vedado Ciudad de la Habana, Cuba.

Smith, Neil (1992). "New City, New Frontier: The Lower East Side as Wild, Wild West," in M. Sorkin (ed.), *Variations on a Theme Park.* New York: Noonday Press.

Stegman, Michael (1988). "Housing and Vacancy Report," Housing Preservation and Development Agency.

Walker, Richard A. (1978). "Two Sources of Uneven Development Under Advanced Capitalism: Spatial Differentiation and Capital Mobility," *Review of Radical Political Economics*, 10/3 (Fall).

Zukin, Sharon (1991). *Landscapes of Power: From Detroit to Disneyland.* Los Angeles: University of California Press.

—— (1992). "Postmodern urban landscapes: mapping culture and power," in *Modernity and Identity*, ed. Scott Lash and Jonathan Friedman (Oxford: Blackwell), 221–47.

# Caribbean Colonial Immigrants in the Metropoles: A Research Agenda

## Ramón Grosfoguel

This article is a proposal for a comparative study of the social, political, and economic conditions of colonial Caribbean immigrants in the metropoles. Specifically, I propose to compare the migration process, modes of incorporation, race and ethnic relations, state institutions and public policies affecting colonial Caribbean immigrant minorities in the metropoles: Puerto Ricans in the United States, Martinicans/Guadeloupeans in France, Surinamese/Dutch Antilleans in the Netherlands, and West Indians in England. This is important for understanding the differences and similarities between colonial Caribbean immigrants in Western European countries and the United States regarding race and ethnic relations, public policies toward these immigrants, and the meaning of citizenship.

A review of the academic literature concerning Puerto Rican migration shows how it is normally compared to the migration from other Caribbean nation-states or to the African American experience (Portes and Grosfoguel, 1994; Massey and Denton, 1989). Although this comparison has provided important insights, it has been insufficient for understanding the peculiarities of the Puerto Rican experience. Puerto Rican colonial migration cannot be reduced to that of migrants from Caribbean nation-states such as the Dominican Republic, Haiti, or Cuba. Migration from a Caribbean colony is significantly different from migration from a Caribbean peripheral nation-state. Contrary to Caribbean migrants from nation-states, Puerto Ricans are US citizens; their migration was organized by a colonial state; and was mostly comprised by the rural lower strata of the sending society (Centro de Estudios Puertorriqueños, 1979; Bonilla and Campos, 1985; Gray, 1966). The socioeconomic conditions of Puerto Ricans in the US are worse than those of many Caribbean immigrants from nation-states. Puerto Ricans are situated among the ethnic groups with the highest number of families living under the poverty level, the highest unemployment rates, and the lowest incomes (Portes and Grosfoguel, 1994).

Emigration patterns surprisingly similar to that of Puerto Rico have occurred in other parts of the Caribbean during the postwar era, namely, French, Dutch, and English Caribbean colonial migrations to the metropoles. They all share citizenship with the metropole; the migration was more or less organized/stimulated by the state; their class/social origin was more rural/unskilled than migrations from Caribbean nation-states; and they all form part of a world-systemic process of colonial labor migration to serve the needs of cheap labor in the core zones of the world economy during the postwar economic boom.

Rather than placing the Puerto Rican migration experience to the US in the spectrum of migration from Caribbean nation-states, it can be understood better in relation to the experience of other Caribbean colonial populations to their respective metropoles during the post-war era. The migration from Surinam (before independence)/Dutch Antilles to the Netherlands; the West Indies (before independence) to England; Martinique/Guadeloupe to France; and from Puerto Rico to the US are peculiar in that these migrants come from colonies of a new type, that is, "modern colonies" (Pierre-Charles, 1979). "Modern colonies," formed after the Second World War, as opposed to old colonies, share metropolitan citizenship, have democratic/civil rights, and receive large transfers from the metropolitan welfare state.

Despite the similarities in the socio-economic origin of these Caribbean colonial migrants, there are interesting differences regarding the modes of incorporation to the labor market, the social contexts of reception, and the cultural/racial dynamics in the metropoles. A comparison of Caribbean colonial migrations during the postwar period of 1945 through 1990 provides a unique opportunity to understand the different racial and social dynamics in France, England, the Netherlands and the United States. This represents an improved strategy to understand the peculiarities of the discrimination and disadvantages these immigrants have confronted. To this date no thorough comparison of the migration processes of these four colonial groups has been done.

## THE FORMATION OF MODERN COLONIES IN THE CARIBBEAN

After the war, symbolic geopolitical strategies became an important structuring logic of the core–periphery relationships in the world system. The defeat of the Nazis changed the geopolitical configuration of the world system. The bipolar division of the world between the Soviet Union and the United States, plus the emergence of newly independent countries in the periphery, were two crucial features that transformed the interstate system. The decline of colonial relations as the dominant means of core control of the periphery increased instability in the system. Both superpowers were afraid that the elites in

the newly independent countries might go with the other side. It is within this context that strategies of symbolic capital (Bourdieu, 1977) to gain "profits" of prestige and honor vis-à-vis their adversary emerged as a central feature of the world system.

Since the first meetings of the United Nations in San Francisco, the Soviet Union and the United States began the struggle to be the champion of decolonization. They accused each other of being a colonial power. The Soviets even raised the case of Puerto Rico to support its claims about American imperialism. It is within this context that we need to understand the political reforms that gave way to the emergence of modern colonies in the Caribbean. The first step was the formation of the Caribbean Commission. This was an international organization composed of core powers such as France, the Netherlands, the United States, and Great Britain. The Commission limited itself to economic and technical cooperation issues. This Commission became a showcase of the goodwill of the West toward the development of the "underdeveloped" world. As Dr H. R. van Houten, Chairman of the Seventh Annual Conference, said:

> In no international organization have I ever felt such an atmosphere of cooperation and goodwill and such a desire to respect the points of view of others and to try to obtain results satisfactory to everybody . . . this organization could serve as an example to many international organizations. Fourteen countries are cooperating to the best of their ability to create happiness and a better way of life for their people. Any person, traveling in this area, will have to agree that enormous results have been obtained. (*The Caribbean*, 2 [December 1957], p. 98)

Thus, after the war, the Caribbean became a laboratory of the core's policies for economic development of the periphery of the capitalist world economy and a showcase of their "goodwill" toward colonial people. The four colonial powers in the Caribbean pursued different alternative statutes for their colonies.

The British established a self-governing federation within an imperial Commonwealth community; the Dutch conceded autonomy; the French annexed the territories; and the US basically concealed its colonial relationship with the semi-autonomous "Estado Libre Asociado" or "Free Associated State."

Despite the diversity of status alternatives, by 1955 the largest of the British West Indies (Guyana, Trinidad, Barbados, and Jamaica), the French West Indies, the Dutch Caribbean, and the United States Caribbean all formed what are called "modern colonies" (Pierre-Charles, 1979). "Modern colonies" are different from classical colonies. In the "modern colonies" the colonial population enjoys civil/social rights; universal suffrage; access to metropolitan state capital through welfare programs or budget transfers; high wages; mass consumption; modern forms of labor processes which leave behind agrarian plantations; and free labor mobility between the colony and the metropole. It can be seen as a form of neo-colonialism without full independence or as a form of colonialism with access to some of the benefits enjoyed by the metropolitan populations. Modern colonies are neither classical colonies nor independent states. A crucial aspect for the emergence of modern colonies was the extension or legitimation of metropolitan citizenship to the colonies. These institutional reforms legitimized or facilitated the transformation of classical colonialism to modern colonialism.

The importance of these changes for our topic is their effect on the integration of the peripheral labor market, creating a "migratory field" between the colony and the metropole. As citizens of the metropole, labor from "modern colonies" had free access to the core labor market. This coincided with a postwar world economic expansion. The upper mobility of white workers to better-paid jobs had created a "labor shortage" at the bottom of the core labor market. The entrance of colonial subjects to the core labor market was not perceived neutrally. After a long history of colonialism, ideological stereotypes in the imaginary of the white dominant groups constructed these immigrants as inferior,

criminals, lazy, dumb, etc. Thus, as racialized colonial subjects, they entered the metropole to perform menial and low-wage jobs.

## THEORETICAL AND HISTORICAL RATIONALE

Recent historical-structuralist approaches to migration address the diverse class composition of migrant populations. This has helped deconstruct the assumption of prior debates, namely that all Caribbean immigrants are poor and illiterate. The historical-structuralist approach also addresses the socioeconomic conditions that explain why certain countries send more migrants than others. According to this approach, Caribbean migrants come mainly from peripheral societies where imbalances were created due to US foreign capital penetration, and are mainly from urban middle sectors of the sending countries (Grasmuck and Pessar, 1991; Portes and Truelove, 1987; Grasmuck, 1985; Bray, 1984; Portes, 1978). This literature is a marked advance relative to the human capital approach and the push–pull theories which conceptualize the migration process as a result of the rational calculation of individual actors in a given national unit. Portes (1978) correctly states that the migration process occurs within a single overarching capitalist world economy wherein world-systemic processes beyond the actors' control condition the migration process. However, the problem of this approach is its overemphasis on the economic aspects of the core-periphery relationship, overlooking the role of the inter-state system as a crucial structuring mechanism of the migration process.

All the Caribbean postwar outmigration correlated to efforts for moving Caribbean economies away from sugar-plantation production toward industrialization, mining, or tourism. The role of foreign capital penetration in the process of development is considered a major cause of international migration in the Caribbean (Sassen-Koob, 1988; Grasmuck, 1985; Maingot, 1992; Portes, 1978). However, if we look more carefully at postwar Caribbean outmigration patterns, although all the islands share the same patterns of transnational capital penetration triggering outmigration, there are major differences among the islands in both the amount and the class/sectoral composition of the migrants, depending on the different legal-political incorporation of the peripheral state within the interstate system.

The spatial/geographical configuration of the Caribbean constrained the possibilities of outmigration. To migrate from an island is in general more difficult than to migrate from a peripheral country that shares a border with a core country (e.g., Mexico). Thus, Caribbean people are more vulnerable to the legal-political institutional context of the interstate system at the time of migration. Whether a given society's incorporation within the inter-state system is that of a modern colony or a nation-state has crucial consequences on the specificity of its migration process in terms of

quantity and class composition. Those societies with a colonial legal-political incorporation (e.g. Puerto Rico, Martinique, Guadeloupe, Dutch Antilleans, and Surinam and Jamaica before independence) have a proportionally larger migration than those societies with a nation-state incorporation (e.g., Dominican Republic, Haiti, and Cuba) (see Table 1).

Moreover, the migration from colonial societies is comprised mainly of rural lower strata while that of nation-states consists of urban middle sectors. The middle-sector migration from nation-states includes mostly educated and skilled workers with household incomes that are higher than the average income of the sending country (Bray, 1984, 1987; Grasmuck and Pessar, 1991; Stepick and Portes, 1986; DeWind and Kinley III, 1988; Foner, 1979, 1983; Kosofsky, 1981; Portes and Bach, 1985; Pedraza-Bailey, 1985; Palmer, 1974). On the other hand, the migra-

---

*Sources for Table 1 (opposite):*

1    US Bureau of the Census, Persons of Hispanic Origin for the United States: 1990, special tabulation prepared by the Ethnic and Hispanic Branch, Washington, DC; 1990 Census of Population, General Population Characteristics, Puerto Rico. US Government Printing Office: Washington DC; 1980 Census of Population, General Population Characteristics, Puerto Rico. US Government Printing Office: Washington DC.

2    Rath, 1983; Bovenkerk, 1987; OECD, Trends in International Migration, 1993 Annual Report, table II. 17, p.85; United Nations World Population Chart-1990, Population Division, United Nationa: New York.

3    Condon and Ogden, 1991; Freeman, 1987; Valentin-Marie, 1993.

4    Condon and Ogden, 1991; Freeman, 1987; Valentin-Marie, 1993.

5    I am including in this category Aruba and the Netherland Antilles. OECD, Trends in International Migration, 1993 Annual Report, Table II. 17, p.85; United Nations World Population Chart-1990, Population Division, United Nations: New York.

6    US Bureau of the Census, Ancestry of the Population in the United States, special tabulation prepared by the Ethnic and Hispanic Branch, Report CPH-L-89, Washington DC: US Department of Commerce. Estimates are that people with Jamaican ancestry are around 65% of the 499,964 total Black Caribbean Population in Great Britain. The total Black Caribbean Population, Table 6 of the 1991 Census, Ethnic Group and Country of Birth, Great Britain, vol. 2, London: HMSO; Maingot, 1992.

7    US Bureau of the Census, Ancestry of the Population in the United States, special tabulation prepared by the Ethnic and Hispanic Branch, Report CPH-L-89, Washington, DC: US Department of Commerce; Maingot, 1992.

8    US Bureau of the Census, Ancestry of the Population in the United States, special tabulation prepared by the Ethnic and Hispanic Branch, Report CPH-L-89, Washington, DC: US Department of Commerce; Maingot, 1992.

9    US Bureau of the Census, Persons of Hispanic Origin for the United States: 1990, special tabulation prepared by the Ethnic and Hispanic Branch, Washington, DC; Maingot, 1992.

**Table 1**  Caribbean migrants in the metropoles

| Country | Year | Home population | Migrants living in the Metropolis | Metropolis | Migrants in the metropolis as percentage of home population |
|---------|------|-----------------|-----------------------------------|------------|------------------------------------------------------------|
| Puerto Rico[1] | 1980 | 3,196,520 | 2,014,000 | USA | 63% |
|  | 1990 | 3,522,037 | 2,651,815 |  | 75% |
| Suriname[2] | 1975 | 365,000 | 150,000 | Netherlands | 41% |
|  | 1980 | 356,000 | 176,000 |  | 49% |
|  | 1990 | 422,000 | 228,722 |  | 54% |
| Martinique[3] | 1982 | 326,717 | 95,704 | France | 29% |
|  | 1990 | 359,572 | 109,616 |  | 30% |
|  |  |  | 175,200 (ancestry) |  | 48.7% |
| Guadeloupe[4] | 1982 | 328,400 | 87,024 | France | 26% |
|  | 1990 | 386,987 | 101,934 |  | 26% |
|  |  |  | 161,806 (ancestry) |  | 42% |
| Dutch Antillean[5] | 1990 | 248,000 | 75,722 | Netherlands | 30.5% |
| Jamaica[6] | 1990 | 2,404,000 | 435,024 (ancestry) | USA | 18% |
|  |  |  | 685,024 (includes illegals) |  | 28% |
|  |  |  | 325,000 (ancestry) | England | 13.5% |
|  |  |  | 1,010,024 | USA + England | 42% |
| Haiti[7] | 1990 | 6,349,000 | 289,521 (ancestry) | USA | 4.5% |
|  |  |  | 689,521 (includes illegals) |  | 10.8% |
| Dominican Republic[8] | 1990 | 6,948,000 | 520,151 (ancestry) | USA | 7.4% |
|  |  |  | 745,151 (includes illegals) |  | 10.7% |
| Cuba[9] | 1983 | 9,771,000 | 910,867 | USA | 9.3% |
|  | 1990 | 10,500,000 | 1,053,197 |  | 10% |

tion from Caribbean colonial societies has a larger representation of unskilled workers with low educational levels who come from low-income households. For instance, Puerto Rico, Martinique, Guadeloupe, Jamaica (before independence), the Dutch Antilles and Surinam (before independence), not only had the largest number of migrants to the metropolitan centers as a percentage of the home population (see Table 1), but also their class composition was more rural and/or lower class (Anselin, 1979; Condon and Ogden, 1991; Falcón, 1990; Bovenkerk, 1979, 1987; Freeman, 1987; Bach, 1985; Levine, 1987; Rath, 1983; Centro de Estudios Puertorriqueños, 1979; Koslofsky, 1981; Roberts and Mills, 1958). Puerto Rico, Surinam, and Martinique are the most extreme cases where the agrarian question became obsolete with the massive exportation of the peasantry to the mainland's urban centers (Grosfoguel, 1994).

Jamaica is an interesting case that illustrates the relationship between migration, the colonial insertion, and depeasantization in the Caribbean. During the 1953–62 period, while Jamaica was still a British colony, 179,049 Jamaicans migrated to Great Britain, of which a large number were unemployed rural workers, urban unskilled laborers, and semi-proletariats (Koslofsky, 1981; Robert and Mills, 1958). After Jamaican independence in 1962 until 1980, approximately 108,843 people legally migrated to the US (Bray, 1987: 85). Due to the 1965 US Immigration Act restraining poor and unskilled migrants, they were mainly of urban middle sectors (Foner, 1979; Palmer, 1974). Therefore, the Jamaican case illustrates how a colonial or nation-state legal-political insertion determines the volume of migrants and their class origin.

Outmigration of lower classes and/or rural population from nation-states like the Dominican Republic has limitations. From 1968 to 1980 an estimated 268,770 middle- and upper-class Dominican immigrants had established in the US (Grasmuck and Pessar, 1991: 22). As David Bray states:

Unlike Jamaica, the Dominican Republic

has not been a colony since the nineteenth century. Hence entry of Dominican citizens into the United States has always been regulated by immigration laws specifically designed to exclude the poor and unskilled. Although many of the rural and urban poor would clearly migrate if they could, it is difficult and expensive to enter the United States illegally from an island . . . those who did leave the Dominican Republic were mostly middle and upper class. (Bray, 1987: 88–9)

One of the most important aspects of colonial migration is the shared citizenship allowing migrants to have direct access to their metropole. As a result, they need no visas to enter the core country and have access to the core's welfare state, making migration more accessible to the poorest sectors of the colonial population and viable for larger numbers, as opposed to the migration from peripheral nation-states where citizenship is not shared with a core country and monetary solvency is a prerequisite to being granted a visa.

Another distinct feature of Caribbean colonial migration is that it was organized, in different degrees, by political elites through state institutions as a so-called "solution" to the unemployment problem or induced through direct labor recruitment (Maldonado-Denis, 1976; Maldonado, 1979; Condon and Ogden, 1991; Koot, 1988; Bovenkerk, 1987; Harris, 1993). For example, the Puerto Rican colonial administration created the Migration Division under the Department of Labor. This Division served as an intermediary between US businessmen and Puerto Rican workers. They identified labor shortages and recruited Puerto Rican labor to fill the need. Inspired by the Puerto Rican example, the French state also fostered an organized migration in the French Caribbean (Anselin, 1979, 42). They created the BUMIDOM (*Bureau pour le développement des migrations intéressant les départments d'outre-mer*) which served a similar role to that of the Migration Division. The BUMIDOM hired thousands of Martinican and Guadeloupean workers as cheap labor for the metropolitan labor market. In Curazao and Barbados, the colonial administration also stimulated the recruitment of workers by metropolitan industries as a "solution" to unemployment (Koot, 1988, 249; Harris, 1993: 40, 42–3).

Overall, the migration experiences of colonial peoples such as the Martinicans, Surinamese/Dutch Antilleans, West Indians, and Puerto Ricans have more in common when compared to the migration processes from Caribbean nation-states. The contribution of this comparative study would be to compare the situation of the Puerto Ricans in the US to that of the structurally similar cases of Caribbean colonial migrations in Western Europe rather than continuing to place them within the context of migrations from nation-states.

The interesting question is: Given the similar class, social and political-legal background, what are the similarities and differences among them once they are incorporated into the metropolitan societies? This comparative study provides an opportunity to understand the peculiarities of the disadvantages and discrimination confronted by colonial migrants in their metropoles. Moreover, this comparative approach can offer insights for the understanding of contemporary controversial issues such as the different meanings and concepts of citizenship; the dynamics of global cities; and national identity, race, and ethnicity as they apply to France, England, the Netherlands, and the United States.

## BRIEF COMPARATIVE SOCIO-DEMOGRAPHIC DATA

Although all Caribbean colonial migrants are incorporated as cheap labor in their respective metropoles, the social and economic conditions are not the same for each of these ethnic groups. As can be seen in Table 2, there are interesting differences in the Caribbean colonial migrants' modes of incorporation to the metropoles' labor markets. The figures in this table reflect different measurement criteria for each country. However, they can give a rough estimate of the relative position of each ethnic group in their respective host society.

The French Caribbeans stand out vis-à-vis other groups in terms of unemployment rates. Their unemployment rates are similar to the French national average. The Martinican unemployment rate is even lower than the French national average. However, this is not the case for the other colonial Caribbean migrants. The Puerto Ricans, Surinamese, Dutch Antilleans, and British Afro-Caribbeans have unemployment rates that are twice or more than the national average. The Puerto Ricans' unemployment rate is double the United States' national average while the Surinamese, Dutch Antillean, and West Indian migrants' unemployment rates are more than double their respective national averages. The labor force participation rates show a different pattern. The Puerto Rican and Dutch Antillean participation rate is lower than their respective national averages, while the other ethnic groups have higher participation rates than their respective national averages. The French Antilleans and British Afro-Caribbeans have a much higher participation rate than the French and British national average. The Surinamese have a slightly higher participation rate than the Dutch national average. It is important to mention that for 40 percent of the Surinamese and the Dutch Antilleans in the Netherlands the principal source of income is state assistance, as opposed to 19 percent for the Dutch national average (Pennix et. al., 119). Thus, the Surinamese and Dutch Antillean labor force participation rates might include high numbers of underemployed workers.

In terms of occupational characteristics, the majority of the French Antillean labor force is incorporated as public employees and only 12 percent are in manufacturing. This contrasts strongly with the French national average, which is 34 percent in public employment and 23 percent in manufacturing jobs. It is important to mention that of the four categories of the French "*agents de la fonction publique*," the French Antilleans are mainly located at the bottom of the ladder in terms of salaries,

**Table 2**   Socio-demographic characteristics of colonial Caribbean migrants in the metropoles

| Colonial population | Unemployment rate % | Participation rate % | Government worker % | Manufacture % | Owner occupier % | Private rented tenant % | Public tenant % | Dweller in main urban centers % |
|---|---|---|---|---|---|---|---|---|
| Martinican | 10.8 | 78 | 55 | 11 | 27 | 25 | 47 | 72 Parisian region (Ile-de-France) |
| Guadeloupean | 12.2 | 77 | 53 | 12 | 26 | 26 | 48 | 75 |
| France | 11.1 | 55 | 34 | 23 | 54 | 25 | 21 | 19 |
| Puerto Rican | 12.4 | 60.4 | 18.4 | 20 | 26 | 74 (rent) | | 35 New York Metro-politan Region |
| United States | 6.3 | 65 | 15.1 | 17.6 | 50 | 50 (rent) | | 7 |
| British Afro-Caribbean | 19 | 73 | — | 17 | 53 | 4 | 34 | 58 Greater London |
| Great Britain | 9.2 | 61 | 8.8 | 18 | 66 | 7 | 21 | 12 |
| Surinamese | 19 | 62 | — | 43 | 14 | 13 | 70 | 59 Randstad Cities |
| Dutch Antillean | 16 | 57 | — | 27 | 16 | 17 | 65 | 32 |
| The Netherlands | 7 | 60 | — | 20 | 43 | 14 | 40 | 13 |

*Sources*: Claude-Valentin Marie, *Les Populations des DOM-TOM nees et originaires, résidant en France métropolitaine, Recensement de la population de 1990* (Paris: INSEE, mars 1993); *Recensement général de la population de 1990, loge-ments-population-emploi, Évolutions 1975–1982–1990, regions-départements, France* (Paris: INSEE, 1991); *Recensement général de population de 1990, population-activité-ménages, La France et ses régions, France* (Paris INSEE, 1992); *1991 Census, Ethnic Group and Country of Birth, Great Britain*, Vol. 1 (London: HMSO, 1993); *1991 Census, Ethnic Group and Country of Birth, Great Britain*, Vol 2 (London: HMSO, 1993); *1990 Census of Population, Persons of Hispanic Origin in the United States* (Washington, DC: US Government Printing Office, August 1993); *Centraal Bureau voor de Statistiek, De leefsituatie van Surinamers en Antillianen in Nederland 1985*, Deel 1: eerste uitkomstem ('s-Gravenhage; Staatsuitgeverij, 1986); Centraal Bureau voor de Statistiek, *De leefsituatie van Surinamers en Antillanen in Nederland 1985*, Deel 2: eerste uitkomsten ('s-Gravenhage: Staatsuitgeverij, 1988); T. J. M. Reubsaet and J. A, Kropman, *Beter opgeleide Antillianen op de Nederlandse arbeidsmarkt* ('s-Gravenhage: Ministerie van Sociale Zaken en Werkgelegenhid [INT], 1985); T. J. M. Reubsaet, J. A. Kropman, and L. M. van Muiler, *Surimaamse migranten in Nederland, deel 2, De positie van Surinamers in de Nederlandse samenleving* (Nijmegen: Instituut voor Toegepaste Sociale Wetenschappen, 1982); T. J. M. and K. J. A. Kropman, *Surinaamse migranten in Nederland; her vetigings- en spreidingsbeleid* (Nijmegen Instituut voor Toegepaste Sociale Wetenschappen, 1982).

benefits, and working conditions. Around 75 percent of the French Antillean public workers are classified in the C and D categories as opposed to 46 percent for the total of French workers in this sector (Marie, 1986: 4). French Antilleans are generally clerks, janitors, drivers, auxiliary nurses, and post-office workers in the French public administration.

The British Afro-Caribbean labor force is employed in manufacturing almost equally to Great Britain's national average. For public employees we have no national data available for Afro-Caribbeans. However, it has been documented that the Afro-Caribbeans have made progress in public administration white-collar jobs. In Greater London 18 percent of their jobs were in public administration, compared to 17 percent for white workers (Cross and Waldinger, 1992: 166). The rest of the ethnic groups show a different pattern. The Puerto Ricans, Dutch Antilleans, and Surinamese are overrepresented in manufacturing jobs. The Puerto Ricans have more public jobs than the United States national average. Probably, this is due to their over-representation in urban areas. The Surinamese have the highest percentage of their labor force in manufacturing jobs, with 43 percent as opposed to the Netherlands national average of 20 percent.

Compared to the national averages of Western European countries and the United States, none of the Caribbean colonial migrants show high percentages of home ownership. Of the Caribbean colonial migrants, the British Caribbeans are the ones with the highest level of owner-occupied households. This contrasts with their situation in the 1970s when the majority of the British Afro-Caribbeans were public housing tenants. This transition may be due to the privatization of public housing during the Thatcher administration. However, these houses purchased by West Indians were council houses in bad condition (Brown, 1984: 71–8). In terms of housing tenure, the French Antilleans, British Afro-Caribbeans, Dutch Antilleans, and Surinamese show high percentages of people living in public housing, amounts far above their respective national averages. It is well known that the Netherlands and France have an important social housing program (Dieleman, 1994; Choay et. al. 1985: 295–304; Preteceille, 1973). And at least until the late 1970s, before the Thatcher administration, so did Great Britain. The figures for public housing for the United States are not available. However, it is well known that, compared to Western European societies, the United States has never had significant public housing programs (Keith, 1973). The United States has relied on private housing as the main source of housing development.

All Caribbean colonial migrants are geographically concentrated in the metropoles' world cities. The French Antilleans are concentrated in the Parisian region better known as Ile-de-France. Most Surinamese and Dutch Antilleans live in the Randstad region which is an urban network connecting the largest four cities in the Netherlands: Amsterdam, Utrecht, Rotterdam, and The Hague. The majority of British West Indians are concentrated in Greater London. One-third of Puerto Ricans live in the New York metropolitan region.

In terms of housing segregation, the Dutch and French cases more effectively disperse these ethnic populations while Puerto Ricans and British Afro-Caribbeans are highly concentrated in urban ghettos (Ammersfoort, 1992; Hamnett, 1994; Body-Gendrot, 1993, 1994; Ratcliffe, 1988; Brown, 1984; Massey and Denton, 1989). Nevertheless, the communities of Caribbean colonial migrants in France and the Netherlands have the potential of becoming ghettos. The Parisian *banlieue* area called Seine-Saint-Denis and the area called Bijlmermeer in Amsterdam concentrate high numbers of migrant workers. Around 20 percent of all the French Antilleans living in Paris are concentrated in Seine-Saint-Denis (Marie, 1993). Approximately one-third of all Surinamese living in Amsterdam live in Bijlmermeer (Ammersfoort, 1992). Recent reforms, shifting social regulation in favor of market regulation of housing provisions in the Netherlands, and the increased racist demands undermining the situation of immigrants in France could lead to the formation of an underclass and the emergence of ghettos. The more the welfare state becomes inscribed in "us and them" racist discourses, the greater is the possibility of cuts in welfare programs. Puerto Ricans in cities such as New York, Chicago, and Philadelphia live segregated in ghettos. Similarly, many West Indians concentrated in Greater London and Birmingham are also segregated in ghettos (Brown, 1984; Rex and Tomlinson, 1979).

What accounts for the differences among the modes of incorporation of Caribbean colonial migrants to their respective metropoles? Why do the French Antilleans have similar unemployment rates and participation rates to the French national average? Why did the Surinamese and Dutch Antilleans show similar or worse economic conditions than the British Afro-Caribbeans and the Puerto Ricans, but do not experience the ghettoization they have? What makes the British and American social systems produce ghettos such as New York's Spanish Harlem, North Philadelphia's Puerto Rican "*barrio*," or the inner London boroughs such as Hackney and Lambeth? What are the prospects for the same occurring in France and the Netherlands? How does the re-emergence of xenophobic and racist discourses against immigrants in Western Europe as well as in the United States affect the future of each of these ethnic groups? What are the differences in the racist discourses of each metropolitan society and how do these differences create important nuances in the peculiar incorporation of each Caribbean ethnic group? What are the social relations of Caribbean colonial immigrants with other ethnic groups? How do the different political and cultural definitions of citizenship affect the incorporation of these Caribbean metropolitan citizens? What changes are occurring in definitions of citizenship in each metropole and how could these changes affect Caribbean colonial migrants? These are complex questions that cannot be answered by looking at a single variable, but rather require an interdisciplinary, world-historical, and multidimensional approach.

## RESEARCH STRATEGY

The migration process can be analytically divided into four subprocesses listed below. The first two are related to the origins and institutional frameworks of the migration experience which explain the historical-structural processes that produced the emigration from the sending country. The last two treat the context of reception and the cultural/discursive impact which address the process of incorporation into the receiving society. These four aspects can serve as a framework to compare Caribbean colonial migrations to the metropoles after World War Two.

**A   Origins:** What are the global capitalist accumulation and geopolitical processes that explain the postwar massive labor migration of the modern colonies to their respective metropoles? What was the rationale for the reforms that transformed these old colonies into "modern colonies" after the Second World War? What were the similarities and differences in their process of transformation into "modern colonies"? How do these "modern colonies" differ from Caribbean nation-states? What was the relationship between the emergence of these "modern colonies" and the massive labor migration experienced after 1950? What are the consequences for the migration flows of the incorporation of the Dutch and the French Caribbean to the European community? What are the race and ethnic differences between the four colonial migrations to be studied?

**B   Institutional framework:** Contrary to the migration from Caribbean nation-states, the migration of these colonial populations was encouraged and institutionally organized by the colonial and/or metropolitan state. Which state institutions and policies were created or were involved in these colonial migrations? How did they differ for each colony? What facilities and regulations were implemented to enable the transportation and the job hiring process of the migrants?

**C   Context of reception:** Once the colonial migrants arrived at their metropolis, how were they received by the core state, public opinon, and the dominant ethnic group? Was their reception favorable or were they discriminated against? Were there historical changes in their reception? What were the specific state policies toward each of these colonial peoples? What kind of rights did they have/not have as citizens of the metropolitan society? Did certain metropolitan states have more successful public policies than others in terms of facilitating the incorporation of these groups into the host societies? How were the migrants incorporated into the labor market? What changes occurred in their labor market incorporation after the 1973 world capitalist crisis? Are women and men incorporated differently into the metropolitan society? What are the dominant features of their household structure?

**D    Discourses and cultural Impact:** What are the discourses of the dominant white ethnic groups and of the metropolitan state used to explain the poverty, difficulties, or disadvantages confronted by these colonial populations? How do racist practices and discourses differ from one society to another, and how have they affected Caribbean colonial immigrants? What are the discourses and strategies articulated by these oppressed colonial peoples in their struggles against poverty and/or discrimination? Are they claiming social equity and cultural rights as a minority group or are they claiming equal treatment as metropolitan citizens? What are the different definitions of citizenship? What is the relationship between these colonial peoples and immigrant groups from peripheral nation-states? Is there solidarity or tension among these groups? Have Caribbean colonial immigrants assimilated into the mainstream language and culture, have they remained insulated, or have their practices been transformed into a border or hybrid culture?

## FINAL COMMENT

This is a call for an expansion of our research agenda. Studies about Puerto Rican migration to the US need a more comparative and global framework. Our experience is different from immigrants coming from nation-states. However, it is not as unique as we usually tend to think. Caribbean colonial migrations to the European metropoles during the postwar era experienced processes similar to the Puerto Rican migration to the US. We have a lot in common and much to learn from this comparison. Due to the colonial relationship between these Caribbean islands and their respective metropoles, the communication between the Caribbean colonial populations as well as between academics has been very poor. We need to break these colonial barriers. Apart from the research topics outlined above, there are other important comparative themes, such as return migration, educational attainment, and health conditions. These questions cannot be answered by a single researcher. This is an open invitation for a transnational research agenda.

## Bibliography

Ammersfoot, H. van (1992) "Ethnic residential patterns in a welfare state: Lessons from Amsterdam, 1970–1990." *New Community*, 18: 439–56.

Anselin, Alain (1979). *L'emigration antillaise en France: Du Bantoustan au Ghetto.* Paris: Éditions Anthropos.

Bach, Robert (1985). "Political Frameworks for International Migration," in Steven S. Sanderson (ed.), *The Americas in the New International Division of Labor.* New York: Holmes and Meier.

Body-Gendrot, Sophie (1993). *Ville et Violence.* Paris: Presses Universitaires de France.

Body-Gendrot, Sophie (1994). "Immigration: la rupture sociale et ses limites. *le Débat,* 80 (mai–août): 168–74.

Bonilla, Frank, and Ricardo, Campos (1985). "Evolving Patterns of Puerto Rican Migration," in Steven S. Sanderson (ed.), *The Americas in the New International Division of Labor.* New York: Holmes and Meier.

Bourdieu, Pierre (1977). *Outline of a Theory of Practice.* Cambridge: Cambridge University Press.

Bovenkerk, Frank (1979). "The Netherlands," in

Ronald E. Krane (ed.), *International Labor Migration in Europe*. New York: Praeger.

—— (1987). "Caribbean Migration to the Netherlands: From Elite to Working Class," in Barry B. Levine (ed.), *The Caribbean Exodus*. New York: Praeger.

Bray, David (1984). "Economic Development: The Middle Class and International Migration in the Dominican Republic." *International Migration Review*, 18/2: 217–36.

—— (1987). "Industrialization, Labor Migration and Employment Crises: A Comparison of Jamaica and the Dominican Republic," in Richard Tadarnico (ed.), *Crises in the Caribbean Basin*. Beverley Hills, CA: Sage Publications.

Brown, Colin (1984). *Black and White Britain: the Third PSI Survey*. London: Heinemann.

Centro de Estudios Puertorriqueños (1979). *Labor Migration under Capitalism: The Puerto Rican Experience*. New York: Monthly Review Press.

Choay, Françoise, Brun, Jacques, and Roncayolo, Marcel (1985). "Production de la ville," in Georges Duby (ed) *Histoire de la France urbaine*. Paris: Seuil.

Condon, Stephanie A., and Ogden, Phillip E. (1991). "Emigration from the French Caribbean: the Origins of an Organized Migration." *International Journal of Urban and Regional Research*, 15/4 (September): 505–23.

Cross, Malcolm, and Waldinger, Roger (1987). "Migrants, Minorities, and the Ethnic Division of Labor," in Susan S. Fainstein, Ian Gordon, and Michael Harloe (eds), *Divided Cities*. Oxford: Blackwell.

DeWind, Josh, and Kinley, David H. III (1988). *Aiding Migration: The Impact of International Development Assistance on Haiti*. Boulder, CO, and London: Westview Press.

Dieleman, Frans M. (1994). "Social Rented Housing: Valuable Asset or Unsustainable Burden?" *Urban Studies*, 3: 447–63.

Falcón, Luis Nieves (1990). "Migration and Development: The Case of Puerto Rico". Economic Development Working Papers No. 18, Wilson Center: Washington, DC.

Foner, Nancy (1979). "West Indians in New York City and London: A Comparative Analysis." *International Migration Review*, 13/2: 284–97.

—— (1983). "Jamaican Migrants: A Comparative Analysis of the New York and London Experience," Occasional Papers No. 36, Center For Latin American and Caribbean Studies at New York University.

Freeman, Gary P. (1987). "Caribbean Migration to

Britain and France: From Assimilation to Selection," in Barry B. Levine (ed.), *The Caribbean Exodus*. New York: Praeger.

Grasmuck, Sherri (1985). "The Consequences of Dominican Urban Outmigration for National Development: The Case of Santiago," in Steven E. Sanderson (ed.), *The Americas in the New International Division of Labor*. New York: Holmes and Meier.

Grasmuck, Sherri, and Pessar, Patricia (1991). *Between Two Islands: Dominican International Migration*. Berkeley: University of California Press.

Gray, Lois Spier (1966). "Economic Incentives to Labor Mobility: The Puerto Rican Case," Ph. D. dissertation. Columbia University.

Grosfoguel, Ramón (1994). "Depeasantization and Agrarian Decline in the Caribbean," in Philip McMichael (ed.), *Food and Agricultural Systems in the World Economy*. Orlando, FL: Greenwood Press.

Hamnett, Chris (1994). "Social Polarization in Global Cities: Theory and Evidence." *Urban Studies*, 31/3 (April): 401–23.

Harris, Clive (1993). "Post-war Migration and the Industrial Reserve Army," in Winston James and Clive Harris (eds) *Inside Babylon: The Caribbean Diaspora in Britain*. London: Verso.

Keith, Nathaniel (1973). *Politics and the Housing Crisis since 1930*. New York: Universe Books.

Koot, William (1988). "Emigración de las Antillas Holandesas hacia los Paises Bajos. Relaciones de Dependencia," in Gerard Pierre-Charles (ed.), *Capital Transnacional y Trabajo en el Caribe*. México: Instituto de Investigaciones Sociales.

Koslofsky, J. (1981). "Going Foreign: Causes of Jamaican Migration," In *NACLA*, 15/1.

Levine, Barry B. (1987). "The Puerto Rican Exodus: Development of the Puerto Rican Circuit," in Barry B. Levine (ed.), *The Caribbean Exodus*. New York: Praeger.

Maingot, Anthony P. (1992). "Immigration from the Caribbean Basin," in Guillermo J. Grenier and Alex Stepick III (eds), *Miami Now!* Gainesville: University Press of Florida.

Maldonado-Denis, Manuel (1976). *Puerto Rico y Estados Unidos: Emigración y Colonialismo*. Mexico: Siglo XXI.

Maldonado, Edwin (1979). "Contract Labor and the Origins of Puerto Rican Communities in the United States." *International Migration Review*, 13/1: 103–21.

Marie, Claude-Valentin (1986). "Les populations

des Dom-Tom en métropole," *Ici La-Bas*, no. 7 (janvier-février).

Marie, Claude-Valentin (1993). *Les Populations des DOM-TOM nées et originaires, résidant en France métropolitaine, Recensement de la population de 1990* (Paris; INSEE, mars).

Massey, Douglas S, and Denton, Nancy A. (1989). "Residential Segregation of Mexicans, Puerto Ricans, and Cubans in US Metropolitan Areas." *Sociology and Social Research*, 73: 73–83.

Palmer, R.W. (1974). "A Decade of West Indian Migration to the Unites States." *Social and Economic Studies*, 23/4: 571–87.

Pedraza-Bailey, Silvia (1985). *Political and Economic Immigrants in America: Cubans and Mexicans.* Austin: University of Texas Press.

Penninx, Rinus, Schoorl, Jeannette, and van Praag, Carlo (1993). *The Impact of International Migration on Receiving Countries: The Case of the Netherlands.* Amsterdam: Swets and Zeitlinger.

Pierre-Charles, Gerald (1979). *El Caribe Contemporáneo.* Mexico: Siglo XXI.

Portes, Alejandro (1978). "Migration and Underdevelopment," *Politics and Society*, 8: 1–48.

Portes, Alejandro, and Bach, Robert L. (1985). *Latin Journey: Cuban and Mexican Immigrants in the United States.* Berkeley: University of California Press.

Portes, Alejandro, and Grosfoguel, Ramón (1994). "Caribbean Diasporas: Migration and the Emergence of Ethnic Communities in the U.S. Mainland," in the special issue on *The Future of US – Caribbean Relations* of the *Annals of the American Academy of Political and Social Science*, 533 (May).

Portes, Alejandro, and Truelove, Cynthia (1987). "Making Sense of Diversity: Recent Research on Hispanic Minorities in the United States," *Annual Review of Sociology*, 13: 359–85.

Preteceille, Edmond (1973). *La Production des grand ensembles.* Paris: Mouton.

Racliffe, Peter (1988). "Race, class, and residence: Afro-Caribbean households in Britain," in Malcolm Cross and Han Entzinger (eds.), *Lost Illusions.* London: Routledge.

Rath, John (1983). "Political Participation of Ethnic Minorities in the Netherlands," *International Migration Review*, 17/3: 445–69.

Rex, John, and Tomlinson, Sally (1979). *Colonial Immigrants in a British City: A Class Analysis.* London: Routledge and Kegan Paul.

Roberts, G. W., and Mills, D. O. (1958). *Study of External Migration Affecting Jamaica; 1953–55.* University College of the West Indies, Jamaica: Institute of Social and Economic Research.

Sassen-Koob, Saskia (1988). *The Mobility of Labor and Capital: A Study in International Investment and Labor Flow.* London: Cambridge University Press.

Stepick, Alex, and Portes, Alejandro (1986). "Flight into Despair: A Profile of Recent Haitian Refugees in South Florida," *International Migration Review*, 20 (Summer).

# Index